"I've never wanted to be a star. I'm much happier just working regularly, having some time to perfect my characterizations. I'm looking forward to growing old. There will be more work for me when I am a few years older. Since I'm primarily a character actress, in a few years I'll be in the running for all the old maiden aunts, sweet old mothers and strange, sweet oddballs that are often found in good productions. And by then that should be just my cup of tea."

—Alice Pearce, 1958

SWEET ODDBALL
The Story of
ALICE PEARCE

Especially for Patti
with appreciation & affection
Fredrick Tucker
July 21, 2021

FREDRICK TUCKER

Sweet Oddball: The Story of Alice Pearce
By Fredrick Tucker
Copyright © 2021 Fredrick Tucker
No part of this book may be reproduced in any form or by any means, electronic, mechanical, digital, photocopying, or recording, except for inclusion of a review, without permission in writing from the publisher or Author.
No copyright is claimed for the photos within this book. They are used for the purposes of publicity only.

 Published in the USA by:
BearManor Media
1317 Edgewater Dr #110
Orlando, FL 32804
www.bearmanormedia.com

Perfect ISBN 978-1-62933-736-4
Case ISBN 978-1-62933-737-1

BearManor Media, Orlando, Florida
Printed in the United States of America
Book design by Robbie Adkins, www.adkinsconsult.com

In memory
CRIS ALEXANDER

In honor
LINDA SUE SWANSON

CONTENTS

PREFACE

My mother recognized her first.

"Oh, that's the first Gladys Kravitz!" she exclaimed. "And that's Abner!"

We had tuned in late to the NBC Saturday night movie, *The Glass Bottom Boat*, already more than halfway in progress. Easily identifiable was the perky blonde lead, Doris Day, but neither of us could come up with the real names for the actors playing her next-door neighbors. To us they were simply "Gladys" and "Abner" from the *Bewitched* television series, then in its seventh season on ABC. How delightful to see them unexpectedly show up here! In the movie's climactic scene, plucky Doris was fleeing an enemy spy in the dead of night, seeking refuge by climbing through her neighbors' bedroom window, only to be trailed by the pistol-wielding agent as he, too, clambered inside. Meanwhile, the reactions from Doris' neighbors (called "Mabel" and "Norman" in this incarnation) were very much like the Kravitzes' responses on *Bewitched*: she, nagging and hysterical; he, blind to the entire fracas. We convulsed with laughter as Gladys/Mabel gulped and tremblingly yanked the bedsheet over her head as each intruder thrust a leg through her open window. And then we got tickled all over again when she frantically whispered an alert to her oblivious husband in the next bed.

It was so enjoyable to see this rubber-faced woman again! She was every bit as funny here as we remembered her from *Bewitched*. But what was her name, I wondered aloud. And why was she no longer on that show? My mother knew the answer to my second question. She said that the "first Gladys"—who had only been in the black-and-white epi-sodes—had died during the run of the show. The "second Gladys," the one with red hair, was the one with whom we had been more familiar the past five years.

When the movie's final credits rolled, we were reminded that the original Gladys/Mabel was named Alice Pearce. Alice Pearce, that's right; that was her name. And, oh yeah, that was George Tobias playing her husband.

As an eleven-year-old that night in 1971, I began to wonder about Alice Pearce. What other roles had she played? What had caused her early death? I tried to recall any specific episodes of *Bewitched* involving the "first Gladys." I had been a faithful viewer of the show for years, but only two faint memories surfaced. One was an episode when Gladys brought a bowl of soup to her neighbor Samantha Stephens who was sick in bed. Although I was only a first grader when that segment ("Take Two Aspirins and a Half Pint of Porpoise Milk") originally aired in 1965, I distinctly remembered viewing it. My second memory of seeing Alice Pearce on *Bewitched* was a scene where Gladys witnessed Samantha diving into a swimming pool, only to lose control when she later peered over the fence to find nothing but a trampoline on the lawn. This episode ("And Something Makes Three") I remembered from the two-year period when *Bewitched* reruns were part of ABC's weekday morning lineup in 1968 and 1969.

Fast forward to 1974. By then I had become a diehard character actor buff. No big surprise there. Since childhood I had always noticed the supporting players in reruns of shows like *I Love Lucy*, *December Bride*, and *The Real McCoys*, but now I was seriously building a personal library of books related to classic Hollywood films and vintage television programs—mainly to pore over the photographs of my favorite character actors. While vacationing that summer, I came in from the motel pool one afternoon to watch "cable TV," a luxury unknown to us at home. Sitcoms being my favorite, I flipped to WRET-TV, broadcasting from Charlotte, North Carolina. Here, in a black-and-white rerun of *Dennis the Menace*, I happily discovered a pre-*Bewitched* Alice Pearce matching wits with Mary Wickes, another favorite of mine. But that day, Miss Wickes was not the draw—I could still catch her frequently on current television shows. Instead, I was absolutely captivated by the departed Miss Pearce, whose television appearances by now were rare jewels, especially since stations in my area chose to air only the color reruns of *Bewitched*. That afternoon, I got a kick out of how she contorted her mouth to give certain lines more of a punch. Her greatest tool, though, seemed to be her nasally voice and how she could shift it instantaneously from the lyrical to the acidulous, or as my fellow Pearce fan Ken Slater once said (better): "Her personality could fold itself down to near-invisibility or explode into Martha Raye bigness." Topping it all off was that cackle—downright maniacal! Needless to say, my curiosity with Alice Pearce was reignited that day.

When I got back home, I looked through my books to see if there were any photos of her. Only one. And that was in John Kobal's *Gotta Sing, Gotta Dance*. So I visited my county library, hoping to find out more about Miss Pearce. There I discovered the *Screen World* annuals by Daniel Blum and John Willis. In the 1967 issue I found an obituary for Alice Pearce which summarized her brief film career. Soon after, I located her *New York Times* obituary on microfilm. Details in that document led to other sources, and quickly I found myself on a long, winding research trail. One early resource, Lawrence B. Thomas' book *The MGM Years*, was a product of the 1970s nostalgia craze. Thomas profiled more than one hundred players in M-G-M musicals, but when he came to Alice Pearce, his affirmation tugged at my heart: "Everyone loved Alice." Whether this statement was merely a generalization or a conclusion based on inside information, it more than ever validated my pursuit. Meanwhile, the more individuals I contacted for interviews or information, the more I realized that Mr. Thomas' assertion was right on the mark. Over the course of the next forty-five years, I devoted an inordinate amount of time, energy, and expense to track down every other bit of information I could find about Alice Pearce. But this was a very private passion, especially in my youth, long before the days of the internet, DVD's, or even VCR's. I wasn't eager to tell my friends or family that I was fascinated with a person once famous but now almost forgotten, someone whose name was unfamiliar to the average person, someone who was neither an athlete, rock star, or sex symbol. Mine was not the typical interest of an American teen, and I knew it.

One particular emotion remained strong as my fascination grew. Looking back, I believe that this feeling was key in fueling my passion. Even though I never met this comical little woman, at times I felt overwhelmingly sad that Alice Pearce had been taken by cancer, just at the height of her fame. Even the irreversible date of her death—March 3, 1966—became burned on my brain. Would I have been so devoted to her memory had she not died so young? I suppose my feelings were comparable to those of the loyal fans of Jean Harlow, James Dean, Montgomery Clift, and others gone too soon.

Whenever I heard Elton John's tribute song (" . . . and I would have liked to have known you, but I was just a kid"), I would think not just of Marilyn Monroe, but of Alice Pearce, who had died when I was in the first grade.

I once dared to show a promotional portrait of Alice Pearce to my grandfather's secretary. I had ordered it from Larry Edmunds Bookshop, all the way from Hollywood. It was my favorite photo of Alice, taken in 1965 at the height of her fame during the first season of *Bewitched*. She was dressed smartly with a mink fur around her neck and sporting a toothy but pleasant smile. The secretary took one glance at the photo and said, "Why are you interested in her, Fredrick? She's ugly." The words stung. To dismiss such a talented comedienne—one that I adored—just because of her looks! It was an assault on both Miss Pearce and me. I knew that Alice Pearce had a receding chin, a hooked nose, drooping eyelids, and teeth that looked too large for her mouth. (Even one of her oldest friends, Cris Alexander, would quip that Alice "was certainly not Jayne Mansfield!") But I didn't care about the Jayne Mansfields of the world. Character actresses were my idols.

It's interesting to note that Alice Pearce's most admiring critics also drew attention to her lack of conventional beauty, calling her "a grotesque comedienne," assigning her the unflattering labels of "goon girl," "parrot face," "walking persimmon," or the gentler, "hokily sophisticated and endearing ragdoll." Similar comparisons followed Alice throughout her career, as she portrayed an array of unattractive females: wallflowers, busybodies, spinsters, fishwives, and halfwits. These archetypes were her destiny, but she knew that better than anyone. And, as writer Axel Nissen has pointed out, "she made them irresistible."

Matt Cimber, who once directed Alice in an off-Broadway production, hit the nail on the head. "The key, I think, to Alice was that she accepted who she was and how she looked," he mused. "And she had the capability of allowing herself to be, not necessarily bizarre, but very, very quirky because of her looks, and therefore she came off very funny. You could say that she laughed at herself before you laughed at her. Many people in the world wouldn't accept themselves—they'd find another route or go get plastic surgery or something. But not Alice. Alice said, 'Hey, this is me, okay? And I know how to make [you laugh], because I start off as funny-looking.' She knew how to *use* [her appearance] and change it into humor, and that meant that she also had to accept it. That made me admire her very much. On top of that, she had great timing. She was a superb comedienne. So, if you mix that attitude with her capabilities, you have something that was supremely professional."

What did Alice think of her typical roles? "I like earthy parts," she told *TV Guide* in 1965. "They're a rebellion against my background." Just a few months earlier, *TV Radio Mirror* reported that Alice had once made a similar statement: "Playing strange, sweet oddballs is exactly my cup of tea." Actually, the *Mirror* had paraphrased part of a 1958 press release, which quoted forty-year-old Alice as saying: "Since I'm primarily a character actress, in a few years I'll be in the running for all the old maiden aunts, sweet old mothers and strange, sweet oddballs that are often found in good productions. And by then that should be just my cup of tea." It's amusing to note that by 1958 Alice was already playing strange, sweet oddballs. In truth, she had been doing so since her college days.

Actually, Alice Pearce was something of an oddball herself. Growing up in Europe as the only child of wealthy American parents, she never had much contact with other children, instead "[living] most of the time in a fantasy world." She was shy and quiet, never really fitting in with either her parents' elite social set or her fellow students at the Belgian finishing school selected by her parents. As a teenager Alice was sent to New York to further her education in an exclusive boarding school but found her non-mastery of English a significant barrier. And when she visited her parents' relatives in the rural Midwest, her sophistication contrasted starkly with the local lifestyle. When she chose drama as her college major, her parents did not understand or approve. They would have preferred that she marry well, i.e., an Ivy Leaguer, and settle down in suburbia, joining the Junior League and the DAR. But Alice confounded them by striking out for New York City, determined to leave her former world behind to establish a stage career. So, if truth be told, Alice Pearce probably felt very much at home playing "oddballs." There is no doubt, however, about her sweetness. In fact, "sweet" was the oft-repeated adjective employed by Alice's friends and colleagues when describing her to me.

As if following a pattern, a certain few of these contacts used descriptions which segued from Alice's physical appearance to her character or personality. Actor Richard Deacon, particularly intimate with Alice during the final four years of her life, shared these thoughts: "Alice had no chin, chipmunk teeth, and very thin hair (hence always a *very* good wig). She was inclined to be a tubby yet she was one of the most beautiful people I have ever known. The more you knew her, the more beautiful she became. Beauty queens couldn't hold a candle to her." "She really was terribly comical looking," insisted Cris Alexander, "but when you knew her, [within] a short time, she was just *absolutely lovely*. And I don't mean she was lovely looking, but she had beautiful skin and beautiful eyes, and what came out of her was just really lovely. You felt very comfortable with her. You didn't get any pretension. She had great delicacy, just an absolutely loving spirit. And everything that she did or touched was just *fun!*" John Lund, Alice's fellow actor when she made her Broadway bow in *New Faces of 1943*, said, "She had a funny face to begin with, and she enhanced it with a wide range of weird grimaces. She had a musical voice which she distorted to great comic effect. But I remember her chiefly for the extraordinary sweetness of her personality. She was always kind, always generous."

"Alice Pearce had a very unusual look for show business," says pop culture historian and author Geoffrey Mark. "[It was] very hard for her to be categorized, which made her stand out, but also it made it hard for her to get work because she *was* so special and unique." Alice appeared in only fourteen feature films, and the last nine of those were made once she permanently moved to the West Coast. For many years she preferred Broadway over Hollywood, a period when her stage work was interspersed with occasional roles on live television shows emanating from New York. All the while, she enjoyed lengthy engagements at Manhattan's chicest supper club, the Blue Angel. "I think she loved the level that she attained in the business and the respect she received," says Matt Cimber. "Alice loved her career," echoes her fellow actor Patricia Wilson. "She cherished it, and she had a right to, because she did some wonderful work, and in her lifetime she brought a lot of people a lot of joy."

Unlike the many spinsters whom Alice played on stage, film and television, she was happily married twice: first to songwriter John Rox who died suddenly during their tenth year of marriage, and then, for the final seventeen months of her life, to actor Paul Davis who survived her. Once, when the topic of physical beauty came up during an interview, as it often did, Alice shared a personal realization, one that remains quite touching. "It may sound corny," she said, "but a woman feels most beautiful when she is loved by a special man. Then you realize that there is something beautiful within you that makes him love you." Her widower, like others quoted here, recognized Alice's essence, not only as a performer but as an individual. "Alice Pearce was unique in a world of many kinds of people," Paul Davis reflected in 1968. "You can always say 'that type' about many people, but you could never put Alice into any category. Her whole way of looking at life was unique. She had a great capacity to love, and I was fortunate to have been loved by Alice. I think this is true of anyone who came in contact with her—for a day or even an hour." In other words, Alice Pearce was a kindhearted individualist . . . a sweet oddball.

Fredrick Tucker
January 14, 2021

CHAPTER ONE
Buckeye Boy

"My parents were Midwesterners ... real down-to-earth people."

By October 1917, the United States had been at war for six months. Soon the first American soldiers would see action on the front lines at Sommervillier, France. In that country on October 15, Mata Hari, exotic dancer turned German spy, would be executed by a French firing squad. Twelve days later, 20,000 suffragettes marched down Fifth Avenue in New York City in a move to convince state legislators to give them the vote, which was accomplished within two weeks. Meanwhile on the Broadway scene, few plays dealt with the war or women's suffrage. That month theatergoers could see Marjorie Rambeau at Maxine Elliott's Theatre in the comedy-drama *Eyes of Youth*, Ina Claire in the charming comedy *Polly with a Past* at the Belasco, George Arliss at the Knickerbocker playing Alexander Hamilton in *Hamilton*, Leo Carillo in *Lombardi, Ltd.* at the Morosco, or Billie Burke and Roland Young—twenty years before they teamed up in the *Topper* films—in *The Rescuing Angel* at the Hudson. Before season's end, sixteen-year-old Tallulah Bankhead would make her Broadway debut, though only as a "walk on," in *The Squab Farm*.

That same fall, one of Miss Bankhead's future colleagues, Alice Pearce, was set to make her own debut into the world. At 595 West 207th Street, located in the Inwood neighborhood on the northern tip of Manhattan Island, her expectant parents were preparing for the birth of their first child. Alice's father Robert Pearce, twenty-eight, was serving his second year as an auditor for the National City Bank of New York, located at 55 Wall Street on the extreme opposite end of Manhattan. With their first wedding anniversary approaching, Robert's wife Margaret, twenty-five, had lived in the city just less than a year.

Robert Eugene Pearce, the youngest of five children, was born in Bellefontaine, Ohio, on August 18, 1889, and spent the first twenty-four years of his life there. At the time of Robert's birth, Bellefontaine—the county seat of Logan County—was home to a little more than 4000 residents, but by the time of his departure that number had more than doubled. Laid out in 1820, Bellefontaine did not prosper much until the advent of the railroad some twenty years later. When Robert was a young boy, the Cleveland, Cincinnati, Chicago, and St. Louis Railroad built a main terminal in Bellefontaine, featuring the largest roundhouse between New York and St. Louis. By 1900, there were six railroad lines converging on the city. "The city is in the center of a rich agricultural country," a 1901 souvenir booklet boasted, "producing all the cereals and raising horses, cattle, sheep, and hogs in great numbers and of the best strains."

Robert, or "Bob" as his family and friends called him, enjoyed a safe, rather conventional upbringing. It was a life shaped by church, school, and civic affairs. In grammar school, Bob excelled in both academics and music, studying the violin from a young age. In 1906, he graduated from Bellefontaine's only high school, an imposing four-story Gothic Revival structure on East Columbus Avenue, then enjoying its last days. Another edifice with keen importance to Bob—and to all the Pearces—was the Bellefontaine Methodist Episcopal Church, completed the same year Bob was born and still standing at the corner of North Main Street and Sandusky Avenue. Bob united with this church two weeks before his tenth birthday; concurrently his father Harry taught a boys' Sunday School class each week.

The Bellefontaine Methodist Episcopal Church, circa 1907.

Harry Pearce, born in 1851 in the parish of St. Keverne in Cornwall, England, was the oldest son of a farmer whose forebears had lived in or near that village for more than two hundred years. Harry was not content to follow that tradition, and at age sixteen he booked passage in steerage on the *Etna*, sailing from Liverpool and arriving in New York Harbor on March 3, 1868. From there he set out for Cincinnati where his father's first cousins, James and Henry Pearce—brothers and partners in a prosperous business manufacturing cotton yarn—had settled with their parents in 1831. For a time,

Harry resided in the home of the widowed James Pearce at 137 Broadway, perhaps helping to care for the elderly entrepreneur who had suffered a stroke. However, Harry's stay in Cincinnati does not seem to have lasted long. Though his motivation remains uncertain, Harry relocated to Bellefontaine, approximately one hundred miles northeast of Cincinnati, where he became a clerk in a dry goods store by 1873. In due time, a Bellefontaine lass—Emma Colton—caught the eye of young Harry Pearce, and a period of proper courtship followed.

Emma, ten weeks older than Harry, was born in Shanesville, Ohio, where her father Samuel had operated a flour mill. Samuel and his wife Eliza Cutforth Colton were natives of Lincolnshire, England, where they married in 1837. Six years later, they, along with their four oldest children, boarded the *Superior* and sailed for America, hoping to find prosperity in their new home. For the next fifteen years Samuel operated flour mills in New York, Ohio, and

Eliza Cutforth Colton, Alice Pearce's paternal great-grandmother.

The Colton Brothers Company, Bellefontaine, Ohio.

Indiana, but he was never satisfied until he reached Marlboro in Stark County, Ohio, where he opened a mill in 1858. He remained in business there—teaching his youngest sons Robert and Joseph the trade—until his sudden death in 1864.

In the spring of 1869, the Colton brothers, still in their twenties, moved their widowed mother and three unmarried sisters, including teenage Emma, to Bellefontaine, which they deemed as an ideal location, given the abundant output of its surrounding farms. Each year the county's farmers produced hundreds of thousands of bushels of wheat, corn, oats, barley, buckwheat, and rye. The brothers bought an old burr mill, operating with their well-worn equipment until 1871, when the mill was partially destroyed by an explosion. Consequently, a new roller process was installed in The Colton Brothers Company on West Columbus Avenue, and subsequent additions would lead to the business being generally recognized as "the largest and best equipped milling property in Logan County." By 1888, the mill had the capacity to produce 500 barrels of flour per day.

Eliza Colton, the widowed head of the family, perhaps felt a bond with fellow Englishman Harry Pearce, an emotion probably shared by her sons. In 1875, soon after Harry married her daughter Emma, Robert and Joseph Colton offered him a position at the mill, one that he held until retiring some forty years later. The Coltons would essentially become Harry's family, for none of his siblings followed him across the Atlantic. Harry and Emma settled on North Detroit Street, not far from the Colton home on South Detroit, which Robert and Joseph had built for their mother and two spinster sisters Lizzie and Anna in 1876. Eventually Harry and Emma Pearce were blessed with three sons: Chester, Wilbur, and Bob—Alice's father. In the Bellefontaine city cemetery lay two additional children who each died before reaching their fourth months. Before Bob's third birthday, Emma also followed her babies to the grave. Though she fought hard and long, tuberculosis claimed her young life on the night of April 7, 1892.

Harry Pearce remarried in the fall of 1894. His bride was Mary Gore, a former resident of

Bellefontaine who had been a milliner in one of the ladies' shops downtown. Mary proved to be a loving stepmother for little Bob. He was at her side when she died following an operation for "nervous trouble" in 1909.

Meanwhile the prosperous Colton brothers had reached a certain level of prominence within Bellefontaine's business, religious, and social circles. While their brother-in-law Harry Pearce had not attained their financial heights—instead investing his earnings in farm acreage and livestock—he maintained just as much respect in church groups and fraternal organizations. Still, Uncle Robert and Uncle Joseph felt obligated to look out for Emma's boys. Chester Pearce assumed a position at the flour mill, and Wilbur, after studying at Ohio Wesleyan University and Ohio State University, became a bookkeeper at the Commercial and Savings Bank. When Wilbur later left his job to become cashier at a neighboring bank, Bob—a special favorite of his namesake uncle—stepped in to become the new bookkeeper.

Bob Pearce found his niche in banking, and in a few years, he was promoted to the position of cashier. He enjoyed associating with others in Bellefontaine's financial circle, including John Inskeep, secretary for Uncle Joseph's building and loan association, and John's brother Clair, a civil engineer. With them he traveled to Europe in the summer of 1912. It may have been that trip that set Bob to thinking more seriously about his future. Both his brothers were married and settled in their careers; his father Harry had chosen a third wife and had moved to her home in nearby Zanesfield. At twenty-four and living with Chester and his family, Bob realized that his high school education was not sufficient to carry him to the heights he aspired. Encouraged by his father and uncles, he enrolled at New York University's School of Commerce, which offered an accelerated track for day students, allowing them to complete a degree in only two years. In September 1913, Bob left Bellefontaine for New York City, and the course of his life changed forever.

Robert "Bob" Pearce, New York University, 1914.

CHAPTER TWO
"Little Dixie" Girl

"We haven't a drop of blue blood in our veins and are glad of it."

"My parents were Midwesterners," Alice Pearce once told a journalist. "Real down- to-earth people. We haven't a drop of blue blood in our veins and are glad of it." Indeed, Bob and Margaret Pearce were products of hardworking families—on both sides of the Atlantic—who lived close to the land, each generation striving to better themselves intellectually, financially, culturally, and socially. Compared to Margaret's lineage, Bob's side of the family was relatively new to America. His father Harry became a naturalized United States citizen in 1879, while his mother Emma was a first-generation American. By the time Bob's maternal grandparents arrived in America in 1843, some of Margaret Pearce's ancestors had preceded them by more than two hundred years.

At separate points before the Civil War, three of Margaret's great-grandfathers had migrated to Missouri from northeastern Kentucky; the generations before them had lived in northern Virginia. James Clark, Alvin Ringo, and William Biggers chose parcels of land in the northeastern section of Missouri, in the bordering counties of Monroe, Audrain, and Ralls, respectively. Their families would become united in 1886 when Margaret's parents Joseph Clark and Sallie LaFrance married in the small town of Perry in Ralls County.

"Everybody from around Perry either came from Virginia or Kentucky," explained long-time Perry resident Dorothy Williams in 2003. "And they call [this section] 'Little Dixie.' We're much more Southern up in this little part than they are in southern Missouri." Indeed, dissertations and even books have been written about the "Little Dixie" belt which stretches across seventeen counties in the fertile river valleys and rolling prairies of upper central Missouri. Historian Gary Fuenfhausen asserts that by 1860, this area had become a "microcosm of the South's plantation hierarchal society, a Southern enclave where distinctive cultural traits and attitudes matched those of the Antebellum South." Furthermore, Fuenfhausen notes that the three aforementioned counties are considered by many scholars to lie within the core zone of "Little Dixie."

Alice Pearce's mother, Margaret Alice Clark—the second oldest of four children—was born in Perry on May 29, 1892. The town was laid out by William Perry Crosthwait and Richard Anderville Mayhall in 1866 and was named for the former, who was the town's first postmaster. Growth was slow; by 1890 the population stood at just over 300. On August 18, 1892, when Margaret Clark was not yet three months old, the town's citizens held a celebratory picnic for the completion of a branch line of the St. Louis and Hannibal Railroad, providing rail service to and from Perry. To commemorate the occasion, newspaper editor Thomas Trimble published on that same day an article—essentially a business directory of Perry—which inadvertently painted a clear picture of Margaret's birthplace. Among the businesses listed were the town's two banks, one operated by Margaret's paternal relatives and the other staffed by members of her maternal side. Like many small towns, Perry was a closely-knit community. Not only were its residents connected by economic or political ties, but by blood or marriage as well. Consequently, Margaret Clark was related to many of Perry's leading citizens.

Margaret's father Joseph Lilburn Clark was born in 1861 on his father's livestock farm near Florida, Missouri, eight miles west of Perry. As a young man, Joe, as he was called by everyone, seems to have lacked the focus and acumen of his successful older brother Alva, who came to Perry in 1876 and quickly established himself

Joe Clark and his granddaughter Alice Pearce at his home in Perry, Missouri, March 1919.

with investments in a drug store and a livery business. By 1886, Alva had disposed of these interests to become cashier of the Perry Bank, subsequently making wise investments in cattle, mules, and swine.

Meanwhile, Joe, very likely aware of living in Alva's shadow, was struggling to find his place in the world. He moved to Perry in 1884 to find more profitable work. At age twenty-five, he married Sallie LaFrance, the daughter of prominent Perry businessman Marcus "Mark" Payne LaFrance who gifted the newlyweds with a home in town. It is not known what type of work Joe found in those early years, but he soon grew dissatisfied with his situation and purchased a farm south of town from Sallie's maternal grandfather. However, in less than four years, he was back in Perry. In 1903, when the youngest of his four children was not yet two years old, Joe pulled up stakes and moved his family 400 miles south to Beebe, Arkansas. Yet in less than three years, the Clarks returned to Perry once again, and Joe set himself up in business as a butcher.

"J. L. Clark is prepared to butcher your hogs and render up your lard at a reasonable cost," ran his 1906 advertisement for the Perry Meat Market. He managed to diversify as well, operating a soda pop factory within the meat market and, as a winter sideline, selling blocks of ice cut from Lick Creek. In November 1911, Joe bought the milling concern of Charles Menke, located near the railroad tracks in Perry. This proved to be his most successful venture, and by September 1913, he was able to divest himself of the meat market. He advertised his new business as "The Elevator Building," which boasted "all kinds of mill feed for man and beast," including wheat flour, corn meal, bran, alfalfa hay, cotton meal, and chicken feed. He reportedly sold livestock feed "by the carload

At left, the newly erected Peoples Bank, Perry, Missouri, 1911. The building at the extreme right housed the Perry Enterprise newspaper office.

Bank, also in Perry. "To this institution he devoted his best energies of his life," extolled newspaper editor Dewitt Masters. "He became its president and remained so until failing health compelled him to relinquish its active management." Two years before his death, Mark LaFrance oversaw the completion of a new Peoples Bank building on the northeast corner of Main and Palmyra Streets, an accomplishment he was said to have regarded as "the real culmination of his business life." Masters viewed LaFrance as "a benefactor to the growth of Perry."

to farmers in Ralls County." Finally, Joe Clark had found his niche.

Margaret's mother and the town of Perry "were of an age," as Shakespeare would say. Sarah Helen LaFrance, whom everyone lovingly called "Sallie," was born in 1866, the same year that her hometown was established. Her mother died two years later, leaving Sallie and her older sister Emma to be reared by an aunt while their father Mark LaFrance was occupied with establishing his dry goods business.

LaFrance, a Pennsylvania native and skillful carpenter, had arrived in the area in 1859. He soon found his services in constant demand, building not only residences for the growing population but also the Lick Creek Christian Church. In fact, LaFrance drew the plans for the church building, and construction began in the spring of 1860. In 1863, he took up farming to supplement his income, and in five years he had accumulated enough wealth to open his own store in Perry. This he operated until 1885, when he joined other men of means in establishing the Perry Bank. He was made cashier and remained with the bank for two years, until he was hired by the newly organized Peoples

Mark LaFrance, Alice Pearce's maternal great-grandfather.

The Entre Nous Club, circa 1914, at the home of Alice Pearce's great-aunt Mrs. Georgia Clark (back row, extreme left). Six other relatives of Alice Pearce are pictured here, including her grandmother Sallie Clark (fourth from the left on the back row.) Sallie's stepmother "Mamma Sue LaFrance" is fifth from the left on the back row.

In 1880, the widowed LaFrance married schoolteacher Sue Belle Fagan, almost twenty years his junior, and together they had four children. Everyone in town seemed to admire "Mamma Sue LaFrance," who was known not only for her wit and wisdom but also for her "remarkably true alto voice." She had a particularly pleasant relationship with her stepdaughters Emma and Sallie, who returned to live with their father and new stepmother until they each married.

By 1900, Joe and Sallie Clark were living on Jefferson Street in Perry. However, in subsequent years they resided in a two-story house which is still standing at 308 South Palmyra Street. Just up the street lived Sallie's father as well as Joe's brother Alva. Sallie's days were busy with the usual chores associated with being a housewife and mother. Besides

daughter Margaret, the Clarks' other children included a son, LaFrance, and daughters Mary Emma and Josephine.

Sallie was very much a homebody, judging from the weekly social columns of the *Perry Enterprise* whose editor monitored the comings and goings of everyone in town. While Sallie's daughters were often reported as visiting relatives in Hannibal, only once in the span of a dozen years does the *Enterprise* mention Sallie accompanying them. Besides attending the Perry Christian Church—of which she and Joe were charter members—Sallie's only other social outlet was the Entre Nous Club.

The Entre Nous Club was organized on January 20, 1900, as a "social and literary club" for married ladies, with a limit of twenty-four members. The club met every other week in members' homes to discuss such diverse topics as poetry, women's suffrage, Shakespeare, women of the Old Testament, labor unions, and "inventors of flying machines." Sallie Clark was a charter member, and she not only helped to draft the club's constitution and by-laws but she also wrote the club song. With a nod to the famous Italian opera star Luisa Tetrazzini, Sallie was once hailed as the club's own "Tetrazzina," when she sang "Where the Flag Is Full of Stars" for a special club meeting. Any other possible resemblance to the vivacious coloratura soprano ended here, for Sallie was by nature a mild-mannered, unassuming woman, much respected by the citizens of Perry. "She was a *lady*," Dorothy Williams declared emphatically, "and her sister was, too." (According to Williams, yet a member of the Entre Nous Club when interviewed in 2003, the club was still living up to its name: "What happens here is between us.")

Sallie apparently passed along some of her musical talent to Margaret, who often sang solos in school pageants and studied piano with Lida Alford, a cousin who lived on Salling Street. At the time, high school courses at Perry were somewhat limited, so in the fall of 1908, the Clarks allowed Margaret to attend the high school at Hannibal, thirty-seven miles northeast of Perry and a ninety-minute train ride away. It was arranged for Margaret to live with Joe's obliging sister, Alice Clark Chowning, who most likely initiated this scenario. As Margaret's namesake, Aunt Alice—who was childless—would also become Margaret's patron, grooming her for a future life.

At fifty-two, Aunt Alice appeared older than she was. Her plump frame stood at five feet, four inches, and her pale face and high forehead were surrounded by her upswept steely gray hair. Behind her spectacles a pair of brown eyes conveyed warmth. Her demeanor revealed a gentility inherited from her Ken-

Alice Clark Chowning, Alice Pearce's great-aunt and namesake, with an unidentified girl in Hannibal, Missouri, circa 1905.

tucky and Virginia ancestry. Aunt Alice was prominently known in Hannibal for her work in women's clubs and in the First Christian Church but was foremost identified as the wife of Dr. Thomas Chowning, a surgeon at Hannibal's Levering Hospital. The Chownings had married in 1885, ten years after the doctor graduated from Missouri Medical College in St. Louis. They had moved to Hannibal in 1892, following the doctor's relatively brief practice in Perry—and a lengthier one before that in the town of Florida, his birthplace. As a physician, Dr. Chowning had followed in his father's footsteps. The senior Dr. Thomas Jefferson Chowning, although he did not live to realize it, would bear the distinction of assisting in the delivery of one of America's most famous sons. On November 30, 1835, that baby boy born in Florida, Missouri, was christened Samuel Langhorne Clemens, better known to the world as Mark Twain.

As Margaret Clark settled into the Chownings' large Queen Anne home, located at 1103 Center Street, she may have been somewhat in awe of her aunt and uncle. In some ways they were more privileged and cultured than her parents; the Chownings had spent the summer of 1908 traveling through Europe. That fall, teenage Margaret had no inkling that she was destined to spend more than a quarter of her own life on that continent. Under Aunt Alice's tutelage, Margaret thrived. She learned social etiquette and practiced the art of being a proper hostess. Meanwhile, she diligently studied advanced courses at Hannibal High School. In the fall of 1910, however, Margaret altered her course. Aunt Alice enrolled her in the Hannibal College of Music, operated by Jon Sheperd Shastid, an Illinois native, and his wife. Professor Shastid taught piano while Mrs. Shastid concentrated on vocal instruction. In Aunt Alice's eyes, education and culture were crucial to the development of young ladies, and she wanted to provide whatever benefits she could

for her niece. During this interim, Margaret accompanied the Chownings on all of their trips, including one to New Orleans and Cuba in 1911. In effect, Aunt Alice and the doctor were her surrogate parents.

On September 12, 1911, Aunt Alice and Margaret alighted from the train at the depot in Columbia, Missouri. Aunt Alice had now decided to send Margaret to her own alma mater, Christian Female College—the state's first women's college—chartered sixty years earlier. Its current president, Luella St. Clair, was one of the first female college presidents in the United States. In the past year, St. Clair had overseen the completion of Dorsey Hall which boasted additional classrooms, laboratories, and a gymnasium. Although Margaret was only enrolled for one school year, she earned a Bachelor of Letters degree on May 20, 1912. Aunt Alice, of course, attended the commencement ceremony, but surprisingly she was accompanied by her sister-in-law Sallie, who made the one-hundred-mile excursion with her.

For almost three years following her graduation, Margaret passed a rather quiet existence with her parents in Perry's bucolic setting. However, in February 1915, the *Perry Enterprise* reported that she had gone to Hannibal to stay with the Chownings and continue her music studies. That summer a cousin introduced her to his college friend who was visiting from Bellefontaine, Ohio.

CHAPTER THREE
Love & Marriage

"My mother was a beautiful woman."

Storm clouds over New York City were threatening on the evening of June 8, 1915, but that did not dampen the spirits of Bob Pearce. He confidently entered the tenth-floor auditorium at the New York University complex to join his fellow classmates for their commencement exercises. Elected as president of the 1915 Day Class the previous fall, Bob was lauded by his fellow students for his courage, diplomacy, and tact. "Bob is a fighting name and true to traditions he has the requisites to go with it," proclaimed the editor of the university yearbook. "Not of a pugilistic nature, but the kind that wins success, the quality that men have who strike out into a new country, where there are no roads or footprints or guide posts or warnings of danger ahead." The editor had no way of knowing that within four years Bob Pearce would indeed strike out into a new country and in coming years would also face one of the most dangerous threats of the twentieth century.

Up to this point, the most serious predicament facing Bob had occurred in the summer of 1914. On Sunday, June 28, he and his first cousin Edwin Colton, then a student at Ohio Wesleyan University, left Bellefontaine for Boston from where they sailed two days later to Liverpool, joining others for a foreign study course in England. The group was chaperoned by Bob's economics professor, Philip B. Kennedy, who was also director of the day class

division at NYU. Aware that Archduke Franz Ferdinand of Austria had been assassinated on the very day they left Ohio, Bob and Edwin did not seriously consider the possibility that England would be affected. "Robert and the party had gone up the west coast of England through into Scotland and had started down the east coast, taking in Newcastle, York," reported the *Bellefontaine Daily Examiner*, before stopping in Lincolnshire to visit their Colton cousins who entertained them royally. They were in Birmingham when Austria declared war on Serbia on July 28. Even after Germany declared war on Russia four days later, they felt safe but wary of following through on their plans to explore the continent.

During the first week of August, when Bob separated from the group to visit his father's siblings and their families in Cornwall, the situation became more real when England declared war on Germany. On August 9, Bob wrote from Oxford to his father Harry: "In every town and city in which we have recently been, soldiers by the hundreds have been saying good-bye to home folks. The Government has called for 500,000 more men and voted $500,000,000 to spend for war purposes . . . The Government has control of the railroads and many trains that leave here have [been reserved] for soldiers and provisions . . . there are hundreds of Americans who are without money and have no tickets home as the boats on which they had return tickets have stopped running." Bob went to four banks before he "could get a penny," trading in British postal orders for nine pounds in gold, "or $45, which I am holding on to pretty tightly." Once in London, the men found it somewhat easier to obtain money from the banks there.

Bob had intended to sail for America on September 12, but ditched this plan because "no vessel was [crossing] at that time." He weighed his options, and, rather than waiting until October and missing the beginning of the NYU fall semester, he booked passage in steerage on the Olympic, sister ship to the Titanic. Edwin stayed behind in Ireland; meanwhile, Bob shared a cabin with seven other men, sailing on August 23. "After the first three days of terrible sea sickness we fared tolerably well," he later told the *Bellefontaine Daily Examiner*. "Dim lights were on the mast poles; all port-holes were screened and the large plate glass windows were painted black and were kept closed all night to shut out the lights within the ship. Heavy papers were over many of the

Bob Pearce, circa 1918.

windows . . . fear of a German vessel chasing us was always imminent." Bob reached New York on August 29, arriving in Bellefontaine the following day. He spent the next three weeks resting before reporting to NYU on September 23, 1914.

Nine months later, the 1915 Day Class, numbering thirty, had completed their studies, becoming candidates for the Bachelor of Commercial Science degree. Meanwhile their nighttime counterparts held day jobs, a situation which necessitated a slower course of study. Bob was fortunate to be a part of the former group, and with diligence and perseverance he excelled. His classmates not only voted him "most likely to succeed," but also "most popular." His position afforded him an individual portrait page in the yearbook. The image shows a serious young man with thick dark hair parted on the left and large dark eyes framed by a delicate pince-nez. From under his starched white collar and conservative waistcoat, a youthful checkered necktie gives a hint that the yearbook editor's estimation—"he has pleased the ladies"—may have been right on the mark.

Bob's closest friend at NYU was Gill Clark, a thirty-four-year-old bachelor banker who had lived in Billings, Montana, off and on since 1902. Following an unsuccessful attempt to study law in Chicago, Gill had divided his time between Billings—where his considerable holdings included both real estate and livestock—and his hometown of Perry, Missouri. Gill's first cousin was Margaret Clark; their fathers Alva and Joe were brothers. Like Margaret, he had once resided with Aunt Alice Chowning when he attended Hannibal High School. Eleven years Margaret's senior, Gill had seen little of her during the ensuing years, except for his brief stays in Perry.

With no immediate employment plans and the entire summer stretching before them, Gill and Bob decided to spend some time in each other's home towns. They arrived in Bellefontaine on June 15 and visited all the Pearce kin. One week later, the men got off the train in Perry, but wasted no time in the little town. The following day they traveled up to Hannibal and crossed the Mississippi over to Quincy, Illinois, where fellow NYU student Rudolph Riggs was summering at the home of his father, also a banker. Bob had planned to be back in Bellefontaine by June 28 at the latest, but he suddenly found a reason to linger in Missouri. For ten days he and his college buddies bounced back and forth between Quincy and Perry. At some point, whether in Perry or at Aunt Alice's home in Hannibal, Gill introduced Bob Pearce to Margaret Clark.

As they got to know one another, Bob and Margaret marveled at their similar backgrounds, particularly the fact that their families were involved in both milling and banking. More importantly, Bob was smitten by Margaret's beauty and charm. And the emotions were mutual. "She was one of the sweetest women, and she was beautiful," recalled Dorothy Williams. "And Bob was one of the most handsome men." As a young man, Bob, at five feet, eight and one-half inches, was not much taller than Margaret, who, like him, had large brown eyes and dark hair. She would gray prematurely, just as her mother Sallie had, but at this point, Margaret's thick and wavy brunette hair was quite striking. Years later, their daughter Alice, reflecting on her own plain looks, countered, "My mother was a beautiful woman."

A fortnight of social activities involving the new couple was followed by a series of seemingly coincidental vacation trips, reported in both the *Perry Enterprise* and the *Bellefontaine Daily Examiner*. Instead of returning to Ohio,

Bob decided to visit his brother Wilbur in Colorado Springs for several weeks. Near the same time, Margaret's maternal aunt Emma Netherland and her family planned a three-week motor trip to the same city. Although Margaret was not mentioned in any newspaper item as accompanying either the Netherlands or Bob Pearce, a curious blurb appeared in the *Enterprise* on August 26: "Miss Margaret Clark returned Friday from an extended trip through the west. She visited Colorado and California... and attended a house party in Seattle, Washington, also a trip through Yellowstone Park." Margaret arrived in Perry on August 20, but the Netherlands did not make it home until three days later. If Margaret had travelled with them, why did she come home ahead of them and alone? Or was Bob Pearce with her? Considering the mores of the time, it seems unthinkable that a proper young lady would have traveled without a chaperone. Moreover, Gill Clark was unavailable to accompany the young couple, as his frequent comings and goings appear in Perry's social columns from mid-July until mid-August. Although this chain of events remains a mystery, it is certain that Bob and Margaret saw each other in Missouri on both the third and fourth weekends of August.

By September 8, Bob was back in Bellefontaine, but not for long. During his stay out west, he had received an offer from Professor Kennedy to become an assistant instructor at the School of Commerce at NYU. Abandoning any thoughts of settling in Colorado, Bob accepted the job and left for New York on September 9. Needless to say, he kept in touch with Margaret Clark, whom he most definitely planned to see again—as soon as the Christmas holidays arrived.

In the meantime, Professor Kennedy realized that Bob's banking experience and accounting expertise were better suited for a career in finance rather than education, so he had no qualms in recommending Robert Pearce to Frank A. Vanderlip, president of the National City Bank of New York, for a position in the auditing department. In early December, Bob resigned from NYU to accept the offer to join the City Bank, with his tenure officially beginning just before year's end. Then it was off to Bellefontaine to spend a few days with his father and brother Chester, who were delighted with this important news. They knew, of course, that the National City Bank, with a capital of $25 million and 800 employees, was the largest bank in the country. They understood, too, a few days later when Bob left for Quincy, Illinois—just across the river from Hannibal, Missouri, where a certain young lady resided with her aunt.

Margaret had been beside herself with excitement for days. On December 9, when she sang the opening solo for the dedication ceremony of Perry's new high school building, she could barely concentrate knowing that Bob was due to arrive in Bellefontaine that very day and would soon make his way to Missouri. He spent most of his Christmas vacation courting Margaret and proposing plans for a future life with her. At twenty-three, she was quite receptive. Two months earlier she had served as bridesmaid for her older sister Mary Emma, who, at twenty-eight, was well past the typical age for a Perry bride.

Over the following four months and with the assistance of the U. S. Postal Service, a long-distance courtship between Bob and Margaret ensued. Their engagement was announced in May 1916, at Aunt Alice's home during a bridal shower for a family friend. The Pearce-Clark wedding was planned for early fall. However, the sunny atmosphere in the Clark home turned to alarm in late June when Mary Emma, now residing in Fulton, Missouri, suffered a miscar-

riage and grew very ill. She battled septicemia all summer, entering the hospital at Hannibal on August 23. Everything possible was done for her, but with no means to combat the infection, she died on September 14.

Bob and Margaret chose Wednesday, the first of November, for their wedding ceremony, to be held in the Clarks' parlor where just one year earlier Mary Emma and Cleve Ward had wed, also on a Wednesday morning. Aside from the day and location, there was nothing similar about the two ceremonies. This time there would be no brightly colored fall leaves draped from the staircase. There would be no bridal attendants descending the stairs, nor any accompanying strains of "The Bridal Chorus" from Wagner's *Lohengrin*. The family thought it best to keep the event informal, considering their recent loss and profound grief. That morning, just before the nuptials began at half past ten, the bride and groom mingled with the assembling guests, who included only the closest family members and a few neighbors. The low-key ceremony was conducted by the pastor of the First Christian Church of Hannibal. A newspaper account of the wedding offered few details, not even the color of the bride's gown. The groom's only relative in attendance was Harry Pearce, who had accompanied Bob on the 500-mile trip from Ohio. At noon he and the newlyweds boarded an eastbound train for Bellefontaine.

Arriving in Bellefontaine the following evening, Margaret was introduced to Bob's stepmother Dora who had been busy with preparations for a large family dinner to be held at the Pearce home the next night. The guests included Bob's brother Chester and his family, his uncles Robert and Joseph Colton and their families, his spinster aunts Lizzie and Anna Colton, and his widowed aunt Mary Bates. The happy occasion would mark the last time

Bob and Margaret Pearce on their wedding day, at the Clark home in Perry, Missouri, November 1, 1916.

that Bob Pearce would see his uncles; Joseph Colton would die within the month, and Robert would follow in 1918.

Back in New York, Bob and Margaret settled into the apartment he had selected for them at 595 West 207th Street in the Inwood neighborhood, a rapidly developing section prompted by the extension of the Interborough Rapid Transit subway line. Nearby on Broadway stood the recently renovated Dyckman Farmhouse, dating from 1764, which three months earlier had been opened as a museum by descendants of the original owner. Even then, the old Dutch colonial stood out among the apartment houses towering over it.

The move must have been quite an adjustment for Margaret. The dazzling contrast of Manhattan's two million-plus inhabitants to Perry's eight hundred was very likely boggling, and the mix of languages, religions, culture, and cuisine certainly exciting. Added to that was the realization that she and Bob—with whom she had spent a relatively meager amount of time prior to marriage—were forging a relationship from the ground up. To compound the situation, America entered the war five months after the Pearces set up housekeeping. Bob Pearce registered for the draft on June 5, 1917, claiming no exemptions for recruitment, but he would never serve in any branch of the military.

Meanwhile, things were going very well for Bob at the National City Bank. Its president, Frank A. Vanderlip, had recognized early on that Bob was a perfect candidate for his newly devised training courses in foreign banking. Even before the advent of the war in Europe, Vanderlip knew that foreign banking was "the new frontier" and that the "profit potential in foreign banking was limitless if one had the proper foreign relations." In 1913, he set the ball in motion by establishing branches of the bank in other countries. When the war disrupted the normal flow of commerce, Vanderlip took advantage of the situation and accelerated his plan. Germany and England—heretofore the major export competitors of the United States—were now essentially out of business. Suddenly there was a demand for both U. S. products and financing. Recognizing this, Vanderlip "capitalized on the misfortunes of Europe." Faced with a shortage of personnel equipped to operate future foreign branches, he designed courses primarily for people already in the banking field to learn foreign banking. Bob Pearce was one of these fortunate men.

Vanderlip assured his transfer to a European branch at some point in the future.

In May 1917, Margaret returned to Perry for a brief visit. Her father Joe was recently home from the Mayo Clinic in Rochester, Minnesota, where he had undergone surgery for "gallstone trouble and appendicitis." Margaret not only wanted to check on her father's recuperation, but she also had a bit of news to share: she was expecting a baby in October.

The National City Bank of New York, 55 Wall Street, circa 1912.

CHAPTER FOUR
Baby Alice

"Alice took her first steps alone [on the day] the Armistice was signed between the Central Powers and the Allies."

Margaret's announcement undoubtedly created great excitement in the Clark home, but probably a bit of concern, too, given her sister Mary Emma's recent pregnancy-related death. This time, however, Joe and Sallie would not be robbed of a daughter or a grandchild. The Pearces chose Dr. Frederic Jellinghaus, a 1901 graduate of Columbia University's College of Physicians and Surgeons, as Margaret's obstetrician. Jellinghaus maintained a medical office at 572 Park Avenue, just five blocks from his residence, also on Park Avenue, but he performed surgeries and delivered babies at the Lying-In Hospital, located at 305 Second Avenue between East Seventeenth and Eighteenth Streets in the Stuyvesant Square neighborhood. This maternity hospital had been built in 1902 with the generous contributions of financier J. P. Morgan.

Light showers fell on Manhattan as dawn broke on Tuesday, October 16, but by nightfall, the autumn sky was clear and starry. Temperatures had remained in the sixties all day, dropping to fifty-nine degrees by nine o'clock that night. Inside the Lying-In Hospital, Margaret gave birth at quarter past nine to a seven-pound, three-ounce baby girl, measuring eighteen inches long. Patiently waiting nearby were Bob and Aunt Alice Chowning, who had made the trip from Hannibal. Aunt Alice had no intention of missing the birth of Margaret's baby, and she came prepared to stay for as long as her niece needed her. Because

The Lying-In Hospital, New York City, where Alice Pearce was born on October 16, 1917.

Aunt Alice had devotedly supported Margaret through the years, Bob and Margaret decided to name the baby Alice Chowning Pearce. The news was telegraphed to Perry in time for it to appear in the weekly edition of the *Enterprise* two days later.

Margaret lovingly recorded every detail of Alice's first year in a silk-covered scrapbook with the words "Our Baby" hand-painted on the cover. From this source, we learn that Dr. Jellinghaus delivered Alice and that the attending nurse was "Miss Kidney," a name that years later surely made Alice Pearce snicker. We know Alice's weight at one-month intervals and that her first outing was on Sunday, November 18, "with Aunt Alice Chowning, Mother and Daddy." On one page, Margaret traced outlines of the soles of Alice's first pair of shoes, noting: "Little white kid pumps, size one. First time she wore them jerked the bow off." Inside a tiny envelope affixed to another page was a lock of Alice's hair, clipped when she was one month old. Another envelope held Alice's first baby tooth: "the left lower front tooth peeped through June 12, 1918." The following day, baby Alice crawled across the room

for the first time. "At age eight months [Alice] could say da-da, ma-ma, bye-bye," Margaret noted, "however, the words had no special significance, merely jabbering. When Alice was one year [she] could say plainly, daddy, hot, bottle, tick tock, baby, bye-bye."

In December 1917, the Pearces moved three blocks east to 31 Seaman Avenue, where they leased a larger apartment. Nearby was a park—ideal for strolling baby Alice—and for when she grew older, a playground.

Grandparents Joe and Sallie Clark finally got to meet little Alice when she was seven months old. On May 16, 1918, they left Perry for New York City, quite an event for Sallie, who was such a homebody. The previous year she had not accompanied Joe to Rochester for his surgery, and of course, it was Aunt Alice, not Sallie, who was present when Margaret delivered. Even more surprising is the fact that Joe returned to Perry after a week or so, but Sallie remained with the Pearces for two months. Meanwhile the Clarks' son LaFrance, who had been clerking at his father's grain elevator, enlisted in the U. S. Army's aviation corps and was shipped to France, where he would remain

Alice Chowning Pearce, age 5 months, April 1918.

Three generations: Margaret Pearce holds baby Alice while Sallie Clark looks on, New York City, August 1918.

until 1919. The Great War would finally end on November 11, 1918, a day Margaret Pearce would never forget. "Alice took her first steps alone [on the day] the Armistice was signed between the Central Powers and the Allies," she wrote in her daughter's baby book. "In two weeks, Alice was walking every place."

1919 was the year of greatest growth for the National City Bank; thirty-three foreign branches were established during those twelve months. These branches, as well as those before and after their creation, were mainly formed to increase America's foreign trade, but the United States government also "wanted to use the bankers and their resources to achieve certain diplomatic policy objectives" in different parts of the world. One of the branches to be opened in 1919 was in Brussels, Belgium, and

Robert Pearce was handpicked to manage it. The plans called for Bob, Margaret, and Alice to move there in April, with the expectation that they would live abroad for several years.

In February 1919, Margaret and Alice arrived in Perry for a lengthy visit with the Clarks. This was the first time that little Alice had met her extended family, including her aunt Josephine, who was set to graduate from Perry High School that spring. Considerable time was passed in Hannibal with Uncle Tom and Aunt Alice Chowning, too. Uncertain of when she would next see her Missouri kin, Margaret wanted it to last. Bob joined Margaret in Perry near the end of her stay; they bid a tearful farewell to the Clarks on March 23. A similar scene ensued in Bellefontaine the following week when their stopover with the Pearces ended.

Once Bob and Margaret were back in New York, their departure for Europe was postponed until summer. In the meantime, they brushed up on their French and enjoyed their final weeks in New York. On April 20, Easter Sunday, they had a nice lunch at the Hotel Holley on Washington Square in the West Village. In May they vacationed at New Dorp Beach on Staten Island.

Meanwhile, Harry Pearce decided that he and his wife Dora would take advantage of the delay and visit Bob and family in New York, remaining until they sailed. Passage had been booked on the *New Amsterdam*, a 1906 steamship which had been built for the Holland America Line. During the war, the ship had been exempted from transporting U. S. troops to Europe because it was reserved for carrying vital quantities of grain from America to the Dutch, who had previously bought the commodity from Germany. By 1919, it was once again transporting first, second, and third-class passengers across the Atlantic. Departure took

Family reunion in Perry, Missouri, March 1919. Kneeling and flanking Alice Pearce are her aunt Josephine Clark (left) and Margaret Pearce. Behind Margaret are her parents Sallie and Joe Clark. Behind Josephine are Sallie's sister and brother-in-law, Emma and William Netherland.

Alice Pearce and her namesake, Aunt Alice Chowning, Hannibal, Missouri, February 1919.

place on July 2 at the Holland America dock in Hoboken, New Jersey. A photograph taken just before the Pearces boarded shows a dapper Bob wearing a three-piece suit and straw boater and Margaret outfitted in a stylish suit and cloche. In his arms Harry holds Alice, dressed in a Peter Pan collar dress and black patent leather button-up shoes. That day, no one could have predicted that this little girl would eventually cross the Atlantic on twenty-three subsequent voyages—and for most of those trips she would travel alone.

Harry Pearce and his granddaughter Alice, New York City, July 2, 1919.

The scene at the Holland America dock on July 2, 1919. Left to right, Bob and Margaret Pearce, Bob's stepmother Dora, and Harry Pearce holding his granddaughter Alice.

CHAPTER FIVE
Belgium

"I never had much contact with other children, so I lived most of the time in a fantasy world."

Alice Pearce was not yet twenty-one months old when she and her family sailed to Europe. With the exception of three extended vacations in the United States, she spent the next fourteen years as a resident of Belgium and later, France. Aside from occasional blurbs in the Perry and Bellefontaine newspapers, these years in Alice's life are sketchy. No transatlantic communications, whether in the form of telegrams or letters, are known to have survived. Therefore, the only documentation of the Pearces' lives from 1919 until 1933 exists in photograph albums and scrapbooks. From these we can piece together, to a certain degree, where they traveled, with whom they associated, and how they lived.

The journey aboard the *New Amsterdam* lasted eleven days, including stops at Le Havre and Rotterdam. The only on-board photograph shows Alice waving an American flag on July 4, 1919. The first photo of Alice abroad, taken that September, shows her "*dans le jardin*" at 95 Rue Defacqz, the townhouse in Brussels' elegant *Châtelain* neighborhood where the Pearces first resided. In this house, which stands today, Alice celebrated her second birthday on October 16. A snapshot shows her seated in her highchair next to a table with paper streamers stretched from its four corners upward to the ceiling.

There are no photographs marked as being taken in 1920, and it is assumed that this period of transition left little free time for Bob and Margaret. However, the Pearces traveled extensively on the continent in the summer of 1921. Margaret's album shows the ruins of Dixmude, a Belgian city reduced to rubble during the war, as well as Kaiser Wilhelm's headquarters in the Belgian resort town of Spa. Happier scenes in Geneva show Alice, not yet four years old, wearing tiny sunglasses, and in Marken holding hands with a Dutch boy dressed in the traditional *klompen* (wooden shoes) and *korte broek* (puffy kneepants). The Pearces also visited Milan's opera house, or *Teatro alla Scala*, and posed on the roof of the Milan Cathedral. In Venice, they toured the Doge's Palace and traversed the Grand Canal.

That same year, Bob became the manager of the branch bank at Antwerp, a city more than twice the size of Brussels. On November 7, Aunt Alice Chowning wrote a chatty letter to her great-niece at her new address, 11 Court Rue d'Argile, asking if she spoke "mainly French or English." The old lady may have been wondering if the Christmas gift she had shipped in 1919 was getting any use. Perhaps to ensure that little Alice be brought up with American literary traditions, she had chosen *The Complete Edition of Mother Goose Rhymes*. However, the nursery bookshelf also held a copy of *Les Fables de la Fontaine*—first published in the seventeenth century—stories which were considered classics of French literature. It's uncertain if Aunt Alice received an answer to her question, but years later Alice

Margaret and Alice Pearce, Brussels, January 1921.

related, "I was taught French before I learned English." Consequently, Alice's English proficiency was lacking throughout much of her youth.

The following year, Alice's extended family had the delightful opportunity to experience her French fluency. Bob was called to America on business and combined the stay with a much-needed vacation in the spring of 1922. The Pearces disembarked the S. S. *Lapland* in New York on Sunday, May 7. While Bob spent the week engaged with meetings at the bank's Philadelphia branch, Margaret and Alice took the train to Bellefontaine, where Bob joined them the following weekend. Bob's brother Wilbur and his family made the trek from Colorado Springs so that all three of Harry's sons would be in town for a family reunion on May 18. The weeks were filled with visits, luncheons, and dinners with family and friends.

The Pearces arrived in Perry on May 29, Margaret's thirtieth birthday, and

Alice Pearce, Brussels, January 1921.

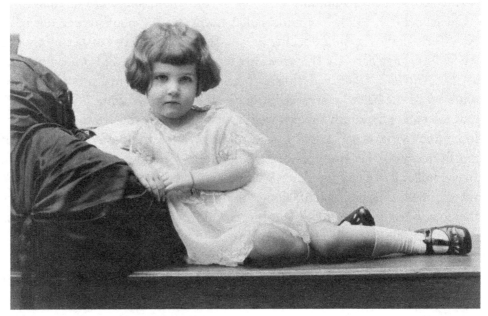

met the same type of reception as they had in Bellefontaine. They were feted by friends and relatives on four occasions, the liveliest one being a Clark-LaFrance family reunion hosted by Sallie's stepmother, "Mamma Sue" LaFrance, on June 16 at the old LaFrance home. "An elaborate two-course luncheon was served at a rose and honeysuckle decorated table with covers laid for twenty-six," reported the *Enterprise*. "The good food was rendered more digestible by the fact that every guest was required to tell a good joke." A bit of impromptu entertainment followed the meal. Mamma Sue's daughter Nana sang, as did Margaret who accompanied herself on the piano. Then Bob, on the mandolin, accompanied his wife on another selection. Not to be left out, little Alice sang several songs in French, much to everyone's delight.

A few days later Bob left for New York, where Margaret and Alice met him in time to sail back to Europe on July 22. Since they were uncertain when they would return to the States, they proposed that their relatives come to Europe for extended visits. Margaret's sister Josephine, twenty-one and footloose, was the first to accept their invitation.

On March 31, 1923, Josephine sailed from New York on the *Lapland*, docking in Antwerp where Bob met her. By this time his tenure at the Antwerp office was finished; he had returned to the bank in Brussels earlier in the year, relocating his family there as well. During Josephine's visit, which lasted fifteen months, the Pearces took her on tours of Switzerland, Italy, Holland, and France. Alice, who was not yet enrolled in school, went along, enjoying the company of her Aunt Josie. They would remain very close for the rest of their lives.

Josephine was nine years younger than Margaret, but she had a more mature face, long and narrow with a high forehead. Her deeply

Best friends for life: Frances Masters (standing, second from left) and Josephine Clark (standing, third from left), members of the tennis club at Perry High School, 1916.

set eyes were dark blue, so dark that they almost appeared to be brown, like Margaret's. Her dark brown hair, almost black, was not yet bobbed, and she wore it pulled back and gathered in a big pouf. Since her college graduation, she had stayed at her mother's side, perfecting her cooking and other homemaking skills. While she was in Europe, Josephine missed attending the wedding of her best friend, Frances Masters, whose father DeWitt was the editor of the *Perry Enterprise*. Because of the girls' enduring friendship, Mr. Masters was always informed of updates involving the Pearces, and without fail he gave such events prime coverage in his weekly paper. Josephine sailed home on July 15, 1924, arriving in Perry on July 30. Little did she know that foreign travel would be an important part of her life in years to come.

Les Tourelles, where Alice was schooled from 1924 until 1931.

ladies, Mademoiselle Eugénie Delstanche, a Belgian, and Miss Dorothy Tungate, a native of San Francisco, who had taught in Europe for twenty-four years.

Each spring Mlle. Delstanche and Miss Tungate presented *Exposition des travaux du trimestre,* a program of musical or dramatic pieces which the students had practiced that quarter. In March 1925, Alice, age seven, dressed in a folk costume including a *capotain* atop her head, performed a Welsh dance. Margaret was so taken with her performance that she had Alice professionally photographed in the costume, just as she would the following spring when Alice and fellow student Simone Blanche donned powdered wigs and eighteenth-century fashions for their *Scene Watteau,* patterned after paintings of bucolic charm for which the French artist Jean-Antoine Watteau was so well known. In another portion of the program, titled *L'Aurore de Jour de Pâques,* Alice appeared with other students demonstrating their calisthenic skills, accompanied by the music of Italian composer Arrigo Boito.

In the fall, Alice's parents enrolled her at Le Pensionnat Les Tourelles, an exclusive girls' school, housed in "an enormous, beautifully furnished mansion" located at 15 Avenue du Longchamp in Brussels. The exterior of Les Tourelles (translated as "turrets") resembled a medieval castle, while the wood-beamed interior favored a hunting lodge. A 1922 advertisement for Les Tourelles described it as "a first-class French Finishing School for Young Ladies of good social standing . . . highest references given and required." It is not certain if Alice boarded at Les Tourelles, because the majority of its students were much older than she. As a traditional finishing school, Les Tourelles focused less on academics and more on the social graces, preparing older teens for entry into fashionable society. The curriculum for older girls included modern languages, music, art, and tennis. They attended lectures and concerts, and there were opportunities for travel as well. After five years of living abroad and becoming quite comfortable financially, Alice's parents saw Les Tourelles as the logical choice, especially since the school welcomed American students. The principals were two elegant

In addition to the annual spring exhibition, Les Tourelles produced two plays each year. During the 1925–26 school year, one production was Moliere's *Le Malade Imaginaire,* a three-act comedy-ballet originally produced in Paris in 1673. Alice, now eight years old, was asked to take the role of Louison, the younger daughter of the character Argan, a hypochondriac. Years later she would laughingly recall that her parents were delighted until they learned that she was playing an illegitimate child. "They nearly fell off their chairs,"

Alice Pearce, age seven, in a folk costume for a musical program at Les Tourelles, March 1925.

Alice (left) and fellow student Simone Blanche in costume for "Scene Watteau," part of the Les Tourelles spring music program, 1926.

remembered Alice, but their reaction didn't faze her. Her comic performance had drawn laughter and applause, and she had suddenly found her niche. In fact, she decided after the first performance that she wanted to be an actress. "I fell in love with the theater [at that point]," she told an interviewer in 1948. Around this time, Alice was also greatly influenced by a Hollywood film star. "As a child,

I adored Charlie Chaplin," she recalled. "He was my idol. I decided then I would like to specialize in comedy characters."

In the summer of 1926, the Pearces made their second trip home to America, arriving in New York on the *Olympic* on July 6. Boarding a train for the Midwest, they first stopped in Bellefontaine where, during their ten-day stay, Margaret was entertained at bridge several times by Bob's cousin Lena JoHantgen. They also finalized plans for Bob's niece Margaret Pearce to accompany them on the return trip to Brussels, where she intended to study music and art. From there they went to Hannibal on July 23 to stay the weekend with Aunt Alice, now living alone since the death of Dr. Chowning the previous September. Once in Perry, Margaret was the guest at four bridge teas; her relatives and friends were eager to hear about life in Brussels. On August 9, the Pearces boarded a train for Colorado Springs where they visited Bob's brother Wilbur for two weeks. Upon their return to Perry, Bob left for New York to attend meetings at the bank's home office, while Margaret and Alice enjoyed more leisurely days with the Clarks and all the kin before sailing back to Belgium on the *Belgenland* on September 18. Bob's niece Margaret would stay with the Pearces for six months, returning to the States in March 1927.

If Margaret had lingered a few days, she would have seen her cousin Alice perform in the spring exhibition at Les Tourelles on April 2. This time, she and Simone Blanche danced as the characters in *Le Loup et L'Agneau* ("The Wolf and the Lamb"), one of Fontaine's fables. Not much is known about the remainder of the year or those immediately following, except for inferential evidence gleaned from the images and captions in Alice's personal photo album. We know that in 1927 the Pearces were living at 19 Rue de Crayer, a Beaux-Arts mansion designed by architect Victor Taelemans and completed in 1912. Its elevation was covered in white stone with elegantly carved ornamentations featuring cul-de-lamp, garlands, and medallions. Prominent was a bow-window on the second floor, surmounted by a small terrace with a balustrade. There were three floors of living space plus a large garret and a full basement.

In 1927, at some point during the spring or summer, or perhaps even early fall, a playground accident occurred, changing Alice's appearance forever. "One afternoon when I was nine, I was playing in a park in Brussels," Alice told a journalist in 1964. "I was showing off on a swing. I think I was trying to impress some boys. I went way up, lost my grip and slipped out of the swing." Alice landed on her chin with such force that its growth was permanently stunted. Helen Tuttle Votichenko, Alice's college friend, recalled being told that the fall actually broke Alice's jaw. "Her jaw was set but didn't grow afterward," Votichenko said. "This is what gave Alice her *look*." For months, Margaret took Alice to various dentists and bone specialists in different parts of Europe, but they could do nothing for the girl. "Her mother worried about [Alice's underdeveloped chin] and thought that it might leave her socially handicapped," explained Votichenko, but actually Alice was already an "excruciatingly shy child." Her demureness is plainly visible in a portrait Margaret commissioned of Belgian artist Marcel Hess, around 1925. And, yes, a touch of sadness is there as well. What was the source of Alice's shyness? That is not something easily determined, but she did insinuate in several interviews that she was overshadowed by Margaret.

"I know that [Margaret] was a very brilliant woman," affirmed Cris Alexander, Alice's close friend and fellow actor. "I never met her, but I know that [Alice] had a rather odd viewpoint about her." "I realized at the age of eight that I was never going to be able to compete with my mother in the living room," Alice revealed in 1965, describing Margaret as "overflowing with wit and charm." It was rare that Alice did not describe her mother's beauty in such interviews, once calling her a "double for Tallulah Bankhead." "I gathered that [Alice] was a shock to her mother and father—that is to say, her appearance," Cris explained, "because she would say herself that both her mother and father were absolute beauties." One wonders if Margaret's obsessive quest to find a doctor to correct Alice's chin compounded her daughter's self-conscious feelings. Although Alice later stated that it was not until she was a teenager when these emotions surfaced, it's quite evident that even as a young child she felt that she failed to measure up to her mother in either personality or looks.

Alice's shyness could also be linked to the fact that she "never had much contact with other children." The family photograph albums substantiate this claim. In hundreds of snapshots taken between 1919 and 1929, Alice appears in exactly three photos with other children, presumably her playmates or children of her father's business associates. They're identified only by first names: Gerald, Sonny, Jane Ann, and Agnes. There are no candid shots which seem to have been taken with any students from Les Tourelles, but most of those girls were quite older than Alice anyway.

From photographs taken in 1928, we know that Alice had a dog named Pierrot and dolls she called Punkie and Rosie. She also had an elaborate three-story dollhouse. That summer the family vacationed in Germany, as there are snapshots of the Rhine River and the Lorelei, a 433-feet high slate rock on the river bank at Sankt Goarshausen. In one pose, they are lunching outdoors with Bob and Margaret hoisting ale mugs and Alice lifting a gob-

Every inch an American girl, Alice is seen in cowboy attire for this candid pose in Brussels, circa 1927. Another snapshot, taken in the same spot, shows Alice in complete Native American attire. By this time she was accustomed to seeing Hollywood westerns at the local cinema.

let. In another charming photograph where Margaret and Alice pose with three Dutch girls, Alice sports a wool coat with cape, knee socks, Oxfords, hat, and a large grin. There's also a happy scene of Alice coasting on sleds with children at the Bois de la Cambre, a public park on the edge of the Sonian Forest in Brussels. Christmas photos taken that year reveal a fresh tree reaching the ceiling, draped in electric lights and with ropes of tinsel wrapping its trunk. Rich draperies and detailed moldings and casings complement the massive antique furniture. On a large chest, the framed 1926 photo of Alice and Simone Blanche in powdered wigs is proudly displayed.

Meanwhile, Alice "lived most of the time in a fantasy world." Since she could not keep pace with her mother socially, she made a conscious decision to "compete on the stage." On March 29 and 30, 1928, she played Mytyl in Les Tourelles' production of *L'Oiseau bleu* (The Blue Bird), a 1908 play by Belgian playwright and poet Maurice Maeterlinck in which Mytyl and her brother Tytyl are aided by a good fairy in their search for the Blue Bird of Happiness.

That May, word came from Missouri that Aunt Alice Chowning had died of heart disease following a five-months decline. The *Enterprise* paid tribute, describing Aunt Alice as a "generous woman, helping in charity, church work, and assisting unfortunates." Alas, Alice had little chance to know her seventy-two-year-old namesake, visiting her only on the occasional trips to the States. The following January a telegram from Josephine arrived, informing Margaret of their father's death. Joe Clark had been convalescing from pneumonia for almost two weeks, but an attack of angina brought on cardiac arrest. "He contributed his share to the civic improvement of our city," declared the *Enterprise*. "For about twenty-five years he served as a member of the Board of Education of Perry Schools. He was vitally interested in the education of our youth." Indeed, Joe Clark saw to it that all four of his children were given the opportunity to become college graduates. His son LaFrance had graduated from Northwestern University in Evanston, Illinois, in 1927. Meanwhile, Josephine had married on Christmas morning, 1927, at her parents' home. The groom was

Perry Christian Church, where Alice attended services when visiting her grandparents in Missouri.

Paul Dillard, a pharmacist from Mexico, Missouri, where the couple made their home.

In June 1929, the Pearces returned to the States for visits in Bellefontaine and Perry, as they had in 1922 and 1926. They arrived in New York on the *Olympic* on June 25 and soon after headed to Ohio. By July 19, they were in Perry, where they were honored with several dinners hosted by family members. On July 28, accompanied by Sallie and Josephine, they left on a "delightful trip through Yellowstone Park" with stops in Colorado and Utah before returning to Missouri on August 9. Bob went to New York to "look after some banking business," leaving Margaret and Alice in Perry until August 29. Alice spent most of her time in the small town with her adult relatives, but sometimes the local children would drop in to play with her. One was Dorothy Hawkinson who was twenty-eight months younger than Alice. Dorothy was one of a foursome of Perry girls who were close in age and practically inseparable. "The Clarks had a large double swing on a frame in their yard," Dorothy recalled, "and we used to sit in it and eat ice cream with Alice." At other times during the Pearces' visit, Dorothy recalled that she and her friends spied on Margaret and Josephine sitting in that same swing. "They were the first women we ever did see smoke," she explained. The Pearces sailed back to Europe on September 7, reaching Brussels in time for Alice to resume her studies at Les Tourelles.

Around this time, a new student from England enrolled at Les Tourelles. Anna Claudia Russell-Brown was six years older than Alice, but if she had been privy to Alice's personal and family history, she may have compared herself to the younger girl. Like Alice, Anna was an only child who had enjoyed a privileged lifestyle, but her domineering mother could not accept her lack of beauty. She had spent the past nine years in a succession of boarding schools which she dubbed "detention camps." At one of these schools, an accident on the hockey field resulted in a fractured nose and cheekbone, which Anna said ruined her "acoustics." Now her "tin voice" was not at all suited for serious music. However, she would go on to become the queen of operatic parody, lampooning the world of classical music, performing at Carnegie Hall and on the Broadway stage—not to mention touring the world—as Anna Russell.

In her 1985 autobiography, Russell describes with pizzazz her delightful year at Les Tourelles. In light of the fact that Alice Pearce left no detailed record her time there, we turn to Miss Russell for some specifics:

> Breakfast was at a civilized nine o'clock, followed by a history lecture by M. Ranci, during which we would sew or knit while he chattered on and gave us historical tidbits, which we never had to remember as there was no such thing as prep. There was literature

with Mr. Ertz, and a gentleman with adenoids would conduct us around the galleries for *l'art*. At all times we were addressed as "mesdemoiselles." There was *l'elocution* and *l'etiquette*, when Miss Tungate held forth on how to enter a room, hold acup of tea correctly, or talk to a duke . . . Our beds were made for us, and we were definitely encouraged to change our clothes and primp about. After lunch we would go for a walk, but only if so inclined, and be fed withextremely rich cakes at some smart patisserie . . . The hairdresser would come in the afternoon to coif us, then, dressed in our best evening attire, off we would go in a limousine to be ushered into our private loge, where we would sit through all the usual operas.

Russell made many friends at Les Tourelles, but one stood out. "There was one darling little girl, much younger than the rest of us, who was sweet, demure, and quiet," wrote Russell. "She turned into that marvelous, mad comedienne with no chin and squeaky voice, Alice Pierce [*sic*], whom I met again in New York. That was certainly a sea change!"

In Alice's case, Les Tourelles left a lasting influence on her life. Years later, many of those who knew Alice Pearce in a professional sense, including actress Elizabeth Montgomery, would remark upon her ladylike demeanor. "I could tell that she was not of a theatrical background, but more of a mannered, good family," recalled costume designer Miles White.

The next few years in Alice's life are rather sketchy. She once again appeared in her school's spring exhibitions of 1930 and 1931. In the latter year, Alice played the lead in Dominique Cladel's adaptation of Romain Rolland's Nobel Prize-winning novel *Jean-Christophe*, the story of Jean-Christophe Krafft, a German musician of

Belgian extraction. In this two-act play, titled *Minna*, Jean-Christophe attempts to teach piano to the coquettish Minna de Kerich, a fourteen-year-old countess, played by Alice, with whom he falls in love. As with all productions at Les Tourelles, the male roles were played by female students. For *Minna*, Connie Nicol took the part of Jean-Christophe. In the makeshift scrapbook documenting Alice's Les Tourelles years, there is a photograph of Alice as Minna, dressed in 1840s style with long pantaloons peeping from under her skirt, leaning on the shoulder of Nicol, also in costume, and looking up adoringly. *Minna* would be Alice's swan song at Les Tourelles; later that year, her father would be selected to manage the Paris branch of the National City Bank of New York.

CHAPTER SIX
The Seine and the Hudson

"I hated living in Europe . . . I never felt I belonged."

"I suppose I had a good education," pondered Alice Pearce in 1965. "For years my French was better than my English, and I can embroider and do a fine cross-stitch." When interviewed by her college newspaper in 1940, Alice admitted that she "never did much work [at Les Tourelles] but had fun with the plays." Without a doubt, Les Tourelles prepared Alice for fashionable society, and it was there that she became fluent in Italian, but it seems that she wearied of the "very artsy-craftsy" school and its successor. "I hated living in Europe," she revealed, "I never felt I belonged. All I wanted was to be an American kid, with the freedom of American kids, walking to the movies or the drug store, without a chaperone." In Missouri, if she wanted a soda or ice cream, she could easily walk from Sallie Clark's house to one of the drug stores on Perry's Main Street. It was this simple convenience that she craved in Brussels and Paris. "To this day," she would later confess, "I look with envy on teenagers here [in America]. I felt cheated."

In October 1931, just before Alice's fourteenth birthday, Margaret enrolled her at the Collège Montmorency in Paris. Like Les Tourelles, it was a girls' finishing school, concentrating on literature, languages, dramatics, and fine arts. According to its 1932 handbook, "American girls are welcomed at the Collège Montmorency and live in an atmosphere that

is truly French." Established in 1920 by Mme. D. A. Perrier, the Collège Montmorency had recently moved into a newly completed facility at 15 Rue Henri Heine. Built in the Art Deco style, the structure stood out among the surrounding buildings as a rare example of cubist architecture, its concrete facade without any ornamentation whatsoever. There were four classrooms, eighteen bedrooms, an infirmary, and a laboratory. On the second floor there was a lounge-library-theater. Here Alice studied drama with Professor Jean Le Goff of the Comédie-Française, founded in 1680 and considered to be the world's oldest active theatre. On June 3, 1932, the drama class of Collège Montmorency staged Theodore de Banville's 1866 one-act comedy *Gringoire*, set in the court of King Louis XI of France. The male roles were enacted by female students, but Alice played Loyse, a seventeen-year-old girl who falls in love with the title character Pierre Gringoire.

Margaret was in her element during this period. Bob's considerable promotion as manager of the Paris branch afforded them an estate called Rosemont, located six miles from the center of Paris in Saint-Cloud, a fashionable suburb on the River Seine. The manor house and gardens required a full-time staff plus part-time workers employed at various times of the year. Margaret was taken with the beauty and history of Paris, not to mention the couturiers and antique shops. Her chauffeur often drove her "into town," as she called Paris, to have lunch with friends, take piano lessons, or treat herself to a facial or massage. In the spring of 1932, she busied herself with preparations for the advent of a very special guest. Alice's grandmother Sallie Clark arrived from the States in mid-June with plans to stay until the following June. During Sallie's visit, the Pearces made certain that the active sexagenarian saw much of France, as well as Lucerne, London, and other places of interest.

Alice did not return to the Collège Montmorency in October when the new term began. Since she yearned to ultimately attend college in the States, it became quite certain that the Parisian finishing school was not sufficient preparation. More importantly, Alice's English deficiency presented a significant roadblock. She was adept verbally, but her written expression was another matter, especially her spelling which Alice described as "something awful." It was obvious that she needed specialized instruction before tackling the curriculum at any American prep school. So, for one year, she was tutored at home by Mr. Kenrick Mervyn Brace, M. A., who regularly advertised as an "English tutor" in the much-respected Paris newspaper *Le Figaro*. Under Mr. Brace's tutelage, Alice studied Latin, algebra, geometry, English literature, and the principles of composition, all in preparation for Margaret's plan to enroll Alice in one of the "right schools" in America for the 1933–34 academic year. Preliminary arrangements began in January 1933, when Alice obtained her passport from the U. S. Consulate General at Paris. That summer, Margaret packed her daughter's trunks and suitcases with a firm anticipation that Alice would be accepted at one of the exclusive secondary schools on her list. Alice was delighted with the plan. (Bob, who was now in charge of the branch bank at Nice in addition to the one in Paris, was busier than ever but planned to

Alice was fifteen when she posed for this passport photo in Paris, France, 1933.

join Margaret and Alice in the States in September.) Mother and daughter sailed to New York on July 5. While aboard the *Champlain* Margaret wrote letters requesting catalogues from various schools including the Masters School in Dobbs Ferry, New York. Mindful of Alice's approaching sixteenth birthday, Margaret requested, "I wish to select a school for her that will permit her to be prepared for college in a year or two at the most without too much burden upon her because of the different systems." Unfortunately, both she and Alice would soon understand just how idealistic this view was.

The Masters School, an incorporated secondary school for girls, was situated on ninety-four acres of high land overlooking the Hudson River Valley. Although easily accessible by automobile via the Henry Hudson and Saw Mill River Parkways, it was a mere forty minutes from Manhattan's Grand Central Terminal via the New York Central Railroad. "Because of this situation, the School can offer its pupils a wholesome country life," boasted the school's brochure, "plus the educational and cultural opportunities of New York City." Founded in 1877 by Miss Eliza Masters, the school "kept a high standard of scholarship and had a very fine reputation." The conservative Miss Masters, serving as headmistress until her death in 1921, combined religion with education and founded her school on the teachings of the Bible. She aimed to produce Christian characters and healthy bodies, as well as "sound habits of scholarship." Her curriculum included literature, history, music, art, languages, mathematics, Latin, and an introduction to science—in other words, a "good general cultural education." Miss Masters abhorred the term "finishing school," and she was "firmly convinced that school girls were not society girls and that the training for society was quickly enough learned after a girl finished school." Consequently, there were "no dances, no sleeveless, low-necked dresses at dinner, no going down to the opera or the theatre, no 'proms.'" She viewed such as interruptions to a girl's school work. Quite a switch from Les Tourelles. By 1933, however, the Masters School had evolved to add a college preparatory course to Miss Masters' "General Course." Margaret Pearce found this quite satisfactory, as she had already registered Alice at Wellesley College, with hopes for admission in the fall of 1935.

In mid-July, while staying with friends in Pelham Manor, New York, Margaret and Alice motored to Dobbs Ferry to meet with Miss Evelina Pierce, current headmistress of the Masters School. They were impressed with both the campus and the curriculum, as well as with Miss Pierce, a "staunch New Englander" and Vassar graduate who had become part of

Margaret and Alice visiting Bellefontaine, Ohio, in 1933.

the administration in 1927. Although they were eager to apply for Alice's admission, Miss Pierce explained that they must first submit the necessary transcripts and references. Since Alice had never taken any standard intelligence tests or college entrance examinations, Miss Pierce found it imperative to rely on documentation provided by Alice's former tutor, Mr. Brace, to whom she wrote right away, asking for grades and details regarding the various subjects taught. While waiting for the paperwork to exchange hands, Margaret and Alice made a brief stop in Bellefontaine to visit Harry Pearce, now eighty-one and widowed for the third time, before moving on to Perry, where they would remain until September 10.

In the meantime, Miss Pierce began checking into the Pearces' background. She contacted Mrs. Gertrude Haff, the mother of a current student, who also lived in Pelham Manor, thinking that she may be able to vouch for the new applicant's family. However, Mrs. Haff sent her apologies. She knew nothing of the Pearces. When Mr. Brace's response arrived, Miss Pierce was dismayed to learn that none of Alice's assignments had been graded, although she had studied Latin grammar and syntax ("the process not quite complete") and had read Caesar, Nepos, and Aulus Gellius, as well as Shakespeare, Milton, and Scott. Brace also reported that Alice had not mastered either algebra or geometry concepts.

Despite this paucity of particulars, Miss Pierce decided to accept Alice's application. In truth, the headmistress found herself in a dire situation. Due to the Great Depression, current enrollment at the Masters School was down, and Miss Pierce was faced with drastically cutting operating costs to meet the school's heavy financial obligations. Just that year, she deemed it necessary to reduce faculty salaries by ten percent. Resident tuition had been lowered from $2000 to $1800 per year.

Receiving Alice's acceptance and expecting Bob's arrival in New York on September 15, Margaret and Alice spent a few days in the city, shopping for clothes and other things Alice would need for school. The Masters School catalogue was very specific about its dress code: "Extremes are to be avoided. No evening dresses are permitted. On Friday evenings simple silk or velvet dresses are worn." Parents were instructed to provide daughters with six to ten "well-selected" dresses and four additional cotton dresses "allowed in spring." During school hours, the pupils were required to wear navy blue serge blazers and skirts, available by order from Peter Thomson, a tailoring house on Fifty-Sixth Street.

Bob and Margaret helped Alice settle into her dormitory at the Masters School in time for classes, which began on September 20. Three adjoining dormitories, completed at a cost of $700,000 in 1930 and known as the Hill Houses, were housed under one roof in an attractive, rambling Tudor-Style structure. These dorms, named Thompson, Strong, and Cushing for former school leaders, were designed to promote a "homelike feeling," so each housed only sixteen to twenty girls under the care of a housemother, with its own living room, dining room, and kitchen, with bedrooms typically shared by two girls. "The view from the Hill Houses is beautiful," a 1941 promotional booklet stated, "looking out as they do on woodland on one side and across the Hudson on the other."

Margaret and Bob returned to France feeling quite satisfied with their selection of the Masters School. "I was sorry not to have seen you before I sailed," Margaret wrote to Miss Pierce from on board the *Washington*. "I had a lovely luncheon at Strong House and enjoyed the day very much. Alice is happy with you and my husband and I are delighted to leave her in your care. My voyage has been most pleasant and each day brings me nearer my home in France, which makes me very happy."

No letters or diaries written by Alice seem to have survived from this period, so we are left to speculate as to her feelings of being alone in unfamiliar surroundings. "In a sense, I left home at about fifteen," she would confess many years later.

The Masters School, sometimes simply referred to by staff and students as "Dobbs," was known as a "strict girls' boarding school." Dormitory rooms were open to inspection

Strong House, Alice's dormitory at the Masters School in Dobbs Ferry, New York.

by housemothers at any time of day. School historian Pamela Vose noted, "On each girl's desk, attached to its spotless blotter, was a weekly chart for tidiness comments." Years later one alumna remembered a remark left by her housemother: "Happy Birthday. Hair in comb." All girls were required to take Bible courses, as well as attend the weekly services at the village church of one's choice. Each evening after dinner, underclassmen were expected to report to the study hall; seniors in good standing were free to make their own plans for daily study.

In the middle of the school grounds stood Masters Hall, built in 1921, a great stone structure housing the assembly hall, study hall, library, classrooms, laboratories, and executive offices. Beautiful leaded windows "appropriate to the purpose of each room" were a distinct feature of Masters Hall. Assemblies were conducted by students two out of five mornings

each week. Mathematics classes were limited to fifteen students, and girls were encouraged to "proceed at their own speed" under individual plans set up by instructors. Designed to minimize "uneven preparation at entrance," even this plan appears to have been insufficient for Alice, who recalled that she "found it terribly hard to do algebra and everything else in English after doing it in French."

Although Alice's first year at Dobbs must have been quite challenging, she was still happy to be in the States. She was not particularly athletic, but Dobbs offered amusements such as tennis, horseback riding, and in winter the tennis courts were flooded to provide a good skating surface. In addition, the hilly campus provided opportunities for coasting and skiing. The town of Dobbs Ferry was just a five-minute walk away, so when permitted, Alice could leave campus to enjoy a soda in the drug store or catch a movie at the Embassy Theatre. There weren't many other sources of entertainment in Dobbs Ferry, besides a miniature golf course, during these lean years. The economic depression kept many local residents home listening to the radio or hanging out in the town's pool hall, where those who couldn't afford to play huddled around a large wood-burning stove—provided they brought along a stick of stove wood. Although Alice must have been aware of such deprivations, she was fortunate not to experience them firsthand. Her parents kept her in spending money, wiring as much as one hundred dollars at a time. And on rare occasions, Alice was allowed to go with groups into Manhattan to tour museums or attend plays and concerts.

Alice doesn't appear to have formed any lasting friendships with the girls at the Masters School. None are mentioned anywhere in Alice's papers at the University of Southern California, nor are there even any snapshots

Perry, Missouri, as it appeared in the 1930s when Alice visited the small town. She seems to have had her pick of places to buy a bottle of ice-cold Coca-Cola.

from this period of her life. She may have encountered a certain amount of difficulty fitting in with the other girls at first, and not just because of their obvious cultural differences.

Alice, recalling her teenage years at Dobbs, said in 1964: "Every girl wants to be beautiful, especially in our society where we put such tremendous emphasis on physical beauty. In our culture, according to the advertisements, to be beautiful is to be automatically happy. Supposedly doors open for you everywhere, men swoon, beauty is the key to success . . . I was brainwashed by this concept, which, of course, made me unhappy." Compounding Alice's insecurity was Margaret's fear that Alice would become socially handicapped. "This left Alice feeling somewhat awkward in situations with people she didn't know well," observed Helen Tuttle Votichenko. Alice herself admitted, "As a teenager I was sent off to boarding school . . . At first, I was self-conscious about my chin. Youngsters can be cruel, and I was afraid my classmates would make fun of me . . . I was unhappy for a while, but I refused to let my chin or lack of one bring me an inferiority complex." Alice was still comparing herself

to her mother, whom she regarded as a beauty. It's true that Alice did not have her mother's thick wavy hair or large brown eyes, instead inheriting her looks from the Pearce side of the family. Her hair was thin, even as a teenager, and her nose, in profile, displayed a prominent hook. And her grin was rather toothy. "But she had beautiful eyes and beautiful skin," marveled Cris Alexander.

Alice also possessed an appreciable sophistication, even as a teenager. In 1933, when she spent the Christmas holidays with her grandmother and aunt Josephine in Perry, her elegant attire made quite an impression on Dorothy Williams, who was then thirteen. "She had on a bright red coat—I never will forget it—and it had black sable fur trim. It was the first tuxedo coat I'd ever seen," Williams enthused. "And she had on high heels, black patent leather." That Sunday, Dorothy and her curious friends followed Alice out of the Perry Christian Church and down the street. "We walked half a block behind her to see how she kept those heels on!" Dorothy snickered. "*We* were still in the 'Oxford stage' or 'Mary Jane' or whatever." Dorothy and her set had never known anyone

Sixteen-year-old Alice, dressed in the latest New York fashions, poses for the camera on Easter Sunday 1934, in Mexico, Missouri, where she visited her aunt Josephine.

Meanwhile, Alice was still keenly interested in studying drama. During her second year at Dobbs, she was inducted into *Le Cercle*, the school's French dramatic society, a natural fit because of her French fluency. *Le Cercle* plays, produced since 1919 and performed in French, opened with a synopsis in English for those audience members who may have not known French. Margaret Pearce's scrapbook includes a review of a *Le Cercle* production, noteworthy as the first critique of Alice's acting ability. On March 8, 1935, the society staged *Le Farce de Maître Pathelin*, a comedy written in the mid-1400s, in which Alice played Aignelet, a dim-witted shepherd who gets the best of an unethical lawyer. "The longest applause was for Alice Pearce as Agnelet [*sic*]," wrote the reviewer for the Dobbs newspaper. "Her high-pitched voice and apparent utter stupidity sent the audience into gales of laughter."

Alice spent the summers of 1934 and 1935 with her parents in Paris, sailing across the Atlantic alone both years, returning to the States in time for the beginning of the fall semesters. The summer of 1936 would be different, however, as Bob and Margaret planned to attend Alice's graduation on May 27, after which she would accompany them home to France. Alice's three years at Dobbs, while never boasting any sort of academic achievement, were a time of personal growth and social development. Admittedly, she graduated in the bottom quarter of a class

who attended a private school, let alone someone whose home was Paris, France, so there was quite the fascination.

of twenty-seven "college prep" seniors—with C's in English, algebra, and Bible, and a D+ in Cicero—but Miss Evelina Pierce saw deeper than academic averages. The Dobbs headmistress notated in Alice's file: "Special ability, French dramatics. Charming and delightful. Considerate of others . . . Innate taste and sharp intelligence."

Though Alice did not know Miss Eliza Masters, the school's founder, she was unquestionably filled with a keen sense of that lady's traditions, including the customary Dobbs graduation attire. On that day, Alice, gowned in a white formal, carried a large sheaf of white chrysanthemums bound with a long red ribbon and joined her classmates to hear the address by Mary Woolley, president of Mount Holyoke College. In those days Vassar and Smith Colleges vied for the large majority of Dobbs' college preparatory girls. With Mount Holyoke, they were members of "The Seven Sisters," a group of elite women-only colleges—parallel to their male Ivy League counterparts—all of which predated the Masters School. By graduation day, however, Alice had chosen not to consider any schools from this esteemed set. Instead, she selected one which had only been around for a scant eight years: Sarah Lawrence College, located about six miles away in Bronxville, New York.

CHAPTER SEVEN

Peeps

"The most unusual thing about me was my chin.
I decided to take advantage of it and become a comedienne."

Soon after the Pearces' arrival in Paris, Margaret set about making plans for an "at-home" reception in Alice's honor, which was held at Rosemont on July 9. Margaret had always delighted in hosting teas and dinners for Bob's business associates and their wives, but Alice, who was still very much a shy eighteen-year-old, was ill at ease with such affairs. However, she dutifully indulged her mother's attempts to provide her with experiences for playing the role of hostess. Of course, Margaret's expectations—and Bob's —extended beyond that. Their established wealth and social standing had brought them a long way from Perry and Bellefontaine. They were focused on providing their only child with a future even brighter than their own circumstances had afforded them. As with many of their social peers, Bob and Margaret were counting on Alice to progress from a "good school" to the Junior League to marrying the right sort of fellow. That summer, Margaret was especially intent on getting Alice into the Daughters of the American Revolution (DAR), then a fashionable pursuit for women with social aspirations. Margaret, with Josephine's help, had joined a Missouri chapter in 1934, but as secretary of the Benjamin Franklin chapter of the DAR in Paris, she oversaw the submission of

Alice's membership application, just two weeks before Alice's summer vacation ended. It is doubtless that Alice, in typical teenager fashion, wasn't very keen on her acceptance into the DAR—accomplished in late October—while it was of the utmost importance to her mother. Alice and Margaret, separated by an ocean for nine months each year, were becoming increasingly less alike with each passing semester.

At noon on September 15, 1936, Alice's train departed the Gare Saint-Lazare station, arriving later that afternoon in Cherbourg where she boarded the S. S. *Bremen*, filled to capacity with tourists returning to America. Her travel plans were detailed in a newspaper blurb, calling her "a well-known American resident of Paris." She was also quite well-traveled; this was Alice's fourteenth trip across the Atlantic, her fourth crossing alone. One can only imagine what was going through her head. Not yet nineteen, this timid girl was about to embark on her collegiate life, leaving her parents behind in Europe and for the second time entering a new school full of strangers.

Alice's unique situation set her apart from the majority of the other students at Sarah Lawrence College. In the premiere issue of the school newspaper that fall, Alice and seven other freshmen—from Hawaii, Mexico, Germany, Switzerland, and Japan—were singled out as having come "from the far corners of the earth." It appears that only two of Alice's 113 classmates had also been members of her graduating class at Dobbs; however, she wasn't particularly close to either. Soon, though, she would make lasting friendships with three girls, each of whom, in years to come, would become privy to Alice's darkest secret.

Alice always maintained that it was the reputation of the dramatics department which drew her to Sarah Lawrence. If this is so, one wonders why it took almost two years for her to get her feet wet. She did not enroll in any dramatics classes at Sarah Lawrence until she was a junior, and she did not appear in any stage plays until near the end of her sophomore year. Nonetheless, Alice was perhaps initially impressed with the college because it was so radically different from the Masters School, which had proved quite a struggle for her. No longer would she have to worry about troublesome required subjects like algebra and Latin literature. At Sarah Lawrence, the emphasis was placed on independent study, and Alice could schedule just the courses she wanted, anything from psychology to sculpting. In fact, the overall curricular structure was entirely individualized, boasting a remarkable ratio of more than one teacher for every five students and with "text books playing little part." Students usually took three courses per year and attended class for a total of three hours daily. The administration believed that individual student conferences with instructors, called "dons," were more valuable than any other type of study, so a half-hour was set aside each week for that. In addition, regular field trips into New York City, a thirty-minute train ride away, were integral parts of most courses. Interestingly, the annual tuition, at $1700, was less than that of the Masters School.

Alice found the atmosphere at Sarah Lawrence quite liberating. "They do not worry about rules," one observer noted, "because there are none...There are no penalties for cutting classes, no rules about smoking, no compulsory chapel." In addition, there were no uniforms like Alice had worn at Dobbs. Sarah Lawrence girls' attire was "comfortably careless." Most enticing to Alice, though, was the fact that narrative evaluations were given in lieu of grades. Despite its progressive methods, Sarah Lawrence College appealed to Bob and Margaret because the trustees and the administration still promoted a central goal from its founding day: "to educate young ladies of good families to take their proper place in polite society."

Sarah Lawrence College was the first liberal arts college in the United States to incorporate a rigorous approach to the arts with the principles of progressive education. Its pedagogy was modeled on the tutorial system of Oxford University and the theories of educator-philosopher John Dewey. It was the brainchild of real-estate and pharmaceutical mogul William Van Duzer Lawrence who, at age 84, planned to establish it on the grounds of his estate in Westchester County and named it in memory of his wife. His unexpected death in 1927 prevented him from seeing the realization of his dream, but already the plan had been set into motion. With Lawrence's hilltop residence, Westlands, as the nucleus of the college campus, his architects designed five dormitories, a refectory, and an auditorium and student activities building. Everything was completed and ready for occupancy in time for the fall semester of 1928.

At the helm in 1936 was college president Miss Constance Warren who had seen to it that the school weathered the Depression, despite a drop in enrollment. She characterized Sarah Lawrence as a "pioneer college" which was attempting "to shift the base of college education from the acquisition of a well-ordered body of information to the flexible use of materials and information for the best development of the individual."

"Westlands," where Alice roomed for her first two years at Sarah Lawrence College.

Faced with selecting courses for her freshman year, Alice steered clear of natural sciences and mathematics. Instead, she enrolled in German, ceramics, and child psychology. The language course, for which Alice showed a strong interest, came fairly easy, given that she was already fluent in French and Italian, but at year's end her instructor noted that Alice was apt to make careless mistakes in written work. The art instructor deemed her work as "very satisfactory" with an approach showing "poise and self-confidence in working out her own ideas." As for child psychology—a curious choice—the professor found Alice's achievement "acceptable for the most part," noting that she took little part in class discussions, a logical consequence given her natural shyness.

During her four years at Sarah Lawrence, Alice spent three Christmases with her parents in France, returning in time for the new semester each January. Her regular trips across the Atlantic, novel even to the Sarah Lawrence girls, always made front-page news in the student newspaper. The crossing in January 1937 was particularly rough when the S. S. *Washing-ton* ran into a storm and "many of the passengers were severely injured and shaken up." Alice's leg was hurt during the bumpy voyage; meanwhile rumors swirled that a sailor who lost his life onboard was actually murdered. Alice downplayed her journey when interviewed for the *Campus* article, wisecracking, "That [was] about all the excitement."

During her sophomore year, Alice was still trying to find her fit—academically and socially. She had happily continued her study of German, with her instructor reporting at year's end that Alice showed "unflagging interest and concentration," yet her "reading and writing need care." She had abandoned ceramics for painting, a move that proved very satisfying. The art professor found that her work had "great charm" and was "the expression of a very individual talent." However, Alice struggled with a philosophy course called "Development of Modern Thought." Her professor asserted that the course material, which included an independent study of the works of French critic and historian Hippolyte Taine, required "more of an intellectual approach than she has been accustomed to," but he concluded that by the end of the course, Alice had "gained much in the way of beginning to think out her own position on social and intellectual problems."

Even though Alice had been active in dramatic productions at Les Tourelles, the Collège Montmorency, and Dobbs, she had not yet taken part in any of the productions frequently sponsored by the Sarah Lawrence drama department.

Instead, her extra-curricular activities were devoted to four clubs—French, German, Italian, and art. Her membership in the French Club fortuitously led to close friendships with three fellow members, girls from distinct backgrounds who, like Alice, had been educated in Europe. Elizabeth "Betty" La Branche, almost one month to the day younger than Alice, was a member of the same class. A native of New Rochelle and a 1935 graduate of Miss Hall's School in Massachusetts, Betty had come to Sarah Lawrence after spending a year at The Center for European Study in Florence, Italy. Betty's father, a New York stockbroker, came from an old New Orleans family of wine merchants. Betty was a born leader; within days of her arrival at Sarah Lawrence she had joined the student council. For four years she held positions on various student committees, as well as serving on the staffs of the school newspaper and yearbook. Not only was she admired for her intellect, but Betty was quite athletic, participating in fencing, tennis, golf, squash, archery, and hockey. Her outgoing nature and varied interests were in stark contrast to Alice's attributes—with one exception. Betty simply delighted in performing for Sarah Lawrence drama productions, often playing male leads in the all-girl casts.

Sisters Fredrika and Helen Tuttle were, respectively, one year ahead and one year behind Alice. The talented pair, who had spent their earliest years in Greenwich, Connecticut, couldn't help but be interested in dramatics because their father was film director Frank Tuttle whose career had begun back in 1922 on the Paramount lot in Astoria where he directed the likes of Clara Bow, Gloria Swanson, and Louise Brooks. By the time his daughters arrived at Sarah Lawrence, Tuttle had been bouncing between Hollywood assignments for a decade, directing Bing Crosby musicals

and George Raft crime dramas. By 1929 he and his wife, the former Frederika Staats, separated, and she relocated to Switzerland, taking the girls with her. Mrs. Tuttle, who was associated with the League of Nations, enrolled her daughters at the International School of Geneva, where Fredrika, known to friends as "Teddy," graduated in 1935. Both Fredrika and Helen enjoyed creative writing, especially plays and skits. Like Betty La Branche, they were very active in drama productions from the time they arrived at Sarah Lawrence. These three, but especially Betty and Helen, bonded with Alice, and it may have been their influence which prompted Alice to finally become involved in dramatics at Sarah Lawrence.

Another young lady may have been partly responsible for encouraging Alice to pursue her desire to act. Mary Holland Gordon, known to everyone as "Dutch," was in the same class with Helen Tuttle. Dutch, a native of San Francisco, was completely unfamiliar with the privileged backgrounds of Alice, Betty, and the Tuttle sisters. She spent much of her youth on her parents' farm in northern Oregon where she attended a one-room schoolhouse. "From the beginning, she was an avid reader," recalled Dutch's daughter Melodie. "Schooling herself on Kipling and Dickens early on, she was teased by her schoolmates who called her 'Book-a-Night-Mary.'" With six children to feed, her parents were unable to give Dutch the education she longed for. So, she was sent east to live with her father's relatives, where she attended a "dangerous and sometimes violent" public school in Queens, later graduating from Prospect Hill Country Day School in Newark. However, the New York State Board of Regents denied her admission to any state-funded college, claiming that she did not have enough credits from the Newark school. "Her future would have been bleak," her daughter asserted,

Betty La Branche.

Helen Tuttle.

Fredrika Tuttle.

"Dutch" Gordon.

"had it not been for a teacher who suggested Sarah Lawrence, a college not governed by the Board of Regents." Dutch was accepted on a full scholarship. From the start, Dutch was an enthusiastic participant in Sarah Lawrence stage productions, building sets, acting as stage hand, but also holding her own as a performer who received consistently good reviews in the student newspaper.

Betty, Helen, and Dutch—soon joined by Alice—were in awe of professor Mary Virginia Heinlein who had come to Sarah Lawrence in the fall of 1933 to teach the college's first full-time drama course or, as it was called, the "Dramatics Activity." The slightly built Heinlein, sporting a boyish curly bob, was characterized by her large brown eyes and delicate, expressive hands. One student, who described her as "brilliantly and sometimes caustically witty," maintained that Heinlein's interest in people was so deep and kind that "she makes you like yourself." A student of the Stanislavski method of acting, Heinlein was prone to choose thought-provoking plays—many of them modern or current and often loaded with symbolism—including *Androcles and the Lion*, *Adam the Creator*, and *Liliom*, or others which were considered controversial like *The Children's Hour*. Often following performances, she led discussions about the plays' messages or themes, eliciting responses—and sometimes animated debates—from audience members.

One such after-session was detailed in the student newspaper's review of Ibsen's dreamlike *When We Dead Awaken*, performed on April 20, 1938, and featuring Alice, now a sophomore, in her first documented role in a Sarah Lawrence production. Dressed in a black robe, Alice played "The Sister of Mercy," a silent mysterious figure who accompanies the character of Irene, equally mysterious but gowned in white, who explains to the protagonist, her former lover, "When we dead awaken, we find that we have never lived." Knowing Alice as the zany comedienne she became, it's challenging to picture her in such a role or in a serious work like *When We Dead Awaken*. But one thing is evident: over the next two years, her working relationship with Heinlein would become a key step in her development as a performer, and she would later count Heinlein as "my dearest, closest friend."

Meanwhile, Alice was looking forward to Commencement on June 11. As a sophomore she would receive a diploma for the completion of two years' study; seniors would be presented with degrees for their four years of coursework. Bob and Margaret arrived from Paris on the S.S. *Europa* on May 17, and Alice spent the following weekend with them in Manhattan before they made the trek out to Ohio and Missouri to visit Harry Pearce and Sallie Clark. Alice did not accompany them, as she had spent the Easter holiday that April in Butler, Missouri, where Sallie was now living with Josephine and her husband Paul Dillard. For Bob, the vacation in the States was an especially well-earned getaway. For the past two years as the Spanish Revolution raged on, he had been serving as an intermediary for the transmission of vital records and communications between the New York office and the branches in Barcelona and Madrid. Meanwhile, as war clouds gathered over Europe, Bob's greatest contribution to the National City Bank was yet to come.

The 1938 commencement ceremony took place at noon on the terrace facing Westlands. Twenty-nine seniors, wearing the traditional black caps and gowns, sat facing the guests. Behind them sat seventy-nine sophomores, dressed in white caps and gowns. As guest speaker Dr. Luther Gulick of Bronxville delivered his address on "regional planning," it's likely that many of the students were instead

Alice during her second year at Sarah Lawrence College, 1938.

thinking of their imminent summer holiday. Teddy and Helen Tuttle were planning a long stay in the Adirondacks while Betty La Branche was waffling between taking a trip to Mexico and gaining some acting experience in a summer theatre.

Alice and her parents would almost immediately board the S. S. *Bremen* for Europe. Before settling in Saint-Cloud for the summer, they planned to spend a long vacation on Lake Lucerne in central Switzerland, where Alice would finally have an opportunity to put her German speaking skills to use. Photographs from Alice and Margaret's albums reveal that the Pearces stayed in the Hotel Schweizerhof, built in 1845, where former guests had included Leo Tolstoy, Richard Wagner, French Empress Eugénie, and Margaret's fellow Mis-

sourian, Mark Twain. The Pearces' accommodations provided easy access to the spacious Lido, where they sunbathed next to the clear blue waters of the lake, framed with a breathtaking view of the Alps. Their visit would not be complete without traversing the steepest cogwheel railway in the world, arriving at the top of the Pilatus, a mountain massif overlooking Lucerne. Snapshots taken on this vacation include two rather comical ones of twenty-year-old Alice, the first being a close-up of her in goggle sunglasses and the other an attempted sultry pose while smoking a cigarette.

However, the final days of Alice's summer vacation were not so lighthearted. Tensions in Europe were growing due to reports of Hitler's planned actions against Czechoslovakia. Since the end of the First World War, when the map of Europe was redrawn, three million Germans had been living in that part of Czechoslovakia called the Sudetenland. Hitler wanted to unite all Germans into one nation, and when protests from the Sudeten Germans incited violence from the Czech police, Hitler saw his chance. He mobilized the military and placed German troops along the Czech border. This concerned the French people because their government had long held an alliance with Czechoslovakia. In the days before Alice left Paris on September 14, the tenseness was palpable. "Everywhere one went in Paris the topic of conversation was the war," Alice told a writer for *The Campus* soon after her return to Sarah Lawrence. "Everyone talked to everyone else, and strangers quickly became friends. The danger of war brought people close, whether ditch diggers or bankers." On September 30, the top leaders of Germany, Great Britain, France, and Italy signed the Munich Agreement, whereby France would not provide military assistance to Czechoslovakia in the upcoming German occupation of the Sudetenland, effectively dishonoring the French-Czechoslovak alliance. Hitler announced that the Sudetenland would be his final territorial claim in Europe, and for a short time, this act of appeasement settled the hearts of those in Paris. Meanwhile, Hitler set his sights on the remainder of Czechoslovakia as well as Poland. On October 16—Alice's twenty-first birthday— a watchful President Roosevelt signed a secret order to expand American air power by 15,000 machines per year.

That fall, Alice continued to seriously study painting, with her work showing "charm and substance." "It is extremely personal painting," estimated her instructor, "having something of the simplicity of folk art." (Alice would continue to paint in that same style for the rest of her life, referring to her works as "primitives" and calling herself a "bad Grandma Moses." In 1965, when discussing her hobby of painting, Alice shrugged, "I please myself and a few friends.") As a college junior, she also pursued her interest in German by signing up for a course in German literature, demonstrating, her professor said, an "unflagging and stimulating" participation in class discussions. By this point, Alice seems to have come out of her shell, perhaps as a direct result of her successful course work. She was elected president of the Art Club, and in that capacity initiated a series of drawing classes, held in the evenings, for club members as well as any others interested in learning to draw.

In the meantime, Alice's name appeared more frequently in the student newspaper, eventually becoming so well known that she was often identified in print only by her nickname, "Peeps." The story of how she was given this curious sobriquet has been lost to time, but it's apparent that it came about during her college days. (It was not a pet name used by her parents because she consistently signed all her letters and telegrams to them as "Monk," perhaps short for "Monkey.") The earliest documentation of "Peeps" appears in a humorous blurb in *The Campus* on October 1, 1938, when it was reported that "Peeps Pearce, with a single room, has two beds—one for guests, she explains—and all her bottles and powders are kept in a cabinet strangely resembling a bar." Lots of Sarah Lawrence girls had nicknames; Alice's dear friend Betty La Branche was known to intimates as "Weenie."

Alice was also recognized on campus for her distinctive wardrobe. When visiting Paris, her mother lavished her with designer fashions, particularly those created by Edward Molyneux whose trademark for "impeccably refined simplicity" made him a favorite of European royalty and trendsetting celebrities like Greta Garbo and Marlene Dietrich. Alice's footwear did not go unnoticed either. "Peeps Pierce [*sic*] has a pair of tan rough suede shoes with wonderful soft and thick soles that she wears," wrote a *Campus* editor, "much to the envy of the rest of us, because she got them in Italy, which makes the possibility of our getting any pretty futile." Not only was Alice known as a *fashionista*, but she was also remembered for frequently purging her clothes closet. "Peeps regularly went through her wardrobe and discarded things which were no longer in fashion or useful," recalled Dutch Gordon's daughter Melodie Bryant. "A good habit to have so young!"

In addition to the German literature and painting courses, Alice enrolled in Miss Heinlein's "Dramatics Activity" class in the fall of 1938. For the first semester's major production, Heinlein chose another controversial drama called *Girls in Uniform* which had run on Broadway for a meager twelve performances during the 1932–33 season. *Girls in Uniform* was an English adaptation of Christa

Winsloe's 1930 play *Gestern und Heute* (*Yesterday and Today*). The story revolved around a group of teenage girls in a strict Prussian boarding school and the relationship one lovesick student developed with a kindly teacher. Suspected of lesbian leanings, the girl is hounded into suicide by the rigid headmistress. The production received an enthusiastic review from the *Campus* editor, who called it "the most finished piece of work [the college has] yet seen." The lighting, scenery, and costumes displayed a "professional touch," while the performances were "real, moving and portrayed more depth and feeling than the usual amateur production." Libby Moore and Felia Ford scored the top acting honors, but Dutch Gordon was praised for stepping in the day of the performance to replace a sick cast member. Alice, too, received a nod for her role of—what else?—the French teacher, Mlle. Alaret.

The following March, Alice joined the cast of *Right You Are (If You Think You Are)*, a three-act play by Luigi Pirandello first produced in 1917. An expressionistic parable set in a small Italian town, *Right You Are (If You Think You Are)* concerned the conflicting versions of truth told by Signora Frola and her son-in-law Signor Ponza. Determining which person is demented—and where fantasy meets reality—is the focus of the play. Signora Frola, played by Alice, explains that her son-in-law went mad when her daughter, his wife, died four years previous, then remarried but now fantasizes that the new wife is his old wife. Signor Ponza claims that Signora Frola could not accept her daughter's death, went mad, and only survives by believing that his second wife is actually her daughter. The ambiguities expand as the townspeople press for more information in their attempts to secure the truth. The student newspaper found Alice's performance "enticing," and Heinlein later recalled that Alice played her role "with

sensitivity and unusually interesting insight." Once again, Alice played not a comic part but a straight dramatic role, one which her future fans would have perhaps never imagined.

Six weeks later, Alice missed another chance to utilize her comic ability when she was not cast in *Twelfth Night*. According to the *Campus*, she was placed in charge of the production's musical accompaniment—presumably recordings—and her selections were deemed as "perfectly keeping [the] mood and scene."

At year's end, Heinlein couldn't praise Alice enough, noting on her evaluation, "In everything she has undertaken—and she has undertaken a great deal—she has shown herself to be a responsible, imaginative and efficient worker." As a final note, and as if with surprise, Heinlein added, "In the rehearsals for the revue she revealed a delicious sense of comedy." This revue, let it be understood, was not a production of Heinlein's dramatics department. Instead, it was written, directed, and performed by students of all departments, produced in conjunction with other commencement activities that June. Informal in nature, its organizers called it "more of a party," while stressing that "strenuous work" had been involved in creating scenery, costumes, and all other components. "It will be the culmination of our thoughts, actions, and wishful-thinking, in this way comprising glimpses of the much-touted world-of-tomorrow as well as the past and the ever-present," predicted *The Campus*. It was called "The Children of '39." Unfortunately, no review of the revue exists because by the time it was presented on June 9, the student newspaper had ceased publication for the semester. However, one person in the audience was so impressed with Alice's comedic ability that his response—without a trace of forethought by him or Alice—created a chain reaction which ultimately led to the launch of her professional acting career.

Ed Seiler, rising senior at Princeton, accompanied his roommate Terry Votichenko to Sarah Lawrence that commencement weekend. Votichenko was the steady boyfriend of Alice's friend Helen Tuttle who was receiving her two-year diploma. Seiler was the newly elected vice-president of Princeton's Theatre Intime, a student theatre created in 1920 which produced its own shows without any university support. Seiler and his fellow Intime members were solely responsible for every aspect of the theatre, from acting to directing, fundraising to administrating. As Seiler watched Alice and Dutch Gordon stir up laughs during the commencement revue, he decided that both girls would be an asset to the Intime, which permitted only male members yet relied on outsiders to fill female roles. He invited the girls to come down to Princeton the following September when tryouts would be held for the fall Intime production. "At the time, we thought little of it," remembered Alice, "and dismissed it from our minds."

Even so, by this time Alice was giving serious thought to a theatrical career. Her experiences during her junior year at Sarah Lawrence had prompted a certain amount of self-reflection. She realized that with her looks she would never be accepted as an ingénue and therefore would never achieve leading lady status, but she felt keenly about becoming a professional actress. "I looked in the mirror one day," Alice recalled in 1964. "I took inventory of myself. The most unusual thing about me was my chin. I decided to take advantage of it and become a comedienne." But, of course, Alice's weak chin was simply a physical trait that enhanced her comic expressions. Her real gifts were an innate sense of comedic timing and an expressive delivery—utilizing both her voice and facial muscles—a surefire combination. "Alice was perhaps not the most academically inclined

Ed Seiler, Princeton University Class of 1940, encouraged Alice to perform for the Theatre Intime, which eventually led to her professional acting career.

but loved theater and very much wanted to be an actress," recalled Helen Tuttle Votichenko. "Among her group of theater friends at Sarah Lawrence she was sociable and could be very funny, something of course that would serve her very well later on."

Alice's final year at Sarah Lawrence would provide many satisfying opportunities for growth as a performer, but first she was obligated to make the customary summer voyage to visit Bob and Margaret, despite the prevalent fear that war in Europe was inevitable. On June 10, 1939, while the commencement ceremony was taking place at Sarah Lawrence, President and Mrs. Roosevelt, seventy-five miles away at Hyde Park, were hosting Britain's King George VI and Queen Elizabeth at the Roosevelt home, an unprecedented and significant visit which did not go unnoticed. Franklin Roosevelt realized the necessity of fostering closer ties between the two democracies, and the monarch's visit would become a key component in developing a stronger political and social alliance between the United States and Great Britain. Alice's fears were with her parents for she and everyone else knew that if Great Britain went to war with Germany so would France.

Despite the growing tensions, Alice and her parents found a few weeks that summer to relax on vacation trips, crisscrossing southern France. First, they visited Saint-Jean-de-Luz, where King Louis XIV married Maria Theresa of Spain, and nearby Hendaye, a popular seaside resort. Crossing over into Spain, the Pearces spent some time in Irun, a city recovering from a heavy siege during the recent Spanish Revolution. From there, on to Saint-Jean-Pied-de-Port, a scenic river town in the Pyrenean foothills. Perhaps most enjoyable was their lengthy stay in the South of France, where they sunned themselves at Cannes, explored the markets of Marseilles, and marveled at the Roman monuments in Nimes and the Palais des Papes in Avignon. Journeying back to Paris, they stopped in Carcassonne to tour its medieval citadel, La Cité, and in Saulieu, a walled town in existence since Roman times. The time spent in southern France may not have entirely been a pleasure trip for Bob Pearce, however. He may have been making important contacts in the event that Paris would be attacked.

Meanwhile, Hitler pushed ahead with his plans to attack Poland. On August 26, French prime minister Édouard Daladier sent a message to Hitler saying that France desired peace but that it would fight for Poland should it be invaded. Five days later, anticipating bombardment, the French government began to evacuate 30,000 children out of Paris. Wanting to keep Alice with them as long as possible yet knowing that the sooner she left for America the better, Bob and Margaret had already booked passage for her on the glamorous S. S. Île de France, set to sail on September 1. When that morning arrived, Bob was unable to leave the bank to go with Margaret and Alice to the train station, so Margaret's friend Eleanor Rowe accompanied them. "The boat train for the Île de France pulled out at 9:45," wrote Margaret in her diary, "leaving us waving a sad goodbye to Alice. Eleanor and I went to Sherry's for Coffee and brioche. On leaving Sherry's, Martin showed us the Paris-Midi saying that Germany attacked Poland at 5:30 this morning." Later that day, Margaret was anxious to verify that the Île de France had sailed as planned, so she had Martin, her chauffeur, to drive her to the bank, where she learned from Bob that the ocean liner had been detained due to the attack on Poland.

The Île de France, which sailed late the next day, was destined to be the last civilian ship to leave France before Great Britain and France declared war on Germany on the morning of September 3. Her 1,777 passengers—400 more than her usual number—were mainly American tourists, clamoring to get out of the country. Besides the overcrowded conditions, the passengers' activities were limited by nightly blackouts. In addition, the complete severance of communications with the world for the duration of the voyage made it a "white knuckle" trip. The Île de France arrived safely in New York Harbor on September 9, but other ships were not so fortunate. Sixteen vessels were sunk by torpedoes, mines, or gunfire while the Île de France was crossing the Atlantic. On September 10, a bank porter from the Paris branch arrived at the Pearces' estate with a cable from Howard Sheperd of the New York office, saying that Alice had arrived safely in the States. Ten days later, they received a letter from Alice, describing the voyage. "Her experience on the *Île de France*," wrote Margaret, "will ever be remembered by her." News of Alice's safe return reached Missouri, too. The *Perry Enterprise* declared in a front-page headline, "Alice Pearce Crosses Safely," citing a letter that Sallie Clark had received from her granddaughter. Though no one could have predicted it, this would be Alice's final crossing. Even after the war ended and travel was again safe, she never went overseas. "I hated living in Europe," she later stated. "I don't even want to go back on a vacation."

That month, while Margaret and her household staff were busy covering their windows with blue paper and blackout curtains, setting up their basement *abri* (bomb shelter), and practicing drills with gas masks, Alice, newly elected president of her senior class, was preparing to emcee a student talent show, to be given in the dramatics workshop on September 23. "Alice Perce [*sic*] . . . was the hit of the show," reported *The Campus*. "Portraying the typical old maid, clubwoman of the self-panicking kind, her remarks, actions, and handling of a six-foot fur piece were clever and amusing enough to keep the program moving."

Later that week, Alice and Dutch Gordon trekked down to Princeton. Some weeks previous, Ed Seiler, true to his word, had mailed them an invitation to attend the tryouts for Theatre Intime's fall production. Finding the letter waiting for them when they arrived for the fall semester, the girls couldn't ignore it: a year earlier, the Intime had been cited by *Stage* magazine as "the best serious undergraduate theater group in the country." Dick Koch, Intime president, was set to direct *The Front Page*, Ben Hecht and Charles MacArthur's 1928 comedy-melodrama about tabloid news-

paper reporters on the police beat. Dutch was given the role of Mrs. Grant, the mother of the play's ingénue, and Alice won the part of Jenny, an imbecilic scrubwoman. "My big moment comes at the opening of the second act," Alice told *The Campus*, "when I am scrubbing the floor with emphasis on characterization!"

Rehearsals began on Sunday, October 1, with six nightly performances beginning October 9. Alice and Dutch planned to commute the seventy-odd miles for part of the first week and stay each night in a boarding house for the remainder. By now, Alice was known for her anecdotes, and she didn't disappoint *The Campus* reporter when she shared one about Seiler and Koch taking Dutch and her to inspect the rooming house that Sunday. "[We] were whisked away through the rain to a lovely boarding-house run by a woman who has an eagle-eye and who was wearing carpet-slippers. [We] were led up a long, dark, winding staircase to a room with three iron beds—[she said] she will bring dressing tables later. 'It is seventy-five cents a night,' the eagle-eye said, 'if you don't mind.'"

Unfortunately, we know more about the shabby rooming house and its proprietor than we do of Alice's performance in the play. Albert Parreno, a reviewer for the *Daily Princetonian*, found the production rather "ragged" and its players "incompetent," adding that it gave the impression that the audience had "walked in on a rehearsal." Perhaps Parreno attended the second night's performance, the memory of which left Alice cringing some eight years later. When the student who played the policeman failed to show up, the stage manager fixed Alice with his eye five minutes before curtain and said, "You learn those lines and go on." Alice protested but retired into a corner and hastily conned the script. When she made her entrance, the amazed newspaper reporters of the cast, who

Alice during her senior year at Sarah Lawrence College, 1939–40. Photo courtesy Sarah Lawrence College Archives.

rence, that worked out fine because the administrators counted *The Front Page* as part of Alice's required "field work."

Meanwhile, Alice was blossoming. Not only was she president of the senior class, but she was also president of the Dramatics Activity, all the while continuing her studies of painting, cultural history, and dramatics. That fall, Alice and classmate Betty Williams were jointly responsible for their senior project, a production of Sidney Howard's 1926 drama *The Silver Cord*. Besides performing in the play, Alice and Williams supervised all details from scenery to publicity, assuming full responsibility for the final production which was staged on Alumnae Day, November 16. Dutch Gordon was cast as the smothering, manipulative Mrs. Phelps—a part readily identified with actress Laura Hope Crews who

hadn't been informed of the change, went up in *their* lines. Alice couldn't help; seeing their confusion, the only line she could remember was, "Do you want some catsup?"

Another reviewer mentioned Alice and Dutch, but only in passing: "They did the best they could with parts which were designed originally as nothing but foils to the main action." Still, Alice made a definite impression on the Intime officers, and they would seek her assistance again before the end of the school year. As for her being absent from Sarah Law-

played the part both on Broadway and film—determined to sabotage her sons' relationships with the women they love. Williams played Christina, the wife of Mrs. Phelps' older son, while Alice assumed the role of the younger son's fiancée, Hester. Williams took issue with the school newspaper's "very general and terribly sweet and gentle" review of the play, writing an editorial in *The Campus*, complaining that the reviewer criticized the playwright ("poor thing") while showering the cast with "empty and unsubstantiated praise." Peeps, however, received the reviewer's most detailed praise: "Alice Pearce accomplished an old Bernhardt trick in her scene with Colin Craig by getting suffused with color in a completely convincing fit of hysteria."

Since the situation in Paris prevented Alice from spending Christmas of 1939 there, she shipped off her parents' gifts—four books and some parlor games—before leaving campus for the holidays. She could have gone to Missouri to stay with her grandmother and aunt, but the situation there was less than ideal. Aunt Josephine's husband Paul Dillard, thirty-six years old, had dropped dead of a heart attack in his Warrensburg drug store on December 6, following a bout with "flu-pneumonia" some three weeks earlier. Josephine and Sallie had since moved back into the Clark home in Perry, and their Christmas promised to be very sad. Alice opted to spend her vacation with Betty La Branche on a skiing party in Sainte-Marguerite, Quebec. Although she professed to be "very, very unathletic," Betty reported that by week's end Alice was "magnificent on skis."

Second semester—Alice's final one at Sarah Lawrence—brought even more opportunities for dramatic exploits. By February 8, when the Dramatics Activity had staged *Love of One's Neighbor*, a 1914 satire by Leonid Andreyev, *The Campus'* drama critic had taken Betty Williams' advice to become more assertive. "The majority of the audience did not understand the play," wrote the reviewer. "There seemed to be no coordinated effort on the part of the actors to draw the group on the stage into a common unit." However, Alice and two others in the cast were singled out for "put[ting] vitality and humor into their roles." One month later, Alice played the pivotal role of clever but uneducated Tony Lumpkin in Oliver Goldsmith's 1773 comedy *She Stoops to Conquer*.

At twenty-two, Alice was keeping busy with school assignments and activities, socializing with her classmates, and preparing for graduation, but one wonders what, if anything, was developing in the romance department. The only mention in *The Campus* of Alice having had a date was when she and Betty La Branche attended the Yale-Army football game with two West Point lieutenants in October 1939. Late in her life, Alice recounted, "While I was in college, I dated boys. Some of them actually phoned for a second or third date, and that was very reassuring to my ego. It proved that the boys were interested in me as a person, in me as a character, not because I had a pretty face." Assuming that Alice, by now well-adjusted to her looks, did not have a steady beau during these years, she nonetheless did not lead a solitary existence. She found great satisfaction not only in her friendships at Sarah Lawrence, but also in the camaraderie shared with the fellows of Princeton's Theatre Intime. These young men were fast becoming some of Alice's closest friends, yet there were no indications that any were interested in dating Alice. For some, that may not have been due to any particular characteristic, physical or otherwise, which Alice displayed. In fact, it's likely that some of these guys were not interested in dating girls, period. Be that as it may, Alice felt comfortable around these fellows. To them, she was Peeps, a sweet girl with a zany sense of humor, and ultimately, someone who understood them.

Winter melted into spring, and the semester's dwindling days were jammed with preparations and rehearsals for events at both Sarah Lawrence and Princeton. First on Alice's agenda was "an intimate musical revue," the Intime's contribution to Princeton's annual "house party weekend," set for April 30 through May 4 on campus at the Murray Theatre. By mid-March, Alice was collaborating

Raise You Five: *Hugh Houghton, Alice Pearce, Bob Perry, and Mary Crichton perform in the "Tobacco Wrath" skit.*

rant such a sketch and that it should be eliminated. Perry, noting that none of the letter-writers had even seen the script or attended rehearsals, shot back, "The Intime is not a radical organization in any way. We are giving an intimate musical revue for pure entertainment. If people are bigoted and prudish, they don't have to stay." Dress rehearsals continued behind well-barred doors of the Murray Theatre, while insiders promised that sex and satire would be the keynote of the extravaganza's twenty-odd skits. Included was "Tobacco Wrath," featuring Alice and containing elements from *Tobacco Road, The Grapes of Wrath,* and other modern literary works, a "realistic drama to end all realistic dramas."

Hailed as "the best production the Intime has given this year," *Raise You Five* played to sold-out audiences

with the Intime on "getting the book started and rounding up potential talent to fill the feminine roles." Assisted by six underclassmen, including newly elected Intime president Bob Perry, Bill Callanan, "Bus" Davis, and Mark Lawrence, Alice and the gang created a "fast-moving satirical extravaganza" titled *Raise You Five.* Advance publicity noting that one number would feature a "rowdy satire on American patriotism" aroused the ire of a few New Jersey ladies who wrote letters to Perry, admonishing that "these troubled times" did not war-

each night. "The mood of the evening is satirical...a resounding smack is taken at everything from Groton, T. S. Eliot and Noël Coward to Steinbeck [and] George M. Cohan," Dr. Carlos Baker of the English department enthused. "A particularly able pair of mimes are Miss Alice Pearce, Sarah Lawrence's gift to Princeton; and the Intime president H. Robert Perry Jr. '41 .. . Whether presenting 14 children to a slightly astonished America, scratching her elbows in a Georgia cracker-box, or playing a fugitive game of rummy behind a Mayfair divan Miss Pearce distinguishes herself, while Perry's lampoon of Cohan's jingoist song-plugging, and his Reginald Gardnerisms are masterful handling of these subtle comic gifts." Another reviewer was equally impressed: "[T]he brunt of the show falls on Alice Pearce of Sarah Lawrence, and co-authors Bob Perry and Bill Callanan, comedians *par excellence*. Callanan's monologue entitled 'The Innate Symbolism of Classical Chinese Drama' was sidesplitting . . . And so with 'Conversation Piecemeal,' offering that sure-fire combination of Pearce and Perry in a broad-lined characterization of [Noel Coward] and [Gertrude Lawrence]."

Winning equal praise with Alice and Perry was blonde-haired, blue-eyed Bus Davis, who, as composer of all the tunes, "eclipsed all his former records." "He has again performed the feat of writing unwhistlable melodies that are a delight to the ear," one reviewer noted. "Literate lyrics are supplied by Mark Lawrence but it is the Davis arranging with those clashing dissonant chords that put them over." Little did Alice or Bus know that their association in musical theatre would continue for many years to come.

Raise You Five drew enough attention to be featured in a photo spread in the July issue of *Mademoiselle*. Alice rated two photos, one with the players from "Tobacco Wrath" and another with Perry from "Conversation Piecemeal," cited as the sparkling revue's hit sketch. "We truly thought the play and the featured players were terrific," Alice enthused, "so I graduated with a certain confidence in my 'talents.'"

Coming down from this high may have been a little challenging for Alice, as it seems to have been the climax of her senior year. Once she was back at Sarah Lawrence full-time, though, the frantic pace almost consumed her. First, she had rehearsals for a workshop production of *Alice in Wonderland*, which would culminate

Bob Perry.

Bill Callanan.

Bus Davis.

Mark Lawrence.

with five performances May 22 through May 24. "I staged *Alice in Wonderland* and played the part of the Mad Hatter myself," Alice recalled. "It was a fat role. The tea party and the court room scenes went on forever." *The Campus* reviewer was impressed: "The funny old Mad Hatter was played by Alice Pearce, and she certainly put him across." Next, there was the commencement weekend revue to ready. Although she was not in charge, Alice was a member of the organizing committee—called "Hits and Misses"—which had been formed the previous fall in response to the hit revue of 1939. Rehearsals for "Opus 1940," written entirely by students, began on May 27 with director Helen Tuttle, now studying at Columbia University, being called in to whip things into shape. "We pick up where *Gone with the Wind* left off," said organizer Helen Wyatt. "Betty La Branche and Alice Pierce [*sic*] play comedy relief." The revue, performed on June 6 and 7, "with its lively skits, catchy tunes, snappy dances, and a monologue by Alice Pearce (under a drier) goes with a bang from the first song on."

Meanwhile, some 3,600 miles away in Paris, Bob and Margaret were ably coping with the dire situation there. Despite Bob's strenuous banking activities, he had found time for important outside associations, and he was "often informally consulted by Allied Military Authorities." He had served as vice-president and treasurer of the American Chamber of Commerce, and continued to serve as director of the American Hospital and trustee of the American Library in Paris. However, his association with the American Club of Paris, of which he was vice-president for three annual terms, had afforded both him and Margaret with indispensable opportunities to meet other Americans living in and around Paris. These friends became their support system not only in the good times but, most importantly, during the turbulent months of the war. Bob found solace in his Sunday golf games with Jack Wright, a longtime executive with the International Telephone and Telegraph Corporation. A lifelong bachelor, Jack often spent weekends at Rosemont, the Pearces' home in Saint-Cloud. To Alice, he was always "Uncle Jack." Other regular visitors at Rosemont were American expatriate and artist Morgan Heiskell and his German-born wife Ilse, who were particularly close to the Pearces. Margaret often lunched with Ilse at places like the Ritz and Maxim's.

The most elite members of the Pearces' social set were Count Jacques Aldebert de Chambrun, who had served for many years as an artillery general in the French army, and his wife, the Comtesse de Chambrun,

General Aldebert de Chambrun and his wife Clara, arriving in America aboard the S. S. Zaandam, September 1939.

occasional visitors in the Pearce home. Général de Chambrun, who retired from military service in 1933, had since become the director of the National City Bank in Paris. His wife, the former Clara Longworth of Cincinnati, patron of the arts and Shakespearean scholar, was the author of some fifteen books, half of which were written in French. Both had connections to Washington, D. C.—the General's birthplace—where his father had been associated with the Embassy of France and where her brother Nicholas Longworth had served

as Speaker of the United States House Representatives. The de Chambruns lived in a posh apartment at 58 rue de Vaugirard, overlooking the Luxembourg Gardens.

Margaret also continued to host DAR members in her home and even found time to take up golf and resume her piano lessons. However, most of her free time outside the home was spent at a nearby church where she made bandages and sewed clothes for refugee children from Belgium and Alsace. She continued to supervise her full-time household staff of cook, maid, chauffeur, and gardener, often joining in by making jam, polishing furniture, and digging in the large garden, which boasted hundreds of jonquils and tulips in the spring and abundant roses and sweet peas in summer. The Pearces' evenings at home invariably ended with a game of rummy or Chinese checkers while listening to radio newscasts.

Even by mid-spring, the war seemed far away to most Parisians. So when Howard Sheperd sent a cable from the bank's New York office on April 29 asking the Pearces to come to the States for a "short visit," they readily agreed. Sheperd lived in Bronxville and therefore maintained a close connection with Alice, and he knew how much it would mean to her and her parents if they could attend her graduation on June 8. The Pearces planned to sail on May 18, and their friends began planning "going-away" parties for them. But on the morning of May 10, when they awoke to sirens and "D. C. A. (*Défense contre les aéronefs*) guns," they knew that something was horribly wrong. Four hours later, they learned from a radio broadcast that Germany had invaded Holland, Belgium, and Luxemburg. "We realize that the war has started," Margaret wrote in her diary. "Elise and Emma heartbroken and my house is in tears. Our trip to the U. S. A. is of course off as Bob can never leave." Yet Margaret remained optimistic; a week later she planted corn in her vegetable garden. The following day, which had been intended for their departure, she wrote, "Sun shining this morning and I feel fine. I am going out to do my work with courage in my heart. The French army is marvelous, and the French people are brave." The next day, Margaret went upstairs to collect Alice's baby clothes and everything else she could spare for the Belgian refugees.

June 8, 1940, was a warm sunny day in Bronxville. At eleven o'clock that morning, graduation exercises took place on the terrace of Westlands, just as it had two years earlier when Alice received her two-year diploma. This time, instead of white caps and gowns, Alice and thirty-four other seniors were dressed in black. The commencement speaker was Stuart Chase, noted economist, social theorist, and writer. His topic, "The Tyranny of Words," was chosen from his 1938 book of the same title, but interestingly not from his most recent book, *The New Western Front*, in which he advocated United States non-interventionism. His remarks were not recorded for the student newspaper, as it had ceased publication before Commencement Day, but one wonders if he did in fact address the war in Europe. Whether or not he did, Alice's mind was fixed on the situation in Paris, wondering the exact location of her parents and what they were doing at that moment. After the ceremony, all around her, the Sarah Lawrence graduates were exchanging hugs and kisses with their parents and even grandparents—bittersweet circumstances for a solitary girl looking on, holding her diploma. The only other memento from the day would be an overexposed candid snapshot showing Alice in cap and gown amid the line of graduates.

CHAPTER EIGHT
New Faces

"If I don't land (and be able to hold) a job soon I'll feel even more stupid and inadequate."

On October 16, 1939, Margaret Pearce wrote in her diary: "Alice's birthday. We have thought of her much of the day. She is twenty-two today. Born during the last great war, her life has been full of the words: *avant la guerre, pendant la guerre, depuis la guerre.* And now again, *pendant la guerre.*" And so it would be for Alice—and for millions of others—for the rest of her life.

The Germans began to bomb Paris on June 3, 1940. Margaret was lunching at Sherry's "while hell broke over Paris." "There is no way to describe the bursting of bombs, you have to hear them," she wrote in her diary that night, " . . . the tales of sorrow, fires and death in the city. The small son of one of the bank men was killed. When will this all end?"

Exactly one week later, Mussolini declared war on France and Britain. When Margaret dropped by the bank that afternoon to see Bob, he informed her that they must leave Paris the next morning. The directors of the National City Bank in New York were concerned that, should the Nazis enter Paris, "certain French directors might be held as hostages and endanger the interests of the establishment." Three months earlier, the bank had arranged for its operations to be moved, some three hundred miles away, to an annex of the Hotel Bristol at Le Puy-en-Velay, an isolated town in southern France, surrounded by high hills and the famous conical volcanic forms of the region. The bank's staff had reserved lodging nearby in an ancient castle overlooking the River Loire. All night long, to the accompaniment of cannon fire and gunfire, the Pearces prepared for the exodus, packing away their most treasured possessions and praying that Rosemont would withstand the bombing during their absence. At 4 a.m. on June 11, they loaded their chauffeured Buick, and, accompanied by their cook, maid, Bob's secretary, and Alice's wirehaired fox terrier Jackie, "[drove] off into the unknown."

"We leave Paris by the Porte d'Orléans and then the long caravan starts," wrote Margaret. "Millions of silent, sad people leaving Paris today, by automobile, truck, bicycle, wagon, horse, donkey, walking. In this long train was every conceivable kind of car and some people had chairs, blankets, bird cages, chickens, sewing machines, big dogs, little dogs, calves, pigs, cats, etc. We move at a snail's pace. You start the car, move the length of the car and stop again. We left Paris at six o'clock in the morning and at six o'clock in the evening after twelve hours we had gone thirty-seven miles . . . The day was hot. However, I must pay tribute to these thousands of French people fleeing from the enemy—many cars were driven by women, including trucks—there was never any anger or confusion other than that caused by congested traffic . . . Planes roared overhead and we prayed that they were French planes. This strange fog, which was over Paris and [over] part of our route, we now realized was artificial and made by the French to protect from bombing the long line of refugees."

The Pearces and their party finally arrived at the Hotel Bristol on the night of June 12. The following morning, after inspecting the castle intended for their stay, they determined it was too far from town and too ill-equipped for their use. Instead they settled on a place nearer Le Puy—the Villa Hermitage—and after four days of cleaning the "dirty, neglected house," they moved in. By this time, German troops had marched into Paris, beginning a four-year occupation of the "City of Lights." On June 22, France signed an armistice with Germany, and the country was split into two parts, with the north being governed by the Germans and the south being under the control of Marshal Philippe Pétain, the head of the French State. "I have decided to close my diary today," wrote Margaret on June 24. "When I started this day-by-day message, my heart was full of hope, and I expected to end this diary on a note of victory and triumph. However, France is defeated, and in some inexplicable way, I have been defeated, too." The Pearces and their comrades would reside in the unoccupied "Free Zone" until it would become necessary for them to return to the States. Bob Pearce would long be commended by the National City Bank of New York for having transported the assets of the Paris branch to the Free Zone, from where they were successfully liquidated.

Alice, in the meantime, was spending part of her summer vacation as the guest of Betty La Branche in the Berkshires. Had the war not come along, she would have perhaps spent that summer in France, but then again, perhaps not. Almost a year previously, she and Betty, dreaming of their futures, had determined that after graduation they would "get an apartment in New York." As for their career plans, well, those were much less firm.

"While [Betty and I] were taking life easy after graduation," Alice said, "we talked about our [apartment-to-be]. Every day we ripped ads out of the *Tribune*, and made a circle around the possibilities and clipped the lists together." In late June, they converged on Manhattan, thinking it would only take a day or so to find and rent a suitable apartment on the east side. When their lists proved unhelpful, they walked down one street to the East River, and up the next street to Lexington Avenue and so on, "stopping in wherever [they] saw an inviting rental sign." After two weeks of this expansive search, "we had lost our sense of values," Alice wisecracked, "and came very close to engaging an apartment with the kitchen in the bathroom." But a week and a half later, they stumbled upon a six-story red brick apartment house, still under construction, at 349 East Forty-Ninth Street. Satisfied that their search could now be concluded, Alice and Betty signed a lease on 2-H, a one-bedroom apartment expected to be ready for occupancy at the end of August.

Earlier that summer, Bob Perry, who had decided to abandon his studies at Princeton and pursue acting full-time, had suggested to Alice that she join him as a member of the Garrick Players, a summer stock group which would open in Maine at the New Kennebunkport Playhouse on July 2. Having performed there the previous summer, Perry assured Alice that he could persuade playhouse owner Robert Currier to take on Alice as an apprentice. She could become familiar with all the workings backstage and in the house, everything from assisting with makeup to handing out playbills. The experience would be worthwhile, Perry told her. That year Currier had worked diligently, sometimes alone and in freezing weather, to convert a 150-year-old barn into a

Manhattan Island, 1940s: the New York that Alice Pearce knew. For more than twenty years, she lived in view of the Queensboro Bridge, upper right.

proper theatre with "three hundred comfortable seats and an excellent view of the stage."

Currier was closely associated with dramatist Booth Tarkington, a longtime summer resident of Kennebunkport and sponsor of the Garrick Players. That summer, he proudly presented his third annual "Booth Tarkington Drama Festival," staging two of the playwright's works, each for a week's run, beginning July 29 and ending August 10. *Magnolia* was followed by *Karabash*, Tarkington's recently reworked version of

his drama *Poldekin*, which had run briefly on Broadway in 1920. Alice met Tarkington on the evening of August 11 when he invited all twenty-six members of the Garrick Players to dinner at his boathouse, "The Floats."

Two nights later, the Playhouse's bill switched to *Cradle Snatchers*, a Jazz Age farce by Russell Medcraft and Norma Mitchell, which had been filmed as a silent with Howard Hawks as director. The plot surrounded three unhappy, middle-aged housewives who teach their philandering husbands a lesson by starting affairs with young college men. Alice and two other actresses, appearing as the "facetious goodtime seekers" cavorting with the husbands, "rate[d] praise for their stage ease and performance." The only other documented production in which Alice appeared that summer was Clifford Goldsmith's hit comedy *What a Life*. When interviewed years later, she never mentioned the Kennebunkport experience very much, except to say that she "paint[ed] scenery and ma[de] intermission coffee."

By the time Alice returned to New York, Betty had secured a job with Macy's, learning quickly that working in the city's most famous department store "was no church bazaar." On her feet six days a week, being shifted from one department to another, and dealing with irate customers would lead Betty to consider the job as a "fifth year of college," with much the same type of problem solving which she had encountered at Sarah Lawrence. When their new apartment became ready for occupancy, it was up to Alice, still not employed, to move their things. "It had turned out quite nicely," Alice quipped, "except we had thought there was to be another window, an extra closet, and four feet more on the living room." When it was time to select colors for the walls, Alice decided Sunset Pink "would be most becoming to our personalities. I chanced to ask the painter if he had any apartment in the same color, and he said he had. Sunset Pink turned out to be bright orange; when I timidly inquired why the paint was not the same shade as the sample, he said—'Oh, the chart—that's faded.'"

That fall, when Alice began to make the theatrical rounds she learned that Broadway was not waiting with open arms for her. "I wore out my shoe leather and my spirits," she sighed. "Peeps says that the number of comediennes, like the number of other type actresses," reported the *Sarah Lawrence Alumnae Magazine*, "is far in excess of the theatrical demand for them." In the meantime, "Peeps" had to support herself. So, in November, Alice, too, joined the ranks of Macy's employees, beginning her career in the "Budget Underwear" department, selling bloomers—a stint she would not pleasantly recall, especially the harried pace of the Christmas shopping season. However, she did so well that Macy's appointed her head of the entire bra and girdle department. Day in and day out, though, Alice fueled her dream of breaking into show business, reassuring herself that one day it would happen.

Meanwhile, Bob and Margaret were not at all happy about Alice's career plan. Some of their distress would be relieved when they were finally instructed by the bank to leave Europe. Sailing from Lisbon on December 20 aboard the U. S. S. *Siboney*—a naval ship originally used to transport troops during the First World War and now chartered to return Americans fleeing Europe—the Pearces arrived in New York eleven days later. For the time being, Bob would be based in the New York office, so he and Margaret soon settled into a rented home at 1 Leonard Road in Bronxville, next door to the Howard Sheperds. Their much closer proximity to New York would afford them the opportunity for serious discussions with Alice about her future.

Even though her parents had been supportive of Alice's study of dramatics, they had secretly hoped that "Sarah Lawrence College would remove the theatre urge." When Alice remained firm in her intentions, Bob and Margaret did not hide their feelings. "They knew so little about the theater at the time," Alice later explained, "that they were wary about it and hoped I might express a desire to do something else." Among friends, Alice voiced concerns about her parents' misgivings. Costume designer Miles White asserted that Margaret, in particular, "did not approve of Alice's theatrical connections," while Cris Alexander mused, "They probably just didn't

Bob Pearce (left) visits his father Harry at 217 North Detroit Street, corner of Pearce Avenue, in Bellefontaine, Ohio, March 1941.

being cared for by a live-in housekeeper. From there they trekked to Albuquerque and on to the Grand Canyon. Never having seen California, Alice joined in them in Los Angeles for a few weeks' stay, during which they toured Yosemite National Park. The trip was destined to become their final family vacation.

Prior to her trek west, Alice had ditched the job at Macy's to resume her rounds to various New York casting offices, all to no avail. The only acting experience she had managed to find was an occasional appearance on *The Experimental Playhouse of the Air*, a local radio program designed perhaps to piggyback on the success of CBS' prestigious *The Columbia Workshop*. *The Experimental Playhouse of the Air* was the brainchild of Alfred Dixon, who also served as the show's director. Debuting on January 11, 1941, on New York's WOV, this program featured scripts "written by English professors at Eastern colleges" and casts made up of nonprofessionals, including "students, clerks, salesmen, beauticians, and secretaries." Dixon taught speech classes at Sarah Lawrence once a week, and given Alice's reputation there, she was perhaps recommended for one of his initial broadcasts.

know what to make of her." As for her parents' desire for Alice to marry well and assume the role of a socialite, Patricia Wilson asserts, "Oh, Alice was much too down-to-earth for that. That was nonsense for her. She was right down there in the nitty-gritty of establishing a career. You would never know that she had a socialite background herself." Meanwhile, Margaret did not hide her disapproval from friends and family. "Oh, how well I know that!" exclaimed Dorothy Williams, who was Sallie Clark's longtime hairdresser. "I remember Margaret and them talking about how they didn't like Alice being on the stage." Neither were the Pearces happy about Alice—a Sarah Lawrence graduate, for heaven's sake—selling panties at Macy's.

As the winter of 1941 neared its end, Bob took a lengthy and well-deserved vacation. He and Margaret planned a train trip out west, stopping first in Bellefontaine on March 15 to visit Bob's relatives. For eight nights they stayed with his aged father Harry Pearce, now

Alice remained very much a presence at her alma mater for the first two years following her graduation. For "Home Talent Night" on September 21, 1940, she and Betty reprised their numbers from the previous spring revue, and they would return to perform in a revue for

Alumnae Weekend the following May. When introduced for the latter, Alice "strolled out intwined [*sic*] in furs and balancing a two-foot feather on her hat. Expressing her sentiments on being an alumna, she ended up by saying, 'Of course I'm a Wellesley girl myself.'"

All the while, Alice maintained close ties with her Theatre Intime friends. Several times during the 1940–41 school year, she traveled down to Princeton to collaborate with Bill Callanan, Bus Davis, and Mark Lawrence on twenty-one skits for *Pick Up Six*, the "revue to end all revues," which would be performed at the Murray Theatre for five nights beginning May 6. Well aware that *Raise You Five* was yet unfaded in the minds of its spectators, the *Pick Up Six* team was challenged with the task of improvement without duplication. Composer Davis and lyricist Lawrence created nine musical numbers which faculty reviewer Carlos Baker would find "less distinguished" than those from the previous year. While Baker singled out "West of the Sierras"—rendered by Alice and sophomore Robert McSpadden—as one of the funniest numbers, he found "But the People Were Nice," performed by Callanan, Lawrence, and Tom Barbour, as nothing short of magnificent. He praised Alice: "[She] fingers a very suburban fox neckpiece with that Helen Hokinson air which has endeared her comedy to Princeton audiences." He was also impressed with cast member Nancy Lawrence, younger sister of Mark Lawrence, who "moves from Brooklynese to Cockney to flat Jerseyesque with the savoir faire of a veteran linguist."

Mark and Nancy were the youngest children of David Lawrence, Washington-based columnist and editor of *United States News*, which later merged with another of Lawrence's publications to become *U. S. News & World Report*. Mark Lawrence, like his Intime cohorts Callanan and Davis, was an English major. Swarthy

yet blue-eyed, Mark was also the newly elected president of Princeton's Triangle Club, a touring musical-comedy troupe. One of the university's longest-standing organizations, the Triangle Club was known for its tradition of presenting an all-male kickline in drag. Under Mark Lawrence, the Triangle Club would produce its first show in a revue format during the 1941–42 academic year, possibly due to the successes of the Intime's revues of 1940 and 1941. Of all the fellows Alice worked with at Princeton, Mark would become the one with whom she was the most closely associated, especially during the postwar years. In fact, their future partnership would give a major boost to her career.

In the meantime, someone else whose very name was synonymous with revues stepped into Alice's life. Broadway producer Leonard Sillman was in the audience for the Saturday night performance of *Pick Up Six* on May 10. Alternately described as colorful, relentless, innovative, and obnoxious, Sillman had been stage-struck since his prepubescent days in his native Detroit. In 1923, at age fifteen and alone, he stormed New York City to study dance at the Ned Wayburn studio, where he learned enough to replace Fred Astaire when *Lady Be Good* went on the road in 1925. Following a vaudeville stint, he arrived in Hollywood where he taught dance to silent film stars trying to break into the talkies. His first revue *Low and Behold*, produced at the Pasadena Playhouse in 1933, was brought to Broadway the following year and became a hit as *New Faces*. Since then, Sillman, always scouting for new talent, had produced four revues on Broadway, one of which—*New Faces of 1936*—was quite successful. Years later, stage and film critic Rex Reed would describe Sillman's modus operandi: "[He] made fierce demands on [his] material, hired the most gifted lyricists, composers

Leonard Sillman, circa 1945.

and sketch writers in show business to execute [his] requests, and then turned the results over to fresh, unique performers who almost invariably became stars." Among those who had been given their first Broadway roles by the frenetic Sillman were Henry Fonda, Imogene Coca, and Van Johnson.

Currently, Sillman—bouncing back from his recent Broadway flop—was planning yet another "small, intimate revue" in the same vein as his previous *New Faces* productions. He was impressed enough with *Pick Up Six* ("one of the best intimate musical revues I've ever seen") to suggest that the Intime take it on the road that summer. At the after-party that night, he made a beeline for Alice, telling her that he thought her "natural instincts and expert timing" were a perfect fit for his next *New Faces* revue. "Talent is not enough," Sillman later said, explaining his method for choosing new finds. "I look for personality that

must come through in a performer." The fast-talking Sillman saw all of that in Alice Pearce, and he asked her to come audition for him, which she did on May 22. She was hired on the spot for a part in his new revue. Dazzled, Alice sighed, "My hopes were high again. My break had come."

What Alice didn't know was that Sillman had no financial backing for his proposed show. This was of no consequence to the plucky Sillman because he was an old hand at raising funds to get a show off the ground. In 1933, during the depths of the Depression, he had faced the same dilemma when trying to find a backer for his first Broadway revue. Then, as now, his show was considered too much of a risk because of its complete cast of unknowns. However, Sillman devised a revolutionary plan. "We would raise our money in small pieces, rather than go for the one big bite from one single Croesus. We would pick up the small pieces from a variety of backers by playing for them not merely our words and music but our whole damned show. From beginning to end. And the entire company would do it." This method, known as a backer's audition, eventually became the standard procedure for raising money in the Broadway theatre, and Sillman was immodest enough to take credit for the idea. "It was never done like that before we did it," he crowed.

Dependent upon the volume of pledges, backer's auditions could go on for months. For Sillman's first Broadway revue—eventually called *New Faces of 1934*—a total of 135 auditions was performed over a period of six months before enough funds were assembled. However, it would take much longer than that for the current revue to achieve sufficient backing. As the summer and autumn months dragged by, Alice began to wonder if her big break would happen after all. The resilient Sill-

The apartment complex which included 31 Sutton Place South, 1939.

man predicted that the revue would open on Broadway in the early months of 1942.

During this lull, Alice was called back to Princeton to appear in a Theatre Intime production. *Three White Leopards,* "a [three-act] play of faculty life" written by Princeton underclassman Lionel Wiggam, opened for a five-night run on December 12, 1941. Broadway actress Katherine Emery, whose best-known credit was the original production of *The Children's Hour,* appeared in the leading role of a college professor's wife while Alice played the family's insolent maid. Student reviewer Phil Quigg praised Alice: "[W]e cannot resist casting a special bouquet of crushed sun flowers to Alice Pearce, veteran Intime trouper and the funniest thing in skirts. In her insignificant role of Agnes, she might easily steal the show, but is satisfied to give the audience the merriest moments of the evening in her all-too-brief appearances."

The bombing of Pearl Harbor occurred during Alice's rehearsals for *Three White Leopards,* and just as Margaret had predicted, Alice would gauge her life using this crucial mile marker. Five of her best friends at Princeton would enlist in the armed services; two of them would not return home safely.

In January 1942, Alice and Betty La Branche moved six blocks north to 31 Sutton Place South, a five-story complex of apartments, built in 1899, where they rented a one-bedroom unit. Situated between East Fifty-Sixth Street on the north and East Fifty-Fifth Street on the south and bounded by the East River, their new home was part of a cozy enclave of writers, jazz musicians, and theatre and nightclub performers. The location also attracted Bob and Margaret who soon made their home in the same building, but in a larger apartment fronting East Fifty-Fifth and commanding a view of the river. On Saint Patrick's Day, Bob was appointed a vice president of the National City Bank, and thus their subsequent relocation from Bronxville was a sensible move. One wonders how Alice, now twenty-four and relishing her independence, felt about having her parents as neighbors after living apart from them for such a long while.

Bob wanted Alice to be certain that an acting career was what she really wanted, while domineering Margaret warned her that "the theatre was an unreliable business and [she] ought to have a trade to fall back on." A compromise—of sorts—was reached. Bob, who agreed to allow Alice to use the family name professionally, suggested that she give the acting field ten years. ("I thought that was an interesting leeway," Alice later admitted.) And Margaret offered to treat Alice to a course in typing. "So I went to a [YWCA] and took shorthand and typing and graduated with a B plus, and I was so proud," beamed Alice.

Eventually, Alice was even prouder because she would never be required to put those secretarial skills to use. But in 1942, she came quite close to it. Although Leonard Sillman

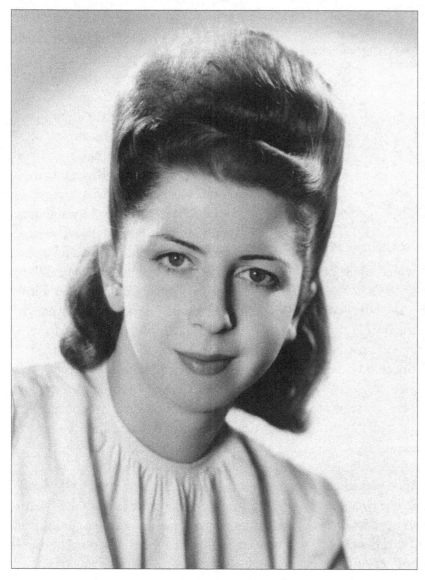

Alice Pearce, 1942, just before her Broadway debut.

was settled last Monday night. I hope rehearsals can start soon because if I don't land (and be able to hold) a job soon I'll feel even more stupid and inadequate. I've been following up job possibilities but nothing has materialized as yet."

Sillman claimed that he spent more than two years searching for his current crop of "new faces," auditioning some 300 young people, covering "every imaginable source of talent ranging from dancing schools and stock companies in tank towns to the smart atmosphere of New York's model agencies." He whittled the list down to fifteen young people. Besides Alice, who was one of the first he had signed, there were several from the nightclub circuit including dancer Tony Farrar and "riff singer" Ann Robinson, as well as radio soap opera actors Ralph Lewis, Laura Deane Dutton, and John Lund. From modeling agencies came Doris Dowling and Marie Charton, who had recently wed Lund. Sillman found Canadian singer Diane Davis working in vaudeville and California native Hie Thompson performing a solo dance act with Jimmy Dorsey's orchestra. Easily, all of these folks had more professional experience in the entertainment world than Alice. She was an authentic "new face."

kept promising that his new revue would begin rehearsals at any time, Alice began to feel as though he was stringing her along. Meanwhile, she tramped up and down Broadway in search of jobs, "flying from one audition to another and 'doing her stuff' for a variety of haughty stage directors, producers' assistants, and other office help." She was consistently turned down. In late October, she expressed her frustration with both Sillman and the job search: "I called Leonard Wednesday and he said 'everything'

After "some 80 tedious auditions," many of which, Alice said, were held in lobbies and rest

The cast of New Faces of 1943. *Bottom row, left to right: Tony Farrar, Dorothy Dennis, John Lund, Alice Pearce. Second row: Laura Deane Dutton, Hie Thompson, Doris Dowling, and Robert Weil. Third row: Kent Edwards, Diane Davis, Ralph Lewis, and Marie Lund. Top row: Ilsa Kevin, Irwin Corey, Ann Robinson, and Leonard Sillman.*

rooms, Sillman finally had enough backers for his long-promised revue. Rehearsals began in early November. In the midst of these frantic preparations, Alice's grandfather Harry Pearce died. Bob and Margaret returned to Bellefontaine for the funeral service, but it was impossible for Alice to leave New York.

Meanwhile, last-minute changes to the revue were ongoing. Sillman had engaged Lund to write the majority of the show, which Sillman had titled, not *New Faces*, but *New Shoes* instead. One month later, Sillman had changed his mind again, renaming the revue *New Faces of 1943*. The sketches were directed by neophyte Lawrence Hurdle, with Charles Weidman and John Wray serving as choreographers. Opening on December 22 at the Ritz Theatre, *New Faces* marked the Broadway

debut of Alice Pearce and all but three of the other fourteen newcomers.

The reviews were, at best, lukewarm. "*New Faces* isn't any fun," *Variety* yawned. "Fresh, eager faces and brisk staging fail to save amateurish material. Only seasoned stars could do that." *Billboard*, calling the show "adolescent and unclever," admitted that the new faces were young and pretty but that they "had no body to hold them up." Rosamond Gilder of *Theatre Arts* deemed *New Faces* as a "sketchy affair more amusing for its ingenious war-time devices for saving money and materials in costumes and scenery than for any brilliant new talents it disclosed." Burns Mantle of the *Daily News* joined *Variety* in its complaint that Sillman was charging top admission prices for a show populated by unseasoned per-formers: "Two dollars as a top figure would work to the show's advantage." (Sillman was charging $3.30 for top seats.) Sillman heeded Mantle's suggestion, lowering the top prices to $2.20, and five weeks later, *New Faces* was still selling tickets, despite *Variety's* prediction of "only a brief stay." Mantle surveyed the situ-ation: "This [current success] may be in part due to the prevailing wartime boom in the-atregoing, but it also can be traced to the fact that the young newcomers have been working hard with their material and are giving better entertainment that it was possible for them to give under the nervous strain of their big-time debuts." Sillman argued that a show like *New Faces*, featuring not only new performing art-ists but also new directors, writers, and scenic and costume designers, "deserved some boost." "If it is true that the theatre needs new blood," he insisted, "*New Faces* is more than doing its share to fulfill that need."

Alice appeared in six of the fourteen sketch-es, including "Tea for Three," which had been written by Bill Callanan and Bus Davis for *Pick Up Six* but slightly amended by Lund. The morning after the opening, she received a nod here and there from the critics. John Anderson of the *New York Journal-American* wrote: "Alice Pearce has a distracted goofiness that is at its best in a burlesque English love affair." Wilella Waldorf of the *New York Post* found Alice "often fun" and that she should "probably be labeled an eccentric comedienne." Meanwhile, *Billboard* gave credit to Alice for "carr[ying] off the comedienne roles with some

ridiculous enough antics, especially in [the sketch] 'The Star's the Thing'," but found most of the skits "embarrassingly unfunny."

More than forty-five years later, fellow actor John Lund remembered Alice best as the prima donna in "Richard Crudnut's Charm School," a miniature operetta he wrote with Lee Wain-er, satirizing beauty-instruction schools. "She was really marvelous," Lund recalled, "flatting and sharping with a kind of insane exuber-ance." Charles Weidman, who choreographed the ballet for this act, considered Alice the best comedian in the show. "She's the female lead," he insisted, praising Alice's singing and dancing ability. "She's a very cute girl who has everything. Everything!"

Viewed then and today as one of Sillman's lesser ventures, *New Faces of 1943* closed after 94 performances. ("We limped through four months," quipped Alice.) In his chatty 1959 autobiography, Sillman spared only two sar-donic paragraphs for the production. "I picked 1943—the middle of the war—as the year in which to produce the third *New Faces*. The timing was peculiarly propitious," he wise-cracked. "No cast ever fought harder—among themselves."

Despite the lackluster reviews, Sillman claimed that on the day after *New Faces of 1943* debuted four of his new talents—John Lund, Ilsa Kevin, Tony Farrar, and Alice—had received job offers, either as replacements in current attractions or for roles in forthcoming plays. In Alice's case, the proposition failed to materialize because she would not be seen on any Broadway stage for almost two years fol-lowing *New Faces*. The majority of Sillman's cast quickly faded from the Broadway scene—even the critics' darlings Tony Farrar and Ann Robinson—while Alice, Lund, and Irwin Corey would go to make names for themselves.

Alice Pearce would remain indebted to Leonard Sillman for being the first to recognize her talent and give her a chance that others could only dream about, but she would also applaud the fast-talking showman for introducing her to another "new face," someone who was too nervous to perform in front of the footlights, someone who had rubbed elbows with celebrities on both sides of the Atlantic, someone who was attracted to her sweet disposition and zany brand of humor, someone . . . who would become the love of her life.

CHAPTER NINE

Johnnie

"I think of you all day (and that part of the night when the pill has worn off) and wonder where you are and what you are doing."

The brilliant sun beat down on the hatted head of Alice Pearce as she maneuvered her way through the sidewalk throng on the afternoon of May 22, 1941. By three o'clock, the mercury would reach ninety-one degrees, making it the hottest day in New York City since the previous July. Alice would later call it "a red-letter day," but not because of the unseasonable weather. This afternoon she would audition for Leonard Sillman's upcoming revue. While it would eventually lead to the beginning of her theatrical career, the occasion burned brightly in her memory for yet another reason—it was the day she met John Rox. Rox, whom Sillman introduced as his associate of almost ten years, had written the music and lyrics for some of the numbers in Sillman's latest Broadway venture, *All in Fun*, a revue which closed after only three performances the previous December.

As she stood there in Sillman's office, chatting with the two men, Alice was instantly attracted to John's slightly rugged good looks, not to mention his natural charisma which shone in sparkling contrast to Sillman's brashness. Standing at five feet, seven and one-half inches, John was not much taller than Alice, but he had a trim physique, greenish-gray eyes, and wavy brown hair. A few creases in his face indicated that he was older than she, but that really didn't matter to her. Alice was smitten. "He was a charmer!"

recalled their friend Cris Alexander. "He was just wonderful! And he was rather handsome . . . he had very good Irish looks."

Even though John had been affiliated with the entertainment industry for fifteen years, he was yet a struggling artist. Like Alice, he was searching for that big break, but he had long abandoned hopes of either an acting or a singing career in favor of songwriting, a hobby which he had pursued since childhood. Twice he had tried to make it as a performer in California, rubbing elbows with many of Hollywood's rich and famous but always seeming to miss the mark. It was during his second stay on the coast that John had met Sillman, for whom he had written several songs for a 1933 revue produced at the Pasadena Playhouse. Since 1937, John had endeavored to make a name for himself in New York. His most noteworthy accomplishment occurred in 1939 with his first publication, an upbeat number which disappointingly had not led to a recording contract. Sillman had used the tune in *All in Fun*, but since so few had seen that flop, the exposure had done John little good. In the meantime, "It's a Big, Wide, Wonderful World" would sit on the shelf for almost a decade.

Although John had held numerous jobs since his college days, he was presently without employment. In fact, a year earlier he had reported to a census taker that he had been unemployed for the past two years. One may wonder how he kept body and soul together, especially in a brutally competitive city like

New York. It seems that periodically throughout his young life, John had been befriended by a succession of benefactors. This is not to say that assembling such a chain of relationships was his particular brand of survival or that John was opportunistic. On the contrary, he appears to have been a very sincere individual in whom others saw talent, worth, and potential. Alice Pearce saw even more, and she was secretly happy to learn that John was unmarried.

In some ways, John Rox remains a puzzle. His scant personal correspondence forces us to rely mainly on scattered newspaper items, which often present conflicting accounts of his movements prior to 1937. His record is further complicated by the fact that he was known by more than one surname. By 1928, John had chosen "Rox" as his stage name. (Many years later he told Broadway columnist Earl Wilson that his professional name was shortened from Roxbury, a surname which had appeared "on his family tree somewhere." This may have been nothing more than a publicity tidbit, as several family historians have failed to locate any such individual among John's lineage.) Prior to adopting "Rox," John was known as John Herring, but that was not his birth name either. When he was born in Des Moines, Iowa, he was christened John Arthur Barber, the only child of Arthur Barber and his wife Ina Brown.

John Arthur Barber, called "Johnnie," poses at age two for a photographer in Des Moines, Iowa in 1904. He was later known as John Herring and ultimately as John Rox. Photo courtesy Linda Swanson.

There is also the issue of John's date of birth. Because no contemporary birth record exists, later records were consulted to determine his exact age. Not a single one of eight official documents accessed by the author bears a date of birth matching that of another. These include John's driver's license, Social Security application, military discharge, marriage license, death certificate, and two separate birth affidavits, one drawn up in Iowa in 1940 and the other notarized in California in 1952. Most agree on the month and day—July 21—but the year ranges from 1902 to 1907. Thanks to the advent of digitized newspapers, the answer was finally found in the *Stuart Herald*, published in the Iowa hometown of John's mother. In that paper, on July 25, 1902, there appeared a birth announcement for John Barber, listing Des Moines as the birthplace and July 21 as the date.

John Arthur Barber was evidently named for his grandfathers, John Barber and John Brown, and for his father, Arthur Grant Barber, who, at the time of John's birth, was employed as a streetcar conductor. Born in Cass County, Iowa, in 1881, Arthur was the youngest of five children. As newlyweds his parents had moved from their native Essex County, New York, to farm in Iowa the year after the Civil War ended. For most of his young life, Arthur had lived with his folks in Atlantic, the county seat of Cass County, working on his father's farm. It's not known how Arthur met his wife-to-be, Ina Maureen Brown, who lived forty miles away in Stuart, but since she had an aunt living in Atlantic, it's likely they met at some social function in that town.

Ina Brown was hardly ever called by either of her given names. To everyone, she was "Dolly," or sometimes "Doll." Like Arthur Barber, Dolly was one of five children, and her parents were not Iowa natives. Her father, Virginia-born John Jefferson Brown, was a merchant who had sold harnesses and the like in Stuart since about 1871. Brown was active in civic affairs and local fraternal organizations, as well as the town's Methodist church. He was called "the life of his home, always cheerful and good natured." His wife, née Alice Cora Barringer, was born in Illinois but came to Stuart at about the same time as John Brown, who was five years her senior.

The Browns' middle child, Dolly, was born in Stuart in 1876. Not much is known about her early life, except an occasional snippet in the local newspaper. We know that in 1899, Dolly clerked for the town's newsstand. And it seems that she and her sisters, Alta and Nelle, were quite social, often visiting relatives and friends in Des Moines and other nearby cities. It is said that the Brown girls were musically talented and that, being very proper young ladies, they never left the house without looking their very best, always wearing hats and jewelry. A photo of these three from around 1900 depicts just that. Atop their stylish pompadours are huge hats bedecked with jewels and feathers.

At some point in the town of Atlantic, Dolly caught the eye of Arthur Barber. A speedy courtship ensued, perhaps prompted by the prior weddings for both Alta and Nelle. Dolly and

Arthur were married in Atlantic on September 7, 1901. Curiously, their nuptials were not reported in the *Stuart Herald*, as Dolly's sisters' marriages had been. It may have been because of a sticky little matter involving Arthur—he was a convicted felon. In 1898, when he was just seventeen, Arthur led two accomplices to commit "highway robbery," taking $135 from a local furniture dealer. Immediately after the crime, Arthur fled to Des Moines but was soon apprehended. Three months later, he was found guilty and sentenced to "five years at hard labor" in the state penitentiary. His sentence was commuted by the governor in March 1901, at which time he returned to Atlantic. Six months later he wed Dolly Brown, and they moved to Des Moines, hopefully to put Arthur's dark past behind them. Ten months later their son John Arthur Barber, whom they called "Johnnie," was born.

What happened next makes one wonder if Arthur Barber reverted to his irresponsible ways. By late 1904, the Barbers' marriage had ended in divorce. Dolly and little Johnnie returned to Stuart, where she assumed her maiden name and lived once again under her parents' roof. John would have very little contact with his natural father from that time forward.

In the spring of 1906, a handsome twenty-one-year-old came to town to clerk in one of Stuart's drug stores. Earl Granville Herring, born in 1884 on a farm near Casey, Iowa, some twelve miles away, had graduated from the normal school in nearby Dexter and had clerked in a pharmacy in Des Moines. Earl was about six feet tall and had brown eyes and thick brown hair. Despite the eight-year gap in their ages, Earl and Dolly began courting and within less than a year's time, they married in her parents' parlor. From the outset, Earl was a strong father figure for John, who was approaching his fifth birthday. In short time, the boy would become

Dolly Brown Herring (left) and her younger sister Nelle McKee, in mourning for their sister Alta, demonstrate their desire to remain inseparable, 1911. Photo courtesy Linda Swanson.

known as Johnnie Herring, but it remains uncertain whether Earl legally adopted Dolly's son. Earl's granddaughter Linda Sue Swanson recalled, "I do know that [John] was like my grandfather's own son." With a nod to his maternal grandfather, he used the name "John Jefferson Herring" for almost twenty years.

During the early years of his marriage, Earl Herring seemingly couldn't settle on a career. He and his family moved four times in the same number of years. They first lived in Sterling, Nebraska, but evidently Earl became dissatisfied there, and by October 1907, he accepted a position as head clerk in a drug store in Winterset, Iowa, a town of about 3000 people. One year later, the Herrings' son Donald was born there. By February 1910, Earl felt the itch to move again. "Mr. Herring has had

special training in the art of butter making and chemistry," the local newspaper reported, "and expects to take up that line of work, but has not yet fully decided on his location." This career switch was short-lived, for the Herrings moved back to Winterset in July 1911 when Earl, now a pharmacist, bought a half-interest in the drug store for which he had previously clerked. In 1913, the Herring family would be complete with the birth of another son, Robert.

As John Herring grew older, he considered Winterset his hometown, as did another famous fellow—Marion Morrison—who was born in Winterset five months before the Herrings first moved there. At one time, the Herrings and the Morrisons both lived on West Court Avenue, but the similarities did not end there. Marion's father was a druggist in Winterset, just as Earl Herring was. And both men, who were born the same year, moved their families from Winterset only to return a short time later. In addition, Marion's mother and John's mother, although not related, shared the same maiden name: Brown. The house where Marion was born is now part of a museum honoring him, for this boy grew up to become the iconic film star John Wayne.

John attended the public schools of Winterset and seems to have enjoyed a happy childhood, except for one notable trauma. He contracted diphtheria during an outbreak at his school when he was seven, and two of his little classmates died. He enjoyed music, poetry, and dramatics, so he was often chosen to perform in events like a 1913 George Washington's birthday celebration, when he recited "The First Flag." In a similar celebration four years later, he dressed in uniform as a Confederate soldier for a recitation of Finch's "The Blue and the Gray." By 1918, John was singing solos in high school assemblies, and the following year, he played the lead in the school operetta.

John Jefferson Herring, age seventeen, at the time of his high school graduation, Winterset, Iowa, 1920. Photo courtesy Linda Swanson.

John's musical talent caught the attention of prominent Winterset dentist Charles Leech for whom music had been a lifelong passion. As director of the Orpheus Club, a local choral organization, Dr. Leech enlisted the sixteen-year-old as one of his baritones. "He is a high school boy who has just commenced to sing," commended the *Winterset Madisonian*, following John's first experience performing with the club, "and his excellent natural voice gives great pleasure."

In addition to his professional duties, Dr. Leech, a well-known organist, also taught private voice and piano lessons. As John's personal voice coach, Dr. Leech took a keen interest in his young protégé. Although twenty-six years older than the boy, Leech—a bachelor who lived with his aged father and unmarried brother and sister—began to spend a lot of time with John, quickly becoming his patron. Over the course of the next three years, Leech provided John with many opportunities he may not have had otherwise. They regularly attended concerts in Des Moines, sometimes staying overnight, exploring the city and visiting friends.

When John had completed his first year of vocal training with Dr. Leech—"sacrificing sports and other fun"—the elder musician decided it was time for John's debut recital. Leech invited a number of intimate friends, mostly musicians from Des Moines, including English-born William Shakespeare, a seventy-year-old voice teacher. Shakespeare pronounced John's voice as "magnificent, a pure Italian tenor in the making." The *Madisonian* concurred: "Endowed with a remarkable voice, good health, intelligence and a love of his work, there would seem to be no limit to his future accomplishments."

Meanwhile, during his senior year at Winterset High, John still found time to perform in school productions. Once he had graduated, Dr. Leech advised that John study voice under Holmes Cowper, dean of the College of Fine Arts at Drake University in Des Moines. Cowper had studied in London, Berlin, Paris, and Chicago before becoming the dean in 1909. John enrolled at Drake University on January 24, 1922, and almost immediately attracted attention. "A new baritone has been discovered at the university," crooned the *Des Moines Capital*, "whose voice, according to critics, offers great promise." On April 21, newcomer John was given a solo to sing at the university's annual spring concert. Meanwhile, he financed his schooling by working "morning and evening" at the Iowa State Bank.

When the spring semester ended, John remained in Des Moines to work at the

Standing, left to right, are John, mother Dolly, brother Don, and stepfather Earl Herring. Youngest brother Bob Herring crouches in the foreground, Des Moines, circa 1925. Photo courtesy Linda Swanson.

bank for the summer. At this point, there was some discussion of his enrolling at Northwestern University in Evanston, Illinois, but for whatever reason, John returned to Drake in September—all the while remaining in close contact with Dr. Leech, who visited him regularly and escorted him to concerts.

At some point during his second year at Drake, John became acquainted with twenty-six-year-old Paul William Zeh, a clerk with the Standard Oil Company. It's very likely that John met tall, slim, brown-eyed Paul at Des Moines' first radio station, WGF, where John made his radio debut on Tuesday, January 16, 1923. Paul was the pianist in a five-piece band called the Melo-Blue Dance Orchestra, which performed on the *Des Moines Register and Tribune*'s weekly radio program each Tuesday night. Formerly a men's clothing salesman, Paul maintained a dapper appearance. He wore

his brown hair slicked back and parted in the middle, accentuating his high forehead. He and John became fast friends. The two young men were often called on to entertain at student parties; consequently they "came to be known as a team, more than as individuals." And in no time at all, John took Paul to meet his grandmother Alice Brown in Stuart.

It's strikingly apparent that John's college plans changed once he met Paul. By semester's end on June 1, 1923, he decided to withdraw from Drake and took a job as an inspector with the Bankers Life Insurance Company in Des Moines. (There was no need for him to move back to Winterset, for Earl Herring, now a traveling salesman for a creamery equipment firm, had plans to move Dolly and their younger sons to Omaha, Nebraska.) John moved in with Paul and his mother, relocating again the following year with the Zehs to an apartment at 1110 Twenty-Ninth Street. John's job at the insurance company was not very inspiring, unless you count the songs he composed while sitting at his desk—one was titled "Quittin' Time." However, because of his day job, John continued to sing on radio programs, especially those on WHO, the Bankers Life radio station.

John Herring, Des Moines, circa 1923. Photo courtesy Linda Swanson.

Eventually the musical pair, eager to break into show business, felt the draw of Hollywood. Encouraged by Dr. Leech to "go west," John, now twenty-two years old, and Paul, twenty-eight, decided to take the plunge in March 1925. They moved to Los Angeles, taking Paul's sixty-four-year-old mother along, and in short time Paul and John were performing their musical act on local radio station KFWB.

Founded by movie moguls Jack and Harry Warner, KFWB was located on the Warner Brothers Studio lot on Sunset Boulevard in Hollywood. From its first day of broadcast on March 4, 1925, Warner Brothers utilized KFWB to promote its film stars and latest releases. During June and July, John and Paul performed a weekly act in the evenings on KFWB, similar to the one they created in Des Moines, with solos by John accompanied by Paul at the piano. The team promoted itself in other ways, such as participating in a benefit performance for disabled veterans, held in Santa Monica that August, but success continued to elude them. After a year of failed efforts to break into vaudeville in the Golden State, John and Paul decided to give their native region a try.

On October 22, 1926, "Herring and Zeh"— calling themselves "The Halfbacks of Harmony"—opened their act at the Strand Theater in Omaha. For seven days, they performed on the movie house stage between screenings of an Adolphe Menjou silent picture called The Ace of Cads. When this gig ended, their act temporarily ran aground but resumed in January with circuit stops in smaller cities in Illinois, Iowa, Missouri, and Nebraska. Before heading back to the coast, John paid a farewell visit to his family in Omaha. His eighteen-year-old brother Don, also dreaming of an entertainment career, joined John and Paul when they left Omaha on March 2, 1927. That spring, John and Paul performed their way across Oregon and northern California. By May, they had reached southern California, where the Riverside Daily Press described their act as a "whirlwind cycle of comedy and character melodies."

By late June, John and Paul were negotiating with Warner Brothers to appear in a Vitaphone short. Vitaphone, debuting in 1926, was a type of sound film system that, according to film historian Roy Liebman, was "one of the epochal efforts that brought forth the talkies." The soundtrack was recorded on phonograph records instead of being printed on the film itself. The discs were played on a turntable coupled to the projector motor while the film was being projected. Many early talkies, including The Jazz Singer, used the Vitaphone system. Gradually, theater owners, especially small movie houses, used Vitaphone shorts to

Paul Zeh, Des Moines, circa 1923. Photo courtesy Linda Swanson.

replace live vaudeville acts they had formerly employed. "Vitaphone was the place vaudeville went to die," said Liebman.

John and Paul's Vitaphone short would essentially replicate their "Halfbacks of Harmony" act—but with one change suggested by the producers. Rather than having two men perform love songs and lighthearted ditties, they thought it advisable to add a female to the team, so the vaudevillian Doris Duncan, a thirty-one-year-old brunette with a toothy smile, was chosen. John and Paul were delighted to learn that, like themselves, Duncan was a native Iowan whose father had made it big as a cattleman in Omaha, of all places. Since 1919, and following a year's study at Stanford University, Duncan had been performing in musical stock companies and vaudeville houses in San Francisco and Los Angeles.

The Vitaphone production, titled *Doris Duncan, Herring and Zeh: "California's Popular Artists,"* was completed in early July 1927. Accompanied by the Vitaphone orchestra, the trio performed four selections. By October, the short would be shown in movie houses all across the country, continuing to appear on bills sporadically until early 1929. John fervently hoped that the short would kick off a career in motion pictures. As for John's professional partnership with Paul Zeh, it must have ended with the Vitaphone production,

for their names are not linked in any subsequent engagements for either.

It is impossible to paint a complete picture of John's years in Los Angeles due to the scarcity of personal correspondence and press coverage. Since his name does not appear in the *Los Angeles Times* or other area newspapers during the 1920s, we must rely on blurbs and articles which appeared in the Omaha and Iowa papers. These notices indicate that John was trying to break into silent pictures. Two separate items mention the completion of a screen test and some "bit work." Although perhaps nothing more than promotional hype, they remain tiny pieces of the John Herring puzzle, offering hints about the circles in which he moved.

The first celebrity connected in print with John Herring is Dolores del Río, then a relative newcomer to the film industry but one of Hollywood's most popular stars by 1927. Six years earlier, she had married the gentlemanly Jaime Martínez del Río, "one of the most eligible bachelors in Mexican high society." Jaime, almost twelve years older than Dolores, also had cinematic ambitions; he dreamed of becoming a screenwriter. Soon after the couple arrived in Los Angeles in 1925, Dolores' career took off, but Jaime's scripts were "turned down over and over." Meanwhile, rumors began to circulate that there was a romantic attraction between the actress and her director-manager Edwin Carewe, who was "pushing Jaime further and further into the background." Of course, none of this strife was reported in an Omaha news piece connecting the del Ríos to John Herring, who, reportedly, "almost immediately found favor in [their] household ... doing scenario work with [Jaime] and singing songs of sentiment and romance

Jaime del Río.

Lloyd Pantages, 1937.

trained singer. As for Jaime and John's collaborative script, nothing came of the endeavor.

Jaime and Dolores del Río socialized primarily with Hollywood's elite. Two of their close friends were Lloyd and Carmen Pantages, son and daughter of theater impresario Alexander Pantages, with whom the del Ríos sailed to Hawaii in August 1927, during the final days of their floundering marriage. Lloyd, who "always wore an ascot, a smile, and a [deep] tan," may have been the one who introduced John to the del Ríos. Like John, Lloyd Pantages wanted to be in pictures, but even with his industry connections, he found it almost impossible. "I was given contracts as an actor at first one and then another studio," the diminutive Pantages explained. "But I guess these contracts were only complimentary because my father owned theaters. For I got my pay checks every week, but I never could get a role." One wonders if John were in a similar situation, or how else did he make ends meet?

John gravitated towards Jaime and Pantages and their coterie. Eventually his social contacts proved profitable, though not in a way that either he or anyone else probably expected. As doors opened quickly for John in the early spring of 1928, he shared an exciting announcement with his mother Dolly who immediately rang up the *Omaha World-Herald.* On April 3, the paper broke John's story which set Winterset and Stuart abuzz. At a party given by screen star Charles "Buddy" Rogers—publicized as "America's Boy Friend"—John was introduced to Harrison Post, identified only as a local millionaire. As the story went, John's "voice interested Post, who became attached

with the lovely Dolores." That John joined the del Ríos in musical entertainment is easily believed—Jaime was a pianist, and Dolores was a

to the boy, and invited him to visit him at his home." In fact, the *World-Herald* revealed, John had been staying with Post for several weeks at the Villa Dei Sogni (House of Dreams), Post's home near Santa Monica. Post, supposedly so impressed with John's talent, offered to finance John's vocal education in Europe, to prepare him for an "operatic" career rather than "fame and fortune on the screen." Quite a sudden switch, but only the first in a series of unaccountable decisions and actions.

On April 12, John arrived in Omaha for a three-week stay in the Midwest. Almost at once he met with a *World-Herald* journalist who the following day delineated a rather incongruous narrative: "John J. Herring is home on his way to Europe, after winning success on the coast as an actor, singer, a member of the movie colony, a friend of millionaires—and last but not least, as a scenario writer. He has passed all the screen tests, and has only to say the word to become one of 'the' film folk. But John intends to put that off for a while for, thanks to a splendid voice and his pen, he is now able to go to Vienna, receive the finishing touches of voice culture and return to America and the picture business as an exponent of its latest development, talking and singing pictures." It's baffling that John would suddenly give up important opportunities and leave the country to study voice, instead of taking advantage of capable vocal coaches in the States.

Even more mystifying is the article's revelation that "just before [John] left Hollywood," he sold a film script for "enough money to pay all of his expenses abroad, give him a view of other European centers, and enough to carry him back to Hollywood and the moonlit sands." If true, this must have been an amazing screenplay, especially coming from the pen of an unknown. Purportedly titled *Blind Man's Bluff*, the story was "purchased by one

of the biggest production companies in the business." Suddenly the source of John's good fortune shifts from a millionaire's benefaction to a novice screenwriter's unexpected business deal. Yet, *Variety* mentions no such script deal, at least not by that title. Moreover, the name John Herring—much less John Rox—never appears in the trade paper during this period of time. Of course, it's possible that John's story could have been bought and never used by the "big production company." Still, it seems a near impossibility that the screenplay was sold in the brief interval between the point that Dolly first reported John's European travel plans and his arrival in Omaha. Compounding the matter is the actuality that John Rox never sold a single subsequent script or story idea to any film studio. If, as a rookie screenwriter, John managed to sell a scenario, why weren't there similar deals later?

The April 13 article states that John came directly to Omaha from the "Uplifters Ranch club at Santa Monica where he has been the guest of Harrison Post, millionaire artist and land owner." The ranch, owned by an exclusive men's club, encompassed 120 acres with a "Spanish Colonial-style clubhouse with tennis courts, swimming pool, trapshooting range, amphitheater, and dormitories." Some members built weekend or summer getaway cottages and lodges on land leased from the club. Evidently, Post had named his residence there the Villa Dei Sogni.

Interestingly, "millionaire" Post, who was only five years older than John, had never earned enough money himself to purchase such a property as the Villa Dei Sogni, much less an additional beachfront home, listed in his name at 905 Palisades Beach Road in Santa Monica. These properties were purchased with funds provided by William Andrews Clark, Jr., of Los Angeles, who had identified Harrison

William Andrews Clark, Jr.

Post as his "ward" on the 1920 United States Federal Census. There is no doubt of Clark's millionaire status; he was a son and heir of the late Senator William A. Clark, an entrepreneur who made a fortune in mining copper, banking, and railroads. The junior Clark, fifty-one years old in 1928, had made his own millions in the Montana copper mines before settling in Los Angeles in 1907. By 1919, he had outlived two wives and had moved Post, almost exactly twenty years his junior, into his home at 2205 West Adams Boulevard, which by 1926 boasted a separate structure—"an elaborate jewel-box Italian Renaissance library"—for Clark's rare book collection. Although Post was regarded by Clark as his secretary and assistant librarian, he was more than that, "as made clear by the gifts Clark bestowed upon [him] including a Mediterranean villa on Cimarron Street

directly across from Clark's own house and a convertible Rolls-Royce."

Harrison Post was actually Albert Weis Harrison, born in Brooklyn, New York, in 1897. One of five children, his parents divorced when he was very young, and after moving to Sacramento, he wound up in San Francisco, adopting the surname Post from a woman he regarded as a foster mother and with whom he lived in 1918. According to William Daniel Mangam, a former Clark employee who wrote a "muckraking page-turner" about the Clark family, Clark and Post met in a San Francisco store where Post was employed. Mangam claimed that Clark was a "binge drinker and a profligate and reckless homosexual and chaser of much younger men."

John Herring was evidently well-acquainted with Post, but we have no actual document tying him to Clark. However, there are strong indications that he knew the millionaire. Mangam's detailed account does not mention John, but he writes of an episode that was allegedly brewing at the time John was staying at the Uplifters Ranch house. According to Mangam, in late 1927, Clark was being investigated by the Los Angeles District Attorney's office because of his suspected homosexual relationships. Jack Oray, an associate of Clark's, whom Mangam identified as a "two-time felon then on parole," gave a statement to the district attorney's office which implicated Clark's valet Richard William Burgess in the matter. Clark then sent Burgess and Post to Paris for an extended stay; he later followed them.

Clark's older brother, prompted by Clark's attorney, became concerned and "hired a special investigator with whose report exposed a group of twenty-four homosexuals associated with W. A. Clark, Jr." Contacted in Paris, Clark was outraged by his brother's interference, promptly fired his attorney, and hired

Joseph McInerney of San Francisco to replace him. McInerney met with Clark in Paris, but Clark refused to see an Idaho attorney whom his brother had sent to Paris. When Clark finally returned home, he and McInerney met with Asa Keyes, the district attorney for Los Angeles County, at which time Keyes signed a document stating that there was no complaint on file against Clark. Mangam insinuated that Keyes was bribed to produce such a document. No part of Mangam's account can easily be substantiated, but a check of New York passengers' lists corroborates that Post and Burgess returned from Paris, docking in New York on February 22, 1928, and that Clark and McInerney disembarked there on April 17. The Idaho attorney whom Clark refused arrived in New York from Paris on May 2.

Meanwhile, John Herring—if we believe the *Omaha World-Herald* article—was occupying the Uplifters Ranch house until around April 10. If indeed it was Post who had the idea of sending John to Europe, it is possible that Post initially met John in March, after the former returned from Paris. However, one wonders if Post could have become well-acquainted enough with John during this brief interlude to feel secure in funding John's travel, accommodations, and education expenses. There is also the possibility that the two had met long before Post went to Paris, with John consequently "house-sitting" at the ranch while Post was out of the country. Alternatively, maybe *Clark* ensconced John at the ranch, either before or after Post's departure to Europe. We will never know for certain. The whole matter involving the district attorney makes one wonder if John was implicated in some way and was therefore sent out of the country by Clark, just as Post and Burgess were. Or John's decision to study in Europe may have transpired just as it was reported in the *Omaha World-*

Herald. Whatever the case, it is apparent that John was comfortable being around Post (and possibly Clark).

William J. Mann, in his landmark study, *Behind the Screen: How Gays and Lesbians Shaped Hollywood*, observed that by the mid-1920s, "the homosexual subculture in the movie colony had exploded," due to more "relaxed attitudes and tolerant experimentation." Judging by the company he kept, John appears to have been a part of this scene. According to Mann, in the Hollywood of this era, "lifestyles were undisguised and rarely apologized for." However, Mann clarifies: "Certain things weren't acknowledged in public, of course, but in a world that both denied and decried their existence, those who lived on the social edge found Hollywood offered authenticity that would have been difficult to achieve anywhere else." This would have included Des Moines, Omaha, and most indubitably Winterset, Iowa.

John's close friendships prior to 1928 provide indicators of his sexual identity. Mann refers to these indicators as "markers," which include: lack of marriage, marrying late in life, lack of children, association with other gays in articles and columns, and census records revealing same-sex partners living together. Taking all of this into account, John's trail of friends follows a definite pattern. Dr. Leech, Paul Zeh, and Lloyd Pantages never married, while Jaime del Río fathered no children. Since no explicit proof of these individuals' homosexuality seems to exist, we must, as Mann points out, weigh "the vast body of gossip, film lore, and legend." On this point, Mann agrees with historian and documentary filmmaker Andrea Weiss, who believes that "rumor and gossip constitute the unrecorded history of the gay subculture," and therefore should not be dismissed as sources of information. With that in mind, it must be noted that del Río endured rumors of his homosexuality, which circulated in both Mexico City and Hollywood. There were similar rumors about Buddy Rogers, in whose home John reportedly met Harrison Post. By this time perhaps—but certainly after John eventually returned from Europe—some of John's own family in Iowa were whispering about the likelihood that he was attracted to his own sex. "In those days, as you know," one relative reflected in 2013, "it was not something that [John] would have professed."

Despite the conflicting details in the *Omaha World-Herald* article of April 13, 1928—titled "Finds the Rainbow's End"—the piece remains the lengthiest news item ever written about John Rox. From it, we gather specifics about his physical appearance ("a pretty good looking boy, with curly movie star hair, even white teeth, and a tan that might be featured in *A Son of the Desert*"), his fashion style ("In his loose knicker suit, polo shirt and low-necked sweater, he is every move a movie star"), and even his coincidental travel mate—the father of actor Harold Lloyd "who carried on to New York to see the opening of his son's new picture *Speedy*." The journalist couldn't omit the obligatory question about John's love life, but all we get from that is: "There is a young lady by the name of Betty Bronson, who is an exceedingly close friend of his." However, the article is most significant because of a tiny detail; it's the first time that John is identified in print as "John Rox."

As if to rationalize John's sudden departure from Hollywood, the film director Rupert Julian is quoted in the *World-Herald* as having advised John to take advantage of his training in Europe in order to "make a name for himself" upon his return to Hollywood. By that time, Julian predicted, the film capital would be producing sound films of "light operas and musical comedies," perfect genres for John's tal-ent. "Everyone . . . has been most kind to me," said John. "I am most tremendously grateful. I can certainly say that I am one who went west to find the foot of the rainbow in Hollywood and came back with [a] pot to hold the gold in, at least! The filling is now up to me."

On the morning of May 4, 1928, a gentle breeze blew across New York Harbor. The day of John's departure dawned with clouds scattered across the sky. Moderate temperatures helped to make it a perfect day to begin an ocean voyage. The previous evening, John had arrived in the city on a train from Chicago. He regretted that his first visit to Manhattan was such a brief one, but his excitement grew with thoughts of exploring much older cities across the Atlantic.

Meanwhile, in Brussels, a ten-year-old American girl was anticipating the end of the school year and her family's plans to tour Germany that summer. Soon Les Tourelles would close its doors for the season, and Alice Pearce would be free to play with her dolls and her dog Pierrot. Likewise, John Rox was dreaming of summertime in Paris, where he would tour art museums and attend concerts with his friend Dr. Leech, who had planned for his vacation to coincide with John's stay in Europe. Thirteen years would pass before John and Alice would meet and perhaps find it remarkable that they had been residents of Continental Europe at the same time.

What we know about John's two years in Europe wouldn't fill a hollow tooth. Aside from two picture postcards, a few snapshots, and a handwritten note to his brother Don, John's surviving niece has no other sources to indicate what unfolded during this important interval. It is known that he resided in Vienna, Paris, and Monte Carlo—most likely in that order—but there is no record of any conservatories he may have attended. Perhaps it was the Imperial Academy of Music and the Performing Arts in Vienna. John left the States with a letter of introduction from writer James Lawrence Campbell to Albert Henry Washburn, the United States ambassador to Austria. He may have been introduced by such means to others in Europe, but given his winning ways, he most likely formed quick and easy ties with many Americans visiting or living on the continent. These were the days of Prohibition, and those who could afford trips to Europe sought its freer atmosphere. In Vienna, John met, among others, recent Pulitzer Prize novelist Thornton Wilder, flamboyant entertainer Mistinguett, known for her risqué routines at the Folies Bergère and the Moulin Rouge, and the androgynous Rocky Twins, Norwegian brothers adored in Paris and Vienna for their drag act impersonating the Dolly Sisters.

By 1929, the allure of Paris, burgeoning at the height of the Jazz Age, must have become irresistible for John. The bohemian capital of France was hundreds of years old, yet it was enchanting and, as writer Gerry Max has noted, "naively young." It was the Paris of Ernest Hemingway, F. Scott Fitzgerald, and Gertrude Stein, and John was experiencing it near the very end of the *Années folles*, an era when American culture had a substantial influence on France. Tennessee Williams, who vacationed there in the summer of 1928, advised, "When you're in Paris, you might as well leave all dispensable conventions behind." It's believable that John did just that. One can imagine that he explored the streets and boulevards, the shops and cafes, the museums and theatres, but also the bars and clubs where lesbians and gays gathered.

Americans were everywhere in Paris, and it's likely that some of John's contacts led him to Monte Carlo where he became chummy with dynamic opera star Mary Garden, who summered there each year for more than a decade. By the time John met her, the Scottish-born lyric soprano kept both a fourteen-room apartment in Monte Carlo and a villa at Beaulieu-sur-Mer, a seaside village on the Riviera some eleven kilometers away. Living life to the fullest, the fifty-five-year-old Garden spent her days in Monte Carlo sunbathing nude on her motorboat and passed her nights in the casino, "having a fling at the green tables."

John evidently frequented the casino as well, according to a story passed down from his first cousin Nellie McKee to her grandson John Higginbottom. "John won three rings in a Monte Carlo casino, a ruby ring, a sapphire, and an emerald," Higginbottom recalled. "He gave the sapphire ring to my grandmother." John also sent McKee's sister a picture postcard from Monte Carlo Beach, showing him and a young male friend grinning at the camera while standing on a wide board being towed by Garden's motorboat. To his mother he mailed a snapshot view from his balcony, with a check mark indicating the newly completed Monte-Carlo Beach Hotel in the distance. Situated on the Côte d'Azur just outside Monaco proper, the pink stucco hotel was flanked by a huge swimming pool, fifty meters long. Both structures had been inspired by roly-poly social maven Elsa Maxwell (and John Rox's fellow Iowan), who, when requested, had advised the prince of Monaco on how to "seduce more rich visitors to [his] vest-pocket country." On the reverse side of John's snapshot he noted that the hotel and pool were part of the "new smart beach club that has just opened and where I swim." Photographs show him as a trendsetter, wearing shirtless bathing trunks at a time when most men still wore one-piece bathing suits which covered their chests. Indeed, John was "living the dream" in the summer of 1929, mingling and partying with Monaco's rich and famous, toning his tanned body with frequent

Dancers Martin Brown and Rozsika Dolly teamed up for an appearance at Keith's New York Palace Theatre, 1914. Brown described his expression as "a little cross-eyed but still sincere."

all in preparation for John's hopeful career in the "talkies."

Garden's bachelor friend Martin Brown, an actor-cum-playwright who had found Monte Carlo an ideal place to write, became another important contact. Since 1922—long before Elsa Maxwell frequented the resort—Canadian-born Brown and his unmarried sister Fredrika, an erstwhile actress, had resided in Monte Carlo. In 1918, at age thirty-four, a heart ailment had ended Brown's career as a dancer in Broadway musical comedies; during his recuperation he had turned to writing. By 1928, he had authored a dozen Broadway plays, including *The Love Child*, *The Strawberry Blonde*, and *Paris*, building a resume that appealed to Hollywood film executives, eager to employ playwrights as screenwriters for the inevitable advent of sound films. In the winter of 1930, Brown agreed to meet with Paramount's Walter Wanger during his upcoming stay in New York, but before leaving Monte Carlo that January, he also assured John, with whom he shared an instant rapport, that they'd be reunited someday.

visits to the club, and, yes, perhaps discovering an occasional romance.

Yet John realized that he must maintain his focus on vocal training, and so he turned to Garden, who, although considered by many as formidable and arrogant, had a generous nature. Impressed with John's singing voice, she recommended that he study with Richard Barthélemy, her favorite accompanist and operatic coach. (Three years earlier, she had made the same suggestion to another protégée, the young opera singer Grace Moore.) Barthélemy, once known as Enrico Caruso's accompanist, divided his time between Paris and Monte Carlo and agreed to coach John for six months,

Meanwhile, John made plans to leave Europe in early summer. On April 3, from his Monte Carlo residence at 40 Boulevard des Moulins, John wrote a congratulatory note to his brother Don Herring in Pasadena. During most of John's absence, Don had lived in Omaha, but by this time, he had once again relocated to California, where he found work as a dance instructor, changing his name to Don Roxy.

On this picture postcard, John Rox identified his Monte Carlo set, left to right, as "Josephine Chapman, Martin Brown, me, an American friend of mine, Fredrika Brown, and an Italian movie actor," 1929. Photo courtesy Linda Swanson.

"Why not Rox?" John mused, enclosing a twenty-dollar bill, saying, "I hope . . . you will tell me if you get too hard up. Yes, it will be great when we get together."

John departed Cherbourg on the *Olympic* on July 1, 1930, arriving in New York six days later. From there he took a train to Omaha, from where a most curious press item emanated, no doubt sparked by his mother Dolly: "John Rox, son of Mrs. E. G. Herring, Omaha, shortly will sail for London where he will play at His Majesty's theater [*sic*] opposite Peggy Wood in *Bittersweet* [*sic*], one of the most successful of the current season's London productions. Rox is here visiting his mother. He is en route to Hollywood where he will appear in talkies until his London contract is received." The illogical sequence of this plan conflicts with John's version, shared much later with publicity agent Stanley Musgrove, who stated that John was signed by *Bitter Sweet* creator Noël Coward to replace leading man George Metaxa, "but he grew homesick and returned to America." As with so many other instances in the life of John Rox, who knows what the true story was? In the case of *Bitter Sweet*, perhaps the real issue was stage fright— John's perpetual stumbling block—which he claimed resurfaced "at the crucial moments."

Yet the biggest mystery of all revolves around John's much-publicized training. It's boggling to note that despite two years of foreign study, John still didn't know how to play any musical instrument or to read music. Nor was he able to write music, according to a friend who knew him two decades later. It's understandable that John had never learned to read music when he was coached by Dr. Leech back in Winterset. In those days, it was common for vocal coaches to teach vocal technique, feeding students a musical piece note by note until they had learned it by rote. The same method may have been used when John was a student at Drake University, but one wonders if such training would have been the norm at a Viennese conservatory. If John attended a conservatory where instructional methods included music theory, then it seems illogical that he never learned to read music. This conditional indicates two possibilities: either John did *not* study in a Viennese conservatory or he studied at a school where sight-reading was not part of the instruction. Given the time he spent in frolic, one wonders just how many of the twenty-six months John spent abroad were actually spent in training.

Now that John was back in the States, he was eager to forge ahead with a musical career. With Dolly and youngest brother Bob in tow, John arrived in Hollywood in time to pal around with Martin Brown, who had spent the spring and summer at Paramount writing screenplays. Brown showed the Herrings around the Paramount lot, taking snapshots of them onboard the riverboat used in Buddy Rogers' 1929 film *The River of Romance*. John and Don, eager to break into pictures, hoped that Brown could help them get their foot in the door at Paramount, which proved more difficult than they perhaps realized. The brothers may have played some bit parts in a few films, but that remains to be proven. "My dad told me that John had a screen test and did quite well," recalled Don's daughter Linda Swanson. "However, he was not happy seeing himself on the screen."

Since performing before the camera didn't pan out for John, he turned to his alternate plan of selling his original songs to film producers, a tactic that also proved unsuccessful. Enter Leonard Sillman, a struggling actor who taught private dance lessons in his home to actresses such as ZaSu Pitts, Bessie Love, and Ruby Keeler. Sillman's feverish desire, however, was to produce a musical revue—a medium with which his name was destined to become synonymous. Explaining his inspiration, Sillman recalled, "In those days Hollywood had a habit of falling asleep—or dying on its feet—after 11 o'clock at night. My notion was to open a late-night spot restaurant where the spectator could eat and drink and watch a stage show all at the same time." Sillman secured enough backers to reopen The Playshop on North Gower Street, bought tables and chairs for about 200 people, and started rehearsals. He chose several of John's songs for *The 11:15 Revue*, which opened on December 31, 1930. In the cast was Sillman's thirteen-year-old "deep-throated" sister June who brought down the house singing one of John's numbers, "I Don't Want One Man."

John and Sillman, together with Viola Brothers Shore, would write *It's All Too Wonderful*, a three-act play, never published but nonetheless copyrighted. At the time, John was living in the Roman Gardens, a deluxe apartment court

John Rox, Hollywood, California, 1931. Not only was John devoted to his brother Don Herring but he was very close to his mother, stepfather, and brother Bob. Photo courtesy Linda Swanson.

built in 1926 and located at 2000 North Highland Avenue in Los Angeles.

In 1931, John signed a contract with Metro-Goldwyn-Mayer, where he wrote dialogue. There was some talk of him winning a part in a Robert Montgomery picture at MGM—probably 1932's *But the Flesh Is Weak*—but if so, his role was uncredited. Such a connection is evidenced by a 1931 photograph of John, clad in swim trunks and standing poolside at P. G. Wodehouse's Beverly Hills home with his old pal Lloyd Pantages and actress Heather Thatcher, Montgomery's co-star in that film. Montgomery and Adolphe Menjou were among the other guests.

At the time of the Wodehouse party, John and his brother Don were living at 635 Sleepy Hollow Lane in Laguna Beach. As they became known for their musical gifts, the brothers were invited to join Laguna's theatrical circles. In the summer of 1932, they co-wrote the book, music, and lyrics for *Fanfare*, a three-act play about a Kansas farmer's daughter, staged as a PTA production at a local school on October 7 and 8. Assisting with rehearsals was former silent film actor Charles Riesner, by then famous for directing comedy greats like W. C. Fields, Buster Keaton, Jack Benny, and Marie Dressler. "The most amazing thing to me," Riesner said, "was the fact that here was a play with book and music written by two Laguna boys, with a cast of Laguna people, and with sets designed and created by a Laguna artist." Don, now calling himself "Rox" instead of "Roxy," won Riesner's praise for his dancing ability and his acting versatility, playing a minister, a Spaniard, and "an old colored mammy." Riesner boasted that if John's melodies had been part of a Broadway show, "they would have become overnight hits." Riesner also related a telling anecdote: "John Rox worked very hard to make this, his first effort, a big success and Saturday night, when a handle broke and the crew couldn't get the dancing stairs on the stage for the finale, poor John almost collapsed. He told me later he just felt a nervous pain in his stomach and rushed out of the stage door." This image of John, perhaps throwing up his hands in distress, gives credence to his earlier experiences with stage fright and discomfort watching his own screen test. It's evident that by this time, John had resigned himself to the fact that a career as a performer was not in the cards. Meanwhile, he would assist with other amateur productions in Laguna Beach for the next two years.

Leonard Sillman bounced back into the picture in 1933 when he hired John to write a few songs for his upcoming "sophisticated" revue *Low and Behold*, which was slated to open at the Pasadena Community Playhouse in May. Sillman had rounded up a group of performers "who made up in youth, charm and enthusiasm what they lacked in experience and visible means of support." The cast of unknowns included a lanky twenty-five-year-old from Mill Valley, California, named Eunice Quedens, who would change her name to Eve Arden; another California native, dancer Charles Walters who later became a top choreographer and director at M-G-M; Kay Thompson, a radio performer who yearned for a movie career; and Sillman's "hunky nineteen-year-old chauffeur, Tyrone Power." Writer Sam Irvin observed that the revue "had a surprisingly progressive queer eye, unabashedly cultivated by its flamboyant creator." Indeed, Sillman had cast a three-hundred pound drag queen, in addition to the Rocky Twins—whose act John had enjoyed in Vienna—"the notorious gay courtesans from Europe." June Sillman sang one of John's songs, "Something Wicked, Unwholesome, and Expensive." The revue, while not the standard fare for the Pasadena Playhouse, was a hit, with the likes of Barbara Stanwyck, Joan Crawford, and Charlie Chaplin clamoring for seats.

Low and Behold morphed into *New Faces of 1934*, the first of Sillman's trademark revues to hit Broadway, opening at the Fulton Theatre in March 1934. Among the new cast members were Imogene Coca, Henry Fonda, O. Z. Whitehead, and Sandra Gould; Charles Walters would be the only cast member of *Low and Behold* to appear in both productions. *New Faces of 1934* ran for 149 performances, not at all shoddy for a Depression-era revue. Sillman later said it closed "in a burst of glory."

Although John Rox was not a part of *New Faces of 1934*, his association with Sillman was far from finished. It may have been Sillman, heady with success, who encouraged John to leave California and try his luck in the east. But then again, maybe not.

Very little can be ascertained about John's movements between 1934, when he disappears from the Laguna Beach newspapers, and 1937, when we find him as a resident of New York City. The strangest clue of his whereabouts is found in a 1941 profile, appearing in the *Des Moines Tribune*: "Rox . . . has done a lot of things besides write songs. There was the time, for instance, back in 1936, when he raised dachshunds in Ithaca, N. Y. When there were finally 44 pups scampering around his kennels, Rox decided his artistic career was on the verge of going to the dogs." It's implied that John soon decamped from the Finger Lakes region to resume his songwriting pursuits, leaving us to wonder why on earth he had ever chosen Ithaca, some 230 miles from Times Square? And dachshunds?

An internet search, jointly composed of city and canine breed, reveals Dr. Lyman Fisher, an Ithaca surgeon whose passion was breeding toy dachshunds and parading them at kennel club shows across the country in the 1930s. A 1928 graduate of Cornell University, Fisher earned his medical degree three years later from Cornell Medical College in New York City, specializing in gynecology. Although John Rox's name appears nowhere in print alongside that of Dr. Fisher, their similarities of location and avocation are too conspicuous to be merely coincidental. With a nod to William J. Mann, Fisher exhibits some very impressive "markers" which cannot be ignored. In 1936, Fisher was a twenty-nine-year-old bachelor, remaining so until his death in 1988. On the 1940 federal census, taken several years after John left Ithaca, Fisher is listed as the head of his household, with the only other occupant being a male "kennel manager" near Fisher's age. It makes sense that a busy physician would need an on-site caretaker for several dozen dogs—perhaps John Rox was the predecessor of the fellow listed on this census record. Since his college days, Fisher had been interested in the theatre. (His "staunch friend" was stage and screen comedienne Helen Broderick.) At Cornell, he was quite a popular performer in the Cornell Masque, the university's drama group. Fisher's specialty? Female impersonation.

Whether or not there was a relationship with Fisher, John abandoned the dachshunds and relocated to the Big Apple. His move may have been encouraged by his youngest brother Robert Herring, then twenty-three years old. Since 1935, Robert, a trained opera singer, had been carving a career for himself in New York City, regularly performing at Radio City Music Hall and on Sunday radio broadcasts. (He would eventually perform in several Broadway shows, including *Du Barry Was a Lady* with Bert Lahr.) Once settled in New York, John found occasional work as a freelance writer. In addition to several short stories he sold to magazines, John also wrote radio scripts, claiming among his credits the popular mystery drama *The Shadow*. However, the work was not very steady, and at this point someone new and exciting came into John's life.

Perkins Hillier Bailey, whom his friends called "Perk," was handsome, debonair, witty, and successful. His affinity for the latest in men's fashions aligned perfectly with his career choice. Employed by the Talon Company, a manufacturer of zippers since the 1920s, Perk had previously worked for the firm in Meadville, Pennsylvania, where its factory was located. Once he became Talon's director of design, he relocated to their offices in Manhattan. A 1928 graduate of the University of Pennsylvania, Perk earned an MBA degree from Harvard in 1934 shortly before being hired by Talon. By 1937, the Ivy Leaguer was living in

Perkins Hillier Bailey, University of Pennsylvania, 1928.

an elegant apartment building at 4 East Sixty-Fourth Street in the Lenox Hill neighborhood on the Upper East Side. About a year later, Perk met John Rox.

Perk was also well-traveled, having spent seven months exploring South America, North Africa, and central Europe in 1929. Once he became established with the Talon Company, Perk's favorite destination appears to have been Bermuda. Between 1935 and 1939, he sailed there four times, accompanied by John on the final vacation trip.

As their relationship developed, John moved into Perk's apartment on the south side of Sixty-Fourth Street between Fifth and Madison Avenues, very near the Central Park Zoo. Once again John had found a benefactor, for

Perk was not just his domestic partner but his sole means of support. John reported on the 1940 federal census that he had been unemployed for the past two years, listing his occupation as "newspaper writer," while Perk reported an annual income in excess of $5,000.

All the while, John had continued to write songs and to keep in touch with Leonard Sillman. The frenetic producer had intentions of using a few of John's creations in his proposed *New Faces of 1940*—ultimately unveiled as *All in Fun*, which Sillman would later call the most expensive flop of his career. Opening at the Majestic on December 27, 1940, the revue starred Bill "Bojangles" Robinson and featured Imogene Coca and Pert Kelton. It closed after three performances. Somewhere among the twenty-five scenes was a number that would (much later) become John's signature piece, "It's a Big, Wide Wonderful World."

It was during the aftermath of this disappointing production that John Rox first met Alice Pearce. They enjoyed each other's company right off; he delighted in her quick wit, and she admired his innate goodness. Besides their mutual love for the theatre, they were delighted to learn that each of them had lived in Paris, and almost concurrently at that. This new connection came at just the right time for both individuals, especially for Alice who was trudging through her post-Macy's unemployment.

It's not certain when Alice discovered the exact relationship that John shared with Perk. (Cris Alexander contended that it was common knowledge among certain circles that the two men were lovers.) Actually, it's possible that their partnership was not discussed because, as one acquaintance explained, "In those days you just *didn't* talk about [homosexuality]." This assertion is corroborated by veteran costume designer George James Hopkins, who, referring to the first half of the twentieth century, wrote,

"Homosexuality wasn't the casual topic of conversation it is today." So, perhaps the situation between John and Perk was just understood, with no need for discussion among their friends and families.

By this point, Alice was already accustomed to the company of gay men, whether their sexual identities were plainly discernible or not. At Princeton there had been Bus Davis whose bawdy ditties had left no doubt as to the sexuality of their creator. (Carol Channing, who regarded Bus as "the greatest musical accompanist in the Broadway theater," recalled that when he was introduced to the voluptuous Marilyn Monroe, he was only interested enough to inquire if she had a brother.) As for Alice's other close friends who were key members of the Theatre Intime, there is no known documentation of their sexual identities. Yet those men displayed common indicators, such as never marrying, never fathering children, or marrying late in life, leaving us to wonder if they, too, were gay. On the other hand, the flamboyant Leonard Sillman prompted one writer to quip: "[Sillman] perhaps had never been asked if he was a homosexual simply because everyone already knew the answer." Throughout the remainder of her life, Alice Pearce would accumulate many male friends who were gay. It was bound to happen—the New York theater was "drenched in gay culture." In today's parlance, Alice was definitely gay-friendly.

And what of Alice's possible exposure to same-sex attraction among women during her years at Sarah Lawrence College? After all, more than one of Miss Heinlein's thought-provoking productions were plays with lesbian themes. As for Alice's classmates, at least one of them was a lesbian, whether that subject was ever broached or not. "Betty [La Branche] was gay in a world that didn't accept it," asserts Melodie Bryant, who knew Betty when she lived in Georgetown, "[but] she had a longtime partner later on in life."

For those individuals like Betty, and for couples like John and Perk, Fire Island, a sandbar and barrier island about thirty-two miles long and a half-mile wide, held a particular appeal. Since the 1920s and the days of Prohibition, Fire Island, located in close proximity to New York City, had been a secluded refuge for "an artistic and high-living cafe society crowd." Summer weekends were an idyllic escape from shoes, cars, and telephones. By the early 1940s, Fire Island was rebounding from the devastating 1938 hurricane, attracting many gay men and lesbians, in addition to artists and writers. Among Alice's papers is a snapshot, presumably taken by her, showing John, Perk, and Betty stretched out under the summer sun on Fire Island. Undated, the image was likely taken in either 1941 or 1942, given that Betty joined the Red Cross in the spring of 1943 and didn't return to the States for four summers. The candid photograph indicates that Alice and John were comfortable being around each other's closest friends.

Years would pass, however, before Alice would meet much of John's family. By the time John knew Alice, his brother Don had remarried Doris Haverstock, the young wife whom he had divorced in 1927. Don, Doris, and their daughter Shirley, almost twelve, had moved to Long Beach, California, in the spring of 1939. The following year, their son Danny was born, to be joined by their youngest child, Linda Sue, in 1944. Alice would never meet John's mother. After suffering with infectious arthritis for twelve years, an exhausted Dolly Herring died in her Omaha home on July 18, 1942.

It is not known when Alice began to develop romantic feelings for John, but they surfaced effusively by the time he was drafted into the army in the fall of 1942. Still unemployed, John,

In June 1941, members of John Rox's family gathered in Omaha. From left to right are his sister-in-law Doris Herring holding her son Danny Herring, his niece Shirley Herring, brother Don Herring, aunt Nelle McKee, and grandmother Alice Brown. Seated is John's mother Dolly Herring. Although none of them knew it then, John had recently met his future wife for the first time. Photo courtesy Linda Swanson.

now forty years old, received Uncle Sam's call on October 13. Nine nights later, as a going-away gesture, he took Alice to hear torch singer Libby Holman perform her sensational new act at La Vie Parisienne. "You did so many nice things before you left," Alice told him. When John came to say goodbye on the afternoon of October 27, Alice instantly regretted her farewell deportment. "I did fall down on your departure," she wrote him three days later. "I so wished I could have sent you off to camp with gay laughter ringing in your ears. I had many things to ask you, and I had some cheerie [*sic*] things I wanted to tell you, but I gagged on all of it; it just took all I could call upon not to break down and ball [*sic*] loudly." Alice had the same reaction when John called the next day from the enlistment office to impart one final goodbye. "When the phone rang, I thought it was you; I was suddenly paralyzed and could only choke out those strange animal sounds. You were sweet to call."

Likewise, Perk Bailey "hit an all-time low" the day John left. When Perk phoned Alice that evening, they only "exchanged disconnect-ed sentences," fumbling to make conversation about the man they both loved. Unfortunately, we don't know John's exact feelings during all of this, for no letters written by him to either Alice or Perk are known to survive. It's clear that he was very fond of Alice, but whether or not he was in love with her by this time is rather hazy.

However, Alice, addressing John in her letter as "Darling," had clearly been bitten by the love bug—most likely for the first time in her life. "I think of you all day (and that part of the night when the pill has worn off) and wonder where you are and what you are doing," she sighed. "Private Johnnie, I miss you very, very much." However, her message was not all sackcloth and ashes; she shared a few witty anecdotes before revealing her plans for their reunion. The previous day a friend had sent over two bottles of champagne—"one to be drunk for your induction into the army, the other for my birthday," she explained to John. "Her timing is poor for both of those events, but I shall save them for such a time when you and I can drink them both at one sitting."

CHAPTER TEN
The Girl with a Cold

"I auditioned for the part of a girl with a cold in George Abbott's **On the Town** *and, having a bronchial condition at the time, I was hired."*

John Rox missed Alice's Broadway debut when *New Faces of 1943* opened at the Ritz Theatre on December 22, 1942. By that time, he was 1900 miles away, in the Colorado Rocky Mountains, serving at Camp Hale near the town of Leadville. Just the day before, John had been promoted to the rank of Technician 5th Grade with the Mountain Training Center (MTC), which was a part of the 10th Mountain Division. The center's mission was to develop procedures and manuals, test equipment, and conduct training in mountain warfare. The environment of Camp Hale, located in the Pando Valley where the mountains averaged 9200 feet, was rather harsh. Temperatures that winter often dipped to thirty degrees below zero and sometimes lower. Accumulated snowfall typically reached twelve feet. Many of the 16,000 recruits had difficulty adjusting to the high altitude and found it difficult to breathe. John was no exception, writing to his brother Bob, then stationed at Camp Adair in Oregon, about the uncomfortably frigid temperatures in Colorado. In New York, Alice's thoughts continuously turned to John, wondering how he was coping and when she would see him again.

Meanwhile, across the Atlantic, the tide was turning in favor of the Allies. The Axis powers were losing ground in both Europe and North Africa by 1943. The war became a little more real to Alice when news reached her that Bob Perry, with whom she had performed at Princeton, had been killed that May. A radioman in the U. S. Air Force, Perry had transferred from Africa to England the previous March. While on a Royal Air Force bombing mission, his plane was shot down over France.

Alice's concerns about other friends and family members engaged in warfare were amplified in September when she learned that her father Bob Pearce was being sent back to Europe by his employer to serve at the London branch of the National City Bank of New York. This time, her mother Margaret would stay behind due to the uncertainty of the situation overseas.

For the previous six months, Alice's career had been at a standstill. The closing of *New Faces* in March of 1943 had ushered in a dry spell which Alice found frustrating, especially since she had lulled herself into thinking that her Broadway debut would open doors everywhere. When that didn't happen, Alice—disillusioned with theatrical agents who "[n]ever did anything but collect commissions on the jobs I got myself"—knew she had to build a network of contacts. She was eagerly receptive to the suggestions of Manhattan nightclub proprietor Herbert Jacoby, who had been impressed by one of her characterizations in *New Faces*. Jacoby, recently partnered with entrepreneur Max Gordon to open The Blue Angel, proposed that Alice develop the character into a nightclub act. Her new objective caught the attention of syndicated Broadway columnist Dorothy Kilgallen, who dropped a small item that summer: "Alice Pearce, daughter of the Chase National Bank [*sic*] exec., is preparing to become a society chantoozie in the East Side boîtes." But that was as far as Alice got. Without her Princeton buddy Mark Lawrence—now serving in the South Pacific—she found it difficult to write enough material on her own. It was even more challenging to find someone to write for her brand of humor.

That fall, as Alice's frustration with inactivity increased, she turned to Leonard Sillman who introduced her to twenty-five-year-old Gus Schirmer, an alumnus of the 1934 production of *New Faces*. Since April, Schirmer, the scion of the famous music-publishing family, had been producing an all-girl musical revue called *Look, Boys! . . .Girls!* for USO Camp Shows in the New York military area. The voluntary revue, featuring Broadway showfolk and nightclub performers, was performed every Sunday at a different camp. Alice signed on in October, joining actress Celeste Holm, most recently of *Oklahoma!*, who had been performing at camps off and on all summer. Alice's first show was at Camp Meade, outside Baltimore.

She wrote about the evening in a letter to her mother, who was then visiting Alice's grandmother Sallie Clark and aunt Josephine in Perry: "It was a wonderful experience. I shall not soon forget it. I think I told you, the show is a revue made up of eight girls. It is written to appeal to service men. It has polite strip teasing, dancing, singing, glamour girls, humor, slapstick, community singing, jitterbug contests with boys from the audience. We met at Penn Station. In our group there were eight girls, our pianist, and wardrobe mistress. A captain, lieutenant, [and] a couple of M. P. sergeants met us with cars at a small suburban station

and drove us to a gym and rehearsal hall. We met the orchestra made up of boys at the camp and we had a quick rehearsal. Some officers took us to their mess hall and we had a delicious meal built around southern fried chicken. At six we were driven in jeeps to the theatre we were going to play in. My first jeep ride and I loved it, though a bit breezy for this time of year. As we were approaching the theatre, we saw a line some ten city blocks long of boys waiting to get into the theatre. The auditorium was a lovely one, a small Radio City. When the curtain went up, all the seats and aisles were filled and boys had to be turned away. What an audience! They screamed and laughed and wanted more and more of everything. During supper a lieutenant had told me that most of the boys were being shipped [overseas] this week. 'They may be a tough audience,' he said, 'because they are blue.' They weren't showing that they were blue and they laughed heartily. When you looked out at this sea of young, eager faces, it was a sight that brought a frog to your throat. They gave me an awfully good hand, and I was very proud. The boy who won the jitterbug contest (boys from the audience came up and jitterbugged with three of the girls) was just about to be discharged from the army for bad feet. As he came off the stage, he said, 'I hope the Doc wasn't in the audience.' After the show, our reception committee drove us back to the station. A very cute M. P. gave me a box of Teaberry gum because he said he had heard it was hard to buy in New York. We received excellent reviews of our show in the Camp Meade paper. The headline across the front page said, '5000 Boys to Go to Bed Happy.' The review went on to say, 'Every girl acted as if her entire career depended on the performance . . . the climax of the show came when Alice Pearce and Celeste Holm sang 'Pistol Packin' Mama.'"

Imogene Coca, New Faces of 1934.

performances in *Look, Boys! . . .Girls!* excelled her work in *New Faces of 1943.* She would be forever grateful to Schirmer, who would prove to be an instrumental friend, more than once rescuing her from unemployment.

Besides Schirmer, Alice made another lasting friendship during the weeks she performed in *Look, Boys! . . .Girls!* Thirty-five-year-old Imogene Coca, whose zaniness and appearance would be compared with Alice for years to come, was yet another *New Faces* veteran. She and Alice instantly bonded. They got a kick out of entertaining at various army camps and hospitals around New York, all the while quite accepting of the fact that they lacked the beauty of other girls in the show. "I don't think we pleased the boys," Alice said in 1964. "At one camp they arrested the men and made them come

A subsequent performance that fall was held closer to home at the Manhattan Beach Coast Guard Training Station, where Alice and the girls had dinner with ex-fighter Jack Dempsey, then serving there as a lieutenant commander. "We had delicious filet mignon, and I told Mr. D. that they were almost as good as you get at Jack Dempsey's in New York," Alice wrote to Margaret. "He was pleased. The Coast Guard gave us bracelets and compacts, and I think they thoroughly enjoyed the show." Years later, Alice would say that she felt that her

to our show. Another time we were walking down a hospital hall to the auditorium and this big soldier in a bathrobe saw Imogene first, and kind of mumbled to himself, 'If they look like you, I'm going back to bed.' When I came trailing along a few yards later, he said to me, 'They *do* look like her and I *am* going back to bed.'"

Alice told that anecdote many times over the years. Her friend, actress Patricia Wilson, whom she met in 1955, laughingly recalled, "Alice always made fun of her looks and how she and Imogene Coca would play USO camps during the war. Their [entrance on stage immediately followed] the bathing beauties in the show. As the soldiers were whooping and hollering over those girls, then she and Imogene would slink out [as if they had the same type of sex appeal]. She made terrible fun of her appearance, but she had the most beautiful complexion I think I've ever seen on a human being."

Wilson's reminiscence demonstrates that by 1943, Alice knew on which side her bread was buttered. Her face was best suited for comedy, as was her personality. In early 1944, encouraged by the roar of the soldiers' laughter and applause, Alice began in earnest to develop her own nightclub act. She spent "all the money she could get her hands on" for material that turned out to be useless.

Nevertheless, she auditioned in New York for Arki Yavensonne, the manager of Boston's Hotel Fensgate, which boasted a small exclusive club called the Satire Room, Yavensonne's own conception. Yavensonne "combs the field of entertainment for satirists," wrote a reviewer for the *Boston Globe*, "and there has been a long procession of them [at the Fensgate]." In those days, an appearance at the Satire Room was "a hallmark that leads a performer to exclusive New York night spots." For instance, Irwin Corey, Alice's fellow cast member from *New Faces*, sprang from the Satire Room to New York's Le Ruban Bleu (and later to the Blue Angel) in the fall of 1943. The immaculately dressed Yavensonne, who always sported a white carnation in his lapel and pearl gray spats, saw potential in Alice, and he signed her for a two-week engagement beginning the final week of February. Her contractual pay was seventy-five dollars per week, a sum equal to approximately $1100 in 2020 dollars.

The Satire Room was indeed intimate; it seated only thirty-eight. "The tables were so close, all I could see were eyes," Alice recalled.

"Eyes staring at me expectantly, daring me to be funny. I was so afraid I couldn't, but when the laughs started to come, it was a triumphant feeling." Boston journalist Joseph Dinneen, who had once denounced "progressive education," changed his tune somewhat after catching Alice's act, devoting an entire column to the novice entertainer. "Progressive education produces fine comedians . . . [Alice] holds a Sarah Lawrence B. A. in dramatics, a singular and rare distinction among comedians, and for my money, she deserves it because she makes me laugh from away down deep, especially when she crawls awkwardly over a grand piano top and dons a fur hat to sing a Russianized American folksong for an imaginary group of Russian guerillas. She understands comedy, especially the contrast of dead-pan [*sic*] with zaney [*sic*] lyrics." Likening Alice to Bea Lillie, Dinneen predicted that "a good deal more will be heard of her from now on." Despite Dinneen's praise, Alice criticized her own act as "weak" and "really terrible." Nonetheless, she continued at the Boston nightspot for a total of eight weeks.

One month after closing the Satire Room, Alice jumped at the chance to join Gus Schirmer's summer stock company in Stamford, Connecticut, especially when she learned that he wanted her for the season opener, supporting Tallulah Bankhead in a revival of the Noël Coward comedy *Private Lives*. Schirmer offered Alice the tiny role of Louise, described by Coward as "a rather frowsy looking girl," the maid of Bankhead's character Amanda Prynne. Louise appears briefly in the third act, set in Amanda's Paris flat. Alice's fluency in French—all dialects, no less—most likely prompted Schirmer to select her for the comic part. It had been four years since she had apprenticed at Kennebunkport, so she relished the opportunity to gain experience in the company of Bankhead

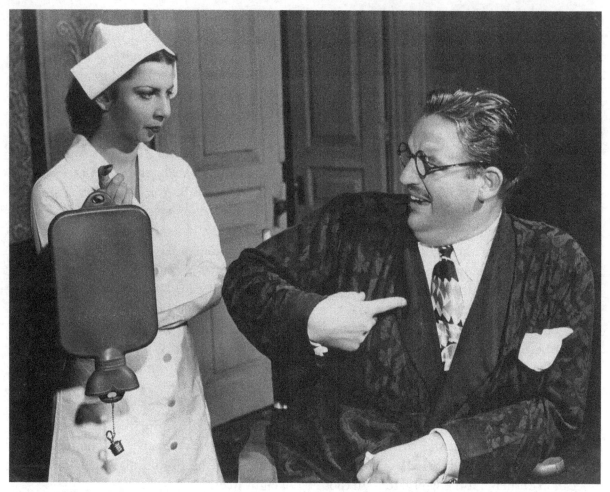

*Alice Pearce as Miss Preen and Laird Cregar as
Sheridan Whiteside in* The Man Who Came to
Dinner, *Strand Theatre, Stamford, Connecticut, 1944.*

and other film stars, each of whom Schirmer
had persuaded to appear at Stamford's Strand
Theatre for one-week engagements.

Rehearsals for *Private Lives* began on June
12, 1944, with British actor Rex O'Malley
directing and John Hoysradt co-starring as
Elyot Chase, the role which Coward himself
had played when the farce premiered in London in 1930. According to the *Brooklyn Daily
Eagle*, O'Malley and Hoysradt were considered
to be "among America's best satirical impersonators" of Coward. On opening night, June
19, the capacity audience included stage and

film veteran Fred Stone, singer Libby Holman,
actress Peggy Wood, and Bankhead's crony
Patsy Kelly. New York critic Robert Garland
was not impressed, describing Bankhead as
"decidedly off key" and declaring the play "not
too far up her alley." However, he declined to
print a "slip of the tongue" she made during
that evening's performance, but columnist Ed
Sullivan was game. The audience "shrieked
happily" at Bankhead's embarrassment, Sullivan reported, when she flubbed a line directed
to Hoysradt: "I'm not jealous. I'm just afraid
you'll fall in love with another *man*." The joke,
perhaps, was really on the audience, for Hoysradt himself was in fact gay.

Garland didn't mention Alice in his review,
but the reviewer for the local newspaper not-

ed: "Alice Pearce received an ovation for her brief appearance as Louise, the voluble French maid." Later that summer, Alice received nods in the *Stamford Advocate* for supporting Gloria Swanson in Harold J. Kennedy's *A Goose for the Gander*, Libby Holman and K. T. Stevens in Joseph A. Fields and Jerome Chodorov's *My Sister Eileen*, Una Merkel in Phoebe and Henry Ephron's *3 Is a Family*, and Glenda Farrell in S. N. Behrman's *Brief Moment*.

Schirmer handpicked Alice for a supporting role in Kaufman and Hart's *The Man Who Came to Dinner*, which opened on July 10. Schirmer had persuaded his friend, Hollywood actor Laird Cregar, to come east to play the title role of Sheridan Whiteside, a vitriolic, blustery egomaniac who fractures his hip at the home of his dinner hosts and makes himself an unwelcome guest for a month. Anyone familiar with the original Broadway production or the 1942 Warner Brothers film will have no problem identifying which character Alice played, simply because of the actress who inaugurated the role on both stage and film, and the one who still remains most closely identified with the part: Mary Wickes. Sharing some physical characteristics with Alice—a hawk nose and a receding chin—Wickes had delighted audiences as Miss Preen, Whiteside's beleaguered nurse whom he calls "Miss Bedpan." Eventually, Alice and Wickes would work together several times in Hollywood, where by then, Wickes had forged a career out of playing caustic nurses, spinsters, and housekeepers "that ultimately defined her," according to her biographer Steve Taravella. It's very likely that at some point Alice saw Wickes perform in the Broadway production of *The Man Who Came to Dinner*, for the smash hit ran for 739 performances between 1939 and 1941. This possibility makes one wonder if she borrowed anything from Wickes' characterization, yet

for those who are familiar with Alice's gifts for timing, especially her ability for a split-second tone-of-voice switch, it's easy to see how Alice could make this part her own.

Variety noted that Cregar lacked the draw of Bankhead, Swanson, and Constance Bennett; only half of the 1600-seat Strand auditorium was filled on opening night. The *Stamford Advocate* found that the production, directed by O'Malley, "lacked the smoothness and rhythm which makes for convincing play-acting due in all probability to limited rehearsal and players quickly thrown together." While Cregar was described merely as "competent," Alice and her fellow supporting players Dudley Clements, Teddy Hart, and O'Malley (as Beverly Carlton) were singled out for their "enjoyable performances, spontaneous and refreshing."

During Alice's eleven-week stint at the Strand, she was trying to keep abreast of developments within her family circle. On May 8, Margaret, accompanied by Josephine, had returned to New York after spending almost three months in Perry. Almost at once, Margaret set into motion a matchmaking plan for her widowed sister, now approaching her forty-third birthday. The matrimonial candidate was fifty-eight-year-old Dr. George K. Strode, whom Margaret and Bob had known in Paris. Strode, a widower for seven years, had recently been appointed director of the International Health Division of the Rockefeller Foundation, with which he had been associated since 1916. In Margaret's eyes, Josephine and Dr. Strode were a perfect match. Josephine, whom her Perry friends called "Jo," was such a "woman of charm and personal magnetism" that Margaret couldn't bear the thought of her being buried in a small town the rest of her life, looking after Sallie and helping her host bridge games and small dinner parties.

"Josephine was one of my favorite people," remembered Dorothy Williams, her former hairdresser in Perry. "She was just as classy as [the Pearces], but she'd always had to work— Margaret never worked. Margaret always had so much more money than Josephine, but Josephine was the best cook, and she gave parties like you could never believe. And that was what Dr. Strode needed: 'the hostess with the mostest.'"

After a whirlwind courtship, the wedding ceremony took place at noon on June 29 at Bob and Margaret's apartment at 29 Sutton Place South. There were no attendants; a small family reception followed. Absent was Bob Pearce, who, earlier in the month, had narrowly escaped a V-1 bomb explosion which partially buried him in his London apartment. These strange new Nazi weapons, which the British called "buzzbombs" or "doodlebugs" because of the loud buzzing sound their pulsejet engines produced, were the world's first operational cruise missiles. First employed on June 13, one week after the Normandy Invasion, the V-1 bombs caused many deaths and injuries, with as many as two hundred per day aimed at London. By late summer, British air defenses were reorganized with increased effectiveness, resulting in most being shot down. Soon after Paris was liberated in August 1944, Bob became one of the first American bankers to return to the city, where he helped to reopen the branch bank after a four-year absence.

As for Alice's relationship with John Rox during this interval, very little can be ascertained. Judging from John's final payroll report at Colorado's Camp Hale, it appears that he left there in March 1943. Yet his honorable discharge papers, drawn up almost two years later, state that John was on active duty until July 3 of that year. By this time, John, almost forty-one, took advantage of a newly created

John Rox, 1943. Photo courtesy Linda Swanson.

army regulation, permitting inductees over thirty-eight years old to transfer to the Enlisted Reserve Corps, thereby releasing them from active duty. John soon returned to New York.

By February 1944, John was working in the "tube shop" at a General Electric plant when Alice sent him a handmade Valentine's Day card. Bound with red yarn, the playful thirteen-page, heart-shaped booklet, was purportedly created by the "My Valentine Agency," proposing that the reader (John) consider Miss Sweetheart Angelface (Alice) as a suitable valentine. Presented as Miss Angelface's "case history," the card contains pasted-in photographs of Alice and her parents at various stages in her young life with Alice's humorous captions written in ink. Years later, Alice revisited the card and made notations in pencil, explaining the actual circumstances behind the somewhat goofy pictures, including one showing her parents and their friends wearing gas masks and relaxing in their *abri*. There is also one of Alice sunbathing topless in Switzerland—photographed from the rear—while leaning over an ornate iron balcony railing, with the caption: "She crossed the ocean, glad to see her *back*." Another shows Alice, in her college graduation cap and gown, scowling at the camera: "She graduated from Sarah Teasdale's School for Touchy Girls." The final page instructs the reader: "If you would like to have Miss Sweetheart Angelface for a valentine, please send 10 cents and a wrapper off of any jar of mustache wax." It's plain to see that Alice was still carrying a torch for John, who was yet quite involved with Perk Bailey. She remained hopeful, though.

Buoyed by her summer stock season at Stamford, Alice returned to New York with renewed confidence and determination. She enrolled in singing and dancing lessons so that she would be prepared for any part that might come her way. In the meantime, she once again made the rounds of the casting offices, hoping to find a role suited to her unique style. Fortunately, her quest was relatively brief. That October, she attended a cattle call audition, conducted by "that granddaddy of the stage," George Abbott, who was set to direct a new musical, one which balanced "classical dance, jazz, farce, and heart." Called *On the Town*, it was the story of three sailors making the most of a 24-hour leave in wartime New York City.

Produced by Broadway newcomers Oliver Smith and Paul Feigay, *On the Town* was a collaboration with four other neophytes—Leonard Bernstein, Jerome Robbins, Betty Comden and Adolph Green, each of whom was destined to become instrumental in shaping the future of the Broadway musical. Earlier that year Smith had designed the set for *Fancy Free*, a production of the Ballet Theatre in which three sailors on shore leave try to pick up girls in a bar. Smith thought the piece could be expanded into a full-scale musical so he approached Bernstein and Robbins, *Fancy Free*'s composer and choreographer, with the idea. They hopped onboard. Bernstein then convinced Smith and Robbins that his friends Comden and Green, at the time performing in a cabaret, would be perfect to write the book for *On the Town*. Although each team member had other projects on tap that summer, work on the musical progressed so rapidly that by September they were searching for a director, hoping to stage their production later that fall. "We were all twenty-five years old, you know, we were nothing but energy then," Bernstein recalled. Actually, the team members, including Smith and Feigay but excluding Green, were either twenty-five or twenty-six years old as the fall of 1944 approached. Alice Pearce, born within one year of everyone except Green, would soon find herself in the esteemed company of these creative geniuses.

The team envisioned *On the Town* as a "whirlwind tour" of New York, with scenes taking place at Times Square, Coney Island, and the Museum of Natural History, a design which allowed Comden and Green to "giddily portray the city they love[d]." When one of the sailors, Gabey, falls in love with a young woman who appears on a subway poster ("Miss Turnstiles"), the three fellows split up to find her, using clues revealed on the poster. They decide to meet at Times Square that night at eleven o'clock, no matter what happens in the meantime. While Ozzie searches the museum, Chip is accosted by an amorous lady cab driver named Hildy, who wants to "take him up to her place." Upon arriving at Hildy's apartment, their passion is suddenly dampened when they find her obnoxious roommate there, nursing a

Lucy Schmeeler (Alice Pearce) surprises Chip (Cris Alexander) and Hildy (Nancy Walker), On the Town, *Adelphi Theatre, 1944.*

cold. This "grand girl," as dubbed by Hildy, is introduced as Lucy Schmeeler. In quick order, Hildy tosses her out, but sniffling wall-flower Lucy shows up later in the action as a potential blind date for Gabey when he's stood up by Miss Turnstiles.

On the day of her audition, Alice showed up suffering from a bronchial condition, fearful that it would be a disastrous impediment. Just the opposite happened. After Alice sang her prepared piece, Abbott surprised her with an offer for a non-singing part—"the girl with a cold." It was perfect casting. Alice's respiratory congestion notwithstanding, she was capable of vocally producing an authentic adenoidal tone, later claiming that she achieved lifelike sniffles by thinking of raw onions. Although the comic role was quite small, "Lucy" was an important break for Alice, thanks to Abbott, a "champion of young talent" who was known to keep many of his protégés steadily at work. Alice considered Abbott "a great direc-

Pitkin (Robert Chisholm) and Lucy (Alice Pearce) blend voices in "I Understand," On the Town, 1945.

tor" who knew "how to make comedy believable." The admiration was mutual. Years later, Abbott, while writing his autobiography, saw fit to praise Alice for her performance in *On the Town.*

Lucy appears so briefly in *On the Town* that critic Rex Reed has called it a "nothing role," noting, "she doesn't even sing." Besides her first-act scene in Hildy's apartment, Lucy shows up in the second act scene at the Slam Bang Club, where she's crestfallen to learn that Gabey, with whom she was promised a date,

has fled to Coney Island to find Miss Turnstiles. Lucy then takes up with the pompous Pitkin W. Bridgework, who's been ditched by his fiancée Claire DeLoone. Pitkin, played by Robert Chisholm, sings "I Understand" while an attentive Lucy lends support between sneezes. Later, in the denouement scene at Coney Island, when Pitkin suddenly sneezes, all eyes turn to Lucy who cackles wickedly.

As Broadway historian Ethan Mordden has pointed out, *On the Town*'s principal cast was "made up almost entirely of unknowns." Com-all along. At twenty-two, Nancy was the youngest of the leading players, yet she had already appeared in three Hollywood films. She quickly became one of Alice's closest friends in the entertainment business and remained so for twenty years.

Another *On the Town* castmate became a constant in Alice's life. "Sainted Alice Pearce was the dearest friend I ever had," enthused Cris Alexander forty years later. Younger than Alice by more than two years, Cris had been trying to make it as a New York actor longer than she had. In 1938, at age eighteen and with the blessings of his widowed and wealthy father back in Tulsa, Oklahoma, he had arrived in the city "because [he] thought that they were waiting for [him]." Cris found a fabulous midtown apartment on West Fifty-First Street and enrolled at the Feagin School of Dramatic Art. He spent his first summer serving as an apprentice with the Manhattan Repertory Theatre Company at the Ogunquit Playhouse in Maine, hopeful he'd

The multi-talented Cris Alexander, circa 1945. Photo courtesy Randy Crocker.

den and Green, who had never set foot on a Broadway stage, created key roles for themselves—Green played Ozzie, and Comden was Ozzie's love interest, Claire. John Battles as Gabey and Cris Alexander as Chip also made their Broadway premieres. Japanese-American ballet dancer Sono Osato played Ivy Smith, or "Miss Turnstiles." Cast as Hildy was Nancy Walker, once described as "that incredible gnome with dead-pan delivery," whom Comden and Green and the producers had wanted

land an acting job in New York. "But it was no soap," Cris lamented. "I made all the right moves, but nobody gave me a tumble." He had always been handy with a camera, so Cris set up a portrait studio on Fifty-Seventh Street. In no time at all, his studies of stage celebrities were appearing in *Harper's Bazaar* and *Town & Country*. Still he wanted desperately to act. Finally, in 1942, Marjorie Jefferson, the director at the Summit Playhouse twenty miles away in New Jersey, invited Cris to join her company.

"That's where I got my first real experience," he recalled.

Meanwhile, Cris studied at the American Ballet School. When his boyfriend John Butler got a job in the dancing chorus of *On the Town*, Cris decided to attend the singing audition, even though he had never sung on stage. That's how he met Alice Pearce. "She auditioned the same day I did," he remembered, adding fervently, "Of course, we became *instant* relatives." In 1994, as the fiftieth anniversary of *On the Town* drew near, Cris reminisced about the company's unique camaraderie: "About some rare productions you hear actors say, 'Oh, we were like one big happy family.' We really were. Everybody in that cast was—and maybe that was part of the chemistry—a definite personality."

The bond between Alice and Cris was especially tight. "I came to know quite soon that she was called 'Peeps.' I don't know who gave her the name," Cris confessed. "Most everybody who knew her called her that. It was very appropriate." When addressing Alice, Cris soon began to alternate between "Peeps" and "Sister," or sometimes just "Sis." Like Alice, Cris was an only child, but he had never wished for a biological sibling. "I'd rather pick them myself," he said, explaining, "You see, Peeps *was* my sister." Alice reciprocated by always calling him "Brother" or "Bro."

Rehearsals for *On the Town* began on November 13, with a ten-day tryout planned for Boston's Colonial Theatre exactly one month later. The typical cuts and additions made for a stressful fortnight in Boston, but ready or not, the musical was slated to open at the Adelphi, located on Fifty-Fourth Street between Sixth and Seventh Avenues. Known as Broadway's "ultimate hard-luck house," the Adelphi was located at the northernmost edge of the theater district and consequently attracted only "the most feeble bookings, all bombs." That all

Best buddies Cris Alexander and Alice Pearce clowning at "some dreary USO outpost for the wounded of Long Island," 1945. Cris Alexander photo.

changed on December 28, 1944, when *On the Town* opened to enthusiastic reviews. *The New York Times* was effusive, proclaiming the show as "the freshest and most engaging musical since *Oklahoma!* Everything about it is right." Walter Winchell called it "a bundle from the musical heavens ... chockfull of flash and zing." Critics across town praised the show's exuberance, energy, and youth. "The main thing was the music," recalled Cris Alexander. "It was so explosive. Most people at a Broadway musical had never heard anything quite like that before. Even at the worst matinee, [the audience] went wild."

Seven months later, during the closing days of the war, folks were still flocking to see *On the Town*, which had moved to more convenient venues twice since June 4. *New York Daily News* drama critic John Chapman, who had essentially panned the show when it opened, revisited it that summer at the Martin Beck

Alice Pearce, photographed by Cris Alexander, in her dressing room at the Martin Beck Theatre during the run of On the Town, *1945.*

Theatre on Forty-Fifth Street. "It looks spick and span and the company is right on the ball," Chapman wrote. "I had no impression that anybody involved was getting the least bit tired of *On the Town*, and an SRO audience was loving it." Alice was in full accord with Chapman, confessing that her part in the musical still thrilled her "to no end." Up until this time, most reviews had not singled out Alice, but Chapman made it a point to add his praise for the show's supporting performers: "Alice Pearce is kept backstage most of the time and her role of Lucy Schmeeler is a very small one in the number of moments on the stage and lines spoken; but these moments and lines, when they come, get laughs—so they have served their purpose."

When *On the Town* closed after 462 performances on February 2, 1946, Alice had only one day of rest before hitting the road for Baltimore, the first stop on the show's national tour. She, along with Nancy Walker, Adolph Green, and a few others from the original cast had signed on for the three-month tour, which included engagements in Philadelphia, Pittsburgh, Detroit, and Chicago.

Living out of a suitcase for twelve weeks on the road could become wearing, but Alice and Nancy, who roomed together, found ways to liven up the dreariest of times, according to an anecdote Alice shared a few years later with a journalist. One night during the tour, Alice and Nancy asked Don Weismuller, a dancer in the company, to drop by their hotel room after the performance. When the conversation withered, Alice had a sudden thought. "Have you ever seen me in my green leotard? Would you like for me to dance for you?"

Changing into her form-fitting attire, Alice wrapped Nancy's fur scarf around her neck, plopped a picture hat on her head, and went into her dance. Without warning, her prank-ish pals pushed her out into the hotel hallway and locked the door. It was three o'clock in the morning, and around the corner of the corridor a noisy convention party was going strong. Alice knocked on the door and begged to be let back in. Suddenly she heard the door around the corner open. "Good night, fellows," came a drunken voice. Alice pounded harder. At that moment, the inebriated gentleman rounded the turn. "No! Oh, no!" he cried at the first look, "Fellows, come, look!" Nancy and Don heard him, softened, and pulled Alice back in and stood behind the door listening. All they could hear was a hysterical voice protesting, "But it was *right here*. I saw it. Honest, I saw it!"

The box-office reaction to *On the Town* was "swell" in all of the cities on the tour, except for Chicago. Even though cordially received by reviewers there, the show did "insufficient business" for its four weeks at the Great Northern, and so the tour ended on April 27. Despite her small part, Alice received good notices, like one from the *Chicago Sun-Times*: "Alice Pearce makes a lot out of the role of a homely wallflower with a bad cold."

In years to come, *On the Town* would be revived three times on Broadway. It would also be staged in London several times, and yet, seventy-five years later, when the name "Lucy Schmeeler" is uttered, the actress who first *achooed* her way across the Adelphi stage comes to mind, hands down. Granted, that identification is boosted by Alice's enhanced replication of Lucy five years later in the film version of *On the Town*— just as Mary Wickes had reprised "Miss Preen" from *The Man Who Came to Dinner*—thereby ensuring Lucy as her signature movie role. (Likewise, Miss Preen will be forever identified with Wickes.) In Alice's case, Lucy would eventually drop to a second-rank position twenty years later, when the plum role of Gladys Kravitz would come along.

CHAPTER ELEVEN
Sutton Place Pixie

"She's crazy to make people happy. She doesn't know she sings off key, that she's bad. She's just having a great time."

Alice soon learned that the pranks pulled by Nancy Walker were amateurish compared to the stunts performed by the irrepressible Tallulah Bankhead, who was set to open a tour of *Private Lives* in Toronto on June 17, 1946. In preparation, Bankhead hand selected a supporting cast including Donald Cook, Mary Mason, Alexander Clark, and Alice, whom Bankhead wanted to repeat the role of Louise, the French maid. The only problem was that Alice had already signed on with Gus Schirmer for a season of summer stock at the Greenwich Playhouse in Connecticut. Since Schirmer wanted Bankhead's *Private Lives* for his season opener on June 24, Bankhead acquiesced—Alice would be hired for the Toronto engagement as well as the two-week Greenwich run, but she would not continue with the tour afterwards.

Dark and handsome Donald Cook, "one the last of the high-comedy matinee idols," played brilliantly opposite Bankhead. One reviewer described their onstage chemistry, noting that they "bring tenderness to their rare placid moments, rowdy roughhouse to their frequent tempestuous scenes." Of course, it didn't hurt matters that the two were having an offstage love affair, something each had been known to do with previous co-stars. The production was so wildly popular in Toronto that the police were called in to handle the crowds of potential ticket purchasers at the Royal Alexandra Theatre.

The tour had its ups and downs, Alice said, due largely to certain eccentricities of Bankhead's maid. Upon arriving in Greenwich, Bankhead had her bags taken directly to the theatre to be unpacked and her dresses pressed. When she herself arrived at the theatre, she discovered that the maid had unpacked all bags except hers and was endeavoring to iron Mary Mason's suit which she had thoroughly doused with water. With the curtain soon to go up, Alice pitched in and pressed the star's Mainbocher gowns, act by act, with Bankhead standing firmly over her—"Get that wrinkle in the second pleat, dahling."

Bankhead drew the largest advance sale in the history of the Greenwich Playhouse. Opening night orchestra seats went for $4.80 each, marking "one of the highest scales ever charged for a summer theater." In the audience that night were Lucille Ball, Vivienne Segal, restauranteur Vincent Sardi, society impresario Earl Blackwell, and members of the fashionable Greenwich colony. Outside, a horde of bobby-soxers clamored for autographs despite the oppressive heat. "Never one to be known as a quiet, retiring missy, La Bankhead romped, snarled, chortled, rolled, and threw things with the passion of a hurricane," gushed critic Vernon Rice, who deemed Cook an excellent sparring partner for Bankhead. Mary Mason and Alexander Clark, Rice said, lifted their characters from "the realm of mere stooges," while

Alice, as the comic French maid, "was both comic and French."

Alice seems to have gotten along well with the volatile Bankhead. According to Alice, the leading lady was so delighted with Alice's brief performance that she got changed in time to stand in the wings for Alice's opening scene, claiming it "put her in a good humor for the whole evening." However, Alice missed a lot of the fireworks that summer when she stayed behind in Greenwich and Bankhead's company trekked back through Canada. In Ottawa, on July 8, Bankhead was reunited with an uncle, a U. S. Embassy diplomat whom she had not seen in seventeen years. After the evening performance, he hosted Bankhead and the cast at a quiet buffet supper at an elegant hotel. Beforehand, Bankhead had beseeched her fellow actors to "be on their best behavior as Americans and as representatives of their often-maligned profession." However, she did not heed her own entreaty. Bankhead got drunk at the buffet, "took off all her clothes, and ran naked up and down the corridors of the hotel."

For the remainder of the summer, Alice was stationed at the Greenwich Playhouse, appearing in such productions as *Angel Street* (as amiable servant Elizabeth) and the revue *Wish You Were Here* (supporting Billy Gilbert). Along with the summer stock engagement and the tours, she had had no choice but to put her personal life on hold.

Indeed, for much of the year, Alice had little chance to see John Rox, who was still struggling to get some of his songs recorded and others published. The foremost contender was "It's a Big, Wide, Wonderful World," which had been used in yet another Broadway show, *Common Ground*, a play by Edward Chodorov, which ran for sixty-nine performances in the spring of 1945. In the meantime, Nancy Nolan,

a singing pianist at the Monkey Bar, a cocktail lounge in the Hotel Elysée, had latched onto the song. For the past several years, "thousands of her fans were haunted by this beautiful hunk of fluff," yet no one had recorded it. Ethel Merman once claimed it as her favorite song, John said, and Judy Garland wanted to sing it in a film but couldn't find its publisher or writer. John's slump dragged on.

Conversely, John's domestic partner Perk Bailey was enjoying a career upswing. In July 1945, he had left the Talon zipper company to become the director of fashion merchandising for *Men's Wear* magazine, a product of Fairchild Publications. Within six months, Perk was named as editor of the trade journal, which served men's wear retailers across the country. In April 1946, soon after his promotion, he purchased a large, old house at 152 Bayview Avenue in Northport, Long Island, to be used as a second home for John and himself—a getaway from Manhattan's hectic pace. Built in the 1870s by Northport master carpenter John C. Smith for George Matthias, the two-and-one-half storied house featured five bays and a flat gabled roof. Right away, Perk had both the interior and exterior remodeled, removing the front porch and giving the facade a Georgian appearance.

Although five years had passed since Alice met John, she evidently still had strong feelings for him, despite his ongoing involvement with Perk. It's uncertain exactly how Alice fit into this equation; those who knew the precise dynamics are long gone. However, in 1944, Alice left a curious notation under a photograph of John and Perk on the beach at Fire Island: "my boyfriends." This indicates that she was not only fond of the pair, but perhaps also quite accepting of their long-term relationship. One wonders, though, how often Alice felt like "the odd man out."

Alice Pearce, 1945.

One person who was not privy to the details of this interrelationship yet felt a definite connection to John was Peggy Watson, a recent Juilliard graduate who, for the past year, had frequented the same studio where John's demos were recorded. John had become good friends with Bill Coburn who managed the Tone-Art Recording Company, and occasionally John would be around when Peggy was recording music for her course work. Bill was attracted to Peggy, but he was too shy to initiate any lengthy conversation. Meanwhile, Peggy had a secret crush on John.

"One night in 1946," Peggy recalled, "the three of us were working in the studio, and John said, 'By the way, when we're finished working, can you come over to the apartment? We're going to have a drink and some refreshments.' And I thought, 'Oh, wonderful! I'll get to be around John longer.' And so, we were standing in the control room after we'd finished about midnight, and Bill looked at me and said, 'Well, we're going over to John's apartment and I guess since you're here we have to invite you, too.' And I got very indignant and I said, 'No, I've *already* been invited!'"

Despite this awkward beginning, Peggy and Bill's lifelong romance began that very night. As her relationship with Bill progressed, Peggy also got to know John and learn little things about his life. "I loved John," she exclaimed in 2014. "Oh, my, he was such a good guy!" Looking back, Peggy recalled that John was not dating Alice at the time she met him. "He was going with Alice part of the time, and then *not* going with her, but *then again* going with her. There was another gentleman, and he was a good friend of John's." When asked if the "gentleman" was named Perkins Bailey, Peggy answered in the affirmative but confessed that she didn't realize that the men were romantic partners. "It doesn't surprise me," she admitted, "but in those days, you just *didn't* talk about it. [Bill and I] never had any feelings about [same-sex relationships] one way or another." Peggy's voice then filled with wonder as she exclaimed, "It's amazing how lives are intertwined! You're very close to these people, but you really don't know anything about them. And it's absolutely fabulous!"

Not only was Alice separated from John for half of 1946, but by midyear she hadn't seen her parents for ten months. In April 1945, Bob Pearce had returned to New York from a nineteen-month stay in Europe. When duties at the Paris bank necessitated his return that September, six weeks after the war's end, Margaret accompanied him on the voyage. They arrived back in the States on July 9, 1946—during the midst of Alice's summer stock stint at Greenwich—with big plans to set down deeper roots. Their brother-in-law George Strode, who owned a summer home in Whitingham, Vermont, had previously pitched the idea that Bob and Margaret should also buy property in the vicinity. Bob, who was now based in New York and anticipating retirement in a few years, seriously considered George's suggestion. The Pearces took a quick trip up to visit George and Josephine and to scout the possibilities. They were immediately attracted to a large farmhouse situated on "Town Hill" in the center of Whitingham Township, overlooking two lakes and offering spectacular views of the nearby mountains. Local historians estimated that the original section of the house dated back to 1833. Eleven red barns also stood on the 300-acre property, of which two thirds were pastureland and the remainder woodlands, which included a sugar maple grove consisting of 1500 syrup buckets. The Pearces offered $50,000 to the surprised owner, seventy-five-year-old Whitman Jesse Wheeler, whose family had lived in the area for generations. Wheeler readily accepted their offer, adding a stipulation that he be allowed access to the main barn and to continue farming part of the land. "They spent a whole winter fixing the house up, and they changed it dramatically from what my grandparents had," recalled Whitman James Wheeler in 2013. The Pearces enlarged the original structure, he said, by attaching an ell constructed from pre-existing sheds which stood in the yard of the house. When completed, the Pearces' impressive new summer home contained over 5,000 square feet, yet it hardly resembled any of the fine homes they had inhabited in Belgium and France.

In the meantime, Alice—still trying to manage her career without an agent—had come to realize that the 1946–47 theatre season was looking rather lean. Her old friend Mark Lawrence, whom she had met at Princeton's Theatre Intime, had come to the same conclusion. Following his military discharge in April 1946, Mark had settled in Manhattan and promptly wrote a musical comedy called *It Sez Here*, for which he envisioned Lucille Ball as its lead. He peddled his creation up and down Broadway that summer and fall, but there were no takers.

Mark commiserated with Alice who felt that the theatre had turned its back on her. By Thanksgiving, she had concluded that "she needed his lyrics and he had decided that he needed her." They devoted this period of unemployment to creating a nightclub act. "I was anxious to rectify the mistakes I had made in my club work in Boston," Alice explained. She knew that Mark was the perfect source for new material. Ever since those Princeton days, when Alice and Mark discovered that their "senses of humor were identical," the pair had felt a strong bond. Over the next five years, Mark would prove himself as Alice's stalwart cohort.

There were other reasons that Alice and Mark clicked. Like Alice, Mark had enjoyed a privileged upbringing. His father's wealth and position in Washington, D. C., had afforded the Lawrence children with a live-in governess, as well as a live-in cook, maid, and gardener. Prior to Princeton, Mark had attended the best prep schools, including the revered Phillips Academy in Andover, Massachusetts.

Mark, three years and three months younger than Alice, was born on January 14, 1921— exactly one year after her pal Cris Alexander was born. Like Alice, Mark had been kissed by the spotlight at a tender age. While she was delighting Belgian audiences in plays at Les Tourelles, Mark was earning laughs in productions at a private school in his mother's home state of South Carolina. At age six, he brought down the house when his trousers ripped while he was portraying an elf. Another ham was born.

Just as Bob and Margaret Pearce had reservations about Alice's career choice, Mark's parents were quite displeased with his plans to pursue writing comedic songs and plays. He received various bitter letters from his mother, and in one of them she wrote: "Some people are born funny. Do you think you are?"

Encouraged to enter the café scene by Herbert Jacoby, proprietor of the swank Blue Angel nightclub, Alice and Mark collaborated during the winter of 1947 and found that they worked together quite smoothly. "When Alice and I decided to become a team," Mark explained, "we knew that to become successful we had to have a different approach, something unusual and catchy. So, the first thing we did was think. For months we kicked around ideas, jotted notes and things, and then it came quite suddenly to both of us. We would act as if we were hicks, a couple of very poor showmen who wanted to entertain more than anything else in the world." Once the pair decided on this format, they wrote a number of skits in no time at all. "I think it took about a week," Mark said. While Alice made suggestions, Mark did the actual writing. "I don't think I'm much of a comedian or actor," Mark confessed, "but I can at least be a part of show business by writing for it." In years to come, one nightclub critic, calling Alice the Mad Hatter, referred to Mark as "her own Lewis Carroll."

Mark also came to realize that the character he had created for Alice needed to be the focus of the act, so his character, accompany-

*Mark Lawrence and Alice Pearce at the Blue Angel nightclub, 1947.
Cris Alexander photo.*

She recognizes this as her big break and gleefully undertakes to give her all, "which might be just like any other girl singers, except for [a few] loose screws."

Mark worked up a repertoire of ten zany songs for The Girl. By this point, both he and Alice felt optimistic about their creation, yet they knew not to put all of their eggs in one basket. So, until they could snag an engagement, they began writing a musical comedy they called *Here's Your Hat*. Meanwhile, Alice was considering yet another option, according to an item that appeared in Dorothy Kilgallen's column in late winter. Kilgallen announced that Alice and Nancy Walker were hoping to launch a nightclub skit "soon after Nancy's next musical *Barefoot Boy with Cheek* debuts." The skit was created by Jeff Bailey who had co-written *Look, Boys! . . . Girls!*, the USO show in which Alice had performed three years earlier. As things turned out, Alice did not need this backup plan.

ing on the piano, slid to the background. Simply called "The Girl," Alice's character was described by Mark as "sort of an extension, to the nth degree, of Alice herself." "She's crazy to make people happy," Alice said of her stage persona. "She doesn't know she sings off key, that she's bad. She's just having a great time." Mark and Alice determined that "The Girl" was a "neglected young person who just happened to be in an alley alongside [a nightclub] as the show began." In desperation, someone poked his head out of the stage door and asked her if she could sing. Whereupon the girl dashed onto the stage before she could be stopped.

By early spring, Alice and Mark felt that their act was polished enough to approach Herbert Jacoby, who offered them a one-night tryout at The Blue Angel on Sunday, March 30. Jacoby evidently smelled success or he wouldn't have encouraged Alice in the first place. He always knew what he wanted, said Portia Nelson, a mainstay performer at his club in the 1950s. "It was his taste that made the Blue Angel," Nelson asserted. Jacoby's judgment was "usually indisputable," thus his acts were the crème de la crème. However, auditioning for the dour Frenchman could be quite daunting. Standing at six foot two, his beaked nose, dark eyes, and gloomy expression intimidated most people. Behind his back, he was called "the Prince of Darkness." Jacoby was actually rather introverted and therefore not given to effusiveness, often glowering during auditions when he was unimpressed. Yet this very serious man had dedicated his career to the discovery of talented unknowns. Very quickly after The Blue Angel had opened in 1943, the club gained its reputation as the number one showcase in New York for "acts that were looking to go places." Alice and Mark felt quite privileged to be sought by Jacoby.

Located at 152 East Fifty-Fifth Street, The Blue Angel was just a little farther than three blocks west of Alice's apartment on Sutton Place South. The building itself had once been an old carriage house. "If you lived in the neighborhood, you could go to a Broadway show and walk home, and maybe stop off at The Blue Angel for a late supper and catch a couple of the acts," recalled Max Gordon, Jacoby's business partner. "We used to get a lot of customers like that." Like Gordon, many people considered The Blue Angel as the greatest nightclub in New York. It would become known nationwide as a "launching pad" for the likes of Yul Brynner, Pearl Bailey, Harry Belafonte, Eartha Kitt, Phyllis Diller, Johnny Mathis, Carol Burnett, Woody Allen, and Barbra Streisand. "But the club itself had an electricity that attracted people regardless of who was appearing," noted cabaret historian James Gavin. "'You've *got* to go to the Blue Angel before you leave,' said many a New Yorker to visiting friends."

Decorated in a "smart, continental manner" by Jacoby and Broadway scenic designer Stewart Chaney, The Blue Angel featured black patent leather walls in the bar. For the main room—a narrow space located behind the bar—the pair chose a red carpet, tufted gray velour walls with pink rosettes, pink leather banquettes along the left and right, and small black marble tables in the center. At the far end was "an adorable tiny stage with a plaster of Paris curtain topped by a little plaster angel [painted blue]." Jacoby had chosen The Blue Angel as the nitery's name because he was a fan of the Marlene Dietrich movie of the same title.

Alice and Mark's tryout on March 30, 1947, proved to Jacoby that they were indeed Blue Angel material: "fine talent with commercial appeal." The following day, Jacoby contracted with Alice and Mark for a four-week engagement at $300 per week—divided between them—to begin on April 28. By signing the contract, they agreed to grant Jacoby's customary option which allowed him to book them for an additional four weeks, in exchange for a bonus of both cash money and food and drinks at the Blue Angel.

The act typically began with Mark calmly entering the stage and placing various objects atop the piano. Among the distasteful props are an exhausted leopard skin, a decrepit black feather fan, a green alligator skin purse, a tattered umbrella, and a splintered banjo. Just after Mark seats himself at the keyboard, the peace and quiet are shattered by "The Girl" scurrying to the piano making gibbering noises to "convey that she is insanely happy to be present." She suddenly plants herself amid the props on the piano, announcing breathlessly, "Our second number will be a request number, a li'l ol' Southern lullaby," done, she says, in answer to two requests—one for a Russian song and another for a Southern song. Giggling girlishly, "The Girl" winds three mink fur pieces into a bandage round her head and begins (to the tune of "Short'nin' Bread"):

Two liddle pahty membahs lyin' in bed,
One was pink and de odder mos' red.
Call for de commissar, he said to me:

Gib dem liddle pahty membahs bublitchki.
Put on the samovar,
Put on the tea,
Mammy's goin' to make
A little bublitchki.

Flinging the minks aside, "The Girl" opens the alligator purse and pulls it down onto her head, informing the audience that next she'll sing Cole Porter's "Night and Day." Since she doesn't like that melody, she will sing it to the tune of *her* favorite song which happens to be the old 1910s standard "Nola"— totally incongruous with Porter's lyrics—producing highly comic results.

Hurling the alligator bag over her shoulder, the pixie prepares for the next number by draping herself in the leopard skin and modeling a crumpled horsehair hat. Bringing two lighted cigarettes out from behind her back, she sings "Two Cigarettes in the Dark," smoking them every time the lyrics call for it and ending up nearly choking to death, "to the screams of a hep audience."

Not only were audiences amused by Mark's lyrics and Alice's delivery, but the peculiar getup of "The Girl" was something with which most Blue Angel patrons were unaccustomed. First there was Alice's "insane" hairdo, parted in the middle and pulled severely against her scalp, with two wisps poking out from either side. Since her teen years, Alice had suffered from hair loss, but instead of adopting some wild wig for her act, she chose a hairstyle which accentuated her thin hair. One critic dubbed it as her "Bikini Atoll hair-do"—a heartless reference to a symptom of radiation poisoning experienced by natives on a small group of Pacific islands called Bikini Atoll, where the United States military began testing nuclear weapons immediately following the war.

Alice was wont to discard out-of-fashion frocks from her personal wardrobe, but there was a Paris original which she had held on to for a decade. "In 1937, Mother had ordered the dress for me from Molyneux," Alice recalled. "It was the first custom-made dress I'd ever had. It was black velvet and floor length then. I wore it to a New Year's Eve party at

"Put on the samovar, put on the tea, Mammy's goin' to make a little bublitchki." Cris Alexander photo.

Maxime's, and I had a wonderful time." She chose it for "The Girl," but not without alterations to make it less chic. Alice had it shortened to ankle length, adding an overlay of black lace and sewing sprigs of paper flowers on the skirt. She borrowed the mink "head bandage" from roommate Betty La Branche, who left it behind when she joined the Red Cross in 1943. Joining Betty's three-piece scarf was an unattached kolinsky which Alice named "Elmer" and a single mink without front feet she called "George," all of which she smooched during the act, cackling like a mad crone. As for the green alligator pocketbook, Alice had bought it using her first paycheck from *New Faces of 1943*. At four years old, it was, for Alice, long passé.

Alice's unique brand of "ladylike lunacy" was an overnight sensation with the open-mouthed elites who packed The Blue Angel night after night that spring. They particularly delighted in a topical number which Mark based on current placards plastered in every pay telephone booth in the city, advising callers to wait for the dial tone before dialing, lest they lose their nickels. It blended two old melodies, "Wait Till the Sun Shines, Nellie" and "Reuben, Reuben":

Wait for the dial tone, Nellie.
Nellie, don't you cry.
You're gonna get your dial tone, Nellie, bye and bye.

Watkins, Watkins, I've been Chickering,
Sweet Lorraine, you're Wadsworth Five.
If Stuyvesant thinks he can Academy,
I'll Butterfield Eight his Riverside Drive.

Another audience favorite was "Aphrodesia McTuttle and Her Fierce Fradou," a satire on the present folk singer craze. It concerned a "wee Scottish lass given to fradous, or fits," especially when she's drunk. (Aphrodesia lures her lovers to the moors and beats them to a pulp.)

During rehearsal at the Blue Angel, Alice poses in her refashioned Molyneux, while Mark Lawrence looks on, 1947.

The chief prop during this number was a "Scottish Fluke," actually a broken-down banjo.

When they could get reservations, Alice's family and friends, like Cris Alexander and Miles White, frequented The Blue Angel. According to Alice, her parents much preferred theatres to night clubs, but still they were quite pleased with her success. Her father, whom Alice said was "so proud he could hardly keep his vest on," regularly brought along his associates from the bank. Bob had always encouraged Alice's ability to "see something funny in any situation." "I'm afraid my mother never understood when Daddy and I winked at each other over private jokes," she confessed.

Meanwhile, Alice and Mark received glowing reviews in the press, as well as nods from Walter Winchell and Ed Sullivan. Bert McCord of the *New York Herald Tribune* was among the first to recognize Alice's performance: "The

Alice, as "The Girl," kisses Elmer, 1947. On her head is the green alligator purse she bought in 1942. Cris Alexander photo.

not share McCord's opinion, calling Alice's act a "weird mangling of song and words," he did admit that it "went over well with the bistro's clientele." Robert Dana of the *New York World-Telegram* confessed: "In a café year that hasn't been particularly distinguished for good comedy, it is heartening to come across a satirist with the effervescence and broad clowning of Alice Pierce [*sic*], who makes her appearance and actions punctuate to a high degree of excellence the clever material written by Mark Lawrence."

The most ardent praise that spring came from George Freedley, drama critic for the *New York Morning Telegraph*, who ordinarily, he admitted, did not venture into "the purlieus of night club life." He was happy to report that "Miss Pearce is even better as an entertainer in a supper club than on the legitimate stage." Regarding Jacoby's "tall supper and drink tariff," Freedley conceded, "However, Alice Pearce is worth what he asks. Asked to describe precisely what Miss Pearce does, this column would be at a complete loss. She uses crazy costumes and props, she sings both off and on key, she grimaces and wriggles; in point of fact, these words could be used to describe many a less talented girl, so we'll just give up and tell you to see Alice Pearce yourself. She is a young Beatrice Lillie, without in any way

most exciting thing about the new line-up at the Blue Angel is the night club debut of Miss Pearce, a saucy and sparkling comedienne whom it is a genuine delight to see and hear ... She camps and cavorts through some wonderfully fresh material that lies somewhere between sophisticated satire and hilarious burlesque. You may have seen this girl in *On the Town*, but until you have seen her at the Blue Angel, you just haven't lived, that's all." While Lew Sheaffer of the *Brooklyn Daily Eagle* did

Alice crooning to Mark Lawrence's accompaniment as part of their Blue Angel act, 1947.

shrewd businessman who always balanced his superb taste with his financial sense"—realized that once successful acts "hit the bigtime [*sic*] coin," they considered themselves too important to return to the spot which gave them their big chance. Jacoby and other club operators felt that too many stars they had launched had gotten away from them. Realizing that Alice Pearce was a hot property—and one without an agent—Jacoby persuaded Alice to sign a personal management contract, his first ever. Jacoby's intent was to maintain control of Alice's act. "After an act's click, performer frequently starts playing opposition spots," explained *Variety*, "and since headliners are too few to be relinquished, bonifaces would like control of bookings." Alice put her pen to paper on June 7, agreeing to pay Jacoby ten percent of gross compensation received by her for the next two years. Mark Lawrence was not left out; Jacoby agreed to "counsel and advise [Alice's] "accompanist, or partner, in all matters which concern [her] artistic and professional career."

imitating the great English star. She is just Alice Pearce and a great darling."

No one was more elated with such accolades—and the business they generated—than Herbert Jacoby. Within a week of Alice and Mark's first performance, he had extended their engagement indefinitely.

Meanwhile, another astute investor also knew a good thing when he saw it. Just three days after Alice's opening, columnist Earl Wilson reported that millionaire Alexis "Lex" Thompson, owner of the Philadelphia Eagles, wanted to buy up Alice's Blue Angel contract. Jacoby scurried into action. Jacoby—"a cold,

As summer approached, Alice's draw among New York's smart set exceeded Jacoby's expectations. The phone at the Blue Angel kept ringing each day with callers asking if Alice Pearce was still performing there. The act had become so wildly popular that it ran for a total of ten weeks, stopping only because the club regularly closed for the months of July and August.

In late May, singer-pianist Phil Gordon, straight from a hit engagement at Chicago's Ambassador West Hotel, joined the Blue Angel bill. Playing by ear, the affable thirty-one-year-old managed to give all his numbers an informal, nostalgic touch, whether they were melancholy ballads or rhythmically wild boogie beats. Jacoby—whose flair for finding talent Gordon considered pure "genius"—deemed the piano "whimsyist" an ideal opener for other club performers like Alice, Pearl Bailey, and Josephine Premice. Gordon was in awe of them, especially Alice, claiming that he always became an audience member when she performed. "She sang in this real high, Mrs. Roosevelt type voice, and she had some of the wildest material you have ever heard," Gordon recalled. "It was awfully left-handed and very New York. I don't think it would go anywhere else . . . I don't mean to be braggadocious, but you had to be *something* to play the Blue Angel. We all complemented each other. I played hot boogie-woogie and was really Southern. I would open the show, and Alice would close it. And in between, [Jacoby] might have Florence Desmond who did imitations—she did a Marlene Dietrich that would scare you to death—and then he'd have Mildred Bailey, the old blues singer. But Alice was a gas! She played up the 'no chin' by painting [with make-up] under there so it would look worse."

Gordon was equally impressed with Alice offstage. "Alice was also one of the dearest, kindest, most likeable (lovable) ladies I *ever* worked with," he wrote. "She had the greatest sense of humor and a true ability to laugh at herself and still keep her self-esteem. She came from a wealthy background—and it showed. She was a delight and one of my better memories."

Late that spring, Alice was photographed for the August issues of *Vogue* and *Mademoiselle*, the latter of which described her talent as "mix[ing] old tunes, words and chapeaux devastatingly." However, the very first photos promoting her act were taken by Cris Alexander, her bosom buddy from *On the Town*. "We must have taken a thousand pictures," Cris

Alice stands on top of the Blue Angel piano holding her battered umbrella, 1947. Cris Alexander photo.

exclaimed. "I could never decide who was my favorite subject, Peeps or Martha Graham." The majority of Cris' photos of Alice wearing the black velvet Molyneux were actually taken on the tiny stage at The Blue Angel. Most poses show her either sitting, standing, or lying on top of the piano, with Mark seated at the keyboard. She holds or wears various props, including the minks, the leopard skin, the alligator pocketbook, the shabby umbrella, and an assortment of taxidermic birds.

Cris posed Alice in other settings, both artful and outrageous, in the early summer of 1947. In one series, she appears in a ruffled nightgown, dancing and prancing like a sprite, on a rooftop with the Manhattan skyline serving as a backdrop. "That was where she used to live on Sutton Place. It was one—sort of grayish—afternoon, and she had me over for lunch, and she made a corn chowder," recalled Cris. "And afterwards we went up on the roof," he said, chuckling, "and *played*."

On the roof of her apartment house, Alice rises on tiptoe while the Chrysler Building looms in the background, 1947. Cris Alexander photo.

Alice, whom Cris Alexander once called an "inspired, absolutely lovely lunatic," prances on the roof of 31 Sutton Place South, overlooking the East River, 1947. Cris Alexander photo.

Another afternoon, Cris was taking some headshots of Alice in his studio on Fifty-Seventh Street, between Fifth and Madison Avenues. "She was wearing my best lace dress," enthused Cris, who collected vintage clothing for his own amusement but sometimes found them useful in photo shoots. "At the time, there was a great big hole in Madison Avenue where they were repairing a sewer. And I just happened to know the man who was in charge of construction—through a very unlikely set of circumstances, not very interesting—but he was a wonderful Italian man whom we called 'The King of the Sewer.' And he was a *camp* if ever there was one! And so, I had arranged with him—I think they shut down [work] at three o'clock—so when we got through working in the studio, I said, 'Sister, you know where we're going?' And she said [*imitating Alice using a mousy voice*], 'Yes, I do, Brother.' And we trot-

ted around the corner, and I threw her in the hole! There's one print where she's looking up, as if from the grave. They used that, much to my surprise, in *Harper's Bazaar*. I used to work for them."

That same summer, Alice was courted by producers Oliver Smith and Paul Feigay for a comic role in Comden and Green's musical titled *Free for All*, set during the Alaska Gold Rush of 1898. Sam Zolotow of *The New York Times* announced to his readers that Alice was the only definite for the cast, but that parts were also being "tailored to fit" George Coulouris and Betty Lou Barto, Nancy Walker's kid sister. Rehearsals were set to begin September 15. However, on July 30, Zolotow reported that plot revisions had made it necessary to delete Alice's part from the show. Alice rebounded quickly. The very next day, Louis

Alice poses in a manhole on Madison Avenue, as if she is emerging from her home to collect her morning paper and milk, 1947. Cris Alexander photo.

Nonchalant Alice appears ready to take a ride in a crane's bucket near the intersection of Madison Avenue and Fifty-Seventh Street, 1947. The Parke-Bernet Galleries is visible on the left. Cris Alexander photo.

Alice serenely "looking up from the grave" in a hole dug on Madison Avenue, 1947. Cris Alexander photo.

Calta disclosed to his *Times* followers that she was "all set" for the George Abbott-Jerome Robbins musical *Look, Ma, I'm Dancin'!*, which would start rehearsing in November. This was especially good news for Alice, who, along with Mark Lawrence, was "not content just to play in nightclubs."

During Alice's summer hiatus from The Blue Angel, she spent two weeks in July at the Ogunquit Playhouse in Maine. *On the Town* director George Abbott, in an effort to appease his starstruck wife, had financed a stock company at the playhouse, where she could be guaranteed some worthwhile roles. Abbott took no part in the playhouse's operation, leaving that to a young Robert Fryer, who would go on to produce such Broadway hits as *Auntie Mame*, *Chicago*, and *Sweeney Todd*. For the week beginning July 14, Alice was cast as Mrs. Draper in *State of the Union*, a Pulitzer Prize-winning comedy still running on Broadway. Faye Emerson was the featured star in the Ogunquit production.

The following week, Alice assumed the comic role of the "blind date," created six years earlier by her friend Nancy Walker in the original Broadway production of John Cecil Holm's *Best Foot Forward*. Featuring Edith Fellows and Harold Lang in leading roles, the company also boasted the musical comedy's composer-lyricist Hugh Martin, who served as the show's musical director as well as a featured singer. "Alice was one of the most charming, sweet, gentle, darling souls I ever encountered in my years in show biz," recalled the soft-spoken Martin in 2003. Although Martin did not remember it, George Abbott paid Mark Lawrence twenty-five dollars so that Alice could sing a few of his songs from their Blue Angel act as a special segment during the second act. It proved to be money well spent. "It is Alice Pearce, however, who really 'runs away with the

show,'" reported the *Wells-Ogunquit Compass* on July 25. "She receives encore after encore after she gives her act, and she is most amusing as one of the characters in the comedy."

One month later, Alice, along with Martin, Fellows, and Lang, repeated their roles in a week-long production of *Best Foot Forward*, presented by the John Drew Theatre in East Hampton, Long Island, closing on Labor Day. While there, she was visited by Arnold Weissberger, renowned theatrical attorney, who was representing Alice and Mark in their upcoming negotiations with Herbert Jacoby for The Blue Angel's fall season. Weissberger, an amateur shutterbug who one day would also live on Sutton Place, snapped photos of Alice and a handsome visitor sunning themselves on a nearby beach one afternoon. John Rox, who by now was spending a lot of time alone at Perk Bailey's second home in Northport, had come back into Alice's life, much to her delight. Evidently, his romantic relationship with Perk had evolved into companionship, albeit a very close one. By January of 1947, Perk, who had spent several weeks in Bermuda or Miami each winter for the past twelve years, had taken to vacationing without John. "They really had fallen apart anyway," observed Cris Alexander.

On August 25, 1947, Alice and Mark signed a contract with Jacoby for a four-week engagement beginning September 4, at $400 per week, not including a $150 weekly bonus for granting Jacoby the option to extend their engagement. Provided things went well, their shared pay for the second four weeks would be increased to $450 per week, followed by a third four-week option period, at $500 per week.

Once again, Jacoby's confidence in his new talent had prevailed. Alice and Mark opened to a "capacity crowd" on the first Thursday in September, and they packed the house every night until their engagement ended the day

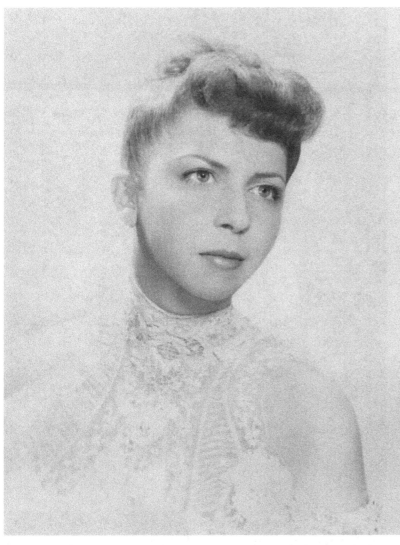

This sedate portrait of Alice, taken by Cris Alexander the same afternoon that she posed in the hole on Madison Avenue, was widely used as publicity for her 1947 fall engagement at the Blue Angel.

ald Tribune, the *Journal American*, and the *World-Telegram*, as well as magazines such as *Cue*, *Harper's Bazaar*, *The New Yorker*, and *Newsweek*. "Once in a blue moon, the night club public is treated to an 'act' that has genuine freshness and originality," crowed *Cue*. "And it is with loud hosannas that we acclaim the return to the Blue Angel of Alice Pearce and Mark Lawrence who definitely belong in the blue moon category. Not since the Revuers, now scattered here and there on the pinnacles of fame (as Judy Holliday, Betty Comden, and Adolph Green) were merrily irreverent and Paula Laurence drew audiences into her own never-never land, has this particular quality of sympathetic insanity been seen."

Those who interviewed Alice found that at home she was as demure as onstage she was possessed. Some found that fact perplexing. "Alice Pearce presents herself as a complete moron with a high, high squeak and a recurrent giggle," wrote *The New Yorker*. "Somehow, I can't follow along wholeheartedly when a young woman like Miss Pearce, who is obviously possessed of great practical intelligence, arbitrarily transforms herself into a flibberti-gibbet." Most journalists, like Jack O'Brian, made much of the fact that both Alice and Mark had come from privileged upbringings. "A couple of youngsters are holding down the fashionable fort who have not permitted mon-

before Thanksgiving. Critics like Bert McCord and Robert Dana who had sung Alice's praises back in the spring were still agog. "Lest you be intimidated by imitations of greatness, let me say simply that here is the funniest girl in town," proclaimed McCord. "After one number, her audiences reach for their sides in an agony of delight." New reviewers helped to transform Alice into a media darling. She was profiled in all the major New York newspapers, including the *Times*, the *Post*, the *Sun*, the *Her-*

ey and good background to keep them from making hilariously blamed fools of themselves," O'Brian wrote approvingly.

With the rave reviews coming in each week, more and more folks could not get into the Blue Angel, despite Jacoby placing extra tables "the size of beauty spots" so close together that, as *Cue* described, "you must love your neighbor as well as your own date." Celebrities, such as Lena Horne, Myrna Loy, John Gielgud, and Dorothy Parker ("ha-ha-ing at *and* with Alice," wrote Walter Winchell), turned out in force.

However, Alice was most touched by the backstage visit of a world-famous playwright who caught her act shortly after it opened that fall. Standing before her that night was Noël Coward, who complimented her by saying he regarded her as "a noble artist." Phil Gordon, who also returned to the Blue Angel that season, remembered Alice's reaction quite well: "She had just gotten back from Fire Island or somewhere, and she had a really

Entertainer Phil Gordon, 1950.

great tan and she had a little dressing room. And when I walked in, she had tears in her eyes. When I asked her what was the matter, she said, 'I just met Noël Coward!' You know, we were all buzzing that night. We used to get Garbo and the Queen of England. We *got* the folks! We got the *real cream*. So, anyway, she was kind of crying like that. And I just laughed. She had a towel wrapped around her, and I said, 'Let's do something dirty.' She said,

'*No*, let's do something *pretty*.' And that was the first time I'd ever heard anybody turn it around, you know, instead of being offended. She had a great biz, and she did it without being crude. She was beauty in every sense of the word. Just a real doll!"

For the new fall season, Alice and Mark employed many of the songs they had performed in the spring. New additions to their thirty-minute repertoire included a satire on stealing from classical music. It began with a symphony about a bottle of Scotch called "Beethoven's Fifth" and ended with Alice playing "The Stars and Stripes Forever" on a comb covered with toilet tissue. As a reverse twist on the French singers who were then trying to sing in English, Alice delivered several numbers which she said "would be in French, but they turned out to be in Masseuse, which is just outside Paris." One of these was "*Un mélange de la Atchison, Topeka, and la Santa Fe,*" sung to the tune of "heaven knows what," reported *The New Yorker.*

Alice continued to wear her Molyneux gown night after night, mending a split in the bodice and remodeling it once again. "I just don't want a new dress," she asserted. Fans sent her some outlandish props, including a tremendous Alpine horn, which Alice spent a day polishing, even though she didn't propose to use it in the act. "As things stand now," she explained, "the horn might knock over people at the front tables." Other donations, Alice found, were in much too good a condition. "I received some fans, but I'm afraid I'll have to trample them considerably before they'll do," she said. Alice preferred props that thrift stores would throw away, and that very thing almost happened after Jacoby hired a new janitor. One morning Jacoby discovered the fellow walking out with a heaping armful of refuse, which turned out to be Alice's entire collection of props.

The main problem with working in a club, Alice discovered, was not the late hours—her first show began at eleven-thirty and the second at one in the morning. In between she lounged in a tiny pink cell upstairs, usually clad in a wrapper and blue mules. She confessed that she didn't get much relaxation there because someone, a friend or an admirer, was always tapping at her door. The worst part of club work, she maintained, was the patrons, whom she found harder to play to than theatre audiences. "Some [customers] look on you as an annoyance," she sighed. "You have to work twice as hard to win them over." And then there were those boisterous ones who'd imbibed too much, like the fellow who stood up and urinated onto the carpet, right in front of Alice.

Despite such misbehavior, Alice considered her nightclub act—totaling thirty-five weeks by 1949—as her favorite work to date. Years later, *The New York Times*, when reporting Alice's death, noted that the best work of her career had been performing in bistros. In truth, her adventure at the Blue Angel had been a sensational personal triumph, particularly because she had helped Mark write some of the material. "Naturally [we] feel much closer to it, a sort of parental pride," she said. With the advent of television, that same material would provide Alice Pearce a lot of mileage in years to come. In the meantime, she was comforted by the roar of applause that nightly greeted her shenanigans. "Next to the roar of the ocean," she ventured, "that's the prettiest roar there is."

CHAPTER TWELVE
Mrs. John Jefferson Rox

"Je suis si heureuse, and it feels so right and fine."

Look, Ma, I'm Dancin'!, like its predecessor *On the Town*, began with an idea conceived by choreographer Jerome Robbins, who wanted to co-author, choreograph, and direct the work which was based on his experiences as a dancer with the Ballet Theatre. However, it was his collaborator, the playwright Arthur Laurents, who came up with the title and created a detailed outline for a musical set in a touring ballet company. The main character is Eddie Winkler, a "brash and manipulative" dancer to whom the most important thing in life is success— a character many have compared to Robbins, including the choreographer himself. Around the time that Laurents abandoned the project in the spring of 1946, Robbins asked Hugh Martin— the "sweet-natured" Alabaman who had written the music and lyrics for "Have Yourself a Merry Little Christmas"—to write the score. Martin recommended that the Los Angeles-based team of radio writers Jerome Lawrence and Robert E. Lee replace Laurents, despite the fact that they had no Broadway credentials. Lawrence and Lee began working on the book, but things stalled when both Billy Rose and Oliver Smith bowed out as potential producers. Months passed while Robbins was consumed with other projects. Finally, in June 1947, *Look, Ma, I'm Dancin'* "sprang back to life, resuscitated" by George Abbott, who proposed to produce as well as direct it.

One year earlier, Nancy Walker had been seriously considered for the supporting role of veteran dancer Lily Malloy, a "tough-talking, tenderhearted, unaffected broad" in love with Eddie. With Walker—long an Abbott darling—still in mind, the veteran director had the librettists transform Lily into a "camped-up caricature of Lucia Chase—a ballet-mad brewery heiress with two left feet who is underwriting a touring ballet company in return for being allowed to perform" in the corps. Robbins' biographer Amanda Vaill wrote: "The role was tailor-made for [Walker's] brand of brassy deadpan humor and her bright, honking voice, and her first entrance, in which the petite comedienne swept onto the station platform clutching the leash of a borzoi the size of a Shetland pony, provided an irresistible sight gag."

Other roles went to performers previously associated with either Robbins, Abbott, Martin, or all three, resulting in a pleasant reunion. The interconnections were noteworthy. Diminutive redhead Janet Reed, an alumnus of Ballet Theatre, was chosen to play Eddie's love interest, even though she wasn't much of a singer, according to Martin who "had to write around her." Martin aggressively pushed for the lithe and nimble-footed Harold Lang to win the role of Eddie Winkler. Lang had been Robbins' old Ballet Theatre colleague, most notably one of the original sailors in the ballet *Fancy Free*, on which *On the Town* had been based. For the male lead in *Look, Ma, I'm Dancin'!*, Lang had the dancing and singing components

Harold Lang, whom Cris Alexander once called "heaven on earth," photographed in 1947.

Alice poses with Harold Lang in a promotional photo for Look, Ma, I'm Dancin'! *(1947). She often wore hats like this when she didn't want to fuss with styling her hair.*

down pat, but when reading lines, his inexperience showed. After a bit of coaching by Martin, Abbott agreed to cast Lang in the male lead. At the time, the short, tightly-muscled, blue-eyed Lang—described by former lover Laurents as hard drinking and notoriously promiscuous—was having affairs with both Nancy Walker and writer Gore Vidal.

Martin also approached Robbins and Abbott about the supporting role of Dusty Lee, the ballet troupe's rehearsal pianist. "Build that part up," Martin pleaded, "and let Kay Thompson play it. Not only is she a dynamite singer, but she also plays piano like a whirlwind and moves like a ballet dancer." Abbott and Robbins were not impressed. "Who's Kay Thompson?" asked Robbins.

Instead, the part of wisecracking Dusty Lee, a "lovely Southern girl" who travels with her pet bird Pavlova, went to Alice who, while not much of a pianist, was then quite a hot property. Her Blue Angel victory notwithstanding, Abbott and Robbins had been well acquainted with Alice's abilities ever since *On the Town*. Still, Alice, like all of the potential cast members, had to prove herself as a dancer—"a revolutionary standard in a business that still . . . condoned dance doubles for features players." She sailed through the audition process, held at the Martin Beck Theatre, in late October 1947. On November 10, Alice signed an Actors' Equity standard contract, guaranteeing her two hundred dollars per week, with December 22 projected as the show's opening date.

Alice and Nancy Walker, each a devoted friend to the other, were thrilled to be working together once again. Their close bond may have been observed by some as a curiosity, given their diverse backgrounds and contrasting temperaments. One was the oldest daughter of a seasoned vaudevillian; the other was the only child of an international banker. One was a product of exclusive private schools; the other was a high school dropout. But running throughout the fabric of each woman's life was a common thread: a burning desire to entertain.

Show business had always been in Nancy's blood. By the time of her mother's death, when Nancy was only eight years old, she had traveled all over the country with her parents, watching practically all of the industry's headliners perform. Nancy quickly developed a sense of deep responsibility toward her father and, despite her young age, began making travel and hotel reservations for their joint tours, spanning the next six years. In 1931, the same year Alice and her parents moved to Paris, nine-year-old Nancy accompanied her father on a tour of Europe. "He would give me money each day," she remembered, "and I would go sightseeing alone, visiting zoos, museums, and palaces." This was a far cry from the parenting skills employed by the Pearces that summer. Although they had lived on the continent for more than a decade, Margaret would not deign to allow *her* teenager to even walk around the corner unescorted.

Their dissimilar upbringings shaped Alice and Nancy into the young women they were in 1947. Alice was ladylike, demure, and tactful; Nancy displayed a "jazzy swagger" and "[spoke] a breezy, highly specialized language," which Hugh Martin described as "wildly profane." Nancy sometimes referred to her father as "my old man," a designation undoubtedly foreign to Alice whenever she mentioned Bob Pearce. And yet, the pair got along famously, making each other laugh over the least little incident. Both actresses also realized that nei-

Alice fairly towers over Nancy Walker in this photo, taken during rehearsals for Look, Ma, I'm Dancin'! *(1947). Photo courtesy Danni Bayles-Yeager.*

ther would win any beauty contests, and they had toughened their skins so that the occasional disparaging remark would bounce right off. (One reviewer referred to Alice as a "bow wow," while another said that Nancy's face "needs only the addition of a cigar to make it the perfect portrait of a tired business man.")

Nancy looked beyond the physical and found Alice's inherent qualities, attributes refreshingly unprecedented in any of her previous working relationships. In fact, through the years as Nancy carved both acting and directing careers, she continued to compare her professional relationships with the peerless one she shared with Alice. Almost thirty years after *Look, Ma, I'm Dancin'!*, she admitted to coming close just twice. In 1976, when she was starring in her own ABC sitcom *The Nancy Walker Show*, Nancy was supported by Beverly Archer, who played her neuroses-ridden daughter. Archer (who, according to one critic, all but stole the show out from under Nancy) received the ultimate compliment from her: "I told her that not since Alice Pearce, have I met anyone who has even come close to the charm Alice had." One year later, following the cancellation of *The Nancy Walker Show* and Nancy's return to a supporting role on television's *Rhoda*, she was confident about her reinstatement on the CBS sitcom. "Not since I worked with Alice Pearce," she smiled, "have I felt the love that is true between Valerie [Harper], Julie [Kavner], and me."

Rehearsals for *Look, Ma, I'm Dancin'!* began on the morning of November 26, the day before Thanksgiving, making it necessary for Alice and Mark Lawrence to temporarily end their Blue Angel act that night. One month later, Abbott and Robbins took their show to Boston for a tryout at the Shubert Theatre, beginning Christmas night. Cyrus Durgin of the *Boston Globe* was not impressed, calling it a "so-so show with a vague and episodic book, negative music, and no good voices to sing it." However, he cited Nancy and Alice as "the only first-rate things" about it. "Alice Pearce, who has made capital of comic awkwardness and become a hot figure in Manhattan night clubs, is on hand to fill up the interstices between songs and dances with her droll delivery of intentionally corny lines."

Alice sings "The New Look" in Look, Ma, I'm Dancin'! *(1948).*

After a bit of doctoring, the show moved on to a second tryout at the Forrest Theatre in Philadelphia, where it was received a bit more warmly. "No critique of *Look Ma, I'm Dancin'!* would be complete without a separate comment on Alice Pearce," wrote the reviewer for the *Camden Courier-Post*, "the zany erstwhile New York night club comic who floats vaguely and comically throughout the show, and eventually reaches her own piece de resistance with 'The New Look.'"

Written especially for Alice by Hugh Martin, "The New Look" was a solo number in which Alice's character Dusty prowled in a trash can and came up with "some ancient and rotting finery" and draped herself in an old shower curtain and a necklace made of linked sausages, calling it "the new look, the new look, the three-months overdue look." Broadway columnist Jack O'Brian would later estimate that Alice's "show-stopping" solo "has nothing to do with anything or anyone but Alice Pearce." Martin was regretful when recalling the number many years later: "It was not really as strong as it should have been. I wish now, in retrospect, that we had allowed [Alice] to do some of Mark Lawrence's special material in that spot." Unfortunately, Alice's rendition of "The New Look" is forever lost because it was not recorded for the soundtrack album. During rehearsals in New York, Martin recalled, the soundtrack was hurriedly recorded before the American Federation of Musicians—then threatening to strike—placed a ban on recordings. At the time, "The New Look" had not even been written.

On January 29, 1948, *Look, Ma, I'm Dancin'!* opened on Broadway at the Adelphi, "with celebrities galore, including Greta Garbo and Truman Capote, cheering us on," Martin wrote. However, most critics found the musical lacking in both book and score. "The book seemed to have been written (or maybe torn apart) somewhere between rehearsals and Philadelphia," quipped Robert Sylvester of the *New York Daily News*. UPI critic Jack Gaver wrote that the show lacked a rousing score, a sentiment somewhat echoed by Martin who later admitted, "I was much too uncritical of my own work." Nancy Walker collected the lion's share of any praise the show garnered, while Alice received favorable nods from Brooks Atkinson of *The New York Times* and Bill Riley of *The Billboard*. Not every reviewer was won over, however. Jack Gaver called Alice "a grotesque comedienne whose appeal is limited." Richard Watts of the *New York Post*, noting that Nancy "still strikes me as something less than a major performer," skewered both comediennes. "It is my morbid and highly ungentlemanly suspicion," he sniffed, "that Miss Pearce's chief value to the show lies in the way she makes Miss Walker seem a prodigy of charm." Evidently, Watts was neither a fan of Alice's Blue Angel act, taking the opportunity to classify her as a "Three-Eye League Paula Laurence."

Look, Ma, I'm Dancin'! did not begin to make any sort of a profit until early April. And then Nancy began losing her voice. "Just at a time when things were beginning to roll well," said Abbott, "night after night we would have to disappoint our audience." Sometimes Nancy would have to be out for weeks at a time. "Had it not been for this unfortunate illness," asserted Abbott, "I think that the play would have been a big hit." Perhaps someone should have listened to critic Robert Sylvester, who made an opening night prediction: "The Adelphi is much too big for a show of this type . . . somebody better move it to a smaller one before the Walker brat tears out her throat." *Look, Ma, I'm Dancin'!* ran for 188 performances, closing on July 10.

Less than three weeks into the run of *Look, Ma, I'm Dancin'!*, Alice felt comfortable enough to double at the Blue Angel, resuming her act with Mark Lawrence on February 17. Despite her familiarity with their repertoire, perhaps there was a greater than expected adjustment of returning to the club after a twelve weeks' absence. *The Billboard* noted: "Maybe it was the butterflies in their stomachs caused by opening night (although all acts were repeats), or possibly the chi-chi mob wasn't in the mood, but the all-over package didn't seem to register as

Alice favored this 1947 portrait by photographer Marcus Blechman so much that she used it for promotional purposes well into the 1950s.

Alice posed for a fan in an alleyway, as she made her way to the Blue Angel, 1948.

solidly as most bills at this bistro. However, individually the acts were deserving of a bigger reward than they received. Alice Pearce, using her full bag of gag-props and slapstick comedy asides, blank-faced her way thru four swell novelty songs. The chirp's high-pitched, bell-clear lung department, coupled with dramatic comedy routining, made for some clever bits which could go over in any type of room. They got off their hands to give her the biggest mitt of the evening, but it rattled no rafters."

Meanwhile, *Variety*, asserting that Alice had been "projected to star proportions for the eastside trade," suggested that she should soon venture across Park Avenue to one of the more mainstream cafes. But Jacoby had made it advantageous for Alice and Mark to remain right where they were, billing her as "The Fun-

niest Girl in Town." With the current gig, *The Billboard* estimated that the partners were splitting $750 per week.

Besides the monetary boost, Alice actually enjoyed the hectic nightly schedule, ending just after two o'clock in the morning when she settled down to remove her makeup. "I'd do a breakfast show, too, if it could be arranged," she crowed. Recalling the twelve weeks she doubled, Alice piped, "I'd come dashing out of the stage door after the show, still wearing my makeup, and bump into people leaving the theater. Sometimes they'd say, 'Hey, where are you going in such a hurry?' And I'd holler, 'To the Blue Angel. Come on.'" Alice was amused when sometimes they actually followed her on the twelve-minute walk. "I felt like the Pied Piper of Hamelin."

As the season progressed, Alice's popularity began to wane. The slide was especially notable in the press, and it's possible that some Blue Angel regulars were also beginning to tire of her repertoire. "Over at the Blue Angel, the only change you'll find in Alice Pearce is that her hats are somewhat less dilapidated," reported *The New Yorker*. She and Mark were using the same songs written the previous year, except for two new ones. Even her old admirer, Robert Dana of the *New York World-Telegram*, was a little less enthusiastic about her standard numbers, admitting that "they don't seem quite as funny as they did the first time." Still, Alice continued to draw in those who hadn't caught her act in 1947.

One first-time visitor to the Blue Angel was not at all amused. Alice's eighty-two-year-old grandmother Sallie Clark was spending that winter in Manhattan with her daughter Josephine Strode. One night, when the Pearces took "Miss Sallie" to the Blue Angel to see Alice perform, they were surprised to see that Alice had added a special segment to her act. As "The Girl," Alice began to reminisce about visiting her grandmother in a small Missouri town. Not knowing what was coming next, Margaret and Bob turned to wink at Sallie. Alice then began to imitate her grandmother performing a common practice from the days before homes had central heating systems, when the only source of warmth was a fireplace or wood stove. "Alice pretended like she was Miss Sallie standing in front of a pot-bellied stove, and then turning around, she pulled up her dress [to warm her backside]," chuckled Perry beautician Dorothy Williams, who during those years went to Sallie's home every Thursday evening to wash and set Sallie's long white hair. "When Miss Sallie came back to Perry, her heart was broken to think that her granddaughter was using her for comedy. She was so upset about it. She was a *lady*."

That spring, Alice was still featured in the local press, although somewhat less regularly. She was among the twenty-two celebrities depicted in caricature for *Cue*'s "New York Easter Parade" montage. Chosen because they had made "amusement news" during the city's 1947–48 season, the Broadway luminaries included Henry Fonda (*Mister Roberts*), Gertrude Lawrence (*Tonight at 8:30*), Wendy Hiller (*The Heiress*), Nanette Fabray (*High Button Shoes*), and Elia Kazan and Jessica Tandy (*A Streetcar Named Desire*). Also walking down Fifth Avenue in the cartoon was Nancy Walker (*Look, Ma, I'm Dancin'!*) and James Stewart (*Harvey*), whose arm Alice's hand was wrapped around. None was without a hat, as was the custom not only of the holiday but also of the era. Alice, whose affinity for quirky chapeaux was now famous, was sketched as wearing a simple toque accented with a towering feather.

Concurrently, a *Variety* reviewer regarded Alice's night club material as "old hat." While he allowed that that she had "tremendous potentialities," he believed that "she indicates a need for 'sock' material. She's always better than the stuff she uses, being the pixie type that brought Imogene Coca to attention in the intimate boîtes. She looks something like Miss Coca, and her general style of working is similar to that of the latter, too, including bits of business with a scrawny furpiece, takeoffs on a dame lush, in all of which she uses plenty of props." Phil Gordon, who worked with Coca in 1950 at the Flame Room in Minneapolis, agreed with that comparison, saying that Alice and Coca ("a *doll*") were "in the same class." More discriminately, cabaret historian James Gavin maintains that Coca "helped pave the way for a legion of singer-comediennes whose stock-in-trade was pointed satire."

John Rox, circa 1949. Photo courtesy Linda Swanson.

in a venue like the Blue Angel. It's also possible that they were introduced by mutual contacts, particularly those associated with an agency called National Publicity Associates, where, by 1947, John was employed an "office boy." Whatever the situation, Bailey was both impressed with John's songwriting ability and sympathetic with his despondency concerning the difficulty he'd encountered in getting vocalists to record his songs, particularly "It's a Big, Wide Wonderful World." It was Bailey's intervention, John believed, that finally opened doors for him. On December 13, 1947, Bailey recorded John's song "Old Man, You've Been Gone Too Long" for Columbia Records.

On Bailey's heels—and much to John's relief—another Columbia artist, Buddy Clark, at last recorded "It's a Big, Wide Wonderful World." Since its publication in 1939, the song had caught on big in New York night spots. (In particular, the team of Harry Noble and Frances King had kept "World" fresh since 1943, making it a standard in their repertoire.) However, the eventual exposure from Clark's recording would make the song John Rox's biggest hit. An upbeat tribute to love, the lilting tune was recorded on December 30, 1947, and was released the following year, climbing up the *Billboard* charts and peaking at the twenty-fifth spot in 1949.

Another revolutionary figure on the supper club scene was singer Pearl Bailey whom Max Gordon brought to the Blue Angel from his other club, the Village Vanguard, in 1944. Gordon and Jacoby, committed to practicing racial tolerance, never barred black customers and hired dozens of black performers like Bailey. Consequently, the Blue Angel became "one of the foremost midtown showcases for black talent." In November 1947, just before Alice went on hiatus to rehearse *Look, Ma, I'm Dancin'!*, Bailey returned to the Blue Angel for six weeks. Soon after, she became a key link to John Rox's success as a songwriter. At some point, either that November or much earlier, John and Bailey had met, perhaps even

It's not exactly known which role Pearl Bailey played in this turn of events, but John was truly grateful. "I know you feel so much better than before, as you have a couple of songs going," Bailey wrote to John in 1948. "Don't you think for once that I am responsible for anything that has happened to you. It's all God's work. He has ways of doing his work."

Another individual who may have had a hand in John's long-awaited success was press agent Phil Bloom, who was the head of National Publicity Associates, located at 208 West Forty-First Street. The most we know about Bloom, aside from sporadic mentions in *Variety*, comes from a twenty-first century blogger who was Bloom's business partner in the late 1960s. In a 2012 post, octogenarian Frank Marshall identified Bloom as a member of a "subterranean community of well-educated and talented men" who were employed in the arts, music, fashion, theatre, and related fields. These gentlemen, whom nonmember Marshall dubbed as the "Society of Tasteful Men," tried to help each other whenever they could, sharing leads about employment opportunities or transacting business with other members, etc. The Society was "discreet, careful, and almost invisible except to its members," because it was made up of homosexuals. "In those days, successful gay men stayed in the closet," Marshall wrote. "Being homosexual was not only criminal in many states, but was considered—even in liberal circles—to be an illness or an unfortunate aberration. Moreover, it was rarely if ever discussed publicly. But, of course, that's how almost all systems work. Gay or straight, it's who you know." Given John Rox's coterie of friends and the fact that he moved in a sophisticated, cosmopolitan world, it's logical to assume that he was a member of Bloom's "society of tasteful men."

While Marshall was writing about the 1960s, his statements apply to the 1940s as well. By 1947, John Rox had lived in New York City for ten years. During that span, the city's homosexual population had witnessed great changes which, according to historian George Chauncey, forced New York's "gay world" into

hiding. In the 1920s and early 1930s, the gay subculture had been very "visible and extensive," but that changed with the end of Prohibition. Chauncey observed, "The revulsion against gay life in the early 1930s was part of a larger reaction to the perceived 'excesses' of the Prohibition years and the blurring of boundaries between acceptable and unacceptable public sociability." As a result, a multitude of "laws and regulations were enacted or newly enforced in the 1930s that . . . censored lesbian and gay images in plays and films and prohibited restaurants, bars, and clubs from employing homosexuals or even serving them."

During the postwar years, anti-gay policing would intensify. Under increased pressure, the police raided gay clubs and bars, especially in the theater district. "Newspapers stepped up publication of the names of people arrested in the raids," wrote historian Sam Abel. "These revelations proved disastrous for public figures and the wealthy, who often lost their careers and social positions when their sexuality became known."

"Senator Joseph McCarthy warned that homosexuals in the State Department threatened the nation's security, and the police warned that homosexuals in the streets threatened the nation's children," affirmed Chauncey. "Federal, state, and local governments deployed a barrage of new techniques for the surveillance and control of homosexuals, and the number of arrests and dismissals escalated sharply." These efforts were largely unsuccessful, Chauncey noted, but "gay life did become less visible in the streets and newspapers of New York and gay meeting places did become more segregated and carefully hidden."

Meanwhile, the gay world continued to thrive at The Blue Angel, where men like John Rox felt right at home. The supper club's regulars—"a rarified breed, very New York, mostly

East Siders, smart, clever, well-dressed," wrote Lorraine Gordon—included a "high quota of homosexual customers." However, Herbert Jacoby, himself a discreet gay, was resolved to keep that element under control, "warning the bartenders not to serve men who seemed to be on the make."

As a freelance songwriter, John probably faced minimal discrimination in regards to his sexuality. Likewise, Alice's gay friends in the theatre enjoyed a rare "port of safety," as the profession has been described by gay historian Michael Bronski. "Nowhere else in popular culture were, and are, gay men so accepted," he asserted. Nevertheless, the same probably could not be said for John's former love interest, Perk Bailey, who, by 1947, was forging a successful career as the editor of *Men's Wear* magazine. To maintain or advance his lofty position, Perk may have felt the pressure to keep his gay life hidden from potentially hostile heterosexual observers. Leading a double life and passing for straight allowed men like Perk to have jobs and status otherwise denied to them.

Advocating the importance of "dressing for success," Perk once said, "Every man is in business for himself. Every day he is selling himself to his boss, his sweetheart, his friends. He is selling his own product—himself." Still single at forty-one, perhaps Perk believed it was time to apply this philosophy to another facet of his life. Perhaps it was time to rid himself of the stigma associated with being a "confirmed bachelor." Perhaps it was time to sell himself as a married man.

In the meantime, while Alice was doubling between *Look, Ma, I'm Dancin'!* and *The Blue Angel* in the winter of 1948, John was living in Perk's house at Northport, possibly to help oversee the final renovations while Perk was vacationing alone in Palm Beach. By this time,

John, too, was weighing options in his personal life. Alice wanted to marry him. She had been attracted to him since that day seven years before when they met in Leonard Sillman's office. She had remained in love with John, despite the forgone conclusions that he was sexually attracted to men and that their dating situation was "on again, off again." Undoubtedly, John was very fond of Alice, but still he was uncertain about a future together. "It took John a long time to decide that he wanted to get married," remembered Peggy Coburn, who questioned John's eventual decision, not because of his sexual orientation but because of his lengthy deliberation. In fact, at the time, Peggy knew nothing of John's past relationships. "People were close-mouthed then. You didn't talk about [same-sex] partners in those days," she said. Even if her husband Bill had known anything about John's sexuality, Peggy said, he wouldn't have told her. "When people shared things privately with my husband, he never revealed them."

By March 1948, John and Alice had decided to make their engagement official. Although they did not want a lot of hoopla, Margaret was determined that their plans should be first announced in *The New York Times*—only to have the item scooped the day before by Walter Winchell: "Alice Pearce (in *Look, Ma, I'm Dancin'*) is betrothed to songwriter John Rox. Her pappy is veepee at Nat'l City Bank." Of all the New York papers that subsequently picked up the announcement, the best coverage was in the *New York Herald Tribune*, revealing that the wedding would take place that autumn. Tucking one of the news clippings into an envelope, John scratched an accompanying note to his brother Don Herring in California: "Enclosed clipping will tell you about my engagement to the most wonderful girl in the world." On April 1, the *Perry Enterprise*, ever faithful to update Alice's Missouri relations, reprinted the entire *Tribune* piece and ran a large photo of Alice on its front page.

The previous twelve months had been the busiest in Alice Pearce's life, but things cranked up even more, once her engagement was announced. Since February, she had been sought by novice producer George Nichols III to appear in *Small Wonder*, a revue to be directed by Burt Shevelove. Nichols had been holding successful auditions, and by April 9, he had almost succeeded in raising the final $50,000 to get the show into rehearsals by July. With an opening proposed for September, Alice realized that the new show would conflict with her wedding plans. Apart from that, her father, now the deputy manager of the bank's overseas division, learned that he would be sailing for Europe in late May, accompanied by her mother. Alice knew that time was of the essence.

As soon as Margaret and Josephine returned from Perry, where they had gone to accompany "Miss Sallie" home, Alice and her mother hurried into action. Alice, moved by sentimentality, chose May 22 for the wedding date because it was the seventh anniversary of the day she had first met John. Once she had chosen her gown, she engaged Marcus Blechman, a Broadway dancer-turned-photographer, to create her bridal portrait. Margaret ably handled all the plans for the ceremony, which was to be witnessed by fifty or so relatives and friends in the Pearces' apartment. A reception and wedding supper would follow. Invitations to the black-tie affair, handwritten by Margaret, went out on May 1.

Margaret's portion of the guest list included eight executives from the bank and their wives, but no relatives from either Perry or Bellefontaine made the cut. John submitted a roster of his closest relatives and friends, including novelist Louis Bromfield whom John had met many years earlier when Bromfield was an expatriate living in Paris. Alice invited three of her Sarah Lawrence friends: "Dutch" Gordon and husband Arthur Bryant, Helen Tuttle and husband Terry Votichenko, and Betty La Branche. From *Look, Ma, I'm Dancin'!*, she included Nancy Walker and her seventeen-year-old sister Betty Lou Barto, who had been Nancy's stand-in during her bout with laryngitis. The remainder of Alice and John's list reads like a roll call for the "Society of Tasteful Men": Leonard Sillman; Herbert Jacoby; Phil Bloom; Gus Schirmer; Broadway producer Gant Gaither; Mark Lawrence and his buddies from the Princeton Intime, Bill Callanan and Buster Davis (the latter coincidentally having been Hugh Martin's assistant on *Look, Ma, I'm Dancin'!*); and Milton Page, organist at the Roxy Theatre.

Meanwhile, a curious twist unfolded. Perk Bailey, grasping the realization that John had chosen him as his best man, quickly proposed marriage to business associate June Kent, an art director for *Women's Wear Daily*, another trade magazine within the Fairchild Publications fold.

June, forty-one, had endured a previous marriage which finally failed, she said, because her husband wanted children while she did not. Instead, June was focused on her career, which she had begun as a fashion artist when she was still known by her birth name, Julia Kuntschke. By 1946, when Perk met June, she had been separated from her husband for years, during which interval she had legally changed her name to June Arys Kent. Upon Perk's proposal, June went to Reno to obtain a quick and easy divorce.

Gone are those who knew firsthand the dynamics affecting Alice, John, Perk, and June in the spring of 1948. Instead, we must resort to microfilmed copies of certified records in order to assemble a chain of events, which ultimately evokes more questions than answers.

Perkins Bailey, June Kent Bailey, Alice Pearce Rox, and John Rox at the Roxes' wedding reception, 22 May 1948.

Alice had known Perk for seven years, but June was a relative newcomer to Alice's realm. It's striking that she would choose June as her matron of honor, when Betty, Helen, "Dutch," or even Nancy, were so close to her heart.

Even more intriguing is the fact that Perk and June applied for their marriage license on May 20, just two days before Alice and John's nuptials. Yet June's divorce had been final for two months. The timing makes one wonder why Perk held off until this precise moment, as if he was waiting to see if John would go through with his own wedding. Conversely, maybe John consented to marry Alice only after June had obtained her divorce and it became more certain that Perk was considering a *mariage de raison*.

Indeed, it's quite possible that Perk and June viewed their marriage as a career move which simultaneously provided greater social mobility and respectability. They knew that it was far preferable to be invited to an industry function as "the Perkins Baileys" rather than as the perennial "Perkins Bailey and date" or "June Kent and date." If indeed the legal bond between Perk and June was a marriage of convenience, it does not preclude their fondness for each other. In the end, their partnership was long and productive, founded on a mutual understanding that usefully enabled both of their lives and careers.

"Rumors are quick about a man who marries late," noted Arthur Laurents when referring to his fellow playwright Moss Hart, who was forty-one when he married Kitty Carlisle. Perhaps similar remarks were circulating about John Rox in the wake of his engagement. Some observers may have considered him on par with Hart or theatre legends Alfred Lunt and Guthrie McClintic, who reportedly maintained "bearded marriages" in order to further their careers. Admittedly, John's career needed a boost, but that doesn't appear to have been his motivation for marrying Alice. Likewise, Alice definitely didn't need a marriage partner to enhance her current position; she couldn't accept all of the offers which were then coming her way.

Some marriages of convenience, such as McClintic's with stage star Katherine Cornell, allowed both partners to maintain various same-sex relationships. In other words, when a gay man married a lesbian, in what was also called a "lavender marriage," each partner acted as cover for the other. Again, this wasn't the case with Alice and John, though some may have wondered. Patricia Wilson, a young actress who met Alice during the 1955 summer stock season and soon grew very close to her, was privy to the details of Alice and John's relationship. Upon meeting John, Wilson—herself married to a homosexual at the time—surmised that he was gay. Alice confirmed Wilson's deduction one day, introducing the subject herself. "Oh, she was very open about John's homosexuality," Wilson recalled casually. "She never denied it." When asked if Alice could have been a lesbian, Wilson responded with assurance, "No. I don't think so at all. No, we lived together on the road and were such close friends. No, no, I don't think there was any of that with Alice at all." Wilson substantiated her belief by citing a clear

memory of Alice's insistence that they go see Charlton Heston's 1955 movie, *The Far Horizons*, in which he appeared shirtless and wearing tight buckskin breeches. "She was madly in love with Charlton Heston!" Wilson chuckled. "She said, 'Oh, we must go see this movie!'"

Some readers may wonder why a biographical subject's sexuality should even be addressed or explored. Gay historians Robert Schanke and Kim Marra have argued: "When acknowledged, the facet of sexuality, considered along with other facets of identity, such as gender, race, ethnicity, and class, changes the shape of the whole and vastly complicates what we see looking through it." Bearing that in mind, Alice Pearce's acceptance of her husband's sexual identity, not to mention her embracing attitude toward her many male friends of the same orientation, demonstrates a key facet of her character. This perspective affected not only her choice of intimates, but also her choice of professional associates, just as John Rox's viewpoint influenced his contacts.

Their individual sexualities notwithstanding, the import of Alice and John's relationship was their devotion to one another. "There's no question in my mind that they did have a bond," asserted John's niece Linda Swanson. "She may have had more romantic feelings and he more of a [respective] fondness. However, he spoke and wrote so lovingly about her." Patricia Wilson, remembering an occasion when Alice was very demonstrative, said, "I do know that she was very, very fond of him. We were at a mutual coach's house one time, and she called [John] from our coach's phone right in front of all of us, and her obvious caring about him was quite wonderful." Cris Alexander perhaps expressed it best: "Oh, how she loved him!"

To have time to prepare for their wedding day, Alice withdrew from *Look, Ma, I'm Dancin'!* on May 15 and ended her Blue Angel

The Collegiate Church of Saint Nicholas, 1946.

Amsterdam in 1728. As a member of the Reformed Protestant Dutch Church, the oldest church organization in the state, the Collegiate Church of Saint Nicholas was where Theodore Roosevelt had worshipped. Waiting inside were Perk, June, and Dr. J. Frederic Berg, temporary pastor of the church. When everyone was in place, the seventy-six-year-old minister conducted a simple ceremony uniting Perkins Bailey and June Kent in marriage. Alice and John signed the marriage certificate as witnesses.

The next evening's clear skies promised an excellent view of the full moon, which was expected to rise one hour past sunset. By six-thirty, the wedding guests began arriving at 503 East Fifty-Fifth Street, assembling in the Pearces' living room and foyer to await the ceremony. At seven, Alice, escorted by Bob, appeared at the top of the spiral staircase. She wore a gown of white lace with matching lace cap and carried a nosegay of lilies of the valley. As father and daughter descended, pianist Buster Davis played Mendelssohn's "Wedding March." The living room was decorated with white peonies, white tulips, and white gladioli. Standing at the improvised altar were John and the Rev. Dr. Theodore Cuyler Speers, fifty-year-old pastor of the Central Presbyterian Church. At John and Alice's sides were Perk and June. Following the vows, the bridal-couple greeted their guests and then sat down to a supper of roast beef, new potatoes, and green peas served in pastry cups. In the center of the bride's table, which seated fourteen, was the two-tiered wedding cake, wreathed in white sweet peas. "I shall always remember my wonderful wedding in every detail," Alice told her parents. "It was so perfect."

run the same night. On Monday, May 17, she and John applied for their marriage license. John listed the Northport house as his address, but he stated his birth year as 1905, thereby subtracting three years from his true age of forty-five. Alice admitted to her thirty years.

Four days later, on the eve of their nuptials, Alice and John made their way to Rockefeller Center. By late afternoon, the mercury had only reached seventy-four degrees, but the air was uncomfortably humid as they climbed the steps of the Collegiate Church of Saint Nicholas, located on the northwest corner of Fifth Avenue and Forty-Eighth Street. A distinct landmark since its completion in 1872, the Gothic Revival structure featured an elegantly tapered spire, thirty-stories high. The massive bell in the steeple had been cast in

John and Alice with Margaret and Bob Pearce, 22 May 1948.

The bride and groom interlock arms for a champagne toast. Photo courtesy Linda Swanson.

John sneaks a kiss from his bride as their wedding guests enjoy the reception in her parents' apartment. Standing to Alice's right and holding a champagne glass is Herbert Jacoby. In the right foreground is June Bailey, who partially obscures Max Chopnick, personal attorney of Leonard Sillman. At extreme right is Howard Sheperd of the National City Bank.

The newlyweds had not planned a honeymoon trip, but instead watched Bob and Margaret sail from New York on the R. M. S. *Mauretania* on May 26, a voyage destined to be the Pearces' final trip to Europe. Three days later, Bob gave Margaret a fifty-sixth birthday party onboard. The menu was fittingly French: *Caviar d'Astrakan*; *Sole, Meuniere*; *Caneton roti, Bigarade*; *Petits Pois, Nouveaux*; *Pommes Chateau*; *Crepes Suzettes*; *Gateau Anniversaire*; *Café*. During their six-week stay in Paris, the Pearces reconnected with old friends like Morgan and Ilse Heiskell and former servants Emma and Jacques. In mid-June, Alice received an excited letter from Margaret, telling of a far-fetched coincidence that left Alice so amazed that she shared the particulars with a *New York Herald Tribune* reporter who wrote: "When [the Pearces] left [France during the first year of Nazi occupation], they weren't allowed to take any francs out of the country with them, so Mrs. Pearce went on a spending spree. Among other things, she bought a set of table silver from an old woman in the public market in the Montmartre. It was complete except for one fruit knife. Last week, seven years and a world war later, Mrs. Pearce again went walking in the Montmartre. Her thoughts turned to the old woman and she wondered if she were still alive. She found her sitting in the same old place. The old woman glanced up as Mrs. Pearce approached. "Ah, madam," she said. "I have that fruit knife for you now."

Alice and John spent their first week of married life in the Pearces' apartment, much more comfortable than Alice's one-bedroom flat, which she and John had decided to keep. Alice called her parents' place "a cabin in the sky, so peaceful and cool." On May 31, she wrote them a long letter: "We have dipped into all your supplies. We drank up the champagne. We have tasted the red wine and tested the bourbon. The Thursday after you sailed was Perk's birthday and Perk and June came over for cocktails. Bill [Callanan], as you know, has been pestering the life out of us to come to dinner. He asked us for Thursday again and we finally gave in. Only Betty [La Branche] was there. I refused a cocktail, and he had cooked a fair meal of chicken and noodles. The four of us went dancing at the Directoire. We had a nice evening. Bill and Betty elaborated on what a wonderful wedding you gave. We have seen many people and we have had nothing but compliments and sincere expressions of the lovely wedding you gave . . . Saturday afternoon we went to the matinee of *Inside U. S. A.*, a great disappointment. Bea [Lillie] is funny, but I don't feel she is worth the price of admission. Phil [Bloom] came to the house for dinner and we opened the champagne at

seven and had our first [week] anniversary celebration. We went nightclubbing after dinner. Yesterday, Sunday, we gave a dinner party and we had Bob and Rae [Herring], Bill Coburn and his fiancée Peggy [Watson], and one of John's musician friends. We had fun fixing for the party and it was a good party. We had more fine compliments about the wedding. I used all your things. We were going to Northport today, but we changed our plans and had a fine lazy day at home. It is eleven at night and we are thinking of going over to the Blue Angel and have a drink to get some air . . . I cannot begin to tell you, and I hope you know, how very much I appreciate the wonderful wedding you gave me. I shall say just, thank you from the bottom of my heart, Mother and Dad, for all you have done for me. No girl has ever had a greater mom and dad. I am indeed an extremely lucky girl. I am crazy about John and I am unbelievably happy. He is a fine, wonderful man and I adore him. I never thought I could be this completely happy. Not a cloud in my sky! Thank you for seeing me through cloudy days. *Je suis si heureuse*, and it feels so right and fine. All our love, Monk *et son mari*."

John was on cloud nine, too. "Alice and I thank you for your good wishes," he wrote to his cousin Marjorie Fitzgerald on June 7. "We are supremely happy." John was also excited that his songs, recorded six months earlier by Pearl Bailey and Buddy Clark, were set for summer releases. He and Alice were anticipating a month's stay in Northport, followed by a week on Fire Island. The only thing bothering him at the moment, he told Marjorie, was that he had received no acknowledgement of his engagement or marriage from his biological father. His letters to Arthur Barber had gone unanswered. "Alice feels badly about it," John told Marjorie, "but we're not going to let that ruin our honey-moon (ha! ha!)." In actuality,

John had been estranged from Barber for a number of years, and it's probable that he didn't know how ill the man was, so ill that death was imminent. On July 6, Arthur Barber, sixty-seven, suffered a cerebral hemorrhage at his Des Moines home and died. Among the survivors listed in his obituary was his son John *Barber* of New York City. The former sewing machine salesman had narrowly missed the chance to hear Clark's recording of his son's biggest hit, "It's a Big, Wide, Wonderful World."

It's possible that Perk and June spent some time in the Northport house while John and Alice were there in June. The Roxes and Baileys clicked. Each member of the quartet was quite career-oriented, most notably Perk, who within the year would begin moonlighting, both as a lecturer at the NYU School of Retailing and as a men's wear consultant for *Look* magazine. All four were creative sorts. Perk held numerous clothing design patents while June excelled as a fashion illustrator in magazines. Alice dabbled in oils; John kept a sketchbook. Alice

In this photo shoot arranged by press agent Phil Bloom, Alice is being fitted by Madame Karinska as John Derro, the costume designer for Small Wonder, *looks on. This image appeared in the October 1948 issue of* Theatre Arts *magazine.*

and June kept abreast of the latest fashions, and both loved stylish hats, particularly quirky ones. John and Perk were known for their sartorial splendor. Neither couple had a desire to become parents. Instead, they relished the cosmopolitan life New York offered folks of their bent.

The newlyweds' summer idyll ended, and they returned to New York, where Alice began rehearsals for *Small Wonder* at the Coronet Theatre on July 26. The music for the revue, featuring seventeen young performers besides Alice and Tom Ewell, was written by Baldwin Bergersen and Albert Selden. Gower Champion made his Broadway debut as the show's

choreographer. The costumes were designed by John Derro and executed by the eminent Barbara Karinska, who had served in the same capacity for *On the Town*'s designer, Alvin Colt. Karinska, an aristocratic émigré "flung westward from czarist Russia by the Bolsheviks" in 1924, had worked with many renowned choreographers, designers, and directors of American stage and film productions, including Agnes de Mille, George Balanchine, Irene Sharaff, and George Cukor.

Being a revue, *Small Wonder* had no plot, but it featured Ewell who wandered off and on between musical numbers, "discoursing earnestly on the failure of the human body to keep up with modern scientific improvements; the possible effects of selling democracy to Europe, in soap opera style; and pantomiming the victim of too much advertising." Alice joined Ewell in some of these sketches.

Tryouts began August 26 with a three-night stop in New Haven at the Shubert, where an oppressive heat wave socked the city. Four nights later, the revue opened at Boston's Majestic Theatre. *The Boston Globe*'s Cyrus Durgin praised Ewell ("his turned-up nose, crackling eyes, and wide-mouthed grin are a source of infinite merriment") as the "normal neurotic," but expressed regret with Alice's contributions ("They haven't done right by her, for she deserves a good sketch all her own"). Elinor Hughes of *The Boston Herald*, praising Alice's take-off on *I Remember Mama*, echoed Durgin: "I could do with more of her, definitely."

Director Burt Shevelove took notice. By the time *Small Wonder* opened at the Coronet back in New York on September 15, gone was a curious number called "Things," in which Alice and Bill Ferguson played "two 'tetched' individuals collecting buttons, newspapers, and string." In its place was "Pistachio," a musical satire on Howard Johnson's twenty-eight flavors of ice cream—written for Alice by Mark Lawrence. As an ice cream saleswoman, Alice hopelessly confuses a customer (Mort Marshall) with her fancy flavors, rattled off in machine-like precision:

HE: (ENTERING) Gimme a dish of vanilla.
SHE: What?
HE: Vanilla.
SHE: What kind of vanilla? Vanilla peach, vanilla marshmallow,
Vanilla raspberry, vanilla pineapple mash, vanilla pecan,
Vanilla. What do you mean vanilla?
HE: Okay . . . chocolate.
SHE: Nog, float, frappe, or fudge?

HE: Just gimme a dish of ice cream!
SHE: Oh! Well, we have (AHEM)
Pistachio
Butterscotch and buttercrunch and butter pecan
And tipsy peach
And chocolate chip, and cherry flip and frozen whip
Banana
Maple Walnut, macaroon,
Or maybe just a little of each.
HE: Could I have a plain dish of plain . . .
SHE: (CONTINUING)
We also have vanilla mousse
And peppermint
And also cocoanut strawberry fudge pecan
And caramel and coffee crunch
And even lemon sherbet
If you are a sherbet man.
Make up your mind . . . decide the kind . . .
The kind of ice cream you prefer.

This goes on for two more stanzas until she asks him what he does for a living. He replies that he's an elevator operator in a large department store, but he's so muddled that when he starts singing a repetitive list of departments per floor, he inserts her ice cream flavors, too. Alice found the fast-paced "Pistachio" the most challenging number in the revue.

Reviews of Alice's contribution to *Small Wonder* were mixed. Critic William Hawkins wrote that Alice "proves herself a splendid pantomimist, garnering big laughs while she stomps grapes in a vineyard, or appreciates her children as a retired messboy." Ward Morehouse was doubtful: "Alice Pearce gets in a good evening's work, but I'm still not overpowered by her ways with comedy." *Cue*'s reviewer asserted that *Small Wonder* didn't make the most of Alice's comic potentialities. Dorothy Kilgallen, who had once referred to Alice as "the weird young nightclub comedienne" was a little more

Bill Ferguson and Alice Pearce pose while rehearsing "Things," a number that was cut before Small Wonder *reached Broadway.*

paper and a functional kitchen. Curled up on a beige satin chaise longue, Alice shared her philosophy of a comedienne's basic requirements: "First of all, a *desire* to make people laugh. Secondly, an understanding of human beings. It's the failings of human nature from which comedy springs. Third, the power to observe. Timing? Oh, well, that comes with experience. You feel it more than anything else. It is never set. The reactions of all audiences differ and you have to adjust your timing to their tempo."

Around the same time, Tom Ewell shared an anecdote with a journalist. "From the producer and the director right through the whole ensemble, the people in this company are young, full of fresh ideas, and ready to work till they drop," he observed. "Alice Pearce has a sense of humor that's all her own. At our first rehearsal, the press department handed her the usual questionnaire. One of the things it asked was, 'Who has the best photograph of you?' 'My mother,' she answered."

charitable: "The *Small Wonder* team is captained by that comical little wren Alice Pearce." The insightful and stalwart George Freedley offered a bit of advice: "Alice Pearce has set her performance at such a pitch that only a happy home life can maintain it. You can't work that hard (incidentally it doesn't show, you just know she must be doing it) and not be happy. Take care of yourself, Alice. You are awfully dear to a lot of people, including this reviewer."

One month into the run, Alice was interviewed in her dressing room at the Coronet, a two-room suite complete with flowered wall-

Forty years later, Ewell was still impressed with Alice. "In my life time I have done, counting everything, over 2200 shows—and worked with more than I can count of fellow players—Alice Pearce was at the top of the list. It's true that out of the hundreds, there was only one that I really disliked. Alice is at the top! She was wonderful to know and tops to work with. I loved her."

By Thanksgiving, *Small Wonder* was showing a steady operating profit; its investors were hopeful to soon make some money. The Roxes were optimistic, too. John, declining a Christmas invitation from his niece Shirley Taylor in California, explained the situation: "It will probably run until next June or even longer. No time off. Six nights and two matinees per week, so, you see, [Alice] is pretty busy what with keeping our apartment and doing a television or radio shot now and then."

Two weeks later, though, *Small Wonder* was beginning to slip. The producer added Sunday performances to the schedule, but that failed to boost dwindling audiences. *Small Wonder* closed on January 8, 1949, having reached 134 performances, a record not even as middling as *Look, Ma, I'm Dancin'!*

However, as it so often happens, one door closed, and another opened. Alice received an exciting offer to appear on television—a proposition she couldn't have accepted as long as *Small*

Tom Ewell and Alice satirize British films in a scene from Small Wonder, *1948.*

Wonder continued. It wasn't a guest shot, though. Alice was set to appear on ABC in her own weekly program called *The Alice Pearce Show*.

CHAPTER THIRTEEN
The Girl with a Cold Goes Hollywood

"I enjoyed working in my first picture so very much.
It was so painless, really such fun."

"In 1945, television was still the stepchild of radio," wrote industry historian Jon Krampner. There were only seven commercial television stations in the United States. The majority of the country's television sets, estimated at fewer than 10,000, were in New York City. Late that year, when she was yet appearing in *On the Town*, Alice Pearce first experienced working in the infant medium. It was not a pleasant encounter.

"I was one of a group taking part in a closed circuit telecast of a fashion show," Alice recalled in 1965. "Things were pretty primitive then and called for the use of a number of huge lights. They were so hot you could only work under them for about five minutes at a time. We were given salt pills—ugh—to overcome their enervating effects. I had on a dress with plastic buttons and my appearance had to be cut short when the lights finally melted the buttons. I can honestly say I've never worked under such difficult conditions."

More than two years would pass before Alice was next seen on the tube—this time as a direct result of her popularity at the Blue Angel. While she and Mark Lawrence had performed part of their act on radio several times during 1947, this was their first time appearing together before the television cameras. *Broadway Minstrels*, a musical revue, had

premiered on the NBC television network on May 10, 1948. Originally conceived to feature an all-black cast, the show was soon retitled *Broadway Jamboree* and thereafter featured both black and white players. On June 28, Alice and Mark were featured on one of the final episodes of the short-lived program. Their half of the live telecast included several songs which had been hits at the Blue Angel.

Among the reviewers was Harriet Van Horne of the *New York World-Telegram* who gushed: "Television couldn't find a funnier entertainer for my taste than Miss Alice Pearce. This chinless gamin, with her hats that ride over the nose, fans that separate in the middle and voice that's first cousin to the loon, has me in stitches without half trying ... With ratty old furs she never goes anywhere without, Miss Pearce cavorted through her 'southern Russian' number, 'Mammy's Little Baby Loves Blubinshki.' And that last word I'm spelling strictly by ear, being neither Southern nor Russian. Most of the time Miss Pearce wears her furs around her head. I'm sorry she omitted the delightful bit of business that used to follow this song at the Blue Angel. Giving a big kiss to the nasty little animals that comprise the scarf, she would throw them into the audience with a shrill mother-hen cry, 'Go play!' As her finale, Miss Pearce sang 'Two Cigarets in the Dark.' Sprawled on the piano, eyes half closed, she plainly meant to tell a sad story, torch song style. But smoking two cigarets (one in each side of her mouth) and coughing like two Camilles, the going was

Perhaps Nancy Walker (left) made a wisecrack, judging by the reactions of pianist-singer Ted Straeter and Alice, but Mary McCarty (who appeared with Alice in Small Wonder*) does not look amused in this candid nightclub shot from 1949.*

a bit tough. You never saw such an agonized expression. Miss Pearce seems to me a young lady of rare talent, and I hope television sees fit to enlist her among the regulars."

Becoming a television regular, however, would have to wait. A few weeks after appearing on *Broadway Jamboree*, Alice jumped into rehearsals for *Small Wonder*, but someone had taken notice of Van Horne's craving.

Producer-director John Heaton approached Alice and Mark with an offer to transform their nightclub act into a weekly television program once *Small Wonder* ended its run. On Friday night, January 28, 1949, *The Alice Pearce Show* debuted on ABC at 9:45 in a fifteen-minute spot, which aired live. On the opening show, Alice delivered several of her familiar nitery numbers—including "Wait for the Dial Tone, Nellie" plus a new one called "I'm In Love with

a Coaxial Cable"—in "her typical dissonant style," observed *Variety*. "Her props are old fur pieces, chapeaux and strange musical instruments which she casually tosses around. Mark Lawrence, accomping [*sic*] at the piano, did a nice job of backing up and handled some solo vocals in straight manner."

Admitting that Alice had an "oblique style of humor that's likely to appeal only to a limited audience," *Variety* predicted that "her stuff will prove either irresistible or irritating, too subtle or too obvious, depending on the point of view." The series lasted six weeks. "It was a little *campy*, I think," remembered Phil Gordon. "Not that it was not funny—*campy*'s the only word I can think of to describe it. It didn't go because some people didn't know what the hell she was doing. But it was light and funny."

It is not exactly known how Alice felt about this short-lived experience. In fact, she had very little to say about her show during interviews conducted in subsequent years. At the height of her popularity during *Bewitched*, she merely described *The Alice Pearce Show* as "a fifteen-minute nonsense of songs, topical skits, and me."

While some may speculate that *The Alice Pearce Show* was cancelled due to poor ratings, there is the possibility that its star pulled the plug herself. During production, Alice received an enticing offer, one she could not refuse . . . a film offer from Metro-Goldwyn-Mayer.

Film historian John Kobal once proclaimed Arthur Freed as "the Ziegfeld of M-G-M, the single most creative and controlling brain in the shaping of the American film musical as we now know it." Since 1939, Freed, a former lyricist, had been a producer at M-G-M. As the head of what would come to be called "The Freed Unit," he "surrounded himself with the finest M-G-M craftsmen" and then tapped "the talent pool of Broadway and Tin Pan Alley," organizing a superior musical repertory company.

By late 1948, Freed had decided to produce a film version of *On the Town*, a project which had been languishing on the shelf for almost four years, ever since the studio had bought the film rights for $250,000—the "first theatrical property to be sold to Hollywood in a preproduction deal." Louis B. Mayer, head of production at Metro when the contract was signed, later attended a performance during the show's run at the Adelphi. He hated it. He thought that Bernstein's score was "too symphonic and too classical," said Betty Comden, "and that

audiences wouldn't understand it." Likewise, Freed considered Bernstein's style avant-garde and thus inappropriate as screen material. Furthermore, Freed disliked the "campy manner" of the book, which he felt would be offensive to film audiences. Consequently, most of the Bernstein score was scrapped, and Comden and Adolph Green were hired to rewrite portions of the book as well as write new lyrics for replacement songs, composed by Roger Edens, an associate producer within the Freed unit.

For much of January 1949, Edens was in New York to lay the groundwork for *On the Town*'s location shoot, yet another milestone in the history of musical films. Edens' mission also included "tidying up loose business ends, such as renegotiating a music contract with Leonard Bernstein." Near the end of the month, he was joined by M-G-M film star Gene Kelly, who was set to co-direct *On the Town* with Stanley Donen. One of their appointments was with Alice, whose performance as Lucy Schmeeler Kelly had not forgotten, having seen the stage version in 1945. Kelly wanted Alice to repeat her role—now enlarged considerably by Lucy's clever creators Comden and Green—in the Technicolor production which would start rehearsing in February. After negotiations, things moved quickly. On February 16, columnist Earl Wilson announced that Alice was "going to Hollywood to play her own part in M-G-M's *On the Town*."

The studio decided to use contract players for the film's leading roles. Kelly, Frank Sinatra, and Jules Munshin, the trio from the previous year's *Take Me Out to the Ball Game*, were perfunctorily chosen as the sailors on leave. This decision created a slight issue for Comden and Green as they began to remodel their original work. "With Gene as [Gabey] and the star of the picture," Comden explained, "the angle of the story had to be changed. He couldn't

Despite the efforts of Lucy Shmeeler (Alice Pearce) to cheer up Gabey (Gene Kelly), he remains glum in On the Town *(1949).*

a striking diversion from Sono Osato's "sensuous, exotic beauty."

Meanwhile, wallflower Lucy—whose surname was changed by a single letter to "Shmeeler" once M-G-M's research department discovered some actual Lucy Schmeelers in the Manhattan phone directory—became somewhat less one-dimensional. Alice, the sole cast member from the Broadway production to appear in the film version, was also the only actress considered for the part. Matt Cimber, who directed Alice in a stage production some ten years later, asserts that no one else could have played Lucy. "Who are you going to replace Alice with?" he proposed, chuckling. "There was no competition. What she was, was correct for the role. There was nobody else who could be more correct." Kelly, Donen, and Freed were obviously of the same opinion. "M-G-M feels it has scored a coup in signing Alice Pearce," the *Los Angeles Times* reported during Alice's first week of rehearsals.

Alice could hardly contain her excitement as she realized she'd be making her movie debut at Hollywood's most prestigious studio, *and* in the company of Gene Kelly and Frank Sinatra. "At the time," Donen later said, "Sinatra was as popular as all four Beatles put together."

Rehearsals began on February 21, but since Alice was needed for only four scenes, she wasn't slated to report at M-G-M's Culver City studios until Monday, March 7. Concluding her televi-

be a helpless, naïve type," as John Battles had been in the stage version. "The whole structure of the story had to be changed to suit the people who were going to play the characters." This included toning down the character of flamboyant Ozzie—now assigned to Munshin—which had originally been tailored "to suit Green's own performance style." As Chip, Sinatra would demonstrate both awkwardness and sweetness, similar to Cris Alexander's characterization in the Broadway version.

The sailors were now written as the main stars of the picture, with the "assertive female voices of the stage production [receding] to become more coquettish." Betty Garrett's Hildy was less brash than Nancy Walker's depiction, and Ann Miller, playing Claire, "radiated a boisterous sunniness that was far afield from the urbane giddiness of Comden." However, the most marked contrast was the casting of Vera-Ellen as revamped "girl-next-door" Ivy Smith,

Alice Pearce, Ann Miller, Betty Garrett, Frank Sinatra, and Jules Munshin sing "You Can Count on Me" to Gene Kelly (right) in On the Town *(1949).*

discovering that Lucy is unexpectedly home with a cold. "Well, what the hell are you doing here?" became "Lucy! What on earth are you doing here?" As Lucy, Alice enters with two loud and very authentic-sounding sneezes. Wearing a drab, oversized flannel robe, she shuffles in, carrying an antique Vapo-Cresolene lamp, which she sets up near Hildy and Chip. Between inhaling the vapor, spraying her throat, and gargling with gusto, Lucy sabotages her roommate's plans for lovemaking. To prevent further interruptions, Hildy

sion series on March 4, Alice, accompanied by John, flew to Los Angeles that weekend. During the next five weeks, Alice rehearsed a total of eighteen days before filming her first scene—which takes place at the apartment Lucy shares with Hildy—on April 8. Almost two weeks passed before she filmed the remaining scenes, which required three full days and half of another before finishing on April 25. Alice's weekly pay was $750, for a total of $6,250. (In comparison, Kelly received a total of $42,000 to co-direct and star in the picture, while Sinatra was paid a flat $130,000.)

For the apartment scene, Comden and Green changed very little of the dialogue they'd previously written for the stage version. The most noticeable alteration was Hildy's line upon

pressures Lucy into leaving to see an "air-cooled movie," promising she'll return the favor someday. "When will you *ever* get the *opportunity*?" the lovelorn Lucy snarls nasally before twisting her mouth into a disgusted farewell to Hildy's sailor: "Goodbye, Mr. Chips!"

In the stage version, Hildy suggests Lucy as a blind date for Gabey once his girl Ivy has fled to her cooch dancing job at Coney Island. But Lucy arrives too late to even meet Gabey who has chased after Ivy. In the M-G-M version, not only does Lucy meet Gabey, but they share three scenes—all filmed in the sequence in which they appear in the final film, an anomaly in filmmaking then, as now. The first two of these scenes take place at the Shanghai Club, where Lucy catches up with Hildy, Claire, and

A tender goodbye between Lucy (Alice Pearce) and Gabey (Gene Kelly) in On the Town *(1949).*

the three sailors. As with the apartment scene, we hear Lucy before we see her—her "achoo" precedes her. Then the camera reveals the rest of her, shot in profile, emphasizing Alice's trademark parrot nose, fadeaway chin, and chipmunk grin. This sight gag is enhanced by Lucy's lack of fashion sense, blatantly contrasted with the glamorous full-skirted gowns worn by Clair and Hildy. Lucy's ensemble, composed of a tight-fitting skirt and a print blouse emblazoned with long-stem roses, is accented by three large pink roses in her hair, green gloves, and flashy earrings dangling down a full three inches. And then . . . Lucy speaks. Her voice is nasal, yet shrill, another blatant disparity between her and the missing Ivy, who's gentle and demure. Coming off as obnoxiously flirty, Lucy's efforts to cheer Gabey fall flat, and he walks into an adjoining bar, brooding over the girl who got away.

To rouse Gabey, Lucy and the rest sing "You Can Count on Me," a pun-filled number designed by Comden and Green to showcase Alice's zaniness. In it, Lucy vamps Gabey, throwing him across a table and cackling while "beckoning him into paradise." Then, trying her darnedest to look sensuous, she wraps herself in a tablecloth, switching the roses from her hair to her teeth, and engages Gabey in a ridiculous tango, punctuated by a piercing sneeze. The number climaxes as all six actors hop onto the table, which promptly collapses as Lucy lets go with one more explosive "achoo."

Despite her antics, we know that Lucy is not a storybook match for Gabey, and he lets her down as gently as possible in the tender scene when he escorts her home. He explains, "Somewhere in the world, there's a right girl for every boy. I guess I found the one for me before I even met you. I tried, but I can't forget her. Don't you worry. You'll find your guy." Kissing her on the cheek, he says, "You're a nice girl, Lucy." She blushes, "You bad boy. Now I won't wash my cheek for a year."

Character actress enthusiast Axel Nissen describes Lucy as "the classic (under) dog—the last girl to be picked for the team, the female nerd, the one who never gets a date, the most unattractive girl in class, with the wrong clothes or glasses or braces or acne or greasy hair or all of the above." In other words, an oddball. "Whether we have been her, persecuted her, or tolerated her, no one has gone through their teenage years without encountering her," he continues. "In the form of Lucy Shmeeler, Pearce brings her back to us, with her disgusting nasal congestion, her hopeless, romantic dreams, her touching neediness, and her exasperating intrusiveness."

Alice had once been in Lucy's shoes. The shy little girl in Brussels had grown into the lonely Paris teenager, only to relive those experiences at the Masters School, where she did not quite fit in. Alice's college years, in comparison, had been happy, but dates with fellows were few and far between.   Now, all of that was long past. Alice's handsome husband was unwaveringly devoted, and her life was enriched by her many friendships, both personal and professional.

Alice's *On the Town* castmates and crew were very supportive of the newcomer. The rehearsal period had been "joyous," Betty Garrett said. This attitude clearly shows in the final print, if one notes the genuine smiles registered by Garrett, Sinatra, Miller, and Munshin as they watch Alice's awkward tango with Kelly. One twenty-first century blogger, praising Alice's performance, observed, "There are moments in the movie [when] you can just sense [Kelly's] joy with her." In 1982, Kelly reminisced, "Alice was one of the loveliest ladies one could know. Off-stage and off-screen, she was the complete antithesis of the roles she played—quiet, very bright, and lovely." Garrett echoed that sentiment, if a bit less eloquently: "Alice Pearce was one of my favorite people. She was as sweet as she appeared on screen, but *not at all* dumb." Frank Sinatra, according to his friend Matt Cimber, "rather adored Alice."

Upon the conclusion of filming, Alice wrote to Arthur Freed: "I am returning to New York today. I am very sorry not to have seen you before leaving. I want to thank you for giving me a chance to be in *On the Town*, and for

taking such good care of me. I enjoyed working in my first picture so very much. It was so painless, really such fun. Thank you for being good [to] me."

Most of the photography for *On the Town* was accomplished by May 5, when the six principal players and crew departed California for the Manhattan location shoot. Once completed, many would consider the film's "stylized musical opening, with its flashes of reality filmed in New York" as its high point. Kelly, Sinatra, and Munshin clowned on the Brooklyn Bridge; they snacked in Chinatown; they sang at the Statue of Liberty; they rode horseback through Central Park; they walked under the Third Avenue el; they sang on Wall Street; they strolled through Rockefeller Center; and they rode a double-decker bus on Fifth Avenue. Their delightful whirlwind tour of the city, accompanied by Bernstein's fast-paced number "New York, New York," was the product of Kelly and Donen's outright desire to make New York a central character in the movie— New York, the city that Comden and Green dearly loved; New York, the birthplace and home of Alice Pearce.

On the Town wrapped on July 2, at a cost of $2,111,250, going over budget by $166,416. Kelly, writing to John Rox the following month, was confident. "Give my love to Alice and tell her that as soon as we preview the picture, which will be in September," he informed, "I'll let her know how big a smash she's going to be." On September 9, the first public preview was held in Pacific Palisades, California, where viewers overwhelmingly approved, a response that echoed on the East Coast. Featured as part of Radio City Music Hall's Christmas show, *On the Town* opened on December 8 to glowing reviews, despite detractors lamenting the loss of most of Bernstein's original numbers. The film was a huge hit with the moviegoing public, the majority of whom had not seen the stage play. Records were set at Radio City. On December 29, an estimated 10,000 people stood in line four abreast, circling the Rockefeller Center skyscrapers for seven blocks. Following its general release on the next day, *On the Town* grossed in excess of $4,400,000.

For her "wistful but unlovely" Lucy, newcomer Alice also received notices describing her performance as "delightful," "hilarious," and "riotous." *The Catholic Weekly* praised Alice's "sizeable contribution" as a "gem of humor," adding, "under the direction of Gene Kelly her comedy develops in sincerity." "A special award is reserved for the inimitable Alice Pearce," pronounced *Cue* magazine, "the adenoidal lass with the most beautiful homely face on Broadway. In her motion picture debut, she shows what the movies have lost by not utilizing long before this her most remarkable talent for comedy."

Interestingly, Alice's contribution is perhaps even more appreciated now. One modern blogger observed, "David O. Selznick noted that it was foolish to economize on bit players. Even if that person is only onscreen for a few moments, for those few moments that actor is the star. There is no better example of that than Alice Pearce in *On the Town*. She steals every scene she is in."

Indeed, Alice made the most of her ten minutes of screen time, practically out-acting the six principals (with Garrett being the most possible exception), even in the subtlest ways. A prime example is her introduction to Ozzie and Gabey at the Shanghai Club. Smiling at Ozzie and employing a voice that's half-head cold and half-chirp, she gushes, "Oh, don't tell me—I *know*—I bet you're Gabey!" When Ozzie corrects her, pointing glumly to his pal, Lucy—for a second—becomes a coquette,

standing straighter, clutching her heart with gloved hand, then inhaling quickly, "*Oh!*" as she gazes at handsome Gabey.

For Alice, *On the Town* was a landmark movie. Her performance as "the girl with a cold" ensured that Lucy Shmeeler would forever be synonymous with Alice Pearce, no matter how many other actresses would later essay the role.

Once Alice's M-G-M assignment was completed, she and John spent an additional week in the Los Angeles area, registering at the storied Garden of Allah Hotel, located at 8152 Sunset Boulevard in what is today West Hollywood. Two decades earlier, silent film star Alla Nazimova had built a complex of twenty-five rental villas around her Spanish-style mansion, situated on two-and-one-half acres of "tropical plants, ferns, fruit trees . . . bizarre birds, and two tall cedars guarding the entrance." Nazimova's efforts at managing a hotel were unsuccessful, and in 1928, she sold the property to new owners who converted the mansion into additional guest suites. Catering to both short-term and long-term guests, the Garden of Allah gained the reputation as a place where Hollywood's famous could conduct their private lives unobserved by the public eye. Among its former guests and residents were Greta Garbo, John Barrymore, F. Scott Fitzgerald, Robert Benchley, Dorothy Parker, Somerset Maugham, and Ernest Hemingway. Gossip columnist Sheilah Graham called the hotel "an oasis for the intellectuals from the East—the Algonquin Round Table of the West."

The Garden of Allah was notorious for its wild parties, fights, pranks, suicides, robberies, and even murder. But the management—disinclined to judge, probe, or interfere—"paid no mind" to the shenanigans. Neither did the guests. Drama critic Ward Morehouse dove into the hotel pool wearing his dress suit. Tallulah Bankhead frolicked naked through the

Newlyweds Alice and John pose with Towzer, a rescue boxer owned by Arthur and "Dutch" Gordon Bryant, most likely during a visit to Steepfields, the Bryants' home near Asbury, New Jersey.

garden. Robert Benchley, who nursed many a hangover at the Garden, walked around the pool wearing a shirt and a leather apron—and nothing else. "The Garden was one of the few places that was so absurd that people could be themselves," said bandleader Artie Shaw. "No producers hung around there, just hip actors and good writers."

John's friend Louis Bromfield had always stayed at the Garden of Allah when he worked in Hollywood. Perhaps John and Alice knew of the place through Bromfield, or maybe John had known of the Garden's reputation during the years he lived in the Los Angeles area. Since the Garden was less expensive than the luxury hotels, it was "ideal for couples or bachelors who were not too rich." John and Alice were also probably attracted to the place because of its bohemian spirit. However, as

Shaw noted, it was always a little shabby and run-down. Playwright Ruth Goetz stayed for only one week in 1948. "The walls were dirty, the furniture was spotty, and there was a dead mouse in the pool floating upside in a fetal position. It was too much like *Sunset Boulevard*."

By the time the Roxes arrived in the spring of 1949, the hotel was undergoing an overdue renovation. It's not certain if they stayed in one of the hotel's nine guest rooms or in one of the villas, which by then numbered thirty. ("No one who was anyone ever stayed in the main house that had been Nazimova's original home," sniffed Graham, noting its gloomy dining room and deserted cocktail lounge.) Permanent villa residents at the time included actors Roland Young, Louis Calhern, and Calhern's ex-wife, actress Natalie Schafer. If truth be told, John and Alice probably felt very comfortable at the Garden of Allah, staying until May 10 when they checked out to make the journey back to New York.

At some point during their western sojourn, Alice met the remainder of her in-laws. Three months later, Alice wrote to John's niece Shirley, who wondered if the Roxes had any plans to return to California, where all of the Herrings had since resettled. "We cannot make plans to go to the coast until we get a call to work there," Alice explained. "I do not forsee [*sic*] any picture commitments, but I am hoping that after *On the Town* comes out, I may get to make another picture (again, I may not). I am also hoping that as the picture is put together, there will be need for retakes. As you see, we are very anxious to get back to the West Coast." The letter was mostly small talk, but Alice did mention Earl Herring: "I loved meeting your grandfather. There is a resemblance between

John and Alice joined Bill Coburn and Peggy Watson to celebrate their engagement, 1949.

well. "Bill and I were invited to social affairs at their apartment in New York, but to tell the truth, I never got to be very friendly with Alice. When she was appearing at the Blue Angel, John made sure that we got to see her act, and it was delightful, of course."

Months earlier, when Bill had been contemplating marriage, John referred him to a Manhattan jeweler, who created a diamond cluster engagement ring for Peggy. On a cold night in February, following Peggy's last show at the Roxy Theatre, Bill proposed during a cab ride to the Roosevelt Hotel, where he had planned a little celebration. "We had a little supper party there with Alice and John, just the four of us," Peggy remembered. "We danced to Guy Lombardo's music at the Roosevelt Grill, and they played John's 'It's a Big, Wide, Wonderful World.' I don't think I ever saw Alice after that night."

Alice was prevented from attending the Coburn nuptials because she had finally landed a two-week guest spot on a new CBS television show. Billed as "Broadway at its best," *The 54th Street Revue*, produced by Barry Wood and directed by Ralph Levy, had premiered in a Thursday night slot on May 5. Hosted by Jack Sterling, the weekly hour-long musical variety show featured new and original songs and dances built around a new locale each week, such as Grand Central Station, Park Avenue, and Central Park. Regulars included comedian Carl Reiner, impressionist Patricia

Mr. Herring and my father. I am afraid my dad has much more of a bay window."

There would be no need for retakes. *On the Town* had ceased production one month previously, and Kelly and Donen had since moved on to other projects. Meanwhile, Alice was having difficulty finding summer employment. Waiting for something to turn up, she and John bided their time, relaxing at Perk Bailey's house in Northport.

In late June, John served as best man for his friend Bill Coburn when he married Peggy Watson in Franklin, Pennsylvania. Alice did not make the 350-mile trip, but she sent a "lovely lace handkerchief," a family heirloom, for Peggy to carry during the ceremony. "I put it inside my little white Bible, covered with white baby orchids and streamers coming down," Peggy recalled. After the reception, Peggy returned the handkerchief, asking John to tell Alice how appreciative she was "to use something that meant so much to Alice." For Peggy, Alice's gesture was touching, especially because they did not know each other very

The cast of radio's The Henry Morgan Show *included Arnold Stang (left), Alice Pearce, and Henry Morgan, 1949.*

the June 23 telecast featured numbers related to "Gay Paree," the episode's locale. The following week, she joined comedians Al Bernie and Mort Marshall in lampooning the ways of Hollywood.

Since late May, Alice had planned to be reunited with a few members of the original cast of yet another former Broadway show. Loren Welch, Katharine Sergava, and Alice had signed on to repeat their *Look, Ma, I'm Dancin'!* roles for a week-long production (starring Kaye Ballard in the Nancy Walker role) at the State Fair Casino in Dallas, Texas, beginning July 18, 1949. According to *The Dallas Morning News*, Alice was still onboard as late as July 10, but one week later, she had been replaced by *54th Street Revue* regular Patricia Bright. It's not completely clear why Alice opted out at the last minute, but most likely it was because she'd been hired for a regular part on a new weekly radio program on NBC in New York.

The Henry Morgan Show, debuting at nine o'clock on the night of July 6, was a summer replacement for the long-running situation comedy *Duffy's Tavern*. Acerbic yet sophisticated, Henry Morgan had been a radio personality for more than fifteen years, beginning as an announcer when still in his teens and landing his own program in 1940. Morgan had become "the darling of his generation's rebels and thinkers" after regularly clobbering his sponsors' products on the air, everything

Bright, baritone Russell Arms, and ten-year-old actor Butch Cavell. Broadway performers guested each week. Skits were written by Max Wilk and George Axelrod, who had written sketches for *Small Wonder*. The duo must have been creating parts with that show's cast in mind, because the season's guest list for *The 54th Street Revue* reads like a *Small Wonder* playbill. Besides Alice, those appearing on the series that summer included Hayes Gordon, Marilyn Day, Joan Diener, Mort Marshall, Jonathan Lucas, and Virginia Oswald.

For the *54th Street* regulars and crew, the success of each weekly live telecast was accomplished only by adhering to a rigorous routine. Songs were assigned on the Friday previous to the telecast, with orchestrations being done over the weekend. The pressure, composer Richard Lewine reported, was "fearsome." An hour's worth of new lyrics, music sketch lines, and dances had to be memorized in five days of rehearsal. Alice's appearance on

from Life Savers candy ("six delicious flavors: cement, asphalt, asbestos, . . .") to Adler Elevator Shoes ("I wouldn't wear them to a dog fight"). Listeners who scorned radio commercials as "odious interruptions" were delighted. By 1949, Morgan, beleaguered by professional setbacks, decided that he had allowed his caustic (and often cruel) wit to be carried too far. It was time for radio's bad boy to reform.

Alice was hired to fill the vacancy left by comedienne Patsy Kelly, who had briefly been a Morgan regular that spring. The writers had hoped that Kelly, playing the man-hunting proprietress of Morgan's favorite cigar store, would help boost ratings, but the plan quickly failed. Cashing in on Alice's *On the Town* persona, the program's writers created the role of Daphne, "the girl with a perpetual cold." Alice would not be the only source of nasality on the program. Returning for his fourth season was scrawny, bespectacled Arnold Stang as Morgan's nerdy Brooklyn sidekick Gerard, a character which had become so popular that Morgan once called Stang "the comedian of the show."

Despite the comic contributions of Alice and Stang, Morgan's reformation led to a ratings decline. Harriet Van Horne of the *New York World-Telegram* noted: "Henry Morgan isn't funny anymore. Alice Pearce, whose talents have delighted me ever since I first saw her in summer stock some three years ago, is utterly wasted on the Morgan show. The lines given her are woefully inept, though she does valiantly by them. With a smart script, Miss Pearce and Morgan should have a rollicking time of it. They both have a keen appreciation of satire."

Alice, in need of the weekly paycheck, stuck it out, and stayed with Morgan for three months. Her final appearance occurred on September 28, the same day that the *New York Herald Tribune*

reported that she was the leading contender for a role in *Gentlemen Prefer Blondes*, a musical comedy adapted from the 1925 novel by Anita Loos. Alice signed on a short time later.

With rehearsals set to begin in less than two weeks, Alice took advantage of her free schedule and, with John, immediately departed New York for a vacation at her parents' second home in Vermont. Situated on a hilltop, the sprawling house, which Margaret had dubbed "Pearce Place," was still under renovation, but there was ample room for the Roxes to relax and enjoy the early autumn weather. Rarely did Alice find time for painting, but here, far from the noise and distractions of the city, the opportunity was irresistible. For several afternoons, Alice happily sat at an easel in her parents' front yard, facing the opposite mountain, aglow with the orange foliage of sugar maples. In the foreground, Sadawga Lake reflected the azure sky. Between the lake and Alice's perch, black-and-white cows grazed in a pasture. Here and there, the roofs of white houses peeked out from behind colorful treetops. Alice added all of these details to her oil painting, which, when completed, strikingly resembled the American primitive style of Grandma Moses. In the lower right corner, she signed: *'49 A. Pearce Rox.*

Rehearsals for *Gentlemen Prefer Blondes* began in New York on October 10. Produced by Oliver Smith and Herman Levin, with music by Jule Styne and lyrics by Leo Robin, *Blondes* was directed by John C. Wilson, a close friend of Anita Loos, who had suggested him to Smith and Levin. Loos had chosen Joseph Fields to help her write the libretto. Rounding out the stellar production team were choreographer Agnes de Mille and costume designer Miles White. Carol Channing and Yvonne Adair, fresh from the revue *Lend an Ear*, were selected as the show's

"Oh, goody! But I can't drink it on deck. Henry might see me," Mrs. Spofford (Alice Pearce) whispers to Lorelei Lee (Carol Channing) who orders a bottle of champagne for the old girl in Gentlemen Prefer Blondes *(1949).*

lead characters, gold digger Lorelei Lee and her wisecracking sidekick Dorothy Shaw.

Set in 1924, *Gentlemen Prefer Blondes* takes place on a luxury liner bound for Europe, with later action occurring in Paris. Lorelei and Dorothy's fellow passengers are an odd assortment, including an older Englishman with a roving eye (Rex Evans); his domineering wife (Reta Shaw); a health-nut zipper manufacturer (George S. Irving); the "button king" sugar daddy (Jack McCauley); a Philadelphia scion (Eric Brotherson) who's smitten with Dorothy; and his pleasure-mad mother Mrs. Ella Spofford (Alice).

The producers had thought Alice, at thirty-two, was all wrong for the part of sixtyish Mrs. Spofford, an age then considered "elderly" by some standards. Aside from that, the actor chosen to play Mrs. Spofford's son was six years older than Alice. So, just for kicks, they allowed her to audition. To her great surprise, Alice got

the part. She had been unaware that Loos, her "biggest booster," was determined to win over Smith and Wilson. "It's hard to realize," Alice later said of the diminutive playwright, "how much she contributes because she never seems to offer an opinion. She's smart and quiet."

However, the role of Mrs. Spofford, "the richest woman in Philadelphia," is inconsequential to the plot of *Blondes*. She merely reacts to those around her, except when she's on the prowl for a champagne cocktail, an indulgence forbidden by her protective son Henry. He insists that she drink only mineral water or Moxie (a popular soft drink in 1924). Lorelei, enlisting Mrs. Spofford's help in setting Dorothy up with Henry, plies the old girl with the firewater she craves, consequently inspiring her to update her wardrobe and bob her hair. Regenerated, Mrs. Spofford ("I don't want to go to bed! I can do that at home!") transforms into a flapper, singing with abandon, dancing a mean Charleston, and giddily riding on the backs of three young men.

On November 17, *Blondes* opened as a tryout at Philadelphia's Forrest Theatre. The *Courier-Post*, calling it "sparkling," predicted that it should "keep ticket agents happy for about two years." Heaping praise upon Channing, Adair, and Brotherson, the reviewer lamented, "The only disappointment of the whole evening lies in the fact that [Henry's] mother, played by Alice Pearce, just didn't have enough to do,

Miles White (center), dressed as a centaur, was a prize-winning sensation at a costume ball to celebrate the seventh wedding anniversary of columnist Dorothy Kilgallen (right) and her husband Richard Kollmar in 1947. Seventy-five celebrities, impersonating their favorite "sinners," romped through the seventeen-room Kollmar apartment for nine hours. Kilgallen's Scarlett O'Hara gown cost $650.

making laughs in *Gentlemen Prefer Blondes* is Alice Pearce. Her playing of Mrs. Ella Spofford, the old gal with the yen for a forbidden snifter, is tops." Even Ward Morehouse of *The New York Sun* surprised his readers: "Finally, I've come around to the admission that Alice Pearce can be funny. She is very funny as the rejuvenated Mrs. Spofford."

Gentlemen Prefer Blondes became a smash hit, and overnight Carol Channing became the talk of the town. "No one will ever forget her," wrote John Mason Brown. "She is not a type; she is the most individual of individuals. Certainly, Broadway has not seen her like before." Most reviewers, accustomed to a petite Lorelei Lee, couldn't get by without mentioning Channing's atypical height. Brown said it was not just Channing's stature, but everything about her. "Take her eyes, for example," he suggested. "They are so big and far apart that they summon memories of the headlights on a Pierce-Arrow. Then there is Miss Channing's walk, which is a short-stepped, hobbled gait decidedly her own. It is all toes and torture, a cross between a slink and a mince." *Newsweek* concurred regarding Channing's individuality, adding that her speaking voice "ranges facilely from the squeak of the distressed to the marshmallow unction of the righteous and, possibly, the vacant-minded."

because for our money she is one of the great comediennes in the theatre today."

That sentiment was repeated after *Blondes* debuted on Broadway at the Ziegfeld Theatre on December 8. Louis Sheaffer of the *Brooklyn Daily Eagle* thought Alice was "whackily humorous," but that she "deserved a more individualized part." United Press drama editor Jack Gaver allowed, "The comical Alice Pearce does as much as she can with the meager material allotted her." Syndicated columnist H. I. Phillips felt compelled to write: "A gal who hasn't had half enough praise for her work in

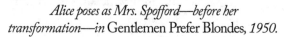

Alice poses as Mrs. Spofford—before her transformation—in Gentlemen Prefer Blondes, *1950.*

Mrs. Spofford (Alice Pearce) becomes a flapper in Gentlemen Prefer Blondes, *1950.*

Newsweek further asserted that during performances even the cast was "slightly overwhelmed by the Channing personality." Offstage, Channing and Alice hit it off. Standing at five-nine in her stocking feet and reaching six feet in heels, Channing towered over her new friend, whom she took to calling "Little Alice." In 1948, Channing had married for the second time—just six months after Alice married John—to Alexander "Axe" Carson, a professional football player turned private detective. During the lengthy run of *Blondes*, the two couples often made time to socialize. "Alice and her husband John Rox were a very definite part of my life," Channing remembered in 1982. In fact, Channing's close friendship with Alice almost matched that of Nancy Walker.

As with her previous stage productions, Alice was popular among the cast and crew. John C. Wilson, remembering the company in 1958, wrote: "We also had Alice Pearce, as brilliant a comedienne as she was sweet." True to form, Alice gravitated to two other gentlemen in the *Blondes* circle—Rex Evans and Miles White—both of whom had impeccable taste in fashion and art. Evans, who played philandering Sir Francis Beekman, had been a cotton broker in his youth but in his twenties began studying acting. In 1928, the six-foot-three actor made his London theatrical debut, followed five years later by his Broadway bow. Prior to *Blondes*, Evans had appeared in small roles in fifty Hollywood films, while moonlighting as an interior decorator.

The masterful Miles White was sought by Wilson to design the costumes for *Blondes*. With over a dozen Broadway shows to his credit—including *Oklahoma!*, *Carousel*, and *High Button Shoes*—White found *Blondes* "great fun to do." According to most critics, it showed. "Miles White's costumes are brilliantly satiric," appraised John Mason Brown, "and show a proper lack of benevolence towards the horrors once thought stylish." *The Commonweal* magazine was equally gladdened: "White [has] seemed to lean over backwards rather than to be authentically in period. Only Alice Pearce, in a character role, gets to wear a real built-on waistline, somewhere down about her knees. And her hats are inspired. Everyone else looks not out of the twenties, nor yet out of the forties, but only rather colorfully out of nowhere."

Before her transformation, old Mrs. Spofford's outfit of baggy layers, a wide fabric choker, and ropes of beads makes her look like a confused crossover from the teens. Perched on her pompadour is a monstrous hat resembling a stork's nest, swathed in net and cradling what looks like buzzard quills. "I hate this hat!" she exclaims to Lorelei, who responds, "I don't blame you! You've got to be the Queen of England to get away with a hat like that!"

Alice was so taken with White's designs that she enlisted Marcus Blechman to photograph her not only in this dowdy get-up but also in Mrs. Spofford's chicest ensemble. Recalling the tipsy Philadelphia dowager, White enthused, "Alice stole the show. A perfect role for her!"

White had previously worked on Hollywood film sets and for Ringling Bros. and Barnum & Bailey Circus but found one aspect missing from those settings. "In the theatre, when you do one show you get to know a lot of people and you travel with them for a while [on out-of-town tryouts] before the New York opening," he explained. "So, you end up with one or two good friends from that show. And then the next show is a whole new set of people to meet. You get some new friends there." During the *Blondes* tryout, White grew especially close to the "charming" Anita Loos ("She became one of my best friends") and Alice Pearce ("She was one of the sweetest women in the world!").

Gentlemen Prefer Blondes ran for 740 performances, providing Alice with a steady income for all of 1950 and for the first five months of the following year. When she received a long-awaited call to return to Hollywood to make her second film, Alice decided to leave the show. Loos was crushed. "I've just heard with the greatest grief that you are leaving *Blondes*," the devoted playwright sighed. "I cannot even begin to tell you how unhappy I am about it and you, yourself know what a loss it will be to the play. However, I do feel so grateful that *Blondes* had you as long as it did, and that your adorable picture of Mrs. Spofford gave so many people so much pleasure."

Alice departed *Blondes* on Saturday, May 26, 1951. After the show closed on September 15, Channing and several members of the original cast, including Adair, McCauley, Brotherson, and Shaw, joined the national tour of *Gentlemen Prefer Blondes*. The following February, Channing wrote to "Little Alice" from Milwaukee: "We talk about you all the time and imitate Alice for everyone in the company. They're so curious about her. Love, Carol."

CHAPTER FOURTEEN
Feast or Famine

"It is very hard to make ends meet in New York . . . It is hardly possible to put away for a rainy day."

For Alice, playing Mrs. Spofford in *Gentlemen Prefer Blondes* was an escape from wallflower roles, yet the old girl was as much of an oddball as Lucy Schmeeler. The laughter and applause she drew eight times a week were a balm for Alice, particularly as 1950 unfolded into a year of anxiety, mishap, and illness.

In March, Bob Pearce had a "nervous breakdown," which rendered him unable to function normally in day-to-day life. The crisis, seemingly brought on by stress, was so severe that Bob was hospitalized for three months. On March 23, Ed Sullivan reported in his "Little Old New York" column that the sixty-year-old was "recuperating" at the Harkness Pavilion in the Washington Heights neighborhood of Manhattan. However, Bob's recovery, beset with reversals, would continue for more than two years. His illness forced his retirement from the National City Bank, and in early June, he and Margaret moved permanently to their vacation home in Whitingham, Vermont. "We were tied down with family all spring," Alice wrote to a relative, recapping the year's trials.

Alice didn't specify the cause of Bob's sudden collapse, but Peggy Coburn believed it was related to a financial issue. By this time, Peggy and her husband Bill were living in a large Victorian house across the Hudson in Englewood, New Jersey. John Rox frequently visited them to obtain Bill's assistance in writing down the tunes inside his head, but he also sought a listening ear. While Peggy wasn't usually privy to the men's confidences, Bill told her that Bob Pearce "got into some sort of difficulty with the bank." Recalling the affair as "very serious," Peggy added, "There was something about some funds, and I think they were even worried about Alice's father being put in prison. The funds were in a bank in Germany, and they had transferred them over here, and it was a mess." Peggy admitted that she "didn't get all the details," but she was aware that the circumstances had greatly upset Alice and her parents.

While no mention of a scandal involving Bob Pearce seems to have made the New York newspapers, neither have any items regarding his retirement. A man of Bob's standing in the world of international finance, not to mention his brave reaction to the Nazi invasion of Paris, would have certainly been recognized after thirty-five years of service to the National City Bank. Perhaps Bob's departure was downplayed due to any stigmas attached to his illness, or maybe Peggy Coburn's hazy recollections were more on the mark than she thought.

Removing themselves from New York and everyone they knew, the Pearces settled into relative seclusion two hundred miles away in bucolic Whitingham, where their only contacts, aside from Margaret's sister Josephine and her husband, were members of the Wheeler family from whom they had bought their home. Although very young at the time and not entirely informed of the nature of Bob's illness, Whitman Wheeler recalled Bob's odd behavior. "He seemed to suffer from what I think was called 'shell shock.' He would not be really a part of conversation. He stood apart."

During Bob's illness and lengthy recuperation, it's very likely that the stress felt by Alice and her mother was compounded by the memory of an event which had taken place twenty years earlier. Bob's brother Wilbur, forty-seven, a bond salesman then living in Colorado Springs, had been found dead in his garage. An apparent suicide, death was caused by carbon monoxide poisoning. All the more reason to relocate Bob to the country—and to remain watchful of him.

Because her only days away from *Blondes* were Sundays, Alice found it difficult to make the trip to Whitingham. So, on the second weekend in June, John went in her place. Soon after he returned to Manhattan, Alice fell ill with appendicitis. Emergency surgery was performed, resulting in a three-week leave from the show. Perhaps she did not realize it, but Alice was genetically predisposed to develop appendicitis. Her grandfather Joe Clark and three of his four children had required appendectomies, all prior to 1929. By summer's end, Alice reported, "I am very well now and feel better than I ever have in my life."

The summer of 1950 did not end without additional disturbance. On Saturday afternoon, August 5, John boarded a six-car passenger train at Penn Station for his customary weekend trip to Northport. Forty-five minutes later, outside of Huntington, a confused young brakeman opened a switch and sent the speeding passenger train onto a siding to crash into a standing freight train. The steam locomotive of the passenger train was ripped from its tracks and rolled over on its side. The first two passenger coaches were derailed and tilted, but

A rare candid snapshot of Alice and John Rox on the tiny patio at the rear of 152 Bayview Avenue in Northport, circa 1950. Photo courtesy Linda Swanson.

did not topple over. Fifty-four persons were injured. "John escaped miraculously," Alice said, "with only a wrenched back." Police said it was "just plain lucky" that the boiler of the passenger locomotive did not explode.

On Monday, August 28, Alice—en route from Northport to Manhattan—took advantage of the train commute to write a long overdue response to John's niece. Providing an update on events of the past six months, Alice wrote, "I tell you all these things not to pour out our troubles but to let you see why you have not heard from us more often. Johnnie found 37 four leaf clovers today and I know everything is going to look up. Johnnie has a new song coming out in two weeks recorded by Burl Ives called 'Pig Pig' (written long before 'Cincinnati Dancing Pig'). Vaughn Monroe has also recorded a wonderful new song of John's called 'Don't Stop My Plane.' This record should be released in a month."

During the run of *Gentlemen Prefer Blondes*, Alice sought to supplement their income by appearing on television in musical variety shows such as *Van Camp's Little Show*, *The Milton Berle Show*, and *The Kate Smith Hour*. Unfortunately, few kinescopes of Alice's early television appearances survive.

One of those preserved is a telecast of *Toast of the Town*, later known as *The Ed Sullivan Show*, which aired on January 29, 1950. Sullivan's other guests that evening were singers Dinah Shore and Vic Damone. Just before Damone's introduction, Alice walks up from the audience to join Sullivan on stage. Employing the persona of "The Girl" from her Blue Angel act, Alice interrupts Sullivan to ask him to introduce her to Damone. "I'm nuts, I'm just nuts for Vic Damone!" she grinningly snuffles, prompting cheers from Damone's young female fans in the audience. When Sullivan asks her name, Alice remains in character, looks straight into the camera and deadpans, "Alice Pearce." The audience responds with applause, and Sullivan pretends he suddenly recognizes her from the film *On the Town*. When asked if she's currently appearing on Broadway, Alice flatly affirms, "Yes, *Gentlemen Prefer Blondes*—I hope Vic doesn't!" Then she jabs Sullivan, giggling.

Later in the show, Alice performs part of her Blue Angel repertoire, its origin perhaps lost on the majority of the studio audience, not to mention the television viewers across the country. The curtain opens to reveal Mark Lawrence seated at the piano. Alice, now completely in character as "The Girl," rushes up, dumping her three minks on the piano lid. When the duo

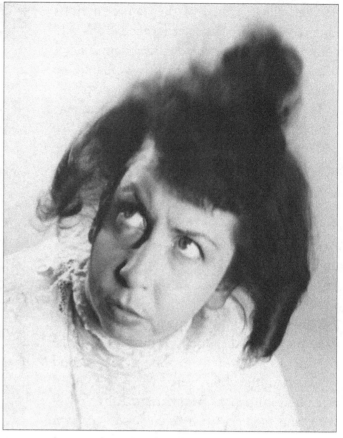

Alice's hairdo on Toast of the Town *was nothing compared to the one she assumed for Cris Alexander's camera in 1947.*

abruptly bursts into frenetic musical gibberish, it's perfectly clear why Phil Gordon said that viewers of Alice's 1949 television series hadn't known "what the hell she was doing."

This brief introduction is followed by a duet of "Constantinople," in which Mark expertly spells the title in rapid repetition while Alice fumbles and stumbles to keep up, *à la* a stagestruck Lucy Ricardo. "The Girl" introduces their second number as "a throaty, sentimental song." The timing of "Two Cigarettes in the Dark," however, seems a little bit off, and the song doesn't garner much applause. Yet, *Variety* was complimentary, noting that Alice "socked across her own particular brand of nitery comedy."

Viewing this segment of *Toast of the Town*, it's easy to understand why some reviewers of Alice's nightclub act tended to mention her hairstyle ("copied from a harried scarecrow," said one). Standing next to the immaculate Sullivan, Alice looks rather bizarre. Her hair is pulled severely across the temples and gathered loosely into a topknot, accentuating her ears, nose, teeth, and absent chin. Her tousled bangs complete the unflattering look, achieving the comical appearance Alice was after.

One year later, when Alice guested on *The Faye Emerson Show*, she imitated her hostess' trademark hairstyle by attaching a large chignon, complete with small black velvet bows. However, any resemblance to the glamorous Emerson—then known as "The First Lady of Television"—ended there. The opening shot focuses on Alice's high-heeled feet propped on a coffee table, panning along her reclining figure and up to her profile as she enticingly takes a drag from a cigarette in a long holder. Exhaling a thick ring of smoke, she faces the camera and promptly demolishes the illusion when she greets the audience with a nasally "Hi!" The camera switches to Emerson who explains that she has given Alice the chance to host the talk show that evening. What followed was a blend of rehearsed and improvised banter between Alice, Emerson, and guest comedian Peter Donald. Getting in a plug for *Gentlemen Prefer Blondes*, Alice appears in a sleeveless 1920s-style shift ("I heard fringe was coming back," she quips) and struggles with the tight skirt to keep her knees covered during the interview. She makes quite a contrast with Emerson, elegant in a black bouffant skirt. Eyeing Alice, Donald capitalizes on the disparity by wisecracking, "She's got a figure eight, but she makes it the hard way—with two fours!" Emerson convulses but Alice, visibly disconcerted, handles it gracefully and

simply smiles. Whether in or out of character, Alice often poked fun at her physical attributes, but her reaction here may indicate that she was unaccustomed to encountering jibes in this type of setting.

Meanwhile, with *Blondes* still going strong, Alice and Mark Lawrence returned to The Blue Angel for a six-week engagement, opening the club's spring show on April 5, 1951. Three years had passed since their last engagement, but they were still getting a lot of mileage out of Mark's old numbers like "Wait for the Dial Tone, Nellie" and "Short'nin' Bread," the latter now slanted toward Alaska where "Mammy's little baby loves blubber soup."

A new Pearce-Lawrence number was one they satirically called "Our Sophistication Song," punctuated with Alice's saliva-ridden raspberries during an otherwise smooth delivery: "Farewell is difficult to say/Just how to say it, I cannot say/Except to say goodbye this way:/If I were as high as a bird in the sky/I would look down on you and say *pfffft!*" Alice then sang the entire song in French, making it all the more hilarious.

In another new number, especially tricky, Alice pantomimed operatic baritone Nelson Eddy's march song "Boots," using a phonograph disk duped from Eddy's original but altered in the recording process with turntable speedups and slowdowns.

Yet another, which Ed Sullivan called "a gem of invention," was a "request number" from an imaginary audience member, a Massachusetts Institute of Technology graduate wanting to hear his school song. "I really don't know it," apologized Alice, "but we'll certainly do our best." As a "girl of courage," she refuses to abbreviate the school's name, inserting the mouthful of syllables into snatches of Yale's "Down the Field," Cornell's "Far Above Cayuga's Waters," and "The Maine Stein Song."

Variety, successfully capturing Alice's essence as a nightclub performer, wrote: "Miss Pearce purveys a brand of comedy that mixes subtle inflections and broad antics for immediate impact ... [she] has natural comedy equipment in her mobile face and off-key pipes. She's an excellent mugger who can switch between high enthusiasm to near nausea with perfect fluidity. This is one of the standard bits with which she hits every time." Syndicated columnist Earl Wilson reported that Alice took twelve bows on opening night.

Just as she had done in 1948 when doubling her nightclub engagement with *Look, Ma, I'm Dancin'!*, Alice left the Ziegfeld Theatre each night after the performance of *Blondes* and headed to the supper club. The six weeks of moonlighting made for a "heavy schedule," John said. The couple never got to bed before five in the morning.

Beginning June 1, the Roxes assumed a much less hectic schedule—and in a new locale. Alice had been chosen for a prime supporting role in M-G-M's musical *The Belle of New York*, so she ended her Blue Angel act on May 16 and left *Blondes* ten days later.

Accompanying Alice and John on the plane trip to California was John's brother Bob Herring, whose singing career and marriage had been sabotaged by his alcohol addiction. In the two years since Bob's divorce, John and Alice had been quite supportive, both emotionally and financially. The trip provided an ideal opportunity for John and Bob to visit all of the Herrings, who by now were living in Anaheim, thirty-five miles southeast of the M-G-M studios.

Derived from an 1897 comic opera of the same name, *The Belle of New York* had been a favorite of M-G-M producer Arthur Freed since his youth. The plot of the original show involved "a Salvation Army lass who reforms a spendthrift playboy." Freed had added *The Belle*

of New York to his production schedule in 1943, envisioning Fred Astaire and Judy Garland as the leads, but Astaire was reluctant because "he would be repeating the fantasy element which had failed" in one of his previous films. The project lagged as a succession of writers overhauled the original book over the next eight years. By that time, Garland had been released from her M-G-M contract, and Vera-Ellen had been cast opposite Astaire. Charles Walters was assigned as the film's overall director, while Robert Alton would serve as director of the dance numbers.

Final screenwriters Robert O'Brien and Irving Elinson shifted the story to 1910, and the film's romance coupled playboy Charlie Hill (Astaire) with prim Angela Bonfils (Ellen), welfare worker for The Daughters of Right. Dependent on his puritanical aunt for his income, Charlie has already left five showgirls waiting at the altar. After falling in love with Angela, he becomes convinced that he is not good enough for her and breaks their engagement. She pursues him by pretending to be a vamp. In an effort to save her from the advances of an obnoxious flirt in a supper club, a brawl ensues, and the couple is reconciled.

The premise of the story depended on the clichéd notion that love is like billowy clouds, and "you walk on air." Utilizing trick photography, this idea is employed at several points in the film as a "fanciful signal of the lead characters' emotional states." (In one scene, lovesick Astaire taps along the top of the famous Washington Square arch.) However, the whimsical concept would "scarcely resonate with movie-going audiences in 1952." Even Walters demurred: "The initial idea was good . . . but [it] didn't work for Astaire, because can he *really* be in love?"

With more than forty percent of the film's eighty-two minutes devoted to dance num-

Fred Astaire, Alice Pearce, and Vera-Ellen pause during filming of The Belle of New York *to consult the script, 1951.*

bers, Walters aspired to inject humor into the remaining scenes. He urged M-G-M to cast Mae West against type as Astaire's wealthy, strait-laced aunt, but the actress "wanted too much money." Marjorie Main, a veteran of thirty-four M-G-M films, was ultimately assigned the part, while her fellow contract player Keenan Wynn was chosen to play Astaire's lawyer and confidant. The remainder of the film's supporting characters were inconsequential except for one: Vera-Ellen's acerbic but good-hearted sidekick Elsie Wilkins, tailor-made for Alice Pearce.

Charles Walters cheerfully supported the selection of Alice for the plain-Jane role. Her impressive performance in *On the Town* made Alice a logical choice, given that spinster Elsie was a transparent copy of cold-ridden Lucy Shmeeler. It also probably helped that Walters knew the Roxes socially. Walters and John had been acquainted since the 1933 production of Leonard Sillman's *Low and Behold* at the Pasadena Playhouse but had reconnected years later in New York.

Intent on a dance career, Walters had moved east several years before John did. He would eventually perform in ten Broadway productions and choreograph four others before accepting a full-time offer from M-G-M as choreographer in 1942. Prior to *The Belle of New York*, Walters had directed six features at the studio, including *Easter Parade* and *Summer Stock*.

During production of *Belle*, Walters leased a beachfront apartment home to Alice and John. Located at 22522 Malibu Road, the rental property was near the home of Walters and his long-time domestic partner John Darrow. "It was in the area of the [Malibu] Colony," recalled Miles White, "but not within the Colony. Chuck Walters had built it as an investment." However, the real estate venture was most likely the plan of Darrow, who had "begun purchasing land around Malibu in 1944," later convincing Walters that they should build a bungalow-style residence at 22506 Malibu Road.

Darrow, an erstwhile Hollywood film actor, had become a successful talent agent after moving to New York, where he and Walters met around 1935. "[They] began a committed relationship," according to Walters biographer Brent Phillips, "about which they were comparatively unguarded." In 1937, the men moved into an apartment on East Fortieth Street in the Murray Hill section. Until 1942, the pair was bicoastal, splitting their time between Manhattan and Hollywood as work dictated. By the time the Roxes became their summer tenants, Walters and Darrow had been living the life in their "sophisticated, bohemian" beach house for three years.

Given their own unconventional marriage— to say nothing of John's previous cohabitation with Perk Bailey— Alice and John found their landlords' domesticity not at all disconcerting. In fact, the Malibu setting, almost twenty miles west of the M-G-M studio, provided a certain amount of privacy, just as The Garden of Allah had two years earlier. Thus, the Roxes' temporary home became an ideal place to entertain their congenial friends, like Miles White who was on the coast that summer to design costumes for Paramount's *The Greatest Show on Earth*. White had rented a small house at Topanga Beach, some seven miles away. "I used to go up on Sundays, usually, to see Alice and Johnnie," White recalled. In addition to hosting their friends, the Roxes were feted not only by Walters and Darrow, but on separate occasions by Roger Edens, songwriter Ralph Blane, and the Freed Unit's music coordinator Lela Simone, once described as "Edens' right hand and Freed's left."

At some point during the summer, Alice and John hosted a barbecue for his brothers Bob and Don Herring and all of Don's family who drove up from Anaheim—an occasion particularly memorable for Don's daughter Linda, then seven years old. "My brother Danny and I were swimming in the ocean along with a celebrity's son," she recalled. "Uncle John and Uncle Bob were standing nearby talking. For some reason there was a bunch of large logs floating in the surf. Danny and I were [behaving like] typical kids, yelling, 'Uncle Bob! Uncle John! Watch this!' Then I got pinned down by a huge log and went under a wave or two. Again, I

yelled their names over and over. Finally, they came running in after me. Uncle John carried me into the house, telling me all the way how brave I was." Linda also remembers the barbecue for a "sweeter" reason: the baked beans Alice served that day. The Herrings had never tasted anything like them. Borrowing her recipe, they prepared them often in the years to come, always calling them "Aunt Alice Beans."

Unfortunately, filming *The Belle of New York* proved to be no such summer picnic. First of all, neither its leading man nor director wanted to make the movie. "The less said about it the better," Astaire later assessed. "That picture was a duty," groaned Walters. "Arthur [Freed] was stuck with the property, and they'd paid a lot of money for it." When Astaire moaned about last-minute script changes and his resulting performance, Walters found it impossible to sooth him. The director discovered that working with Vera-Ellen ("like a piece of moving putty") was even less enjoyable. "I couldn't stand Vera-Ellen," he openly confessed. "I would talk with her about a scene, and she'd be doing pliés. That's the kind of concentration you got." Citing the pathetic reactions from his lead players, Walters said that his job "was like putting a gun to your head every day."

Meanwhile, Freed was "noticeably preoccupied" with *Singin' in the Rain*, which began production the very same day as *Belle*. Some believed Freed's lack of attention had an adverse effect on the picture. "There were no conferences; there were no set meetings, nothing," sighed Lela Simone. "[*The Belle of New York*] just sort of wandered along." Such heedlessness partly explains why Alice's projected employment of six weeks swelled to sixteen.

Alice reported to the studio six days in June but was only needed for a total of less than nine hours, and some of those were taken up with wardrobe fittings. Considering that the

"I confess that I want to care less than Eva Tanguay!" Elsie (Alice Pearce) warbles during her reprise "Naughty but Nice" in The Belle of New York.

Marjorie Main (center) struggled to dominate her scenes with Alice (right) in The Belle of New York *(1952).*

script changed almost daily, perhaps Alice wondered how her character would be affected. But on June 21, Edith Gwynn reported in the *Los Angeles Mirror* that Alice's role would be "built up because of the way she's coming through [in rehearsals]." Alice was given a song-and-dance number, actually a parodied reprise of Vera-Ellen's solo, "Naughty but Nice." Then suddenly the production bogged down, and Alice wasn't needed again until mid-July.

When things cranked up again, Marjorie Main joined the rehearsals. Walking about the set with what writer Damon Runyan described as "a section boss stride" and speaking with a "voice like a file," Main had been a fixture at M-G-M for more than a decade. As for her walk, Main said she copied it from "aggressive rural type women" she had known growing up in Indiana. "Character actors are best," she believed, "when they portray characters that give them a chance to draw on their own experiences, backgrounds, and observations." She added that she couldn't imagine herself playing a "society woman," an admission that made her casting her as Astaire's philanthropic aunt in *Belle* all the more inconsistent.

The sixty-one-year-old Main was at the height of her fame, thanks to her signature role of rough-and-tumble Ma Kettle in loan-outs to Universal, and she wanted nothing—or no one—to cloud her popularity, particularly a relative newcomer. "Marjorie Main was always afraid of Alice Pearce, of what she might be doing behind her back," recalled the film's assistant director Al Jennings. "Main was scared to death that Pearce would steal a scene from her." Perhaps the older actress was also disconcerted that a musical number designed especially for her had been dropped, whereas Alice's role had been enlarged so much that her eventual screen minutes doubled that of Main (or Wynn).

Alice's final day of filming was September 12, but she was required to remain on the coast for a few weeks in case she was needed for retakes. On October 3, *Belle* closed thirteen days behind schedule, at a cost of $2,606,644. Following its release on February 22, 1952, it failed to make a profit, grossing $1,993,000. Nor was it a critical success. Bosley Crowther of the *Times* described the script as "dramatically boneless," while Annie Oakley of the *Windsor Star* accused its "drab atmosphere" of "overwhelm[ing]" its tunes. Wanda Hale of the *Daily News* noted that the film's "entertainment and humor are jolted up and down," blaming Walters for not "spark[ing] it with any brilliance."

Alice received mixed reviews for her performance, several of which singled her out as the film's chief supporting player—although billed below Main and Wynn. "The show is stolen quite handily by Alice Pearce, a plain but merry tambourine thumper," cheered Wood Soanes of the *Oakland Tribune*. "Alice Pearce contributes a nice little comedy bit," observed Jean Walrath of the *Democrat and Chronicle*,

"but Marjorie Main might just as well have handed her part over to a lesser lady of the screen. They didn't need her for this part." Philip Scheuer of the *Los Angeles Times* chimed in, "Alice Pearce turns out to have more comic value here than Miss Main or Wynn." Others were far from impressed, like John Rosenfield of the *Dallas Morning News*: "Alice Pearce might be described as a homely Judy Canova. She is supposed to be funny." A reviewer from the *Journal Herald* in Dayton, Ohio, shrugged, "Alice Pearce [is] agreeable in [a] lesser role, though about all she does is beat a great big drum."

Over the years, *The Belle of New York* has been roundly dismissed or overlooked by film historians. Astaire scholar John Mueller, while impressed with *Belle*'s three dance duets, cited the film's whimsicality as a chief problem, asserting that its "efforts at impish fancifulness sometimes become a bit coy." Furthermore, he considered its characters as "cartoonish" and "empty-headed," as they "wander as best they can through various difficulties." Perhaps most perceptive is his critique of the film's "somewhat elusive" humor: "much of the dialogue is very funny, but it is often understated and delivered in a throwaway manner." Still, Mueller reserved a bit of praise for Alice: "Considering the brevity of the film and the length of the musical numbers, there is little time to develop characters other than the principal two. Nevertheless, Alice Pearce . . . makes the most of her opportunities. Although she sometimes overdoes her characteristic cackling, she delivers most of her comedy lines with open-eyed innocence and apt timing."

As essayist (and strict devotee of *Belle*) Douglas McVay once noted, Alice's "Elsie" is a "companion portrayal" to her "Lucy" of *On the Town*. Indeed, the similarities between the characters are rather blatant; at times both spinsters can

"Quick! Look sophisticated!" Elsie (Alice Pearce) instructs Angela (Vera-Ellen) in the supper club scene in The Belle of New York.

be uncouth yet charming. (Elsie even erupts with a "Lucy Shmeeler" sneeze.) The biggest difference in the two is that Elsie actually helps to move along *Belle*'s feeble storyline. When the romantic leads reach an impasse, Elsie shows her "best-friend mettle" by cooking up a scheme to reunite them. Dressed alluringly, the girls visit the supper club where Astaire is waiting tables and the reconciliation is ultimately realized.

In preparation for their night out, Elsie and Angela splurge on finery, everything from frilly garters to feather boas. As she dresses in the privacy of her boudoir, Angela performs a solo song and dance ("Naughty but Nice"), which in the following scene is comically reprised by Elsie. Dance expert Mueller, writing in the 1980s, was less than pleased with Alice's solo ("the comedy is heavy and badly timed"), branding it "a lumpish parody." However, Ken Slater, a twenty-first century blogger who professes that Alice's performance is one of his "all-time favourite supporting turns," counters

that Alice could "mug without offending, be broadly funny and still adorably human." Both Mueller and Slater agree that Alice was quite touching in the wedding rehearsal scene where Elsie stands in for the bride. "It's one of those moments where the director lets the spotlight shine gently but firmly on Pearce," writes Slater. "As she walks down the aisle, Elsie becomes more and more overwhelmed by the moment. It's hard not to love her as she melts from cheerful hubbub mode into hushed wonder."

Given all of *Belle*'s faults—from its "featherweight plot" to its uneven editing—the fact remains that *The Belle of New York* ultimately provided Alice with more screen minutes than any of her other films, as well as her only song and dance solo—an attainment that not even the more polished *On the Town* could claim.

During *Belle*'s lengthy production delays, Alice was careful not to rest on her laurels. She promptly signed with John Darrow's agency in hopes that he could secure future film and television roles for her in Hollywood. (Earlier in the year, while still performing in *Gentlemen Prefer Blondes*, she had engaged the enterprising Barron Polan, then representing Carol Channing, as her New York agent.)

In addition, Alice and John hired Stanley Musgrove as a publicity agent, a decision which would prove more worthwhile, if only in the short run. While Alice was on the coast, Musgrove made certain that her name appeared in several *Variety* blurbs announcing future gigs, none of which ever came to fruition. First, there was an item in Mike Connolly's column that Alice would transition from *Belle* to a Los Angeles-based stage production of *Lend an Ear*, performing the role which Carol Channing had originated on Broadway. Two months later, an even more improbable notice touted Alice's nightclub debut on October 1 at Ciro's in London. However, the project with the most promise—yet ultimately as unlikely as its title—was *Helen Goes to Memphis*.

Described as a "musical burlesque in the French manner," *Helen Goes to Memphis* was the creation of John Rox's friend, the Pulitzer Prize-winning novelist Louis Bromfield. In February 1951, Bromfield claimed to have enough backers for the show to open on Broadway that fall. At the time, he and co-writer Herbert Cobey were "dickering" with performers they had envisioned for various roles, including Pearl Bailey as the Queen of Sheba, Sono Osato as a dancing lead, Reginald Gardiner as the pharaoh, and Alice as the pharaoh's sister. "All that Bromfield and Cobey need at the moment, it seems, is a star to play Helen," wrote Robert Sylvester of the *Daily News*. "The script is finished and about three quarters of the score," Bromfield said. "I think it has turned out well and Alice's part as Fatempora the Menace . . . is about as good as any actress could want." Six months later, when Alice was still working on *The Belle of New York*, Walter Winchell reported that Bromfield was "renovating" his musical, with plans for it to premiere "at a London music hall." That never happened, and *Helen* soon disappeared from any further mentions in the press.

In late September, as Alice was preparing to leave California, she learned of yet another possible stage role, though not through either of her agents. From New York came a letter from Anita Loos, whose adaptation of *Gigi* was being produced on Broadway that fall by Gilbert Miller. *Gigi*, the story of a young Parisian girl being groomed by her grandmother and great-aunt for a career as a courtesan, had been written by French novelist Colette in 1944. For Miller's production, Colette herself had chosen a twenty-two-year-old unknown for the title role—a British chorus girl named Audrey Hepburn. Constance Collier and Cathleen Nesbitt, both veterans of the London stage, had been signed as the grandmother and great-aunt, but the part of Gigi's errant mother Andrée, a music-hall actress with "no talent and no brains," had not yet been cast. "It would be wonderful to have you in the zany role of Andrée," Loos wrote to Alice. "I'm sure you'd make the very most of it and be just as divine as you were [as] Mrs. Spofford. Andrée is supposed to be about 30 and, as you will note, she can best be described as a 'slob.' But she certainly *is* funny and the last act curtain depends on her completely." Alice immediately wired Loos of her definite interest in meeting with Miller soon after her return to New York on October 3.

George Cukor, after a twenty-three-year absence from the Broadway scene, had been set to direct *Gigi*, but due to the delay in finding an actress for the title role, he was now committed to direct a film for M-G-M. On October 1, Miller returned from Paris with Cukor's replacement, Parisian director Raymond Rouleau, who spoke not a word of English. Collier conversely spoke not a word of French and promptly bowed out. The language difference was no barrier for Loos, Nesbitt, or Hepburn, whose French was in perfect order, and neither would it have been of any consequence for Alice—had she been chosen to play Andrée. Instead the part went to British musical comedy star Doris Patston, thirteen years Alice's senior. (It is not known if Alice even met Miller. In fact, it's entirely possible that

Alice reunites with The Belle of New York *director Charles Walters (right) at a New York party honoring him in October 1951. Posing with them are party-giver Earl Blackwell (left) and journalist Michael O'Shea.*

some of Walters' friends who had worked with him on Broadway or in Hollywood, among them, Garland, Rosalind Russell, Van Johnson, Ginger Rogers, Ann Sothern, and Bert Lahr. "Ralph Blane and Hugh Martin played and sang and really got the party going," reported Michael O'Shea of *Gotham Guide* magazine. "Judy Garland began to sing from her table. She moved to the center of the floor and finally joined the boys at the portable piano. Then everyone got into the act with a community sing that made it a memorable night." The party lingered until the wee hours, with Alice and John being among the last to leave.

With no stage or film roles in the offing, Alice turned to television, which heretofore had proven to be a somewhat limiting medium. Up to this point she had appeared only on variety shows, usually performing numbers from her Blue Angel act.

Miller had signed Patston before arriving in New York.)   By now, Alice well understood the ups and downs of show business. Sometimes being hired for a show or film was all about timing.

Two weeks after returning to New York, Alice and John found themselves among Hollywood royalty at an impromptu party given by society impresario Earl Blackwell for Charles Walters, who was in town to stage Judy Garland's act at Broadway's famed Palace Theater. Blackwell hosted the supper party at the Pen and Pencil restaurant on East Forty-Fifth Street, inviting

The pattern continued that fall. Alice appeared twice on each of three series telecasting live from New York: *The Kate Smith Evening Hour*, *The Garry Moore Show*, and *Faye Emerson's Wonderful Town*.

The industry had grown tremendously since the brief run of *The Alice Pearce Show*. By 1951, the number of television sets in America had reached almost twelve million. "The young medium was starting to attain critical mass," wrote historian Jon Krampner. "The coaxial cable carrying TV signals now crossed the United States, making television a truly national medium." It was a time like no other in the history of television, a time of live electronic theater based in New York, a time considered by Krampner (and many others) as a golden age. The current crop of live dramatic anthologies emanating from New York included *Studio One, Goodyear Television Playhouse, Kraft Television Theatre*, and *Robert Montgomery Presents*, each one prestigious in its own right. In time, Alice Pearce would perform on all of them.

However, her first appearance on a live anthology series was a telecast of *Lux Video Theatre*, also originating from New York, on November 26, 1951. "Dames Are Poison," starring Nina Foch and William Eythe, centered around a nurse (Foch) who is forced to make a sharp real estate deal when her roommates leave her holding the bag—and the lease—on a huge house. Cast as the flighty tenants were Alice and Peggy Cass, a budding comedienne with whom Alice would cross paths many times in the coming decade.

The following week, Alice supported Dan Morgan and Patricia Breslin in "Money to Burn," a story about a well-meaning counterfeiter on NBC's acclaimed *Goodyear Television Playhouse*, directed by Delbert Mann and featuring actor David White, two gentlemen with whom she was destined to work again.

The competition for roles in these hour-long dramas was stiff. According to a 1952 *Theatre Arts* article explaining the difficulties faced by television writers and actors, the CBS casting department interviewed 150 applicants each week—auditioning "more players than any other organization in television"—a total of 7800 per year. Of that number, it was estimated that about seventy-eight actually got jobs. Most television producers and directors, working against time constraints in a fast-paced industry, preferred those players who had worked with them before. Therefore, actors like Alice found that their chances of employment were limited. "The trade consensus," *Theatre Arts* reported, "is that most actors of non-featured or non-starred status land no more than one [television] job a month."

In Alice's case, the statistics were even more brutal. For all of 1952, she performed in only one prime-time television episode, a dearth not at all due to a busy schedule of stage and film projects, but instead just the opposite. Aside from a brief return to Broadway early in the year, Alice sat around for months waiting for the phone to ring.

However, 1952 had dawned with great promise. In early January, a surprising proposition came from the writer Truman Capote whom Alice had known casually since 1947, when he was "the darling of half of Manhattan." Capote, part of the glitterati who flocked to the Blue Angel that year to catch Alice's act, was a fan. Now adapting his most recent novel, *The Grass Harp*, for the stage, Capote thought Alice an ideal choice for a comic role in the second act.

The Grass Harp, described by one reviewer as "a Southland fable," is the story of Dolly Talbo, a gentle, childlike spinster who hears "a harp of voices telling a story," as the wind blows through the grass. "It knows the stories of everyone," she says, "and when we are dead it will tell ours, too." Dolly lives with her sister Verena, another old maid but of a different type, stern and businesslike. The sisters share their home with a young cousin, an orphaned lad named Collin, and a "blunt-talking Negro woman [named Catherine] who likes to pretend she's an Indian." When Verena pressures Dolly to disclose the formula of her home-brewed dropsy cure for commercial exploitation, Dolly refuses and leaves home, accompanied by Collin and Catherine, to live in a treehouse in the woods. There they are joined by an eccentric ex-judge who wants to "find out who he really is." The foursome's effort to escape infuriates most of the townspeople whose "conventionality demands that all conform." In a scuffle with the sheriff's posse, Collin is shot in the shoulder, an accident which reconciles the two sisters.

Six months before Capote's novel *The Grass Harp* was even published, theatrical producer Saint Subber approached him with a "crazy proposition," offering the writer "option money in the event that [he] ever [wrote] a play." Short on cash, Capote eventually accepted Subber's offer. By August 1951, with the novel yet to appear, the twenty-six-year-old was hard at work writing the stage adaptation from his home at the Niagara, an apartment building on Park Avenue. Capote had realized that "substantial changes needed to be made to make [the piece] work dramatically." He sharpened some characters while eliminating others. To replace the humorous Sister Ida, a wandering evangelist with fifteen children, Capote created a brief spot in the second act for a new comic character, a "traveling cosmetics saleswoman he named Miss Baby Love Dallas."

Capote stipulated that *The Grass Harp* must be a "top-flight production." Soft-spoken Subber accepted Capote's want list without protest: the insightful Peter Brook to direct, the exquisite Cecil Beaton (and Capote's close friend) to design the sets and costumes, the respected Virgil Thomson to compose the incidental music, and Alice Pearce to play Miss Baby Love Dallas. Subber and Capote also believed that the Gish sisters, Lillian and Dorothy, as Dolly and Verena, would ensure a hit. All, except Brook who had other commitments, consented to join the production.

After reading only the first act, but finding it "charming, fanciful, funny, and moving," Broadway veteran Robert Lewis enthusiastically agreed to direct. While waiting for Capote to finish the second half of the play, Lewis and Subber proceeded with casting, but not without a few speed bumps. Mainly, Lewis did not want the Gish sisters. Subber, "taking the recommendation of an experienced director over that of an inexperienced playwright," dropped them from the cast list. The key role of Dolly went to the masterful Mildred Natwick, the part of Verena to Ruth Nelson. Rounding out the cast of eighteen were Georgia Burke as Catherine, Johnny Stewart as Collin, Russell Collins as the retired judge, Sterling Holloway as a mincing barber, and Jonathan Harris (later known as Dr. Smith on television's *Lost in Space*) as an unctuous swindler. Rehearsals began on February 18, 1952, with a tryout scheduled for Boston's Colonial Theatre.

The set for Dolly Talbo's dining room was an elaborate Beaton creation. The designer made extravagant purchases at Madison Avenue antique shops, filling the room with Rococo Revival pieces and red velvet draperies for the windows. Even Alice was skeptical. "Honey, you [will] know," she said to Georgia native Andrew Lyndon, Capote's pal who was hired as Lewis' assistant. "Is that what a [dining room] in the South looked like?"

More impressive was Beaton's atmospheric set for the treehouse scenes, dominated by the "biggest [tree] ever yet constructed on any stage." Twenty-four feet in height, with its branches spreading thirty-four feet, the tree took up an entire stage. "Because we were opening in Boston, and the tree was tremendous," recalled Virgil Thomson, "we held no dress rehearsal in New York. We gave, however, to an invited group of some two hundred Broadway professionals, a last run-through in street clothes, on a bare stage with only worklights. The play was touching; everybody wept. After we had got into our scenery in Boston, nobody out front ever wept again."

Following the Boston opening on March 13, *Variety*—citing its feeble storyline—found Beaton's sets as "the perfect background to more vital doings." Declaring that Capote lacked the technique required for the stage, the reviewer issued a fateful prophecy: "Without a pretty extensive rewrite, the sound of *The Grass Harp* will probably not be long heard in the land of Broadway."

All the while, Lewis had been perturbed with Beaton's overpowering scenery, but he had also strongly argued against Capote's addition of Miss Baby Love Dallas. "Her scene was a capricious vaudeville turn," he said, "having nothing to do with the rest of the play, and out of style with it. This fault was compounded by the casting of Alice Pearce in the part of Baby Love. She, too, was a dear friend of Capote's and a favorite cult comic of small but swank nightclubs. I tried to warn Truman that everything that was good in Alice as an eccentric entertainer would only serve to make this section of the play seem even more of an interpolated number. At the first run-through, I conveyed to Truman my conviction ... that the first act seemed to work fine, but the overall mood and style of the performance was interrupted by Baby Love's cavortings in the second half, and the play never got back on its tracks again."

Capote promised to change the scene if it didn't work in Boston. "Well," Lewis recalled, "Elinor Hughes in the *Boston Herald* hit the nail squarely on the head: 'Miss Pearce had about as much to do with the play as a passing butterfly lighting on Mr. Beaton's tree.'"

Lewis then confronted Capote, who responded, "Tell y'what, Miss Baby Love Dallas is really New York humor. Wait, you'll see."

The Grass Harp opened on March 27 at the Martin Beck Theatre. Brooks Atkinson of the *Times* couldn't have been more enthusiastic

"We mustn't give up hope. I can beautify anything," *Miss Baby Love Dallas (Alice) tells Dolly Talbo (Mildred Natwick) in* The Grass Harp, *1952.*

about it, but most critics sided with George Jean Nathan who found the play "pleasing to the eye but less than satisfactory to the ear." "The final impression," Nathan assessed, "is of a slim volume announced on the cover to be verse which, when opened, is found to consist mostly of blank pages." Walter Kerr of the *Herald-Tribune* was equally metaphorical in his summation: "Seeing it is like coming across a handful of flowers in an old scrapbook. The flowers have been pressed into attractive patterns, but they are quite dead."

Nathan, too, addressed the "disruptive" Miss Baby Love Dallas: "Alice Pearce, arbitrarily incorporated into the play as a vendor of cosmetics, performs what is nothing more but a revue skit." Kerr concurred with Nathan but added that Alice did it "with fierce, and very funny intensity." "Maybe it was New York humor," Lewis later conceded, "but it was not *Grass Harp* humor, and the fragile play, in my view, instead of building steadily to its rightful, moving denouement, slowly went down the drain." On April 26, *The Grass Harp* closed after thirty-six performances.

Although Alice appeared on stage fewer than five minutes, she impressed other critics. "Miss Pearce has a welcome bit in a travesty of a traveling saleslady," wrote William Hawkins of the *World-Telegram & The Sun*, "which she plays with breadth and style." Moreover, syndicated journalist Carl Jacobs cheerfully singled her out: "Mildred Natwick, Johnny Stewart, Russell Collins, and Georgia Burke give creditable performances in the principal parts. But the acting honors go to Alice Pearce, an exceptional comedienne, who does something enchanting with the small part of Miss Baby Love Dallas, an itinerant peddler of beauty preparations."

Alice's reaction to less favorable critics, such as Hughes and Nathan, remains a mystery. Nor is it known if she was privy to the blame Lewis laid at the feet of Miss Baby Love (and Capote). The playwright, however, would later fault Lewis for the production's failure, saying the director "had never understood his work at all."

If nothing else, *The Grass Harp* kindled a mutual fondness between Alice and Capote, evidenced by letters they exchanged for the remainder of 1952. Eager to return to Sicily for an indefinite stay, Capote sailed on the *Île de France* without waiting to see how long his play would eventually run. "You were angels to come to the boat," he wrote to Alice and John eleven days later from Meudon, outside Paris. "It was a great comfort. Thank you, Alice precious, for the music box and the jellybeans: I could've wept—I was homesick before we were a hundred miles to sea."

Capote and his lover Jack Dunphy settled in Taormina, on the east coast of Sicily, where Capote—stage-struck despite the failure of *Harp*—intended to write a stage adaptation of his short story "House of Flowers," an amusing tale about a Haitian bordello. "I want you to be in *Flowers*," said Capote, writing to Alice from Taormina. Since she and John had tentatively planned to accompany Perk and June Bailey to Europe that summer, Alice broached the possibility of meeting with Capote to discuss her role, but he put her off, saying, "I don't think I would have anything to show so early as July."

Despite her enthusiastic interest, Alice expressed an uncertainty about accepting a part in *House of Flowers* because she was counting on reprising her role of Mrs. Spofford for Jack Hylton's London production of *Gentlemen Prefer Blondes*, scheduled for September and starring Carol Channing. Capote, in no rush to finish his script, felt certain that the "two jobs would not conflict," adding, "I think you should take *Gentlemen*, especially since it would be such a good chance for you to introduce yourself at a cabaret in London. You will have the most tremendous success there, I know."

None of it was to be. In August, plans for the London production were scrapped after Channing learned that she was pregnant. Meanwhile, Capote, sidetracked by his social life, waffled between finishing his play and writing short stories. He would not complete the first draft of *House of Flowers* until October 1953, and by that time he had long deleted the role intended for Alice. Moreover, John and Alice did not make the trip to Europe with the Baileys when they sailed in August 1952. They simply couldn't afford it.

"If only we had some money," John wrote to his brother Don in September. Don had asked for advice regarding their brother Bob—"such

Alice, perhaps in an attempt to escape her madcap persona, favored this somber 1949 portrait which she used for publicity throughout the 1950s.

a good guy underneath"— who needed medical attention due to, John said, either alcoholism or the effects of an old boxing injury. "This has been our worst year . . . Alice hasn't worked for months (except for a small summer theatre thing for try-out), and my royalties have been just enough to keep us from going hungry. Things are looking up a bit. Alice may go into a play in November. And I have possibilities of two new recordings. Maybe we can help later . . . after the first of the year . . . We feel so helpless."

Yet, the Roxes' financial difficulties seemed not to test their marriage. If anything, it appears to have made their partnership stronger. "Oh, they had a very good marriage," attested Cris

Alexander. "John and Peeps really were a wonderful team. They just seemed always to be *so* happy together." Frequently, Alice had been the chief breadwinner, but she never measured that against John's contributions. "She was very proud of him, you know, proud of his work and the fact that he wrote so prolifically," remembered Patricia Wilson. "She was always thrilled to be able to talk about John's songs." Future gossip columnist Liz Smith, once a gofer for Gus Schirmer, had been introduced to Alice and John during this era. When Alice revealed to Smith one of their annual customs, it made an indelible impression. "Every New Year's Eve since, I've thought of Alice and her husband John, in bed drinking champagne and eating caviar," she recalled in 2000. "This introduced me to a new concept of celebrating."

During the past decade, Alice had striven to remain financially independent of her wealthy parents, always conscious that, no matter how proud of her accomplishments Bob and Margaret might be, they still did not entirely approve of her career choice. Now, with her father incapacitated and no longer employed, her resolve was even more solidified.

Tallulah Bankhead, when once contrasting the English theatre business to that in the States, proclaimed that the summer theatre had always been a "life-saver" for American actors. Likewise, Alice was keenly aware of the merits of the straw-hat circuit. As *The Grass Harp* limped along during the early spring of 1952, Alice could see the handwriting on the wall. She turned to her old friend Gus Schirmer, who was still directing and producing summer productions, just as he had been in

1946 when Alice supported Bankhead in *Private Lives*. The ever faithful Schirmer found a spot for Alice in a revue he was staging at the Westport Country Playhouse; however it was only a one-week engagement. Alice couldn't be choosy; she signed on.

In early July, she boarded a train for Connecticut to begin rehearsals for *Three to One*, a compilation of material from three previous Broadway revues, going back to 1939. Her fellow headliner was twenty-six-year-old Kaye Ballard, a Blue Angel alumnus on the cusp of making her Broadway debut. Following the opening night performance on July 7, they each received good notices in the local newspapers, particularly for Ballard's song "My Sam" and Alice's sketch "The Story of the Opera," in which she played a woman attempting to summarize Wagner's opera *Die Walküre*. A reviewer from the *New Haven Evening Register* assessed not only Alice's talent ("probably tied with Imogene Coca for the title of best comedienne in America") but also her looks ("With the startling exception of Miss Pearce, the cast is a strikingly handsome group of young people"). Nor did this critic reserve barbs just for Alice; he found *none* of the youngsters in "fine singing voice—they quavered, slurred, and more than a few times were painfully flat." Alice later complained to Truman Capote that her week in Westport was "miserable."

For the remaining five months of the year, Alice was hired but once for a prime-time television appearance, and that was for a segment of *Broadway Television Theater,* produced locally by WOR-TV in New York. The only other television exposure Alice enjoyed that fall was on two fifteen-minute daytime shows, *Mike and Buff* and *The Al Capp Show*. The former was a talk show hosted by husband-and-wife team Mike Wallace and Buff Cobb. The latter—written by confrontational cartoonist Al Capp (*L'il Abner*)—afforded Alice a jolly good time of mugging in two satirical skits. In the first, she and pint-sized Mort Marshall played doleful Eisenhower supporters who had voted for the president-elect's opponent Adlai Stevenson—to spare "poor Ike" the "kicking-around he's going to get from the thirty-six million people who voted *for* him." The second skit lampooned gossip columnist Dorothy Kilgallen and her like who, said Capp, hide behind their "cowardly little phrases" in perfect safety while murdering "the dignity, decency, and privacy of their victims."

Bedecked in a lace-and-satin peignoir, Alice becomes Dorothy Spillbeans who boasts that it's "hideously easy" to get away with printing such innuendos. When she sets out to sully the reputation of a Fifth Avenue furrier to avoid paying for a $5000 mink coat, her husband-secretary (adroitly played by Larry Blyden employing a Southern accent) turns the tables on her. Threatening to sue him for using her petty cash to purchase a silver cigarette case, her husband slyly issues a counter warning that if she pursues the matter, he'll tell her editor's wife the real reason that the columnist and editor went out of town together. Spillbeans cowers, wondering "where he ever learned about stuff like that." Both skits, particularly the latter, are right on par with those produced twenty-five years later on NBC's *Saturday Night Live*.

While it's not known what Alice was typically paid for a single television appearance during television's early days, a contemporary source offers some insight. According to a 1952 *Theatre Arts* article, the "average good actor" in the television industry drew "somewhere between $3,000 and $7,500 annually, sums which would inspire no great envy in the hearts of competent plumbers or waiters."

"It is very hard to make ends meet in New York," Alice had once warned John's niece Shirley, who was contemplating a move to the metropolis. "Prices are extremely high. It is hardly possible to put away for a rainy day in this city."

The reality of the Roxes' financial situation weighed heavily on Alice during the latter months of 1952. She had thought that exposure from *The Belle of New York* would open up possibilities of other film assignments, especially with John Darrow representing her on the coast, but that didn't happen. Likewise, her return to Broadway in *The Grass Harp* had ended up a major disappointment, despite the illustrious production team. Added to this were the multiple letdowns when prospective stage productions evaporated. Unable to rely on either of her agents, Alice knew that it was time to seriously strategize.

CHAPTER FIFTEEN
Recovery

*"If they gave me more money, I wouldn't care
if I bowed at all."*

In 1953, New York's "great era of nightclub entertainment still flourished," says cabaret historian James Gavin, "and nearly everyone, regardless of budget, could take part in it in some way." The Blue Angel yet held sway as the city's most prestigious supper club, with Le Ruban Bleu on East Fifty-Sixth Street maintaining a close second. Herbert Jacoby continued to preside at the former, while his significant competitor Julius Monk managed the latter. Although they had known each other in pre-war Paris, their business association began in 1939 when Jacoby, then managing the exclusive Ruban Bleu, had hired Monk as a pianist and substitute emcee. The tall, flamboyant Monk, whose speech was once described as a blend of "an upper-class North Carolina drawl and a type of Oxonian," had charmed not only the club's staff but its patrons as well. Soon customers began to associate the club with the suave Monk instead of the dour Jacoby, who, following a hostile showdown, turned the club over to Monk. An enduring rivalry began when Jacoby opened the Blue Angel in 1943.

Both impresarios were inclined to pilot new acts that "East Siders would have never ventured into Harlem or Greenwich Village to see," asserts Gavin. As a logical consequence, "the Blue Angel and Ruban contingents generally stayed faithful to the club that had launched them." This was certainly true of Alice Pearce. After debuting at the Blue Angel in 1947, she never performed in another New York club. Furthermore, Alice stood apart from other noteworthy artists such as Imogene Coca, Pearl Bailey, Wally Cox, and Eartha Kitt, who had performed first in other Manhattan clubs before moving uptown to the more distinguished Blue Angel or Ruban Bleu. But Alice had gone straight to the top, thanks to Jacoby. For the most part, his good judgment was undeniable. "He exuded an authority that comes only to those who are sure that their decisions are impeccable," says Gavin, "and when everyone around is too frightened to question them." In 1950, the *Herald Tribune* had named Jacoby "King of the Intimaries." As his loyal (and down-on-her-luck) subject, Alice asked to return to the Blue Angel as soon as he could accommodate her. The king granted his permission.

When Alice, along with stalwart Mark Lawrence, opened their act for a seven-week run beginning January 8, 1953, *The New Yorker* proclaimed: "This showstop has returned to its palmiest days now that Alice Pearce is again its Mad Hatter. Mark Lawrence, her own Lewis Carroll sings in tandem with her from his piano."

Such praise was more than welcome, but Alice realized that her competition was stiffer than it was five years earlier. In her absence from the Blue Angel, a cadre of singing comediennes had distinguished themselves at the prestigious club, including Charlotte Rae, Alice Ghostley, and, to a lesser degree, Jane

Alice Ghostley, circa 1948.

Dulo. Soon Pat Carroll would join their ranks. Like Alice, most of them were short on sex appeal but cleverly used their imperfections to their advantage. "They were a tough breed of women," Gavin observes, "struggling to succeed in a field where men did the hiring and made their business decisions. They fretted constantly over whose act was the best, who received the longest bookings for the highest fees, and who made the most frequent TV and theatre appearances."

Charlotte Rae, after studying drama and voice at Northwestern University, had moved to New York at age twenty-two to break into the business, although she had no real plan of action. In 1948, she found inspiration in Alice's nightclub act, just as she would the following year when she saw Wally Cox's routine at the Blue Angel. "They were great and I said I'm a very good character actress," Rae recalled

in 1979, "so I thought I would do satirical character sketches, [too]." A stint at the Village Vanguard led to Rae's debut at the Blue Angel in 1951.

Alice Ghostley, a last-minute addition to Leonard Sillman's *New Faces of 1952*, had studied at the University of Oklahoma before coming to New York in 1944. For several years, she had teamed with George Wood in nightclub acts and musical revues before they landed a 1951 gig at the Bon Soir, a Mafia-owned cellar club in Greenwich Village. In the summer of 1952, during Ghostley's Blue Angel engagement, she met "sweet Alice Pearce," whom she fondly recalled as a "wonderful artist." In years to come, there would be television viewers who occasionally confused the two comediennes, perhaps due to the first name they shared as well as their separate appearances on the sitcom *Bewitched*.

On May 11, 1953, Alice returned to the Blue Angel for a five-week engagement but without her accompanist Mark Lawrence. The previous year, the former free-lance writer—who had also written material for Dean Martin and Jerry Lewis, Elaine Stritch, and Jack Carter—had joined the advertising agency of McManus, John, & Adams as a radio-television production manager. Moonlighting at the Blue Angel during the winter of 1953 had proved too difficult for Lawrence. Now a new father, he had other responsibilities. Lawrence would never again perform professionally.

Nevertheless, Alice once again trotted out Lawrence's standby numbers, which pleased *The New Yorker*: "That redoubtable and penetrating comedienne Alice Pearce is heading the bill at the Blue Angel, and it's hard to think of any better news than that." *Variety* was equally approving: "Alice Pearce goes with the lease, a very funny gal who may yet achieve the TV break she deserves . . . her hybrid French versions of Yank pops, her MIT college nonsense, parodies like 'Wait for the Dial Tone, Nellie,' etc., as she is hoydenishly perched on the piano make for the same socko returns as heretofore."

Alice, like other nightclub performers, found that intermingling so closely with the public was often more challenging than working in theatre or television. "In nightclubs, [patrons] often bring their emotional problems and with the help of a few drinks take them out on the first person they see," Imogene Coca once explained. "Usually, it seemed to be me." "Saturdays were the worst," recalled Pat Carroll, "because everyone seemed to have had their champagne cocktails before they came." One night in 1953, during Alice's spring engagement, the actor Wendell Corey—seated in the audience with his wife—almost slugged a noisy patron who began to insult Alice. "The inebriated customer was willing to pick a fight until [Corey] stood up," reported journalist Danton Walker. "That stopped everything. The show went on with no further interruption."

Despite the ups and downs of her career, there were many occasions when Alice felt honored to be in her profession. In late spring Alice was invited to Waltham, Massachusetts, to be a part of Brandeis University's five-day Festival of the Creative Arts (its theme to be "Comic Spirit"), under the direction of Leonard Bernstein. Alice was the only female chosen to join the group of humorists and performers—including Fred Allen, Irwin Corey, pantomimist Jack Gilford, and writer S. J. Perelman—who each gave illustrations of their comic art on the evening of June 10. In light of the campus setting, she thought it apropos to perform the well-worn yet still amazing MIT song.

Her 1953 nightclub engagements notwithstanding, Alice was once more experiencing the dry spell of the previous year. By late April, she had appeared on only three television programs, and she'd had no local theatre prospects whatsoever.

Once again, Gus Schirmer came to her rescue. As the New York representative for the State Fair Musicals in Dallas, Texas, Schirmer made certain that Alice was cast as the blind date in the Fair's production of *Best Foot Forward*. Opening for a two-week run on June 22, the show starred the unlikely Joan Bennett, who had never before sung in a musical ("and it is not quite fair to say that she showed why," admitted a critic following the opening night performance). The reviewer also touted the talents of twenty-one-year-old Texas native Debbie Reynolds (M-G-M's "camera-bred star who is aware of the audience every second and has a sixth sense of how to reach it"). The *Dallas Morning News* called Alice "an audience darling . . . with an asymmetrical physiognomy, a humorously weary voice and a species of madness in song."

Rehearsals had become uneasy after Reynolds received a phone call from a deranged fan who said he had come to Dallas to shoot her. "We were all so frightened," Alice recounted six years later when visiting the city. "Of course, we hoped nothing would happen to her, but we weren't really rooting for him to be a bad marksman either—not with us as secondary targets. Even in rehearsals nobody stood too close to Debbie. On opening night there were plainclothesmen backstage. And others sat with the orchestra with bows in one hand, guns in the other. There was a scene where a loud noise was needed and earlier in the week one of the crew had come up with the idea of shooting a pistol into a bucket of water. He did it on opening night and the poor man was surrounded and almost shot before he could

184 Sweet Oddball: The Story of Alice Pearce

Alice Pearce shares a moth-eaten raccoon coat with Debbie Reynolds who brought it to Dallas from M-G-M's costume department. When Best Foot Forward *closed, Reynolds presented the coat to her as a gag, but Alice later used it as a very expensive prop, insuring it for $1,000.*

very tender." Although they would not see each other again for almost a decade, Alice and Reynolds stayed in touch. (When Reynolds married Eddie Fisher in 1955, Alice was invited to the ceremony, but she was unable to attend.)

Still believing that she would be prominently featured in Truman Capote's *House of Flowers* that fall (yet very much unaware that the playwright had already excised the role intended for her), Alice sought solid summer employment to see herself through to Labor Day. In a move that must have left the imperious Herbert Jacoby fuming, she aligned herself with Julius Monk, who promised her top billing in a new revue to be produced in Hamilton, Bermuda. Monk, a frequent visitor to the islands, was "invited by some admirers to put together a show for a limited run at the Bermudiana Hotel." Joining Alice were several of Monk's Ruban

explain what he was doing." Eventually, Alice said, the troubled stalker was caught.

Alice and Reynolds hit it off during the two weeks in Dallas. "I was hardly alone in loving Alice," Reynolds recalled. "Everyone loved her. She was a rare person, one of God's very special people. What was she like? Well, she was like a little hummingbird, very sweet, very busy,

Bleu regulars, including Bill Dana, Bibi Oster-wald, and Jack Fletcher. Most of Alice's numbers paired her with Fletcher, a bespectacled character actor whose career would alternate between stage and television roles for almost forty years. They rehearsed at both the Village Vanguard and Spivy's Roof—formerly a midtown club—before taking off for Bermuda.

Stock in Trade, with words and music written by Bud Redding and Bud McCreery, opened for a seven-week run on July 10. The revue was a great success. Though Alice's recollection of working with Monk had gone unrecorded, one wonders if she felt as warmly as Pat Carroll did. A novice performer, Carroll found his support amazing. "He had a great sense of humor, so whenever he gave you notes about why your material might not be working, he was so amusing that your feelings were never hurt . . . and he was the most elegant gentleman I'd ever seen. He always dressed in such a dapper fashion, and the way he carried himself was exquisite."

Meanwhile, Alice had become disenchanted with both her agents, John Darrow in California and Barron Polan in New York. In the past two years, she hadn't received any film offers from Hollywood, a situation that would linger for yet another two years. "[Her agents] didn't push her at all," mused Cris Alexander when considering Alice's slim outputs. Alice's sporadic film appearances made her so unfamiliar with audiences that the theatrical trailer for *The Belle of New York*, featuring a clip of her solo, identified her as "Alice Pearce—Remember her in *ON THE TOWN?*"

As for Polan, Alice may have empathized with Kay Thompson who had dropped him as her agent in 1951. According to Thompson biographer Sam Irvin, Polan's devotion to client-singer Julie Wilson, "in addition to his ever-expanding list of other female clients, was a bit too much competition for Kay." Whatever her own reasoning, Alice terminated her contracts with both Polan and Darrow in 1953. In their stead, she signed with her faithful friend Gus Schirmer—and that fall, the job offers steadily flowed in.

Occasionally Alice also received propositions from friends in the industry, as she did in 1953 when approached by Buster Davis, who had been recruited to cast singers for a rather curious (and rash, some said) experiment. Sam Vitt and David Brown, young men employed in the advertising industry, had invested $10,000 in recording a musical score written by their fellow ad writer, David Lippincott—even though the musical had not yet been produced, let alone written. Their project was titled *The Body in the Seine*, a collection of twelve songs comprising "a musical tour de force through Paris." Released in 1954, the purpose of the disk was to introduce Lippincott's tunes, hoping to spark someone who could adapt the songs into a story for Broadway. Lippincott, a Yale alumnus who, the *Times* said, "was obviously an admirer of the works of an older Yale alumnus, Cole Porter," for he wrote in a "persistently pseudo-Porter manner." Musical director Davis not only selected the vocalists but created the choral arrangements and directed the orchestra as well.

Alice headed the cast, which included her former fellow players George S. Irving (*Gentlemen Prefer Blondes*) and Don Liberto (*Look, Ma, I'm Dancin'!*). She and Irving, playing lovers who each blamed the other for their break-up, sang the mildly racy "Did You Really Have to Do That?" When Irving sniffed, "At least, the places I go, I don't pick up impetigo," Alice countered, "There's a little girl in Corning, who feels sick now every morning—now did you really have to do that?" In Alice's solo, "Dirge," she played a French chanteuse who prefers Hungarian gypsy tunes over the ballads demanded by her American patrons. Grudgingly, she trills an audience favorite about a woman who murders, then buries her philandering lover ("Fresh cee-ment on ze old cel-lar floor! One more guy who won't leave me no more!").

Regular cast members of ABC's Jamie *included Ernest Truex, Brandon De Wilde, and Polly Rowles, 1953.*

In the fall of 1953, Alice returned to television, marking her second appearance in a situation comedy. ABC's *Jamie* was the story of a wistful orphan who moves in with his aunt and grandfather. Premiering on October 5, the show quickly became the most popular of the network's new programs. Produced by Julian Claman and directed by Dan Levin, the live series blended humor and poignance as Jamie (played by eleven-year-old Brandon De Wilde) and his grandfather (veteran stage actor Ernest Truex) find escape from their loneliness together. In return for the old man's love, Jamie manages to resolve the recurring crises that descend on the household, including the episode which introduced Alice as a semi-regular. In "Aunt Laurie's New Assistant," telecast on November 2, Alice plays Annie Mokum, who adds complications to Aunt Laurie's catering business instead of making things easier. Bumbling Annie would be highlighted later that season when Jamie, playing Cupid, becomes her confidant and adviser in "Love Comes to Annie Mokum."

Two nights after the *Jamie* episode, Alice appeared in the debut of another live ABC sitcom, *Take It from Me*, also known as *The Jean Carroll Show*. *Take It from Me* starred stand-up comedienne Jean Carroll as an "average" New York City housewife, complete with a "slob of a husband" (comedian Alan Carney) and an awkward daughter (Lynn Loring). Carroll opened each show with a monologue—typi-

Santa Claus (Alan Carney) finds he has bumbled up the holiday plans for the Carroll family as daughter Lynn Loring unmasks his Christmas deception while mother Jean Carroll waves her off in Take It from Me, *1953.*

cally centered around being driven crazy by her husband, daughter, or neighbors—then spiced the night's sketch with comic asides to the audience. The action took place in the couple's apartment and the surrounding neighborhood, which, though never identified, was presumably located in Brooklyn or the Bronx. Alice appeared as one of the talkative neighbors in a scene set in the apartment building's laundry room—the show's only segment, said *Variety*, that bogged down. Even so, the trade paper singled her out: "Alice Pearce sparked the supporting players here but in all the thespers were better than their lines." Little is known about *Take It from Me*. No kinescopes seem to exist. According to television historian Tim Brooks, the network's files from this period were not preserved, but it is believed that Alice was a one-time guest and not a series regular as other historians have apparently presumed. Carroll, who felt that Carney was "dreadfully miscast," quickly became disenchanted with the series and, after only eleven episodes, announced to ABC that she no longer wished to continue.

Although Alice's typical work schedule for shows such as these can no longer be determined, it's certainly possible that she experienced the same situation as fellow *Jamie* castmate Ernest Truex, who once described the unique strain of live television for journalist Jack Gaver: "You don't have the sort of rehearsal time you do for a stage show, for example. If you're lucky, you have ten days for an hour-long show; less than a week for one that runs a half hour. There can be no prompting from the wings as there is on the stage. You have just one chance to give the performance you want to give." *Jamie*'s cast, performing live on Monday evenings for viewers on the East Coast, rehearsed all day on the previous Fridays and Sundays, as well as the day of the actual broadcast. Kinescopes, to be aired for other time zones, were created as the program aired lived from New York.

The local live series *Broadway Television Theater*, to which Alice returned that same November for its production of "The Bat" starring Estelle Winwood, usually rehearsed its plays for eight days or longer. Actors on that trailblazing show were paid by the week, similar to performers in stage plays, as opposed to being paid for a single television appearance. WOR-TV producer Warren Wade was responsible for the revolutionary programming concept of *Broadway Television Theater*, which presented yesteryear's top plays in their entirety. The same play was performed live for five consecutive nights, so that viewers could choose whichever evening suited them best.

At NBC, *Kraft Television Theatre* was one of the medium's most prestigious showcases, winning top ratings and many awards and becoming a Wednesday night institution. Alice's first appearance on *Kraft* occurred on December 2, 1953, in "The Rose Garden," an original teleplay by twenty-three-year-old Meade Roberts. Silent film star Enid Markey, also making her *Kraft* debut, starred as widowed Rose Frobisher, a self-described dramatic coach whose own film career never eclipsed her "ten-second close-up in *The Broadway Melody*." Rose operates a Hollywood rooming house—flanked by a rose garden—for aspiring ingénues, whose dreams reflect Rose's former self. The landlady yearns to achieve through a protégée the distinction that escaped her, but her unphotogenic, plain daughter is not at all interested and an attractive boarder attempts suicide after being rejected once again for a film role. A spectator to all this angst is the comic character Maxine, played by Alice, who has been waiting twenty years for her first break. With no job offers on the horizon, Maxine usually sleeps until mid-afternoon, then plops herself in a lounge chair

Alice Pearce as Maxine in "The Rose Garden," a segment of Kraft Television Theatre, *1953.*

to either read movie magazines or use a sun reflector to build her tan, often bursting into songs like "You Ought to Be in Pictures." At the program's conclusion, when Rose's daughter finds escape from her controlling mother by marrying a much older bachelor, Maxine becomes Rose's only source of comfort.

Alice's final television appearance of the year came four weeks later when she joined the distinguished cast of "The Thirteen Clocks," an hour-long presentation of ABC's *The Motorola Television Hour*—yet another anthology series, though a rather short-lived one. The evening's live production was a musical adaptation of James Thurber's fairy tale starring John Raitt as the good Prince Zorn, Basil Rathbone as the evil Duke of Coffin Castle, and Sir Cedric Hardwicke as the Golux, an enigmatic character "on the side of good." In his castle—so cold that its thirteen clocks have frozen at

ten minutes to five—the Duke holds captive the beautiful princess Saralinda (opera star Roberta Peters) whom many suitors have failed to win. Before the Duke will allow Zorn to court Saralinda, the prince must bring him a thousand jewels within ninety-nine hours—and he must arrive precisely when all of the clocks are striking five. At the Golux's suggestion, Zorn and the Golux set out to find Hagga (played by Alice with characteristic cackling), who has been given the magical power to weep jewels instead of tears. Two days later, they encounter Hagga, who explains that she has been made to weep so much in the past that now she is no longer able to weep at even the saddest stories. The pair try and fail to make Hagga weep, but as they cast about for further sad stories, they find an oaken chest filled to the brim with jewels. Hagga tells them that these are the "jewels of laughter," beautiful but of no use to the prince as they last but a fortnight, unlike the jewels of tears which last forever. In desperation, the Golux and the prince try to make Hagga laugh and fail at this also. Then suddenly she goes into hysterics over her own jokes about two traveling wayfarers, laughing uncontrollably until her hut is ankle-deep in jewels. Prince Zorn and the Golux gather one thousand jewels and return with them to the duke's castle, where Saralinda's warmth has started the thirteen clocks, freeing her to escape with the prince.

"The Thirteen Clocks" met with mixed reviews. "Thanks to the deft acting of an all-star cast, a gently melodic score by Mark Bucci and Thurber's elfin epigrams," wrote *Life* magazine, "the production achieved real distinction. Audience and critics, feeling it was high time TV got this far, began looking with renewed hope to the new year for more Thurber, more fantasy and many repetitions of 'The Thirteen Clocks.'" *Variety*, however, found the production lacking in "charm and warmth," due to the "rather harried pace the video version took on." While disappointed with the performances of Hardwicke ("stumbling") and Rathbone (unable to "make his character jell"), the reviewer was impressed with Peters, Raitt, and Alice's "good bit" as Hagga.

As much as she was grateful for these occasional appearances on television, Alice strived to find steadier work in the theatre, even if it meant accepting parts "too small for a comedienne of her stature." Such was the case with *John Murray Anderson's Almanac*. Staged by

Weeping gems as she goes into hysterics over her own jokes, a bewitched old Hagga (Alice Pearce) helps the cause of the prince (John Raitt), left, and the Golux (Sir Cedric Hardwicke) in "The Thirteen Clocks," a presentation of The Motorola Television Hour, *1953.*

veteran producer John Murray Anderson—whose professional credits also included that of actor, dancer, songwriter, director, screenwriter—*Almanac* was a fast-paced revue which bore the distinction of introducing Hermione Gingold, Billy De Wolfe, Harry Belafonte, and Polly Bergen all to Broadway. Upon its debut at the Imperial Theatre on December 10, 1953, the show was a smashing success. Anderson, asserted the *Brooklyn Daily Eagle*, had managed to blend the contributions of a "small army of composers, lyricists, and sketch writers" into a "single personality, to give the show a uniform style of glossy smartness." Esteemed critic Walter Kerr agreed with most others that *Almanac* found "its greatest strength where most revues falter—in the comedy [sketches]," which were directed by Cyril Ritchard. The

show-stopping Gingold and De Wolfe became media darlings.

Comic actress Kay Medford had been hired not only to appear briefly in four of the sketches, but to also serve as Gingold's understudy. However, during tryouts she was being considered to support Mary Boland in the forthcoming stage production of *Lullaby*. Since she'd been rehearsing *Almanac* since early October, Medford remained with the revue for two and a half weeks after its opening at the Imperial. When Alice heard about Medford's planned departure—perhaps through Buster Davis who was the show's musical director—she auditioned and was chosen to replace Medford as both performer and Gingold's understudy. Seeing that Alice was already committed to appear in "The Thirteen Clocks," it was arranged for her to join *Almanac* on December 30, the day after the telecast. Despite her relatively small part in the revue, Alice would remain with *Almanac* until its end on June 26, 1954, receiving billing on the playbill's title page—a perk which had escaped Medford.

At one point during *Almanac*'s run, there were major changes in the order the stars took curtain bows. Some of them, "jealous about who bowed after who and before who," got slightly temperamental about it. When asked if she cared when she bowed, Alice quipped, "If they gave me more money, I wouldn't care if I bowed at all."

One of the sketches teamed Alice with comic Orson Bean and dancer-singer Carleton Carpenter. Called "Don Brown's Body," the lampoon crossed the dramatic reading style of "John Brown's Body" with the literary excellences of Mickey Spillane. Carpenter, who was renting a tiny apartment on Fiftieth Street and Second Avenue, would come to consider Alice and John Rox as dear friends. "While we were doing *Almanac*," he recalled, "we would decide with great deliberation what sort of drink we'd share after the curtain came down. We'd always have dinner together between shows on matinee days, most often at Jim Downey's on Eighth Avenue. I think the lightweight special, a delicious steak dinner, cost $1.75 or $2.25, something ridiculous like that. We'd chow down quickly and head back to the theater for a nap."

Almanac was somewhat of a family affair as it featured one of John's songs, "The Earth and the Sky," sung by Bergen near the end of the second act, marking the third time that one of his original numbers had been used in a Broadway production. John was still struggling to create another hit song like "It's a Big, Wide Wonderful World," which earned him $3,000 to $4,000 annually in royalties. That past May,

Eartha Kitt had recorded John's "Two Lovers" as an RCA Victor release, but it had not been well received. One reviewer called the song—and the chanting Kitt—"far-fetched." John, too, dismissed it. "'Two Lovers' is not worth listening to," he told his brother Don. "It was a bad recording and I'd just as soon you didn't hear it." On the same label that October, Vaughn Monroe's recording of John's ballad "I Know for Sure" boasted a rhumba beat and memorable lyrics, but it didn't prove very popular either.

However, by the time *Almanac* opened that December, radio listeners were flocking to record stores to buy copies of John's latest, "I Want a Hippopotamus for Christmas," a bouncy novelty number recorded by a ten-year-old Oklahoma City girl named Gayla Peevey. Discovered by Columbia Records' pop-music impresario Mitch Miller, Peevey had never had any vocal training or coaching. The song's popularity was boosted by Peevey's performance on Ed Sullivan's television show in November. Eventually, "I Want a Hippopotamus for Christmas" climbed to the twenty-fourth highest spot on the *Billboard* chart, one place higher than "It's a Big, Wide Wonderful World" had reached in 1949.

John continued to crank out tunes, but he had yet to learn how to compose them on paper, relying instead on his steadfast friend Bill Coburn to complete the creative process. John frequently visited the Coburn home in Englewood, New Jersey. "My husband wrote a lot of [John's] music for him because John did not write music down," recalled Peggy Coburn, chuckling. "John would whistle [the melody], and my husband would write the notes down. And then Bill would play chords, and John would say, 'No, that's not what I'm hearing in my head. I don't want that chord there.' So, they worked on the chords that would be behind the melody. It was kind of interesting, really."

One month before the end of *Almanac's* run, Sarah Lawrence College alumnae hosted a gala event on campus to raise money for their scholarship fund. Employing an *Alice in Wonderland* theme, the party was advertised as "Alice and the Mad Hatters: A Mad Hatters Party Starring Alice Pearce." Guests were encouraged to wear "mad hats" of their own design to be judged by John Pico John, the famous milliner known as "Mr. John". To accommodate Alice's schedule, her portion of the evening's entertainment—called "Songs Through a Looking Glass"—was reserved for the second half, which began at midnight. Sitting atop a grand piano, she used a tambourine to accentuate her renditions of her familiar nightclub numbers while accompanied by pianist Bud McCreery.

Given their shared name, it was inevitable that Alice would be associated with Lewis Carroll's famous heroine. Since childhood, admirers had given Alice copies of *Alice in Wonderland*—so many, Alice told journalist Margaret Mara, that the volumes filled an entire bookshelf in her apartment. As Alice's penchant for offbeat characterizations developed, the identification with Carroll's work became even more appropriate.

Now that *Almanac* was a closed book, Alice was again unemployed, but she unashamedly utilized the system set up for those in her situation. Carleton Carpenter found himself in the same boat. "Peeps had convinced me to sign up for unemployment," he recounted, "making it sound like a great game. Every week she'd pick me up in a taxi and we'd set off for the office on East Forty-Second Street. We'd stand in line, sign up, and then go have a lavish lunch, giggling like idiots. Her nickname for me was 'Lucky,' and that's how I felt having her, John and their dog Roxy as friends."

Alice spent much of July relaxing while considering her options for the new Broadway season. Producers Charles Bowden and Richard Barr were keen on bringing a revival of George Kelly's *The Torch-Bearers*, a popular 1922 satire on little theatre groups, to Broadway in the fall. They envisioned Alice in a leading role, alongside Mary Boland, who had appeared in the original, but now, at age 72, was most likely being considered for the role which Alison Skipworth had played some thirty years before. Unfortunately, the production never left the planning stage.

However, another prospect—which one year previously had been but a mere possibility—suddenly came to life. *One Minute Please*, a live prime-time game show imported from Great Britain where it had proved quite popular on the BBC for some years, had been telecast as one-time "tryout" on the DuMont television network on September 29, 1953. The show featured six celebrity panelists, three women versus three men, who were required to talk extemporaneously for one minute on an outlandish topic without repetition, hesitation, or straying from the point. Successful panelists scored a point for his or her side, but the opposing team had the power to challenge the speaker's right to continue for any reason. The tryout featured John McCaffrey as the host, and the panelists were Alice, actress-writer Hildy Parks, author-editor Agnes Rogers, comedian Morey Amsterdam, and writers Cleveland Amory and Jimmy Cannon.

When the weekly series eventually premiered July 6, 1954, on DuMont, Alice, Amory, and Cannon, returning as panelists, were joined by comedian Ernie Kovacs and actresses Hermione Gingold and Anne Burr. Reviews were generally positive. "*One Minute Please* could be an immensely amusing program," offered Jack Gould of *The New York Times*, "because it does

That old devil Time seems to stump DuMont's One Minute Please *panelist Alice Pearce while eliciting smiles from fellow-panelist Hermione Gingold and producer-director David Lowe, 1954.*

put a premium on inventive humor conceived on the spur of the moment." Gould, however, felt that Cannon and Kovacs "strained too much to come up with boff gags." Syndicated columnist Bob Mack found the panelists "a witty, urbane and more-than-ordinarily extroverted lot—and they acted as if they had been

Gingold, said Gould, "caught the spirit of the game" and was an "inspiration to her distaff colleagues." When asked to talk on glass blowing, Gingold launched into the following explanation, all in a "fearfully British" accent:

"I have blown glass for *yeahs*. When I am out of work, I do practically nothing else but blow glass. I blow little vases, toys, and chandeliers. If you have asthma, I beg you don't take up glass blowing." Alice's first topic was "King Farouk and I," and Gould complimented her "oblique approach" to discussing the former ruler of Egypt.

Alice appeared as a regular panelist for the next three Tuesday evenings, sandwiched between rehearsals for a four-week summer stock tour of F. Scott Fitzgerald's only published play, *The Vegetable*. The production was a collaborative effort between three close friends, all of them actors, who, the previous winter, had planned it as an opportunity to work together. The most famous of the trio was comedian Wally Cox—then starring in NBC's hit television series *Mister Peepers*—who, they decided, would be the lead player. Acting as director, in addition to playing a supporting role, was Peter Turgeon, who had served as best man at Cox's wedding that June. Supervising the entire production was William Redfield, who was younger than either of his collaborators but possessed more professional stage experience, having made his Broadway bow at the age of ten. By the summer of 1954, Redfield had racked up eleven Broadway credits. Together the men assembled a cast of friends they had known either from previous shows or other connections, including Alice, Peggy Cass, William LeMassena, and Cox's new bride Marilyn Gennaro.

Fitzgerald's curious title was inspired by a quotation he supposedly read in a 1923 magazine: "Any man who doesn't want to earn a million dollars or at least park his tooth brush in the White House hasn't got as much to him as a good dog has. In fact, he is nothing more or less than a vegetable." *The Vegetable*'s hero, Jerry Frost, is a business failure whose nagging wife thinks he does not have enough "push," that he ought to strive to be president of the United States, but the meek little fellow really yearns to be a postman. The "sophomoric flop" had run only briefly when it was originally staged in Wilmington, Delaware, back in 1923, leaving many in 1954 to wonder why anyone would take the trouble to revive it, despite the touted revisions made by Cox and company.

After *The Vegetable*'s opening at the Marblehead Summer Theatre on August 2, the *Boston Traveler* appraised it as "all right" as a summer showpiece for a popular television star, but cited its "cracks about the Roosevelts and [Senator] McCarthy imitations" as being incongruous for a satire set during the Prohibition era. The *Boston Daily Record* agreed that the play needed "considerable alteration," but found favor with Cox ("wonderful") and Alice ("matchless . . . "one of the funniest women alive").

From August 9 through August 21, *The Vegetable* was performed for patrons of the Salt Creek Summer Theater in Turgeon's hometown of Hinsdale, Illinois, twenty miles west of downtown Chicago. Sydney J. Harris of the *Chicago Daily News* dismissed the play's author as "bitter, boorish and infantile," adding that Cox "labored diligently with material that simply would not stand the test of time or mature judgment." His opinion of Alice's performance was somewhat brighter: "Alice Pearce is a superb comedienne who manages to project her personality beyond the confines of Fitzgerald's narrow characterization. She, too, is ultimately defeated by her lines and deserves a play more worthy of her rich inventiveness."

By the time the troupe returned to Boston for a week at the New England Mutual Hall, Turgeon and Redfield had given up any wild hopes they had to invade Broadway with *The Vegetable*. Rod Nordell of *The Christian Science Monitor*, reporting on the production's opening night in Boston, echoed the Chicago critics. "Mr. Cox and Miss Pearce contribute more to the occasion than Mr. Fitzgerald does . . . [their performances] are well-nigh unerring. He has refined his deliberately anti-climactic delivery to a point of expertness. She seems able to give any line a sardonic, or gleefully sardonic, twist."

In 1992, Turgeon reminisced about the burden he felt while directing, producing, and acting in *The Vegetable*. "I found myself suffering from a severe case of insomnia for the first time in my life," he recalled. "Knowing that Alice traveled with a little black bag filled with various pills, I implored her to come to my rescue. She dove into her satchel and brought forth a small, pink capsule as well as another which resembled a mothball. Having a scant

Peter Turgeon, who once said that Alice Pearce was one of the most beautiful human beings he had ever known. Photo courtesy Wendy Turgeon.

knowledge of drugs, I asked her to explain the difference. Patiently, she pointed out if I took the pink pill it would seem as if a nun had tip-toed into my bedroom and quietly lowered the blinds. When I inquired about the mothball, she cooed, 'Dearie, that would have the effect of a mother superior hitting you over the head with a baseball bat!' I took the pink one."

Alice became especially good friends with tall, slim, blue-eyed William "Bill" LeMassena, whom Turgeon had recruited for a dual role in *The Vegetable*. Turgeon and Bill, both former G.I.'s, had been in the national touring company of *Call Me Mister* in 1947. A native of Glen Ridge, New Jersey, Bill traced his dramatic aspirations back to 1927 when, at age eleven, he saw a play in nearby Newark. "It was *Dracula*, and it scared hell out of me," he recalled, "but that one look at the stage and I determined I wanted to be an actor. I

fixed up a theater in our barn in Glen Ridge and never stopped playing at acting until I became a professional." Bill's parents "staked [him] to four years majoring in drama at NYU," where he graduated in 1938, staying on for a post-graduate course and acting with the Washington Square Players. In 1939, he read in the *Times* that Alfred Lunt was holding an audition at the Guild Theatre for parts in a tour of *The Taming of the Shrew*. "Fifty-Second Street was jammed with actors when I got there," he said. "We all tagged into the theater after Mr. Lunt and then he gave a little speech. There were only two parts to be cast, he said, but he'd listen to as many of us as he could. I walked over while the readings were going on and tugged at his sleeve, 'I'd like to do the pedant,' I said. 'Don't be silly, young man. The pedant is an eighty-year-old man. You're just a kid,' he said. And before they got a chance to call me, Mr. Lunt was ready to end the try-out. I ran over and grabbed a script. 'You will hear me read the pedant,' I announced. And I started reading." Bill's brashness paid off. Lunt gave him the part, and thus began a close association with Lunt and his wife Lynn Fontanne, whom Bill would call his "second parents," that would last for more than forty years. He would go on to appear with the Lunts—"the most powerful people in the theatre at that time"—in four Broadway productions.

Bill and Alice found that they had other things in common besides an early desire to act. Like Alice's parents, Bill's prominent family had "considerable doubt about his choice of profession." His maternal grandfather—a wealthy steel merchant—had been born in Sheffield, England the same year that Harry Pearce, Alice's grandfather, had been born in Cornwall. Both Alice and Bill had traveled extensively through pre-war Europe. And they

Wally Cox (left) and Bill LeMassena rehearse The Vegetable *with Alice Pearce in the background, 1954.*

Alice as Wally Cox's nagging wife and Peggy Cass as her loud, gum-chewing, movie-mad sister-in-law in The Vegetable, *1954.*

were each delighted to be identified as character actors, providing masterly support for some of Broadway's biggest stars. Once again, there was something there that clicked, drawing Alice to Bill, who, like most of her male friends, happened to be gay.

During her weeks touring with *The Vegetable*, Alice had been studying lines for a role in yet another production, one that came with a guarantee of opening on Broadway that fall. For two months, Tallulah Bankhead had been making the usual summer stock rounds in *Dear Charles*, a piece with a rather checkered past but now proving its audience appeal—thanks to its dynamic star. Gus Schirmer, whose friendship with Bankhead went back more than a decade, had suggested Alice for a small part at the end of the last act, but she was already committed to Turgeon and Redfield for the month of August. As soon as *The Vegetable* closed in Boston, Alice raced up the coast to Ogunquit, Maine, just in time to join the final week of Bankhead's tour.

In *Dear Charles*, Bankhead was cast as Dolores Darvel, a Parisian novelist with three young adult children who believe that the portrait hanging over the drawing room mantel represents their father, "dear Charles." The truth is that Dolores has never been married, and furthermore her children were all sired by different men. When the eldest two children announce their plans to marry into a stuffy commercial family, Dolores decides to make their heritage more respectable. She tells them the whole truth and promptly invites the three former lovers to her home, instructing her children that they shall decide which man she should marry and pass off as their father. This plan is to coincide with Dolores' introduction to Madame Bouchemin, the prospective mother-in-law of Dolores' two oldest children. Just before the Bouchemins arrive, Dolores comes

Madame Bouchemin (Alice) drops a bombshell on Dolores Darvel (Tallulah Bankhead) in Dear Charles, *1954.*

to her senses and abandons her ruse. Happily, Madame Bouchemin is not at all the ogre she has been built up to be, and Dolores is compelled to confide in her—only to be beaten to the punch when her visitor reveals that she, too, is an unwed mother.

The part of Madame Bouchemin, although nothing but a bit, reads as if it had been written expressly for Alice. When introduced to Dolores' friend, who is a doctor, she realizes she already knows the man. "*Ah le docteur*—but of course," she says. "He was once brilliant with a kidney of mine." And then we learn that the lady's given name is Eglantine, an appellation ranking right up there with Lucy Schmeeler and Gladys Kravitz.

Dear Charles opened at Broadway's Morosco Theatre on September 15, 1954. Critics found the play "sluggish" but cheered Bankhead's knockout performance. "Batting those big eyes with the long lashes, undulating around the furniture, grinning, roaring, putting saucy inflections into innocuous lines, she plays with gusto and wit," said Brooks Atkinson of the *Times*. "Trust Alice Pearce," he added, "to be grotesquely funny as a bourgeois French woman worried about respectability." Others saw fit to give Alice a nod, including William Hawkins of the *World-Telegraph & Sun*, who admitted, "I found more pleasure in Alice Pearce's deceptive matron than in all Miss Bankhead's relatives, by marriage or otherwise." Walter Kerr of the *Herald Tribune* chimed in, "And I felt that Alice Pearce, on for only five minutes, was in complete command of the nonsense handed her." *Dear Charles* ran for 155 performances, ensuring Alice steady employment for five months, before closing on January 29.

Although Alice rarely mentioned Bankhead in interviews, it is believed that the two got along, both on and offstage. The uninhibited star was famous for her hysterical tirades, whether under the influence of alcohol or not. Bankhead's biographer Joel Lobenthal noted that for the bulk of the *Dear Charles* run, her "behavior was good." Only once did she show up drunk for a performance—and that was rectified by an unperturbed stage manager who stripped off her clothes and held her under a hot shower until she sobered. Bankhead dreaded being alone at night, and after performances, she was always hopeful that someone would invite her to join them at a restaurant or club. "She often had cast members back to [her suite] at the [Hotel] Elysée," wrote Lobenthal, and those may have included Alice and John Rox. Although the impetus is now lost to history, it's certain that John, at least once, offered some assistance to the frightfully needy Bankhead. Among his papers is a brief note written on her letterhead: "On my own I want to thank you, kind sir. Love, Tallulah."

Alice chose to forego Bankhead's road tour of *Dear Charles*, one columnist reported, to return to the television panel of *One Minute Please*—a rather unlikely game plan, considering that the quiz show was on its last leg. Its network, DuMont, ranked fourth behind NBC, CBS, and ABC, and losing money every day, would drop the program on February 17, 1955.

Actually, Alice skipped the road tour in anticipation of a return to Hollywood that winter. Producer-director Nunnally Johnson had handpicked her to play an oddball character in *How to Be Very, Very Popular*, a 20th Century-Fox production intended for Marilyn Monroe.

CHAPTER SIXTEEN
Goodbye, Sutton Place

"No girls ever get jealous of me. A physical handicap like this [chin] makes you very, very popular—no woman thinks of me as competition."

By 1955, Hermione Gingold was snooting all Broadway offers. "I prefer television," the eccentric redhead informed an interviewer. Although Gingold would later call *One Minute Please* a "silly show," the self-admitted chatterbox found a new public through the medium of television, progressing from the quiz show format to talk shows and even dramas. Her outrageous personality led to her being called "the British Tallulah." "Bosh," Gingold snorted. "Tallulah's the American Gingold!" Still, she remained incredulous when *Pageant* magazine estimated that her 1954 performances on *Omnibus* and *Toast of the Town* had been seen by almost fifty million television viewers, "so many times more than had ever seen me in all my years on the British stage," she said.

Alice Pearce was also keenly aware of television's impact, but, like Gingold, found it difficult to simultaneously nurture a career in the new medium and remain active on the Broadway stage. The majority of New York-based television programs were still telecast live, and that greatly limited opportunities for stage actors whose only free evenings were Sundays.

As *Dear Charles* neared its finish at the Morosco, Gingold asked her *Almanac* and *One Minute Please* co-star Alice to join her in a sketch to be performed on the *Toast of the Town* telecast on

Sunday night, January 16, 1955. Simply called "Hats," the skit had been written by Denis Waldock for the 1941 London revue *Rise Above It*, featuring Gingold and the other comical Hermione, Miss Baddeley. "[We] played two self-centered old dowagers trying on a variety of hideous hats in a millinery shop," Gingold explained, "as we kept up a banter of silly gossip about ourselves and the war."

Gingold updated Waldock's sketch, essentially making Alice "the straight man" while reserving the best lines for herself.

ALICE: My dear, I do believe you're thinner!
HERMIONE: My dear, of course I'm thinner. It's my new diet.
ALICE: Do tell me what it is.
HERMIONE: Just worry—sheer worry.
ALICE: What about?
HERMIONE: Anything, anything. Sometimes I worry about my diamonds being old fashioned and sometimes I just worry about moths.

Exposure via the small screen was fine, Alice thought, but she could not reject an unsolicited offer from a motion picture producer like Nunnally Johnson who was set to direct his own screenplay of *How to Be Very, Very Popular*, loosely based on Howard Lindsay's 1933 Broadway hit *She Loves Me Not*. Just before production began, Marilyn Monroe, stating she was "tired of the same old sex roles," refused to make the picture, thus beginning a year-long battle with 20th Century-Fox. Sheree North replaced Monroe when the cameras began to roll on February 21, 1955. Betty Grable, Bob Cummings, and Charles Coburn joined North as the film's leading players.

In *How to Be Very, Very Popular*, Grable and North are San Francisco burlesque chorines on the lam after they witness the murder of a fellow stripper. Seeking refuge in a college town, they are hidden by three college students in their fraternity house until the murderer is caught. Grable falls in love with Cummings, a man who has put off graduating for seventeen years, so that his inheritance money will keep coming. North falls for Orson Bean, a dimwit who is in college only by virtue of his father's money. Coburn is the much put-upon college president who will accept anyone with the right amount of cash.

Miss Sylvester (Alice Pearce) enlightens Mr. Marshall (Fred Clark), the father of a college coed, on panty raids in How to Be Very, Very Popular *(1955).*

Alice was cast as the fraternity's amiable, addlepated housemother Miss Sylvester, whom the boys call "Miss Syl." The starry-eyed spinster has been bitten by the classics and quotes soulfully from Longfellow and Thayer at the slightest provocation. However, her key scene arrives when she delicately explains campus hijinks to a frat boy's father. "A panty raid," she begins politely, "is a new phenomenon in this country in which the boys of the school—bless their innocent hearts—are stirred by youth and the first touch of spring in the air to move *en masse* on the girls' dormitories and demand certain *tokens* of gallantry." Using a wide range of vocal tones and facial expressions during this discourse,

Dr. Tweed (Charles Coburn) becomes flustered by the poetic language used by Miss Syl (Alice Pearce) in How to Be Very, Very Popular *(1955).*

Alice demonstrates a brand of subtle humor far removed from Lucy Schmeeler in *On the Town* or Elsie Wilkins in *The Belle of New York*. The refreshing interplay between Alice and the consummate Charles Coburn is among the few highlights in *How to Be Very, Very Popular*—its first half often resembles a third-rate sitcom without a laugh track, uncomfortably silent after the feeble punch lines are delivered.

Released in July, less than four months after its completion, *How to Be Very, Very Popular* charmed few critics. "A better description of this film might be 'How to beat a gag to death,'" quipped the *Chicago Tribune*, nevertheless praising Coburn and Alice as "far better than any of the principals." *Variety* thought that Johnson's screenplay "waxes a little thin, but some of his cracks are so funny and the overall mood is so cheerful one forgets its empty moments," while commending North's torrid dance number, Coburn's "delightful" contribution, and Alice's "standout" performance.

Onscreen in *Popular*, Alice looked very fit and trim, a fact not lost on journalist Harold Heffernan who visited her on the set. "This five-foot-two actress has beautiful blue eyes, milk-white skin, a 35-25-35 figure many a glamor gal would envy," Heffernan wrote, "but the curvaceous dimensions are usually disguised in dowdy duds." When the talk turned to the beauty of sex symbols Grable and North, Alice shared the childhood tale of how she wound up with a fadeaway chin. She was quick to explain that her defect was not a deficiency—producers take one glance and cast her in weak-brained portrayals, she said. "One thing about it," Alice chuckled, "no girls ever get jealous of me. A physical handicap like this makes you *very, very popular*—no woman thinks of you as competition."

Since her stay in California that winter would be brief, Alice had traveled without John. In the evenings, when she finished work at the studio, Alice looked up friends she had made during her previous stay on the coast. One night she joined M-G-M screenwriter Leonard Spigelgass and his much younger Australian boyfriend Brendan Toomey at a Los Angeles nightspot called The Keyboard. Spigelgass, whom Alice had met at Malibu in 1951, was "very well connected, very influential and very respected," reported their mutual friend Miles White. No doubt Alice felt comfortable in his company, despite his tendency to become "outrageous" or "melodramatic" after a few drinks. According to historian William J. Mann, Spigelgass "stood apart from the status quo." He was a "homosexual and a Jew in an industry and a town that was committed to making sure America saw neither," yet he passionately guarded his position within the system. As they talked shop, Alice filed away facts in her head for future reference. Despite her strong ties to New York, she was becoming interested in a more active Hollywood career.

Alice was equally delighted to spend another evening with her in-laws in Anaheim. John's niece Shirley Taylor hosted a family dinner in late March, shortly before Alice returned to New York. "Alice said she had the most beautiful time with you that day," John later wrote to his brother and sister-in-law. "She thought Susie and Danny were wonderful and that Dad looked well. She appreciated so much you coming all that way in town to get her." This was a rare visit—Alice had only seen her in-laws three times—but they also kept in touch by telephone. "Danny and I spoke to Aunt Alice and Uncle John several times on the phone when were just kids," remembered Linda Sue Swanson, who was eleven-year-old Susie in 1955. "We would always ask her to use her 'funny' voice. Alice would then go into her high-pitched comedic voice and make us

Patricia Wilson, circa 1956.

Gus Schirmer, circa 1959.

both laugh. Uncle John had a very soft, mellow voice. I remember that he used the [endearment] 'Honey Child' a lot when speaking to us, which I liked."

Upon her return to New York, Alice began scouting for stage and television work. Gus Schirmer phoned to report that he had found a summer theatre production of *Best Foot Forward* in Pittsburgh. It was easy money—by now, Alice could have played "the blind date" role blindfolded. At the time, Schirmer also managed Patricia Wilson, an up-and-coming young singer whom he helped win the part of Ethel in *Best Foot Forward*. "Knowing that he had booked both of us into Pittsburgh to do that show," Wilson recalled, "Gus said, 'You and Alice should room together, save some money.' I said, 'That's great if she'd like to.' And that's how we met. She was a very exceptional lady. Everybody loved Alice Pearce. She

was just unbelievable with her friendship. She was so loyal. When Shirley Jones was cast in the movie version of *Carousel*, Alice was *furious* with Rodgers and Hammerstein. In fact, I think she even contacted them directly to vouch for me, to say that I should be playing the part of Julie, that I had the acting chops and the singing voice to do it. Alice was like an advocate. She wasn't afraid of people; she didn't *care* whether they were annoyed by her bothering them or not! And Gus Schirmer loved her dearly—what was not to love?"

Since 1951, Schirmer had operated his own theatrical agency single-handedly. Wilson considered him one of the most unique people she ever met. "He was blunt, sentimental, irascible, tasteful, generous to a fault, and masculine, but candidly gay in a time when 'politically correct' was forty years in the future," Wilson wrote in her 2009 memoir *Yesterday's Mashed*

J. Pat O'Malley, Arthur Shields, and Alice Pearce in "The Ticket and the Tempest," an episode of Kraft Television Theatre, *1955.*

ed to return twice to the NBC set of *Kraft Television Theatre.* "Flowers for 2-B," telecast on May 4, 1955, was an original story by Edward DeBlasio. Written with warmth and believability, it featured Virginia Vincent as a tenderhearted, self-sacrificing spinster whose family obligations conflicted with the attentions of a gentleman caller. Even more appealing was "The Ticket and the Tempest," airing on November 9, an original story written by novice Frank Kulla about two Irishmen engaged in a donnybrook over a sweepstakes ticket worth $28,000. Film actor Arthur Shields played Sean, who bought the ticket but wrote in the name of his old friend Liam, played by J. Pat O'Malley, on a lucky hunch. The tumult arises when Sean can't collect the money, and Liam won't claim it without receiving a good-sized chunk of the total. Liam's wife, played by Alice, refuses to let him take the money because gambling is immoral, she says. The nest egg eventually goes to buy a new stained-glass window for the church. "The wrangle over who should get what made for bright entertainment with good, brittle lines," wrote the *Times*, "and very little of the sticky stuff that so often sticks to authors' fingers when writing dialect drama." Shields, O'Malley, and Alice "went through their paces ably and joyfully under the brisk direction of Richard Dunlap."

Drawing more media attention was Maurice Evans' production of "Alice in Wonderland," a ninety-minute color presentation of the *Hall-*

Potatoes. "He had a built-in radar for talent, and one of the biggest hearts I've ever encountered in show business."

On July 18, a terrific rainstorm forced the cancellation of the opening night performance of *Best Foot Forward* at the Pittsburgh Stadium. After things got off the ground the following night, the *Pittsburgh Post-Gazette*, unimpressed, called the show "a poor man's *Charlie's Aunt*," noting that Alice was a "great comedienne who fairly cries for better material." Her tried-and-true "Blubber Soup" version of "Short'nin' Bread" was successful with the audience, but the *Pittsburgh Sun-Telegraph* couldn't be fooled, calling her well-worn rendition "vintage comedy."

For the remainder of 1955, Alice concentrated on television appearances. She was delight-

mark Hall of Fame, which aired live on NBC on October 23. Adapted by Florida Friebus, the production's large cast included Eva Le Gallienne, Elsa Lanchester, Reginald Gardiner, J. Pat O'Malley, Tom Bosley, and Alice Pearce, all wearing "costumes that hued to the spirit of Sir John Tenniel's famous illustrations for the original tome." The *Daily News* praised its "essence of Carroll's humor and whimsy," while gratefully noting that the production did not "attempt to 'modernize' the story by marring it with loathsome vulgarities"—a thinly veiled reproof of *Kraft*'s version of the story which had been telecast the previous year. *Broadcasting* magazine lauded NBC's engineering staff for the show's special effects yet lamented the loss of "the inherent simplicity of the Lewis Carroll stories."

While a black-and-white kinescope of *Hallmark*'s "Alice" survives, modern viewers may likely find the primitive camera tricks and the characters' bulky masks a detraction, especially the latter which often hampers the actors' speech. However, Alice, as the Dormouse, gives a delightful performance.

Alice's talents were wasted on two other shows that year, both of which coincidentally featured Australian actor Cyril Ritchard. In an episode of NBC's hit series *Mister Peepers*, the program's star Wally Cox travels to England for the reading of his late uncle's will. He's most interested in his uncle's insect collection, but it has been bequeathed to the housekeeper, played by Alice. Ritchard plays a "social parasite" who offers to help Peepers obtain the set by charming her. It's a pity the setting was not France, for Alice's attempt at a British accent falls as flat as the humor in this episode.

Alice is given even less to do in "The Spongers," an installment of the CBS anthology series *Studio One*, in which a nefarious couple (Ritchard and Alice) latch on to a wealthy old man (Ernest Truex) and firmly entrench themselves in his household. The wry fantasy was a showcase for Ritchard and Truex, but Alice's character— nothing more than Ritchard's puppet—was confined to the sidelines.

Meanwhile, Alice remained hopeful that she would soon star in a Broadway show. *The New York Times* reported on September 4, 1955, that she had been signed "to head the feminine contingent" in *The Nine O'clock Revue*, to be produced by actors David Brooks and Ted Thurston who had reportedly acquired sketches by Ira Wallach, Sheldon Harnick, and Ronnie Graham. Several of John Rox's songs were to be used, but none were well-suited for Alice. "It seems I can't write anything good for her," John confessed to columnist Earl Wilson. Rehearsals were expected to begin near the end of October with a Broadway opening planned for December. However, as the holiday season neared, the project remained in limbo.

In previous years at Christmas time, Alice had often been tied up with a Broadway show, which prevented her from spending the holidays with her parents in Vermont. The Christmas of 1955 was different. She and John, accompanied by Perk and June Bailey, spent several days at her parents' spacious home in Whitingham. By this time, Alice's grandmother Sallie Clark was a permanent resident of the community, having moved from Perry in 1953. The eighty-nine-year-old was yet quite spry, dividing her time between both daughters' homes. While she greatly missed her old friends and kinfolk back home, "Miss Sallie" made the best of the present arrangement. At least the idyllic environment of Whitingham was more reminiscent of rural Missouri than the constant commotion of New York City, where she had spent several previous winters.

Bob Pearce's physical and emotional health were now greatly improved, although he and

Margaret chose not to mingle very much with the locals. "I never remember going to the general store and seeing them down there," recalled Whitman Wheeler, who grew up in the area and whose grandfather had sold the Pearces their home in 1946. "I'm sure they ordered all of their groceries delivered. They never drove much. They had a 1949 or '48 Oldsmobile Hydra-Matic in the garage. I don't think it had 10,000 miles on it."

Before Bob's illness, Wheeler said, the Pearces had great intentions for their country home. "You know, they were going to be gentleman farmers. They had an orchard, but it never turned into anything. They did grow a garden. For the first ten years, they mowed the lawn themselves—they had an electric lawnmower. I can see them both out there. One would rake and one would push the mower. And it was a fairly good-sized lawn, and [mowing] would take up quite a bit of time."

Looking across the valley, the Pearces could see the home of Margaret's sister Josephine and her husband George Strode on the opposite hill. In 1951, when George retired from the Rockefeller Foundation, the Strodes had relinquished their Manhattan home and made Whitingham their year-round residence. As active members in several clubs, George and Josephine were much more social than either Bob or Margaret Pearce. George, being "civic-minded," was appointed to fill the unexpired term of a selectman who had moved out of the town. He also chaired Whitingham's Medical Committee which for two years studied the prospects of establishing a town medical center. George was also friendly with the area children. "He was a relatively small man," observed Wheeler, "and I remember he gave us kids all his formal clothes—top hats and tails and all that—which was great fun to play with in those days."

However, Wheeler's family had very little contact with Alice, who visited her parents "probably once or twice a year." "I met Alice only two or three times," Wheeler recalled. "Obviously, Vermont was not where she wanted to be. She wasn't very attractive, sort of puffy cheeks, and even in real life she had a fairly high-pitched voice. I never had enough engagement to remember anything about her personality."

John Rox made more of an impression on Wheeler, who was then a preteen. "John was totally charming. He used to pass me money—two-dollar bills, two or three dollars. Certainly, you would call him urbane and very suave. I think John liked coming to Vermont. He could sort of get in with the Yankees and have relaxing conversations with them."

To Wheeler, there was no doubt about who ruled the roost at Pearce Place. "Margaret was domineering," he asserted. "She and Bob were both chain smokers, but the thing I remember about Margaret was that she'd always say, 'Bobby, Bobby, get me a drink, Bobby,' and she would talk with the cigarette in her mouth and never take it out. And it would go up and down as she talked. For a kid, that was quite fascinating to see." Wheeler also recalled that Margaret, as well as Josephine, had a fiery temper. "Margaret used to wear a [crinoline] petticoat under her skirts, and she always wore makeup and was attractive, [whereas] Alice was like her father. But Jo Strode was more attractive than Margaret."

In 2013, more than fifty years after the Pearces had lived in Whitingham, Wheeler still remembered a conversation in which Bob Pearce had discussed Alice's acting career. "He told Alice that if she wanted to become an actress, she had to get a profession. So, they sent her to [school] to learn how to be a secretary." Even after Alice had proved herself on

Margaret Pearce, Sallie Clark, and Josephine Strode on Christmas Day, 1955, at Pearce Place in Whitingham, Vermont.

stage and screen, her parents had yet to completely accept her career choice.

"Alice never mentioned her parents to me," Patricia Wilson reflected. "It's kind of interesting because I was close to my parents, and they would sort of follow me wherever I [performed], but I don't think Alice ever talked about her parents." Cris Alexander was somewhat more aware of the situation. "I know that Alice was not close to them by any means," he said. "I never met her mother, but I know that Peeps had a rather odd viewpoint about her. It wasn't like [*affecting a cheerful tone*], '"Oh, Mom's coming over.'"

Soon after the Roxes returned to New York, Alice received a call to come straight to Boston, where Nancy Walker was appearing in a revival of Noël Coward's *Fallen Angels*. Produced by Charles Bowden and Richard Barr, the show was slated for a Broadway opening on January 17, 1956. Walker thought Alice a perfect choice to replace character actress Pauline Myers, who had relinquished the role of Jasmine Saunders during the previous tryout in New Haven.

For just a bit Alice found herself in a quandary. She had been standing by, hopeful that *The Nine O'clock Revue* would be her chance at stardom. "It's so hard to find the right material," she explained, "and I thought [this revue] would be just right for me." However, her hopes had begun to fade once the revue's new producers, Herbert Jacoby and Harry Rigby, had deleted certain sketches for which Alice had a soft spot. "It's no longer the same little show," she sighed. So, off to Boston's Plymouth Theatre she went.

Arriving on Tuesday, January 3, Alice had four days before the Saturday matinee to learn lines and blocking while watching the understudy perform each evening. Ten days later, *Fallen Angels* would open at the Playhouse Theatre on West Forty-Eighth Street.

Actually, Nancy Walker had started the ball rolling. The previous spring, while appearing in the revue *Phoenix '55*, Walker had been tagged by the *Times* as "a low comedienne of the highest grade." Yet, she longed to be considered "an *actress* of the highest grade," and therefore approached Bowden and Barr with a notion that Coward's *Fallen Angels* was just the right vehicle. However, *Fallen Angels* had been a Broadway flop back in 1927, and the producers knew that it would require "retooling" to display Walker's talents which—per the *New York Times*—were more apt for vaudeville than a drawing-room comedy. In July 1955, Bowden flew to Jamaica to pitch the idea to Coward, suggesting Maureen Stapleton as Walker's co-star in the revival. "They are both good actresses," admitted Coward, "so I have said yes. It's an old play and if it's a flop it doesn't matter much and if it's a success, which it might be, so much the better."

Fallen Angels is a piece about two bored housewives who learn that a Frenchman with whom both women had a premarital affair is coming to town. With their husbands away on a golf trip, they invite their former lover

Fallen Angels producer Charles Bowden presents Nancy Walker with a birthday cake while Margaret Phillips (left) and Alice look on, May 10, 1956.

for a dalliance and get rip-roaring drunk in the process. Disaster ensues in the third act when the husbands return. Welsh-born actress Margaret Phillips, instead of Stapleton, ultimately became Walker's co-star, and William LeMassena and William Windom played their husbands. Rounding out the cast were Efrem Zimbalist Jr. as the Frenchman and Alice as Walker's newly hired maid Jasmine Saunders, an erudite wonder. The setting was moved to Manhattan, and the characters' names were Americanized. Critics remained skeptical. "It is surprising that anyone would think of reviving it," wrote syndicated columnist Jack Gaver, "even with some added Coward dialogue."

On January 17, the New York audience greeted the show with gales of laughter. Though Brooks Atkinson of the *Times* conceded that Walker "radiate[d] comedy," he had little regard for the piece itself: "There are times when the original play shows through, and it is awful." Coward, with Marlene Dietrich in tow, was in the audience the following night. The producers assembled the cast onstage after the final curtain and waited for the playwright to appear. "Ladies and Gentlemen, you are all geniuses, of course," Coward announced. "I wrote this comedy thirty-two years ago. Tonight, I recognized only seven minutes of it, and I wasn't upset. So, you really must all be geniuses." Coward noted in his diary on January 22: "Strange to say, [*Fallen Angels*] is a hit . . . the audience rolled in the aisles, and everyone was delighted." *Fallen Angels* ran for

239 performances before closing on August 11.

Alice received kudos all round for her performance. "A walking persimmon named Alice Pearse [sic] makes the eternal housemaid—with her profound knowledge of golf, musical tone, and the only right way to prepare gin—a fresh delight," said Walter Kerr of the *Herald Tribune*. "Alice Pearce is a joy as a resourceful maid, graduate of a parochial school," wrote Robert Coleman of the *Daily Mirror*. "She knows her French, can correct an errant pianist, or tutor a duffer at golf." The *Daily News* observed: "Miss Walker and Miss Phillips get fried on champagne while the maid, Alice Pearce, looks on askance. If you want to take a lesson on how to look askance, just study Miss Pearce."

Other critics took notice, too. On the evening of May 26, 1956, the Outer Circle, the official organization of New York theatre critics for out-of-town newspapers and national publications, held its annual awards ceremony at Theodore's Restaurant on East Fifty-Sixth Street. Alice received a special citation for her performance as Jasmine Saunders in *Fallen Angels*. Other winners that year included actor Anthony Franciosa for *A Hatful of Rain* and scenic designer Peter Larkin for *No Time for Sergeants*. The *Diary of Anne Frank* and *My Fair Lady* received awards for the best play and best musical, respectively, of the 1955–56 season.

The congenial cast of *Fallen Angels* made it a delightful seven months for Alice. "We have an absolute ball backstage," said Margaret Phillips. "Alice Pearce has the dressing room

Jasmine Saunders (Alice) plunks out a tune while Julia Starbuck (Nancy Walker) attempts to sing in Fallen Angels, *1956.*

next to mine and she's a divine girl. We shout from dressing room to dressing room, chat, tell jokes. We all get there early—Nancy, Alice and myself. Of course, Nan is absolutely wonderful, and Alice sings for us—sometimes whole scores from shows. Then, too, people drop in to visit, which makes it gay. The boys, Windom and LeMassena, sit and play hearts when they're not on stage."

Once the production was running like a well-oiled machine, some cast members secretly decided to liven up the routine. For her part of Jasmine, Alice was required to sing in French while playing the piano. "I can't really play

Bill LeMassena, 1955.

well," she admitted, "so I have arrows marked on the piano pointing to the right keys. Nancy is always threatening to move the arrows. But I can get even if she does. She has to play a few chords before I make an entrance, interrupting her. She has only memorized a certain number of chords and if I delay my entrance, she's trapped."

Walker made good on her threats, according to William Windom. "Nancy Walker and our stage manager Edmund Baylies, both stern disciplinarians, re-marked Alice's keys for one matinee," Windom recalled. "Alice caught on during her solo, but too late to avoid hysteria—heaven! I'm proud to say that we were colleagues, Alice and LeMassena and I. Usually, we enjoyed a post-performance supper together."

Alice was delighted to be working with the witty Bill LeMassena again. He was a happy

man, content with doing the work he loved with "no big dream of an ideal role or play." "I love working in the movies, and I've enjoyed doing television," Bill confessed during the run of *Fallen Angels*. "Last winter, as a labor of love, I worked in the off-Broadway production of *Thieves' Carnival* for $26 a week. But I must admit that, to me, the most exciting theater is that which is the most commercially successful. As Dorothy McGuire once put it, an actor's dream is being a hit within a hit."

Since 1948, Bill had lived in Greenwich Village, first at 132 Bank Street. Eventually, he purchased several houses in the neighborhood, a wise investment which provided rental income during lean theatrical times. "I get more calls about apartments than I do about jobs," he shrugged in 1956.

Three weeks into the run of *Fallen Angels*, Bowden and Barr permitted Alice to take a brief leave of absence to film a role for M-G-M's *The Opposite Sex*. "Alice left yesterday for the coast," John informed his brother on February 6, 1956. "She will only be gone a week or ten days. Her understudy is taking over, but [the producers] are afraid business will suffer unless Alice gets back in the show as soon as possible." As it turned out, Alice was in California for eighteen days, and most of those were miserable.

Producer Joe Pasternak assembled an all-star cast for *The Opposite Sex*, an adaptation of Clare Booth Luce's 1936 Broadway hit *The Women* and the M-G-M film of the same title released in 1939. Filmed in Cinemascope, the picture starred June Allyson, Joan Collins, Dolores Gray, Ann Sheridan, and Ann Miller, but unlike prior versions it featured both men and musical numbers. Allyson plays a theatrical producer's wife who inadvertently learns from a garrulous manicurist (Alice) that her husband is having an affair with a sexy showgirl (Collins). Allyson

Across the manicure table, Kay Hilliard (June Allyson) gets the latest gossip from manicurist Olga (Alice Pearce) in The Opposite Sex *(1956).*

picture loses a lot of bite and bile in the transformation," Harold Cohen asserted. "Joan Collins has the face and figure for the part of the wily vixen, but she plays it without any style or strumpetry. Dolores Gray comes off best as the poisonous false friend, and handsome Ann Sheridan is likewise excellent as a caustic, level-headed playwright."

Alice demonstrates remarkable range as Olga, from acerbic ("Sometimes I think if I gotta look at another hangnail, I'll throw up") and artificial ("Oh, my, what interesting hands") to philosophical ("I always say you can tell a person's character by their hands") and rational ("Crystal's terribly clever and terribly pretty—at least you know what you're up against"). It's one of her finer bits on film.

Meanwhile, John scored with "Change of Heart," a song which had recently been chosen for inclusion in the revue *New Faces of 1956*. The previous year, Dean Martin had recorded it for Capitol Records as the flip side to "Memories Are Made of This," a fortuitous opportunity for John because the latter reached number one on *Billboard*'s Top 100 chart, eventually becoming one of Martin's biggest hits. "It was a lucky break for me having that record," John told his brother. "I'll be able to pay off the [beach] house come next year." In the summer of 1955, when John and Alice were spending a weekend at the Fire Island home of actor John Conte and his wife Ruth, they happened upon a cottage for sale just five doors down.

discovers if she wants to win her man back, she must adapt to the predatory ways of women like Collins.

The part of Olga, the gossipy manicurist, was crucial. Alice was confident that her scenes couldn't be cut from the film's final print because her character "starts the whole plot rolling, and without it there would be no picture." But things went awry almost as soon as she arrived on the set. Allyson burned her arm just before she was to film her scene with Alice, and they had to wait over a week for the injury to heal. Meanwhile, Alice worked on her other scene which included Gray and Sheridan. "The part was small, but it was a rat race getting it all in, and it was long hours of work," Alice explained to her Anaheim in-laws. "To go along with the work, I had a touch of the flu. This has not been my favorite trip!"

Upon the release of *The Opposite Sex* on October 26, 1956, many critics compared the picture unfavorably to the earlier film version. "The

The oceanfront home was located on Great South Beach near the Davis Park section of the island, accessed only by ferry from Patchogue, Long Island, about four miles away. Owning it was a dream come true for Alice and John, who loved spending every spare moment on the beach.

While the Roxes gained one home, they were about to lose the other. Shortly after Alice returned from filming *The Opposite Sex*, they received a six months' notice to vacate 31 Sutton Place South. The entire row of "black-and-white" houses in their block was set for demolition to make way for a twenty-story apartment building. It was difficult for Alice to give up her home of fourteen years, eight of which she had shared with John. "Her Sutton Place apartment was *so* charming," Cris Alexander recalled. Alice had filled the small space with French antiques and period paintings. She and John shared their quarters with a parakeet, which John said "made enough noise to fill the Grand Canyon," and a forty-pound male boxer mix named Roxy. Adopted by the Roxes in 1950, when he was still a puppy, city-bred Roxy spent most days sitting on a needlepoint chair, looking out the window. He never missed certain neighbors who walked their female beagle thrice daily.

It was not just their tiny apartment that Alice would miss, but the neighborhood itself, which one former denizen, reminiscing in 1975, called "an uptown Greenwich Village." Identified only as "the old curmudgeon" by a columnist in *The New Yorker*, he waxed nostalgic: "It was a wonderful neighborhood—unbroken river view, and if you got tired of that there were all those tennis courts for playing on from dawn to dusk. And those little bits of three-story houses! John McNulty [who wrote for *The New Yorker*] used to live there, in a fine old row. Alice Pearce, who was so funny in *Gentlemen Prefer Blondes*

lived around the corner." Other residents, he said, included Herbert Jacoby, "the great Julius Monk," singers Lee Wiley, Hugh Shannon, Gigi Durston, and Julie Wilson, plus jazz pianist Barbara Carroll and concert pianist Earl Wild. "I probably knew forty to fifty after-dark people within a ten-minute walk. There were one or two parties every night, and a little plaza by the river, and if you felt lonely you could walk out there and see who else didn't have a dinner engagement—just like the Village."

Alice and John wanted to remain in the neighborhood and thus began a stressful search to find nearby yet affordable housing. Added to the strain was John's hospitalization in April. His exact need for medical treatment is not fully known—or if he underwent surgery—but it is believed it may have been cardiovascular in nature. Whatever the case, it was serious enough to cause Alice great alarm, according to Cris Alexander, who related a most intriguing account shared with him at some point following John's discharge from Midtown Hospital.

"One afternoon, Jan Sterling and Peggy Cass had come to our apartment for lunch," Cris remembered in 1987. "And Jan, who has always been *extremely* interested in the supernatural, said, 'Oh, I have the most amazing story to tell you about Alice Pearce.'" Sterling went on to recount that some months back Alice, merely out of curiosity, had sought the services of a rather reputable "fortune teller." "And, so the story was," Cris continued, "that this person had said to Alice, 'As a rule, I don't tell anybody if I see a real tragedy in the wind, but having talked to you, I sense that you are somebody who would really want to know. In six months' time, your husband is going to be dead.' And so, Alice was, of course, upset beyond measure and asked if there was anything she could do to avert this, and the person said, 'There is not one thing that can be done. It is going to happen within six months. He won't suffer.'"

Bearing in mind that Cris was a talented raconteur, there is more than an ample chance that with the passage of thirty years, his account may have been somewhat embellished. However, documentation exists which indicates that Cris may have leaned more toward fact than fiction. Among Alice's papers is an eight-page handwritten document created on August 29, 1955, by astrologer Charles A. Peacock of Tarrytown, New York. The report, based on Alice's date and time of birth, bears no indication that Alice had previously met or conversed with Peacock. In fact, it had been mailed to her home address. It is not known how Alice became acquainted with the services of Mr. Peacock, or if he had previous knowledge of her career.

Peacock's horoscope reads like a rolling stream of consciousness. "Please pardon if I write disjointedly," he explains to Alice. "I write things down as they come to me." Whether by coincidence or not, the horoscope contains some elements which notably correspond with events in Alice's past, present, and future.

First and foremost, he identifies Alice as an actress. "There are many signs of this," Peacock states, citing examples. "The moon is on an actor's degree, so is Uranus on an actor's degree. Then there is the aspect of Venus to Jupiter so often found in the charts of actors and actresses. Along with this, is a *strong* sign that you are interested in and believe in Astrology . . . I see writing ability too and great sensitiveness. There is taste for music, a gift for poetry, indeed any form of artistry comes easily to you. You are one with great ability to entertain others. There is [a] great gift for humor in your chart."

"You have been, will always be a storm center," Peacock writes. "It started early in life . . . you want attention, you become in some way the center of attention . . . there is an excess of

feeling that must in some way manifest itself, be released . . .you make a better impression away from home than in your home." Some may say that this observation not only correlates to Alice's childhood desire for applause and laughter but also indicates her parents' disdain for her theatrical career.

Other aspects of Alice's horoscope were somewhat more specific and linked to actualities, both present and future. For instance, Peacock noted that "right now money can be a problem—you may feel a shortage." At the time Peacock prepared Alice's chart, she had been employed only four weeks out of the previous seven months. He also discerned that "1949 was a year that marked a change of status of some sort." That year was indeed important, if for only two reasons: Alice starred in her own television series and made her film debut in *On the Town*. "There is a danger from scalding and burning," Peacock warned. "Be careful when you handle hot liquids." One morning five years later, when hosting a reporter in her apartment, Alice prepared coffee for her guest. When the coffee pot suddenly exploded, her thumb was badly burned.

Peacock also noted that Alice would "suffer in some way in connection with love, law, foreigners, and travel." However, he was most specific regarding her love life. And the most outstanding prediction lies within those paragraphs. "I see an inhibition against *lasting* love. It does not deny happiness in love, but it does limit it to, say, seven years. I will give examples of the way it works—there is the girl with a mother to support—there is the early death of a husband (this is shown in your case, I think)—love not returned is another form. Clark Gable has an aspect similar to yours. His chart shows one true love removed by a tragic death. His search goes on. Over and over again a constant restless seeking for a love that cannot be ever

Clockwise from the left are Ethel Waters, an unidentified friend, Alice and John Rox, Mike Rayhill, and recent newlyweds Charles Lowe and Carol Channing enjoying a night out at the lavish Latin Quarter. This is one of the last, if not the last, photo of Alice and John together.

found." (The reference to Gable alludes to his third wife Carole Lombard—and many say his one true love— who was killed in an airplane crash in 1942.) Elsewhere in the horoscope, Peacock notes "the loss of a partner."

Alice's reaction to Peacock's chart seems to have gone unrecorded, but certainly the prediction of a spouse's early death would give one cause for concern, especially if the recipient believed in astrology. It is logical to think that upon John's hospitalization Alice may have given thought to Peacock's prediction, and she could have been greatly relieved when John recovered quite nicely. Since Cris Alexander's "fortune teller" account varies from Peacock's document, we can only take it at face value. For the record, Cris said that "Alice lived on

tenterhooks" preceding and throughout John's hospitalization. "Alice was scared to death and thought something's going to go wrong and that will be it. John Rox came home from his operation and was just dandy, and Peeps breathed a sigh of relief and thought, 'Well, [the individual] misread that.'"

In late summer 1956, Alice and John moved into Apartment 14-B on the topmost floor of 400 East Fifty-Ninth Street, a leisurely five-minute walk from Sutton Place South. Constructed in 1929, the building faced the Queensboro Bridge on the north and First Avenue on the west. Cris, who later visited Alice there, observed, "There wasn't too much opportunity to make it as charming as her other place. But lots of actors lived there. George Gaynes and his wife Allyn Ann McLerie lived there for a while." Eventually, Herbert Jacoby would move in, as well as Alice and John's friend, the pianist Baldwin "Beau" Bergersen.

Meanwhile, Alice's schedule was filled with semi-regular appearances on NBC's late-night talk show *Tonight!*, as well as other programs like *Camera Three*, *Omnibus*, and *Studio One*. On December 2, she was included in the ensemble cast of "Merry Christmas, Mr. Baxter," a colorcast of NBC's *The Alcoa Hour*. Based on the book by Edward Streeter and adapted for television by William McCleery, the story is about George Baxter who loses his Christmas spirit when bombarded with holiday commercialism. Baxter, played by Dennis King, visits Prescott's Department Store to find a footrest for his wife, but instead he accumulates other purchases, including a negligee, a bottle of perfume, and a folding kitchen stool, all foisted on him by pushy saleswomen. Alice's brief appearance as the fast-talking housewares saleslady is a tour de force, alternating between sugary insincerity during her sales pitch and vinegary annoyance when challenged by Mr. Baxter. She's triumphantly smug when the weary shopper walks away with a "Jiffy Boy" ice cream maker.

Alice appeared twice that year on *Omnibus*, trumpeted as "the most outstanding and longest-running cultural series in the history of commercial network television." Hosted by Alistair Cooke, the aptly titled series presented everything from dramas to ballets to documentaries; each program contained several segments. The Ford Foundation financed the ninety-minute program, enabling the producers to devote the full time to program content—there were no commercials on *Omnibus*. The live telecast of January 1, 1956, included Alice singing Ogden Nash's parody of "The Twelve Days of Christmas."

Almost a year later, on December 9, Alice, dressed in a sequined formal and feather boa, opened the live telecast by singing three old standbys, including the hilarious "If I Were as High as a Bird in the Sky." A surviving kinescope of the broadcast reveals a few mishaps. During the MIT song, when all is silent as

Alice pretends to drink from a stein, soft murmurs off camera are audible. Then, when Alice prepares to lip-sync "Boots," she has to repeat her cue to Cooke, who's manning the turntable, to engage the phonograph needle. Such distractions and pauses did not go unnoticed by New York reviewer John Crosby: "As to Miss Pearce, I have one word of advice for *Omnibus*. No monologuist [*sic*] and no patter singer of this sort should ever be put in front of a camera without an audience. The audience for an entertainer of this sort is part of the act and even if *Omnibus* could dig up no more than twelve people, it would make all the difference in the world." (Alice's future colleague Mary Wickes had once similarly observed: "There's nothing so crushing to a comedienne as to play to a couple of cameras and a bored crew.")

Two weeks later, columnist Jack Anderson, espousing the merits of *Omnibus*, announced its upcoming projects, including one involving Alice. She was to team up with Carol Channing for a parody on theatrical sister acts, but the idea seems to have remained just that.

Earlier that fall, Alice had become a semi-regular on Will Rogers, Jr.'s *Good Morning!* series on CBS, appearing as television's "first comic weather forecaster." Unfortunately, no kinescopes of her meteorological contributions seem to have survived. Even more regrettably lost is her rendition of John's "I Want a Hippopotamus for Christmas," which she sang on Rogers' show on Christmas morning, 1956.

Two years previously, John had written another children's Christmas song, "Santa Claus Is Coming in a Jet," intended as a record release for Kaye Ballard. Although that never happened, John was still hopeful for the song's future when interviewed by Earl Wilson in the fall of 1956. Explaining his typical method of songwriting, John revealed, "I get fascinated by titles, and then, of course, I have to write songs around them."

John told Wilson about another recent creation, similarly inspired, called "One More Sunrise," a song about a man condemned to death.

"It excites me," said John, "but it frightens my wife. She keeps muttering, 'How could you!'" Perhaps the lyrics were a little too close to home for Alice. Perhaps they evoked other unsettling words—the words of Charles A. Peacock.

CHAPTER SEVENTEEN
Challenged to Adjust

*"If I hadn't been working, I would have lost
my sanity."*

On February 25, 1957, Alice returned to the Blue Angel for her seventh engagement. It would prove to be her final appearance at Manhattan's toniest club. "Alice Pearce, a very funny young woman who has been missing from the night-club scene for a few years, working on the stage and in the movies, is back at the Blue Angel," announced *The New Yorker*. "Where else? Miss Pearce has the distinction of having appeared in no other night club since she took up this line of work, some ten years back, and it suits me that I always know where to find her, and don't have to go running off to the Copacabana or Las Vegas or somewhere in search of her. Anyway, she wouldn't be caught dead in that sort of place."

Likewise, the flavor of Alice's act was no surprise. Once again, she gave the impression of being an "essentially quiet" girl who, downing the first drink of her life, suddenly decides to entertain everyone. "This girl happens to know several old songs of doubtful value—things like 'Constantinople' and 'A Tulip Told a Tale'—and although she has mastered none of them, she essays them all with wonderful verve," extolled *The New Yorker*. "She has a deep affection for 'If I Were as High as a Bird in the Sky,' a kind of rallying song for disillusioned lovers. You've probably heard her do most of these numbers before, but hearing them again may restore your faith in the world of night clubs."

Nevertheless, the Blue Angel audience was tough. They expected witty special material, and Herbert Jacoby—still reigning as the club's manager—demanded that comics work hard to be funny every night, no matter the audience. "It was a scary thing to stand up in a place like that with a top reputation and a show-me audience," said Ben Bagley, whom Jacoby had recently hired to select material for comics and singers. "In the '50s the customer was God. Doormen opened doors, and waiters were subservient. In a bank you could be fired if you didn't smile all the time. Usually if the Angel crowd didn't like you from the start you were out on your ass."

Yet the glamour of clubs like the Blue Angel was something of an illusion, according to historian James Gavin. "They were hard work," he says, "offering less money and exposure than television, theatre, or recordings." Alice knew that firsthand, but at the time, there seemed to be no alternative. 1957 was beginning to look like the nadir of 1952.

When Alice's engagement ended on March 27, it marked her fifty-eighth week at the Blue Angel—reputedly an all-time aggregate for the club. (Nine years later, many of Alice's obituaries would erroneously report her record-breaking total as *sixty-eight* weeks. The discrepancy apparently dates back to a typographical error on Alice's 1961 career resume.)

One week after closing at the Blue Angel, Alice was reunited with some of her fellow players from *Fallen Angels* during a two-week run at the Palm Beach Playhouse in Florida. Nancy Walker and Louise Hoff, who had understudied Alice in the Broadway production of *Angels*, played the leads in the Coward comedy for a week beginning April 8. Alice assumed her old role of Jasmine Saunders. The following week, Alice played the comic role of the deaf domestic Janet Mackenzie in *Witness for the Prosecution* which featured Margaret Phillips in a leading role.

As May approached, Alice had no summer plans, except for a return to the State Fair Musicals in August. "There's nothing quite as strange as casting for summer stock productions," she told the *World Telegraph and Sun* in late March. "I just signed a contract today to play in *Rose Marie* in Dallas. But that's not half the story. We're all supposed to sing on ice—and I've never done any ice-skating."

Alice and John spent the first three weeks of May at their cottage on Fire Island, getting it ready for the summer. Meanwhile, John anticipated that several of his songs would be chosen by recording artists. One was a ballad titled "Unbelievable," which Dot Records was considering for the Hilltoppers, a pop vocal quartet. More definite was a release of "Where's the Boy I Saved for a Rainy Day?," which John had written with Beau Bergersen for the 1940 Broadway flop *All in Fun*. Well past middle age, John was keenly aware that he needed to keep up with the changing trends in music. Elvis Presley, Buddy Holly, and Jerry Lee Lewis were the hottest recording artists that year. "I'm trying to get in the Rock 'n' Roll groove," John admitted to his brother Don.

John and Alice had planned a leisurely summer without interruption until Alice was due in Dallas. However, as June approached, the producers of a new musical began negotiations with Alice to fill one of its supporting roles. David Craig had co-written the book

for *Copper and Brass* as a starring vehicle for his wife Nancy Walker. If successful enough to reach Broadway, the production would team Alice with her best friend for the fourth time. Intended for a New York debut in October, late-summer rehearsals for *Copper and Brass* would conflict with her Dallas engagement, so Alice opted out of the two-week run of *Rose Marie*.

John and Alice returned to their beach retreat at Davis Park in early June, as did other beachcombers who flocked to Fire Island to relax in its relatively untouched (and automobile-free) environment. Davis Park, the easternmost community on the island, now sported an enlarged marina which could accommodate up to two hundred boats. The Leja Beach Casino, despite its name, was not a gambling venue but served as Davis Park's only restaurant, with its bar doubling as a nightclub in the evening. That summer, Leja Beach—on the western end of Davis Park—would be chosen by "beachologist" Hans Koningsberger as one of the world's top ten beaches. "Leja Beach on Fire Island would be a great beach anywhere in the world," Koningsberger wrote in the *New York Times*, "and considering its relative closeness to New York, its unspoiled beauty is miraculous." For the Roxes, it offered an ideal getaway.

The summer of 1957 was a season of drought for the entire Long Island area, lasting for more than seventy days. A violent thunderstorm passed through on July 29, bringing an inch of welcome rain, but things soon dried out again. By Monday, August 5, the temperature had dropped into the comfortable seventies.

Early that afternoon, John went outside to fill his birdbath. While pumping water from the well, he was stricken with a massive heart attack and died within a few minutes. He did not suffer. The coroner, based at Patchogue, was promptly summoned from across the bay to

Alice and John Rox's Fire Island cottage, 1956. Photo courtesy Linda Swanson.

pronounce death. No autopsy was performed, but John's death certificate listed "coronary atherosclerosis" as a contributing cause—a condition perhaps brought on by heavy smoking. Two weeks earlier, John had turned fifty-five years old.

Alice was numb. Before leaving for New York, she made calls to her parents and close friends. When she phoned the Herrings in Anaheim, John's seventy-two-year-old stepfather Earl Herring, who loved John "like his own son," wept, asking why God hadn't taken him instead.

Word of John's death spread quickly. Bill and Peggy Coburn, who had moved to the Los Angeles area in 1956, were vacationing in Michigan when they heard the news on a radio broadcast. Patricia Wilson remembered being in the studio of musician-coach Kenny Welch when he told her of John's sudden passing. "I called Alice immediately," Wilson remembered, "and I said, 'Is there anything I can do?' But she was sobbing and said, 'No, there's nothing anybody can do.'"

"Of course, Peeps was just demolished," Cris Alexander recalled in 1987. Recounting Alice's horoscope, he declared, "It was one of the most astonishing things I've ever heard *and* the only time that I have ever heard in advance that someone's death had been predicted. So, when John died, everyone who had previously known about the prediction was in awe. This [astrologer] must have had some strange gift."

John Rox's funeral was held at two o'clock on the afternoon of August 8 at the Frank E. Campbell Funeral Chapel on Madison Avenue at Eighty-First Street. For almost sixty years, the respected firm had arranged funerals for such luminaries as Enrico Caruso, Rudolph Valentino, George Gershwin, Arturo Toscanini, and William Randolph Hearst. No details of John's funeral service have come to light, but that afternoon Alice was surrounded by friends like Nancy Walker, Oliver Smith, Miles White, and Perk and June Bailey. Don Herring was the only member of John's family who was able to attend. Following the service, John's body was sent to the Ferncliff Crematory in Hartsdale, New York, for cremation.

John's obituaries, without fail, cited "It's a Big, Wide Wonderful World" as his signature song but neglected to name any of his other works. Years later, a journalist insisted that John would remain among "a surprisingly large number of [songwriters] whose reputations have been founded on just one song." In 2000, William E. Studwell, author of *They Also Wrote: Evaluative Essays on Lesser-Known Popular American Songwriters Prior to the Rock Era*, was quite dismissive of John's contribution to the music world, calling him an "obscure one-hit wonder" and labeling "I Want a Hippopotamus for Christmas" as "unimportant." Studwell's estimation, of course, preceded the resurgence of the novelty Christmas number. Some modern observers may argue that the popularity of "Hippopotamus" has eclipsed "Wonderful World."

Charles A. Peacock had predicted that one day Alice would be "challenged to adjust" to unhappiness, and now she was dealing with the harsh reality of life without John. To provide immediate comfort and assistance, Nancy Walker stayed at Alice's apartment for a week or so "while she endeavor[ed] to recover from [her] loss." Naturally, her friends soon returned to their regular routines, and Alice—bereft in her small apartment on Fifty-Ninth Street—quickly realized that she needed professional help. Ultimately, she sought counseling at Manhattan's Reich Clinic.

Besides coping with her grief, Alice was faced with settling John's affairs, a task compounded by the fact that he had died intestate. Nancy and other members of the *Copper and Brass* cast hoped that strenuous rehearsals—beginning two weeks after John's death—would be the best possible distraction for Alice. Alice rarely spoke of her personal tragedy in interviews, but near the end of her life she confessed, "If I hadn't been working, I would have lost my sanity."

In 1956, David Craig and Ellen Violett had completed the libretto for *Copper and Brass* to capitalize on Nancy Walker's recent Broadway successes *Phoenix '55* and *Fallen Angels*. David Baker, who had written the music for *Phoenix '55*, once again collaborated with lyricist Craig. Rounding out the team were director Marc Daniels (known for directing the first season of *I Love Lucy*) and choreographer Anna Sokolow, a former student of Martha Graham.

The show's producers were Lyn Austin and Thomas Noyes.

Nancy's custom-made role was Katey O'Shea, a Staten Island native whose "career guidance" tests indicate that she is ideally suited to become a policewoman. Her first assignment as a rookie cop is a school crossing. Opposite the schoolhouse is a jazz cellar to which the school principal Miss Winowna Crane (played by Alice) naturally objects. Persuaded by the principal to order the musicians to silence their instruments during school hours, Katey instead falls in love with "cool cat" clarinetist George the Second. Inadvertently she generates his arrest, wins a promotion, and becomes miserable with regret. When George refuses Katey's help, she enlists the students who dote on George's music. To prove that the kids are music lovers and not being led astray by a sinister pied-piper, Katey suggests they invite the police commissioner and her captain to their school prom and petition the authorities to release George. Katey is successful, and at the block party celebration, George proposes marriage. The "copper" in the title, of course, refers to Katey, while the "brass" alludes to jazz.

Besides Nancy and Alice, the original cast included Dick Williams as George, Alan Bunce as the police captain, and Joan Blondell as Katey's wisecracking and very young mother. Rehearsals began in New York on August 19, followed by a month of tryouts, first in New Haven and then in Philadelphia.

After *Copper and Brass* opened at the Erlanger Theatre on September 25, the *Philadelphia Inquirer* reported that "both metals gleamed only fitfully," with much of the proceedings falling on "the dull side." Nevertheless, the reviewer noted that the block party scene—in which the characters played by Blondell, Bunce, and Alice reminisce about the popular dances of their youth—was "merry

The cast of Copper and Brass, *1957. Foreground: Norma Douglas, Peter Conlow, and Nancy Walker. In the background are Laurie Franks, Joy Lane, Ernie Furtado on bass, Frank Rehak on trombone, Dick Williams on clarinet, Hank Jones on piano, Alan Bunce, Doug Rogers on drums, and Alice Pearce.*

and bright." The same had been observed in New Haven a week earlier: "One of the funniest bits in the show is a part of the triad which includes the Blondell 'Sweet William' number. As they remember the dancing of quaint days gone by, Alice Pearce turns her comic talent to 'Argentine Tango' with the delightful assistance of Alan Bunce. They literally stopped the show Monday night. [Their characters] enjoy a belated and mildly coy romance inspired by their exposure to modern rhythmic music. Their tango is the acme of drollery."

However, Elliot Norton of the *Boston Daily Record* took producers Austin and Noyes to task, calling Nancy's casting as "the mistake of the century." "This little comedienne with the jutting jaw, who swings her arms from her shoulders like a fullback when she walks, isn't the romantic type," said Norton. "To make her the subject of a musical comedy love story is not only silly, it is embarrassing." Neither was he happy about Alice's limited role: "Alice Pearce is wasted in this musical. One of the strangest comediennes in the world, she has a craggy face that slopes away from her nose and a shrill voice, and when they give her a really funny line or song, she smiles with a kind of celestial lunacy and belts it out as though she had just discovered the whole truth about everything. In *Copper and Brass*, she charges into the story

"Alice Pearce is loyal as a public school principal under a bird's nest wig," wrote critic Walter Kerr of Alice's role in Copper and Brass.

occasionally as a city schoolmarm who is usually marshalling her tough pupils from one activity into another, when she isn't heckling the police for failing to close up the jive joints."

During the Philadelphia tryout, Blondell and Bunce became unhappy with their roles when "extensive changes" were made in the musical's book. As a result, both withdrew. Blondell was replaced by Benay Venuta, while Bunce was coaxed to return to the show in time for the New York opening at the Martin Beck Theatre on October 17.

New York critics were far from impressed. Ward Morehouse deemed *Copper and Brass* a "noisy and negligible musical." He was unstirred by the "Remember the Dancing" number—performed by Alice, Bunce, and Venuta—denying that it produced a nostalgic feeling. "It's all more in the mood of the honky-tonk that Times Square is today," he shrugged. Brooks Atkinson of the *Times* rejected the show's "breathlessly unfunny book, uninteresting music, [and] unlovely ballets." "You would think that nothing in the field of musical comedy had changed," he groaned, "since the theatre went bankrupt in the Nineteen Thirties . . . Even a dull show represents a lot of hard work and hope. This column dutifully salutes the intentions. Alice Pearce, who seems to have less chin every season, shrieks and shoves her way through the book as an amusing school principal . . . But there is no use pretending that *Copper and Brass* is of any use to Miss Walker or to the members of her Association. Something will have to be done." One month later, Atkinson got his wish. *Copper and Brass* closed on November 16 after thirty-six performances.

If nothing else, *Copper and Brass* provided Alice with a steady income for three months and a temporary diversion from her profound grief. Yet the stark reality of her situation was ever present in her mind—widowed at thirty-nine after only nine years of marriage. John's royalties alone would never provide enough income, and while she still relished live theatre, flops like *Copper and Brass* ultimately kept her on the lookout for alternative means of support. Alice would have readily agreed with Jan Sterling—widowed at thirty-eight in 1959 when actor Paul Douglas died suddenly—who insisted, "You have to be a grown-up to take widowhood."

Alice found it particularly distressing that she had found no television work for eleven consecutive months. Live television drama was dying, as were television series originating from New York. *Broadway Television Theatre* was long gone, and *Robert Montgomery Presents* ceased production in the spring of 1957. The prestigious *Kraft Television Theatre* would follow suit in October 1958. *Goodyear Television Playhouse* moved its production to Hollywood in June 1957—followed by *Studio One* six months later—because that's where the talent was. Besides that, the facilities for production were better than in New York. "The decline of the live 60-minute dramatic showcase," noted *Variety*, "comes as a major blow to legit talent in New York [where] performers have come to rely more and more on TV assignments in carrying them through the slack periods on Broadway."

Faced with this challenge, Alice responded by parting with Gus Schirmer, hoping that a new agent would be more beneficial. She chose Milton Goldman, then head of his own agency, but soon to be bought out by the Ashley-Steiner Agency. Goldman was the domestic partner of attorney Arnold Weissberger whom Alice had known for more than a decade. However, after two years Alice became dissatisfied with Goldman's Fifth Avenue agency and signed as her personal manager Bob Kohler, whose office was in Hell's Kitchen. Kohler, one of the first agents to represent non-famous black artists, was privy to theatre circles and A-list parties yet rejected any discussion about his status. "Don't make me out to be a big shot," he later said; "I was an independent agent who worked my ass off." Kohler's efforts notwithstanding, Alice abandoned him after one year. Then she signed with General Artists Corporation—which had offices on both coast—in hopes of increased film work. This revolving-door of agents would do little good for Alice's career, outside of several theatrical assignments.

To make ends meet, Alice resorted to making television commercials for products such as Ajax cleanser, Scotkin Napkins, and Oxydol laundry detergent. In October 1957, she filmed a twenty-second commercial for Scotch Brand tape at the MPO Studios on East Fifty-Third Street, receiving a one-time payment of $750 for one day's work. In 1960, long before Nancy Walker hawked the "Bounty" brand on television, Alice advertised for a new regional product, Hudson Paper Towels. Her gimmicky plug quickly became a favorite among her East Coast fans. "Alice Pearce is perfectly cast," wrote Ralph Porter of *The Magazine of Creative Advertising*. "The entire feeling from her desperate whisper 'spongeability' to the victorious gush of water that is wrung out create the 'big spoof.'" Hudson Pulp & Paper Corporation, which had recently put 75% of its media budget into television advertising, was tickled with the results. "With the battle cry of 'spongeability' from the mouth of comedienne Alice Pearce," *Sponsor* magazine proclaimed, "Hudson moved in one year to a sizable share of the paper-towel market."

Meanwhile, Alice didn't limit herself in the advertising world—she also posed in print advertisements for products like Chatham Blankets and the newly released prescription drug Ritalin. Originally marketed to treat chronic fatigue, narcolepsy, and depression, Ritalin was yet to be prescribed for students diagnosed with Attention Deficit Disorder. One Ritalin pamphlet distributed to physicians depicted Alice as a comically lethargic candidate in three separate poses—morning, noon, and night—with the slogan, "She'll be active again on Ritalin."

Still, Alice sought opportunities in the legitimate theatre. On December 23, 1957, she joined the cast of *Bells Are Ringing* as a temporary replacement for supporting actress Jean

Alice Pearce and Eddie Lawrence in Bells Are Ringing, *1958.*

Stapleton, who took a four-week leave to try out a new play in Miami. By this time, the Theatre Guild's successful production of the Comden and Green/Jule Styne musical starring Judy Holliday had been playing at the Shubert for thirteen months.

Alice assumed the role of Sue Summers, the owner of "Susanswerphone," an answering service which employs her cousin Ella Peterson (Holliday) as one of the operators. Ella is that rare breed who feels that people should care about one another every day, not just in times of crisis. She puts her philosophy into practice by trying to help her unseen subscribers, much to the annoyance of Sue, who maintains a cool and impersonal manner when she's at the switchboard. Nonetheless, sensible Sue

is duped by J. Sandor Prantz (Eddie Lawrence), a con artist who plans to use Susanswerphone as a front for his bookie ring. The role of Sue was not sizable, but it afforded Alice a lively duet ("Salzburg") with the consummate Lawrence.

At the same time, friends and acquaintances came to Alice's assistance. Late-night talk show host Jack Paar, who had taken over NBC's *The Tonight Show* after Steve Allen's departure, invited Alice to be a guest three times in the fall of 1957. Their association went back to the spring of the previous year when Alice had guested on Paar's daytime talk show on CBS. Paar enjoyed surrounding himself with offbeat performers like Genevieve, a chanteuse whose fractured English pivoted her into a comic personality, and Dody Goodman, a former Broadway dancer with a quavery voice whose approach to comedy was to make quirky, off-kilter remarks. For Paar's 1957 New Year's Eve show, the hefty lineup included Goodman, Genevieve, Alice, and Carol Burnett, a dynamite combination that must have been a feast for fans. Unfortunately, no published reviews or kinescopes of this live telecast appear to exist.

Frank Sinatra—hearing that Alice was strapped for cash—arranged for her to make a guest appearance on his ABC television series in early 1958. For most of that season, the crooner's musical variety show had proved as unsuccessful as his first series, which sputtered out in 1952. To boost his low ratings, Sinatra—diverting from his usual film format—planned a much-publicized St. Valentine's Day program to be telecast live from the El Capitan Theater in Hollywood. "Romance is in the air, and three loves have I," said Sinatra that evening as he announced his guests, "sweet and lovely Shirley Jones, funny and lovely Alice Pearce, and little and lovely Tina Sinatra."

To set the scene for Alice's solo number, character actor Jesse White appears as resident heckler Clifford whose girlfriend—"Alice Pearce"—wants an autographed picture of Sinatra for Valentine's Day. If she doesn't get her wish, Clifford says, she's going to break up with him. Sinatra agrees to meet the bashful girl, but when she's introduced, she becomes a giggling, uncouth prattler, much like Clifford. Sinatra kindly offers to pose with Alice for a photo and exits to arrange the shoot. Meanwhile, Clifford and Alice have a

Frank Sinatra, Alice Pearce, and Jesse White share a laugh during rehearsal for The Frank Sinatra Show, *1958.*

tiff over the half-eaten box of candy he's given her for Valentine's Day. When Clifford storms off, Alice sings her old standby, "If I Were as High as a Bird in the Sky." *The New York Times* panned the episode, observing, "Only Alice Pearce succeeded in smiling through the dull cloud of insipid banter."

Outspoken television critic Janet Kern, however, dreaded the evening's telecast. In a syndicated release that morning, she groused, "This week's Sinatra show will boast among its guests a comedienne named Alice Pearce, of whom I more than had my fill during TV's most pioneering, 7-inch screen days, when she was one of the few 'performers' available to the then experimental medium. Why Sinatra is unearthing Miss Pearce again, I cannot imagine. And why he should combine Miss Pearce with his 9-year-old daughter 'Tina' (whom I'd rather LIKE to see) is particularly difficult for this Pearce-averse viewer to comprehend." If

Kern tuned in that night, she must have been even more disgusted because little Tina got stage fright at the last minute and didn't appear in the brief segment set aside for her at the program's conclusion.

If Kern's words stung Alice, then an unexpected note she received soon afterwards furnished the perfect balm. "One of those garrulous and theatre-wise cab drivers paid you the ultimate in compliments the other day," actor Hume Cronyn wrote to Alice. "We were discussing actors, particularly comedians, and he came out with this: 'Y'ever see Alice Pearce? Boy, is she funny. I could pee my pants over her.'" Cronyn added, "I felt such a tribute should not be kept from you."

That summer, Alice returned to the Paar show for the first of six appearances. While never achieving the rank of Paar's frequent semi-regulars—chatterers like Elsa Maxwell, Jonathan Winters, Hermione Gingold, and

Alice appeared in a series of publicity photographs for her guest appearance on The Frank Sinatra Show, *including this zany full-length pose.*

Peggy Cass—she was still a favorite of the talk show host as well as an early fill-in for his recently demoted sidekick Dody Goodman. One year earlier, Goodman had been hired by NBC as a regular to "sit and talk" during Paar's nightly program. Her distracted air and hesitant, befuddled delivery quickly made her more popular with viewers than Paar. In December 1957—without any communication from Paar—Goodman read in the newspapers that her appearances were to be cut from five nights to one or two nights per week, as Paar saw fit. The change did not make good press

for Paar, whose feuds with columnists Dorothy Kilgallen and Walter Winchell soon became famous.

Television hosts like Paar, Steve Allen, and Ed Sullivan looked to nightclub performers like Goodman and Alice to help fill airtime on their shows, a practice which had been in place since the late 1940s. Consequently, this exposure had "alerted the nation" to the existence of intimate clubs such as the Blue Angel and Le Ruban Bleu. No longer were these Manhattan night spots "local secrets hidden away in cellars or down side streets."

Within a decade, however, the same medium which had promoted Manhattan night spots also contributed to their decline. "By 1959, Herbert Jacoby was having trouble booking acts," notes James Gavin. "Many of his past headliners now earned up to five times their weekly Blue Angel salaries for a single TV appearance." Jacoby was forced to hire a "distressing number of folk singers and mediocre comics." Angel perennial Portia Nelson cited rock and roll as another culprit: "People wanted to hear the rock singers and the noise and something they could shout along with . . . being still, quiet, just went out of fashion." "Not only had the Angel failed to attract a young crowd," observes Gavin, "it had also lost much of its older one to the suburbs and the TV set."

Alice noticed the changes in the wind, too. Privately, she conceded the validation of Janet Kern's strong words—the songs that Alice and Mark Lawrence had written a decade earlier were indeed threadbare from overuse. Yet, she dragged them out year after year, like an old coat. In 1958, during a guest appearance on *The Jack Paar Show*, Alice sang "Blubber Soup" and the M. I. T. song, and the studio audience just sat there, embarrassingly silent. Only when Alice cackled shrilly at her own jokes did they halfheartedly join in. By 1960, Alice would never again sing her old numbers on television.

Due to the lack of preservation of early variety and talk shows, Alice's songs have almost faded into oblivion. With the passage of time, kinescopes have been lost or destroyed, and network videotape collections have been erased. Only a few shows featuring Alice singing her own compositions survive, but they're not readily available to the general public. They are either in the hands of collectors or maintained in libraries or archives located in New York, Los Angeles, or Chicago. These rarities remain a hidden facet of Alice Pearce's twenty-five years in the business.

On April 14, 1958, Alice rejoined the Broadway production of *Bells Are Ringing*, this time as a permanent addition to the cast. (Jean Stapleton had relinquished the role of Sue to film *Damn Yankees* at the Warner Brothers studio in Hollywood.) "She was playing at the Shubert at the same time I was playing right across Shubert Alley at the Broadhurst in *Auntie Mame*," recalled Cris Alexander. "We'd meet for lunch every so often."

Working six days per week that spring and summer provided little time for Alice to enjoy her place at Fire Island, but for the time being that was just as well. The cottage evoked painful memories of John's sudden death. Nor would she spend any free time with Perk and June Bailey in Northport. Perk had decided to sell the house at 152 Bayview Avenue. It, too, was a house closely associated with John, whom they all missed terribly.

Meanwhile, the Baileys' individual careers with Fairchild Publications were continuing to thrive. In addition to their primary jobs, June had become an art consultant for *Vogue* and *Harper's Bazaar*, while Perk had gained recognition as consultant to many of the country's best-known menswear manufacturers. Their recently acquired four-story brownstone at 171 East Seventy-First Street was a next-door twin to Number 169, prominently featured in the 1961 film *Breakfast at Tiffany's* as the home of Holly Golightly, played by Audrey Hepburn.

Meanwhile, up in Vermont, Alice's parents became more reclusive. "They sort of banged around in that big house," recalled Whitman Wheeler, who, as a teenager, mowed their lawn in summer. "They hung their laundry in the basement. There was a lot of upkeep to the house. And even though it was totally renovated, it still must have been a dog to heat."

Winters in rural New England were particularly hard on Bob and Margaret. Since they rarely ventured out in the snow, they were often isolated until the arrival of spring. They kept their garbage in a large chest freezer until Margaret's sister Josephine Strode could drive across the valley in her jeep to pick it up and dispose of it.

"I think they watched a lot of television," said Wheeler. "They had a huge picture window, and once a bullet came right through that glass and narrowly missed them. The house was decorated with beautiful European antiques. Over the mantel was one of Alice's paintings which she'd [created while] sitting outside the house one year."

Although Bob and Margaret had lived in Whitingham full-time for almost a decade, they had made no effort to accumulate friends. Aside from Reginald and Elaine Maynard, a young couple who lived across the road, the Pearces' only contacts were the Wheeler family. "We'd pretty much just see them in passing," Wheeler said. "Then once a year at Christmas, we'd either go to their house or they would come to our house and exchange gifts." The Pearces' current situation was vastly removed from the social whirl they had relished in pre-war Paris—a contrast completely unknown to their Vermont neighbors.

"Alice did not come up very much after John Rox died," Wheeler noted. Bob and Margaret, he remembered, went down to New York "about twice a year" to shop and visit Alice, especially just before Christmas when they would "stay for a week or so." For these trips, the Wheelers always took the Pearces to the train station and then picked them up upon their return.

In October 1958, the Pearces' brother-in-law George Strode died after battling bladder cancer for four years. Josephine had long been the primary caregiver for Alice's unassuming grandmother Sallie Clark, but to lighten her load during George's illness, "Miss Sallie" had temporarily made her home with the Pearces. Although she had a heart condition, the widowed Josephine insisted that their mother once again reside with her. Approaching ninety-three, Sallie Clark retained her keen mind and general good health, except for a bad fall in the spring of that year. Meanwhile, two hundred miles away, in the shadow of the Queensboro Bridge, Sallie's granddaughter was gracefully fighting her own battles—just as an astrologer had predicted.

CHAPTER EIGHTEEN
Bosom Buddies

"I remember her telling me that New York was where it was at . . ."

As Alice adjusted to widowhood, she not only depended on her career for diversion, but she also relied on her friendships, both old and new. In the summer of 1958, she reconnected with twenty-eight-year-old actor-singer Mike Rayhill whom she had known casually two years earlier.

Rayhill, a native of Utica, New York, had found only marginal success in the entertainment world, despite a romantic singing voice and a polished appearance, perfectly fitting the "tall, dark, and handsome" stereotype. By this time Rayhill's credits included brief stints in Paris nightclubs, unbilled bits in two Hollywood films, and a gig as Fernando Lamas' understudy in the Broadway musical *Happy Hunting*. Since 1956 when he relocated from Hollywood, Rayhill had been seen squiring an assortment of female celebrities around New York, including Ethel Merman, Christina Crawford, and Ethel Waters. According to Dorothy Kilgallen, Rayhill drove to and from the Majestic (where he eventually replaced a singer in *Happy Hunting*) in a Rolls Royce, but had it "parked a couple of blocks from the theater so no one [would] notice how madly rich he is."

It's possible that Rayhill's wealth was derived not from his middle-class Catholic parents, who owned an aluminum siding business in Utica, but from a Manhattan benefactor. In Hollywood, he had been the boyfriend of

Mike Rayhill, 1957.

television producer-director Ralph Levy, with whom he shared an apartment at the fabled Chateau Marmont on Sunset Boulevard. Levy, who had previously directed more than eighty episodes of *The George Burns and Gracie Allen Show* as well as the pilot for *I Love Lucy*, was then Jack Benny's boy-wonder director. Rayhill's relationship with Levy appears to have ended in the spring of 1956, when the director left the States to film episodes of *The Jack Benny Program* on location in Europe. Failing to make it in Hollywood (despite being a discovery of the notorious agent Henry Willson who launched the careers of Rock Hudson and Tab Hunter), Rayhill had settled in New York.

Not long after his arrival in the city, Rayhill met Alice and John Rox through mutual friends. After John's death, Alice and Rayhill continued to socialize from time to time, sharing their life stories and finding a common ground. Impressed with Rayhill's musical talent and experience, Alice asked him to help her write a musical comedy, utilizing some of John's unpublished songs. Work was underway by August 1958 when Dorothy Kilgallen reported that the pair hoped to have the venture completed within a month. For whatever reason, the project fizzled, and Rayhill disappeared from Alice's world. Not a shred of their collaboration can be found among Alice's papers.

Conversely, lanky and good-natured Bill LeMassena had remained Alice's crony since they were introduced in 1954. (Had Alice not departed *Gentlemen Prefer Blondes* in 1951 to film *The Belle of New York*, she and Bill would have met that summer when Bill replaced actor Irving Mitchell as decrepit Mr. Esmond.) Both were so entrenched in the New York theatre scene that the anecdotes came tumbling one after another in their conversations. Theirs was an enthralling friendship.

During Alice's eleven consecutive months with *Bells Are Ringing*, she and Bill, one year her senior, often met for a late supper or relaxed together at a club. Sometimes Bill hosted suppers in his bachelor apartment at 132 West Eleventh Street in Greenwich Village. Known by all his guests as a gourmet cook, Bill had been taught by the best: Alfred Lunt.

Alice and Bill began to spend so much time together that their friends grew hopeful of a budding romance. Whispers made their way to columnist Walter Winchell who announced in early May 1959: "Alice Pearce, femmedian, plans to keep Wm. LaMassena [*sic*] laughing all the way to the church." Unfortunately, neither Alice nor Bill seems to have left any documents confirming their marriage plans. In 2015, when Bill's only niece was informed of Winchell's intimation, she was incredulous. "But my uncle was *gay!*" she protested. Likewise, in 1959, other insiders who realized the couple's true inclinations—Alice's attraction to homosexual men and Bill's sexual orientation—may have shrugged off Winchell's teasing hint. But there may have been more truth to the matter than anyone knew. In 2003, Tom Monsell, a retired high school English teacher and theatre devotee then living in Greenport, Long Island, recalled a conversation he once had with Bill. "The late William LeMassena," Monsell said, "told me that he and Alice Pearce were engaged. Nothing came of it."

The timing of Winchell's announcement remains curious, considering that by that point, Alice and Bill had not even seen each other for two months. On March 7, 1959, *Bells Are Ringing* ended its Broadway run, and Alice immediately left the city as a member of the show's touring company. She did not return to New York until September, and in the interim, there was no opportunity for Bill to visit her on the road because he was enjoying a successful Broadway run in the musical *Redhead*. Perhaps being apart for six months gave either of them time to reconsider the possibility of marriage. In the end, maybe they thought it best to remain buddies without any legal or romantic attachments. Whatever the case, it was just as Monsell said— nothing came of their "engagement."

Early in 1959, Alice became chummy with two late additions to the *Bells Are Ringing* company. In January, Paul Davis assumed

Bill LeMassena, Alice Pearce, and an unidentified friend enjoy a drink at a neighborhood bar, circa 1958.

the position of assistant stage manager, and the following month, Ralph Roberts replaced Heywood Hale Broun in the role of a police detective's dopey assistant. The previous fall, confirmed bachelors Roberts, forty-two, and Davis, thirty-six, had each been linked in gossip columns to the show's lead Judy Holliday, fresh from her romantic break-up with co-star Sydney Chaplin. First, columnist Earl Wilson coyly identified Roberts as Holliday's "stage door Johnny." Then, Danton Walker and Dorothy Kilgallen each implied a romance between Roberts and Holliday—the former claiming that the couple frequented the Left Bank, a club owned by Kilgallen's husband. Walter Winchell only added confusion to the mix. In October 1958, he named Roberts as "Judy Holliday's new big secret," only to announce one month later that Holliday had replaced Chaplin with her "old flame" Davis. To insiders, such drivel carried even less weight than Winchell's suggestion of an impending marriage between Alice Pearce and Bill LeMassena. Plainly, Roberts and Davis were merely

serving as escorts for Holliday, just as Mike Rayhill had done for Ethel Merman.

It's quite likely that Holliday, in turn, was instrumental in ensuring both Roberts' and Davis' placements in *Bells*, just in time for the two men to be included in the production's upcoming tour of Washington, D.C., Los Angeles, and San Francisco. Holliday especially wanted warmhearted Ralph Roberts—a licensed masseur—along because his therapeutic sessions would prepare her for its rigorous rehearsals and performances. Ralph, a husky 215-pounder, standing six feet, three inches tall, kept in shape with weightlifting routines at a local gym. A shock of wavy dark hair crowned his head, and his rugged profile "looked like the Indian on the old buffalo nickel."

In 1946, after serving five years in the army, Ralph had settled in Greenwich Village. He was full of determination to study acting, a dream he'd nourished for more than a decade. However, stage assignments were sporadic, with Ralph usually typecast as policemen, sailors, and bodyguards, but he didn't mind. He was grateful for any experience he could gain. "I really wanted to be an actor," he said, "but how do you make a living?" Ralph needed a job that would allow him free time for speech, dance, and French lessons. He had always enjoyed receiving massages, so he decided to get trained as a masseur. Massage therapy, he reasoned, would take little time yet produce the income needed for the "in-between" times when he wasn't acting.

Ralph Roberts, circa 1976. Cris Alexander photo.

After nine months of training, Ralph hung out his shingle. In a relatively short span, he became one of New York's most outstanding masseurs. By the time he joined *Bells*, Ralph's regular clients included Holliday and Davis, as well as others within Alice's circle, like Imogene Coca, Betty Comden, Adolph Green, Gloria Safier, Milton Goldman, and Arnold Weissberger. Ralph was respected not only for his skillful therapy, but also for his "solid reputation as a Southern gentleman in the classic mold, soft-spoken, compassionate, and courtly."

Like Ralph, Paul Davis had been seriously interested in theatre from a very young age. The eldest of four children, he was born on September 6, 1922, in Dorchester, Massachusetts, a neighborhood comprising six square miles within the city of Boston. When he was only thirteen, Paul began collecting actors' autographs outside stage doors in Boston's theatre district. Soon he would become one of three ringleaders in a gang of fifty-five autograph hounds who frequented first nights and Wednesday and Saturday matinees.

In 1939, when interviewed by the *Boston Globe*, Paul explained their technique: "We give [the actors] gifts. We make scrapbooks for them—we clip from all the newspapers and magazines pictures and stories of each star, file them away in envelopes, and when we read of a star's coming to Boston, we take out all the clippings we have on that particular person and paste them into a scrap book." As the actors arrived at the theatre, Paul and his fellow fans brought forth the scrapbooks, a ploy that usually gained them entrance into the lobby. Quite often, they accompanied the stars to their dressing rooms where they were given complimentary tickets to the show.

Branching out, Paul and his two cohorts hitchhiked to New York at least twice each winter to collect autographs on the Great White Way. There, in 1938, Paul had his photograph taken when he was leaning through the window of Joan Crawford's limousine. "He treasures it like a passport, always has it with him," the *Globe* reported. One night, Paul got a ride with Katharine Hepburn from her hotel to the theatre. "She just couldn't get rid of [me] any other way," he beamed.

Collecting autographs was tied to Paul's fervent dream of becoming an actor. When he finished high school, he enrolled in Boston's prestigious Bishop-Lee School of Theatre, where he was befriended by fellow student Ruth Roman who was destined to make more than fifty films in Hollywood. When Roman left New England to forge an acting career in New York, Paul followed. "Paul and Ruth Roman had done summer stock together," recalled Paul's sister Renee Summers, "and they were very close friends for many, many years—I think from the time he was eighteen. But I

Twenty-year-old Pvt. Paul Davis, right, and Pvt. Jackie Harrington check out the day room's supply of current hits at Fort Eustis, Virginia, May 1943. Prior to induction, Harrington played one of the Days in the stage production of Life with Father, *and Paul was heard as Homer Brown on radio's* The Aldrich Family.

was only a *baby* when he left home, you know, when he first went off to see the big world. I was, what, six? I never knew him very well. His life in the theatre was all his own."

By 1942, Paul had moved to Manhattan, where he pounded the payment, making the endless rounds to various casting agents. Finally, in March 1943, he landed a job as an assistant stage manager for George Abbott's comedy *Kiss and Tell* featuring Joan Caulfield, Jessie Royce Landis, Richard Widmark, and Frances Bavier (later "Aunt Bee" of *The Andy Griffith Show*). Although Paul did not perform onstage, he always listed this show as his Broadway debut. The experience, however heady it may have been, was short-lived. Less than a month into the play's run, Paul was drafted.

No details regarding Paul's military service have surfaced, except for his participation in USO productions, both in the States and overseas. When he returned to New York in 1946, Paul found it even more difficult to pursue an acting career—on either coast. Finally, in 1950, he made his debut on the Broadway stage as a member of an ensemble of "townspeople" in *The Devil's Disciple*. When this production closed three months

Paul Davis, left, attended the Hollywood premiere of the Warner Brothers film Breakthrough *on November 8, 1950. He accompanied Alfred Hitchcock's daughter Patricia (third from left), along with his old friend Ruth Roman and her soon-to-be husband Mortimer Hall.*

later, he decided to give Hollywood a try, but that ended nowhere.

In 1955, Paul sailed for Europe where he spent several months in England, Italy, and Greece. While there he won a bit part in the Dino De Laurentiis film production of *War and Peace*. The following year, Paul appeared as the laconic Sgt. Gregovich in the national touring company of *The Teahouse of the August Moon*, opening at Boston's Colonial Theatre where twenty years earlier as a starstruck lad he had worshipped his idols.

Despite his career struggles, Paul still yearned to achieve leading-man status, listing himself as such in both industry casting bibles, *The Players' Guide* (published in New York) and the *Academy Players Directory* (published in Hollywood). Physically, he was perhaps more suited for character parts, although he had a rather handsome face. His blue eyes and thick wavy light brown hair, combed straight back, were his best features. Standing at five feet, nine inches, Paul's barrel-chested physique carried a few more pounds in 1956 than it had a decade earlier.

In 1957, with New York's live television dramas on the decline, Paul returned to Los Angeles. Lady Luck continued to bypass him, but he did win a small role in Warner Brothers' *Auntie Mame* starring Rosalind Russell. Paul shines as a frustrated stage manager during the scene of Mame's calamitous acting debut. When she accidentally remains in front of the curtain after it's summarily rung down, Paul reaches through the folds, grabs her by the bustle, and yanks her out of view.

Unfortunately for Paul, his brief exposure in a hit movie didn't offer much of a career boost. "Paul Davis couldn't find a job in Hollywood," gossip columnist Mike Connolly explained, "so he went back to New York and got himself a job with Judy Holliday—as a *real* behind-the-scenes stage manager of Judy's Broadway stage

musical, *Bells Are Ringing*." Paul, like everyone else in the entertainment industry, knew that networking was key to building a career, but when he joined the *Bells* company in 1959, he had no clue that connecting with one of its cast members would eventually alter the course of his life. Nor did Alice Pearce.

Thirteen years had passed since Alice had last been a member of a national tour, and while *On the Town* had been a thrilling experience, it could not match the sixteen weeks she was on the road with *Bells Are Ringing*. When the show opened on March 10 at the National Theatre in Washington, D.C., the audience was not only studded with familiar social figures but also included the entire staff of Courtesy, Inc.—thirty-five telephone answering girls. The show proved to be a huge success, selling standing room at every performance. Washington tourists were amazed that they couldn't get into the theatre, but the five weeks were largely sold out before the show opened. It was predicted that the production would leave town with a "tidy total of $280,000 taken in at the box office."

On March 21, first lady Mamie Eisenhower attended a matinee performance. "That day the interest was in the audience, not on the stage," wrote Rose Post of the *Salisbury Post* (Ralph Roberts' hometown newspaper in North Carolina). "Someone in the cast had an eye on her every minute. When the performance was over, they compared notes and found that they had a minute-by-minute report—including the instant when she blew her nose."

The Washington run of *Bells* was interspersed with a steady rehearsal schedule, during which Holliday—one observer noted—had been the hardest worker, boosting the morale of the rest of the company. When the engagement ended on April 11, most of the cast and crew (including Alice, Paul, and leading man Hal Linden) went back to New York to rest for a couple of days before flying out to Los Angeles to begin the second leg of the tour. Meanwhile, Ralph Roberts, massage table in tow, drove cross country in his sports car.

The opening at the Philharmonic Auditorium on April 20 was a gala affair. "Hundreds of dinner parties lured first-nighters out early to exclusive clubs and hotels," gushed Elizabeth Goodland of the *Los Angeles Times*. "The attire was lovely—furs, brilliant jewels, impeccably-arranged coiffures and the prettiest theater dresses created a most sophisticated look in the audience." Goodland's fellow staff writer Albert Goldberg focused instead on the show: "Judy Holliday has a magnetic way with a song though not much voice, and she contrives to be the constant center of attention while not seeming to work at it." He gave a few nods to the supporting cast members like Eddie Lawrence ("has a fat part and does it with fine gusto"), but he lumped third-billed Alice with a group of players "who come in for momentary notice." Similarly, Jerry Pam of the *Valley Times* noted, "Alice Pearce is excellent and deserved more lines." Indeed, the part of Sue was rather lackluster, except for her schmaltzy duet with Sandor (played by Lawrence). Still, many felt that Alice had enlivened the role more than her predecessor Jean Stapleton had—including Lawrence, who called Alice a "very funny woman."

One Saturday night during the Los Angeles engagement, Alice arranged for her brother-in-law Don Herring to bring his family to the show, inviting them to join her afterwards for a nightcap. It was the first time Don's family had seen Alice since John Rox's death. "Alice took us to the cast's hangout," recalled Linda Swanson. "I remember it was a club or a pub of sorts, and we were able to see all of the cast members milling about." Linda, then fifteen, was agog, asking her aunt for the inside scoop on her favorite movie stars. "I remember her telling me that *New York* was where it was at—referring to the stage and the great training that makes real actors, rather than Hollywood flashes-in-the-pan." (Alice would have probably beamed had she known that many years later Eddie Lawrence would describe her as "a Broadway person.")

Alice's response to Linda is noteworthy. Besides revealing Alice's bias, it also may have reflected an issue that stuck in her craw. Earlier that month, columnist Mike Connolly had reported "heartbreak backstage" at the Philharmonic when the actors heard a bit of scuttlebutt pertaining to M-G-M's casting plans for its film version of *Bells*. "I learned that the MGMoguls want Big Name Stars," Connolly eye-rolled, "for comedienne Alice Pearce's part as the phone-answering service boss and for Eddie Lawrence's as the literate bookie—such as Thelma Ritter and Milton Berle!"

It's easy to wonder if Alice was disillusioned with Hollywood by this point. She hadn't forgotten how M-G-M's *On the Town* had ended up bearing only a slight resemblance to what had been so dynamic and groundbreaking on the stage. And she shuddered to recall how *The Belle of New York* had dragged on for months during its multiple script alterations. While Alice had endured her share of Broadway flops, she still preferred the sound of live applause, the kind that enveloped her at each curtain call. Most likely, she would have concurred with Jared Brown, biographer of the Lunts, who proposed: "Most good actors also enjoy the challenges that only the stage can provide. There is almost no margin for error in the theatre; a performance must be carefully built because each moment is a finished product; a scene cannot be repeated if the timing misfires or a line is misread or an accident occurs . . . The financial reward is not nearly as great as that provided by the electronic media, and the celebrity status the stage can confer does not begin to compare with the kind of fame created by exposure in film and television." Had Alice desired greater fame or fortune, she would have deserted the theatre long before 1959. Perhaps at the root of it all was New York City, the place she loved so much.

In San Francisco, where *Bells* opened on June 1 at the Curran Theatre, Alice received nothing but praise from the critics. Theresa Loeb Cone of the *Oakland Tribune* found Alice "marvelously funny." William Glackin of the *Sacramento Bee* declared, "The priceless Alice Pearce is, as usual, priceless as the sister [*sic*]." Hortense Morton of the *San Francisco Examiner* cheered, "I couldn't be happier that clever Alice Pearce, proprietor of the answering service, runs amuck innocently, of a horse track bookie operation."

For the five-week run at the Curran, Alice, Ralph Roberts, and Paul Davis rented an apartment together several blocks away. Sixty years ago, those outside the theatre world may have frowned on a young widow sharing rooms with two bachelors. However, Alice saw no cause for concern. By this time, the threesome was known among the *Bells* company for their simpatico relationship. Besides that, from all indications her male roomies were members of "the society of tasteful men," although quite discreet. Therefore, the housing arrangement offered Alice both security and congeniality.

After *Bells* closed on July 4, Alice returned to Los Angeles, where she had previously agreed to make a guest appearance on the successful ABC television series *The Real McCoys*. She was cast in the role of Emmy—yet another lovelorn spinster—who was quite comparable to Annie Mokum, the character Alice had played six years earlier on TV's *Jamie*. Both girls were sweet but inept in the kitchen, and they each had an overweight boyfriend who was matrimony-shy. Emmy's intended was played by Stafford Repp, who would later gain fame as Chief O'Hara on the *Batman* television series. As Emmy, Alice attempts a countrified/Southern accent, but the show's regulars Walter Brennan, Richard Crenna, and especially Kathy Nolan run circles around her in that department.

Character actors like Alice were contractually required to furnish their own wardrobes for film and television appearances. Since she hadn't been back to her New York apartment for months, Alice used some of her regular traveling clothes for Emmy, like a heavy corduroy coat and a checked dress. But for Emmy's dowdy hat, she went straight to a thrift store, just the type of place she loved to haunt. Her closets in New York were bursting with hats of every description, many of which she used in her nightclub act. According to a blurb in a Los Angeles paper a few weeks prior, Alice's collection of hats—an astonishing 2,000—rivaled Hedda Hopper's. (In 1953, when Alice spent the summer in Bermuda, each Friday she spent part of her weekly paycheck to buy a certain style of hat until she had purchased one of every available color, and usually shoes and purse to match.)

Alice left Los Angeles shortly after filming the spot on *The Real McCoys*, arriving in Dallas to repeat the role of Sue in the State Fair Musicals production of *Bells Are Ringing*, opening August 17 for a two-week run. Rehearsals were easiest for Alice—coming straight from the tour—but even so, a positive aura almost immediately filled the music hall. By the second day, everyone knew their parts, scripts were put away, and the company settled into a relaxed and fast-moving routine. Veteran stage and television comedian Phil Leeds, playing Sandor, fretted, "I just can't stand it. I don't like it all. Everything is too perfect, and everybody is too wonderful."

The production reunited Alice with chatterbox Peggy Cass, whose main concern as the lead player was adjusting to the Dallas air conditioning. The pair of comediennes hadn't worked together since the 1954 tour of *The Vegetable*. "Peggy played my sister," Alice explained to the *Dallas Times Herald*, "and we have been sisters ever since." (Cass would echo that sentiment two years later when she told journalist Martin Cohen that Alice was one of her four closest friends.)

As the final show of the summer season, *Bells* was one of its most popular. Alice received good notices, but not without a backhanded compliment from John Rosenfield of the *Dallas Morning News*: "Miss Pearce manages to give a dizzy, chinless impression on the stage. In a tête-à-tête, she really is a good-looking girl even if her features are more pleasing than photogenic."

Alice received better press two weeks later after opening the fall season at a Dallas night spot called the Tree Club, owned by interior decorator Norwood Ballow, and housed in his restaurant, the Twin Tree Inn. "Since everybody in the world already loves Alice Pearce, there really was no worry how she would do in opening a two-week stand," wrote Don Safran of the *Dallas Times Herald*. "Alice, of course, is magnificent. But then she has the advantage of almost not being a real live person like the rest of us. Alice could have been created by Walt Disney or put together with feathers, bubble gum and sugar plums." Noting the restrictions of Alice's straight role in *Bells*, Safran rejoiced that Alice was "now herself in free form," cackling and singing her old standbys like "Boots"

Alice Pearce, 1959.

and "Night and Day." Alice's material, he estimated, was secondary to the performer. "She is a comedienne like few around ... she has made the Tree Club a Wonder in Alice-land."

While Alice was in Dallas, word came that Jean Stapleton had been cast as Sue in the M-G-M film version of *Bells Are Ringing*, which would be directed by Vincente Minnelli. Having more screen experience than Stapleton, Alice may have been disappointed that she was not chosen for the part. As things turned out, such regrets probably withered quickly. Screenwriters Betty Comden and Adolph Green had overhauled the stage musical's original script, making necessary deletions and additions. Sue and Sandor's duet "Salzburg" did not make the cut, effectually eliminating the one bit of humor allotted to the colorless Sue. Moreover, the production became "one constant struggle." Judy Holliday, plagued by insecurity and health issues, was miserably unhappy throughout the filming.

Bells Are Ringing would be released in June 1960. "We watched as it sank like a stone outside New York," Minnelli later observed. "Am I allowed to say [Holliday] was too urban to fit into middle America?"

Leaving Dallas, Alice returned to New York in time to see the leaves change color in Central Park. After being away from home for six months, she relished the opportunity to relax in her favorite city.

For Alice, the social event of the season must have been the Mayfair Supper Dance, held at midnight on Halloween in the Terrace Room of the Plaza, six blocks from her apartment on East Fifty-Ninth Street. The members-only midnight dance was a benefit for the Actors Fund of America. Those attending the costume gala were invited to impersonate someone from the theatrical past or to come as a character in a movie or play. The Meyer Davis Orchestra obliged with several medleys of tunes from Broadway productions in which the assembled stars had appeared. Donald Dun-

can of *Ballroom Dance Magazine* noted that "in the mixture of café society and theatre folk, the ones in show business were far better as ballroom dancers."

Among the celebrities judging the costumes were Helen Hayes, Claudette Colbert, Ethel Merman, Vincent Sardi, Walter Pidgeon, and Sir Cedric Hardwicke. Irish actress Siobhan McKenna turned up in the guise of a sleepwalking Lady Macbeth, while Gloria Vanderbilt imitated "Auntie Mame." Lillian Gish, as Lucretia Borgia, looked as if she had procured her authentic costume from the wardrobe of one of her old silent films. Celeste Holm came as Madame Butterfly, and Peggy Wood was a dead ringer for Laurette Taylor in *The Glass Menagerie*. Alice, escorted by Milton Lyon, donned 1880s finery— complete with vintage bonnet perched atop a frizzy red wig—as "Vinnie Day" from *Life with Father*. Lyon, the thirty-six-year-old director for Princeton's Triangle Club productions, dressed as the rabbit from *Harvey*.

That fall, Alice's professional calendar was relatively empty, but her schedule for 1960 was dotted with several stage and television assignments—and a last-gasp nightclub engagement.

CHAPTER NINETEEN
Bicoastal Interlude

"I wear a hat morning, noon, and night . . ."

On November 29, 1959, NBC telecast the National Academy of Recording Arts and Sciences Awards on *Sunday Showcase*, a presentation previously recorded on videotape in Los Angeles. Hosted by Meredith Willson, this second annual Grammy Awards ceremony was the first to be aired on television. Included in the nominations, but not among the winners, was *Monster Rally*, a novelty album which twitted the horror craze. In August 1958, Alice had teamed with veteran actor Hans Conried and a ghoulish chorus to record a medley of twelve whimsical numbers, including "The Dracula Trot" and "I'm in Love with the Creature from the Black Lagoon." Of Alice's four solos, most appealing was "The Thing," a jaunty rendition for which she combined a juvenile register with a nasal twang, similar to that of Lily Tomlin's "Edith Ann" character of the 1970s.

To kick off the release of *Monster Rally*, Alice and Conried appeared at a promotional cocktail party at the Round Table in Manhattan in early March 1959. Wearing a frilly hat that resembled a head of cabbage, Alice sat next to Conried and sipped from a glass embossed with a skull-and-crossbones and labeled "strychnine." When a journalist asked why the pair had taken part in the album, Conried cringed dramatically. "Honey!" he exclaimed. "What do you think was the reason? They paid me money, of course." Without a doubt, Alice's motivation corresponded with her colleague's.

The record, aimed at youngsters, was received fairly well by the public, despite the fact that *Variety* thought it was a "good idea carried to extreme lengths." Today, *Monster Rally* is a collector's item, if only for the imaginative cover design by noted artist Jack Davis.

Another common denominator shared by Alice and Conried was the controversial late-night talk show host Jack Paar, then at the peak of his popularity. Conried was a member of Paar's "salon of eccentrics," a crafty device which had helped to make Paar's show such a success. One critic—clearly not a fan of Paar—once described semi-regular Elsa Maxwell, the inveterate party-giver, as "a blabbermouth who can talk for hours about anything from kings and queens to hors d'oeuvres, jodhpurs, fox hunting and opera." Why should Paar exert himself, the critic asked, when he could find such windbags as Maxwell and sit and listen while they entertained his audience.

As an interviewer, Paar was droll, incisive, and highly emotional. His show was all about "intelligent, literate conversations that veered from witty repartee to the serious, and from barbs to bonhomie." It also featured stand-up comedians, singers, musicians, and skits. "By television standards then and later," asserts Maxwell biographer Sam Staggs, "the show was sophisticated . . . the stay-up-late time slot—11:15 P.M. to 1:00 A.M.—appealed to the hip and excluded early-to-bed squares."

Perhaps inspired to draw a wider late-night audience, Paar produced a special primetime variety show to be aired on NBC's *Startime* on January 26, 1960. The hour-long color telecast, previously videotaped in New York, would feature Broadway singer Pat Suzuki, dancer Harry Mimmo, pianist Jose Melis, singer-comedienne Betty Bruce, and in the comedy sketches, Jonathan Winters and Alice Pearce. It was called "The Wonderful World of Jack Paar," a title, groaned Jack Gould of the *Times*, that "was to prove an agonizing misnomer."

Most critics agreed with Gould. Percy Shain of the *Boston Globe* estimated that forty million viewers tuned in to watch Paar "pour the special magic of his midnight stanza into the variety show mold, [but] it couldn't be done." Cynthia Lowry of the Associated Press lamented: "Maybe Jack was trying too hard for the day people ... the sketches, even those with Jonathan Winters and Alice Pearce, just didn't come off."

In one poorly executed skit, Paar, playing himself, was a passenger aboard Birdland Airlines. Alice, as simpering stewardess Emmy Lou Pride, punctuated her puerile lines with a trademark chortle—but with embarrassingly awkward results. The reviewer for the *Journal-American* criticized Alice for "regularly cackling off in her maniacal screech of a laugh about which, as Damon Runyan said about something else, all we can conscientiously say about it is, you can have it." Even Winters' ad libs were too infrequent to salvage the airplane sketch. In another skit, "Baby Face Paar," a disc jockey imprisoned for accepting payola, played tunes for his jail-mates, including "Songs for Shut-Ins" and "I Was Having a Ball 'til They Added the Chain."

Allen Rich of the North Hollywood *Valley Times* proved to be the only dissenter, praising the show for its "delightful whimsy and satire." "It was all high good fun," Rich allowed, "save for a song by Alice Pearce, which was in bad taste." Alice's ditty remains unidentified, but we know what she wore for her objectionable solo, thanks to Margaret Pearce who snapped Polaroids of her television screen that evening. As convict Number 36-26-36, Alice sported a kinky red wig and an ill-fitting, horizontally striped décolleté gown with matching elbow-length gloves.

"The Wonderful World of Jack Paar" marked one of Alice's final network television appearances produced in New York. Aside from a subsequent appearance on Paar's late-night show and a dramatic role in a *Camera Three* telecast, Alice would not secure any other network assignments based in Manhattan until late 1961. The handwriting was on the wall; if she wanted to pursue employment in television, Hollywood was her most viable choice.

Since there was nothing brewing on Broadway in the winter of 1960, Alice agreed to appear with Paul Hartman and Carol Bruce, both well-known in the musical comedy field, in the revue *Angel in the Wings*, opening in Miami on February 23. The escape from New York's sleet and snow made the undertaking even more advantageous. The mercury in Miami hit eighty degrees the day rehearsals began at the Coconut Grove Playhouse.

Hartman and his wife Grace, assisted by Hank Ladd and Ted Luce, had co-written the revue's sketches for *Angel*'s original 1947 Broadway production. For the two-week engagement in Miami, there were eighteen scenes, including two sketches spotlighting Alice. "Up Early with the Upjohns" was a satire of cheerful early morning radio broadcasts, with Hartman and Alice playing married hosts who are disenchanted with their daily schedule. "Salina Select Garden Club" featured Alice as a sedate club president—reminiscent of the Helen Hokinson type she had played so adroitly two decades earlier at Princeton—who winds up dancing wildly with guest anthropologists Hartman and Bruce, following their lecture on primitive fertility rites. "Alice Pearce brings down the house," wrote Ethel Tombrink of the *Miami Herald*, "both in her skits with Hartman and her solo number." Herb Kelly of the *Miami News* chimed in, "All [Miss Pearce] has to do is whine and the audience doubles up."

That week, *Miami Herald* fashion editor Beverley Wilson profiled Alice and revealed a good deal about Alice's current tastes in clothing. "She either appears in a bright red wool unbelted tunic over skinny black tights, or in the most understated outfit she can find," reported Wilson. "Much of the time . . . she shops with an eye to 'very simple clothes—just good lines but no extremes, no fussy pockets and things.'" Alice, a follower of Chanel and Dior, had developed a "burning interest" in fashion as a girl in Paris. "I wonder what Molyneux would say about my black tights?" she grinned. But the focus of Wilson's piece was Alice's love for hats. "I wear a hat morning, noon, and night—mostly the kind that fit snugly all around my head," Alice admitted, "to cover my hair completely, don't you see, because I hate to fuss with a fancy coiffure." Essentially, Alice was confessing that she wore hats—in place of wigs—to cover her thinning hair. Her favorite hat designer was Mr. John who had once created a mink bonnet which, he told Alice, was "so you." She confided, however, that she preferred hats in shades of purple, lavender, and pink. Most of them had a "kooky little touch," offset by her unobtrusive frocks.

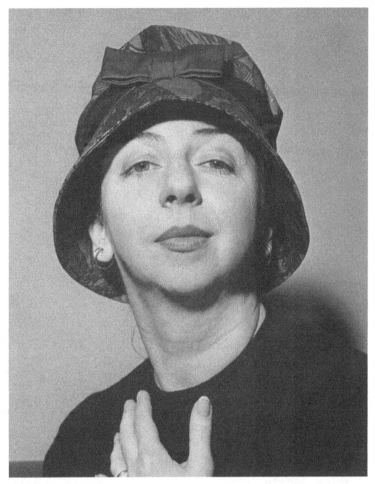

Photographed in February 1960, Alice said she found this Swedish-designed cloche of purple cotton "all alone" on a bargain counter. "Nobody wanted it but me," she said. "They didn't understand it." Later that year, she wore it for a guest appearance on the CBS sitcom Angel.

One month later, Alice returned to Florida with Hartman to reprise *Angel in the Wings* at a small supper club—the "Plantation Room"—inside the Colonial Inn at St. Petersburg. As she surveyed the venue and its retiree patrons, Alice couldn't stop thinking about the halcyon days of the Blue Angel, when the elegant and famous had packed its back room to see her impersonate "The Girl." That girl was long gone now, but her modern-day portrayer still attempted to amuse, singing "Night and Day" to the tune of "Nola" and lifting her stein in a toast to the Massachusetts Institute of Technology. The old folks adjusted their hearing aids, laughed, and applauded politely. The *Tampa Bay Times* reviewer misspelled her name, compared her to Patsy Kelly, and touted *New Faces* as her most famous work. Shaking her head, Alice knew it was time for an overhaul. She became determined to write a new act for herself as soon as she got back to New York.

To accomplish her goal, Alice enlisted Mark Lawrence, who was still employed full-time in the advertising industry but nevertheless interested in writing for the stage. Concurrently, she undertook another daunting project—one without a collaborator. "I'm writing an intimate revue," she told journalist William Peper, during an interview in her apartment in early May. "I think the Broadway revues lately have been too big. Does anyone really care about all those production numbers? I think the people just want to laugh."

Lady Umbridge (Philippa Bevans) criticizes her guest Mrs. Oxslip (Alice) in The Ignorants Abroad.
Lady Umbridge: "The manner in which you dressed was an obvious signal that it was not to be an occasion for restraint."
Mrs. Oxslip: "And what was wrong with my dress?"
Lady Umbridge: "Nothing really, except there is a difference, you know, between being well turned out and turned well out."

However, Alice wasn't writing it with herself in mind. She had planned it for Nancy Walker, "the finest clown we have."

Ultimately, a new acting venture took precedence over either project. After frequenting the Broadway stage for more than seventeen years, Alice, now forty-two, was set to make her *off-Broadway* debut—amid a production team of men in their twenties and early thirties. The previous year, Robert Cavallo, a theatrical attorney, had become the managing director of Theatre East at 211 East Sixtieth Street. He was soon joined by industry newcomer Matt

Cimber as the theatre's artistic director. For the 1960 spring season, they partnered to present *The Ignorants Abroad*, a three-act comedy written by another neophyte, William Guthrie, a postgraduate of the Yale School of Fine Arts, where the piece was first staged in 1951. The costumes, lighting, and set were designed by Patton Campbell—the only member of the team with Broadway credits—who had created the costumes for *Fallen Angels* in 1956. Alice and Philippa Bevans, forty-seven, were cast in the leading roles.

The Ignorants Abroad, written in the artificial literary manner of Oscar Wilde, is the story of brash Texas oil millionairess Mrs. Oxslip (played by Alice) who endeavors to marry her daughter Agatha to the young lord of Abbotts Crumbling, an ancient manor house in England. Standing in her way is the lord's imperious but impoverished mother, Lady Valerie Umbridge (played by London-born Bevans) whose condescending epigrams are the focus of the piece. "Enthusiasm," she instructs her son Anthony, "is the root of vulgarity, just as indifference is the flower of refinement." During the course of the play, Lady Umbridge and Mrs. Oxslip volley other "trifling paradoxes back and forth like middle-aged ladies on a tennis court." In fact, Guthrie had given his characters a great deal to say but not much to do, as James Lynn of the *Long Island Star-Journal* observed: "Some of the epigrams might be worth hearing if Mr. Guthrie had bothered to write a play around them."

Manners (Howard Morton) the butler makes a play for Mrs. Oxslip in The Ignorants Abroad.
Manners: "I offer you my heart on a tray. Take it. Naturally this may not be just the way you envisaged your life. This is fate. After all, what does it matter if you compromise a little here and there?"
Mrs. Oxslip: "A woman who has been compromised here and there has certainly given in more than a little."

"I think it was the first comedy I had ever tackled," recalled Matt Cimber, who was only twenty-four years old at the time. "We actually tested it up at Yale first, but without Alice. It was a battle between the two ladies about cultural differences. The job—actually, the staging—was to keep it moving so that it didn't settle down into 'talking heads.' That was part of the challenge, and of course, we were doing it on a very small stage. It was a very intimate theatre, in fact the perfect theatre for that play because you felt right in there with [the actors] and therefore, if they got a little conversational, it was okay because you weren't at such a distance that it became a bore."

Most critics disagreed with Cimber's assessment. Judith Crist, who felt that Guthrie's clever lines had at once enchanted and ensnared him, noted: "Cimber has permitted the lines to hold the actors captive, too; they just sit or stand and exchange them." *Variety* was somewhat more charitable: "Accepting the script,

This pose of Alice was used to promote The Ignorants
Abroad *in New York newspaper ads with the caption:*
"Pearce a Panic!"

with its built-in limitations, the production is very good ... it is a skillful imitation, concocted by a writer of talent. It would be interesting to see what Guthrie would do under less restrictive circumstances." "The dauntless Miss Bevans often puts splendid distaste into her strokes in the tennis match," allowed James Lynn, "and Alice Pearce, a redoubtable comedienne whose homely face is a closely printed catalogue of laughable expressions, serves some winners herself when Mr. Cimber's clogged staging gives her a chance."

Brooks Atkinson of the *Times* faulted *Ignorants* for having a plot not equal to the dialogue. In addition, he noticed that Lady Valerie and her butler, played by Howard Morton, have the best lines—"in a style of antithesis which goes beyond cleverness"—while Mrs. Oxslip is allowed only an "occasional earthy wisecrack." "If the contrasting characters were more evenly balanced," Atkinson prescribed, "the war

of words might yield a heartless humor that would result in a verbal victory. If the performance were icy, that is." Yet he pointed out that Alice gave her best effort, playing "in the style of middle-class obtuseness and excitement that has long endeared her to theatregoers in this town."

Judith Crist also gave Alice a nod: "Alice Pearce, screechy voice and glittering eye and all, is a fine comedienne—but her triumphs of the evening are her silences as she attempts to digest a crumpet or simply gapes at the flood of insults directed at her and her daughter as the American upstarts." Dorothy Kilgallen called Alice "a riot," but couldn't resist a catty detraction: "One of the critics who panned [*The Ignorants Abroad*] was really part of the show opening night; he fell asleep early in the performance and snored so loudly the audience was paying more attention to him than to the stage."

When interviewed prior to the opening on May 23, Alice conceded that *Ignorants* was not the most original idea for a comedy but that its "crazy quality" had reminded her of Georges Feydeau's farce *Hotel Paradiso.* "There are so few straight comedies on Broadway anymore," she explained. "And I thought audiences might like to laugh a little this summer." After playing in big musicals, Alice was a little startled at the smallness of the stage at Theatre East. "It's about the size of that carpet," she said, gesturing across her apartment. "And as for my salary, it's the same size as the one I got in *On the Town* about fifteen years ago. Now, that's what I call progress." However, she said her friends had pointed out that the theatre's close proximity to her apartment would save her lots of taxi fares. "It's a thought," she admitted, "and I do love the play."

June Harding, cast as Agatha Oxslip, made her New York stage debut in *Ignorants.* With two seasons of summer stock experience, she had arrived in the city the previous fall. "I had worked with other professional actors," Harding recalled, "but Alice was the first professional I worked with on the New York stage—and she was impressive. She was bossy, quite set in her ways. She knew what she wanted. She was entitled to that, don't you agree?"

Cimber concurred with Harding to a degree, but he understood Alice's perspective and position. "I was a fledgling director, and Alice sensed that, but I never felt that she was bossy," he said. "I heard her giving suggestions and saying she wanted to play this and play that. Everything she did seemed to make very good sense. *I* learned from it! She had such great comic timing, you know, and I had never done anything where I had that kind of performance value and so, I was learning from it as well."

During the weeks of rehearsals and performances, Harding sent letters to her mother in Virginia, which offer a behind-the-scenes glimpse of the production. "Dear Mama," Harding wrote on May 20, 1960, "As the opening night draws closer and closer, more people are becoming jittery. Our character man was quite temperamental yesterday during our rehearsal. We all thought he might even take a swing at the director!"

Offstage, a friendship grew between Alice and Harding. On opening night, Alice presented her with a wooden cricket in a cage. The attached card read: "Dearest Daughter: You're going to have a wonderful career, and I am so proud to be Your Mother." On the reverse side, another note from Alice: "This is not the roach Valerie passed on the stairway. This is a Japanese cricket: I hear they bring good luck. All my love, Mom."

Alice's thoughtfulness did not end there. She looked through her closets and gave Harding several of her dresses she no longer wore, including a pink tucked organdy. "I worked on the hem of the dress Alice gave me," Harding wrote to her mother, "beautiful material, so nicely made. Also she gave me a gray cotton, also beautiful and a perfect fit. She seemed so happy that they fitted me so well. She really is a marvelous person. She is leaving the show in two weeks to accept another job out in Texas, just for the money, she said. So, the director is busy looking for a replacement, and then [when one is hired] we will have to hold rehearsals in the afternoons. I sure hate for Alice to leave. She is great to work with."

For weeks, Alice had had a contingency plan, in the event that *Ignorants* had only a brief run. She had signed to appear in another State Fair Musicals production, which would begin rehearsals on June 27. When it appeared that *Ignorants* might run through June, she gave her notice, although that soon proved unnecessary. On June 18, her off-Broadway venture closed at the end of its fourth week. That evening, after the performance, Cavallo gave Alice, Bevans, and Harding each a red rose with a note of thanks. Over champagne, Alice brought out another wardrobe extraction—a black coat for Harding. "Alice made me promise to call her, and said if I didn't, then she would call me," Harding wrote to her mother. "I got to be real fond of her. She said I was indeed 'quite professional' . . . and that in itself is a supreme compliment."

The termination of *The Ignorants Abroad* brought Alice a little free time to study her lines for *Redhead*, a musical production which would open in Dallas on July 11. Although Gus Schirmer was no longer her agent, they had remained steadfast friends. As the director of *Redhead*, he had offered Alice a role in the show. When *Redhead* opened on Broadway in February 1959, it had created a virtual sensation among theatregoers, mainly because of

June Harding, Alice Pearce, Philippa Bevans, and Raymond Myles in The Ignorants Abroad, *1960.*

For the 1960 Dallas production, Finnish dancer Taina Elg, cast as Essie, was paired with six-foot-four baritone Peter Lombard, making his stage debut as the strongman Tom Baxter. Alice and Honey Sanders, as Essie's chirping spinster aunts who own the waxworks, were highlighted in "Behave Yourself," a number in which they offer Essie opposing bits of advice on romance. Elg drew lukewarm reviews in the *Dallas Morning News*—compared to Lombard who "had the animal magnetism of L'il Abner, an aplomb and expansiveness of gesture to go with a looming presence." The *Denton Record-Chronicle* summed up the production with a shrug: "When the show tries to be clever, it only seems flat. When it tries to be a bit ribald, it only seems obvious." Alice's performance went unnoted by either paper, but the *News* saw fit to mention a twenty-one-year-old college kid who "handled his incredibly long form with grace, control, and power." His name was Tommy Tune.

the overpowering personality of its star, Gwen Verdon. However, without her, the Dallas critics were not so certain that lightning would strike twice.

Described as a "rollicking murder mystery set to music," *Redhead*—Tony winner for best musical—was set in an eerie wax museum in Victorian London. Essie Whimple, a plain and awkward sculptress, has reached the age of twenty-nine, "the gateway to spinsterhood," with only wax figures to hold in her arms. In spite of her hovering, protective aunts, she directs all her foolish adoration upon a brawny American vaudevillian, a weightlifter with a local theatre troupe. The story cranks up when the American tries to rescue Essie from the maneuverings of a mysterious strangler intent on murdering her for having pictured him too accurately in one of her wax figures.

When Alice returned to New York, she expected to soon begin rehearsals for *Midgie Purvis*, a new play starring Tallulah Bankhead and intended for an October opening. But the project met with extended delays, so Alice decided to interview for openings in television productions based in Hollywood. This venture proved most successful. Alice spent five weeks in Los Angeles and worked the entire time, eventually appearing on five series.

In mid-October she joined the cast of "The Reluctant Dragon," an episode of *The Shirley Temple Show*, videotaped in color at NBC's Burbank studio. A musical adaptation of Kenneth Grahame's 1898 short story, the whimsical fable centers on a young boy who befriends a docile, poetry-loving dragon who lives in a cave outside a medieval English country town. When the townsfolk discover the beast, they blame it for all their troubles—from the elopement of a young couple and to bread loaves that failed to rise—and send for brave St. George to slay it. After he arrives, the boy convinces the knight to interview the dragon about these accusations. St. George and the dragon agree not to fight and instead stage a fake joust. As the "winner," St. George proclaims that the dragon is reformed, and the villagers then accept him.

Shirley Temple played the boy's older sister who is also convinced of the dragon's harmlessness. John Raitt appeared as St. George, and eleven-year-old Charles Herbert played the boy. The veteran supporting cast, including Jack Weston, Grady Sutton, Dabbs Greer, Lester Dorr, and Barbara Pepper, brought charm and humor to the proceedings. Alice, as village baker Rebecca Free, twisted her rubber face this way and that with comic effect, rallying the townsfolk to summon St. George. Jonathan Harris provided the mincing voice of the reluctant dragon, but inside the pink and purple dragon costume was dancer Don Weismuller, whom Alice had known since 1944, when they performed together in the Broadway version of *On the Town*.

In early November, Alice secured contracts for three other prime-time television productions, but in the midst of those she appeared on a daytime soap opera for the very first time in her career. *Full Circle*, a CBS serial broadcast live from Hollywood, was set in Crowder, Virginia, and starred Dyan Cannon as wealthy widow Lisa Crowder whose had husband died under mysterious circumstances. She falls for a sexy drifter (played by Robert Fortier) who finds himself caught up in the intrigue of the town and its first family. The program featured character actors Byron Foulger, Amzie Strickland, and Jean Byron in supporting roles. It is not known how Alice's character fit into the melodramatic mélange, and it's possible that she may have appeared in only one segment. By this time, the soap was already struggling in the ratings, despite a strong lead-in from *As the World Turns*, then the most popular daytime serial on television. *Full Circle* left the air in early March 1961.

More suited to Alice's comic abilities was a guest spot on the CBS sitcom *Angel*, a new entry that season. Created and produced by Jess Oppenheimer, who had produced *I Love Lucy* for five seasons, *Angel* was often compared to Oppenheimer's previous show—and not just because it was filmed with three cameras before a live Desilu audience. The title character, played by Annie Fargé, was a pretty, young, scatterbrained Frenchwoman married to an American (played by Marshall Thompson). With her distinct—and sometimes indistinct—accent, Angel Smith gets into various predicaments with the culture, language, and customs of her new country. Although *Angel* featured less slapstick comedy, the show's plots were akin to both *I Love Lucy* and *December Bride*, another Desilu production. The latter comparison is not surprising, given that *Angel*'s script consultant was Bill Davenport, one of *December Bride*'s writers. To top all of that off, many of the talented supporting actors appearing on *Angel* were alumni of one or both of the other two Desilu sitcoms—folks like Doris

Singleton, Gale Gordon, Joseph Kearns, Herb Vigran, Madge Blake, Howard McNear, and Mary Wickes.

For her guest segment on *Angel*, Alice played Cassie Turnbull, an inept waitress who is fired after three hours on the job. As a patron witnessing the calamity, Angel feels sorry for Cassie and suggests that she become her housemaid. Cassie's husband and brother are so grateful for Angel's kind offer that they volunteer to serve as butler and violinist for an evening in the Smith home. That night, the situation gets a bit sticky when John's reptilian boss drops in. Mistakenly suspecting John of embezzling, the man assumes the Smiths are using the missing money to employ three servants.

The script, titled "Angel of Mercy," called for Alice to employ a cockney accent, which she accomplished much more skillfully than she had on a *Mister Peepers* segment five years earlier.

At this point in her career, Alice Pearce remained somewhat of an unknown among regular sitcom viewers, simply because her home base of New York prevented frequent appearances on situation comedies, produced predominantly in Hollywood. While she fit perfectly within that particular genre, she was not yet ready to give up opportunities to appear in Broadway productions.

During the third week of November, Alice reported to CBS Television City in Los Angeles to rehearse and film an episode of that network's popular series *The Twilight Zone*. "Static," a teleplay by Charles Beaumont, is the story of Ed Lindsay, an embittered bachelor living in a boarding house, who is dismayed over the mindless programs and commercials aired on the television set shared by the home's residents. He retrieves from the basement an old radio which, in his younger days, he enjoyed as a source of relaxation. Installing it in his bedroom, Ed is elated to hear the radio receiving broadcasts from the 1930s, but when other residents come in to listen to Ed's radio, all they hear is static. Meanwhile, Ed retreats into the past, becoming obsessed with his radio and the hope that life can return to a happier time. Dean Jagger, as Ed, and Carmen Mathews as his former girlfriend, deliver topnotch performances. Alice plays the boarding house proprietor Mrs. Nielson who finds Ed's obsession quite annoying. "He's gone completely psychological," she gripes to another boarder.

Alice was due to begin rehearsals in New York for *Midgie Purvis* the day after Thanksgiving, but just before leaving Los Angeles, she squeezed in a ninety-second bit on *The Ann Sothern Show*, another sitcom produced at the Desilu studio. Sothern starred as Katy O'Connor, assistant manager of the plush Bartley House hotel in New York. Previously that season, veteran character actor Jesse White had joined the show's regulars as slimy Oscar Pudney who operates the hotel's cigar stand. In the episode "Operation Pudney," he conceives a money-making scheme when he takes charge of buying Katy an expensive watch, intended as a surprise gift from hotel employees. When Katy's misled to believe that the collection is for a newly engaged hotel maid named Ethel, she offers her congratulations. Confused, Ethel (played by Alice using her most adenoidal tone) responds, "I've been married to my Herbie for twenty-two years—he's a creep, but after twenty-two years, what difference does it make?"

Alice's sojourn in Los Angeles provided a beneficial opportunity for networking. She made favorable impressions on both Ann Sothern and William Asher—then producer of *The Shirley Temple Show*—who would remember her when suitable roles materialized in future productions. In fact, Alice's success that fall laid the groundwork for her permanent move to the coast, a major shift which would transpire within two years.

In the meantime, Alice's previous engagement—a supporting part in the play *Midgie Purvis*—took precedence. The whimsical piece, starring Tallulah Bankhead in the title role, was written especially for her by Mary Chase, author of the 1944 runaway hit *Harvey*. Bankhead had agreed to do the play back in March, and soon afterwards Alice was approached to join the production. It's quite possible that Bankhead herself suggested Alice for the role. If instead it was the producers' choice, then Bankhead, who had final say-so, would have readily approved. After all, she and Alice had a history; *Midgie* would mark their fourth production together.

Producer Robert Whitehead brought Burgess Meredith on board as director when José Ferrer bowed out due to other commitments. (Meredith had "considerably less directing experience" but had known Bankhead since their romantic fling back in 1935.) Colorful sets and elegant costumes were designed by Ben Edwards and Guy Kent, respectively. Enacting Chase's houseful of zany characters were seasoned professionals like Clinton Sundberg, William Redfield, Nydia Westman, and John Cecil Holm. Seven-year-old Pia Zadora, making her Broadway debut, was chosen as one of the three children in the cast.

Midgie Purvis was the story of a wealthy woman whose serious-minded son, on the eve of his wedding, is embarrassed by what he regards as her unbecomingly youthful eccentricities. Hurt by his disapproval, she goes away, disguises herself as on old crone and becomes a babysitter but retains her juvenile attitude. In the back room of a candy store, she creates an enchanting hideaway for herself and her three young charges. Midgie's hoydenish pranks cause all sorts of complications, which are finally resolved by her son's changed attitude. Alice was cast as Dorothy Plunkett, the mother of the bride-elect whom the mother of the groom has no desire to meet.

Unfortunately, *Midgie Purvis* was illogically constructed. "The play wasn't right from the beginning," said Bankhead biographer Lee Israel, "and it could not be made right." Although possessing "one of the most original comedy minds," Chase produced works that were customarily "disorganized and needed to be put together." Despite numerous revisions during both the New York rehearsals and the out-of-town tryouts, *Midgie* was doomed to become, as critic Howard Taubman put it, a work which "started with a germ of an idea that must have seemed happy to its author . . . but in the translation to the stage somehow grew into a gross, unmanageable plant."

Burgess Meredith praised Chase's "sharp wit and offbeat imagination," yet he maintained that the play didn't work because its "individual scenes were fine, [but] they didn't add up." Meredith demanded rewrites, but Chase's subsequent efforts confounded Meredith even more. "She would create not a new sentence, not a new paragraph, but a whole new scene—overnight." The reams of new material overwhelmed and confused the actors, and this sort of thing continued throughout the tryouts in Philadelphia and Washington, D. C.

Henry Murdock of the *Philadelphia Inquirer* deemed the play "only intermittently funny" when it opened there on December 26, 1960. Blaming Meredith, he thought the pace was too frantic and the volume too high as characters popped in and out of doors, chasing each other about. Ernie Schier complained in the *Evening Bulletin* that Chase was "almost totally lacking in a sense of direction." Jerry Gaghan of the *Philadelphia Daily News* simply said *Midgie Purvis* didn't "seem to be long for this world."

Midgie Purvis (Tallulah Bankhead), second from left, meets her prospective in-laws Luther Plunkett (John Cecil Holm), Dorothy Plunkett (Alice Pearce) and Vivian Stubbs (Janice Mars) in Midgie Purvis, *1961.*

mother-in-law but now his prospective (snoopy) mother-in-law, but also her castmates John Cecil Holm and Janice Mars who played her character's stuffy husband and inseparable sister. They, along with Bankhead and William Redfield (as Canfield), were required to learn an entirely new scene in one day and play it that night.

Chase, above all, realized their frustrations and delivered handwritten apologies to each of them. "Dear, dear Alice Pearce," she wrote from the Jefferson Hotel in Washington, "I believe you know how much delight you give me as an artist—me and everyone else who sees you. But I also want you to know how much I appreciate your beautiful spirit these last two weeks in absorbing rewrite after rewrite, making a moment work—only to lose it. I thank you for your patience—and I only ask for it a little longer."

Meanwhile, Bankhead, suffering from both emphysema and an insecurity related to her role's physical stunts, grew testy. "She continued to accept new material," says her biographer Joel Lobenthal, "but in her dressing room on tour she heatedly told Meredith that the rewrites were making this the most grueling pre-Broadway experience of her career." Meredith maintained that Bankhead's loss of confidence resulted in an unfriendly attitude toward the rest of the cast. "Everyone's perfor-

By the time the play opened at the National on January 10, 1961, its three acts had been reduced to two, but critics were still left wondering what Chase's message was. Jay Carmody of Washington's *Evening Star* suspected that the playwright's imagination was "running away with her or from us." With the New York opening less than three weeks away, Meredith insisted on a drastic change. In Chase's original script, all of the action took place in one evening, with Bankhead dressed in her old lady's garb from the beginning scene until very near the play's conclusion. The revised beginning introduced a glamorous Midgie not yet inspired to disguise herself as the aged babysitter. Another important change was that Midgie's son Canfield, who had been married in the original version, was now merely engaged to be married. This alteration affected not only Alice, formerly playing Canfield's snoopy

Janice Mars, circa 1960.

mance suffered," he said, "and it was difficult to develop any esprit de corps."

Others remembered things differently. "I thought she was terrific," Pia Zadora recalled in 1991. "When I met Tallulah for the first time, she looked down at me, and said, 'How long have you been in show business, young lady?' I looked at my brand new Mickey Mouse wristwatch and said, 'Exactly twenty minutes.' Tallulah let out one of her loud throaty laughs, and I was her pet from then on."

"I remember being surprised at how nervous Miss Bankhead was," said Janice Mars. "She had a severe problem with her eyes, being afflicted with a frequent tendency to bat her eyelids rapidly, in addition to slight facial tics. These symptoms she managed to control onstage. Once, during a rehearsal she made an exit up some onstage stairs. There was a ter-

rified shriek. A stagehand had neglected to put up the backstage high platform for her protection. She was much afraid of heights, and it really upset the poor lady. I felt, so did others, very sorry for her because she tried so hard to put on a brave front and was always kind and courteous to her supporting cast."

At the time, Mars was best known for her nightly performances as a singer in her own small Sixth Avenue club, the Baq Room, "a dark, dank little box in the back of a rowdy Irish pub called the Midtown Bar." Although she and Alice shared a common friend—Beau Bergersen, Mars' nightclub accompanist—Mars admitted that she was never well acquainted with Alice. However, as a fellow performer, Mars knew her as "a frank and honest person, friendly and kind—she was very well liked by everyone."

During their stay in Washington, John F. Kennedy was inaugurated as the nation's thirty-fifth president. "It was bitter cold," Mars recalled. "The theatre was located close to Kennedy's inaugural proceedings and we could hear and see a little of it from the theatre lobby."

Two weeks later, on February 1, Bankhead's usual claque seated themselves among other opening-night theatregoers at the Martin Beck Theatre. As the curtain rose, revealing a grand staircase, they breathlessly awaited their idol's entrance. Then came Bankhead's "unmistakable singing voice from offstage tremulating 'Yes! We Have No Bananas.'" At the top of the stairs she appeared in a dazzling white satin evening ensemble, unable to speak her next line for several minutes while her fans indulged in a frenzied welcome. The wild catcalls were amplified when she gleefully slid down the banister.

Alice, the master of the snarl, with John Cecil Holm in Midgie Purvis, *1961.*

costumes, were to get entangled in a long telephone wire in the Purvis mansion." It seemed that whole purpose of *Midgie*'s supporting characters—excluding the children—is to be made fools of, but as the *Evening Star* noted, "it comes off too easily here to be altogether the effect needed."

A couple of critics singled out Alice, but barely. "Except for Pia Zadora, the remainder of the cast contribute little that's standout," *Variety* allowed. "Alice Pearce manages to pull an occasional laugh, but it's a struggle." Walter Kerr observed: "The [play] wastes time on a batch of snoopy [women] who aren't worth the cost of their costumes (except for Alice Pearce, who is worth every bit of the purple hydrangea that she wears on her head and that seems about to devour her if she doesn't stop snarling)."

However, the New York critics, in general, were not as enthused. John McClain of the *Journal-American* noted that the opening scene gave promise of a delightful evening, but "suddenly the play seemed to run away with the author, and from then onward it raced downhill on its meandering and diffuse course." Walter Kerr of the *Herald Tribune* called Bankhead's Midgie her "best performance in years." Still, most reviewers agreed with McClain that Bankhead "was great, but the play ain't."

Several reviewers criticized Meredith's "weak" staging, particularly a scene involving Alice and her sidekicks. "Mr. Meredith implied it would be pretty hilarious," grumbled Frank Aston of the *World-Telegraph & Sun*, "if Alice Pearce, John Cecil Holm, and Janice Mars, all of them indignant and all looking stylish in Guy Kent

Two days after the play opened, a weekend blizzard dumped seventeen inches of snow on New York. Traffic was at a standstill. Due to the weather and the equally brutal reviews, *Midgie Purvis* largely sank without a trace. It had lasted for only twenty-one performances, marking Alice's briefest time treading the Broadway boards. "The play was rather charming," Janice Mars admitted, "but the humor was a bit light for the tough New York audiences. We did close pretty quick, and I never met Alice Pearce again." Ted Hook, who at the time was Bankhead's secretary/companion, insisted that "if Buzz Meredith hadn't made poor Mary Chase change [the play] so much and if José Ferrer had directed it, it probably would have been Bankhead's] swan song classic." While the closing sent Tallulah Bankhead into a deep depression, Alice Pearce—having seen the handwriting on the wall—resiliently finalized plans to return to the coast for more television work.

In the meantime, two amusing photographic projects—one for profit, the other for pleasure—had occupied part of Alice's free time during the *Midgie* fiasco. First, she modeled for *Look* magazine photographer Douglas Kirkland for a one-page feature on electric can openers. In three comical poses, Alice employed her rubber face to best advantage as she tested various models, while dressed appropriately for each design. For instance, Alice donned white evening gloves and thick coils of pearls and rhinestones to open a tiny tin of truffles using a gold-plated can opener, complete with clock and timer.

In a similar vein, but far more ridiculous, Alice had a high old time posing for her friend Cris Alexander whose enthusiastic mission it was to provide more than 150 uproarious photographs for Patrick Dennis' latest book, *Little Me*.

Cris had first met Dennis—whose real name was Edward Everett Tanner III—back in 1956 when the author made an unexpected appearance at the first rehearsal for the Broadway adaptation of his wildly popular novel *Auntie Mame*. "It wasn't until Pat [Tanner] took to materializing at the Philadelphia tryouts that I began to know and marvel at this amazingly sensitive and kind man," Cris recalled in his preface for the 2002 re-release of *Little Me*. "We would gravitate to the same bar after performances and soon found that we shared enthusiasms for many more things than vodka."

Meanwhile, Tanner learned that Cris was truly a Renaissance man whose talents included portrait painting and photography, both of which were self-taught. (Cris, affecting the accent of his Mississippi kinfolk, confessed in an interview in 2003, "I never had no trainin' nowhere!") Visiting Cris' studio one day, Tanner paid a visit to the toilet where he marveled at the campy photos which plastered its walls. The seed for a "phony autobiography of a rotten movie star" was planted that day, but it would not be until 1960 that Tanner got serious and asked Cris to create the photos for what would become *Little Me*.

Billed by E. P. Dutton & Company as a "dead-pan parody of the typical star's typical autobiography," *Little Me* is the tale of lovably rapacious Belle Poitrine whose climb from the "wrong side of the tracks" in Venezuela, Illinois, carries her to the dazzling lights of Times Square and Hollywood—a journey hilariously punctuated by multiple marriages and love affairs, triumphs and failures, and a murder trial.

Cris suggested his friend Jeri Archer, "a sometime actress and 'model,'" to portray the voluptuous Belle. "Pat had surrounded our star with so many other fascinating characters that I feared we might end up with a cast of thousands," recalled Cris, who rounded up his photogenic friends to fill the roles. Included were his "five best pals from shows past," including Alice (*On the Town*), Jan Sterling (*Present Laughter*), Kaye Ballard (*That's the Ticket*), Dody Goodman (*Wonderful Town*), and Peggy Cass (*The Amazing Adele* and *Auntie Mame*). Pat Tanner's wife, son, daughter, and the children's nanny were also recruited to pose, as well as Cris' domestic partner Shaun O'Brien, a successful dancer with the New York City Ballet.

"The whole thing was marvelous fun for all of us," O'Brien recalled. "There was always a bottle of Scotch or something around, and Pat would be carrying on, and we'd all come up with ideas and start laughing. Pat would say, 'Get me a cute blonde!' and I'd go to some girl at [the ballet] and say, 'Do you want to be in this book, just for fun?' We did all the casting like that."

*Alice as a revamped Winnie, "Principessa
Pizzicato," in* Little Me. *Cris Alexander photo.*

*Jeri Archer and Alice pose as Belle Poitrine and Winnie Erskine,
fellow inmates in a "boarding school" in Patrick Dennis'
outrageous book* Little Me. *Archer was born in Summit, New
Jersey, exactly three months before Alice was born in Manhattan.
Cris Alexander photo.*

"Many of the pictures were taken against a
blank wall," explained Cris, "and then superimposed onto an appropriate background." Some
sessions were shot on location, however. Much
use was made of the Tanner townhouse, as well
as Cris and Shaun's top-floor apartment at
134 East Sixty-First Street. For Cris, matching photos with the text's absurdities was the
proverbial field day, from beginning to end.
Little Me, published in October 1961, got great
reviews and remained on the *New York Times*
bestseller list for nine months.

By late February 1961, Alice was
back in Los Angeles where she rented
a unit at the Montecito Apartments, a
ten-story Art Deco structure which had
originally served as a hotel. Located
on Franklin Avenue at the base of the
Hollywood Hills, the Montecito had once been
the home of such stars as Ronald Reagan and
Mickey Rooney, but by the late 1950s, it had
become somewhat run-down. "The place was
inhabited mostly by New York actors who had
come out to work or, between shows, to look
for jobs," explained Carleton Carpenter, who
had lived there for a spell in 1958. "One and all
called the Montecito 'the poor man's Chateau
Marmont,' referring to the posh, star-filled residence on Sunset Boulevard." Nevertheless, the

Montecito would be Alice's West Coast base for the next three months.

Almost as soon as she unpacked, Alice reported to the NBC studios in Burbank to film another episode of *The Shirley Temple Show*. "The Princess and the Goblins," adapted from an 1872 story by British author George MacDonald, followed the basic plotline of the original but glossed over the darker elements to play primarily as a comedy. The tale was set in a legendary kingdom where the ruler's discontented subjects (who "frowned too much, quarreled too much, loved to hate, but hated to love") were banished by him to live below the ground where things only worsened over time. Known as the goblins, these exiled creatures sprout horns and tails, loathe sunshine, and

Shirley Temple surrounded by goblins Alice Pearce, Arthur Malet, Jack Weston, and Barbara Perry (extreme upper right), among others, in "The Princess and the Goblins," a segment of The Shirley Temple Show, *1961.*

go berserk when poetry is recited. After nine years underground, they vow to harm the king's only daughter Irene (Temple) before her eighteenth birthday. Their plans are thwarted by the princess' guardian spirit Esperanza (Irene Hervey) via a handsome young miner named Curdie Peterson (Jack Ging) who has fallen in love with the princess. The goblins are forgiven their evil deeds and reform.

The band of grumpy goblins has as its king Jack Weston—almost unrecognizable behind the "Munsters-like" makeup created by John Chambers—and Alice as his strident wife who

steadfastly clutches a stuffed white owl, symbolic of mythology's underworld messenger-bird.

Although predating *The Munsters* by three years, the ironic humor employed by writer Richard DeRoy mirrors that of the iconic CBS sitcom. The king, hoping to marry off Prince Gripe (Arte Johnson) to Princess Irene, enticingly suggests to his son, "You could look forward to a lifetime of misery with that girl." But Gripe shudders and says that he'd be ashamed to be seen in public with the blonde beauty—à la Marilyn Munster. "I'm in love with Zelda Snide," he winks, nudging his father, "Y'ever seen her figure? Like a pretzel!"

Meanwhile, Alice amplifies her grotesque appearance with her typical facial contortions and grating nasality. Near the conclusion, when the goblins confess that they really don't enjoy being so negative, Alice socks Arte Johnson, saying, "Do you think I like popping you all the time? Why, it hurts you more than it hurts me!"

"The Princess and the Goblins" reunited Alice with Temple and Weston and introduced her to the talented Mary Wickes, who lent trademark touches to Princess Irene's fretful nurse Lootie.

Two weeks later, Alice returned to the Desilu studios on North Cahuenga Boulevard for another guest role on *The Ann Sothern Show*, now in its third season. However, the reunion was bittersweet because the episode happened to be the series finale. In February, Sothern's show, owned jointly by her and Desilu, had been dropped by its sponsor, General Foods. For its first two seasons, the program had done nicely in a Monday night slot, but when the sponsor switched it to Thursday nights at the beginning of the third, it had slumped steadily in the ratings.

In those days, it was quite rare for a sitcom to end production with a special episode which wrapped up any unsettled business. Most final episodes gave no hint that the series would not return the following fall. But *The Ann Sothern Show* broke new ground. Since the first season, there had been somewhat of a romantic undertone in the relationship between Sothern's character Katy and her boss Mr. Devery. However, few sitcoms risked rocking the boat by having leading characters marry each other—that very thing, some said, had helped kill off NBC's *Mister Peepers* back in 1955. Since Sothern's show was already cancelled, the producers figured it wouldn't matter now to make Katy and Mr. Devery an official couple.

The final episode's title—deliberately ironic—was "The Beginning." Katy's office sidekick Olive believes that Devery cares for Katy and urges Katy to make him aware of it in order to get him to propose. Olive's husband warns Devery, who remains doubtful that Katy would stoop to such scheming. When coincidences make it appear to Devery that Katy may be up to something, he plays right along, acting nonchalant even when she decides to take a six-months leave from work. Finally realizing that she's serious, Devery rushes to share his true feelings with Katy who has already boarded a plane for Rio. Seated between them is passenger Lahoma St. Cyr (played by Alice), who at first sides with downcast Katy but then is swept up by Devery's sincere proposal. Lahoma looks on with approval as Katy accepts and the plane leaves the ground. In an atypically subdued performance, Alice is warm yet comical.

Alice's next characterization was even more of a departure. She was chosen for the straight role of Hilda, the nurse to a wheelchair-bound girl (Angela Cartwright) in the Warner Brothers production of *Lad: A Dog*. Adapted from the 1919 novel by Albert Payson Terhune, *Lad* is the sentimental story of a collie which is "less dog than a canine miracle worker." Among other feats, Lad wins a dog show which is fixed in favor of a jealous neighbor's pup, protects his farm from poachers, and rescues his mistress from a burning barn.

In between these heroic acts is a climactic scene involving Hilda and her charge Angela, a girl whose shock from her mother's death has left her unable to walk. Angela is smitten by her neighbors' collie Lad, much to the irritation of her wealthy father (Carroll O'Connor), a real blowhard. One afternoon, when they're visiting Sunnybank Farm, where Lad lives with his owners, Hilda settles Angela on a blanket under a shade tree while she goes to

Alice Pearce and Angela Cartwright in the Warner Brothers production of Lad: A Dog *(1962).*

Beautiful spring weather and the picaresque setting made *Lad* a pleasant shoot, despite a few mishaps. On Alice's first day of filming, she fell and hurt her knee, a relatively minor accident treated with first aid. A week later, Peter Breck, who played Lad's owner, sustained a deep abrasion under his kneecap, an injury also treated onsite. Most shooting days at the ranch were long—sometimes twelve hours—with the morning commute from Burbank beginning at 6 o'clock. Principal photography wrapped on May 19, only four days behind schedule. Alice and Angela Cartwright were each paid $500 per week, while Carroll O'Connor's weekly pay was four times theirs.

fetch the child a drink of water. Meanwhile, a copperhead emerges from the rushes and slithers toward the girl, but Lad pounces on it. Angela's screams bring Hilda running, mistakenly thinking the dog is attacking the girl. As Hilda beats Lad with her umbrella, Angela is so stunned by her nurse's fury that she rises and walks to defend her savior.

Alice began filming her role for *Lad: A Dog* on April 21, 1961. Of the ten days she was required on the set, all but one were spent at the Golden Oak Ranch, twenty-three miles north of Warner Brothers' Burbank location. Commonly called the "Disney ranch," the 315-acre spread had been purchased by the Walt Disney Studios two years earlier but was frequently leased to other studios. The lakefront house serving as the home of Lad's owners had been used the previous summer as Brian Keith's house in Disney's production of *The Parent Trap*.

Lad: A Dog was released on May 1, 1962. Most reviewers panned it as being too saccharine. "The plot is as soggy as a dish of dog food and becomes patently preposterous as it chugs to its ending," said Kevin Kelly of the *Boston Globe*. "There's neither bark nor bite in the acting, but there are some nice Technicolor shots of Lad." With reviews like that, it's not surprising that the film turned out to be a dog at the box office, despite a rather natural performance from Breck and a skillful turn by O'Connor, still a decade away from his signature role of Archie Bunker on *All in the Family*. Alice, almost unrecognizable under a drab wimple and enveloped in a voluminous gray cloak, did her best to give some life to the humorless Hilda. It would remain the oddest bit of casting in her film career, and, thankfully, one not to be repeated—all because of the guiding hand of a new friend.

CHAPTER TWENTY
Broadway Swan Song

*"First they cut her hair, then they cut her part
and then they fired her."*

George Morris was a whiz. That's how actor Christopher Plummer remembered him. In 1953, George—a "chubby sheepdog of a youth"—was a New York-based television agent partnered with Jane Broder, one of the entertainment industry's most respected theatrical agents. That summer George had wangled a leading role for Plummer, then a twenty-three-year-old unknown, in an episode of *Studio One*. Following that broadcast, television work "began to come thick and fast" for the newcomer. George had a gift for enabling the careers of actors like Plummer—an energy he channeled following his own unsuccessful attempts at making the rounds a few years before.

George had hankered for an acting career since the early 1940s during his high school days in Aurora, Illinois. He attended Northwestern University "for a few minutes," hated it, and quit to join the military. "George went to New York almost immediately after his discharge from the Army Air Corps in 1945," recalls his niece Carolyn Roesner. "He got a small flat on Forty-Second Street and used his GI benefits to pay for [tuition at] the Neighborhood Playhouse." Despite George's training and several years of experience in summer stock, he never became a successful actor. However, according to his lifelong friend Jack Denton, George followed the motto "Never

George Morris, circa 1950. Photo courtesy Carolyn Roesner.

regret!" and eventually "peeled off into agenting and got a real kick out of it."

George's senior partner Jane Broder eschewed the medium of television, so those assignments were delegated to him. By late 1959, he had become so adroit that he decided to go out on his own, which meant relocating to Los Angeles where most television series were produced. Early the following year, George rented and furnished an office at 9490 Brighton Way in Beverly Hills. "And [then he] sat there," related Denton. It was tough for a long while, but

George "hustled and told the truth and started selling clients and succeeding."

George's specialty was landing perfectly suited roles for character actors, and that got Alice Pearce's attention. She had switched agents three times since dropping Gus Schirmer in 1957, and now, four years later, she was eager to sign with someone on the coast who could find more television and film roles for her. Alice was impressed with George's stable of uniquely talented clients who "swore by him." At that time, they included Ed Begley, Robert Emhardt, John Fiedler, Margaret Hamilton, Doro Merande, and Jean Stapleton—as well as Alice's future *Bewitched* castmates Marion Lorne and David White. So, during the production of *Lad: A Dog*, Alice contracted with George, and right away he prepared her first-ever resume and updated her entry in the *Academy Players Directory*. After completing *Lad*, Alice immediately returned to New York, confident that she had made the right choice. She had gained not only a seasoned agent but, as time would tell, a trustworthy friend.

Alice remained in the east for the next eleven months, a circumstance which would prove to be the final stretch in her native city. The month of June was relatively free, and it provided her with a rare opportunity to reconnect with a young fellow whom she'd known since the day he was born. Channing George Lowe, an eight-year-old with curly light brown hair and an enthusiastic grin, was the only child of Alice's friend Carol Channing. Everyone called him "Chan."

"My mother told me that Alice was one of the people who, along with John Rox, came to visit us in her hospital room on the day I was born," says Chan of that spring day in 1953. His father was Alexander Carson, whom Channing would divorce in 1956. That same year she married Charles Lowe who later adopted Chan. While Channing once referred to Alice as Chan's godmother, Chan recalls that his parents called Alice his "love aunt." "The 'love' part is certainly accurate," he affirms. "It flowed from her, and it was returned in full measure."

Since Channing was often on the road with engagements, Alice saw Chan—who accompanied his mother on tours—only occasionally. When their paths intersected in Manhattan, Alice would suddenly appear to take Chan out on a "date," during which he was treated exactly as though he were an adult. "My memories of her," Chan explains, "are colored by the emotions, fantasies and intensity of a small boy experiencing many things for the first time."

"I don't remember exactly how it happened," Chan says, "but when I was about five, we developed a secret 'pact.' (Her word. She had to explain to me what a 'pact' was—a sacred agreement.) This involved the color green, and it was understood that whenever we went out together, we would each wear green on our person. In her case, this consisted of bright green lipstick and green nail polish—I have no idea where she found these items in the late 1950s. When we were apart, we would send each other lengthy letters. She would sign (or should I say, 'smear') hers 'Love, Aunt Alice' with the green lipstick."

While Alice's motivation for these green adornments lacks proof, fans of her friend Pat Tanner would readily endorse Mame Dennis as the inspiration. Tanner's most famous protagonist "Auntie Mame" wore green nail polish upon meeting her orphaned nephew Patrick for the first time—both in print and on the Broadway stage. Anyone familiar with either version knows that free-spirited Mame is a flamboyant and exuberant woman who lovingly exposes her nephew to the world of her eccentric, bohemian friends. Who knows, perhaps Alice Pearce secretly imagined herself

Chan Lowe and his mother Carol Channing, 1960.

tiny bar, and a large grand piano tucked in the corner that Goldie would play in the evenings. I felt very grown up sitting there with Alice, toasting her with my Shirley Temple while she sipped her martini. Goldie and other sundry types would drop in on us during the meal, and afterward Goldie would invite us up to his living quarters above the restaurant for drinks. For a young boy, it was the height of sophistication and urbanity. To Alice, my age was irrelevant."

"Another fond memory," Chan continues, "is when I spent the whole day with Alice, when I was around eight. She showed up one morning to pick me up, and said she'd take me anywhere I wanted to go. I suggested we climb to the top of the Statue of Liberty, and sure enough, we got on the ferry, cruised over, and poor Alice and I hiked all the way up to the crown. Afterward, we bought ingredients for a picnic and spread it out on a tablecloth in Central Park. It was a magical day. When she brought me home that evening, Alice was exhausted. My parents were apologetic. She laughed, [saying] that that was what Chan wanted to do, and by God, we were going to do what Chan wanted."

Alice's idyllic interlude with Chan, however, took place on the brink of the most bitterly disappointing experience of her theatrical career—one that she did not see coming. Nineteen years a stage professional, Alice had earned the respect of producers and directors like Leonard Sillman, George Abbott, and John C. Wilson. She was the darling of playwrights Anita Loos, Truman Capote, and Mary Chase. Designers Oliver Smith and Miles White counted her among their dearest friends; likewise the composers Hugh Martin and Baldwin Bergersen. Even stage managers became her fans. Most

as an "Auntie Mame" figure in the life of little Chan Lowe. His memories of her certainly suggest that.

"When I was seven years old, my family moved to New York City, where Aunt Alice also lived," recalls Chan, "so our 'assignations' became more frequent. She lived in the same apartment building near the East River as the legendary Broadway composer Charles Gaynor (also a family friend), with a view of the Fifty-Ninth Street bridge from her window. She got a kick out of taking me to the House of Chan restaurant and telling the waiters that I was the owner—she said it would get us better service."

"Aunt Alice would also take me, on occasion, to a small dive owned by the restauranteur Goldie Hawkins. You had to descend a flight of stairs from the sidewalk to get into Goldie's. It comprised only about five tables, a

of all, Alice's fellow performers depended on her support, candor, and good humor—especially Tallulah Bankhead and Nancy Walker who more than once saw to it that she had a role in their vehicles. "Everyone loved Alice," recalled actor Richard Deacon, "*except* Noël Coward, and they disliked each other much."

Prior to 1961, Alice and Coward had met casually at least twice, but their mutual aversion did not materialize until after theirs became a professional relationship. That year, in late winter, Alice had successfully auditioned for Coward who was in New York to cast the much-heralded production of *Sail Away*, for which he would write

Elinor Spencer Bollard (Alice Pearce) dictates her latest novel to her niece Nancy Foyle (Patricia Harty) in Sail Away: *"Page 56. Chapter 5. Sylvia galloped into the paddock, her hair flying in the wind."*

the music, lyrics, and book, as well as direct. Determined to succeed, Coward would put more into this project than any other in his forty-year career.

Sail Away took place on a British cruise ship sailing between New York and the Mediterranean. Alice was cast as passenger Mrs. Elinor Spencer-Bollard, a famous American novelist, described by Coward as "a well-disposed megalomaniac and the ideal of women's clubs from San Francisco to Portland, Maine"—an appropriate addition to Alice's repertoire of oddballs. Although she appeared and reappeared throughout both acts, Mrs. Spencer-Bollard was more or less an incidental role, rather like Mrs. Ella Spofford in *Gentlemen Prefer Blondes* only a bit more substantial. From her deck chair, the old frump dictates "old-fashioned heart-throb trash" to her niece-secretary. Her dictation is interspersed with derisive com-

ments—laced with quotes from Keats and Wordsworth—about fellow passengers.

Sail Away's lead characters were brassy Mimi Paragon (played by Elaine Stritch), who as cruise hostess is in constant trouble with the tourists, and Verity Craig (opera star Jean Fenn), an unhappily married passenger who falls in love with a younger man (James Hurst). Patricia Harty was cast as Mrs. Spencer-Bollard's niece Nancy, and Grover Dale signed on as Nancy's love interest.

Coward found it very tricky to keep all three stories balanced. "The danger of writing musicals, often, is that the book gets in the way," he explained in a *Theatre Arts* interview. "I've tried to keep the dialogue down to a minimum." The show's seventeen musical numbers, not counting reprises, left Coward with "no time to develop the characters"—a consequence which would eventually prove detrimental to *Sail Away*. His fellow playwright William Marchant estimated that Coward had not attempted "anything even half so ambitious for longer than a decade."

When rehearsals began at the Broadhurst on July 10, 1961, "a sense of something very important and of the highest quality informed the mood of the participants." At week's end, a triumphant Coward wrote in his diary: "I don't remember, since *Bitter Sweet*, being so completely happy with a company. There is not one of them that I don't like ... the whole thing is quite obviously headed for enormous success. There will probably be a few minor dramas and miseries but I do not envisage serious ones." Coward's prophetic powers turned out to be both a hit and a miss.

"Before Alice went into rehearsals," asserted Cris Alexander, "I remember she said, 'Imagine, imagine how wonderful really being in a show of Mr. Coward's— I'm so thrilled!' But it really wasn't very long before she *dreaded* him. She didn't too much explain why, but as you can well imagine—not to say that she was limited—there was really only *one* way, if she was going to be good [in the part], that Alice could have done anything. It wasn't like, you know, 'Would you like it sweet or sour?' It was just how it came out. And he apparently had quite some different ideas and really just kept practically chewing her out. He got a thing about her and was not gentlemanly!"

Such misbehavior was evidently not noted by Don Ross of the *Herald Tribune* when he observed Coward directing a scene between Alice and Patricia Harty one morning in July. "Coward, the kind of director who shows the actors what he wants by doing it himself," wrote Ross, "flung himself onto the sofa where Miss Pearce sat, put her black handbag on his right arm and rattled off her lines in the rattle-brained way he wanted them rattled. Miss Pearce got the point and gave an inspired per-

formance of Noël Coward imitating a silly lady novelist. 'Lovely,' Coward breathed. 'Lovely,' Miss Pearce breathed." Alice obviously felt at ease with Coward at this point, hence her final bit of parroting "The Master," down to the last syllable. A few days later, any and all rapport between them would be shattered.

William Marchant, though not an intimate of Coward, was yet allowed to "attach himself unofficially" to the production in order to observe his mentor in action from *Sail Away*'s earliest stages straight through to its Broadway premiere. Marchant, regarding Coward as "the [world's] best confectioner of light entertainment," relished the opportunity and later recorded an insider's history of the show in his 1975 memoir *The Privilege of His Company*.

Marchant noted that despite the musical's overabundance of songs, not a single one included Alice—an exclusion which made her most unhappy, and understandably so, given that heretofore she had sung in every musical and revue of her Broadway career. "From time to time this lack had been pointed out to Noël," wrote Marchant, "who said, 'There simply isn't *room!*' and she had to be content with that." But frustration got the better of Alice, according to Marchant:

> One hot July Sunday afternoon, the day before the production was set to leave for its trial run in Boston, the show was performed from beginning to end without interruption before a handful of invited spectators. It went remarkably smoothly, all things considered, and very much as planned except for a series of novel exits made by Miss Pearce that had never been rehearsed and that surprised the members of the company every bit as much as it did Noël. She had a number of brief scenes throughout the action,

each one terminated with a slow and plodding march on uncertain legs from one side of the stage to the other. That afternoon each of her exits was embellished with an operatic delivery of the first line of one of Noël's famous songs, from "I'll See You Again" to "Mad About the Boy," an interpolation that was not at all the amusing invention she had hoped it would be. There were audible groans from the auditorium and here and there a shocked, nervous laugh. But Noël smiled benignly on the proceedings and showed nothing of his displeasure. He reserved that until the very end, when, after hearing the usual theatrical courtesies from those who had seen the run-through, he went directly backstage and climbed the stairs to Miss Pearce's dressing room. The entire backstage area of the Broadhurst Theatre rang with vituperation and abuse. The word "unprofessional" was used several times. He had searched his long memory and in it could find, he said, no single example of equivalent insubordination or impudent mockery. It was he who had insisted on her being cast in the role over the objections of others because it was rumored that she needed the job. Deliberately to introduce snatches of his songs from other shows as if he were apologizing for the quality of the new songs he had written for *Sail Away*, and at the same time reminding the audience of his past successes, was expressive of a vulgarity and self-advertisement unparalleled in his experience. There may have been tears, for Noël's voice reduced its volume suddenly. Most of the company stood about with looks of deep embarrassment and worry: Miss Pearce was a great favorite with them all ...

The episode was misunderstood. Many in the company, particularly the singers and dancers of the chorus, sided with the comedienne and were unable to conceal their championship of her. One or two of them may have said a few ill-chosen words on the subject to the stage manager or other representative of the management. The disagreement was magnified into a *cause* that was soon said to be a feud. Noël always disliked backstage warfare, and stood above the battle like a disinterested spectator, but in this fray he was nominated as the principal belligerent. It was largely for this reason, I think, that for the rest of the theatrical life of *Sail Away* he never exchanged more than simple courtesies with Alice.

Marchant's account appears to be the only specific source of the discord between Alice and Coward. Richard Deacon did not provide details of their mutual animosity. Cris Alexander's reminiscence—given that he was not a part of the production—may have included a fair amount of assumption. Elaine Stritch, when contacted in 1989, elected not to reveal any distinct memories of Alice: "I can only tell you she was the dearest, not to mention funniest, lady I have ever known. I adored her and MISS her." In 2018, dancer Grover Dale, who also declared a love for Alice, was "surprised that she had issues with Coward." Alan Helms, cast in a small role as one of the passengers, was equally clueless: "I recall [Alice] as cheerful, witty, and cooperative, and also a

Cruise director Mimi Paragon (Elaine Stritch) attempts to persuade Mrs. Spencer-Bollard (Alice) to give a talk to the passengers one evening during the voyage in Sail Away, *1961.* New York Herald Tribune *critic Walter Kerr said Alice "flicked her blue and red crystal beads to handsome effect."*

one and only Alice Pearce," Coward told her that Alice could make "pass the mustard" sound funny.

Marchant, who professed a fondness for Alice, felt that she had been "merely unwise" to alter her performance, just that once. Unwise or not, such a display took guts. Surely by then, Alice had heard of Coward's legendary arguments with "nearly every star of one of his plays," especially those who dared to embellish his "pristinely perfect" dialogue. Once, he had even torn Tallulah Bankhead's performance to shreds, inciting a three-year rift between them.

One critic, after reading Marchant's memoir, determined that Coward was "a brittle man, imprisoned by his public image and enthroned in self-enclosed majesty." Perhaps after his tirade in Alice's dressing room, she shared that opinion. At the very least, Coward was no longer the same gentleman whose praise had moved Alice to tears at the Blue Angel fourteen years earlier. "She went through some unpleasant times," Cris affirmed, "and I remember her saying that it was such a blow to her because he had just been one of her idols." Amazingly, Coward didn't fire Alice. Despite the underlying strife, she stuck it out and remained with the show for its entire run.

During the Boston tryout, which began on August 9, Coward realized that the focus of *Sail Away* was divided. While the energetic Stritch received raves, the romantic duo of Fenn and Hurst were saddled with a storyline that slowed down the entire show. Still, the production was a sell-out for "four solid

great favorite in the company. I knew nothing about any unhappy experience with Noël."

Neither Alice nor Coward seems to have left any record of the incident Marchant describes or any other difficulty between them. Coward's uncensored diaries, published posthumously, are filled with blistering critiques of both friends and enemies, yet the name of Alice Pearce is absent. In fact, he seems to have mentioned her only twice in published interviews, once in passing when listing *Sail Away*'s cast in the *Theatre Arts* interview and again upon the company's arrival in Boston for the initial tryout. When Peggy Doyle of the *Boston Evening American* inquired about "the

weeks in the full blazing heat of summer." Famous faces in the audience included Judy Garland, Kay Thompson, Alfred Lunt and Lynn Fontanne, and Eleanor Roosevelt who dined with Coward before the show on August 15. Two nights later first lady Jackie Kennedy arrived at the Colonial Theatre, causing more commotion than any other celebrity. The company (including Alice) was introduced to both presidential wives.

Alice's *Sail Away* notices were good. "She is greeted by warm applause," observed the *Boston American*, "by theatregoers to whom she is a welcome old friend." But Cyrus Durgin of the *Boston Globe* lamented, "Alice Pearce needs funnier lines." On that point, playwright-novelist Edna Ferber

Mrs. Spencer-Bollard (Alice) discovers that her niece (Patricia Harty) has been daydreaming of romance with a fellow passenger instead of taking dictation in Sail Away, *1961.*

admonished Coward: "No woman writer ever talked like that. No woman writer ever wrote like that. If you say that you know a woman novelist who dictated her books while perched on a bit of Parthenon ruin, I'll apologize."

The tryout in Philadelphia, opening at the Forrest Theatre on September 5, coincided with Jean Fenn's final performance. Coward had come to regret casting the opera star, who, he said, was "far from convincing" as an actress. In addition, frictions mounted over Fenn's trademark hairstyle (a ladylike French twist) and wardrobe ("linen iron lungs," Coward repeatedly groused). He mistakenly thought a chic bob and gowns by Mainbocher would do the trick for Fenn. "First they cut her hair, then they cut her part and then they fired her," Alice observed.

The morning after the Philadelphia opening, the show's choreographer Joe Layton, who had

become Coward's right hand, approached the director with a revolutionary solution: delete Fenn's part entirely and allow Hurst to play the love story with Stritch. Coward readily accepted Layton's proposal: "there was nothing against the idea and everything in favour of it." *Sail Away* played to packed houses for three weeks and broke the house record.

Sail Away debuted on Broadway on October 3. The performance, said Coward, was "magnificent" and the enthusiastic New York audience "chic to the point of nausea." Howard Taubman of the *Times* raved about the musical, but the majority of critics agreed with Walter Kerr of the *Herald Tribune* who said that "it looks like vanilla ice cream, slides about as smoothly as though it were melting on the plate, and has no particular flavor. From this general lazing-about in the holiday sun let us exempt Elaine Stritch." Faulted for its "passé plotting" and "ancient gags," *Sail Away* also suffered at the hands of *Variety* ("an empty show about hollow people") and Dorothy Kilgallen who slammed it on her radio program.

The critics praised Stritch to the skies, and Alice received some of the best notices of her career. "Listen hard," instructed *Theatre Arts*, "whenever Alice Pearce strides onto the stage, for she doubles the value of every amusing word she has been given to say." "Some of the comic lines work," confessed *The New Yorker*, "especially those given to Alice Pearce, who is, as always, one of the right people. Cast as a lady novelist, she thumps around the deck, cackling merrily and quoting tender bits from dead poets. (Her large, gaudy striped pocketbook is the prop of the year.)" Howard Taubman of the *Times* chimed in, "Looking like an irascible macaw, Alice Pearce plays the old girl with the timing of a faultless comedienne." Walter Winchell also remained a fan: "*Sail Away* got jumbled notices from the middle-aisle mandarins, but any show with Alice Pearce in it can't be all bad."

Yet some reviewers, siding with Edna Ferber, could not be charmed by Elinor Spencer-Bollard's speeches. Barbara Rhodes of the Mt. Kisco *Patent Trader* observed: "Margalo Gillmore [playing Hurst's haughty mother] and Alice Pearce struggle professionally with unformed characterizations." *Variety* found Alice only "mildly funny."

Despite the critics' carping, Coward was optimistic that the show would run for two years even though he admitted that the show was "not quite the immediate smash" he had expected. Two weeks later, he was resigned to the hard truth that the show probably wouldn't last beyond May or June. Privately, Coward confessed that "there is something about *Sail Away* that doesn't satisfy me." He was proud of the music and the lyrics but not the book. The

show stumbled along into the new year. A few days before it closed on February 24, Coward wrote, "I am sick to death of poor *Sail Away*." Perhaps Alice Pearce shared those same feelings.

On the night of the New York premiere, a note had been delivered to her dressing room. It read:

> Dearest Alice,
> Gallop into the paddock with your
> hair streaming behind you
> All my love,
> Noël

While the playwright had cunningly borrowed a bit of dialogue describing one of Elinor Spencer-Bollard's heroines, one wonders if it may have been intended as a barb: in one of the show's scenes, an obnoxious boy passenger tells his mother that Elinor "looks like a horse."

Without a doubt, Alice's experience with Coward definitely left a lingering bitter taste. "She said that she had never been so disappointed about anyone in her life," sighed Cris Alexander.

Syndicated columnist Mel Heimer had advised his readers in November to see *Sail Away*. "For those of us who love Alice Pearce, the comedienne, it's one of our few chances to see her on the stage," he said. "She plays all too few roles these years." Perhaps some of Alice's fans harkened to Heimer's words. Those who procrastinated may have been regretful later—*Sail Away* marked the final stage performance of Alice Pearce.

Another finality Alice associated with the production was her grandmother's unexpected death which came during the Philadelphia tryout. "Miss Sallie," at ninety-five, had been in relatively good health, but her daughter Josephine Strode had had a heart attack earlier in the year. Consequently, they thought it best to move nearer to the area hospital. In late June 1961, Josephine had sold her 140-acre property in Whitingham, Vermont, and relocated with her mother to 44 Western Avenue in Brattleboro, twenty-five miles away. On the night of September 12, Sallie suffered a heart attack at home and died about thirty minutes later. She had outlived her husband by more than thirty years.

Alice, in the midst of *Sail Away*, was not able to accompany her parents and Josephine to Perry for the funeral service. The *Perry Enterprise* eulogized Sallie Clark in a lovingly detailed obituary on its front page. More importantly, over the years its editors—numbering only two since the paper's establishment in 1899—had chronicled her long life with frequent mentions in their weekly editions. Tracing the social columns, we learn not only when "Miss Sallie" hosted bridge luncheons but what refreshments were served at her table. We know every occasion that she sang solos for the Entre Nous Club meetings and when she hosted picnics for her Sunday School class. Her small-town life greatly contrasted with those of her daughters and granddaughter, but until the end "she possessed a beauty of mind and facial features not dimmed by age."

After Sallie's death, Bob and Margaret Pearce could not bear to think of spending another snowy winter sequestered in their cavernous house at Whitingham, especially without their helpmate Josephine. Before the killing frosts arrived, they listed their home with a realtor, packed their bags, tightly shut up Pearce Place, and joined Josephine in Brattleboro.

Weeks before the final curtain had fallen on *Sail Away*, Alice had begun to rethink her career. Although the musical's run—including rehearsals and tryouts—had provided her with thirty-three weeks of steady income, she was weary of the tentative nature of stage productions. In the

first place, they were dependent on too many variables, including the script, the direction, and the timing. Poor reviews had doomed shows like *Midgie Purvis* and *Copper and Brass*. "When a show closes, all actors are sure they'll never work again," Alice once said. "I don't feel exactly that way, but I certainly don't enjoy the strain of always being in search of work. Nothing lasts in the theater. Every few months, or every year or so, you're always looking for another job." Maybe it was time, Alice thought, to seriously consider a television career.

Alice's close friend Peggy Cass had just completed a twenty-six-week contract as one of the leads on *The Hathaways*, an ABC sitcom produced in Los Angeles. At the outset, Peggy had rationalized, "[The contract] means something you don't have in the theater. I mean, even if we get poor reviews in the beginning, we still have the chance to improve ourselves." Alice was envious. She wanted to be a series regular, but that would require relocating to the coast, a move she was not quite certain about.

In January 1962, while weighing her options, Alice won a supporting role in a television pilot being filmed by CBS at the Ziv-United Artists studio in New York. *Acres and Pains*, produced and directed by Perry Lafferty and written by Harvey Yorkin and Dave Schwartz, was based on S. J. Perelman's 1942 series of stories spoofing suburban living. The script expanded on Perelman's theme: the tribulations of a New York City writer who tries homesteading in Bucks County, Pennsylvania.

Walter Matthau, then appearing on Broadway in *A Shot in the Dark*, and Anne Jackson, starring in the off-Broadway production of *Brecht on Brecht*, were cast as the writer and his wife. Irked by urban life, the couple makes a fast deal on a country farmhouse, sight unseen. When they arrive with their vanload of furniture, they discover its ramshackle condition—

Patrick Tanner, Alice, and playwright James Kirkwood pose for Cris Alexander in early 1962. "They were just up for an afternoon," remembered Cris. "I think we all had lunch and we came up to my apartment. And I said, 'You sit here, Peeps. Boys, take your pants off.'" In lieu of underpants, Tanner wore specially made shirts with long tails which could be pulled up between the legs and buttoned.

"a far cut above many a comedy series now on television," noting its deftly written script as well as Matthau and Jackson's fine comedic performances. "It is such an amusing, warm, and at times hilarious comedy [that] it makes you wonder why the pilot was grounded." However, Ogden Dwight, the television critic for the *Des Moines Register*, estimated that the roles of the "difficult" writer and his "cunning" wife were characters which "may look funny on paper but won't bear weekly watching." Alice, who didn't catch *Acres and Pains* until it appeared as a rerun in 1965, similarly theorized, "Perelman just doesn't seem to translate to TV. He's like Thurber, you've got to read him to fully savor him."

As spring slowly approached, Alice became available to participate in two concurrent projects headed by Pat Tanner and Cris Alexander. Following on the heels of *Little Me*, Tanner planned a similar mock autobiography called *My Thirty Days Upstairs in the White* House—the title itself a parody of presidential maid Lillian Rogers Parks' 1961 memoir *My Thirty Years Backstairs at the White House*. Tanner's new work was the reminiscences of fictional Martha Dinwiddie Butterfield, first lady of the United States for one month in 1909. Eventually the title would be changed to *First Lady*, with the original choice now serving as a subtitle.

Mrs. Butterfield's life story, as told to Patrick Dennis, would begin in her native Pellagra County, where her family manufactured

and the stubborn tenants who refuse to vacate. The city slickers try to outwit the country bumpkins but wind up spending the night in the back room of a bowling alley. Alice and character actor Philip Coolidge were featured as the farm couple, Maude and Jud Ledbetter.

Production was completed by mid-February, but *Acres and Pains* failed to attract a sponsor. Instead of becoming buried, the half-hour show aired as a segment of *General Electric Theater* on CBS on May 13. *Variety* found it

Lohocla Indian Spirit Water (190 proof and guaranteed to kill or cure). This miracle decoction would wash the Butterfields into the White House by one vote, only to swept out again when the missing vote turned up in Lohocla's Brooklyn warehouse.

"These parody memoirs are a cinch," Pat Tanner enthused, explaining to the *Saturday Review* that he and Cris began with an outline and a list of accompanying photographs. "The pictures are more important than the text, yes they are. If Cris comes up with a very funny picture, I'll change the text to fit it. Cris does all the casting for the stories. He's much better at it than I. The people who pose get one dollar and all the refreshment they can hold."

Cris chose Peggy Cass to depict the first lady. "I had a wonderful time doing [the photo shoots]," she recalled. "We went to the Brooklyn Museum costume department, and I got to wear all kinds of wonderful Worth gowns." For the rest of the large "cast," Cris recruited friends from the theatre world for chief supporting roles. Dody Goodman and Harold Lang appeared as Martha Butterfield's siblings Clytie and Bubber, while William Martel portrayed her husband George. Perhaps with a wink toward Teddy Roosevelt's eldest daughter, Alice Pearce became the Butterfields' daughter Alice. Kaye Ballard, Jan Sterling, Portia Nelson, John Battles, and the 1950s television personality Dagmar— along with Cris and Pat's relatives—filled lesser roles.

Cris employed the same process to create *First Lady*'s outrageous photographs as he had for *Little Me*. "Many of the pictures were

The wizardry of Cris Alexander is displayed in this delightful composite image, created in early 1962, of Peggy Cass and Alice Pearce as mother and daughter trying out an exercise class in Patrick Dennis' book First Lady.

taken against a blank wall and then superimposed onto an appropriate background," Cris explained. "The images I used for these backgrounds came from a remarkable and friendly shop, now closed, called Brown Bros., where one could climb a ladder and find, stacked deep on dusty shelves, photographs of nearly anything taken since the invention of the camera."

One composite photograph, an amusing scene showing George Butterfield and his brothers skinny-dipping in a swimming hole, presented a slight problem. Cris couldn't find enough male models to pose nude. "Peeps and I were having dinner, which was not our habit because we didn't do that a lot, but we did occasionally," Cris recalled in 1987. "We were having dinner at 21, and I was saying to her, 'I've got to find nine nice looking, but goofy looking, boys to be the Butterfield brothers.' So, she

Alice jokingly leers at male model Robert Locklin during a photo shoot for
First Lady, *1962. The following day, he propositioned both her and the
photographer. Cris Alexander photo.*

said, 'Oh, I see one right across the room.' She was like that! And so, he really was a character, and he looked very attractive, very approachable. He happened to be with an old acquaintance of mine, a man who ran an antique shop in Manhattan and someone that I had always unusually dreaded. But I went over and sort of broached the subject, and on their way out they came by and spoke, and so I introduced them to Peeps. Anyway, this boy was under the antique dealer's roof at the time, and he agreed to pose. So, it happened that I was shooting pictures of Peeps and him on the same evening, although they weren't going to be in any scenes together in the book. It was a rather unusual circumstance, and we were having vodkas and 'laughing and scratching.' The boy was great fun. And the next day he called me on the phone. He had heard us say 'Brother' and 'Sister,' which is usually what we called each other—'Bro' and 'Sis.' And so anyway, he called

on the phone and said, 'I'm sure you won't mind, but I would really love to go to bed with you and your sister at the same time.' So, I couldn't wait to get on the phone and give Peeps the invitation, and I thought she'd *croak* laughing. She said, '*Well*, I think he's *awfully* cute.' And I said, 'Well, should I tell him he could go to bed with the *sister*?' And she said, 'Oh, no, no, I don't do that.' He thought she was very attractive which gave her a charge, you know. But the idea just convulsed us!"

"Those two books with Pat were a riot in the making," Cris recalled in 1986. "He was a genius! He adored Alice—as did everyone who ever knew that inspired, absolutely lovely lunatic. He wrote a musical for her aimed to open in London—for her and Dody Goodman. It was a great idea that never got off the ground."

The first draft of this musical, for which Pat wrote both the lyrics and the book, was created in early 1962, while Cris was working on the photos for *First Lady*. "The story was not very complicated," chuckled Cris. "It was about this girl who had won a contest by writing a jingle for a soap company. The prize was two tickets to Europe, but this unpopular girl, who was so selfish and stuck-up, couldn't get anyone to go with her. This really would have been quite a character for Dody to play, but she would have been wonderful. Anyway, she couldn't get anyone to go with her, except poor Cousin Alma, who was Peeps, of course. They went all over Europe together and had all sorts of adventures. In the end, an English nobleman whom they had met—I think, in the Louvre—took a great shine to Cousin Alma, while Dody was doing everything she could to lay hands on him. And Cousin Alma became a noblewoman, and Dody was sent back to the United States."

Pat engaged Cris to pose Alice and Dody—à la *Little Me*—in a set of cut-and-paste photographs featuring famous backdrops such as Versailles, Notre Dame, the Paris Métro and the Venetian canals, designed as "a kind of pre-packaged publicity" which Pat could present to backers in England, rather like a storyboard. At the time, the project lacked a title, so Cris simply identified it as "Cousin Alma."

Appearing in the publicity photos as the nobleman was Pat Tanner's friend Hal Vursell, a managing editor at the publishing house of Farrar, Straus and Giroux. Tall, lean, dapper, and sporting a Clark Gable mustache, Vursell was the embodiment of nobility. Described as "cosmopolitan" and "intellectually sophisticated," the well-traveled Vursell was famous among his colleagues for his acid wit and fluent French. The nobleman's protégé was portrayed by actor and mime Sterling Jensen, who would soon help to found Manhattan's Roundabout Theater. A young character actor named Dal Jenkins was recruited to play a Venetian street urchin. "He was an *amazing* creature," Cris sighed. "He was fascinating—and he was Charlton Heston's first cousin."

In the spring of 1962, Cris Alexander posed Alice (as the nouveau noblewoman) and Walter Pistole (as her chauffeur) on the street outside his Manhattan studio. Later, he literally cut and pasted their images and the Rolls-Royce against a background photo of Versailles to create a scene for the "storyboard" promoting Pat Tanner's projected musical, first called High Life *and later* Fancy Me.

Cris Alexander's first "storyboard" scene for High Life *shows the contest winner (Dody Goodman), right, and her cousin Alma (Alice Pearce) as they depart for Europe.*

The girls visit a marketplace furrier (Pat Tanner, at left).

Wearing her new fur stole, the contest winner calls at the House of Dior with Cousin Alma.

In the Louvre Museum, Alma looks askance at the Venus de Milo while her cousin charms a foreigner (Sterling Jensen). His impeccable companion, the nobleman (Hal Vursell), waits nearby.

Poor Alma lacks charm and grace, but the nobleman comes to her aid while her cousin remains oblivious to her plight.

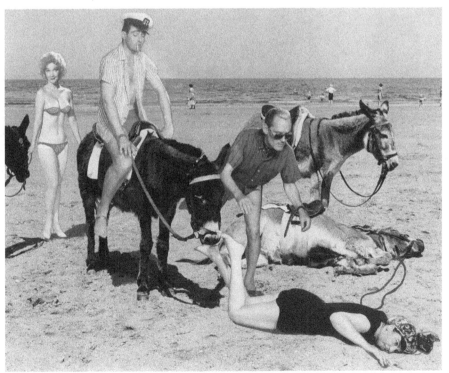

Again the nobleman rallies round when Alma's donkey conks out, and again her conceited cousin stands idly by.

In Venice, Alma—with her trusty camera—scopes the canal for photo opportunities while her cousin hopes to pass through the "tunnel of love" with her foreign suitor.

When a local urchin (Dal Jenkins) leads the girls down a murky Venetian alleyway, the nobleman charges to their rescue.

Now an "item," Cousin Alma and her debonair swain plan a travel vacation together.

"Dody and Alice very much admired each other," Cris continued, "and after the little bit of rehearsing that they'd been doing, they were terribly good together—as you could imagine. It was Pat's plan, and I think a very good one, to have it produced first in London, because of the many American comediennes who had gone there and made big hits. Dody had never performed there, nor had Peeps. It was kind of a natural plan, because he figured that they would just eat them up." Pat explained his choice of venue to columnist Earl Wilson: "It's a friendly country, the costs are low—and if it falls on its posterior, the word doesn't get back here right away."

Pat hired composer Harry Percer to write the music for the show, by then titled *High Life*. Percer was the domestic partner of Walter Pistole, "an old pal of mine," said Cris. "Walter had been an editor at *Harper's Bazaar*, a very, very bright man." Percer and Pistole accompanied Cris and the Tanners to England in the summer of 1962. "Pat took [*High Life*] around to investors, and he *damned* near, *very* nearly, got it on," exclaimed Cris. "He contacted one of the main agents there, and there was a lot of interest in it. And the music was from good to fair. Pat had done all of the lyrics, and most of them were, for the time, pretty outrageous. The trouble was that this was not Pat's best written piece of work. As was true with many of his lesser things, there were always hilarious places where you just burst out laughing, but overall, it didn't really hold up."

When Pat returned from Europe that September, he put *High Life*—in need of a rewrite—on the back burner while he tackled the manuscript for *First Lady*.

By that time, Alice had long completed her photo sessions for both of Pat's projects and was no longer in the loop. In late winter 1962, Alice's agent George Morris had phoned, assuring that if she relocated to California, he could find film and television roles suited to her talents. There might be opportunities, he said, to appear in another television pilot which could lead to a regular series. In the past five years, television production had shifted from New York to Hollywood, pumping new blood into the film colony. "It's like a New York convention," Walter Smith, manager of the Montecito Apartments, told *Newsweek* in 1957. "There has never been anything like this," said another "bedazzled" observer. "This is the gold strike. There are more actors working here now than at any time in history." The time was right, George said, for Alice to join the mighty migration.

"I [had become] discouraged and disenchanted with Broadway," Alice later explained, "because supporting actors suddenly stopped getting paid [enough]. I think I blame [producer] David Merrick for that. His theory is to pay actors less and they'll do it anyway. On Broadway, it's harder for a character actress than for a star because producers will settle for second or third best to save money. So I moved west."

Still, the thought of packing all of her bags and leaving her New York friends behind was rather daunting for Alice. Peggy Cass had compared it to "stepping off a dock into the water, when you don't know whether it's going to be shallow and warm or deep and icy." But Alice was resolute. Deep in her heart, she felt that the move was worth the risk, so she gave George the go-ahead to begin searching for more oddball roles.

CHAPTER TWENTY-ONE
California Whirlwind

"I have been bouncing back and forth so much between here and New York that I am beginning to feel like a yoyo."

George Morris was as good as his word. Alice's film assignments for the spring and summer began to line up rather quickly. On March 14, 1962, she signed a contract to appear in Paramount's romantic comedy *My Six Loves*, Gower Champion's attempt to transfer his directorial skills from stage to screen. Alice's prospects were augmented by the fact that the film's star and its producer were her old friends—Debbie Reynolds and Gant Gaither. Although Gaither had produced six Broadway shows, none had been successful. Like Champion, this was his first film effort. Besides Alice, Gaither and Champion chose a few more New York-based actors to round out the veteran cast, including Eileen Heckart as Reynolds' wisecracking secretary, John McGiver as an astute judge, and Alice Ghostley as Reynolds' haughty housekeeper.

Based on a novel by Peter Funk, *My Six Loves* is the story of glamorous actress Janice Courtney (Reynolds) who, on the verge of a nervous breakdown from the publicity hubbub that engulfs her, is ordered to rest up for a while at her Connecticut retreat. When she discovers six homeless siblings living in an abandoned greenhouse on her property, she takes them in for a spell and soon learns to adore them—and in the process falls in love with the local minister.

Alice's role was that of a harried school bus driver. She could handle the harried part, but the other half proved to be something of a challenge. Alice didn't know how to drive. As a teenager, she had been chauffeured all over Paris by her parents' driver. At the Masters School and Sarah Lawrence College, she either walked or took the train wherever she wanted to go. Even after she and John married, they had not owned an automobile, relying instead on trains, taxis, and ferries. She had once lost a part because she couldn't drive. "It was offered to me, and I didn't admit I couldn't drive," Alice confessed. "I tried to learn. I applied at all the accredited driving schools in New York and found they had waiting lists for months. So I had to resort to a black-market driving academy. Their technique was to put me in the driver's seat and turn me loose on Second Avenue during heavy traffic. When I saw the instructor starting to jump out, that was all I needed."

Alice's inexperience was discovered soon after she arrived on the *My Six Loves* set on May 4. Debbie Reynolds recalled, "Well, in her first scene— she'd never told the director she couldn't drive—she was supposed to take the bus a certain distance and stop short. But Alice kept going until she ran into a wall. Out she came with that laugh of hers: 'There are two pedals down there, and I've forgotten which one is the brake.' On the next take, she was to push a button that opened the bus door. She fiddled around and finally quipped, 'I must

Debbie Reynolds, Alice Pearce, and Eileen Heckart struggle to load a bunch of unruly children onto a school bus in My Six Loves *(1963).*

have lost my buttons.' Finally, they put a man in the bus and had him lie on the floor to push the brake and button. But *then* she shifted gears without putting in the clutch! Anyway, by the time they finished I was whooping so hard all my makeup was spoiled and had to be redone."

When the ordeal was over, Alice sighed, "Better I should walk." Nonetheless, Reynolds insisted, "Her timing was perfect. When you were in a scene with her, you just *resigned* yourself to having it stolen from you."

When *My Six Loves* was released in April 1963, most critics agreed with Henry S. Humphreys of the *Cincinnati Enquirer* who dismissed it "as syrupy-sentimental as you

Debbie and Alice were delighted to be working together again on the set of My Six Loves *in the spring of 1962.*

can get." That was a shame, he said, "because it could have been a good, lively romp, what with six lively children and a cute bewhiskered dog that was intelligent enough to ignore the script and bark his own lines." Judith Crist noted: "Eileen Heckart as a latter-day Eve Arden type, Alice Ghostley, Alice Pearce, and Jim Backus offer moments of satiric relief, but the sweetness, light, and loving teardrops glue even them into the goo." *The New York Times* went as far as to say that "the real loves here are not the six nice enough waifs, but six expert comedians who bring up the sidelines and rear. Count 'em: Alice Ghostley, Jim Backus, Hans Conried, Mary McCarty, Alice Pearce, and Eileen Heckart. These hardies put the real spice and fun into this tame but genial showcase for Miss Reynolds." Producer Gaither later summed up the picture regretfully: "Debbie Reynolds, six children, and a dog. Nearly did me in." He would not attempt to produce anything, on stage or film, ever again.

Alice made practical use of the interval between *My Six Loves* and her next assignment. In the words of Peggy Cass, Alice was quite ready to "step off the dock"—but not without a life jacket. In order to remain a legal resident of New York City, Alice decided to keep her apartment on Fifty-Ninth Street, just in case things on the coast didn't work out. Then she began scouting for an apartment in the Hollywood area and shopping for its furnishings. Since she did not drive and had few close friends in Los Angeles, these chores were more of a challenge. Still, Alice found it all exciting. She settled at 8629 Holloway Drive in West Hollywood, south of the Sunset Strip, close to where Santa Monica Boulevard runs into Sunset Boulevard. The immediate area was a colony of quaint bungalows, built in 1937 and 1938, and there were eateries and shops within walking distance.

"West Hollywood was like a small, comfy village," recalled Carleton Carpenter, who had lived there for several years before Alice took up residence. "Short blocks connected and shot off from one another, and most of the residents were in the 'biz.'" Carpenter lived on Norma Place, about a mile from Alice's apartment. His neighbors included actresses Dorothy Dandridge, Estelle Winwood and Nina Foch, actor John Dall and his partner Clement Brace, and writer Dorothy Parker and her husband Alan Campbell. Alice's neighborhood didn't boast as many familiar names as those at Norma Place, but the esteemed character actor Vladimir Sokoloff (*For Whom the Bell Tolls, The Magnificent Seven*, etc.) had lived five doors away at 8624 Holloway until his death in February 1962. A few years prior to Alice's occupancy of 8629, her apartment had been the home of cinematographer Ernest Haller, who had won an Academy Award for his work on *Gone with the Wind*.

It is believed that Alice's friend Paul Davis, then dividing his time between New York and Los Angeles, steered her to choose West Hollywood as a suitable neighborhood. Paul knew the area well. In July 1959, when the national tour of *Bells Are Ringing* ended, he had rented a home at 833 ½ Sweetzer Avenue, located about one mile southeast of 8629 Holloway Drive.

Paul had become part of the "television invasion." New York-based writers Paddy Chayefsky and Rod Serling, directors Delbert Mann and John Frankenheimer, and actors Steve McQueen and Jack Nicholson had all made the move west. "That whole freer, more theatrical sense from New York was brought out here," recalled Charles Williamson, who moved to Los Angeles in 1958 after finding limited success as a young stage and television actor back east. Hundreds of gay men, like Williamson, settled in West Hollywood, particularly in its west end where both Alice and Paul had their apartments.

Soon after Paul moved into his new place on Sweetzer Avenue, he reconnected with veteran actor Francis Lederer, whom he had first met twenty years earlier when he was a young autograph collector in Boston. One summer evening Lederer invited Paul to dinner at his West Hills home where he introduced Paul to Lucille Ball.

Earlier in the year, Ball—attempting to fill the void left by her crumbling marriage to Desi Arnaz—had established the Desilu Workshop Theatre as a means to develop new talent for the film industry. The Workshop employed "a stock company of resident contract players" under Ball's personal supervision, including Dick Kallman, Robert Osborne, and Carole (née Mildred) Cook. Ball confided to Lederer and Paul that her most recent ambition was to produce a musical revue aimed at Broadway, featuring some of the young performers under her wing. There was one tiny little problem. Never in her twenty-five years as an actress had Lucille Ball appeared in a Broadway production. "Lucy was very naïve about the stage," explains Carole Cook, whose own experience by then included productions both on and off Broadway. "Lucy needed someone with stage experience to help her with the revue." Paul Davis' theatrical background fit the bill. Two days after meeting Ball, he signed a contract as her assistant on the workshop production of *The Desilu Revue*, which would eventually run for four weeks beginning October 6, 1959.

Around this same time, Paul—with a nod to his ethnic heritage—temporarily adopted "Pesha Darshefsky" as his professional name. "Paul loved to be called Pesha (pronounced "Pay-sha")," says Cook. "That was the Russian name for Paul, I assume. We all called him Pesha." The origin and meaning of the name

"Pesha" vary according to the source consulted, but in Paul's case the best explanation seems to be that "Pesha" can be used as a diminutive for "Pavel," which is "Paul" in Russian. "Paul was named for a man whose nickname was Pesha, but growing up he was never called that at all," asserted his sister Renee Summers. "He took the name Pesha *later on* because he liked the sound of it. He liked the idea of something more exotic than 'Paul.'"

Paul's Massachusetts birth certificate bears the name "Paul *Dashefksy*"—minus the "r" which Paul later inserted. As a first-generation American growing up in Depression-era Dorchester, Paul was part of an ethnically diverse community populated with immigrants (and their descendants) from Ireland, Poland, Russia, and Italy. Paul was the grandson of Ukrainian-Jewish immigrant Chaim Dashefsky who narrowly succeeded in bringing his wife and four young sons to Boston just months prior to the atrocious pogroms which rocked Kiev in 1905. "My grandparents came to this country at the turn of the twentieth century, spoke little English and struggled so that their children and grandchildren could have a better life," wrote Paul's brother Milton Davis in 2005. By 1930, Paul's grandfather, father, and uncles were all using the anglicized surname "Davis."

"Paul always wanted to be a successful actor," Milton recalled. However, by the time Paul was thirty-seven, it was painfully clear that his dream was not going to materialize. "I got to know Pesha very well," says Carole Cook. "He was a nice guy and all that, but I always had the opinion that he was too old to 'find himself.' I thought he wanted to be associated with Lucille Ball so that it would lead to something else, bigger things." Cook maintains that Paul wanted to direct *The Desilu Revue*, but that didn't happen.

In November 1959, when Ball decided to transfer the revue to television as an episode of *The Westinghouse Desilu Playhouse*, Paul missed his chance again. "Lucille did everything for this show," insisted producer Bert Granet. "She chose the people, directed, produced, and renovated the theatre." Cook says, "I've always thought that Pesha was disappointed that he wasn't given the job of director of the television show. Aside from Lucy, the choreographer [Jack Baker] had the most to do with the show." When the program aired on Christmas night, Paul watched it at his parents' home back in Dorchester, Massachusetts. Near the end of the final credits, he was listed as the show's "associate producer"—not as Pesha Darshefsky but Paul Davis. Noting the name change, columnist Mike Connolly quipped, "Proof-readers all over the country will be happy!"

After unexceptional reviews for both the stage and television versions of *The Desilu Revue*, Ball "soon forgot her workshop as her marriage collapsed." The workshop group disbanded in 1960, and soon after Paul's professional relationship with Ball ended. Paul later shared details of that experience with Jonathan Oppenheim, the young son of his friend Judy Holliday. "I was just a kid, but I spent a lot of time with Paul," Oppenheim recalled in 2018. "The adults in my childhood talked a lot around me. I was probably nine years old when Paul told me that Lucille Ball was very difficult and demanding." Paul and Ball continued to socialize occasionally, however, especially during 1961 when she was appearing on Broadway in *Wildcat*.

In mid-August 1960, Paul left Los Angeles to join the cast of *Laurette*, a three-act drama starring Holliday as theatre great Laurette Taylor. Holliday had arranged for Paul to fill an incidental role, but mainly he would serve as her "secretary and general factotum" during

Carole Cook and Paul Davis visit Lucille Ball during the filming of "The Ricardos Go to Japan," an episode of The Lucy-Desi Comedy Hour, *October 1959.*

the production. Rehearsals were plagued by the play's flimsy script, its lackadaisical director, and— most regrettably—its insecure star. An ill-fated tryout opened in New Haven on September 26 but closed a week later due to Holliday's sudden illness. A thorough examination revealed breast cancer. A mastectomy followed, sending Holliday into a prolonged depression. For the ensuing months Paul remained in Manhattan, available to occasionally lend a hand with Jonathan, who would soon turn eight.

"I was very close to Paul," says Jonathan Oppenheim. "He was sort of like a surrogate uncle, at least that's how he functioned for me. He would take me to the movies. I would stay over at his house sometimes. My grandmother, for some reason, didn't like him. But I felt very connected to him."

An unfortunate incident would further strengthen the bond between Paul and the young boy. On May 2, 1961, Jonathan and his grandmother Helen Tuvim were waiting for a taxi outside their home at the Dakota Apartments on New York's Upper West Side. Suddenly a parked car in the building's driveway rolled down a slight incline, throwing Tuvim to the ground and pinning her for several minutes. The accident caused both Holliday and Oppenheim great distress. "I freaked out," Oppenheim recalls. "I remember Paul taking me to the Empire State Building to sort of distract me. He was very much a presence for me during that trauma."

Despite their thirty-year age difference, Paul and Jonathan Oppenheim continued to enjoy each other's company for the next two years. "Paul was very warm and fun," Oppenheim asserts. "I enjoyed hanging out with him. He was very involved in antiques, or rather he had friends in the antique business. I would go with him to antique shops. I was very interested in movies, and Paul encouraged my interest in a way. He was a very lively person, especially when he was sharing his interest in the stage. Paul had a lot of ambitions—he wanted to direct. He took me to this theatre where he was directing something called *Infidel Caesar*—he was developing it."

Actually, *Infidel Caesar*, a version of Shakespeare's *Julius Caesar* set in modern-day Cuba, was developed by actor-director Gene Wesson. According to *Variety*, Paul served under Wesson as a production supervisor. The cast boasted Ramon Navarro, Michael Ansara, James Earl Jones, and John Ireland, as well as two exiled actresses from Havana. Scheduled to open at the Music Box Theatre on May 1, 1962—foregoing the customary out-of-town tryouts—the show closed after only one preview performance. It was obvious to everyone that *Infidel Caesar* needed much more work than the production budget would allow.

Out of work once again, Paul found it necessary to give up both his New York apartment and his place in West Hollywood. By this time, Alice was filming *My Six Loves* and scouting other career opportunities in Los Angeles, so she offered Paul the use of her apartment, located on the fringe of the Upper East Side.

In June 1962, Alice was handed a plum role for an episode of the CBS sitcom *Dennis the Menace*, then beginning its fourth and final season. "You Go Your Way," expertly written by John Elliotte and Clifford Goldsmith, provided a showcase for the unique talents of Alice and series semi-regular Mary Wickes. When Dennis (Jay North) overhears and repeats part of a conversation between John and Eloise Wilson (Gale Gordon, Sara Seegar), rumors of their break-up fly through the neighborhood. With the belief that John is now single, man-hungry Miss Cathcart (Wickes) and Miss Tarbell (Alice) vie for his attention with the help of an unsuspecting Dennis.

By this time, both Alice and Wickes had handled more than their share of wallflower roles, but *Dennis'* madcap spinsters allowed the veteran pair to pull every trick from their bags. Employing a full range of vocal tones, Alice coos, gulps, titters, snarls, and cackles as the giddy Miss Tarbell. Likewise, the body language of the masterful Wickes is purely a study of carefully timed business. Producers Winston O'Keefe and Harry Ackerman were so pleased with the finished product that they instructed John Elliotte to create another episode featuring Miss Cathcart and Miss Tarbell. In mid-October, Alice and Wickes were called back to appear in a segment in which their characters compete to "lasso [their] sugar cookie"— this time setting their sights on police sergeant Harold Mooney (George Cisar). Unfortunately, this outing—secondary both in sequence and quality—resorted to forced slapstick instead of the snappy dialogue of "You Go Your Way."

Dennis the Menace was a production of Screen Gems, the television subsidiary of Columbia Pictures Corporation. Screen Gems operated out of Columbia's Hollywood studios at 1438 North Gower Street, a lot that covered fourteen acres and contained fifteen sound stages. It was supplemented by the Columbia Ranch, a 36-acre tract in Burbank with five sound stages. While filming her *Dennis* guest appearances, Alice had no idea that she would soon be a regular at the Ranch. Two years later, *Bewitched* would join the Screen Gems stable. (The façade used for exterior views of Samantha and Darrin Stephens' *Bewitched* house is plainly visible in the background as Miss Tarbell enters the front gate of the Wilson house in "You Go Your Way.")

Tammy and the Doctor was the third and final installment in a series of "Tammy" films produced by Ross Hunter, who immediately clicked with Alice after hiring her for a somewhat sizeable role as a wisecracking but gentle nurse. This offering transported backwoods Mississippi sprite Tammy Tyree (Sandra Dee) to Los Angeles where her elderly friend (Beulah Bondi) is hospitalized, awaiting heart surgery. To be close to the old lady, Tammy takes a job as a nurse's aide. Her lack of sophistication gets her into trouble with the doctors and nurses, but compassionate Millie Baxter (Alice) always bails her out. Meanwhile, Tammy falls in love with a young intern (Peter Fonda, in his film debut).

Production for *Tammy* began July 9, 1962, at Universal Studios, where "one of the largest interior sets used in several years" had been constructed. Visiting doctors claimed that the complete hospital set was so authentic that it could be used for actual surgery in an emergency. Patterned after a recent addition to the Hollywood Presbyterian Hospital, the set included an admitting room, doctors' offices, patients' rooms, operating room, and a maternity ward, with nurses' quarters on another set. Filming was completed by mid-August at a total cost of $730,000.

Tammy and the Doctor premiered in Dallas on May 29, 1963. Reviews were lukewarm to negative. *The New York Times* simply called it "a bore." *Variety* criticized Harry Keller's direction ("doesn't aid matters much"), Russell Metty's photography ("too dark to see the lack of expression on some of the actors' faces"), and Oscar Brodney's screenplay ("slight and limp"). Neither did the performers escape reproach. Dee was "too chic to be a hick chick," Fonda was "artificial," and Bondi, Reginald Owen, Margaret Lindsay, and MacDonald Carey were collectively deemed "not much better than adequate." "Alice Pearce has a funny moment or too," shrugged *Variety*.

Ross Hunter countered all the carping by insisting that if the few pictures of the "Tammy" genre weren't made, "kids wouldn't have anything else to see. There's plenty of blue in the world already." William J. Mann, author of *Behind the Screen*, paints a clear picture of Hunter: "a fiercely determined producer" who couldn't bear to see the studio era and its "old-style Hollywood glamour" slip away. Many of Hunter's films, such as *All That Heaven Allows*, *Imitation of Life*, and *Back Street*, were arguably "overblown, artificial, and playing to sentiment." Yet they were moneymakers. Hunter believed that the real problem besetting the film industry wasn't television—it was the "lapsed commitment to the ideals" of its founders, men like Irving Thalberg and Louis B. Mayer. He didn't care that a movie like *Tammy and the Doctor* was dismissed as flimsy or shmaltzy. It was entertainment for the folks in small towns who bought tickets.

Sandra Dee explains the benefits of drinking river water to a befuddled Alice Pearce, a skeptical Joan Marshall, and a curious Mitzi Hoag in a scene from Tammy and the Doctor *(1963).*

Alice's characterization of Millie Baxter is like no other in her film or television careers. Devoid of mugging (except for one awkward instance), her performance is natural, restrained and at times quite subtle. There is no shrill laughter, no strident speech. Instead, there is sincerity and a touch of refinement, perhaps our best glimpse of what Alice Pearce must have been like offscreen. Two years before his death, actor Richard Deacon, who knew Alice both professionally and privately, reflected: "I was a great fan of hers and am delighted when I catch a movie like *Tammy* in which she was warm *and* funny."

While Alice was grateful for any film roles that came her way, she still had her heart set on landing a regular role in a television series. Late that summer, George Morris, knowing that she had appeared twice on *The Ann Sothern Show*, alerted Alice that Sothern was filming a new television pilot. Aimed at the

1963–64 season, *Atta Boy, Mama!* was produced by Mark Goodson and Bill Todman, in association with NBC. Written by Mac Benoff and directed by Ida Lupino, the comedy was filmed at M-G-M the week of September 17, 1962. The premise was rather implausible. Sothern, fifty-three, played Molly Maguire, the widowed mother of four children—ages twelve to five—who juggled her parental obligations with her duties as a small-town mayor while courting a handsome young doctor. Alice was assigned the negligible role of Molly's next-door neighbor Annie Miller. Others in the cast included Martin Braddock, Arthur Peterson, and Sothern's daughter Tisha Sterling, who played a babysitter. It was not the most pleasant set. According to Walter Winchell, there were tensions between Sothern and Lupino. Most sources report that *Atta Boy, Mama!* failed to attract a sponsor, but Sothern later claimed that "[the pilot] reeked and I just walked away from it although [the network] wanted to go ahead."

More prestigious but curiously atypical was Alice's next acting assignment, which got underway the following week at the Revue Studios at Universal City. "The Hands of Danofrio," an hour-long segment of the ABC dramatic anthology series *Alcoa Premiere*, was directed by three-time Emmy winner George Schaefer. Connecticut art dealer Caleb Burlington (played by John Williams) believes that he has catalogued the complete works of Danofrio, an Italian sculptor believed to have been killed in an explosion during World War Two. Now he discovers a new work—a pair of hands—done in Danofrio's unmistakable style, which the owner (Beulah Bondi) claims was recently given to her by a local stone cutter named Lombardi (Telly Savalas). When Burlington and his auctioneer friend (Joseph Campanella) finally gain Lombardi's confidence, the artist confesses that he is actually Danofrio. He explains that in the wreckage of the explosion another man's unidentifiable body was mistaken for his. To escape his unhappy marriage, Danofrio secretly started a new life in America where he remarried and fathered a daughter. Now widowed, Danofrio does not want daughter Rosa (Janet Margolin) to know that he was a bigamist or that he is the world-famous sculptor. Shortly after his confession, Danofrio dies. Burlington respects Danofrio's wishes and auctions off his remaining works as those of Lombardi. Unaware, Rosa sighs, "He'll be famous—if only he could have known."

Alice played Burlington's private secretary Isis Flemington, the embodiment of decorum.

In each of her three scenes, she is beautifully coiffed and smartly dressed. In the final auction scene, Alice wears an A-line evening coat of hot pink silk which she bought off the rack at Lord & Taylor. The coat would become her go-to garment for private and professional wear for another three years.

"The Hands of Danofrio" was so well-received that for a brief time Revue Studios considered promoting it as a television pilot. Schaefer was intrigued by the idea, mainly due to the diminishing output of NBC's *Hallmark Hall of Fame*, with which he had been closely connected for years. "We need to have something running to keep our organization together," he said. "Furthermore, the series is an interesting idea, built around an antique shop. I'd enjoy doing it." However, the idea remained just that, and Alice lost another chance to join a series.

She went directly from shooting "Danofrio" to memorizing lines for an episode of *The Many Loves of Dobie Gillis*, a CBS sitcom produced at the Fox Film Corporation studio at the intersection of Sunset Boulevard and Western Avenue in Hollywood. In this segment, naïve college disc jockey Dobie Gillis (played by Dwayne Hickman) finds himself duped by a "lowdown bunch of sharpies" in "And Now a Word from Our Sponsor," written by Arnold Horwitt and directed by Rod Amateau. In their seedy rented room, Mom Baker (Alice) convinces her son, ex-con Eddie (Lennie Weinrib) that they can return to "Moolah Road" if they find "some drippy college disc jockey what never heard of payola." Mom wants Eddie to push the recordings of their old friend Fifi LaVerne, now posing as folksinger Patience Virtue (Carole Cook).

A copy of Horwitt's script, dated September 20 and marked "final draft," is included among Amateau's papers in the UCLA Library's Special Collections but differs greatly from the eventual film. The opening scene requires "crusty" and "hard-bitten" Mom Baker to talk with a cigarette hanging out of her mouth. Whether or not it was Alice's decision to dispense with the cigarette is not known, but on film there's not a single smoke in sight. (Off-screen, Alice had been only an occasional smoker. When interviewed in her apartment in 1960, she offered the journalist a cigarette from her refrigerator, where she stored them to maintain freshness.)

Alice's casting as Mom Baker is equally curious. She doesn't exactly demonstrate "crustiness" or "hardness," at least not like other character actresses known for those qualities—Marjorie Bennett comes to mind. And her twang sounds nothing like that of Bronx-born Weinrib. Nevertheless, Alice is at her nasal best.

Added to the mix is the folksy accent of Texas native Cook. Originally Joyce Jameson was slated to play Fifi/Patience; however at the last minute she was replaced by Cook. "I felt that was the dumbest casting I've ever seen," Cook exclaimed in 2019. "I'm not a dumb blonde!" The script requires Patience to sing "Sweet Betsy from Pike," but the filmed version has Cook screeching a tune called "Call Out the Dogs and Let's Go Huntin'."

Cook first met Alice in New York in the fifties. "I knew her socially, I saw her at parties," Cook remembered. "An absolutely fabulous woman—the nicest person I've ever known! She was one funny woman. And she was funny on 'not funny' lines. The lines weren't that funny sometimes, but she was hysterical saying them. That was the day when somebody could become a real staple on Broadway, and she was *that*. She and Alice Ghostley—they were big names. Alice Pearce would walk onstage and people would *applaud*. She was always so vulnerable. I thought, 'You can't act that.' She just *was*. And I thought, 'My God, that's a

wonderful quality to have!' I knew she came from *wealth*, but she didn't talk about it. She was private about it—not ugly about it—but it just didn't come up. Looking back now, I'm sure that was class-related. I also knew that her mother was domineering, but I certainly didn't talk with her much about her beginnings."

As soon as Alice's gig on *Dobie Gillis* wrapped, she returned to Screen Gems for her second guest spot on *Dennis the Menace*. In between commutes to the studio that week, Alice began packing for a quick trip to New York. Although she had been in the Los Angeles area for more than five months, she had not taken the opportunity to visit her in-laws, the Herrings, in Anaheim. On their end, they knew nothing of Alice's schedule or her exact whereabouts, so their letters were mailed to Alice's Manhattan address and then forwarded to her in West Hollywood. On October 15, the day before Alice's forty-fifth birthday, she was reminded of Don Herring and his wife Doris who both shared her birthday. They had not seen her since 1959. It was high time to let them hear from her.

"Dear ones," Alice wrote. "I have been bouncing back and forth so much between here and New York that I am beginning to feel like a yoyo. When you receive this, I shall have one foot on the plane for the East, but I shall be back just as soon. And then I hope we shall, at long last, have a visit ... I was thrilled to hear of Susie's engagement. Please ask the family to have patience with old Aunt Alice. I promise to get to my desk soon. Meanwhile, I send you all, all my love, and to my dear brother and sister a very happy birthday and many x x x, Alice."

Traveling to New York with Alice was Paul Davis, who had been visiting her in California for the previous three weeks, during her back-to-back television assignments. Alice's motivation for returning to New York—for a mere three weeks—remains a mystery. There is one curious possibility. It seems unlikely, but certain pieces of the puzzle fit.

Alice's old friend Oliver Smith, while already juggling a heavy fall schedule including restyling the ballroom of the Waldorf-Astoria Hotel, had decided to co-produce and design *Tiger Tiger Burning Bright*, a new play by Peter Feibleman. Rehearsals would begin in early November, followed by a Broadway opening on December 22. Listed in the show's playbill, directly under the heading "Staff for Mr. Smith," is a production coordinator identified as "Alice Pearce." Below her are Smith's design assistant and production assistant, an indication that the coordinator may have kept records of the activities, materials, or supplies of these other two. Could Alice have handled this position? "It doesn't seem likely to me that she would get herself into such a capacity or *want to*," suggested Cris Alexander. "Oliver was a dear, sweet man, but I don't know—she may have contributed something to it."

A survey of the name "Alice Pearce" in the Manhattan telephone directories from 1942 through 1960 reveals only one—the actress. Moreover, only once does the name "Alice Pearce" appear in a non-performing capacity in the esteemed *Theatre World* annuals covering the years between 1944 and 1990—and that is for the production *Tiger Tiger Burning Bright*. Similarly, the performer Alice Pearce is the only individual listed by that name on the Internet Broadway Database. If Smith's production coordinator was indeed actress Alice Pearce, then whatever work she performed would have been completed prior to November 7, 1962, when she returned to California. Among Alice's papers at USC is a playbill for the December 31 performance of *Tiger Tiger Burning Bright*, which may have been forward-

ed to her by Smith or perhaps saved by Paul Davis who may have seen the play that evening.

In the meantime, Ross Hunter's film production of *The Thrill of It All* had kicked off at Universal's Revue Studios. Whenever possible, Hunter hired friends for supporting roles in his films. Alice became a member of that privileged group with her induction into *The Thrill of It All* subset, which also included Hayden Rorke, Alex Gerry, and Sandra Gould (whose bit part as a salesclerk would be deleted from the final print). Alice's role—considered by some as a cameo—was that of a shrew stalled in a traffic jam in the comedy's climactic scene. Surely the devoted Hunter was responsible for her prominent screen billing: eighth in a cast of more than fifty, outranking numerous others with significantly greater screen minutes.

Directed by Norman Jewison, *The Thrill of It All* was Carl Reiner's first-ever screenplay, and a terrific one at that. Housewife Beverly Boyer (Doris Day) is suddenly thrust into fame and wealth—to her gynecologist husband's chagrin—as a TV spokesperson for "Happy Soap," a product manufactured by the father-in-law of one of her husband's wealthy patients, Mrs. Fraleigh (Arlene Francis). Beverly is forced to spend more and more time away from home, and trouble erupts in the Boyer household. Her husband Gerald (James Garner) schemes to get even by pretending to also be too busy to spend time at home. The couple is reunited in the backseat of Mrs. Fraleigh's Rolls Royce, and there Gerald delivers her baby during a traffic jam. Overjoyed, Beverly decides to quit her job and return to her role as wife and mother.

Hunter's production, as customary, featured "an expensive, glamorous sheen," with music by Frank De Vol and gowns by Jean Louis. Reiner, said *Variety*, slipped in "some sharp and substantial observations" that American film audiences would appreciate. "Reiner's scenario

Jane Dulo, Richard Deacon, Alice Pearce, and an unidentified friend enjoy a night at The Crescendo, a West Hollywood jazz venue on Sunset Boulevard, December 1962.

. . . is peppered with digs at various institutions of modern American life. Among the targets . . . are television, Madison Avenue, and the servant problem." Mildred Stockard of the *Houston Chronicle* observed, "The lines and situations are fresh and funny and all the players, from stars Doris Day and James Garner down to Alice Pearce who has a bit part as the mercenary wife of a stalled motorist, romp through their roles as if they were enjoying them."

Following its premiere at Radio City Music Hall on August 1, 1963, *The Thrill of It All* was a "smash grosser," just as *Variety* had predicted. The film became one of the top moneymakers of the year.

During the busy summer and autumn months of 1962, Alice reconnected with a few old friends who were now based in Los Angeles. Character actor Richard Deacon, then enjoying his second season on *The Dick Van Dyke Show*, was delighted that Alice was once again in California. "We met through a mutu-

al friend a long time ago in New York City," Deacon recalled in 1966. "[Alice] was the type of human being that nice people insisted on passing around as a favor to other nice people. They introduced her as if they were conferring an honor. And it was. She had a genuine genius for friendship."

Deacon's longtime pal was actress Jane Dulo, who had also known Alice many years before in New York. Dulo had been Nancy Walker's understudy in the Broadway version of *On the Town*. "The first night I had to step in for Nancy," Dulo recalled, "Alice was as excited as I was. She couldn't have been more helpful."

Out of touch with Alice for numerous years, Dulo was thrilled that Deacon brought them back together for occasional dinners out and a bit of club hopping. Dulo found Alice to be just as she remembered her from their early days together. "Alice was crazy about antique and thrift shops," said Dulo. "She never felt completely dressed without a hat, usually one with a kooky little touch. She was also one of those people who manage to be proper without being stuffy." Echoed Deacon, "Alice was one of the few ladies out here to wear a hat and gloves."

When Alice was settling into her home on Holloway Drive, Dulo volunteered to help. "Since Alice didn't drive," she explained, "I told her she should call on me any time she needed to go shopping or for an interview. But, as I expected, she didn't call. She hated to impose on people. She simply took taxis . . . A dear, absolutely feminine, womanly woman . . . But basically, I'd say she was a loner, in spite of the love she inspired in all sorts of people."

Jane Dulo's summative observation is ironically comparable to Carole Cook's unprompted impression of Paul Davis: "I don't mean that he was a loner in a reclusive way, but he just really was kind of by himself, you know. During the time we worked together on the Desilu Workshop, he would go to lunch with us—and he was fun—but I never got the feeling that he had a lot of people around him, or lots of friends."

This pair of independent appraisals, although separated by a span of fifty years, may provide significant insight into the mutual attraction of Alice and Paul—and the solemn pact that they, as lonely individuals, would one day form.

CHAPTER TWENTY-TWO
Settling In

"I never thought I'd say this, but I love living in California."

The flurry of film work that fell Alice's way in the second half of 1962 flickered out just as the new year began. Demand for film roles was definitely greater than supply. Alice found herself competing with the four hundred other comediennes and character actresses listed in the 1963 quarterly issues of the *Academy Players Directory*.

Even so, she had succeeded in making her comedy technique so distinctive that directors and producers began to refer to "Alice Pearce" types. "It doesn't do any good sometimes," Alice told Hal Humphrey of the *Los Angeles Times*. "I remember going to read for a part and when the script was passed around to about ten of us in the waiting room, we noticed it described the character as 'an Alice Pearce type.' Well, the other girls said, 'Why are we wasting our time? Alice is here.' They waited, though, and it's a good thing they did. I read, but didn't get the part."

When the offer for another television pilot came along in late January, Alice snapped it up. Edward Montagne, the producer of the hit ABC series *McHale's Navy*, was eager to capitalize on his success by creating a comedy series about WACs. His inspiration was a television episode produced by a rival network. In October 1962, character actress Ann B. Davis—soon to be known as "Alice" on *The Brady Bunch*—had filmed a guest segment as a WAC sergeant on *McKeever and the Colonel*, a Four Star television production which aired weekly on NBC. Now Davis, thirty-six, was to star in the spinoff pilot with Alice Pearce as her WAC captain. Another "plain Jane," twenty-nine-year-old Beverly Wills, was also signed for the all-female cast. "[Wills] and I were sharing a dressing room at a wardrobe fitting or something one day," said Davis, recalling Wills in 2004. "And she said, 'I'm not used to being the pretty one,' which I thought was kind of sweet of her. She was the ingénue, and the rest of us were character types."

The pilot, originally called *Get with It*, was filmed in two days, beginning February 4, 1963. Just before production started, the title was changed to *Shape Up, Sergeant!* "The more undisciplined members of the crew," Davis remembered in 2013, "referred to the pilot as 'Knockers Up, Sergeant!'" Like Alice's previous pilots, it eventually failed to attract a sponsor.

By this time, Alice had decided that her move to California would be permanent. Realizing this, her parents expressed an interest to relocate to the West Coast in order to be closer to her. Bob Pearce was seventy-three and not in the best of health. The Pearces' large house in Whitingham had finally sold the previous December, so they reasoned that the time was right. In late winter they flew to California to scout possible locations for a new home.

On March 12, Alice wrote to Cris Alexander from La Jolla's La Valencia Hotel, thanking him—belatedly—for his Valentine's Day card.

"Dearest Bro: Have not been able to get to my desk because my mother and father have been in California looking for a home (for themselves). We found a place in La Jolla, and everyone is happy …Shall do better than this card as soon as I ship the parents back to Vermont. All is well. Give my love to Shaun and the dear Tanners. My love to you, Sister Peeps."

The Pearces bought a four-bedroom Spanish-style house at 6101 Avenida Cresta in La Jolla, more than a hundred miles from the metropolis of Los Angeles—much closer to Alice than New England yet far enough away for her to lead her own life. Bob and Margaret moved in to their new place on May 15. Their home would provide a happy getaway for Alice when she had free time.

With no job prospects on the horizon, three quarters of 1963 for Alice was just that: free time. Yet, when Alice was invited to attend the wedding of John Rox's niece Linda Sue Herring in Anaheim that June, she sent her regrets. "Your wedding invitation was forwarded to me," Alice wrote to Susie. "I wish I could be with you, but there is not a chance that I can get away. My thoughts will be with you and I wish that you and Charles may be as happy as John and I were." The Herrings—still not privy to Alice's West Hollywood address—were required to write to her in care of her New York apartment. It seemed as if she was keeping them at arm's length, and they found that so puzzling, so unlike the Alice they had previously known.

That same month, Alice met with Dody Goodman who was in town to film a role for Universal's *Bedtime Story* starring Marlon Brando. She caught Alice up on the latest with *High Life*, the musical which Patrick Tan-

Linda Sue Herring, circa 1962.

ner had written expressly for them. Actually, the project was in limbo. For six months Tanner had been a patient at a psychiatric facility in White Plains, New York. His attempted suicide in December 1962 had brought on "a major depressive episode."

Just prior to his illness, Tanner had revised parts of *High Life*, now retitled *Fancy Me*. "Patrick had rewritten a section for Peeps, who was to play the Cousin Alma role," explained Cris Alexander. "And anyway, he had written a couple of new songs for her. Later, while he was detained at White Plains, there were a couple of numbers that needed changing. And I had the gall to write new lyrics for some of them, one being a song for Alice called 'Wahoo,' which I sang [in her place] on the demo record, cut while Patrick was still in the hospital." Dody and some of Cris' other friends—Harold Lang, Allyn Ann McLerie,

George Gaynes, and Barbara Cason—also sang Tanner's songs on the demo. "None of it, I must tell you," Cris admitted, "was really awfully good, except for the number Barbara sang in that very deep, remarkable voice of hers. It was a Russian song, in a gypsy tavern, and it just kind of sticks in my mind because I think I've never heard anything as gross. I remember just one little bit: 'They *adore* your *odor*—drives them *simply* mad!'"

Cris dispatched Dody with the demo record to get Alice's reaction. "She never said anything negative about it to me—she was too sweet—but Dody and she talked about it when Dody was on the coast. When Dody got back to New York, she came to me laughing. She said that when Peeps heard the demo, she asked incredulously, 'You're not really going to *do* this, are you?'"

As far as *Fancy Me* went, Alice had nothing to worry about for the immediate future. By the time Tanner was released from the psychiatric hospital on August 1, 1963, Dody had already committed to do a Broadway show for the fall. Meanwhile, Tanner remained hopeful for the future of *Fancy Me*, announcing in November to *The New York Times* that Dody and Alice would "appear in the offering next October in London under the auspices of Walter Pistole." Again, Alice had no reason to fear. Tanner's plans were eventually aborted.

Conversely, his book *First Lady*, featuring ridiculous photographs of Alice, Dody, Peggy Cass and Cris' other willing models, came to fruition in August 1964. "It was a big, lavishly produced extravaganza," wrote Tanner's biographer Eric Myers, "but it could not begin to compare to the fresh outrageousness of its predecessor, *Little Me*." Most critics agreed with Russell Martz of the *Pittsburgh Press*: "What should have been one of the highlights of the literary year has turned out to be one of the most disappointing . . . the photographs are really more entertaining than [the] text."

Since film assignments continued to elude Alice during the summer and early fall of 1963, she reached out to friends for sources of amusement. As a gag, she sent Ross Hunter, fresh from producing *The Chalk Garden* in England, a "welcome-home" message penned on the back of a vintage photograph of a grinning woman wearing an elaborate 1920s bathing costume and raising an American flag: "I hope you had a happy Fourth. As you can see, I did. I long to see you."

In June, Alice flew to Las Vegas with Richard Deacon to see Mitzi Gaynor perform in her smash nightclub act at the Flamingo Hotel. Later that summer, her agent George Morris invited her to dinner at his antiques-filled home in Studio City where she reconnected with actor John Fiedler, also represented by George. Bald and bespectacled Fiedler, famous for his "helium-high" voice, had known Alice only casually in New York. "I first met her at an audition," he recalled. "We went in, and we read for something. Then I didn't see her again until she came to California. After she became George's client, the three of us became great friends and spent a lot of time together." Alice even took Fiedler to La Jolla to meet her parents, a rare honor not afforded to most of her show business friends. "Everybody loved Alice," Fiedler said.

The long list of admirers included George Morris, who, his niece said, "had many lifelong friends, and with his typical passion he loved everyone deeply." This characteristic would become obvious when George's client Ed Begley broke new ground with his acceptance speech at the Oscars ceremony, held on April 8, 1963, at the Santa Monica Civic Auditorium. In those days, agents were often the butts of nightclub jokes and largely overlooked by

Alice and Richard Deacon catch Mitzi Gaynor's act at the Flamingo in Las Vegas, 1963. She's wearing the hot pink silk evening coat from Lord & Taylor which she had first worn on camera in "The Hands of Danofrio."

noting that "she never suggests by even the flick of an eyelash that she doesn't believe in the inane business, and displays the same quality of personal radiance and projection that gave added dimension to *Bells Are Ringing.*" However, the star's valiant performance was not enough to save the show, and it closed in late May, marking the end of her career. At the time, Holliday was unknowingly experiencing the first stages of throat cancer that would later claim her life.

In the meantime, Paul realized he was never going to make it either as an actor or director in New York. Since 1959, Holliday had been his main lifeline, but now it was time to release that tenuous grasp and seek new opportunities in Los Angeles. Before leaving New York, Paul turned Alice's apartment over to her friend Gant Gaither who had asked to borrow it for the summer and fall. Gaither, too, was done with show business. After his stressful turn as producer of *My Six Loves*, Gaither "wanted to do [his] own thing," which turned out to be original animal paintings gently mocking human antics. After showing a few of his creations to the proprietor of a New York gallery, Gaither was promised an exhibit if he could produce enough pieces to fill four walls. He closed himself up in Alice's apartment and painted 124 canvases in ten days. Immediately after his showing, Gaither's art career took off. Celebrities such as Anita Loos, Helen Hayes, and Princess Grace began collecting his origi-

award-winners when publicly acknowledging associates. Begley, who won as best supporting actor for *Sweet Bird of Youth*, surprised the audience and evoked a few knee-jerk snickers with his soon-to-be famous thank-you: "But *most of all*—and this is from the heart—my *agent*, George Morris—really and truly—this man had faith in me that I didn't have myself. I never dreamed that I would get that part, but he had faith in me and he kept after it, and I got it!" George would prove to be just as tenacious on Alice's behalf.

In mid-July, Paul Davis returned to California after finally giving up his flagging stage career. Since January, he had been employed as an assistant to the producers of *Hot Spot*, the doomed musical comedy starring Paul's pal Judy Holliday. After weeks of various attempts to salvage the disorganized show, *Hot Spot* had finally opened on Broadway on April 19. *Variety*'s review paid compliments to Holliday,

nal works. Eventually Gaither's whimsical creations—he called them "Zoophisticates"—were reproduced on wallpaper, scarves, teapots, and the like.

Unfortunately, instant success did not happen for Paul Davis. Staying with Alice that summer on Holloway Drive, there was ample opportunity for him to commiserate—she had not found any acting jobs since February. Together they began plotting a new television series they titled "The Groupers." Presumably a sitcom, no other information about this project has surfaced over the years.

Meanwhile, Alice had kept her name on waiting lists with the casting directors of television commercials. She had long given up the notion that appearing in advertisements would damage her professional status. By 1963, most commercials were high quality productions, and the residuals were hard to refuse. Many casting directors preferred to cast actors instead of models and "real people" because "a talented actress with home appeal and no more than a paid interest in the product may get across the feeling of truth more effectively." They were looking for experienced actresses who were able to employ movement, facial expressions, and character development. Alice had all that down pat. While glamor types continued to be cast in ads for cosmetics, shampoos, clothing, and cigarettes, the "true-to-life" approach had taken a strong foothold in the realm of household products. True-to-life, Alice Pearce, check. Other character actors currently populating the "slice-of-life" ranks were Gertrude Berg (for S.O.S scouring pads), Wally Cox (Salvo detergent), and a pre-Palmolive Jan Miner (Goodman's Noodles).

Auditioning for commercials could be very trying, whether the competition was stiff or not. Allen Swift, who specialized in trick voices, explained the situation to *Television Maga-*

zine: "The performer hates himself for sitting there nervously waiting, hoping. But the truth is, he desperately wants the job." Commercial performers like Alice worked for scale partly because the residual system made it worthwhile and partly because ad agencies were reluctant to pay over-scale. In 1963, under the terms of the Screen Actors Guild and the American Federation for Television and Radio Artists, an on-camera performer working for scale received $95 for a straight eight-hour day. With residuals it was possible and "not particularly unusual" for a single well-used spot to bring the performer $12,000 a year.

In August 1963, Alice landed a contract for a series of two commercials for Gleem toothpaste. Cast as the strident mother of a chubby boy who gorges on cake, she frantically chases him to the school bus, screaming, "Chester, you forgot to brush your teeth!" Chester was played by seven-year-old Ken Weatherwax, later known as Pugsley on *The Addams Family* sitcom. (Previously, Jean Stapleton had appeared as a weary mother in a Gleem commercial but with much less pizzazz than Alice.)

The Gleem ads featuring Alice and Weatherwax proved to be very popular with viewers, airing continually for two years. "I had no idea the Procter & Gamble people would run those for so long," Alice sighed. "I leave the room myself now, when they come on." The commercials brought Alice more recognition from people on the street than anything she'd previously done, but she grew weary of it. "I couldn't stand that thing," she said. "People would come up to me and say, 'Oh, you're Chester's mother!' I was just a face. Nobody knew *me*." Alice didn't grouse much about the pay, though. In the first year, the residuals totaled $8,000.

In December 1964, the makers of Gleem approached Alice about filming additional commercials. "I decided that if the first two were good enough to run that long, they should pay me more money," Alice explained. "I wanted double the residuals each time the commercial ran, but they said no, and I must say I'm glad." Paul Burggraf, the director of the commercials, decided it would be foolish to try to replace Alice, so character actor Hal Peary was cast as Chester's father.

After shooting the spots for Gleem, Alice was chosen by Broadway composer Michael Brown for a small part in his musical revue *The Wonderful World of Chemistry*, to be performed in DuPont's circular pavilion at the upcoming New York World's Fair. The half-hour presentation would combine singers and dancers working interchangeably with life-sized actors on film. In one of the filmed portions, a flamboyant Marge Redmond (playing "Mrs. Weston," a nod to her real-life husband actor Jack Weston) is joined by giddy Alice and deadpan Bobo Lewis as they expound on the wonders of Dacron and Lycra fashions. In another segment, the trio demonstrates the wonders of Freon by playing a comical rendition of "The Blue Danube Waltz" using aerosol cans fitted with whistles. *Cue* magazine deemed the production "noteworthy even for the small glimpse of delightful Alice Pearce." *The Wonderful World of Chemistry* would run an unprecedented 14,600 times, or forty times a day, during two six-month seasons in 1964 and 1965. Thus, Alice was exposed to more than five million fair visitors, many of whom during the 1965 season would recognize her from *Bewitched*.

Now that Paul was permanently fixed in Los Angeles, he served as Alice's steady escort to plays, movies, or parties. One summer event was particularly noteworthy. On August 6, 1963, Paul accompanied Alice to the West Coast premiere of *The Thrill of It All* at the Village Theatre in Westwood. Sixty film celebrities were expected to attend, including Alice's fellow *Thrill* players Doris Day, James Garner, Edward Andrews, Reginald Owen, Carl Reiner, and Hayden Rorke. Others on the list—Irene Dunne, Ray Milland, Ronald Reagan, Mickey Rooney, and Barbara Stanwyck—represented Hollywood's Golden Age. Tippi Hedren, Suzanne Pleshette, and Peter Fonda were among the industry's newcomers attending the showing. The gala occasion marked Alice's first opportunity to be a part of the Hollywood debut of one of her own films.

As autumn got underway, Alice's professional calendar began to mirror her busy fall schedule of 1962. First, she returned to Columbia to film an episode of *The Donna Reed Show*, a plodding segment called "A Touch of Glamour" in which Reed gets a beautiful formal gown, loses it, and then gets it back. Alice, playing a wealthy doctor's chirping wife, is the only bright spot in the drab affair, especially in a scene where she merrily munches on finger sandwiches. To make herself look older, Alice chose a new wig interspersed with strands of gray. Noticeably heavier than a year earlier, her extra weight augmented the frumpiness of her character.

In mid-October, Alice relished a departure from her typically silly characters by accepting the role of odious Haila French in "Good-Bye, George," an episode of *The Alfred Hitchcock Hour*, a CBS series filmed at Revue Studios. Haila is a caricature (the script's "most devastating," noted one reviewer) of notorious Hollywood columnist Hedda Hopper, right down to the absurd hats Alice pulled from her own wardrobe. The story centers on film star Lana Layne, an Academy Award winner who sees her career about to go down the drain when the ex-convict husband she thought was dead turns up ready to cash in on her success. During an argument, Lana (played by Patricia Barry) strikes the man with an award statuette, killing him instantly. Turning to her manager-boyfriend Harry Lawrence (Robert Culp) for help, she agrees to go along with his scheme to bury the dead man at Harry's remote cabin outside Los Angeles. But first they invite Haila—who demands to know their honeymoon plans for her exclusive—to their quickie Tijuana wedding and then rebuff her by driving away (with the corpse stuffed into a wardrobe trunk) for a purported vacation in southern Mexico. After tooling along for an hour, they turn around and head back to the cabin in California. As the newlyweds drag the body inside, they are mortified to discover Haila and her photographers waiting in the dark to surprise them.

For this assignment, Alice disguised her weight gain with voluminous outfits, including the hot pink coat from Lord & Taylor. She seems to have had greater difficulty hiding her automatic adenoidality. On the voice track are several blatant dubs where Alice was evidently instructed make Haila sound less "witchy" and more "bitchy." In the final scene—when Haila yells "Surprise!"—it's not Alice's voice at all but that of another female artist. Nevertheless, Haila French was a role Alice could really sink her teeth into.

Meanwhile, Alice was thrilled about her return to the big screen in the Martin Manulis production of *The Out-of-Towners*, an original screenplay by Tad Mosel to be filmed by Warner Brothers and directed by Oscar winner Delbert Mann. The title referred to the lead characters, two strangers who meet at a New York City luxury hotel during a postmasters' convention. "Jack Warner said *The Out-of-Towners* was the worst title he had ever heard," Mosel recalled, "and he made us change it. Henry Mancini asked me what kind of song I wanted for the movie's signature, and I said a 'letter' song, since the story dealt with postmas-

ters. He came up with the lovely "Dear Heart," and that became the name of the picture."

Mosel and Mann, who both studied at the Yale School of Drama, had become close friends during the previous decade when hour-long teleplays were still being produced on shows like *Goodyear Television Playhouse*. Mosel, one of the genre's leading dramatists, was also associated with Manulis who produced the *Playhouse 90* series. Color television shows were yet to be the norm, and this reality may have benefitted the production of *Dear Heart*. "The producer and director and I all thought it was a 'black-and-white' story," explained Mosel. It turned out to be a convincing decision.

Geraldine Page was cast as Evie Jackson, a gentle, compassionate spinster who often unwittingly covers her inner beauty with an air of nonsensical prattle. Nonetheless, she wins the attention of Harry Mork (played by Glenn Ford), a recently promoted greeting card salesman who is just a few days away from marriage to a widow with a teenage beatnik son. Nadine Edwards, writing a review of *Dear Heart* for the *Hollywood Citizen-News*, perhaps summed up their love story best: "Two essentially lonely people who know what they want from life but aren't just certain how to go about achieving it—until they meet each other. And then her façade of the bright, gay, prattling woman slips away, while his rather worldly veneer disappears and they discover what they've been looking for—each other."

Manulis and Mann built a solid supporting cast, headed by Angela Lansbury as the determined widow; Michael Anderson Jr. as her precocious son; Barbara Nichols as a brassy magazine stand clerk; and Patricia Barry as a seductive card designer. Besides Alice Pearce, the film abounds with gifted character actors such as Ruth McDevitt, Richard Deacon, Neva Patterson, Peter Turgeon, Mary Wickes, and

Tad Mosel who wrote the screenplay for Dear Heart *(1964).*

the private histories of people coming and going, meeting and parting." That October morning, sunlight filtered down through the "soot-encrusted windows" of the busy station. Its Grand Staircase and steel-and-glass concourse roof would provide a backdrop for the movie's opening and closing scenes. Less than four weeks later, a demolition crew began jabbing at the thick granite walls with jackhammers. In a small way, *Dear Heart* managed to preserve a bit of American architectural and rail history.

The remainder of the film's scenes were shot in Hollywood at the Paramount-Sunset studios, due to an overflow at the Warners studio in Burbank. "Geraldine Page arrived for filming," Mosel recalled, "and announced that she was three months pregnant, which meant redesigning her complete wardrobe, and in some scenes, shot late, having her peer out from behind columns or hold objects in front of her. And Glenn [Ford] showed up for filming with a sty, and I commented to Martin Manulis that this must be the only picture ever made with a leading lady who could only be photographed from the neck up, and a leading man who could only be photographed from the neck down. She was so thrilled to be playing opposite a glamorous movie star, and he was so gallant and professional that the filming was sheer delight from beginning to end."

Ken Lynch. Even bits, like Barbara Luddy's disinterested hotel bookkeeper, shine under Mann's careful direction. During his previous association with the *Goodyear Television Playhouse* and the *Philco Television Playhouse*, Mann had directed Barry, McDevitt, Patterson, Turgeon, and Alice in various productions, so their inclusion in *Dear Heart* is no mystery.

Production began on October 2, 1963, with two days of location shooting for Page, Ford, and Barry at New York's majestic Pennsylvania Station, then in its final days of operation. Almost two years earlier the ailing Pennsylvania Railroad had decided to save itself by sacrificing Penn Station. Despite an outcry from preservationists, the end was very near. "A half century of emotion hung in the air," wrote historian Lorraine B. Diehl, "texturing it with memories of two world wars, a worldwide depression, and

Production was completed four days ahead of schedule on November 22, 1963, the day of President Kennedy's assassination. During post-production composer Mancini sat through the film five times before writing its score. When finished, he still had no title or lyrics for the lilting theme song. Johnny Mercer wasn't available so Mancini called in Jay Livingston and Ray Evans, who read the script, considered Page's character, and came up with the title "Dear Heart." Although he still thought *The Out-of-Towners* was the best title for the picture, Mancini then told Warner that if the film's titled had to be changed, why not use "Dear Heart." The song, which Mancini called "a waltz right straight down Middle America, with a bow toward the South," was released prior to the motion picture and became an instant hit.

The official premiere for *Dear Heart* would take place at the newly renovated Radio City Music Hall on March 8, 1965, but in order for it to be considered for Academy Award nominations, Warner Brothers rushed its release into Hollywood's Paramount Theatre on December 3, 1964. The *Los Angeles Times* called it "funny and touching." The *Valley Times*, praising Mosel's script as "human without being sentimental," labeled it as a sleeper. *Variety* noted that Ford and Page "play[ed] their respective parts for a peculiar brand of comedy with serious undertones, and here is where the film especially excels." "It received rave notices all around the country," Mosel affirmed, "but when it opened in the major cities—NYC, LA especially—it was thoroughly trounced." Bosley Crowther of *The New York Times* was particularly venomous, calling the film "stale, dull and humorless" and blaming everyone involved: Mann ("lusterless direction"), Mosel ("embarrassingly feeble and flat" dialogue), Page ("too elaborate, artificial, and improbable"), and Ford (as charming as a "punctured tire, losing air"). In 1991, Mosel confessed, "I take the blame for it, because I tried to be funnier than I am capable of being, and much of the comedy fell flat. But I still treasure the performances and love the actors for giving so much of themselves to it."

As for Alice, the film finally provided an opportunity to work with her pal Richard Deacon, who was cast as the officious post-master heading up the convention. Their lively late-night scene in the hotel bar—which took three days to film—pits their abstinent characters against a roomful of drunken postmasters. Its conclusion affords Alice a comical close-up as she begs the raucous revelers to quit drinking and go to bed. This scene is noteworthy to *Bewitched* fans for its brief exchange between Alice and Sandra Gould, both destined to play Gladys Kravitz on the hit television series.

In other scenes, the film spotlights McDevitt, Wickes, and Alice as a triumvirate of straitlaced spinster postmistresses who disapprove of Page's attempts to escape their fate. "They're after me, you know," Evie tells Harry, "for a fourth at bridge and getting tables in restaurants. There comes a time when women band together. Sometimes they don't even call each other by their first names—because they're not even friends!"

The trio of seasoned actresses presented quite a visual contrast. Lanky brunette Mary Wickes—who insisted that she was 5' 9¾" but actually may have been slightly taller—towered over dumpy, gray-haired Ruth McDevitt. Somewhere in the middle was Alice whose stooped shoulders and slightly bowed head made her appear a tad shorter than her official height (5' 3"). "We cast the roles very much for the individual characteristics which each lady brought to her role. Perhaps eccentricities might be the better word," explained Delbert Mann. "The chemistry between them worked so I didn't have to do a lot of 'directing' in the way of molding or changing what each had to give. Staging them to take advantage of them was about what happened. Ruth was getting along in years at that time so I sort of set the pace of things to her."

New York-based Ruth McDevitt, sixty-eight, had previously appeared in five Hollywood films while Mary Wickes, fifty-three, had racked

Miss Moore (Alice Pearce), Miss Tait (Ruth McDevitt) and Miss Fox (Mary Wickes) grow jealous of Evie Jackson (Geraldine Page) and her escort Harry Mork (Glenn Ford) in Dear Heart *(1964).*

up seven times that. Wickes and McDevitt would work together again in a 1970 television episode of *Here's Lucy*, but *Dear Heart* marked the final time that Wickes would perform with Alice. In 1982, when asked to share any memories of McDevitt or Alice, Wickes responded tersely, "I knew them only briefly those few times. They were both older than I and our professional backgrounds were entirely different." Granted, McDevitt was the oldest of the three, but Wickes was seven years Alice's senior. More curious is Wickes' assertion regarding disparate "professional backgrounds." A little fact-checking makes her claim rather questionable. Before joining summer stock companies, all three actresses had acquired theatrical experience during their college years. Wickes and Alice were the same age—twenty-five—at the time of their respective Broadway debuts, in 1936 and 1942. Arguably, late-bloomer McDevitt was of the same era, landing her first Broadway role in 1937. In the late 1940s, they had each helped to usher in the infant medium of television. Furthermore, all three enjoyed bicoastal acting careers for a number of years before eventually settling in Los Angeles. With such significant commonalities, why would Wickes be so dismissive?

Dear Heart's *director Delbert Mann.*

Steve Taravella, who authored the 2013 biography *Mary Wickes: I Know I've Seen That Face Before*, offers a possible explanation: "This is simply how Mary responded whenever anyone compared her to women whom she felt were less attractive or whose age was known. She went to great lengths to create the perception that she was younger than she was, and to distance herself from colleagues who were older or homely. She hated being compared with ZaSu Pitts, for instance." (It's likely then that Wickes cringed in 1973 when reading a review of her current play which identified her as having played the nosey neighbor on *Bewitched*. If she were alive today, she'd still be cringing, contends Taravella, because she and Alice Pearce continue to be confused.) Interestingly, Taravella's standpoint is substantiated by Wickes' completion of a Warner Brothers

employment form during *Dear Heart*'s production—she lopped ten years off her true age.

Professional backgrounds aside, it's interesting to note other parallels shared by Alice and Wickes, parallels that each woman almost certainly never discovered about the other. Both actresses were only children whose doting parents kept baby books and career scrapbooks for them. Wickes maintained a closer relationship with her mother's side of the family, as did Alice with the Clarks. Like Alice, Wickes took a post-college stenography course in the event that an acting career was not in the stars. During their young-adult years in New York, both women were separated from their parents by great distances, the Pearces in Paris and Wickes' family in St. Louis. Born with a sense of propriety, both Alice and Wickes rarely wore slacks, especially not in public. Perhaps most interesting is the reality that from the very beginning of Wickes' career, "those who showed greatest interest in her company . . . were gay men." In fact, Taravella says, three of these men were among "the most important people" in the actress' life. Like Bill LeMassena, Richard Deacon, Ross Hunter, and some of Alice's other gay buddies, Wickes' homosexual friends were motivated by "a strong desire to keep secret something they had good reason to believe would hurt them professionally." This factor—and Wickes' naivete at the time—may have caused her to "[think] of some of them as suitors far longer than a young woman might today." (Here is where the actresses' common avenue diverges. Although Alice may not have discussed her buddies' gay identities, she certainly didn't seem to consider them as "suitors," even those she knew many years earlier at Princeton.) Finally, and most importantly, both actresses' appearances shaped their careers. Their common attributes—pronounced noses, receding chins—"drew the notice of casting directors" but limited them to roles as nurses,

Mary Wickes, attractively photographed by Marcus Blechman, New York, circa 1948.

that she didn't apologize for her singularity, she exploited it." Carole Cook is more blunt: "Mary Wickes was a character, a tough lady! She was just cantankerous. She was prickly. She was funny and good [at her craft], but I didn't much care for her." In his biography, Taravella carefully explores possible reasons for such impressions, concluding that Wickes lived behind many walls of privacy, secrecy, and fear. No doubt Alice maintained walls of her own, but their existence seems not to have negatively affected her interactions with friends and coworkers.

During the production of *Dear Heart*, Alice sandwiched in yet another television pilot. *My Boy Goggle*, produced by Filmways and filmed at M-G-M during the final week of October, was based on a 1955 book by Bentz Plagemann. Jerry Van Dyke starred as the father of Cameron "Goggle" Wallace, an eight-year-old boy who is accused of biting his music teacher and turning his clay sculpture into a "hostility-oriented" blob. Eight-year-old Teddy Eccles (who had been one of the waifs in *My Six Loves*) played tone-deaf Goggle. Goggle's sincere attempts at singing "Forgive Us, Noble Red Man" evoke laughter from the students, but the teacher Mrs. Audubon (Alice) mistakenly thinks he's trying to disrupt her class. When she grabs him around the neck to drag him to the principal's office, she feels a sharp pain in her arm and assumes she's been bitten. In the final scene Mrs. Audubon, realizing the pain was instead produced by her bursitis, apologizes to Goggle and his parents.

My Boy Goggle was planned as a CBS series for the 1964–65 season, but no sponsors would touch it. Eccles and Pamela Dapo, playing

domestics, gossips, nagging wives and, as in *Dear Heart*, old maids.

In terms of personality, Alice Pearce and Mary Wickes were polar opposites, according to some who knew them both personally and professionally. While Alice is uniformly described by colleagues as "congenial" and "sweet," it appears that the same compliment is not often reserved for Wickes. "She wasn't a warm and cozy person," admitted Wickes' friend Anne Kaufman Schneider. "Her angularity put one off a little." Director Jack O'Brien noted, "Mary never pushed a button that asked for affection . . . she didn't project any physical, any human complicity of any kind. She was extraordinary by dint of the fact

Goggle's precocious classmate, stole every scene from the adult actors, but *Goggle* was a puny offering. It was also the fourth failed pilot that Alice had filmed in less than two years. "They all seemed so terribly funny on paper, such good comic ideas," Alice said. "But when I saw them later, I could understand why they didn't work. There was no chemistry—even the one with Walter Matthau, whom I love."

In late November, during the time of President Kennedy's assassination and its aftermath, Alice filmed "Hot Potato à la Hazel," a segment of the NBC hit series *Hazel* which united Alice with Shirley Booth whom she had known back in New York. In this episode Alice plays Miss Elsie—another rattled reject of romance—a mender of china who secretly breaks items in a bachelor's antique shop to keep him coming back to her for repairs. To increase Miss Elsie's chances, Hazel assumes the role of matchmaker, insisting that the spin-ster update her wardrobe. In the process, they are mistaken for con artists by the proprietors of a local dress shop who find $500 missing from their till. The segment adroitly showcases the talents of Alice and Emmy-winner Booth, as well as Alice Frost and Hope Summers who play the dress shop owners.

As 1963 drew to a close, Alice was beginning to feel very much at home on the West Coast. Down in La Jolla, her parents were content with their new place, and Alice was happily forming new friendships and rekindling old ones in Los Angeles. Professionally, her crossover from Broadway to Hollywood seemed to be satisfactorily complete. In a matter of months, Alice would admit, "I never thought I'd say this, but I love living in California. I don't miss New York at all. It's nonsense, all that baloney about Los Angeles being a cultural desert. You pick your own friends. You bring your own books."

CHAPTER TWENTY-THREE
The Ultimate Challenge

"I've split my dress because I've gained too much weight, too . . . so, let's make a bargain. Neither of us will remove our coats and we'll eat like sparrows tonight."

By early 1964, the Gleem toothpaste commercials featuring Alice Pearce seemed to appear on every channel of the dial. Not only did the ads provide Alice with more exposure but they also drew attention to the chubby little boy who played her son. Ken Weatherwax had no prior experience as a child actor, but he came from a show-business family. His aunt was film star Ruby Keeler, his uncle was Lassie's trainer Rudd Weatherwax, and his half-brother Donald Keeler was one of the original cast members of the *Lassie* television series. "Ken wanted to do television because of his brother," his mother explained. In February 1964, Weatherwax auditioned for *The Addams Family*, a television pilot based on Charles Addams' cartoons in *The New Yorker*. "Kenny got the role [of Pugsley] because of his exposure on the Gleem commercials. He tested with Carolyn Jones and got the part."

Coincidentally, Alice tested for the *Addams* pilot, even though the character was a wizened old woman. Alice didn't mind playing older or unattractive characters; she had recently made herself frumpish for *The Donna Reed Show* and *Dear Heart*. All she desperately wanted was to be a regular on a television series. But, at forty-six, she was told that she was too young for Pugsley's "Grandmama." Her competition had

included character actresses Minerva Urecal, who was sixty-nine, Marjorie Bennett and Blossom Rock, both sixty-eight. Rock got the part.

Just prior to this audition, Alice had played a "senior citizen" in "Auntie Up," an episode of *The New Phil Silvers Show*, a first-year CBS sitcom filmed at 20th Century-Fox Studios. This follow-up to Silvers' popular series *You'll Never Get Rich* (aka *The Phil Silvers Show*, aka *Sergeant Bilko*) cast him as Harry Grafton, a factory foreman who was always whipping up get-rich-quick schemes. By mid-season Silvers' new show was in trouble, leaving its star to admit that it was "just a watered-down version of Sgt. Bilko." Trying to save the series, Silvers decided to concentrate on Grafton's home life, adding a sister, niece, and nephew for his abrasive character to badger. It was all in vain. On January 28, 1964, four days before any of the newly formatted episodes aired, the network decided not to renew the show for the next season. When Alice arrived on the set the following week, *The New Phil Silvers Show* was like a dead man walking.

Despite its nonsensical plot, "Auntie Up" turned out to be—according to one reviewer—"one of the show's funniest outings." Alice's sizeable guest role cast her as Aunt Minnie, a sweet old lady whom Grafton hires her as a temporary housekeeper. Actually, the old girl is the operator of a floating gambling den. Each day while Grafton's family is away, Aunt Minnie breaks out the cards, poker chips and liquor, and invites her regulars in for one-hour

Phil Silvers and Alice Pearce in "Auntie Up," an episode of The New Phil Silvers Show, *1964. Photo courtesy Steve Cox.*

and direct rapport with the audience, this showcase was played as if the camera was following Goulet around on a "typical" day—rehearsing, talking to a college drama class, performing in a club, etc. During one segment, Goulet was "interviewed" at the Brown Derby by columnist Earl Wilson. Seated at the next table were Alice, Albertson, Veazie and comedian Terry-Thomas (in drag) as former college pals—an odd bit of casting since Albertson and Veazie were a generation older than Alice— arguing over how to split their luncheon check. Alice's character Francine, who had consumed only boiler-makers, was zonked out for most of the tedious exchange. Critics roundly blasted the entire production for its forced and artificial efforts at informality.

sessions of black jack and poker. When Grafton becomes wise to her racket, he determines to "out-little-old-lady the little old lady." Disguising himself as "Gladys Crump," he joins the other players, beating Aunt Minnie at her own game. Six weeks later when the segment aired, a syndicated reviewer observed, "Most of the laughs come from Alice Pearce [who] adds another great job to her list of credits."

During the week of February 17, Alice joined fellow character actresses Mabel Albertson and Carol Veazie for a taping of *An Hour with Robert Goulet*, a television special which would air on CBS the following season. Instead of the usual format: star as emcee with singing stool

After living in Los Angeles for almost two years, Alice was beginning to receive an increasing amount of recognition in the press. One contributor was Mike Connolly, whom *Newsweek* had once identified as "the most influential columnist inside the movie colony." Since 1951, he had written the successful "Rambling Reporter" column for the daily trade paper *Hollywood Reporter*. Connolly, *Newsweek* reported, was the one writer "who gets the pick of the trade items, the industry rumors, the policy and casting switches." Publicity agents wanted producers and casting directors to see their clients' names in Connolly's column because, as one press agent said, "Everyone in the industry reads Mike. But not everybody reads [Hedda] Hopper or [Louella] Parsons." By 1964, Connolly was at

Columnist Mike Connolly, 1956.

the height of his fame; his column was syndicated to 191 newspapers. To be mentioned in his "Rambling Reporter" column delivered much-coveted status.

Connolly's best sources were his best friends. Number one on that list was publicist Stanley Musgrove who happened to represent Alice Pearce. From time to time Alice's name cropped up in Connolly's column. "Much of the column was filled with press agents' expectations for their clients," explained Jack Bradford, Connolly's successor at the *Hollywood Reporter*. Oftentimes these expectations never came to fruition, like a project Connolly—employing his trademark alliteration—mentioned in his column on February 9, 1964: "The silly-season singing sister trio tapped by Sultan and Worth Productions for 'One More Time,' a musical special, consists of comediennes Alice Pearce, Phyllis Diller, and Nancy Walker, doing a dizzy takeoff on the Andrews Sisters." For more than a year, producers Arne Sultan

and Marvin Worth had been promoting their doomed screenplay—a satire of the recording industry—futilely hoping to lure pop recording artists to fill cameo roles in a film release.

One month later, Connolly reported that he was a guest at the wedding of actors Tom Troupe and Carole Cook at the First Baptist Church of Beverly Hills on March 7. Lucille Ball, Cook's only attendant, was the matron of honor. "'Twas strictly one of those it-could-happen-only-in-Hollywood weddings," Connolly rhapsodized:

It was like a script for one of Lucy's TV shows. First off, comedian Jack Weston, one of the ushers, showed me to my pew. Then, looking around, I spotted almost every comedienne in town, from Barbara Nichols and Lucy herself to Alice Pearce and Collette Jackson (that kook from *Seven Days in May*)—and all-weeping like embryo Barbara Stanwycks! Then suddenly, clank! The unmistakable sound of a wedding ring falling to the floor made all the weeping comediennes start giggling. The ring-dropper, all of us neck-craners discovered, was the six-year-old ring-bearer, Christopher Troupe, the groom's son by a previous marriage. After some scrambling, during which Lucy got down on her hands and knees to help Christopher find the ring, the bridal procession continued with Christopher at the head of it once more, head up, eyes straight ahead, unsmiling, holding the cushion that held the ring. But firmly this time. And with Lucy keeping a careful eye on his every step. And then, clank! Christopher hit a too-smooth section of the newly-waxed middle aisle and went down for the long count, all 30 pounds of him. I looked at Lucy. She was the only one there who wasn't laughing uproariously. And with good reason, as she explained later at the reception: "I couldn't decide which was most important—to pick up Christopher or look for the ring!" As it happened, ushers Weston and Ray Stricklyn solved Lucy's problem: one picked up Christopher and dusted him off, one found the ring and gave it a quick re-polish by blowing on it.

Since Paul Davis' return to Los Angeles the previous July, he had reconnected with the savvy and witty Carole Cook, his former Desilu Workshop crony. Occasionally, he and Alice socialized with Cook, yet she wasn't aware that Alice and Paul may have been sharing the apartment on Holloway Drive. "I would always see them together, but I never got the feeling that they were living together as a romantic couple." Paul had never mentioned any former love interests, Cook says, but she surmised that he was either gay or bisexual. "And if you'd told me that they lived together but there was no sexual attraction, I would have said, 'Oh, that's nice,' because there are women who live with men who are gay, and they are really joined at the hip." As for Alice's perception of the situation, Cook is emphatic: "She was *not* a dummy, so she would have known about [Paul's sexual identity]!"

Jonathan Oppenheim, the only child of Judy Holliday, knew Paul far better than he knew Alice, although he found Alice "very likeable." To Oppenheim, Alice was simply "a friend of a friend." Paul, however, who spent the majority of three years—August 1960 to July 1963—in New York, frequently passed time with Holliday and her family.

During this interval Oppenheim, maturing from seven to ten years old, was frequently privy to conversations between the adults in his life. In fact, they spoke rather freely around him. "One thing that I heard, and possibly from my grandmother, was that Paul was gay," says Oppenheim who hastens to add, "People were very open with me, but I didn't necessarily process this type of information fully." In fact, this revelation left Oppenheim somewhat confused because he knew that Paul loved Alice. "He made that very clear to me, even though I was a young person. He talked about her a lot, using the pet name he'd given her—Alicia. There was something that really drew Paul strongly to Alice. I felt that she was somebody he really aspired to have a relationship with."

There are those who would argue that perhaps "friendship" is a more authentic term than "relationship." Consider this intriguing nugget which appeared in Mike Connolly's column of January 2, 1960: "Desilu actor Pesha Darshefsky changed his name, proof-readers all over the country will be happy to know, to Paul Davis and proposed to comedienne Alice Pearce." At the time, Alice was still based in New York, and Paul—in from the West Coast—was spending the holidays with his parents in Massachusetts. It is possible that he could have detoured to Manhattan and popped the question to Alice before returning to California, but there is nothing to substantiate such a side trip. Connolly's tidbit doesn't mention Alice's response, nor is it revealed in any subsequent column.

Studying Connolly's typical techniques provides a possible reason for reporting this curious item. First of all, the columnist's biographer Val Holley—extolling his subject as "a virtuoso of the gorgeous properties of the English language"—admits that Connolly may have fabricated much of what appeared the "Rambling

Reporter." Secondly, Holley maintains that Connolly's column, "for those who knew how to read between the lines, was a remarkable daily chronicle of gay goings-on." Although Connolly lived openly with a male partner, he was cautious not to write about that aspect of his life, bowing to the Hollywood protocol of the day. In fact, he sometimes falsely promoted himself as a skirt-chaser. "He rendered the same service to other homosexuals," says Holley, "assuring his audience . . . that Cesar Romero, Sal Mineo, Tab Hunter . . . and other gay actors had been spotted . . . with opposite-sex dates." In this way, Connolly demonstrated that Hollywood's homosexuals were "meeting society's requirements."

If those of Connolly's readers (who had *not* the ability to read between the lines) were waiting for an exclusive description of Paul and Alice's wedding or reception, they eventually abandoned their expectations. Only one month after announcing that Paul had proposed to Alice, Connolly dropped this jewel: "Ruth Roman's not-so-ever-lovin' mate, Budd Moss, finally moved out of their home, following their separation of a month ago. And Paul Davis is now romancing Ruth." The great majority of Connolly's readers may not have even known who Paul Davis was, much less that he was an old schoolmate of Roman's with no romantic interest whatsoever. Over the years, Paul had frequently escorted Roman to movie premieres and other events in Hollywood—much like confirmed bachelor Cesar Romero had perpetually squired friends like Agnes Moorehead and Barbara Stanwyck to various functions. Those in the know realized that coupling Paul and Roman was both meaningless and typical-Connolly. Carole Cook, who professed to know Paul quite well at this point in his life, never heard him speak of any emotional attachments at all. Perhaps

Paul, intent on finally becoming successful by following all of Hollywood's rules, had hired Stanley Musgrove to feed the two tidbits to Connolly.

Paul remained on the coast for much of 1960 while Alice was doing her own thing in New York. As time went on, others began to realize that Connolly's item about their pairing of Paul with Alice carried as much weight as Walter Winchell's 1959 vague hint that Alice and Bill LeMassena would soon marry.

"I think that Alice and Paul were just buddies," insists Cook, who never visited Alice's Holloway Drive apartment but occasionally met them with her husband for dinner out. "I think that he was her best friend." By late 1963, Alice and Paul were almost inseparable.

Cook was among the first to visit Paul's new framing shop, which he had opened that fall. Pesha's Framing Studio was located at 8568 Melrose Avenue in West Hollywood, less than a mile south of Holloway Drive. Paul offered custom framing, but he also sold oil paintings, Svedborg drawings, framed theatrical posters and commemorative stamps. Alice shopped there, too. For Christmas that year, she sent Debbie Reynolds a framed set of show business stamps. "Alice dear, your gift was exquisite," Reynolds wrote from Palm Springs on January 8, 1964. "I have one more week of looping and stills on *Molly Brown* and then old Mother will be-a-callin' for a dinner date, as I have missed seeing you and we think [of you] so very often and cherish your sweet friendship dearly."

Early in 1964, Carole Cook and Tom Troupe were in Pesha's when Alice came in. "I remember it to this day," says Cook, "because it was rather shocking. She walked in, and I swear to God, the only thing I can tell you is that her stomach was quite distended. It was very noticeable. She said, 'I'm just worried about my stomach. I can't hold it in anymore.'" When

Cook suggested that Alice should ask her doctor about it, she and Paul both revealed that they had no regular doctor in the area. Cook and Troupe insisted that Alice go see their trusted personal physician, Hilard Kravitz, a general practitioner who was also their good friend. (Dr. Kravitz had given Cook away on her wedding day.) Alice agreed to get an appointment and to let Cook know the results.

"I always wondered why she didn't go sooner—but that's not for me to say—because it was *painfully* obvious that something was wrong," Cook says. In truth, there were indications of an irregularity months earlier. While Alice "was naturally inclined to be a tubby," as Richard Deacon once noted, her weight had drastically increased in 1963. One evening that summer when Deacon arrived at her apartment, he discovered that the seat of his pants had split. "I was pretty embarrassed—not only because of my pants splitting but because I'd gained weight and none of my clothes fit! And, as it happened, that was the night we were to fly to Las Vegas for an opening. Alice, I might add, was dressed to kill in a blushing-pink dress with matching coat. As we were leaving for the airport, Alice saw that I was still feeling embarrassed. So she said, 'Look, Deke, I want to show you something.' Then she took off her coat and showed me that her lovely dress was entwined from neck to waist with white shoelaces. 'I split my dress because I've gained too much weight, too,' she told me. 'And this is how I've fixed it for tonight! So let's make a bargain. *Neither* of us will remove our coats and we'll eat like sparrows tonight.'"

That fall, when Alice filmed *Dear Heart*, she chose a loose-fitting dress suit for the drunken postmasters scene, but her abdomen was still visibly distended. In another segment, her too-tight suit jacket didn't meet, emphasizing her expanding waistline. For her final scene in the movie, Alice resorted to the voluminous pink coat she'd worn to Las Vegas. Ill-fitting clothing, weight gain, and a distended abdomen were all signs of a condition that she should not have ignored.

When Alice finally saw Dr. Kravitz, he knew immediately that there was a serious medical issue. "Alice called me," Cook remembers, "and she said, 'It's a little more of a problem than I thought. He's sending me to another doctor.' She never mentioned the words 'cancer' or 'hysterectomy' to me."

Alice's new doctor was thirty-two-year-old Thomas E. Jacobson, who was also a clinical instructor at the UCLA medical school. He recommended surgery to determine the exact problem. Alice agreed but requested a delay since she had two film assignments already lined up for April. While she was concerned for her health, she was also realistic regarding the effect these new developments could have on her career. "Alice wanted to keep working and was afraid if people knew she was sick that they wouldn't hire her," says Terry Votichenko, the son of one of Alice's college friends, Helen Tuttle. In the meantime, Alice confided the details of her upcoming operation only with Paul.

First on her schedule was a small comic part in *Bus Riley's Back in Town*, a B-grade picture budgeted at $550,000 and filmed in less than six weeks at Universal City. William Inge's screenplay was an expanded version of his one-act play. The title character is a young, athletically trim male who returns to his small town after a three-year stint in the navy. Picking up the pieces of his life—while trying to resist the seductive charms of an old flame who's now married—he attempts to make something of himself. Although an excellent auto mechanic, Bus (played by Michael Parks) is recruited by hot-shot salesman (Brad Dexter) to be his assistant, selling vacuum cleaners door-to-

Novice salesman Michael Parks watches the cleaning contraption as his boss Brad Dexter watches the customer, Alice Pearce, in Bus Riley's Back in Town *(1965).*

door. On Parks' first day, Dexter shows him how to charm lonely housewives into buying their product. Alice plays a gullible, apple-munching customer who has an eye for the husky Dexter, subtly stroking his jacket lapel as he explains their company's "atomic method" for cleaning average houses. When Dexter and Parks set off an "atomic mist bomb" to rid her home of "bacteria, germs and larvae," the ensuing explosion propels the shrieking woman into Slocum's protective arms. She then exits to prepare the men some coffee, and Dexter, snapping his fingers, announces to Bus, "Sold!"

Alice filmed her scene during the first week of April. By the end of the month, *Bus Riley* was in the can. Or so Inge thought. "When we signed Ann-Margret [as the old flame], she wasn't quite a big star," he explained to *Variety*, "but in six months she was, and Universal became very frightened of her public image.

They wanted a more refined image of her." In January 1965, the studio ordered many of Inge's scenes rewritten and re-shot to glorify Ann-Margret. (A few original segments were sacrificed for the inclusion of these new scenes. One that landed on the cutting room floor featured Natalie Schafer—soon to become known as "Mrs. Howell" on television's *Gilligan's Island*—as one of Parks' prospective vacuum cleaner customers.) Suddenly bumped up from supporting player to name-above-the-the-title star, Ann-Margret became the focus of *Bus Riley's Back in Town*. Chagrined that his original story had been altered without his input, Inge asked that his name be removed from the film's credits.

Bus Riley's Back in Town opened in Los Angeles on March 24, 1965. Promotional ads displaying Ann-Margret's curvy underwear-clad frame steered attention away from Inge's title character, but the critics were not fooled. Howard Thompson of *The New York Times*, thoroughly dismissed Ann-Margret's sex kitten role. Winking at Inge, he found most of the picture "exquisitely written," yet missing its target when Parks "uncorks a set of James Dean mannerisms that minimize his dilemma—young man without hope." The "beauty and backbone" of the picture, said Thompson, was its gallery of small-town characters, including Kim Darby as Bus' spunky and wistful younger sister, Janet Margolin as her sensitive young friend, Crahan Denton as a lonely, aging gay mortician, and Brett Somers as a high-strung spinster schoolteacher.

Alice's second film assignment—scheduled to follow closely on the heels of *Bus Riley*—was equally perfunctory but far more noteworthy . . . and controversial. Billy Wilder's sex comedy *Kiss Me, Stupid* boasted Dean Martin, Kim Novak, and Ray Walston as its leads plus a lush musical score by André Previn and three previ-

Bearing a petition to close down the local honky-tonk, Mrs. Mulligan (Alice Pearce) and Reverend Carruthers (John Fiedler) solicit a signature from Zelda Spooner (Felicia Farr) in Kiss Me, Stupid *(1964).*

Belly Button. When Dino starts romancing Polly, Orville throws him out of the house for molesting his "wife." Meanwhile, Zelda gets so drunk at The Belly Button that she's taken to Polly's trailer out back to sleep it off. Dino arrives at the bar looking for a hook up and is directed to the trailer, where Zelda pretends to be Polly. Weeks later, Orville becomes bewildered when he sees Dino singing one of his songs on television. Turning to Zelda for an answer, she simply smiles, "Kiss me, stupid."

ously unreleased songs by George and Ira Gershwin. Wilder and fellow screenwriter I. A. L. Diamond loosely based their script on an Italian farce, transporting their characters to a small Nevada town called Climax. Smooth crooner Dino (Martin), a hard-drinking womanizer en route from Las Vegas to Hollywood, stops there for gas and encounters oafish mechanic Barney Millsap (winningly played by Cliff Osmond), an unsuccessful amateur songwriter whose collaborator is piano-teacher Orville J. Spooner (Walston). Barney sabotages Dino's sports car and persuades him to stay at Orville's house for the night in hopes that he might buy some of their songs. Orville is worried, though, that his attractive wife Zelda (Felicia Farr) might become one of Dino's conquests. Orville provokes an argument with Zelda so that she will leave the house and replaces her with Polly the Pistol (Novak), a hooker who moonlights as a cocktail waitress at a roadhouse called The

A wealth of comic actors filled small roles in *Kiss Me, Stupid*, including the inimitable Doro Merande as Farr's acidic mother, Howard McNear (Floyd the barber on *The Andy Griffith Show*) as Merande's longsuffering husband, and a tarted-up Barbara Pepper (soon to be Doris Ziffel on *Green Acres*) as Big Bertha, proprietor of The Belly Button. Alice's close friend John Fiedler appeared briefly as the local minister, the leader of a little band of prim parishioners—including Alice—intent on shutting down the Belly Button. Alice shines brighter, though, in another short scene as a patient of jokester-dentist Mel Blanc who elicits her trademark cackles.

Ray Walston was not Wilder's first choice—or even second—to play the insanely jealous Orville. He had initially intended for Jack Lemmon to play the part but had to settle for British film comic Peter Sellers when Lemmon became unavailable. Principal photography with Sellers began on March 6 at the

Goldwyn Studios in West Hollywood. One month into production, Sellers had a heart attack or a series of heart attacks, depending on the source one consults. Doctors advised six months of recuperation, so back to England he went. Wilder quickly replaced Sellers with Walston, who had previously appeared in Wilder's *The Apartment*. "Alice and I were just about to report to the studio for our scene, and Sellers had his heart attack so we never filmed with him," John Fiedler recalled in 2003. "Our shooting date was postponed." This deferment also delayed Alice's planned surgery, adding more anxiety to her unsettling situation.

Meanwhile, Wilder had his own problems to worry about. "At issue was the intentional coarseness of the humor Wilder and Diamond were playing with," says John M. Miller of Turner Classic Movies. "They were going to be testing the limits of censorship organizations in America, and they must have known that a fight was looming." During an October sneak preview of the film, many audience members stalked out, but surprisingly *Kiss Me, Stupid* received approval from the Production Code Administration. "Though Wilder's film treated its vulgarity with an in-your-face brashness few other directors would have attempted," wrote Frank Miller for his 1994 book *Censored Hollywood*, "it really was no worse than other pictures [the PCA] had felt compelled to pass." Wilder had already turned down a request from the PCA to change a key scene near the end of the movie which left no doubt that Farr's character had cheated on her husband with Dino, but he began to have second thoughts when the studio expressed embarrassment. To appease the Catholic Legion of Decency, Wilder called Martin and Farr back to reshoot the scene, slightly cleaning it up. It did no good—the Legion slapped *Kiss Me, Stupid* with a "C" (Condemned) rating

and advised the nation's forty million Catholics to stay away. United Artists immediately announced that it would not release the film, then "it quietly turned the picture over to its subsidiary, Lopert Pictures, for nationwide distribution."

By the time *Kiss Me, Stupid* opened in Los Angeles on December 18, 1964, everyone in Hollywood seemed to be following the story. Reviews were generally negative. *Variety* allowed that *Kiss Me, Stupid* was not likely to corrupt viewers but criticized its "cheap" and "crude" handling of a "contrived double adultery situation." *The New York Times*, noting the film's condemnation, opined that its "exceedingly larger stigma [is] being pitifully unfunny." *Life* deemed it "a titanic dirty joke, an embarrassment to audiences, the performers and the industry which produced it." Wilder defended his film, calling it "a comedy . . . which deals with human dignity, with the revolt of the little man." Conceding that many of his pictures had dealt with sex, he reasoned, "What the critics call dirty in our pictures, they call lusty in foreign films. This is not a French film or an Italian film. It is a Hollywood film. Automatically it goes under the microscope as very suspect . . . Audiences have grown up. One can do almost everything. It depends on how you do it."

Alice's reaction to the furor went undocumented, but her fellow castmate John Fiedler, almost forty years afterwards, recalled: "When it came out, it was the biggest flop. Billy Wilder was at the top of his game, but they had to kind of clean it up because of morality issues. In the original script, there was no question that [Farr] went to bed with Dean Martin and so forth. They had to pussyfoot around that. I thought that the script they started with was much funnier. Nowadays, that kind of Puritanism doesn't exist, but it did then."

In May 1964, very soon after Alice completed filming her scenes for *Kiss Me, Stupid*, she entered the hospital to undergo exploratory surgery. The surgeon had but to take one look, and the fearful fact was revealed—Alice had ovarian cancer. Most devastating was the harsh reality that very few treatment options existed for ovarian cancer patients, especially if the cancer had metastasized. Alice was informed that her disease was incurable.

Only a few weeks before, Dr. Albert B. Lorincz, chairman of the department of obstetrics and gynecology at Creighton University School of Medicine in Omaha, had addressed the Clinical Congress of Abdominal Surgeons in Chicago. Lorincz reported that an estimated 9,000 American women would die that year of ovarian cancer, the highest death rate of all pelvic cancers and one of the highest among cancers generally. The average age at diagnosis was fifty years old. "Delay in ovarian cancer diagnosis is reprehensible," said Lorincz, "with the blame shared by physicians and patients." Another speaker at the same conference reported that a recent study of Americans who underwent delayed surgeries showed that 47 percent of them had not realized they needed operations, 10 percent could not bear the expense and 11 percent had been "just plain negligent."

It's difficult to say exactly how Alice's particular case fit with these percentages. It's probable that she showed ambiguous symptoms—or perhaps no symptoms at all—for quite a while, as is characteristic of ovarian cancer. There are also indications that Alice may have been neglectful. After Alice's death, rumors of her delayed response began to circulate, including one shared by her former agent Barron Polan. Writing from New York to an ailing Agnes Moorehead in Wisconsin, Polan admonished: "But it is important to guard that greatest of possessions, your health. I guess poor Alice Pearce must be a lesson for all of us, for I was told that she was warned, but did not take the time out to see." Carole Cook cannot forget the day in Paul's shop when Alice asked for advice. "I remember thinking then, 'I can't believe she hasn't gone to the doctor,'" Cook says. "I was stunned. I really was. And that stayed with me."

Alice's doctors were unsure how rapidly the disease would progress, informing her that she may have only months to live, a few years at the most. Alice was astounded by the prognosis. She was only forty-six years old, beginning a new life, building a film career after years of devoting her attention to the stage. How could this be happening to her, she agonized. Her parents were in their seventies and in relatively good health. And Grandmother Clark had reached ninety-five. As she tried to come to grips with her own mortality, Alice's thoughts turned to her beloved husband John who had died without warning shortly after his fifty-fifth birthday.

The initial numbness Alice felt was followed only briefly by a sense of helplessness. These emotions quickly gave way to an iron-like determination to get on with life. Alice's immediate concern was two impending film assignments, one of which was particularly choice. She knew that if she suddenly turned them down without a logical explanation, questions would be asked. On the other hand, if she were forthcoming about her illness, producers in the entertainment industry may consider her employment as a risk.

Not willing to jeopardize her career, Alice chose to say nothing about her current situation, even with her agent George Morris. Besides, it was against her nature. "Although very warm and congenial, Alice was always a *very* private person," actress Jane Dulo recalled in 1984. Moreover, Alice had always hated gossip. "She once told my mother that Hollywood was a very small community," says Terry Votichenko, "and that whatever you said about people could very easily get back to them and make it difficult to get jobs or to be able to work with them later on. As a result, Alice was often very circumspect. Unless she knew people well, she was often hesitant to open up to them." Votichenko's mother Helen, one of Alice's oldest friends, was among the few to whom Alice disclosed her diagnosis. To her friends in the entertainment industry, she said nothing.

Although Alice's type of surgery usually required six to eight weeks of recovery, she could not allow herself that luxury without arousing suspicion. She was back to work by June 3, after only three weeks of rest. Her brief role in 20th Century-Fox's *Erasmus with Freckles* would require just one day's work.

Produced and directed by Henry Koster, *Erasmus with Freckles* was based on John Haase's satirical novel of the same title. The film version centered around an absent-minded but brilliant poet/college professor Robert Leaf (played by James Stewart) who lives with his family on a houseboat in Sausalito, California. His son, eight-year-old Erasmus (ten-year-old Billy Mumy), is a mathematical genius who writes love letters to the international film star Brigitte Bardot. After the boy wins a small fortune handicapping horse races, he and his father travel to France to meet Bardot in the flesh.

The climactic scene with Bardot was actually filmed first. Stewart, Mumy, and the crew flew to Paris on May 15, and shooting began three days later on a set designed to resemble Bardot's real home. Sandwiched between the Paris segment and a location shoot at Sausalito was a two-week stretch at the Fox studios near Beverly Hills, where Alice's ninety-second scene was filmed.

Stewart's character, after quitting his teaching job, checks in at the state employment bureau and is greeted by Alice, playing a chipper, wisecracking office clerk, just the type of earthy part she enjoyed. With a minimum of mugging and just a tad of chortling, Alice makes the very best of her screen time (much like she had for her small part several years earlier as the store clerk in "Merry Christmas, Mr. Baxter" on *The Alcoa Hour)*. When Stewart explains his literary talents, she quips, "Oh boy, this morning so far, I've had an oyster-opener, a balloonist, a circus fat lady who claims she went on a diet and lost her job, and now I got me a poet!" Stewart attempts to prove his authenticity with a poetry anthology bearing his name, but Alice is unimpressed. Plunking a hefty directory on the counter, she responds, "See this? My name's in this book—that don't make me a telephone!" Alice—afforded the closest "close-up" of her movie career as she flirts with Stewart—looks better than ever and without a hint of her recent trauma.

During post-production the studio changed the film's title to *Dear Brigitte*, despite previously making a pact with Bardot that her name would not be used in any publicity. The finished product, opening on January 27, 1965, in New York, did not elicit much praise. Bosley Crowther deemed it "synthetic," and Margaret Harford of the *Los Angeles Times* branded it "a cliché-ridden comedy for the family, innocuous and predictable." Meanwhile, straitlaced Jeanne Miller of the *San Francisco Examiner* condemned its vulgarity ("an eight-year-old boy's raging passion for Brigitte Bardot") but startlingly concluded on a complimentary note: "The film's funniest sequence is a vignette by Alice Pearce, who plays a marvelously amusing bureaucratic clerk."

James Stewart and Alice Pearce compare books in
Dear Brigitte *(1965).*

The day after Alice finished work on *Dear Brigitte*, she signed a contract to appear in *The Disorderly Orderly*, a Paramount production starring Jerry Lewis. The comedy would be the eighth and final Lewis picture directed by Frank Tashlin whose slapstick films had been influenced by his previous work as a Warner Brothers animator. "Tashlin had played a pivotal role in the evolution of Lewis' life and art," asserts essayist David Ehrenstein. However, Tashlin's *Disorderly Orderly* screenplay, says film scholar Ethan de Seife, deviates significantly from his typical technique in that "it contains minimal amounts of two of his most important stylistic calling cards: sexual humor and satire." Unlike *Kiss Me, Stupid*, the Production Code Administration considered *Orderly* a "very 'clean' film."

Production began on Monday, June 8, 1964, with a lengthy location shoot at the Greystone Mansion in Beverly Hills, not much more than a mile away from Alice's apartment. Completed in 1928, the 55-room Tudor Revival mansion and its lovely grounds served as the exteri-

or setting for the film's Whitestone Sanitarium & Hospital. Also known as the Doheny Mansion, Greystone had been a private residence until 1955. Since then, the 16-acre property had been occasionally leased to film studios. The previous summer, Greystone was used in the Bette Davis film *Dead Ringer*. Immediately following the completion of *The Disorderly Orderly*, the mansion and its grounds were heavily featured in M-G-M's *The Loved One*.

The plot of *The Disorderly Orderly* is rather simple. Lewis plays title character Jerome Littlefield, a medical school dropout who suffers from "neurotic identification empathy," a condition which causes him to suffer the pains of his patients. His overanxiety to help them produces mayhem throughout the exclusive sanitarium, but its administrator Dr. Howard (played by Glenda Farrell) is too fond of him to fire him. Although nurse Julie Blair (Karen Sharpe) is in love with Jerome, he falls for Susan Andrews (Susan Oliver), a bitter young woman who's hospitalized following a suicide attempt. When Jerome takes on extra duties to pay for the young woman's hospital stay, she offers him her love out of gratitude. However, their first kiss is unmagical, and Jerome concludes that he must be in love with Julie, whom he ultimately wins back.

The Disorderly Orderly abounds with stand-alone sight gags which have nothing to do with the narrative. In one comic segment, Lewis drinks from a fountain marked "Pure Mineral Water." As he swallows, we hear what sounds like rocks rattling around in a metal can. Another gag occurs when Lewis bites into an apple while in a quiet zone, and "the ensuing crunch brings all nearby activity to a halt." Yet another, involving Barbara Nichols as an irritable film vixen, is an example of impossible comedy. When Jerome attempts to repair her staticky, or "snowy," television screen by opening up the set,

Jerome Littlefield (Jerry Lewis) gags as Mrs. Fuzzyby (Alice Pearce) describes "bile mixing with the stomach acid" in The Disorderly Orderly *(1964).*

a roaring blizzard erupts from inside, filling her hospital room with real snow.

Alice's scenes—shot in the formal gardens of the Greystone Mansion—are among the few comic segments which actually advance the plot. Cast as Mrs. Fuzzyby, an entitled hypochondriac, Alice gives a superb film performance, second only to Lucy Shmeeler in *On the Town*. As Jerome wheels Mrs. Fuzzyby around the hospital grounds, she stops to chat with other patients, rhapsodizing about her ills and operations. Poor Jerome reacts with nausea to her brilliantly detailed description of her leaky gall bladder, dripping its bile into her stomach and mixing with acid before it rises into her throat, gagging and choking her. He also endures her "broken leg story," complete with eighty-nine stitches and dried-up marrow, but when Mrs. Fuzzyby begins her oft-repeated saga of her weak kidneys, he desperately tries to distract her. As he blabbers on, her cool condescension advances to eye-rolling annoyance before she finally roars, "WILL YOU BE QUIET?!"

Mrs. Fuzzyby appears again near the end of the film when Jerome, thinking his love frustration is resolved, tests his ability to withstand her graphic miseries. Charmed that Jerome is now interested in her digestive tract, Mrs. Fuzzyby smiles broadly and boasts, "My intestines are like a blast furnace in August!" Jerome sails through with flying colors, even surviving the "weak kidney" epic, and dashes off to find Julie, his true love.

According to Tashlin's preliminary script, he designed the roles of Mrs. Fuzzyby and those eventually filled by Jack E. Leonard and Barbara Nichols for three "cameo guest stars." Nichols and Leonard received billing as such, but Alice—evidently not perceived as part of their echelon—did not. Tashlin (and Lewis) may

have considered bigger names for the part of Mrs. Fuzzyby, but it's difficult to imagine who else could have matched the artistry of Alice Pearce. She inhabited the role. Writer Gary Brumburgh recognizes Alice's segment as "the one comic moment critics invariably mention when recalling *The Disorderly Orderly*." *Variety* called Alice's performance a "standout," and *The New York Times*, citing Alice's scene as one of "only two hilarious bits," found her "screamingly funny."

Clocking in at only eighty-nine minutes, *The Disorderly Orderly* wrapped on August 24. Even though it was the last of Alice's 1964 films to be completed, *Orderly* was rushed into release ahead of *Bus Riley's Back in Town* and *Dear Brigitte*, opening in Seattle on December 18, the same day *Kiss Me, Stupid* premiered in Los Angeles. As moviegoers howled at Jerome Littlefield's attempts not to wet his pants while Mrs. Fuzzyby rattled on about her weak kidneys, they remained unaware of the scene's irony. The lively little actress in the wheelchair gave no indication that she herself was seriously ill, that she was yet reeling from the recent prognosis which gave a prophetic meaning to one of her lines: "But I guess I'll live long enough to suffer even more."

After *Orderly*, Alice's freed-up schedule allowed her time to contemplate the future and to put her house in order. Most significantly, she signed papers to make her confidante and best friend the sole beneficiary of her pensions with the Screen Actors Guild, the American Federation of Television and Radio Artists, and the Actors' Equity Association. "I made a pact with Alice—and with myself—that I would never leave her," Paul Davis later explained. "We didn't know if it would be three months or three years."

CHAPTER TWENTY-FOUR
Gladys Kravitz

"Now, I'm Gladys Kravitz and people are even beginning to know my real name."

TV Guide hailed the 1964-65 television season as "the year of the chuckle." Of the ninety-six network shows to be aired during prime time, forty-six were comedies, almost half of which were new series. "We have funny sailors, funny soldiers, funny Marines and funny Waves," the magazine announced. "Silly monsters, fey witches, zany newlyweds, madcap castaways, a droll robot and many other comedy characters are being added to a schedule already rocking with the ludicrous antics of a teenager, a Martian, oil-rich hillbillies, lovable sheriffs, and a number of kooky civilian families." The bumper crop of new "escapist sitcoms" included *The Addams Family*, *Bewitched*, *Gilligan's Island*, *The Munsters*, and *My Living Doll*.

Earlier in the year, before her terminal diagnosis, Alice had lost a chance to join the cast of ABC's *The Addams Family*. Now she thought that may have been for the best. Under the present circumstances, there was no certainty that she would be able to complete an entire television season. In fairness to any interested television producers—and to their shows—Alice reasoned that she should instead concentrate on the short term and hope for guest spots on some of the season's new offerings. After all, she still needed to support herself, and she was determined to pursue her acting career for as long as her health would permit. At the same time, Alice continued to guard her dire secret. In fact, it's likely that she still had not even confided in her agent George Morris. Without a hint of any troubles, Alice attended auditions suggested by George, just as she had before her surgery.

In July 1964, Alice won a guest role on the new CBS sitcom *Many Happy Returns*, starring character actor John McGiver as the head of "adjustments and refunds" at Krockmeyer's Department Store in Los Angeles. Created and produced by Parke Levy—whose earlier sitcom successes *December Bride* and *Pete and Gladys* had aired on the same network—*Many Happy Returns* had been touted as a hit by CBS executive Hunt Stromberg even before any post-pilot episodes had been filmed. "It's not the type of show we have been doing," Stromberg told *Variety* in May. "It's more of a return to sentimental comedy which we think the audience is ready for."

Nevertheless, by the time Alice reported to the show's set at M-G-M Studios on July 28, the series was in turmoil. Production had been shut down for the past month in order to edit the three previously filmed episodes, including the pilot. During the layoff, CBS bigwigs and representatives of General Foods (the show's sponsor) ordered Levy to reshape storylines and change the lead character Walter Burnley (played by McGiver). Levy, as sole owner of the show, dug his heels in. Henceforth, the executives led "a running feud over creative control" with Levy—an unhappy affair which carried over to the work environment. "That was a mean set," recalled Stanley Cherry who directed a number of the show's episodes.

Alice's episode—"A Date for Walter"—was intended to get *Many Happy Returns* back on track. Levy brought in veteran director Marc Daniels to handle the script created by long-time partners Ray Singer and Dick Chevillat, most recently known for their work on *The Lucy Show*. The story aimed for the type of sentimentality extolled by Stromberg but unfortunately missed the mark. Walter's subordinate Joe Foley (played by Mickey Manners) is threatened with dismissal for tardiness and sleeping on the job. When Walter investigates, he learns that Joe has been trying to propose to his sweetheart but the girl's mother Mrs. Walsh (Alice) will not leave the room, no matter how late Joe stays. Walter phones the mother with a fictitious story about her winning the nonexistent title of Krockmeyer's Queen for a Night contest. To get Mrs. Walsh out of the house so that Joe can spend time alone with the daughter, Walter takes her out on the town. However, she becomes extremely obnoxious by getting tipsy and running up the bill.

The finished product was such a disappointment that CBS shelved "A Date for Walter," reserving it for a late-season telecast in March of the following year. By that time, the fate of *Many Happy Returns* had long been determined. On December 18, 1964, CBS cancelled the show when Levy abandoned negotiations with both the network and sponsor. "I refused to give them creative control," he stated flatly when interviewed by *Variety*. The experience left Levy—"the only comedy writer in the millionaire class"—with such a bitter taste that he essentially relinquished his thirty-year show business career and retired comfortably. In the meantime, Alice Pearce moved on—to a rewarding, life-changing venture.

The very week that Alice Pearce filmed "A Date for Walter," a three-member team at Screen Gems began discussions to cast supporting roles for the studio's new television series *Bewitched*, scheduled to premiere on ABC in September. The show's leading roles had been cast nine months earlier when the series pilot was produced. Elizabeth Montgomery and Dick York were set to star as newlyweds Samantha and Darrin Stephens, with Agnes Moorehead as Samantha's mother Endora. The sitcom's premise was simple. Samantha was a perky, attractive modern-day witch who preferred not to exercise her craft but was often forced to do so when her wacky relatives and mortal husband got themselves into trouble. Her domineering mother, also a witch, viewed the mixed marriage with unwavering contempt.

Harry Ackerman, William Asher, and Danny Arnold—the creative forces behind *Bewitched*—each brought his own expertise to the table. As Screen Gems vice-president of production, Ackerman had supervised numerous programs for the past six years, becoming "almost single-handedly responsible for the success of the studio's sitcoms." Asher, a television pioneer, had directed more than one hundred episodes of *I Love Lucy*, as well as dozens of other television series and motion pictures. Newly married to Montgomery when he directed the *Bewitched* pilot, Asher would continue as the series director, yet—in the words of one *Bewitched* historian—he "was essentially a silent producer." Arnold was a former film editor-comedy writer-director who had graduated to producer (*The Real McCoys*). Hired by Ackerman as *Bewitched*'s official producer and story consultant, Arnold possessed a versatility which *Variety* estimated as "a few cuts above most comedy producers."

During pre-production, Arnold edited the over-long *Bewitched* pilot—which would air as the series' first episode—to fit the allotted thirty-minute time slot. His position also required him to engage writers for subsequent episodes. "A writer-turned producer has a distinct advantage," Arnold maintained. "He can not only protect the scripts he writes but can doctor the others. In most cases it's the producer who provides the story line. I get two drafts from the writers and then go to work on them."

Barbara Avedon was hired to write the script for *Bewitched*'s second episode, "Be It Ever So Mortgaged," in which the Stephens buy a new house and become suburbanites. An early draft—dated May 20, 1964—lists Arnold as a co-writer. The episode introduces befuddled neighbor Gladys Kravitz who witnesses new landscaping and furniture appearing and disappearing at the Stephens house as Samantha and Endora use magic to try out various decorating ideas. Also present is Gladys' dubious husband Abner who always happens to view the scene only after the magic has been reversed, which frustrates Gladys to the point of hysteria.

Although the Kravitzes were not initially planned as series regulars, the triumvirate of Ackerman, Arnold, and Asher viewed their castings as important as their selections of Montgomery, York, and Moorehead, whom Arnold called "glove-fitted for their roles." On July 28, 1964, Ackerman drew up a list of character actors as possible choices for the roles of Abner and Gladys, many of whom were familiar to him as veterans of various Screen Gems productions, like *Father Knows Best*, *The Farmer's Daughter*, and *Grindl*. The eighteen candidates for Abner—ranging in age from 39 to 63—ran the gamut of stereotypes, from the authoritative (Frank Maxwell) to the bombastic (Parley Baer) to the gnomelike (Phil Arnold) to the

Harry Ackerman, executive producer of Bewitched, *in a 1959 photograph.*

grotesque (Maurice Gosfield). The role was eventually offered to the oldest fellow on the roster, stage and screen veteran George Tobias. According to Tobias, *Bewitched* producers chose him after seeing his performance in *The Seven Little Foys*, an unsold Universal Television pilot which aired as a 1964 segment of *Bob Hope Presents the Chrysler Theatre*.

Ackerman's list of actresses considered for the role of Gladys featured a wider age range—41 to 75. A few were currently inactive, including Helen Hatch, Gladys Hurlbut, and the gravely ill Cheerio Meredith, best known as the town hypochondriac on *The Andy Griffith Show*. Others were stereotypically incorrect for the role, like Helen Kleeb who often played lowkey secretaries and the elegant Eleanor Audley who excelled in parts which she once categorized as "Mrs. Rich-Bitch." Septuagenarians Enid Markey and Doro Merande, the stars of the 1960–61 sitcom *Bringing Up Buddy*, both made the list despite their widely-known offscreen hostility toward one another. Comical-looking Jesslyn Fax, whom Ackerman had once cast for television's *Our Miss Brooks*, was unavailable, having already signed on as a regular on *Many Happy Returns*. Perhaps most well-known to Ackerman were three alumni of his production *Dennis the Menace*: Irene Tedrow, Mary Wickes, and Alice Pearce. The handsome Tedrow had played prickly Mrs. Elkins in twenty-six episodes during *Dennis'* four-year run, while Wickes had enlivened ten episodes as man-hungry Miss Cathcart. Alice had appeared only twice as Miss Cathcart's rival Lucy Tarbell but had also sparkled in Screen Gems' *Hazel* and *The Donna Reed Show*. Ackerman placed Alice fourth on his list—just above Wickes—before submitting it to Asher and Arnold. The team quickly agreed that there was a standout. Of the fourteen actresses, only one was suited to personate the excitable yet vulnerable Gladys Kravitz.

Soon afterwards, Bill Asher called Alice, saying that he wanted her to play "a kooky neighbor who realized something was fishy with [Samantha Stephens] but couldn't figure what." He explained that it was only for two guest appearances, but Alice happily agreed to do it. "Alice was offered the part of Gladys without auditioning," Ackerman explained, "because her talents were very well known to producer Danny Arnold, director Bill Asher, and to me as executive producer." It was a heady experience for Alice. *Bewitched* was already considered as "the most promising pilot and most fought-over show for the new season." And now she was part of the excitement.

Production on the series began on Monday, August 10, but without its star who was home recuperating from the birth of her first child. Until Montgomery joined the cast and crew a week later, Asher shot around his wife's scenes for both "Be It Ever So Mortgaged" and "The Witches Are Out," an episode with a Halloween theme. It's likely that Alice's scenes for "Mortgaged" were among the first to be filmed since Gladys does not share the screen with Samantha in that episode.

Alice was a little surprised when she opened the "Mortgaged" script and read her character's name. She instantly thought of Dr. Hilard Kravitz, the physician referred to her by Carole Cook. Careful not to reveal her medical secret with anyone in the *Bewitched* company, Alice was still eager to share her personal connection with the surname. She devised an amusing anecdote which reversed her true association with Dr. Kravitz. "When I first heard I was going to play a character called Gladys Kravitz," Alice told *TV Radio Mirror*, "I couldn't understand how they could invent such a nutty name. Well, the day before I was to report on the set of *Bewitched* for the first time, I came down with one of those minor upsets and I needed a doctor fast. A friend recommended someone. His name? Doctor Kravitz." Even though Alice fudged the actual circumstances, it made for good press and no one was the wiser.

Two weeks after Alice filmed "Mortgaged," she was called back for her second guest appearance on *Bewitched*. "Mother Meets What's His Name," written by Danny Arnold, provided her with an even better chance to shine. As a member of a "welcome wagon" committee, nosy Gladys gains entry to the Stephens house, determined to learn the identity of the redhead—Endora—she's seen with Samantha ("Do you have a maid with a large, curly head around? Do you have a gardener that works in pajamas?"). In this episode, Gladys becomes a stooge of her fellow committee members who are planning a protest ("Nobody asks me—

Gladys Kravitz (Alice Pearce) reports strange goings-on to her husband in "Mother Meets What's His Name," her second appearance on Bewitched, *1964.*

they just say, 'Gladys, go sit down in front of a cement mixer!'") but she's also victimized when no one else will pay attention to her suspicions ("There's something *funny* going on with *that house!*"). Alice demonstrates impeccable timing and uses her rubber face to maximum advantage, especially when Gladys realizes that she spoke with Abner over the Stephens' new telephone—even though it's never been connected for service.

It didn't take long for the *Bewitched* production team to realize that the Kravitzes—and

their portrayers—were comedy gold. Barbara Avedon was engaged to include the pair in a third episode already in the works, "Little Pitchers Have Big Fears," filmed during the week of September 14. In this outing, Gladys briefly shows her obnoxious side when bragging on her little-leaguer nephew and disparaging his awkward teammate whom Samantha has befriended. At this time Alice and her TV husband George Tobias were still employed as freelance performers, but as *Bewitched*'s debut approached—and predictions of its success abounded—Alice began to hope that her services would be needed on a regular basis.

Meanwhile, her personal life was fraught with pivotal decision-making. As the only person in Los Angeles who knew of Alice's mortal crisis, Paul Davis had previously agreed to remain loyal and support her until the end came. In return, Alice had completed the legal paperwork to ensure that Paul received her death benefits. Now, three months later, Alice and Paul began discussing the possibility of marriage as a means to further substantiate and reinforce their pact.

According to Kathleen Post who wrote a memorial to Alice in *TV Radio Mirror*, there had been discussions of marriage prior to Alice's surgical diagnosis. Without going into detail, Post disclosed that Alice had "somehow never felt ready for a second marriage." This sheds a glimmer of light not only on her mysterious engagement to William LeMassena but also uncovers a facet about her relationship with Paul. Both men were undoubtedly enamored with Alice, but she may have had serious reservations about entering into another marriage with a gay man. (Paul would later claim that Alice and he had "always planned to be married" but that his financial instability was the real deterrent.)

Things were different now. Alice knew that her illness would soon threaten her independence. As her fondest and closest friend in the city, Paul was trustworthy and loving. Alice needed him. Similarly, yet conversely, Paul was at a new place in his own life, gaining independence by becoming a business owner the previous year. It seems clear that the pair gravitated toward marriage as a result of their previous agreement but also as a token of their devoted friendship.

Alice was inclined to reticence, especially when her parents were involved, so it's uncertain just how informed Bob and Margaret Pearce were of this arrangement. In fact, at this point they may have not even known that Alice had cancer. Prior to their marriage, Paul said, only Alice's doctors and he knew that Alice was fighting a terminal illness. That was the way Alice wanted it.

When Alice announced her wedding plans to her parents, Margaret immediately offered to host the wedding reception and assume all of the plans, including ordering the wedding announcements. However, that was the last thing Alice wanted. On September 11, she explained her feelings in a letter to Bob and Margaret:

> Paul and I have had long discussions about our wedding plans. We have come to the decision that there is no way to have a small wedding reception. Too many friends, and family, would feel hurt that they were being left out. We do not want a large wedding because at "our age" it would be a travesty. So we have decided that, as far as our friends and Paul's family are concerned, we are going to "elope." But what we are actually going to do, if this meets your approval, is to be married by a judge in Los Angeles, with George [Morris] and Johnny [Fiedler] as our witnesses, and then fly to La Jolla for a glass of champagne and a piece of cake with you. Then we will proceed from La Jolla to the Coronado Hotel for a honeymoon.
>
> I would very much like Josie [Strode] to be with us on our wedding day. I shall finish my work by the middle of this coming week (I am doing another *Bewitched* T. V. show). Paul can get away at this time, so we have decided to be married a week

from Sunday, the twentieth of September. I hope you can see your way to approving of this plan . . .

Paul and I have had a wonderful time this week making plans for our wedding, and I am very happy. I shall be calling. All my love—Monk.

It would seem that the issue of "our age" would apply more to Alice that to Paul. Soon to be forty-seven, she was not a "starry-eyed" young bride facing a bright future. After all, John Rox was forty-five when he married the much younger Alice in 1948, which was not uncommon at that time. Now she was marrying a man closer to her own age, forty-two-year-old Paul, and they approached marriage as a mature couple. For whatever reason, Paul did not inform his parents of his marriage plans until after the ceremony had taken place, and even then, by indirect means. "They phoned me from San Diego and asked me to notify the family about their wedding," recalled Paul's youngest brother Milton Davis.

On Sunday, September 20, at half past noon, a limousine picked up Alice, Paul, George Morris, and John Fiedler in Los Angeles and transported them to the courthouse in Santa Monica, where Alice and Paul exchanged wedding vows at one o'clock in a brief ceremony within the judge's chambers. Alice was dressed in a two-piece suit of ecru linen, accessorized with beige pumps and matching purse, which was embellished with a nosegay of exotic white flowers. In characteristic fashion, she had chosen a rather distinctive hat from the millinery department at the May Company on Wilshire Boulevard. Designed by Cathay of California, the wide-brimmed cloche of gathered apricot satin featured a beige velveteen underbrim. To this Alice added her own quaint touch by pinning a large beige silk rose on the top of the crown. Paul, beaming, sported a new

Alice and Paul Davis shortly after their marriage ceremony, Santa Monica, California, September 20, 1964.

Margaret and Bob Pearce pose with Alice and Paul at the Pearces' home in La Jolla, September 20, 1964.

blue serge suit with matching tie. After posing for snapshots outside the courthouse, the foursome motored to the Skyview Restaurant at the Los Angeles International Airport for brunch. Afterwards the bride and groom caught a plane to San Diego, arriving at the Pearces' home in La Jolla around five o'clock that afternoon.

"The most perfect part of our wedding day," Alice later wrote to her parents, "was our reception, and being with you, at Avenida Cresta. The house looked so beautiful filled with white flowers. I loved seeing all your beautiful linen laces and silver. A bride never had a more magnificent wedding table. And I truly never saw a prettier wedding cake. I saved some of the rice that was caught in my hat for good luck. To my mind, it was the most perfect reception, with the dear people I love most."

Alice and Paul spent their week-long honeymoon at the famed Hotel de Coronado, a majestic resort set between the sparkling Pacific and the sheltered Glorietta Bay, less than twenty miles from the Pearce home. The Coronado had reigned as monarch of Western resort hotels for three-quarters of a century. "We have the most beautiful suite overlooking the ocean, a perfect honeymoon retreat!" Alice exclaimed to her parents. The newlyweds spent their vacation soaking up the sun and taking long walks on the shore. Each day, Alice dove into her copy of Charlie Chaplin's newly released autobiography. As a child she had adored his movies and often remarked that Chaplin had inspired her to become a comedienne.

The highlight of the week was a call from George Morris who phoned Alice to tell her that the *Bewitched* producers wanted to place her (and George Tobias) under contract as series regulars. The particulars would be discussed, George said, when she returned to Los Angeles. Alice was elated. After almost giv-

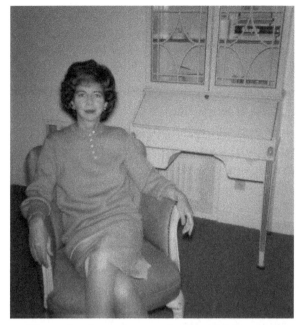

Alice on her honeymoon at the Hotel del Coronado, September 1964.

ing up on becoming part of a television series, she had finally gotten her wish. The call from George had made her honeymoon all the more eventful.

Bewitched premiered three days before Alice's wedding ceremony and became a phenomenal hit with both viewers and critics. "This is the one to watch," proclaimed *Variety*. "Miss Montgomery distinguishes the show with a bizarre charm and restrained artistry, York has the face and talent as her ever-loving and, resultantly, *Bewitched* should have the home lookers lapping at their eccentricities as a weekly diet." During its first two weeks, the show lived up to its advance acclaim and nailed down second place in the Nielsen ratings with only one-half point out of the lead held by *Bonanza*. *Bewitched* would hold on as the industry's number-two series all season long.

Alice's first episode, "Be It Ever So Mortgaged," debuted while she was honeymooning, and it, too, was well received. *TV Guide*'s resident reviewer Cleveland Amory, declaring himself "bewitched by *Bewitched*," cited the show as a standout exception to a "dangerous" trend. "Like so many new shows we've seen this season, the pilot, or first episode, was far ahead of the next episodes . . . and then, when they don't deliver on the next shows, disappointed audiences are going to pack up and go elsewhere . . . Fortunately, in the case of *Bewitched*, the second episode was saved by the appearance of the inimitable Alice Pearce and her almost equally adept 'husband,' George Tobias. Both are wonderful, and any episode thereafter without them was the poorer." A reviewer for the *Arizona Republic* echoed Amory, calling Alice and Tobias—after having seen them as the Kravitzes only once—"our favorite other people's neighbors."

Harry Ackerman was listening. He had already requested of Charles Fries, Screen Gems' executive production manager, to commence contract negotiations with Alice and Tobias. On September 29, Fries reported back that the company's casting department could make deals with both performers for seven out of thirteen episodes. For each segment, Alice and Tobias had settled on $1,000 and $900, respectively—quite a large increase over the previous "if available" agreement which had been in place since September 4. "I believe we should review very carefully making any commitment to these people, especially in the light of our present budget position," Fries advised Ackerman. "If we are receiving outside pressures from [the advertising] agency or network, possibly they will consider increasing or giving us some contribution for the additional cost per film." When Fries expressed his concern to Jackie Cooper, newly appointed Screen Gems vice-president in charge of West Coast activities, Cooper readily supported the new contracts for Alice and Tobias. "While I realize the costs on this show are far in excess of what

we hoped they would be," Cooper rationalized, "it is extremely necessary we insure ourselves with everything that is good for the pictures."

On October 9, Alice signed a memorandum of the terms of her forthcoming contract with Screen Gems. This document would serve as a binding agreement until a formal contract could be prepared and executed. In addition to Alice's initial contract year, Screen Gems held options on her services for four subsequent years. Her compensation per "picture," or episode, for the 1964–65 season was $1,000. The terms also specified that Alice would appear in a minimum of seven-thirteenths of the next nine episodes, which the Screen Actors Guild mandated to be five out of nine. In the event that she was used in less than five episodes, Alice agreed to waive payment for those in which she did not work. (Tobias contractually refused to permit Screen Gems this waiver.) Additionally, Alice agreed to make commercials for *Bewitched*'s sponsors at double the SAG minimum pay. Lastly, Screen Gems honored Alice's request to either suspend or reduce her contract in order for her to appear in the Warner Brothers motion picture *Inside Daisy Clover* for which she had a tentative commitment.

On October 19, Alice and Tobias reported to the studio to begin filming their fourth episode, "And Something Makes Three." That same week, columnist Louella Parsons named the pair as welcome additions to the guest list for a cocktail and dinner party in the private room at Chasen's, hosted by the show's sponsor Quaker Oats to celebrate *Bewitched*'s top ratings. According to Army Archerd of *Variety*, Asher told the troupe that night that "there'd be no Christmas hiatus for 'em—they have to shoot sans stop to meet their close deadline."

It's logical to assume that Paul Davis attended the party at Chasen's, but it may have gone unmentioned by Parsons and Archerd simply because Alice's remarriage was yet to be widely publicized. During their stay at the Coronado, Alice had phoned Mike Connolly to inform him of her wedding, which he announced in his syndicated column on October 3. "It's a lovely place for a honeymoon," Alice told Connolly, "but for a fast few minutes after we arrived I thought we were both on hallucinogenic mushrooms—until I realized we're sharing the hotel with a convention of 400 gynecologists!"

Even though Alice was far removed from the New York society of her youth, she still bowed to the rules of etiquette. "As long as this is an 'elopement,' she assured Margaret, "it is conventional to send out the announcements within a month to six weeks after the day of the wedding." Many of Alice's friends, especially those in New York, were caught unawares by the announcement. Miles White and Cris Alexander had never heard Alice mention Paul, even during the period that both she and Paul lived in Manhattan. "I really didn't know anybody who knew him," said Cris, "except one person—Portia Nelson—and she wasn't on good terms with him at all." Likewise, Paul's friend Carole Cook didn't see it coming. "When they married, I was kind of surprised," she says. "Now they were together *a lot*, but, see, I thought they were just *really close* friends."

Alice's godson Chan Lowe, at eleven years old, initially found the news from Aunt Alice difficult to accept. "It took Chan two days to adjust," his mother Carol Channing wrote from the St. James Theatre, "but he is very happy now. I have no idea what he wrote you, but he keeps reminding me we were the first to know which seems to make all the difference. I'm supposed to be napping in my dressing room, just before the show, but wanted to send my

one note for the year. All love and welcome to Paul. I think of you always, Little dear Alice."

On November 3, Alice wrote to share her news with former brother-in-law Don Herring, whose Orange County family she mysteriously continued to keep at arm's length. "Paul is a great guy and, at long last, I am happy again," she said. "We will settle in L. A. because I am now a permanent member of the *Bewitched* series, and Paul has an art gallery in L. A. I am going to give up my New York apartment. But the next few weeks, until we know where we will settle, I can best be reached through my New York address. I shall let you know, Don, where we will finally settle. I owe a letter to Shirley and one to Suzie [*sic*]. I hope they will find it in their hearts to forgive my silence. These past months have been madness! I promise to improve my writing habits. All my love, Alice."

Don's wife Doris hastened to reply, sending a congratulatory greeting card and updating Alice on all of the Herrings. "We are very happy for you," Doris wrote. "We were wondering why we hadn't heard from you for so long. So glad you won't be alone anymore. We enjoy *Bewitched* very much. We also see you on the Gleem commercials." Encouraging Alice to phone or visit them in Anaheim, Doris also requested Alice's Los Angeles address, not knowing that all along—for more than two years—Alice had been living on Holloway Drive in West Hollywood.

Although Mike Connolly scooped all other reporters, the news of Alice's marriage began to appear in various columns in papers across the country. Soon after the couple's engraved announcements were mailed out, Louella Parsons cheered, "Alice Pearce made the happiest move of her life when she left New York to make her home in Hollywood. First, she married Paul Davis . . . then she lands the job as a regular on *Bewitched*, top rated TV series." More than likely this item was written by the aged Parsons' longtime assistant Dorothy Manners, who was soon due to take over the column. Manners had recently met Alice and Paul for the first time at a small party given in their honor by producer Ross Hunter. "It was one of the laughing-est evenings I have ever spent," she declared. "We knew Alice had been in the hospital (but not for what reason). And she kept us hilarious with story after story of the 'amusing' things which befall a patient. No one laughed more at her nonsense than Paul. Until the tears rolled down his face, actually."

Manners began to note the Davises' comings and goings. On November 13, she reported that they had recently attended publicist Rupert Allan's late afternoon cocktail party for actress Inga Swenson, then wowing Los Angeles audiences in a stage production of *110 in the Shade*. Other guests included George Segal, Steve McQueen, Hugh O'Brian, Dorothy McGuire, Susan Strasberg, and Olivia de Havilland ("in one of the new very low-cut cocktail dresses"). The "very aristocratic and very socially connected" Allan—a Rhodes scholar—was an intimate friend of Marilyn Monroe, Ava Gardner, and Princess Grace. His star clients included McQueen, Bette Davis, Rock Hudson, and Gregory Peck. Invitations to Allan's grand home at 1455 Seabright Place overlooking the Beverly Hills canyon were particularly coveted. Alice and Paul had truly arrived.

A press agent of Allan's ilk surely had a hand in the publication of "Alice Pearce: The Chinless Wonder," an exclusive article which appeared on October 11 in *Parade* magazine, a Sunday newspaper supplement with a circulation of 13 million. Given the fact that Alice's second episode of *Bewitched* had aired only three days before, Lloyd Shearer's article—at first glance—would seem to be a timely piece,

an inspired tactic to promote television's top sitcom via the actress who played its most comical character. However, *Bewitched* is mentioned nowhere in the feature. The omission may be explained by the fact that *Parade* operated on a "six-week closing date, or deadline for its feature material," indicating that the article was likely prepared sometime in August, when the *Bewitched* crew was scrambling to complete its earliest episodes. This timeline makes sense except for one tiny detail. Shearer included a brief paragraph revealing that "last month Alice Pearce got married again," an event that occurred exactly three weeks before the issue hit the newsstands. Shearer's last-minute insertion is likely due to a publicist working on Alice's behalf or to the journalist's own tenacious curiosity. In either case, Shearer—once described as "a genius for understanding popular culture"—had scooped both Parsons and Walter Winchell. Unfortunately, his article was not printed without two glaring errors. Shearer mistakenly wrote that Alice played opposite Fred Astaire in her debut film *On the Town* and misidentified Paul Davis as "a former Broadway director."

One month after her wedding, Alice returned to the *Bewitched* set looking healthier than she had in August and September. During the rest period, she had regained some weight and rethought her wig, eliminating the unflattering "flip" for a more pleasing pageboy. During October and November, she filmed only three episodes. "It's Magic," completed during Thanksgiving week, revealed Alice's artistry in a story involving Zeno, a down-on-his-luck magician whom Samantha engages for her club's benefit bazaar. Gladys, manning the kissing booth ("only on coffee break"), has no customers until Darrin drops by looking for his wife. She agrees to tell him if he buys a kiss. As closes his eyes and puckers up, the comely

Gladys (Alice Pearce) once again tries to convince her husband Abner (George Tobias) that Samantha Stephens has magical powers in "A Vision of Sugar Plums," the Christmas episode from the first season of Bewitched, *1964.*

relaxation but one of stress and sorrow. First, Paul required Alice's assistance in his tiny, cluttered framing shop. Soon after Christmas ads for Pesha's Framing Studio ran in *Variety* and other publications, customers took advantage of the studio's extended holiday hours, some arriving on nights very near the nine o'clock closing time. The shop also featured a small art gallery. "I'm learning about soft-sell and all that jazz," Alice told Mike Connolly. "A plumber came over to unplug the sink in the back of the store, and I sold him a canvas of a nude!"

In the midst of all the Christmas bustle, Alice's aunt Josephine Strode died somewhat unexpectedly on the night of December 12. Although she had been diagnosed several years previously with mitral valve disease, Josephine, at sixty-three, had continued to lead an active life. Since the 1961 death of her mother, Josephine had rented an apartment at 7 Oak Street in Brattleboro, Vermont. On December 4, when her symptoms of congestive heart failure became too great to ignore, she checked into Grace Cottage Hospital, a small facility in Townshend, seventeen miles north of Brattleboro. The one-doctor hospital was a sprawling complex of Victorian clapboard structures, featuring homey patients' rooms decorated with framed prints and floral curtains at the windows. Although Josephine received good care, her condition deteriorated and she lingered barely a week.

Samantha suddenly replaces Gladys, kisses Darrin, and generates a string of eager customers. As Samantha and Darrin exit, Gladys sails alongside the line of men, snatching their dollars and announcing gleefully, "Gentlemen, this booth does *not* give refunds!" Later, during two scenes featuring Zeno, Gladys suspects Samantha of "magically" assisting the bumbling magician and grows more annoyed with Abner when he refuses to believe her. Throughout this episode, but particularly during the magic show sequences, Alice is a study in facial expressions.

Alice was not required on the set for three weeks following the completion of "It's Magic," but the break proved not to be a period of

Josephine had requested to be buried near her parents and first husband Paul Dillard in the Lick Creek Cemetery in Perry. During the two decades following her second marriage, she had visited Perry more often than Margaret, maintaining close contact with distant cousins and old friends. In fact, Josephine had retained her membership in both the Perry Christian Church and the D. A. R. chapter in nearby Mexico, Missouri. Margaret, her heart filled with grief, made the funeral plans from her home in La Jolla, while Alice secured round-trip plane reservations to St. Louis for herself and her mother.

Friends met Margaret and Alice at the airport to drive them the 120-mile distance to Perry. Alice had not been to Missouri since 1938 but found its small towns much like she remembered them. The friendly folks in Perry went out of their way to make the California visitors comfortable during their short stay. Over the years, they had kept up with Alice and the Pearces through updates Josephine provided to Burney Fishback, editor of the *Perry Enterprise*. Now that Alice was appearing on a hit television series, the locals were even more proud of her. When Alice heard someone mention Iva Leake's delectable sugar-cured hams, she bought one from the farmwife to take back to Los Angeles for Christmas. Both Alice and Margaret knew that this would most likely be their final trip to Missouri—Josephine had been their last link to the rural communities of their ancestors. Now, as they said goodbye to her, they were especially grateful that Josie had been a part of Alice's wedding celebration just three months earlier.

Alice had no sooner returned to Los Angeles than she received word of the death of eighty-year-old Earl Herring, John Rox's stepfather, who lived in Anaheim with his son Don. "He is not very well," Doris Herring had written to Alice six weeks earlier. "He can't do anything but sit all day. The television is a lifesaver for him. The doctors want to perform heart surgery, but he is reluctant." On December 22, Alice sent a telegram with her condolences. "Because of my own loss," she wrote, "I have not been able to attend to holiday greetings and so I send love and best wishes for the new year to each and every one of you."

As 1965 neared, Alice—still showing no outward signs of her illness—contemplated the busy year ahead. Since the Kravitzes were slated to appear in a greater percentage of *Bewitched* episodes, Alice's work schedule was about to ramp up. In addition to those duties, she learned that Josephine's will, executed in December 1962, named her as both executrix and primary heir. This responsibility would necessitate a trip east to settle her aunt's affairs, but that would have to wait until spring when *Bewitched* went on hiatus. Meanwhile, Bill Asher was as good as his word. The *Bewitched* crew did not take a lengthy Christmas break. By December 31, Alice had filmed two more episodes, "Ling Ling" and "Red Light, Green Light."

Alice was quite pleased to be under contract to Screen Gems. "I've always wanted a series," she confessed to journalist Harold Stern during an interview at the Villa Frascatti on the Sunset Strip. "I made so many pilots that never materialized that I thought I'd never do one … I hear actors complaining about being tied to a series, but I love it. I love the security of a long run, even in the theater. I like playing the same part year after wonderful year." Alice also relished the challenges of being a television actor, maintaining that she found it "just as stimulating as the stage." Even though her experience with the medium stretched back to 1945, when the punishing studio lights melted the plastic buttons on her dress, Alice confessed, "I still have a lot to learn about it."

Elizabeth Montgomery and Alice Pearce in "Little Pitchers Have Big Fears," a season-one episode of Bewitched.

Adjusting to the *Bewitched* shooting schedule was particularly challenging. Quite frequently the production crew filmed more than one episode at a time, especially when last-minute script changes dictated or when "pick up shots" were needed. Consequently, the normal state on the set was a swivet. Agnes Moorehead aptly summed it up: "This is the treadmill. This is TV. Mad, hectic. No time to relax. Every second counts." A typical *Bewitched* episode was completed in three and one-half days, but the days were long. "I would drive [Alice] to the studio at six in the morning," Paul said. "Then I would leave for a while to go to the shop. Then I'd go back to the studio for lunch with Alice, then back to the shop—then back to the studio and wait until she was finished with the day's shooting." Some nights, the company didn't call it quits until eight o'clock.

Despite the frenetic pace, Alice developed a valued friendship with Elizabeth Montgomery. "I felt closer to Alice than to anyone I'd met in a long time," Montgomery said in 1966. "She was so dear, so outgoing . . . [Bill Asher] and I felt particularly near to Alice and Paul because they were married after we met her. It had the effect of making us feel part of their lives."

According to Paul, the two women hit it off because they were very much alike—"both smartly dressed, beautifully educated, and well brought up ladies." Like Alice, Montgomery had attended schools in Europe when her father was producing films there. She later attended the exclusive Spence School on Manhattan's Upper East Side, making her society bow at the Debutante Cotillion and Christmas Ball at the Waldorf-Astoria in 1951 when she was eighteen. The actresses' similar backgrounds contributed much to their relationship, said Paul, but primarily "they liked each other because both had depth, warmth, and courage."

"When *Bewitched* first opened," Paul remembered, "someone did a story on [Montgomery and Asher] and called them 'cloying.' They hadn't been married long at the time, and it kind of offended Liz . . . Alice and I were on the set [that] day. She was looking not too happy, and we walked over, asked her what was the matter, and she showed us the article. Alice just said, 'Well, that's all right. You're the REAL McCloys.'" After that, Alice and Paul always called the Ashers the McCloys.

Alice's rapport with Montgomery was no exception. According to Harry Ackerman, Alice "got along splendidly with other cast members." Likewise, Dick York observed her aura: "It was impossible, no matter how down the company was feeling, *not* to be cheerful around Alice." As for Agnes Moorehead, Alice had little chance during the show's first season to get to know the "fabulous redhead." The characters of Endora and Gladys shared only six of the thirty-six episodes, none of which allowed them to interact or even meet.

Moorehead biographer Charles Tranberg maintains that the actress didn't want to play Endora on a weekly basis. "If Endora was the conflict each week the show would begin repeating itself and lose its originality," he explains. "This gave the writers the opportunity to develop other characters which kept the show fresh." This proved advantageous for Alice and George Tobias but also for David White, who played Darrin's boss Larry Tate, and Marion Lorne, perfectly cast as dotty Aunt Clara. Most of Alice's scenes were shared with Tobias. Professionally, the pair radiated a delightful chemistry, but curiously neither seems to have mentioned the other in interviews. Apparently, they were compatible off-camera. Asher once noted that the talented *Bewitched* cast was "a peculiar mix of people who all seemed to like each other."

Fourteen first-season episodes of *Bewitched* were filmed between January and April of 1965. Alice appeared in eight, two of which—"Abner Kadabra" and "Illegal Separation"—moved Gladys Kravitz from the sideline into the primary plotline. The former, in particular, was a showcase for Alice Pearce's talents, prompting one reviewer to note: "Miss Pearce makes all of her lines and bits of business seem funnier than they are." When Gladys catches her neighbor performing a magical stunt, Samantha uses more witchcraft to convince Gladys that she is actually the one who's gifted with the power of "mind over matter." Unstoppable Gladys then attempts various tricks, like turning on the stove without touching it, but her failures make life miserable for her husband. Abner appeals to Samantha, who reasons that the only way to "cure" Gladys is to stage a séance and "scare the daylights out of her." However, Samantha's plan proves only to exhilarate Gladys and terrify Abner. When Gladys orders him to "dry up," Samantha instantly turns Abner into a pile of dust. Gladys, filled with remorse, swears to renounce her magical ability, and Abner is restored to his old self. The standout scene, however, is one where Gladys wills her lawn sprinklers to turn on automatically. When a sudden rain shower develops, an exuberant Gladys, soaking wet, dances a jig and waves the sprinkler key like a magic wand, laughing maniacally.

In "Illegal Separation," Abner moves in with Darrin and Samantha after he and Gladys have a ten-round fight. While not as sharply written as "Abner Kadabra," this episode features amusing snippets of Gladys as she tries to win Abner back—first as a pouty blonde in a black lace negligee and then as a poor man's geisha girl. Both episodes veered from the more formulaic use of the Kravitzes, demonstrated in an earlier segment, for instance, when Gladys fails to persuade Abner that she saw a woman in a fur coat on all fours lapping milk like a cat. Even the most predictable scenes worked because of Alice's expert use of her adenoidal vocality and bug-eyed, slack-jawed expressions.

Bewitched, as the ratings phenomenon of the season, provided Alice more screen visibility—and more recognition on the street—than ever before. Likewise, customers in the framing studio eyed Alice with expressions that said, "Haven't I seen you someplace before?" Alice was delighted. "I've been in show business for over twenty years, and now, for the first time in my life, people recognize me wherever I go," she chirped. "Even door-to-door salesmen seem surprised and confused to find me—or should I say 'Gladys.' Many actors dislike being identified as only one character, but I love it."

Alice was particularly relieved to be identified less and less as "Chester's mother" on the Gleem commercial. It had become annoying when fans yelled across the street, "Hey, did you brush your teeth?" "I was just a face," Alice complained. "Nobody knew *me*. Now, I'm Gladys Kravitz and people are beginning to know my real name." (An amusing exception was the young boy who spotted Alice in a restaurant and shouted, "There's a bewitched!")

"I'm playing someone who's going over big with kids," Alice told *TV Radio Mirror*. "They stop me and want to know if I can wiggle my nose, like Liz Montgomery. And they like my snooping and poking around. The more frenzied my reactions are and the louder my 'eeeks' get, the better."

Recognition and fame aside, the greatest benefit from *Bewitched* was significantly more tangible. For the first time since making the move to California, Alice had a steady income. "Bless my series," she said gratefully. "May it last a long time." Before *Bewitched* came along, Alice was earning between $20,000 and

Abner (George Tobias) administers medicine to his bewildered wife Gladys (Alice Pearce) in "Ling Ling," a segment of Bewitched, *1965.*

$30,000 per year, which included the royalties—about $5,000 annually—she drew from John Rox's compositions. Unfortunately, between paying rent on both her Manhattan and West Hollywood apartments—not to mention satisfying the property taxes on her Fire Island beach cottage—Alice had amassed little reserves to even consider buying a house in California.

However, the chain of events during the second half of 1964 permanently altered the course of Alice's life. Soon there would be extra income from the trust left by her aunt, as well as the bonus liquidation of Josephine's valuable antiques collection. Induced to finalize her own affairs, Alice decided to divest herself of the Fire Island property. Its sale, she reasoned, would afford her the ability to buy a West Coast home for Paul and herself. The little house on Great South Beach, of which John Rox was so proud, was snatched up rather quickly. The sale was completed on March 9, 1965, with the understanding from the new owners that the Davises would not be free to remove the furnishings until the following month. Meanwhile, Alice finished up *Bewitched*'s first season and booked reservations for a mid-April flight to New York. Things moved quickly from there.

On April 2, Alice and Paul—as joint tenants—purchased a home in the Hollywood Hills, described by syndicated journalist Margaret McManus as "a small house, made of adobe brick, with a view of the city below, enough land for privacy, and a separate studio where Miss Pearce can paint." Located at 8242 Hillside Avenue, only a mile and a half from their Holloway Drive apartment, the property had been on the market for almost a year. Built in 1947, it had become the home of writer John Weaver and his wife Harriett the following year. Weaver, the West Coast editor of *Holiday* and *Travel and Leisure* maga-

zines, called 8242 "a little cement-block house" which his wife had "remade in her own radiant image." "She wove wall-to-wall wool carpeting for the living room, built a desk for my workroom, and laid the bricks for three patios," Weaver wrote in *Glad Tidings*, a collection of letters written between him and fellow author John Cheever.

When the Weavers moved from Hillside Avenue in 1964, Cheever lamented, "I can't think of a place more intimately associated with two people than Hillside Avenue. I know that Harriett made the rugs but I've always felt that she spun the grass and roses and I cannot yet see her on another terrace with another view." Weaver later shrugged, "It was more difficult for John than for Harriett and me to give up 8242 Hillside Avenue." In point of fact, the Weavers had moved to a roomier home on Beverly Grove Drive, with a 180-degree view of the city and a living room that "looked across a draw to Cary Grant's place."

During negotiations pertaining to the sale of 8242, Weaver learned that Alice had known Cheever's wife—the former Mary Winternitz—when they were both students at Sarah Lawrence College. Alice evidently told Weaver of Josephine's legacy, judging by Cheever's exaggerated response to his friend: "Alice Pearce has millions of affluent aunts and she is also affluent. I did not know she had a husband."

In the meantime, Alice and Paul flew to New York, intent on tackling the necessary chores for completing their move from east to west. When Alice and Paul weren't sorting and packing possessions in her Fifty-Ninth Street apartment, they each made appointments to visit old friends, perhaps for the final time. At the Dakota Apartments, Paul's pal Judy Holliday, now in the final stages of throat cancer, was confined to her bed and received few visitors. Holliday's illness was no longer a secret in

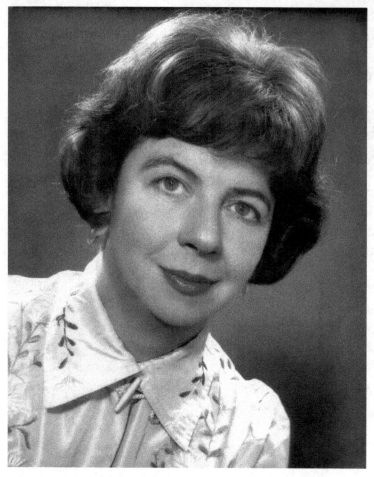

A portrait of Alice Pearce made during her last photo session with Cris Alexander, 1962.

me long to be back here. I love the comfortableness of California, and I love the continuity of a television series. It makes you feel so secure to have guaranteed work." Although she didn't say it, Alice was doubly secure with Paul at her side in Los Angeles, but especially on this trip to New York when there were so many plans to maneuver. In between the necessary chores, they enjoyed seeing other shows during their stay, including Neil Simon's *The Odd Couple* which featured their friend John Fiedler in the supporting role of Vinnie.

Alice also phoned Cris Alexander and arranged a private reunion with him. "She took me out to a very posh dinner at a place that we used to go to every so often," Cris recalled. "And I remember the occasion very well because she was just particularly herself. One wouldn't have—or *I* certainly didn't *dream*, *suspect*, or *imagine* that she wasn't her very self. We put away lots of martinis and *steak au poivre*, which was her favorite—which is amazing, considering her condition. She *never* gave a *hint*, let alone a hint you wouldn't have suspected, that she was ill." However, Alice knew that their evening together would be the final time that "Bro" and "Sis" would meet.

show-business circles, but Alice continued to mask her own disease as she enjoyed reunions with those whom she had not seen in more than two years.

She greatly anticipated a visit with Carol Channing, then the toast of Broadway in her comeback role of Dolly Levi in *Hello, Dolly!* She and Paul attended a matinee of the show, afterwards catching up with Channing in her dressing room. That same evening, Alice and Paul took twelve-year-old Chan Lowe out to dinner. "It's all very nice, going to the theater and going out to dinner and feeling the crackle of the electricity," Alice told syndicated columnist Margaret McManus, "but it doesn't make

From New York, Alice and Paul traveled to Brattleboro where Josephine's effects had been stored since her death in December. Alice had asked Paul's brother Milton Davis, twenty-eight, to accompany them and assist Paul with any physical chores, but he found it impossible to fit a trip into his schedule. "By then, I had two children, and I was working at New York

Hospital in New York City," Milton Davis explains.

Back in February, Alice had been appointed by the probate court of Marlboro County, Vermont, as the executrix of her aunt's estate. Her immediate duties were to return a "true and perfect" inventory of the estate within three months and to render an account of her administration of the estate within one year. Josephine's will specified that Alice was to inherit all of her "tangible personal property," including household furniture, personal effects, jewelry, and any automobiles. In addition, Josephine named Alice as the sole beneficiary—"for the duration of her natural life"—in a trust maintained by the Vermont Bank and Trust Company of Brattleboro.

Alice disposed of Josephine's old jeep, but she arranged for the removal of her aunt's French antiques, as well as her own furnishings from both the Manhattan apartment and the Fire Island beach cottage. All were to be shipped to Hillside Avenue. "It will be one glorious chaos when the vans arrive," Alice admitted to McManus. "We can only guess what might fit into what corners, but consider the excitement of it. Will the sofa from Fire Island fit the fireplace in Hollywood? What will we do with the oak sideboard from Vermont? You will simply have to turn in next week."

The final stop was Boston. On the evening of Saturday, May 1, Alice was introduced to Paul's family at a celebration held in their honor in the suburb of Milton. "It was like marrying my wonderful Paul all over again," Alice said, describing the wedding cake and all the fixings. "There were about fifty-five at the party, and we had such a jolly time," she told the *Boston Globe*. "It was 3 a.m. Sunday before we headed for our hotel. Sunday afternoon the festivities continued on Withington Street in Dorchester, where Paul's parents reside."

Alice was especially taken with the "delightful little children" who attended both celebrations. "There are so many of them," she said. Paul's nephew Dana, eight, was in the process of losing one of his baby teeth. "He wanted a memento of Alice's visit and her autograph to show to his friends," remembered his mother Renee Summers. "Her immediate response was to sit down and write a note asking him to save his front tooth for her. He was a proud and happy youngster, running around, showing all of his friends the note from his Aunt Alice."

"Oh, Alice was very lovely, very sweet to me," Renee Summers recalled in 2013. "You know, I was Paul's sister so she couldn't be anything but nice. My mother loved her." Sarah Davis, sixty-one, was pleased that Paul—the oldest of her four children and the last to marry—had chosen such a charming wife. Alice's new mother-in-law, born of Jewish ancestry in London, immigrated to America at age two with her mother, then eight months pregnant with her second child. They joined Sarah's Polish-born father in Brooklyn where he had established himself as a tailor. At eighteen, Sarah—by then living in the Bronx—married Max Dashefsky whose father was also a tailor, but in Revere, Massachusetts. How the young couple met is unknown, but they settled in Dorchester where Paul was born thirteen months after they wed.

Like Sarah, Max had immigrated to America at a very young age, via the port of Boston in 1905—but without either parent. His Ukrainian father had arrived in the United States in 1900, but four years later when he sent for his wife and four sons to join him, two of the boys were sent back. "They were caught up in the deportations for eye infections and returned to England," explained Summers. Several months later, these sons— one of whom was Max—were joyfully reunited with their family in Massachusetts. By the time Max was introduced to his new daughter-in-law Alice, he had been employed as a truck driver for more than forty-five years, delivering the *Boston Globe* all over the city's neighborhoods.

Alice made quite an impression on Paul's parents and sister during that fleeting weekend—the only time that they enjoyed her company. "Listen, I don't think you'd find anybody that didn't love Alice," Summers recalled. "She was very charming, *very charming*—I think that would be the word for her. She wasn't a 'second banana' when you saw her in person."

"I'm looking forward to a longer stay in Boston on the next visit," Alice cheerfully told the *Globe*, but in her heart, she sensed that her in-laws had hosted a "hail and farewell" celebration.

Alice and Paul's busy schedule on the East Coast carried over to Los Angeles upon their return. First, there was the task of moving everything from the Holloway Drive apartment to Hillside Avenue, but the biggest challenge came a week or so later when the moving vans arrived from New York and Vermont. They fit as much of it as they could into Alice's "separate studio," which was actually a detached garage. The next step was to get Josephine's antiques appraised by a local expert so that they could eventually sell the pieces they chose not to keep.

In time, Alice hoped to set up her home studio and get back to painting. "It's the first time I've had plenty of room for an easel," she said. "Before, I've always had to drag it in and out of a closet." There were other adjustments. Harriett Weaver had left behind artfully designed flower beds surrounding the terraced patios, but Alice readily admitted that she knew nothing about gardening. In time, perhaps that skill could be nurtured, too, but for now Alice was simply thrilled with 8242 Hillside Avenue. "It's the first real home I've ever had," she told everyone.

CHAPTER TWENTY-FIVE
Valiant Lady

*"People look beautiful when they are happy.
That's why I like to make people laugh."*

In late February 1965, when Bill Asher told *Bewitched* producers that his wife Elizabeth Montgomery was again pregnant, they "let out a screech you hear halfway around the world." Asher could hardly blame them. "When Liz was pregnant last year with our first," he said, "the production schedule on *Bewitched* was so far behind, everyone connected with the series had to work fifty hours a week to catch up in time to meet our deadline for kicking off the show." Asher calmed their panic by suggesting that for the show's second season they should make Samantha Stephens pregnant as well.

Asher also came up with a way to avoid another production delay. Seventeen episodes would be filmed between May and September, with production resuming in December, once Montgomery had fully recuperated. "Our TV cast had expected eight weeks' vacation," Alice explained to the *Boston Globe* in early May, "but the time was shortened as we must tape through the summer . . . we'll have time off in the fall." The situation mirrored that of Lucille Ball's pregnancy during the second season of *I Love Lucy*, which Asher also directed. Noting Asher's similar plan for *Bewitched*, Alice promised, "He won't wear viewers down by stringing out the episodes. He'll have only about a half-dozen segments on the new arrival, thus keeping Samantha busy with other wifely duties."

Alice would appear in seven of the first seventeen segments, including the second-season premiere episode, "Alias Darrin Stephens," in which Samantha attempts to break the news of her pregnancy to Darrin. However, just before that happens, bumbling Aunt Clara accidentally turns Darrin into a chimpanzee dressed in Darrin's tuxedo and plaid golf cap. Gladys later captures the chimp ("Around the eyes, he looks familiar," she tells Abner), and turns him in to the local zoo. Eventually Samantha undoes Clara's spell and returns Darrin to his human form. In the closing tag, when Gladys drops in on the Stephenses, she notices that Darrin is dressed in the same outfit which the chimp had worn. She gulps, whimpers, shrieks, and flees in typical fashion. Although the Kravitzes were only a cursory addition to this episode, it bears the distinction of being the only one in the eight-year history of *Bewitched* to feature all of the first season's key supporting characters: Endora, Larry Tate, Gladys, Abner, and Aunt Clara.

In "Alias Darrin Stephens"—filmed on May 18, 1965—Alice looks much as she did at the end of the first season: chubby chipmunk cheeks, plumpish figure, sparkling eyes. Six weeks later, when she filmed "My Grandson, the Warlock" and "A Strange Little Visitor," the camera captured a noticeably different figure. Now Alice was so much thinner that her wardrobe, especially the necklines, didn't fit properly. By the time "And Then I Wrote" was produced in late July, Alice's dresses—both of which she'd worn in the previous season's shows—had been taken in to allow for her shrinking form. Alice appeared even more gaunt in August when she completed two additional episodes.

"She never admitted to anyone the onslaught of cancer," said Harry Ackerman, "although it was painfully obvious to all of us that she was losing weight rapidly." Paul's daily presence at the studio also aroused suspicions. "Husbands do not usually spend so much time where their wives are working, especially on a busy film set," observed an industry journalist. However, no one said a word, especially Montgomery whose affection for Alice grew daily.

Alice's weight loss was perhaps more astounding to regular viewers of *Bewitched*. That fall, Alice's first seven episodes were not telecast in the order of their production, with the exception of the season opener "Alias Darrin Stephens." Five weeks after "Alias" aired, "Take Two Aspirins and Half a Pint of Porpoise Milk"—which was filmed twelve weeks after "Alias"—was telecast, revealing a radically changed Alice Pearce. Viewers were further confused when earlier filmed episodes followed "Take Two Aspirins," giving the false impression that Alice's weight was alternately increasing and decreasing during the fall season.

Despite her declining health, Alice remained upbeat, especially concerning her present employment. "After appearing in a dozen Broadway plays, as many movies and five times as many television shows," she said, "it's nice to have a home like *Bewitched*. The show gives me a chance to plant some roots and maybe even grow a few potatoes." "Miss Pearce loves her series," reported Margaret McManus, "loves the star, Elizabeth Montgomery; loves the rest of the cast." And she loved her role. "Playing Gladys," Alice said, "has given me the greatest self-satisfaction and the most rewarding expe-

Alice and Paul Davis pose outside the second location of Pesha's Framing Studio, fall 1965.

riences I have ever known." As she submitted data for her inclusion in the 1966 edition of *Who's Who in the Theatre*, Alice listed Gladys Kravitz as her "favorite part."

When not working on *Bewitched*, Alice often joined Paul at Pesha's Framing Studio. "I'm [there] every minute I have off from the show," she said. "It's a nice balance for the television series." Although her experience selling bloomers at Macy's twenty-five years earlier was arduous, Alice admitted, "I always wanted to be part of a shop. I don't try to impose my taste on customers. I like a plain gold frame—but, of course, that isn't at all good for the business." Pesha's celebrity customers included Lucille Ball, Henry Fonda, Debbie Reynolds, and Tom Tryon. "Raymond Burr has an art gallery," Paul said, "but I do most of his framing.

Henry Fonda does beautiful watercolors and oils. Shirley Booth is a very good artist. She works in oil and does portraits and landscapes. Alice is a first-rate painter. She exhibits her work [here] and sells some of it." "He's got some now that he can't unload," Alice quipped. On display, but not available for purchase, was Alice's 1949 oil painting of the Vermont countryside, a favorite with Margaret Pearce. Paul also dabbled in painting. Once he and Alice settled into 8242 Hillside Avenue, several of their works adorned the walls.

In the meantime, the moving vans bearing Josephine's antiques collection arrived. Paul and Alice stored it all in their small house until they could get it appraised—which took three months. "Now that they know its worth," said Hedda Hopper, "they plan to sell quick." The Davises' intentions were to open a second shop—to be called "Alice and Pesha's"—marketing the pieces which wouldn't fit either spatially or compatibly in their new home. That plan may have been abandoned due to Alice's decline. Nevertheless, that fall Paul relocated Pesha's Framing Studio from its cramped quarters to a larger space across the street at 8583 Melrose Avenue. Antiques may have been sold from this location, but Alice retained some for Hillside Avenue. Richard Deacon, who visited Alice in the summer of 1965, recalled, "Her home was furnished with eclectic furniture, French and country American."

Alice and Paul took advantage of *Bewitched*'s fall hiatus to celebrate their first wedding anniversary in Hawaii. "We're going to one of the small islands," Alice told Dorothy Manners, "just hanging a sign on our shop, 'We've gone fishing, and surfing and suntanning. Be back when we damn please.'" However, that version of their vacation plans conflicts slightly with the one Alice reported to Agnes Moorehead: "Paul gave me an anniversary present of two weeks in Hawaii. We are staying in Maui the whole time." During their stay, she sent dozens of postcards to friends, including columnists. She wrote Manners more than once, telling her that she and Paul "spent their time painting up a storm." Mike Connolly reported that Alice and Paul were "dining out every night and discovering [that] delicious Mahi Mahi just had to be their dish. Curiosity won out and when Alice learned it was porpoise [*sic*], she dropped her fork, stood up: 'Since *Flipper* is my favorite, you have made a dire mistake!'"

Alice and Paul arrived home just in time for her to appear at the tenth annual Thalians Ball, held on October 2 at the Beverly Hilton Hotel. The Thalians—a group now numbering 150—had formed in 1955 to prove "that charity work can be fun as well as highly rewarding." Taking their name from the muse of comedy in Greek mythology, the Thalians had ambitiously pledged to Cedars-Sinai Medical Center one million dollars, earmarked for a new clinic to serve emotionally disturbed youngsters. Their 1965 fundraising ball, designed by board chairman Debbie Reynolds and president Donald O'Connor, would put them near the halfway mark. Called "The Cloak and Dagger Ball," its theme was linked to the current popularity of international intrigue in films and television. "We'll combine the James Bond-*Man from U.N.C.L.E.* type of fare into every aspect of the ball," explained Reynolds.

The sizable $100-a-plate audience—including film stars Judy Garland, Greer Garson, Elizabeth Taylor, Hugh O'Brian, and June Allyson—was an autograph hunter's dream. The evening's emcee was Richard Burton. Entertainment was provided by a number of television actors from current hits, such as Jim Nabors (*Gomer Pyle, U.S.M.C.*), Carolyn Jones (*The Addams Family*), Jim Backus (*Gilligan's Island*), Robert Vaughn (*The Man from*

U.N.C.L.E.), and Agnes Moorehead and Alice Pearce (*Bewitched*). Moorehead joined Raymond Massey, Angela Lansbury, and Sam Jaffe for a dramatic reading "derived from the work of Ian Fleming, which could have been called 'James Bond's Body.'" The spritely ninety-minute show closed with a series of "do-it-yourself" skits, remakes of classic films with an espionage twist. Robert Vaughn and Rod Taylor performed "Father No" (combining *Going My Way* with *Dr. No*), while Backus and Jones converted Arthur Miller's Willie Loman into a failed spy in "A Shot in the Kishkes." In a subtle nod to Gladys Kravitz, Alice became "Gold Poppins," a governess who gives *spying* lessons to her puppets O'Connor (dressed as Little Lord Fauntleroy) and Reynolds (a very lifelike "Baby Jane Hudson" doll).

Alice winked and smiled whenever someone commented on her smaller figure, never letting on that she was ill.

Reynolds, then filming *The Singing Nun* with Garson and Moorehead, noticed Alice's loss of weight during rehearsals for their Thalians skit. "I said that she was looking like a young girl, all trimmed down," Reynolds remembered. "She winked at me and said, 'Yes, I'm out to become the newest sex symbol in Hollywood.'"

Alice's self-deprecating reply was automatic; she had had much practice deflecting similar comments through the years. (When asked by Boston tabloid reporter Anthony LaCamera if she regarded herself as strictly a comedienne, she replied sweetly, "No, I consider myself a sex symbol. It just happens that I get funny parts.") Now, as her illness advanced, Alice was using this skill to steer even her dearest friends from the topic of her health.

Alice remained philosophical about her looks even as her frame diminished, accenting even more her stooped shoulders and disappearing chin. "Being beautiful has never been one of my problems," she said with a twinkle when interviewed by actress Arlene Dahl, whose syndicated newspaper column featured beauty tips and advice. "There are compensations, though. If you don't start out being beautiful, you don't have anything to lose . . . Pretty ladies have to get in so much earlier at night, to get their beauty sleep, and I can play. And they have to wear girdles, and I can be comfortable!"

Although Alice joked about her situation, Dahl found her to be a woman with a "warm personality and genuine insight." "If you don't fit in the regular mold," Alice told Dahl, "you have to be resourceful. And then you learn that physical beauty is really not that important. There are other things that make people beautiful, too. Like peace of mind and joy of living. People look beautiful when they are happy. That's why I like to make people laugh."

Alice also offered a few interesting tips for Dahl's readers. "You need taste, not money to be 'chic'... I never use anything for what it's meant for. I use pine oil and a box of baking soda in my bath water instead of soap, for instance. It makes my skin very soft. I figure it costs me about eight cents a tub. And instead of taking castor oil in a spoon, I spread it on my face for a few minutes each night. It's a cure-all! I use a green liquid athlete's foot remedy as an all-over astringent. It's wonderfully soothing and stimulates circulation. Of course, I look like the 'jolly green giant' until I wash it off."

Alice and Paul discuss framing options with a customer at Pesha's Framing Studio, fall 1965.

Dahl noted Alice's smooth complexion, but she also observed: "Alice dresses mostly in beige, her favorite color. It complements her clear, blue-gray eyes and light auburn hair, which she wears in a soft, casual bob around her face." If Dahl could have peeped into Alice's closet, she would have been further impressed with the actress' flair for fashion. Most of Alice's suits were made of fine Italian wool, simply but smartly tailored. She eschewed flashy jewelry and accessories, rarely wearing more than gold loop earrings and her wedding band.

Meanwhile, as the cancer inside Alice's body grew in virulence, she remained astoundingly objective, recording her thoughts in a journal she had begun as a means to track her symptoms and bodily reactions to the drugs she was taking. "I feel the progress of the disease in my case is unusual because of my mental attitude," Alice wrote. "I am a supremely happy woman. I have never been beautiful, but I have been blessed with a rich career and the love of two fine men. The strength I have found in the devotion of my dear Paul is beyond measure. Even when he is gone, I do not feel the black helplessness or hopelessness usually associated with my condition. In truth, I do not associate myself with my condition. I do not attempt to think happy; I *am* happy, blessed with a love which comes to the few, not to the many. I am humbly grateful for my beautiful life."

During *Bewitched*'s fall hiatus, Alice trekked to San Francisco twice to tape appearances on Gypsy Rose Lee's syndicated talk show. Although the former burlesque queen lived in Beverly Hills, she regularly commuted to the Bay City's local ABC affiliate to record interviews with notables in the entertainment industry. During Alice's first segment, fashion designer Else Tyroler—enlisting the help of Alice and actress Pat Carroll—demonstrated alterations to make slacks fit, a curious topic since Alice preferred skirts, as well as a potentially touchy subject, given her recent weight loss. One month later, during the first week of October, Alice joined fellow guest Mei Mei Quong, a young Chinese-Hawaiian dancer-actress, in a discussion of witches and warlocks for a segment which would air near Halloween.

The following week, Alice began filming *The Glass Bottom Boat* which would become her fourteenth and final motion picture. She had come full circle. The Everett Freeman farce was filmed at M-G-M where Alice had rollicked with Gene Kelly and Frank Sinatra in *On the Town* sixteen years earlier. Co-produced by screenwriter Freeman and Martin Melcher, *The Glass Bottom Boat* starred Melcher's wife Doris Day.

Day plays Jennifer Nelson, a conscientious public relations worker at a space laboratory where co-star Rod Taylor, the engineering genius heading the facility, has invented a device both the U. S. government and the Soviets want. He falls for Jennifer and contrives to have her write a biography of him so she'll always be nearby. Jennifer gets caught up in the world of espionage when security officer Homer Cripps (brilliantly played by Paul Lynde) notices her calling up her dog Vladimir on the phone (the ring cues his exercise) and burning all papers as instructed. Other actors in the excellent supporting cast included Dick Martin, Dom DeLuise, and Edward Andrews.

The Glass Bottom Boat reunited Alice with Frank Tashlin who had expertly directed her in *The Disorderly Orderly* the previous year. Production had begun on August 3 and, like *Orderly*, had dragged on for eleven weeks

by the time Alice was required for her brief scenes. Although *Variety* would not report her involvement with the film until October 20, Mike Connolly had scooped every other publication by announcing in mid-August: "Alice Pearce and George Tobias are taking time out from acting bothered about their *Bewitched* neighbors to act bewildered at Doris Day's carryings on as a mermaid in Metro's *Glass Bottom Boat*." Once again, Alice and Tobias would play neighbors to an attractive blonde, this time the forty-three-year-old Day. While many have speculated that Freeman capitalized on the popularity of Abner and Gladys Kravitz by creating their doppelgängers Norman and Mabel Fenimore, there seems to be no written evidence of this. However, the similarities are blatant—Mabel is meddlesome and nagging, while Norman is alternately unconcerned and irritated by his wife's actions.

Tashlin scholar Roger Garcia suspects that the director may have had a hand in editing Freeman's original screenplay, inserting bits of business and dialogue here and there. An examination of cinematographer Leon Shamroy's preliminary copy of the script (dated July 20, 1965) proves that changes were indeed made during filming. In one scene where a disguised Homer Cripps flees Jennifer Nelson's home, his fake beard falls off and, according to the script, lands under Norman's lawn mower. However, in the filmed version it's shrieking Mabel who's pushing the mower, leaving us to wonder if Tashlin thought it would be funnier for Alice to employ a "Gladys Kravitz" reaction here. A similar change was made during the film's hectic chase finale when Jennifer is pursued by an enemy agent. Following her into the Fenimores' house where she has sought refuge, the spy awakens Norman who, in the original script, clobbers him with a golf putter. However, in the completed film, Norman remains

Homer Cripps (Paul Lynde) flees in disguise from Jennifer Nelson (Doris Day) when he is caught snooping. Neighbors Norman (George Tobias) and Mabel (Alice Pearce) are puzzled witnesses in The Glass Bottom Boat (1966).

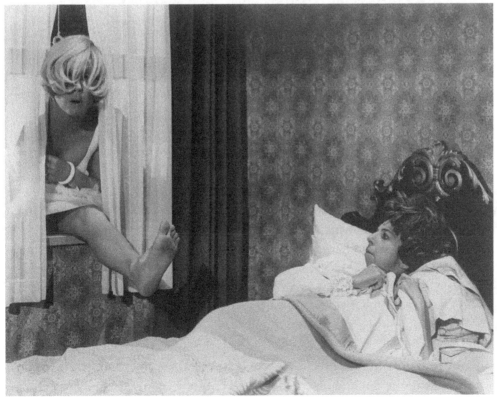

Mabel Fenimore (Alice Pearce) reacts to Jennifer Nelson (Doris Day) as she seeks refuge in the Fenimores' house in The Glass Bottom Boat (1966).]

BEFORE / **AFTER**

A Coty Cremestick turned Alice Pearce… into Joey Heatherton.

And you thought lipsticks weren't important, eh?
Another Cremestick trick: they're moisturizing,
but they're never greasy.
And zip! They're on in a stroke.
Ask Alice Pearce.

Some luscious Cremestick colors:

The Coty advertisement which appeared in the April 1966 issue of Cosmopolitan *proved that "Alice Pearce" was finally a household name.*

oblivious while frail but gutsy Mabel saves the day by crashing a lamp onto the intruder's head. Again, this switch seems to be a product of the Tashlin touch which, according to Garcia, embraced "a cynicism that nothing and no one are what they seem." Tashlin's possible contribution notwithstanding, Freeman gets credit for an exchange between Mabel and Norman that is typically Kravitzian. As Jennifer is chased into the Fenimores' guest room, Mabel alerts a disbelieving Norman. "There are two people in this house!" she whines. "Yeah, and one of 'em is *nuts!*" he barks, pulling the covers over his head.

Alice's expressions—as Mabel reacts first to Jennifer's bare foot, and then the spy's shoe poking through her bedroom window—are

priceless. Trembling with fear, she pulls the sheet over her head as each one enters and exits, then lowers it to whisper an alarm to her husband. Frozen with fear, she is unable to speak at all, emitting only strangled gasps. Just then, Vladimir bounds through the window, barking. "Shut up, will ya?" Norman growls, "You sound like a dog!"

By October 20, Alice and Tobias had completed their brief scenes in *The Glass Bottom Boat.* The next day, she purchased plane tickets for a hastily arranged—and financially motivated—trip to New York. Although Alice often made light of her physical charms, she continued to capitalize upon her deficits. In what turned out to be her final visit to her native city, she posed for Madison Avenue ad man George Lois in an unlikely two-page advertisement for a beauty product. Years later, Lois explained his motive for choosing Alice.

"On the assumption that most women saw most lipstick ads as the usual cosmetics con job," he said, "I did a Coty campaign that spoofed instant glamour in a *totally* outrageous way." In a four-color spread, the left-hand page said "Before" with a close-up photo of bewigged Alice unevenly smearing on lipstick. On the right-hand "After" page was a close-up of seductive blonde dancer Joey Heatherton peering through half-opened eyes, her tongue inching out of her full, pouty lips. The ad copy read, "A Coty Cremestick turned Alice Pearce . . . into Joey Heatherton." "Alice Pearce was a lovely, funny lady," Lois said, "but no looker (she made a living playing a bow-wow), and her tortured face caught the comic pathos of all the desperate women of the world, yearning to be beautiful."

Further explaining his choice, Lois said, "We're all suckers for a famous face. A celebrity can add almost *instant* style, atmosphere, feeling, and/or meaning to any place, product or situation—unlike any other advertising 'symbol' . . . I use celebrities for the pleasant shock of their seeming irrelevance to the product, for unexpected juxtapositions . . . for a marriage between myth and marketplace." The Coty ad proves that "Alice Pearce" was now a household name, thanks to *Bewitched*.

By the time the ad ran in the April 1966 issue of *Cosmopolitan*, Alice Pearce was near death. Lois had wanted to use her in a follow-up television commercial—to be photographed by Richard Avedon—with her face dissolving "werewolf-style" into Heatherton's, but Alice died before it could be arranged. "Finding a replacement for a beautiful woman would have been a piece of cake, but there was only one Alice Pearce," lamented Lois. "So, I sadly cast Alice Ghostley, another beautifully talented nonbeauty."

Alice's weight loss was very evident in December 1965 when she returned to the Bewitched *set following its fall hiatus. Photo courtesy Herbie Pilato.*

In the meantime, production on *Bewitched* resumed in early December 1965. When Alice arrived on the set, the cast and crew were saddened to see that she had become extremely emaciated during the four-month hiatus. By now, the familiar auburn wig framing her pitifully drawn face looked positively outsized. It was painfully obvious to everyone that Alice was suffering—yet silently. "At all times, good or bad, she held steadfastly to a show of good cheer," Paul later said. "I knew she did this for me and for her friends—to spare us unnecessary anguish." Paul was a constant presence at the studio, administering Alice's medication

On January 7, 1966, George Tobias, Alice Pearce, and Elizabeth Montgomery playfully posed on the Bewitched *set during the filming of "Samantha the Dressmaker."*

when necessary. "It was thrilling just to see them together," said Agnes Moorehead, "he so attentive, she so glowingly proud and happy that this much-admired man was hers." Dick York pointed out, "She never brought any problems to the set. Her illness would have given her every right to be irritable. But she never was."

Amazingly, Alice managed to perform several physical stunts during her final episodes. In "My Baby, the Tycoon," she took a pratfall when the script required that she bump into Elizabeth Montgomery who was carrying a bucket of water for baby Tabatha's bath. Although the shot was edited to zoom in on Alice's feet, it's plainly visible that her stick-like figure lands rather hard onto the carpeted floor of the set. In "Fastest Gun on Madison Avenue," she wrestles with a bulky, oversized cardboard box—purportedly filled with exercise dumbbells—to manipulate it through a

doorway. And in "Samantha, the Dressmaker," Alice scampers about searching for dresses that magically disappeared.

In each segment, Alice attempted to conceal her weight loss as best she could. For the "Dressmaker" episode in which Gladys Kravitz is the focal point of a fashion show for "the average American woman," Alice again resorted to the hot pink evening coat from Lord & Taylor, even though it now engulfed her. To remedy its gaping neckline, she purchased a matching feather boa from I. Magnin to wind around her neck. For the episode's final close-up where Gladys playfully twirled an open parasol over her shoulders, Alice added a delightfully comic touch by blowing at a feather that was caught on her bottom lip.

For "Baby's First Paragraph," filmed during the third week of January, 1966, Alice was finally granted a very special wish—her first scene with Agnes Moorehead. The previous spring, she had revealed that she was a big fan of the legendary actress. "But I have never worked in a scene with her," Alice shrugged. "[Gladys keeps] seeing [Endora] through the window, but that's as close as we get. I keep hoping that we'll do a scene someday."

Due to a lack of opportunity, it's plain that Alice had not become as intimate with Moorehead as she had with Montgomery. When she wrote Moorehead from Hawaii in September 1965, she signed the postcard "Love, Alice P." As an afterthought, she wrote "Pearce" in parentheses below, denoting her uncertainty that Moorehead would instantly identify the sender.

Ironically, Alice's final film session may have been the scene in "Baby's First Paragraph" which she shared alone with Moorehead. "Alice worked to the day she could no longer stand on her feet," attested Jerry Davis, who by this time had replaced Danny Arnold as producer. "We were all aware by then that she was sick, but never discussed it with her because we realized that was the way she wanted it. She appeared before the cameras for the last time on January 21." Even though that date coincides with the completion of "Paragraph" as it is listed on Screen Gems' "production summary" records, a discrepancy definitely exists.

A studio call sheet, listing actors required for filming on Thursday, January 27, includes Alice. On that day, her scenes for both "Baby's First Paragraph" and the subsequent "Disappearing Samantha" were scheduled for Stage 4, which contained the Stephens house set. For certain, Alice did not appear in the telecast of the latter episode, but her copy of the "Disappearing" script includes her own handwritten notes which specify that she would be needed for filming January 19 through January 21, resuming on January 26 until the episode was completed. A call sheet for February 4, when additional scenes for "Disappearing" were planned, notes that Alice would be notified if needed. Whether Alice ever filmed any of her brief scenes in "Disappearing" is not known. The Screen Gems production summary shows a January 27 completion for "Disappearing," but the call sheets prove that filming may have extended beyond that date. Whatever the case, by February Alice was too ill to work.

In short order, Gladys Kravitz had become Alice's signature role—and her most providential, arriving at a time when her days were clouded by financial uncertainty and inexorable mortality. Its abundant rewards, not the least of which were monetary, had sustained her for the past eighteen months. Alice had finally "hit TV paydirt," noted one observer who cited the benefits of residual income. In addition, her success on *Bewitched* had led to a motion picture role, appearances on talk shows, and lucrative commercials—not only for the show's sponsor Chevrolet but for independent advertisers as well.

Equally satisfying was the media exposure, particularly a feature article in the Christmas 1965 issue of *TV Guide*, proclaiming Alice as "Finally the Center of Attention." Without a doubt, Alice was grateful for Gladys, confessing to *TV Guide*, "I like earthy parts. They're a rebellion against my background." In an ABC news release, prepared that same week, Alice further delineated her character: "Gladys Kravitz is an enigma among television characters. She's a nosy neighbor with too much time on her hands. A devoted pryer. Yet there is empathy. Viewers who instinctively dislike people like [her] still feel sorry for Gladys. They know she really sees Samantha practicing 'twitchcraft.'" (Even Samantha and Darrin sympathized with Gladys, most notably in the tag scene for the second-season episode "A Strange Little Visitor." When their departing visitors vanish almost before an incredulous Gladys, Darrin and Samantha consolingly surround her and gently guide her into their house, promising her a "scoop of sugar." It's a particularly touching image, especially since we know Alice's physical condition at the time.)

Cancer, however, didn't define Alice Pearce. Courage did. In the final twenty-one months of her life, she seized all the opportunities available to her: completing three films, remarrying, accepting a regular role on a television series, taking part in a business venture, overseeing the dispersal of her late aunt's effects, vacationing in Hawaii, and buying her first home and decorating it.

Now it was time to slow down. Knowing that she would never work again, Alice settled into 8242 Hillside Avenue to make final preparations for the inevitable. Paul secured the services of attorney Edythe Jacobs, who lived next door, to draw up Alice's new will which she signed on January 30. In addition, Jacobs was entrusted with preparing certain documents required of Alice as Josephine Strode's executrix. During the past twelve months, Alice had failed to make any headway to settle her aunt's estate, not even returning the preliminary inventory of Josephine's assets which had been due in May 1965. Now the one-year deadline to apply for an extension to settle the estate was fast upon them. Jacobs hustled to accomplish as much as possible before Alice's expected death.

Paul persevered to honor his pact with Alice. Over the course of the next month, he ensured that she was kept as comfortable as possible, ordering extra bed sheets, pillow slips, towels, pajamas, and warm socks from Saks Fifth Avenue on Wilshire Boulevard. For the first three weeks, Alice was able to function on her own, but she spent most of her time in bed. At night, Paul propped himself up in Alice's queen-size bed, watching television shows with her—sometimes until dawn. Paul also oversaw her numerous medications and learned to administer the pain-killing injections. Even though Alice was on intravenous therapy, her weight continued to drop. The *Hollywood Reporter*'s Radie Harris revealed Alice's decline in her "Broadway Ballyhoo" column: "Alice Pearce's loss of weight has her countless friends greatly worried. She's down to seventy-seven pounds."

"During the last month of Alice's life, I don't think she was seeing many people," Milton Davis recalled. Alice's friend Miles White was visiting the West Coast at the time. "Alice wouldn't allow me to come to the house," White said. "I realized later that it was because she didn't want to be seen." She had refused to discuss her illness even with Richard Deacon, but he had long suspected the worst. He tried to find reasons to send her flowers as often as possible. Alice, he said, always played the game of not understanding what he was up to. The last ones Deacon sent her were for Valentine's Day. "I addressed the card 'To My Valentines,' which would include Paul," he explained. "He, too, played the game and never let on for a moment that her illness was terminal. Two days later, I received a thank-you note from her. It was dated February 16. Think of that greatness. How did she ever find the strength and resolution to attend to such a small matter when she knew death was so near? But then, of such quality Alice was made. She was a lady through and through."

Word of Alice's dire situation reached her friends in New York, many of whom were caught unawares. After hearing the news from Cris Alexander, Kaye Ballard felt compelled to drop Alice a line: "I just want you to know that even though I don't write you many letters, I love you very much and think of you often." Ballard, as usual, signed her first name with a cartoon face substituting for the letter "a." This time, copious tears dropped from the face.

One person who did gain entry to 8242 Hillside Avenue was Alice's college friend Mary "Dutch" Gordon, then living in Connecticut with her second husband, the writer Max Shulman. Dutch flew out to Los Angeles expressly to say goodbye to her beloved Peeps. By then, Alice was confined to bed. "My mother told me," says Gordon's daughter Melodie Bryant, "that Peeps' devoted husband stayed in his bathrobe 24/7 and kept the lights low so Peeps wouldn't feel the passage of time." When

Alice and Paul Davis posed for a final photo session four months before her death.

Paul's sorrow became so great, he retreated to his own bedroom so that Alice would not see him crying.

Margaret Pearce hired and dispatched a private duty nurse to care for Alice during the final two weeks of her life. Helen Farrell, a fifty-four-year-old widow, had become a registered nurse in New Hampshire many years before. Moving to California in 1960, she quickly became a reputable caregiver in the La Jolla area.

By February 27, Alice's condition had worsened significantly. Paul kept Bob and Margaret updated with phone calls to La Jolla. On March 2, he and Mrs. Farrell realized that they could no longer care for Alice at home—she had wasted away to seventy pounds. That night, at forty minutes past nine, Alice was admitted to Cedars of Lebanon Hospital on Fountain Avenue. There was nothing to be done except to make her final hours as comfortable as possible. At a quarter past four the next morning, Alice Pearce died peacefully with Paul Davis at her side. "Alice never went into coma," Paul said. "She said goodbye to me just before she died."

Later that day, various West Coast newspapers announced Alice's death in their afternoon and evening editions. As some of those papers hit the Hollywood stands, seventy-nine-year-old actor William Frawley—of *I Love Lucy* fame—exited a movie theater on Hollywood Boulevard. While waiting for a friend to arrive, Frawley was downed by a fatal heart attack. The next day, on March 4, papers across the country would print joint obituaries for William Frawley and Alice Pearce. Invariably, they erroneously listed Alice's home as her place of death. Only one newspaper in the nation got her age right. "Alice Pearce Dies at 48" ran the headline on page eight of the *Los Angeles Times*.

Even up to her death, Alice had managed to keep her condition a secret from some of her friends, especially those based in the East. "I couldn't believe it when I read in the *New York Times* that she had died," remembered Alice Ghostley. "I was on my way there from California (on the train!)." Patricia Wilson also learned of Alice's death via her obituary. "I remember the *shock* I had at her passing," Wilson says, "because we were in touch after her move to California, but I did not know she was ill. She kept it from me." William LeMassena, who had opened in the off-Broadway drama *The Coop* on March 1, pasted Alice's *New York Times* obituary into his overstuffed career scrapbook. He shook his head at its ironic subheading: "A Favorite of Noël Coward." In an effort to fortify its tribute, the *Times*—ignorant of the enduring rift between playwright and actress—had pulled quotes from its 1947 feature article on Alice's Blue Angel act, attended by then fan Coward.

At Alice's request, there were no funeral services. Pierce Brothers Hollywood Mortuary handled the cremation on March 4, but there are varying accounts of the remains' disposal which took place on March 8. Kathleen Post's tribute to Alice in the June issue of *TV Radio Mirror* verges on the romantic: "Still following Alice's wishes, Paul rented a plane and, with shaking hands, scattered her ashes over the billowing Pacific, in the direction of Hawaii, where they had spent a belated honeymoon. She had always loved the sea, finding it both mysterious and calming." Peter Turgeon's version, included in his 1992 collection of theatre anecdotes, is perhaps more accurate: "One thing Alice disliked over all others was water in any form, lakes, ponds, rivers … She left instructions that she be cremated and her ashes sprinkled over the film capital, but a new city ordinance forbade any additional substance to be added to the smog-clogged atmosphere. Her executor decided to hire a plane in which he and a number of her close friends could fly out over the Pacific to dispose of the remains. Armed with the canister and a bottle of vintage champagne, the mourners took to the sky. Finally, when the pilot indicated they were legally far enough off shore, the wine was uncorked, a toast delivered, and a window opened to consign Alice to the sea. Of course, she was having none of this! The ashes immediately blew back, turning the cabin and its occupants into an airborne Pompeii!"

While friends may have smiled or laughed at this story, their sorrow was still great. "Alice Pearce was one of my closest friends," said John Fiedler. "Her death was a real loss to those who loved her. She was a warm, lovely woman who was more fun to be with than almost anyone I know." Debbie Reynolds echoed Fiedler's sentiments: "She was the perfect lady with a most special and unique sense of humor. I cherish having been her friend. She was here on earth much too short a time, and she is sorely missed by all of us." Jane Dulo, who had known Alice since the waning days of World War Two, recalled their friendship: "Knowing her

was a joy as she was so witty, and bright, and extremely—for want of a better word—'classy,' something rarely found these days. She had impeccable taste in everything and I am happy to have been part of her life."

Alice's *Bewitched* colleagues were particularly affected by her death, having witnessed her brave efforts to continue playing Gladys Kravitz even though suffering greatly. "Alice and I had many things in common," Agnes Moorehead reflected. "For one thing, she was an eccentric, and so am I. I've always felt that it is wrong to hold back on eulogies until after people are dead. Why not tell them how you admire, respect or love them while they are still able to appreciate it? In the case of Alice, I *do* believe she knew how we felt about her, and this goes for the crew as well as the cast. She was always kind and considerate of everyone."

No one on the series was more impacted by Alice's passing than Elizabeth Montgomery and Bill Asher. "They were devastated in losing her," says Montgomery biographer Herbie Pilato. Alice's demeanor made an indelible impression on Montgomery who later said of her, "One of the few true-blue ladies I've known. The word 'lady'—like the word 'nice'—has lost all its meaning, I regret to say. I don't mean aristocracy by the term either. I mean it in the wider sense." Perhaps Montgomery would have agreed with another industry insider who noted, "Ladies are a rarity in Hollywood, where too many stars had to fight their way up from unfortunate backgrounds." In her own final fight, Alice Pearce retained her dignity. "She was never bitter," Paul recalled. "One day she said to me, 'God closes one door only to open another.'"

In February, when the *Bewitched* producers had realized that Alice would never return to the set, they gave the matter careful consideration. Since scripts for future episodes fea-

Bill Asher and Elizabeth Montgomery.

turing Gladys had already been written, they decided not to immediately recast the role but instead create a surrogate to serve in a similar capacity. The scripts for "Follow That Witch!"—a two-part story to be telecast during consecutive weeks in April—were revised on February 7 to introduce the character of Harriet Kravitz, Abner's sister, who would explain that Gladys had gone away to visit her mother. Character actress Mary Grace Canfield, then playing a recurring role on the CBS sitcom *Green Acres,* was hired to play Harriet without ever reading for the part. Like Gladys, Harriet would witness strange happenings, but Canfield's reactions lacked the comic liveliness

created by Alice Pearce. The magic was definitely missing.

In fairness to Canfield, she may have been directed to play the role with less intensity. She would film only three episodes, two of which were completed after Alice's death. "I was dropped and never told why," Canfield recalled in 1986. "There was an air of uncertainty on the set and a lot of melancholy. In addition, they were working with a different director [Jerry Davis], and Dick York was not well. It was not the happiest of occasions." According to *World Telegram and Sun* columnist Al Salerno, there were discussions—at least for a brief time—to also drop George Tobias, particularly if Screen

Gems ultimately "decide[d] against giving him a kooky sister to take Alice's nosy-next-door-neighbor place." Citing Alice's untimely death, Salerno observed, "Now, one's misfortune may affect the future of the other."

In the midst of this gloom, the episode "Baby's First Paragraph" aired on Thursday, March 10, one week after Alice was gone. "All of us watched it," recalled Jerry Davis. "All of us wept."

Spirits rose, however, on April 26 when the eighteenth annual Emmy Award nominees were publicly announced by the National Academy of Television Arts and Sciences. *Bewitched* garnered five nominations in the comedy category, including best series, best director (Asher), and best actress (Montgomery). Both Alice and Agnes Moorehead were nominated for the "outstanding performance by an actress in a supporting role in a comedy," along with Rose Marie of *The Dick Van Dyke Show*. Academy president Rod Serling informed Paul of Alice's nomination, inviting him to attend the "most gala ceremony in our seventeen-year history" in anticipation of "saluting her achievement, even though, sadly, it must be posthumous."

A "blue-ribbon" panel of industry peers—whose identities were not made public—viewed "several episodes" of nominated programs telecast between May 1, 1965, and April 10, 1966, before voting to select the winners. Award presentations were made on Sunday evening, May 22, 1966, during a live CBS telecast—the first Emmy ceremony to air in color—jointly from the Hollywood Palladium and the Americana Hotel in New York. The program's producer had been widely quoted beforehand that it "would be handled as an event, and not as an entertainment special." He was as good as his word. There were no musical numbers and "very few awkward stage waits," noted the *Hol-*

lywood Reporter, calling the ceremony "probably the most zippily paced awards show in either Emmy or Oscar history."

That evening the standing-room-only audience at the Palladium included Art Carney, Henry Fonda, Lee Grant, Roddy McDowall, and Barbara Stanwyck. Shortly into the ceremony, emcee Danny Kaye introduced actress Barbara Parkins as she descended a flight of stairs to reach the podium, her *Peyton Place* series theme song swelling in the background. Parkins had been selected to announce the best supporting comedy actress. Seated at a round table just below were Elizabeth Montgomery, Bill Asher, and Paul Davis. To Paul's right was Alice's agent George Morris, and to Paul's left was Debbie Reynolds, there to accept the Emmy for the absent Agnes Moorehead in the event that she won. At the same table was Don Knotts who moments before had been presented his fourth Emmy for his role on *The Andy Griffith Show*.

The presentations coincided with Parkins' twenty-fourth birthday, and in an impromptu move, Kaye asked the audience to join him in singing "Happy Birthday" to the actress. Parkins got on with her duties but abruptly stalled after opening the envelope and viewing the name of the winner. Awkwardly turning from the audience, she asked, "Mr. Kaye, would you please present this, please?" As Parkins backed out of camera range, Kaye took the podium and with downcast eyes somberly announced, "In Hollywood, ladies and gentlemen, the winner is Alice Pearce." A few shouts rang out—most prominently from the enthusiastic Morris—as the audience broke into generous applause. As Paul rose from his seat to accept the award, a beaming Reynolds reached out to pat his knee. Onstage, Parkins handed the Emmy statuette to Paul, who paused for the ovation to subside while he swallowed hard before speaking. "I

Paul Davis poses with Alice Pearce's Emmy statuette during the awards ceremony on May 22, 1966.

teary-eyed, smiling broadly and shaking her head in exclamation.

The *Hollywood Reporter* called Alice's win "the most dramatic point" of the ceremony, while the *Valley Times* regarded Paul's acceptance as the evening's "most touching moment." Many reviewers noted Parkins' passing the baton to Kaye, assuming that she was overcome with emotion or even "frightened and confused." However, a few journalists—smelling staginess—observed that the actress' face registered nothing of the sort. Syndicated columnist Dick Kleiner revealed, "She was just following instructions. Director [of the telecast] Dick Dunlap had told her, before the affair, to call for Danny [Kaye] if Miss Pearce was the winner."

However, there was no exaggeration in the many notes Paul received from industry officials during the days immediately following the awards ceremony. Rod Serling, representing the academy, wrote: "Your loss is shared by the many, many millions who delighted in your late wife's comedic sense and in the warmth of her spirit. We hope that this award is both a satisfaction and a consolation to you." Chevrolet advertising executive Carl Uren expressed bittersweet thoughts shared by many of Alice's fans: "If the recognition of a grateful industry can alleviate your sense of bereavement, it must indeed have been a proud and happy moment for you to accept the posthumous Emmy Award for your wife, Alice. It is regrettable that she could not have known of this distinctive honor which was so genuinely deserved by her wonderful portrayal of Gladys Kravitz in the *Bewitched* series. We at Chevrolet have always been most appreciative of Alice's talent for comedy and her tremendous contribution to the success of the series." Dominick Dunne, then the vice-president of Four Star Television, had been introduced to Alice by *Small Wonder* director Burt Shevelove in New York

think the best thing we could do," he proposed, "if you all join me sometime this evening in drinking a toast to a *wonderful* actress, *great* human being, and the *most delicious* wife a man could have ever had. Thank you." Holding back tears, Paul quickly exited the stage. Just before the cameras cut to a commercial break, they caught an applauding Montgomery, also

many years earlier. He felt compelled to write to Paul: "I cannot tell you how touched and moved I was by your lovely acceptance speech for Alice last night at the Emmy Awards. I am so very happy that Alice won, and I know that there could be no better tribute to her than the one you paid last night." In perhaps the greatest tribute of all, Screen Gems took out a full-page ad in *Variety* on May 26, which read: "ALICE PEARCE, our lasting affection."

Alice's name continued to appear in newspapers for several months as the television season wound down and summer reruns began. On June 9, 1966, the thirty-eighth and final episode of *Bewitched*'s second season aired. "Prodigy"—filmed almost a year earlier—featured Jack Weston as Gladys Kravitz's maladjusted brother, a former child violinist who elicits sympathy from his overprotective sister. With Alice's Emmy win still fresh, many television listings highlighted the episode as Alice's last appearance on the series. (One even headlined: "Alice Pearce Stars in *Bewitched*.") Of course, "Prodigy" wasn't the final episode Alice filmed; it was the last of her episodes to be telecast.

Some modern-day fans have surmised that this segment was held back as a posthumous tribute to Alice—a claim which is totally inaccurate. "'Prodigy' was one of those incredible experiences that sometimes befall a television series," Harry Ackerman explained in 1986. "It was written by two master comedy writers, Larry Cohen and Fred Freeman, and when it was filmed on stage the lines and the comedy business continually broke up the cast and crew. However, when I ran the first cut of the picture it seemed to me a disaster. When I so informed our series director (Bill Asher, who did not direct that particular episode), he couldn't believe me, but when we ran it together the next day, he was in complete agreement with me that we had a disaster on our hands.

That led to our decision to 'bury' the picture and air it as the last episode of the season, when audience viewing would be down anyway."

That fall, after the new television season began, members of the Entre Nous Club gathered for their monthly meeting at the home of Mrs. Hiram Biggers in Perry, Missouri. The program topic was Alice Pearce, whom locals had long claimed as one of their own, even though she was an infrequent visitor to the small town. Following notices in the *Perry Enterprise* over the years, they had kept informed of Alice's many accomplishments, from her earliest performances at Princeton to her nationwide fame as Gladys Kravitz. They had read of her personal triumphs and sorrows, her marriages and widowhood. Many had memories of Alice as a girl, attending services at the Christian Church or enjoying a soda at the drug store. Some even remembered when her mother was a girl in Perry. Others reminisced about her grandmother who had helped to organize their club more than sixty-five years earlier. But that day, the Entre Nous members paid tribute to Alice—in their own simple but sweet way—by reading aloud several published articles about her. They were proud of their native daughter, Broadway actress and Hollywood star.

Gladys Kravitz, the last in a long line of sweet oddballs, brought immortality to Alice Pearce. Today, through the wonder of the internet and cable television, her legacy lives on as she attracts new fans, many of whom were born long after her lifetime. Alice's ingenious and endearing characterization of Gladys leads some admirers to discover more of her film performances—but especially one who knew firsthand the lady's real character. "I recently watched *On the Town* which I had never seen before," says Chan Lowe, Alice's godson. "In it, Alice played the kooky, odd-looking roommate of the principal actress, and her character had developed a crush on Gene Kelly, a sailor at liberty. At some point in the movie, he has to gently explain to Alice that he's not romantically interested in her, and she keeps a brave face, but breaks down after they part. There was something about the vulnerability and the loving heart that dwelled beneath the comic exterior that brought tears to my eyes. That was Alice."

Epilogue

Soon after Alice Pearce's death, Bill Asher approached Alice Ghostley about assuming the role of Gladys Kravitz, but she promptly declined. Ghostley felt uncomfortable about it because she and Alice had been friends for many years. "I just couldn't do it," she told Herbie Pilato in 1988. So, the search went on. According to *Variety*, more than sixty actresses read for the role, and seven of these tested for it.

Among them was forty-nine-year-old Sandra Gould, a widow of five months. "I was so numb and withdrawn [then] that I hardly knew what was going on about me," Gould recalled in 1967. Then one night, George Tobias, who had known Gould for more than thirty-five years, phoned to ask her to read for the part of Gladys. "He kept on insisting, saying that if I didn't come back to earth and get my feet on the ground, I would be a total mental wreck in no time at all." Gould agreed to read for Harry Ackerman. "They had already read sixty actresses, and I read with fourteen or fifteen," Gould recollected. "Then they wanted me to test, and I was still reluctant. But I tested with five others, and I didn't hear anything for a while until one day they called and said, 'Come down and sign your contract.'" Gould was hired on May 5, 1966.

In years to come, Gould would be quoted as saying that her initial reluctance to play Gladys Kravitz stemmed from her "very close" friendship with Alice Pearce. However, there is no indication among Alice's papers that such an intimacy ever existed between the two actress-es. Closer to the truth was a statement Gould made about Alice in the fall of 1966: "We shared a dressing room while making the movie *Dear Heart*. She was an enchanting, lovely gal." Most likely, their association was restricted to those two days in 1963 when filming the drunken postmasters scene.

Once Gould joined the cast of *Bewitched*, however, there were grievous issues. "Elizabeth Montgomery was still heartbroken over losing her friend Alice Pearce," says *Bewitched* historian Herbie Pilato, "and she was not one hundred percent behind the casting choice of Gould as Gladys." In fact, Pilato says, "Elizabeth did not like Sandy at all." There was also strife between Gould and Bill Asher, especially whenever the director absentmindedly called her "Alice," provoking Gould's angry flight to her dressing room. According to Pilato, Montgomery found Gould "too abrasive" in the role.

Gould's grating voice coupled with her native Brooklynese accent made her a known commodity, says pop culture historian Geoffrey Mark, "but what she could not do was bring warmth to the part that Alice had done . . . Sandy's portrayal of Mrs. Kravitz was all one-note. Shrill and angry." Therefore, Mark says, the producers were forced to use the Kravitzes less often. Sandra Gould and George Tobias would appear in twenty-nine and twenty-six *Bewitched* episodes, respectively, over the course of seasons three through seven. (Neither Gould nor Tobias were seen during the show's eighth and final season.) Alice Pearce had appeared in a total of twenty-seven episodes during her two seasons on the show.

On June 9, 1966, three months after Alice's death, *The Glass Bottom Boat* opened at Radio City Music Hall, followed by a general release in July. Reviews were mixed. *The New York Times* called it a "frantic failure." Philip Scheuer of the *Los Angeles Times* admitted, "[It's] one of those insane comedies that won't amuse anybody but us lowbrows ... I enjoyed it for the presence of a boatload of funny comedians." *Variety* was somewhat more generous: "Given to sight gags and frenzied comedy performances, much of the humor of the Panavision-Metrocolor film is contrived in a loosely-developed plotline but builds into a slambang laugh ending." Many reviews noted that it was Alice Pearce's final film, most notably the one in the *Los Angeles Times* which featured an amusing shot of Alice's reaction to Doris Day climbing through her bedroom window.

Meanwhile, Paul Davis, as Alice's executor, continued to dispose of Josephine Strode's antiques collection, which he made available for sale at Pesha's Framing Studio. One customer was Dominick Dunne, who had occasionally run into Alice after she made the move to Los Angeles. "Alice was from what we used to call 'a good family,'" the inveterate namedropper recalled in 2003. "I remember that her parents were friends of friends of my mother, and I used to hear about Alice before I ever met her. She had some lovely French furniture. After her death, I bought a small eighteenth-century table with a marble top. It was first in my house on Walden Drive in Beverly Hills and later, after my divorce, in my apartment in Beverly Hills. It was a beautiful table, or commode, and I invariably said when it was admired, 'That belonged to Alice Pearce,' as opposed to its historical provenance. When I went broke at the end of the seventies and

had to sell all my possessions, I sold it to Dodi Fayed who bought it for an actress girlfriend of his—name forgotten—who lived in my apartment complex on Spalding Drive . . . now I wish I hadn't sold that beautiful French table."

Paul eventually sold his framing business to Tommy Sand who subsequently moved the shop to 7966 Melrose Avenue. (In 1983, Sand was still operating Pesha's Framing Studio but lamented the demise of area small businesses. He had recently moved to yet another location on Melrose because the rent soared from $850 to $3000 a month. It is not known how long Sand stayed afloat after that.)

In the meantime, attempts to settle Josephine Strode's estate dragged on until 1973. Her will stipulated that the trust set up for Alice would terminate at Alice's death and that the residue would be divided equally among George Strode's nephews and nieces. However, that trust was never established because Alice, as executrix, had died without having fully administered the estate. A twofold legal struggle ensued. First, Margaret Pearce and her brother LaFrance Clark, as their sister's next of kin, contended that two-fourths of the residue was not bequeathed and was therefore intestate property. The court later overruled this claim, but Margaret appealed. (Her brother had died in the interim.) Secondly, the Strode legatees objected to certain disbursements which Paul claimed were due Alice's estate for the twelve months of her executorship. The court eventually allowed all these compensations, but then the legatees appealed. Finally, both sides agreed to withdraw their appeals.

"After Alice died," says Carole Cook, "Paul kind of went into seclusion. I mean he didn't hang around in the same group here in Los Angeles." Cris Alexander recalled, "I was never in touch with him afterwards. I wrote him and got a lovely note back from him, declaring, you know, that we would be in touch . . . well, we weren't." Of that dark period, Paul said: "Everyone was wonderful to me after Alice's death. Everyone was shocked; they all felt her loss. But Liz [Montgomery] and Bill [Asher] are the ones who actively *did* something . . . They asked me one day what my plans were, and I said I wanted to get back into the business, back into directing. And they said okay—just like that." The Ashers waited for a good script, one that they felt Paul could handle well. "It's Wishcraft," directed by Paul, was filmed in February 1967. That October, Paul also directed the *Bewitched* episode "McTavish," but his directing career seems to have ended there.

Paul's final professional acting credit appears to have been a small role in *Dinah East*, a low-budget film co-produced by Paula Stewart and its screenwriter-director Gene Nash. Released in 1970, the controversial film—*Variety* called it a sexploitation—centers on a 1950s transvestite who fools the world into believing he is a she—a glamorous movie diva. Paul played a Hollywood agent. Viewed today as a camp classic, *Dinah East* was virtually lost for years due to a quagmire of copyright and legal hassles. Upon its original release—carrying an X rating—the federal government had shut it down and confiscated all prints of the film due to unpaid withholding taxes. Following its 2010 DVD distribution, one blogger proclaimed *Dinah East* as "far ahead of its time in its empathetic depiction of gays, lesbians, and transgender."

Paul never remarried. "After Alice died, I never knew Paul to have a long-lasting relationship that I was conscious of—a gay relationship, that is—because I saw him less and less," says Carole Cook. Indeed, little is known about Paul's final years, except that he remained at 8242 Hillside Avenue until his death. In 1980, when the home's former owners John and Harriett Weaver visited Paul, they discovered very few changes in the house. "The view was as magnificent as ever," John wrote to a friend, "but the rooms seem to have shrunk. Harriett was surprised to find that the counter tops in the kitchen are still covered with the black linoleum she'd intended to replace fifteen years ago. The shutters she'd hung there were still in place and her brickwork has held up nicely, except for the intrusion of roots from trees we'd planted."

Paul's health began to deteriorate in 1983. "My wife and I took care of him during the last six months of his life," says Milton Davis. "Paul phoned me once when he was very ill," Renee Summers recalled, "and I asked him how he was and he said, 'Ah, my back's bothering me.' But I didn't know that he had called to say goodbye. My other brother never told me that he was dying—I didn't know that—but then, I wasn't that close to Paul. There was a big difference in our ages." A biopsy revealed that Paul, a smoker since his youth, was suffering from lung cancer.

Even though the protraction of Josephine's probate case had also delayed the closure of Alice's estate, Paul evidently procrastinated in settling his wife's affairs for another other ten years. Facing his own mortality, he finally initiated the paperwork for the final distribution—which transferred all of Alice's assets to Paul—on December 21, 1983. Two months later, on the night of February 20, Paul died at home. He was sixty-one years old.

Cancer would also claim the lives of Alice's *Bewitched* castmates Elizabeth Montgomery (in 1995), Agnes Moorehead (1974), and George Tobias (1980). Dick York died in 1992, following a long battle with emphysema. Marion Lorne suffered a heart attack and died in New York City on May 9, 1968, ten days before winning an Emmy Award for playing Aunt Clara.

In 1969, Alice's agent George Morris died of heart attack one morning as he was preparing to leave home for his office. The previous fall, he had introduced Jean Stapleton to producer Norman Lear who was casting a pilot called *All in the Family*. The rest, as they say, is history. When Stapleton won her first Emmy for playing Edith Bunker in 1971, she thanked George on nationwide television. "He was a wonderful man," she said, "and he worked very hard to get me the part. It was all George's doing."

Perk Bailey and his wife June, who had been best man and matron of honor at Alice and John Rox's wedding in 1948, seem to have practically vanished from Alice's life following John's death. In 1965, the Baileys moved to Palm Beach, Florida, where they bought an elegant home and joined a circle of well-heeled retirees who were interested in art, fashion, and civic affairs. On September 22, 1977, Perk died at age seventy-one after a month's illness. June later divided her time between Palm Beach and New Orleans. Eventually the nonagenarian settled in Naples, Florida. "She was a character," said her friend Anne Richards. "She saved everything, and her guest bathtub was full of stuff!" Feisty until the end, June died in a Naples nursing home two months after her one hundredth birthday.

Alice's three most intimate college friends all reached their nineties, surviving Alice by more than forty years. Betty La Branche died at ninety-two in 2010, Mary "Dutch" Gordon Shulman died at ninety-five in 2014, and Helen Tuttle Votichenko died at ninety-eight in 2018.

Alice's closest friends in the entertainment industry are all gone now, too. Richard Deacon died suddenly in 1984. Alice's former agent Gus Schirmer, who had moved to Los Angeles in 1972 to become a booking and casting director, died of congestive heart failure and uremia in 1992. Both Nancy Walker, sixty-nine, and Bill LeMassena, seventy-six, died of lung cancer in 1992 and 1993, respectively. Peggy Cass was seventy-four when she died of heart failure in 1999. Although battling cancer at age eighty, John Fiedler continued to provide the voice of Piglet for Walt Disney Productions until the end came in 2005. Dody Goodman, who had gone on to create zany characters for *Mary Hartman, Mary Hartman* and *Grease*, died at ninety-three in 2008. Health enthusiast Carol Channing almost made it to age ninety-eight; she died of natural causes in 2019.

Three weeks after Alice Pearce died, Cris Alexander opened in the off-Broadway production *The Madness of Lady Bright* at Theatre East where Alice had appeared in *The Ignorants Abroad*. This would be his final professional appearance on the New York stage. "My [photography] studio was going so well then, and I had so much to do that I never really tried out for anything [else]," he later explained. Cris was the official photographer for the New York City Ballet for many years, as well as chief photographer for Warhol's *Interview* magazine from 1980 until his retirement in 1986. He was noted for his many photographic portraits of celebrities—among them Vivien Leigh, Leonard Bernstein, Andy Warhol, Nancy Reagan, Mother Teresa, Gloria Vanderbilt, and her teenage son Anderson Cooper. However, his first gallery show was not until 1980 when a small collection was exhibited in Saratoga Springs, New York. In 1973, Cris and his longtime partner Shaun O'Brien had bought a twelve-room Victorian house in Saratoga, gradually filling it with choice antiques and Cris' paintings. After their permanent relocation from Manhattan in 1991, the pair became an integral part of Saratoga's artistic community and soon found themselves hosting historians who sought out the pair to discuss the illustrious circles in which they had traveled. "I must say, I have been very close to some of the most wonderful people who ever have lived in our time," Cris told *Show Music* magazine in 1994. "Our life is just the greatest life imaginable." After living as partners for sixty-one years, Cris and Shaun married in Saratoga Springs on November 23, 2011. By that time, eighty-six-year-old Shaun was very ill. After Shaun died on February 23, 2012, Cris—brokenhearted—literally pined away. He died at home on March 7. Cris was ninety-two.

Following Alice's death, Bob and Margaret Pearce continued to live a very quiet life in their La Jolla home. In 1967, when Margaret's distant cousin Edward Alford wrote to her regarding their shared genealogy, she responded: "These Clark papers I am sending you, you might as well keep. My daughter Alice has left us. How I miss that dear girl every day of my life! I kept these papers for Alice. I hope they will give you some information, and, what you don't want, burn . . . I am getting older and slower, but still can take care of myself and my house."

By this time, Bob Pearce, weakened by a previous heart attack, was in a fragile condition. In the summer of 1971, he suffered a cerebral blood clot and lingered five days. Bob died at Scripps Memorial Hospital in San Diego on August 23. He was eighty-two years old.

Margaret subsequently moved to Los Angeles to be nearer Paul Davis who helped take care of her until his death. Paul's brother Milton took over those duties but found it frustrating. "Mrs. Pearce is an eccentric old woman who has no desire to hear from anyone," he said in 1984. "She refuses to take phone calls, will not even read letters or cards from her family and friends and has no desire to be reminded of the past. She focuses on her daily life in the here-and-now and reads in several languages to keep her mind active."

On April 22, 1986, Margaret Pearce, then a patient at the Brotman Hospital in Culver City, died of cardiac arrest brought on by coronary artery disease. She missed her ninety-fourth birthday by one month. "It is amazing that she reached that age," says her former neighbor Whitman Wheeler, "considering how heavily she smoked." Strong-willed Margaret had survived Alice by twenty years.

Acknowledgments

No work such as this is ever entirely the author's own. I am obliged to the many individuals who shared their insights and knowledge and sometimes their own archives. I cannot say "thank you" ardently or respectfully enough.

I begin by expressing my thanks to the following individuals who offered advice or provided assistance early in my research—more than forty-five years ago: film historian James Robert Parish, Leonard and Alice Maltin of *Film Fan Monthly*, film critic Judith Crist, Eddie Brandt of Eddie Brandt's Saturday Matinee, Robin Smith of Larry Edmunds Bookshop, Muriel Hamilton of Hampton Books, Jack Simon of Wide World Photos, Jo Anne Wazny of Columbia Pictures Television, and Paul Myers, curator, Lincoln Center Library for the Performing Arts.

When just a teenager, I wrote to Alice Pearce's widower Paul Davis but never received a reply. Nine years later, his brother Milton Davis phoned from Los Angeles to notify me that Paul had recently died. Among Paul's files, Milton had found my letter. He graciously offered me a small portion of Alice's mementos, informing me that the bulk of her papers and photographs would be donated to the Cinematic Arts Library at the University of Southern California.

Years passed, but finally in 2002, I began researching the Alice Pearce Collection at the Cinematic Arts Library, returning for follow-up visits in 2004 and 2013. I am indebted to Edward "Ned" Comstock, senior library assistant *extraordinaire* whose guidance and accommodations made researching the collection a relaxed and pleasant experience. As many have said, Ned is a credit to his profession and a gift to any author. Additional accommodations were provided by Sandra Garcia-Myers, director of the Archives of the Cinematic Arts Library.

Additionally, I thank the following for their professional assistance: Mark Quigley, Research and Study Center (ARSC), UCLA Film & Television Archive; Amy Wong, Library Special Collections, Charles E. Young Research Library, UCLA; Jonathan Auxier, Warner Brothers Archives, USC School of Cinematic Arts; Jeremy Megraw and John Calhoun, Billy Rose Theatre Division, New York Public Library; Carol Bowers, Leslie Shore, John Waggener, and Piper Thompson, American Heritage Center, University of Wyoming; Bruce Tabb, University of Oregon Libraries; Matt Reeder, Seeley G. Mudd Manuscript Library, Princeton University; Jane Klain, Research Services, The Paley Center for Media, New York; Val Almendarez, National Film Information Service, Margaret Herrick Library, Academy of Motion Picture Arts and Sciences; Kevin LaVine, Music Division, Library of Congress; Susan Halpert, Harvard Theatre Collection, Harvard University; Karen Lyons, Local History Room, Knowlton Library, Bellefontaine, Ohio; the Logan County (OH) Historical Society; the First United Methodist Church of Bellefontaine, Ohio; the Local History and Genealogy Department,

Hannibal (MO) Free Public Library; Mary McCollum, Monroe County (MO) Historical Society; Susan Dunham, Marlboro Probate Court, Brattleboro, Vermont; the Office of the City Clerk, New York, NY; Nancy R. Miller, University of Pennsylvania Archives; Lauren Lessard, Alumni Relations, Harvard Business School; Shawna Woodard, Dayton (OH) Metro Library; Rebecca Jewett, Thompson Library Special Collections, Ohio State University; Brittney Falter, Special Collections Research Center, George Mason University; Kirsten Camp, Kennebunkport Historical Society; Stella Stevens, Whitingham (VT) Historical Society; Mary Huelsbeck, Wisconsin Center for Film and Theatre Research; Claire Henrich, Films Media Group; Matthew Nye, Special Collections, San Diego Public Library; K. J. McCoy, Walter J. Brown Media Archives, University of Georgia; and Molly Dotson, Robert B. Haas Family Arts Library, Yale University.

For help regarding the educational backgrounds of Alice and her parents, I'm grateful to Susie Mackay and Amie Servino, directors of Alumnae/i and Parent Relations, The Masters School, Dobbs Ferry, New York; archivists Valerie Park, Abby Lester, and Lauren MacLean, Sarah Lawrence College; Alison Lotto and Bernadette Siddiqi of the New York University Archives; and Stephanie DeLaney and Jordy Staley, Registrar's Office, Columbia College, Columbia, Missouri.

For information related to John Rox and his background, I acknowledge Kevin Moenkhaus, Mark Stumme, and Katherine Lincoln of Drake University; Mary Hart of the Madison County (IA) Genealogical Society; Keli Schmid of the 10th Mountain Division Resource Center, Denver Public Library; Rebecca Fenning Marschall of the William Andrews Clark Memorial Library, UCLA;

Steven King of the Northport (NY) Historical Society; and Brown family historian John Higginbottom whose grandmother Nellie McKee Rupp was John's first cousin.

Sincere thanks are extended to Betsy Tolley and Keyonna Brown of the Interlibrary Loan Department of the Spartanburg County Public Library who eagerly and patiently filled my many requests for newspapers on microfilm, chiefly the invaluable *Perry Enterprise.*

I am especially indebted to Alice Pearce's friends and colleagues who shared memories of her: Harry Ackerman, Kaye Ballard, Mary Grace Canfield, Carol Channing, Matt Cimber, Carole Cook, Bob Cummings, Grover Dale, Ann B. Davis, Doris Day, Richard Deacon, Jane Dulo, Dominick Dunne, Tom Ewell, John Fiedler, Betty Garrett, Alice Ghostley, Phil Gordon, June Harding, Patricia Harty, Alan Helms, Gloria Henry, Mitzi Hoag, Hope Holiday, Ross Hunter, Gene Kelly, Chan Lowe, John Lund, Delbert Mann, Janice Mars, Hugh Martin, Tad Mosel, Jonathan Oppenheim, Debbie Reynolds, Liz Smith, Elaine Stritch, Renee Summers, Louise Tanner, Helen Tuttle Votichenko, Miles White, Mary Wickes, Patricia Wilson, William Windom, and Efrem Zimbalist, Jr.

Additional assistance, whether in the way of information, photographs, or recordings, was provided by Danni Bayles-Yeager, David Bennett, Tommy Bishop, Jay Blotcher, Ronnie Bowling, Tim Brooks, Liz Brown, Gary Brumburgh, Melodie Bryant, Joseph Buonocore, Dann Cahn, Mark Cocanougher, Norman W. Cook, Steve Cox, Randy Crocker, Nancy "Brucie" Cummings, Bill Dedman, James Gavin, Dot Goodwin, Phil Gries, Ed Gross, Bo Gunn, Linda Biesele Hall, John Harrington, James Harris, Laurence Holzman, Laurel Huber, David M. Inman, Alix Jeffry, Lynn Kear, Sammy Keith, Gary Levine,

Eddie Lucas, Thomas Monsell, Mary Lou Montgomery, John Mueller, Robin Mukerji, Eric Myers, Marian Smith Nee, John Nelson, Laure Passemier, Brent Phillips, David Pierce, Herbie J Pilato, Michael Rayhill, Adam Redfield, Anne Richards, Sandra Robnett, Carolyn Roesner, Guthrie Sayen, Nancy Schlick, Stephen M. Silverman, Mark R. Simpson, Merrill Sindler, Ken Slater, Jeffrey Smith, Donna Spencer, Sam Staggs, Charles Stumpf, Steve Taravella, Charles Tranberg, Wendy Turgeon, Frank Vlastnik, Terry Votichenko, Thomas J. Watson, Alfred A. Weinrib, George H. Werner, Michael Whitton, Neil Wilburn, Mark Willoughby Wood and Eric Woodard.

A huge thank-you goes to Ron Leake, the Perry, Missouri historian who led me to the delightfully spunky Dorothy Hawkinson Williams (1920-2009) whom I met in 2003. Self-proclaimed as "the oldest call girl in the county," Dorothy at that point had a part-time job answering the phone at an appliance store in Perry. Formerly a hairdresser in that small town, she had intimately known Alice Pearce's grandmother, aunt, and mother, as well as other extended family on the Clark and LaFrance lines. I spent two delightful afternoons with Dorothy, and those hours remain the highlight of my trip to Missouri.

Barbara Alford Torbjornsen, Alice Pearce's third cousin once removed, generously provided copies of Clark family papers and offered encouragement along the way. Others who shared details about Alice's family background were Biggers family historian Barbara Vaughn (author of *Lick Creek Beckoned*), LaFrance cousin Claire Helferich Woods, Colton cousin Fran Wood Jenkins, and Pearce relation Mary Barbara Squires. As longtime residents of Whitingham, Vermont, Reginald Maynard and his wife Elaine, as well as Whitman Wheeler, offered amusing anecdotes about Alice's parents during their residence on Town Hill Road. The gentlemanly Dana Friedman (1938-2007), who owned the Pearces' former home, graciously conducted a tour and introduced me to his neighbors, the Maynards, when I dropped in unannounced one evening in 2004.

A curious item among the papers of John Rox's niece Linda Swanson led to the serendipitous discovery of a sprightly nonagenarian named Peggy Coburn, residing in Agoura Hills, California in 2014. Peggy effusively recalled details about Alice and John's relationship, facts she knew firsthand and through her late husband Bill. Linda and I only knew Peggy for the final eighteen months of her life, a brief relationship we view as nothing short of providential.

A big salute to Victor Mascaro—a magician if there ever was one—who beautifully restored and enhanced several photos which appear in this book, including the colorized photograph on the cover.

Warmhearted thanks go to Ben Ohmart and Stone Wallace of BearManor Media for their enthusiastic support and excellent guidance during postproduction of *Sweet Oddball*. Ben's sincere interest in this work goes back more than a decade.

Without the lively Cris Alexander I would have never been amply inspired to write a biography of his dear friend Alice Pearce. Cris' boundless generosity afforded me not only the rarest of photographs but the wittiest recollections to flesh out our "absolutely lovely lunatic." I'll miss him the rest of my life.

No one has shown more enthusiasm and encouragement for this project than Linda Sue Herring Swanson, niece of John (Herring) Rox and Alice Pearce Rox. For every request I made of her, Linda cheerfully complied, often contributing help beyond the call of duty. She not only shared her family's archives, but she also volunteered to do follow-up research using the Alice Pearce Collection at USC, proving herself to be quite a meticulous researcher. And she has become a faithful friend as well.

My good-natured editor Tony Waters—as stalwart as Lindsay Woolsey was to Mame Dennis—gave support and sage advice, guiding this book every step of the way.

I also take my hat off to my parents who long ago indulged my passion by driving me to libraries, ordering photos of Alice Pearce from faraway memorabilia shops, and prevailing upon their cable television-subscribing friends to allow me to take over their living rooms to watch an Alice Pearce movie on the late show.

Notes

Abbreviations Used in the Notes:

APC   Alice Pearce Collection, Cinematic Arts Library, University of Southern California

APSF   Alice Pearce Student File, The Masters School, Dobbs Ferry, New York

BDE   *Bellefontaine Daily Examiner*

DP   *Daily Princetonian*

FT   Fredrick Tucker

LSC   Linda Swanson Collection

OWH   *Omaha World-Herald*

PE   *Perry Enterprise*

SH   *Stuart Herald*

TC   *The Campus* (Sarah Lawrence College student newspaper)

WM   *Winterset Madisonian*

WN   *Winterset News*

Preface

ix   **"Her personality could fold itself":** "I'm Out with the Belle of New York," *Canadian Ken On . . .*, https://canadianken.blogspot.com/2013/07/im-out-with-the-belle-of-new-york.html, accessed 13 January 2021.

ix   **"Everyone loved Alice":** Thomas, *The MGM Years*, p. 115.

x   **"was certainly not Jayne Mansfield!":** Myers, *Uncle Mame*, p. 200.

x   **"hokily sophisticated and endearing ragdoll":** *Newark Star-Ledger*, 4 November 1971.

x   **"she made them irresistible":** Nissen, *Actresses of a Certain Character*, p. 157.

x   **"The key, I think, to Alice":** Author's interview with Matt Cimber, 25 June 2014.

x   **"I like earthy parts":** "Finally the Center of Attention," *TV Guide*, 25 December 1965, p. 14.

x   **"Playing strange, sweet oddballs":** *TV Radio Mirror*, September 1965, p. 16.

x   **"Since I'm primarily a character actress":** "Funny Valentine," ABC Television Network Feature (press release), 6 February 1958, author's colletion.

xi   **"[living] most of the time":** *TV Guide,* 25 December 1965, p. 13.

xi   **"Alice had no chin":** Letter from Richard Decon to FT, 30 August 1982.

xi   **"She was terribly comical looking":** Author's interview with Cris Alexander, 24 September 1987.

xi   **"She had a funny face":** Letter from John Lund to FT, 24 October 1989.

xi   **"Alice Pearce had a very unusual look":** Ed Gross, "Here's What Happened to *Bewitched* Actress Alice Pearce," *Do You Remember?, https://doyouremember.com/126352/what-happened-mrs-kravitz-from-bewitched*, accessed 12 November 2020.

xi   **"I think she loved the level":** Cimber interview.

xi   **"Alice loved her career":** Author's interview with Patricia Wilson, 17 August 2019.

xii   **"It may sound corny":** Arlene Dahl, "Alice Pearce: Beauty Is Making Others Laugh," *Cedar Rapids Gazette*, 26 September 1965, p. 54.

xii   **"Alice Pearce was unique":** Jan Landy, "Elizabeth Montgomery Saved My Life!", *Movieland and TV Time*, October 1968, p. 83.

Chapter One

1   **That month theatergoers could see:** Bordman, *American Theatre*, pp. 65–79.

1   **"The city is in the center":** *Bellefontaine, Ohio,* 1901 souvenir booklet, Logan County Historical Society collection.

2   **Robert united with this church:** Bellefontaine First United Methodist Church membership roll, 1897-1904. Rev. Charles C. Peale became the pastor of this church in 1913. His famous son, the Rev. Norman Vincent Peale, was a 1916 graduate of Bellefontaine High School.

2   **his father Harry taught:** *Bellefontaine Republican*, 21 November 1899.

2   **Harry Pearce, born in 1851:** The earliest baptism records for St. Keverne show the spelling of the family surname as "Pearse," which was pronounced as "purse," according to the article "When Hand Pumps Were Used by Our Firemen," *Cincinnati Enquirer*, 22 April 1923. Harry Pearce (1851–1942) was the oldest child of Henry Pearce (1828–1874) and his wife Elizabeth Nicholls (1828–1902).

2 **Harry was not content:** "Harry Pearce Dies," BDE, 19 November 1942; New York Passenger Lists, 1820–1957, Roll 291, www.ancestry.com. James Pearce (1803–1875) and Henry Pearce (1824–1884) were two of the ten children of Thomas Pearce and his wife Elizabeth Pearce Pearce, the sister of Alice Pearce's great-great grandfather James Pearce (c. 1794–1857). According to the *Cincinnati Enquirer* (22 April 1923), Thomas and Elizabeth and their family of ten arrived in Cincinnati in 1831, only for a cholera epidemic to take the lives of both parents and three of their children the following year. In 1842 James Pearce, the oldest child, opened a factory at the corner of Fifth and Lock Streets, making his brother a partner and naming it James Pearce & Brother. They manufactured machinery which spun and braided cotton into yarn. Five years later they entered a partnership with C. H. Gould, renaming the business Gould, Pearce, and Company. Following the Civil War, the company abandoned production of these machines and committed itself to sell braided cotton. It evolved into what is currently Atkins & Pearce Manufacturing of Covington, Kentucky, specializing in industrial twine, coated insulated sleeving, and candlewick.

2 **Samuel and his wife Eliza:** *Logan County Index*, 15 November 1900. Eliza Colton was the only grandparent Robert Pearce ever knew; his grandfathers died before he was born, and his paternal grandmother Elizabeth Nicholls Pearce died in Cornwall ten years before he first crossed the Atlantic. Eliza Colton was born March 19, 1810, in Lincolnshire, England, where she joined the Methodist Episcopal Church in 1835. She was the mother of nine children, seven of whom lived to reach adulthood. She died from the effects of pneumonia on November 10, 1900, at the family home on South Detroit Street. The *Bellefontaine Daily Examiner* eulogized her with these words: "When the weather would permit, she was in her [church] pew, an attentive and intelligent listener to the last. Though well past 90, her faculties were unimpaired, and she was interested in and perfectly conversant with the affairs of the day."

3 **They bought an old burr mill:** Hover, p. 120.

3 **Though she fought hard:** *Logan County Index*, 14 April 1892.

3 **Harry remarried:** BDE, 5 May 1909.

4 **Meanwhile the prosperous Colton brothers:** Hover, pp. 120, 122. Robert Colton, while still serving as president of The Colton Brothers Company, was also the president of the Commercial and Savings Bank. In addition, he was an officer and stockholder in the Bellefontaine Bridge and Iron Company and the Bellefontaine Carriage Body Company, not to mention president of the board of trustees of the M. E. Church and treasurer of the board of trustees of the Bellefontaine Carnegie Library. Joseph helped his brother organize the Commercial and Savings Bank, remaining on the board of directors until his death. He also served as president of the Building and Loan Association, a member of the city school board, and the recording secretary for the M. E. Church.

4 **Chester Pearce assumed:** BDE, 31 October 1930; BDE, 10 December 1956. For twenty-seven years Chester Pearce was a miller for Colton Brothers, ending his association with the family business when he opened an insurance agency which he operated until his retirement in 1955. In 1899, he married Carrie McDonald, and they became the parents of two daughters, Thelma Pearce White and Margaret Pearce Ransbottom Wayne. Following Carrie's death, Chester married Thelma Detrick, twenty-one years his junior. In 1956, he died of a sudden heart attack one Sunday morning after shoveling snow preparatory to leaving home for church services. Wilbur Pearce married Mary Graham in 1908, and their only child was Barbra Ann Pearce Squires. Wilbur and family left Bellefontaine in 1913 to settle in Colorado Springs, Colorado, where he became a bonds salesman. He was found unconscious in the family garage on October 30, 1930, and he soon died of carbon monoxide poisoning, an apparent suicide.

4 **Harry had chosen a third wife:** BDE, 29 September 1932. On October 1, 1912, Harry Pearce married Dora Alice Henry Wickersham, a childless widow who claimed American patriot Patrick Henry as an ancestor. After the first two years of their marriage, they moved into Harry's house on North Detroit Street in Bellefontaine. Dora died of heart disease in 1932 at age 74.

Chapter Two

5 **"My parents were Midwesterners":** Charlotte Barclay, "Comedienne Talks of Her Audiences," *New York Herald Tribune*, 10 October 1948.

5 **"Everybody from around Perry":** Author's interview with Dorothy Williams, 1 March 2003.

5 **"microcosm of the South's plantation hierarchal society":** Gary Gene Fuenfhausen, *Missouri's Little Dixie*, www.littledixie.net, accessed 19 November 2020.

5 **The town was laid out:** "Ralls County Place Names, 1928–1945," *The State Historical Society of Missouri*, https://shsmo.org, accessed 16 April 2018.

5 **a celebratory picnic:** PE, 17 August 1944.

6 **Margaret's father Joseph Lilburn Clark:** PE, 31 January 1929. Martin Judy Clark (1825–1906), the father of Joseph Clark, married Mary Elizabeth Ringo (1834–1907) in Tallula, Illinois, in 1851, and moved to Missouri in 1852. From *A History of Northeast Missouri* (1913), we know that Martin was "an authority on all classes of livestock and it was his enthusiasm for mules that inspired the farmers of Monroe County to engage extensively in the industry. His connection with the sales stables of Edwards, Irvin, & Clark, of St. Louis, covered a long period of years and being an auctioneer, his was a leading part in the conduct of the firm . . . He had an attractive personality, was always well dressed, a splendid conversationalist and a speaker of much force and ability. His physique was vigorous, above the average of avoirdupois, and he sat a horse like royalty itself." Martin Clark died at the home of his daughter Alice Chowning in Hannibal, Missouri. His widow, an invalid for eight years, died the following year in Mrs. Chowning's home.

6 **older brother Alva Clark:** PE, 14 June 1923.

6 **Alva had disposed:** PE, 20 May 1909. James Alva Clark (1853–1923) was educated at Westminster College in Fulton, Missouri. He became the vice-president of the Perry Bank in 1909. Both of his sons became bankers. Alva's considerable real estate holdings in Monroe, Ralls, and Audrain Counties afforded him the luxury of wintering each year in warmer climates such as California and Florida. He died in Long Beach, California, in 1923.

6 **He moved to Perry:** Williams, *A History of Northeast Missouri*, p. 1820.

6 **pulled up stakes:** PE, 18 June 1903.

6 **"J. L. Clark is prepared":** PE, 15 November 1906.

6 **soda pop factory:** PE, 25 July 1912. The paper reported that Joe Clark's only son, LaFrance Clark, was injured "yesterday afternoon at the Clark & Carter soda pop factory. He caught the fingers of his right hand in a line shaft, and cut the ends off of the third and fourth finger."

6 **selling blocks of ice:** PE, 11 January 1912. "Clark & Carter finished yesterday putting up 200 loads of nice 10-inch ice in their house near the railroad track. The cakes are 10 inches thick and 22 inches square, and weigh on an average 180 lbs."

6 **"The Elevator Building":** PE, 24 July 1913.

6 **"by the carload":** PE, 23 April 1914.

7 **Her mother died:** In 1863 Sarah Margaret "Maggie" Biggers married Marcus Payne LaFrance, by whom she had two daughters, Emma Jane and Sarah Helen. Upon Maggie's death in 1868, the girls went to live with Maggie's sister Mary Emmarine Myers. In 1887 Sallie LaFrance would name her firstborn, Mary Emma Clark, for the aunt who took her in. Although Sallie LaFrance Clark had little or no recollection of her mother or either of her grandmothers, she did know quite well her great-grandmother Matilda Harrison Biggers, who lived until 1886 when she was ninety-four. According to George Wolfe Fagan, whose reminiscences appeared in the *Perry Enterprise* in 1922, "Granny Biggers rode horseback over the neighborhood visiting relatives and neighbors when she was eighty-five to ninety years old."

7 **Lick Creek Christian Church:** It was named for its proximity to a tributary of the Salt River.

7 **LaFrance drew the plans:** Vaughn, *Lick Creek Beckoned*, p. 286. The Lick Creek Christian Church, about one mile south of Perry's Main Street, was the parent of the Perry Christian Church, which was organized in 1891 when parishioners wanted a worship place closer to the center of town. According to the 1966 Perry Area Centennial souvenir booklet, the Lick Creek building sat abandoned for a number of years before it was sold and dismantled in 1927, with the proceeds to benefit the endowment fund of the Lick Creek Cemetery Association. The cemetery, adjacent to the old building, was only seven tenths of a mile from the Joe and Sallie Clark home on Palmyra Street. Five generations of Alice Pearce's maternal ancestors are buried at Lick Creek Cemetery.

7 **he took up farming:** Williams, p. 1716.

7 **he joined other men of means:** PE, 18 December 1913.

7   **completion of a new Peoples Bank:** *Ibid.*

7   **"a benefactor to the growth of Perry":** PE, 11 January 1912. Marcus Payne LaFrance was born March 5, 1838, in Susquehanna County, Pennsylvania, but spent his boyhood south of there, in the town of Pittston in Luzerne County. At nineteen, he heard the call of the west, and in 1857, with his father's blessing, boarded a train for Chicago. He continued by rail until reaching the terminus at Kewanee. Staying in Illinois   for about a year, he was in the right place to hear Abraham Lincoln make a campaign speech in the fall of 1858. He moved on to Missouri the following year, and there he lived until his death in 1913. Alice Pearce and fellow *Bewitched* castmate Marion Lorne, though they probably didn't know it, both had a connection to Pittston, Pennsylvania. Alice's great-grandfather M. P. LaFrance and Lorne's grandfather John MacDougall were both residents of that town in the 1850s. Lorne was born across the river in West Pittston in 1883.

8   **"remarkably true alto voice":** PE, 7 November 1940. Sue Fagan moved from Hannibal to the Lick Creek area in 1859 and remembered dancing a jig, accompanied by her father on the violin, to entertain some Confederate soldiers who stopped in their home as they were passing through the area. She began teaching when she was only fifteen years old. Mamma Sue LaFrance's four children, and hence Sallie Clark's stepsiblings, were Nana LaFrance Turner, William, James, and John LaFrance. Longtime Perry resident Dorothy Williams fondly recalled in 2003, "Everybody in Perry called her 'Mamma Sue,' and she wore a black velvet band with a cameo around her neck." For sixty years she lived on Palmyra Street in the old LaFrance house, directly across the street from one of her nieces who "got drunk every afternoon at 4 o'clock and took off all her clothes to stand in an upstairs window for everyone to see." Mamma Sue would rock in her chair, thoroughly disgusted at this display. On the day of Mamma Sue's funeral, all businesses in Perry closed for one hour to allow everyone to attend the service.

8   **the Clarks' other children:** All of Joe and Sallie Clark's children were born in Perry. Mary Emma, born in 1887, was the oldest. LaFrance Robert Clark, the only son, was born in 1895, and the youngest child Josephine followed in 1901.

8   **The Entre Nous Club:** PE, 1 May 1913. Other charter members of the Entre Nous Club were Sallie's stepmother Sue LaFrance, Sallie's sister Emma Netherland, and Sallie's cousin Lorena Roselle. As of this writing, the Entre Nous Club is still active and is believed to be the oldest women's club in northeastern Missouri.

8   **diverse topics:** PE, 18 March 1909, 15 April 1909, and 29 April 1909.

9   **"She was a *lady*":** Williams interview. Sallie's sister Emma Jane LaFrance married William Richard Netherland eight months before Sallie married Joe Clark. Netherland clerked in Mark LaFrance's store as a young man, later holding a position at the Peoples Bank. From 1901 until 1908 the Netherlands lived in New London and then in Center but returned to Perry where Netherland became president of the Peoples Bank. They built a two-story house on Martin Street in 1909, where they lived until retiring to Fort Lauderdale, Florida. Netherland died in 1942 while visiting in Perry. In 1948, his widow Emma died at age 84 while visiting her daughter Gertrude Helferich in Scarsdale, New York.

9   **Margaret, who often sang solos:** Margaret's older sister Mary Emma was musical as well, but by 1909 her efforts were concentrated on her teaching career, having served several years in a rural school before becoming a fixture at the Perry school, where she taught third graders, including her youngest sister Josephine.

9   **Margaret's namesake:** Margaret Alice Clark was named for both her maternal grandmother Margaret Biggers LaFrance and her paternal aunt Alice Clark Chowning.

9   **stood at five feet, four inches:** U. S. Passport Application, Certificate #53050, Alice R. Chowning, 14 April 1908; www.ancestry.com.

9   **They had married in 1885:** *Hannibal Evening Courier*, 9 May 1928; *Hannibal Courier-Post*, 16 September 1925.

10   **The senior Dr. Thomas Jefferson Chowning:** Wecter, *Sam Clemens of Hannibal*, p. 43. Thomas Chowning, Sr. was born in Henry County, Virginia, in 1809 and died in Monroe City, Missouri in 1854.

10   **Chownings had spent the summer:** PE, 21 May 1908. The Chownings sailed home on the ill-fated Lusitania in September 1908.

10   **advanced courses at Hannibal High:** PE, 26 November 1908.

10   **Hannibal College of Music:** PE, 10 November 1910.

10 **Education was very important to Aunt Alice:** Joe Clark was keen on education, too; he served on Perry's school board for twenty-five years. He saw to it that his three other children had the opportunity to earn college degrees.

10 **Aunt Alice and Margaret alighted:** *University Missourian*, 13 September 1911.

10 **Aunt Alice had decided:** Like her Clark and Ringo forbears, Alice Chowning was a staunch member of the Christian Church (aka "Disciples of Christ"). She graduated from Christian Female College in 1875, per the 1896–97 annual catalogue.

10 **Christian Female College:** A posthumous tribute to Sallie Clark, appearing in the *Perry Enterprise* on 21 September 1961, would claim that she, too, had attended Christian Female College, but in 2014 the college registrar could find no records verifying that. Moreover, Sallie was not listed among the school's former graduates in the 1896-97 catalogue.

10 **Luella St. Clair:** "Christian College, Columbia, Missouri, Records, 1836–1986," *The State Historical Society of Missouri*, https://shsmo.org, accessed 23 April 2018.

10 **Bachelor of Letters degree:** Christian Female College diploma of Margaret Alice Clark, 20 May 1912, APC; *University Missourian*, 21 May 1912. Notable alumni of Christian Female College (now Columbia College) include singer-actress Jane Froman, actor-writer-director Arliss Howard, and notorious fan dancer Sally Rand.

10 **accompanied by her sister-in-law Sallie:** *University Missourian*, 25 May 1912.

Chapter Three

11 **"Bob is a fighting name":** *The Commerce Violet* (yearbook), 1916, page 133.

11 **he and his first cousin Edwin Colton:** BDE, 27 June 1914.

11 **"Robert and the party":** BDE, 31 August 1914.

11 **Bob separated from the group:** BDE, 15 August 1914.

11 **"In every town and city":** BDE, 22 August 1914.

12 **"no vessel was [crossing] at that time":** BDE, 31 August 1914.

12 **"most likely to succeed":** *The Commerce Violet* (yearbook), 1916, p.138.

12 **thirty-four-year-old bachelor banker:** *Billings Gazette*, 1 April 1902; PE, 26 December 1912.

13 **They arrived in Bellefontaine:** BDE, 17 June 1915.

13 **fellow NYU student Rudolph Riggs:** *Quincy Daily Journal*, 23 June 1915.

13 **"She was one of the sweetest women":** Williams interview.

13 **"My mother was a beautiful woman":** Lloyd Shearer, "Alice Pearce: The Chinless Wonder," *Parade*, 11 October 1964, pp. 10, 19.

13 **Bob decided to visit his brother:** BDE, 2 August 1915.

13 **Emma Netherland and her family:** PE, 26 August 1915.

13 **"Miss Margaret Clark returned Friday":** PE, 26 August 1915.

13 **Bob and Margaret saw each other:** PE, 26 August 1915; *Quincy Daily Journal*, 27 August 1915.

13 **a position as an instructor:** BDE, 8 September 1915.

13 **Professor Kennedy realized:** BDE, 11 December 1915. The National City Bank boasted a stellar list of former and current customers, including President Martin Van Buren, President Grover Cleveland, Admiral George Dewey, John Philip Sousa, Enrico Caruso, Lillian Russell, and Will Rogers.

14 **sang the opening solo:** *Quincy Daily Whig*, 10 December 1915. Margaret's solo selection was "My Heart Is Singing" by Gertrude San-Souci.

14 **He spent most of his Christmas vacation:** PE, 30 December 1915.

14 **she had served as bridesmaid:** PE, 21 October 1915. Mary Emma Clark married veterinarian Dr. Harry Cleveland Ward in the Clark home at Perry on 20 October 1915.

14 **Their engagement was announced:** PE, 4 May 1916.

14 **suffered a miscarriage:** Mary E. Clark Ward, Certificate of Death, Missouri State Board of Health, File #31776, 15 September 1916. Mary Emma's funeral was one of the most largely attended ever to be held in Perry. The high school students sat in a body and likewise marched behind the casket to Lick Creek Cemetery.

14 **The family thought it best:** BDE, 28 October 1916.

14 **the bride and groom mingled:** PE, 2 November 1916. Besides Harry Pearce, the out-of-town guests included Aunt Alice and Uncle Tom Chowning, Bob's friend Rudolph Riggs, Cousin

Alice Armstrong and her daughter Edna, and the Clarks' son-in-law Dr. Cleve Ward. A check of marriage licenses at the Ralls County Courthouse in New London, Missouri, revealed that Robert and Margaret obtained their license (#1584) on 23 October 1916, and were married two days later. However, both of their hometown newspapers stated that the ceremony actually took place one week later on 1 November 1916. Furthermore, Margaret listed the November date on Alice Pearce's DAR membership application (National Number 298118) in 1936.

14   **a large family dinner:** BDE, 3 November 1916.

15   **would see his uncles:** BDE, 4 December 1916; BDE, 18 June 1918. Joseph Colton died on 3 December 1916, after battling multiple sclerosis for eight years. Robert Colton suffered from chronic colitis and anemia and passed away on 17 June 1918. His obituary included these words: "The sons of the sister, the late Mrs. Harry Pearce, were also very near and dear to Mr. Colton and he concerned himself in their welfare from childhood to adulthood."

15   **Dyckman Farmhouse:** Located at 4881 Broadway, it is still operated as a museum in the city's only remaining Dutch colonial farmhouse.

15   **registered for the draft:** U. S. World War I Draft Registration Card, New York, Manhattan City, Form 14492, No. 147 (www.ancestry.com).

15   **"the new frontier":** Mayer, *The Influence of Frank A. Vanderlip and the National City Bank on American Commerce and Foreign Policy*, p. 109.

15   **"capitalized on the misfortunes":** *Ibid.*, p. 117.

16   **"gallstone trouble and appendicitis":** PE, 3 May 1917.

Chapter Four

17   **Dr. Frederic Jellinghaus:** *New York Sun*, 23 April 1946.

17   **Lying-In Hospital:** "Lying-In Hospital," *Weill Cornell Medicine, Samuel J. Wood Library*, https://library.weill.cornell.edu/lying-hospital, accessed 29 April 2018.

17   **seven-pound, three-ounce baby girl:** "Our Baby" scrapbook, APC, Box 1.

18   **Alice Chowning Pearce:** *Ibid.* Alice Pearce's middle name appears in primary sources quite rarely, leading one to wonder if she disliked it. The only places the author has seen it written are in the baby book and as part of an inscription in

a children's book given to Alice by Aunt Alice Chowning. This middle name, nor its initial letter, is not included in any of Alice's school yearbooks or records, her two marriage licenses, or her 1936 DAR membership application. Her passport, issued in 1933, identifies her as "Alice C. Pearce."

18   **31 Seaman Avenue:** Small leather-bound photo album, APC, Box 2, File 1.

18   **finally got to meet little Alice:** PE, 16 May 1918; PE, 3 August 1918.

18   **LaFrance:** PE, 2 August 1917; PE, 1 November 1917; PE, 9 January 1919.

19   **"Alice took her first steps":** "Our Baby" scrapbook, *op. cit.*

19   **1919 was the year:** Mayer, p. 122.

19   **"wanted to use the bankers":** *Ibid.*, p. 197.

19   **lengthy visit with the Clarks:** PE, 13 March 1919; PE, 27 March 1919.

19   **Harry Pearce decided:** BDE, 5 July 1919.

19   **the *New Amsterdam*:** "Captain Albert's Blog: Nieuw Amsterdam (I) of 1906," *Holland America Line*, https://www.hollandamerica.com blog/albert/holland-line-ships-past-and-present/the-nieuw-amsterdam-i-of-1906/, accessed 29 April 2018.

Chapter Five

22   **no transatlantic communications:** It is very likely that if such documents endured Bob and Margaret's move to California in 1963, they were destroyed by Margaret following Alice's death.

22   **ruins of Dixmude:** Margaret Pearce's photo album, APC, Box 2.

22   **"mainly French or English":** "Our Baby" scrapbook, *op. cit.*

22   ***The Complete Edition of Mother Goose Rhymes*:** Arranged by Logan Marshall and published in 1917 by the John C. Winston Company, Philadelphia, Alice's well-worn copy of this book is now in the author's collection.

23   **"I was taught French before I learned English":** Gilbert Swan, "Banker's Daughter, Noted Editor's Son Win Fame as Broadway Comedy Team," *The Circleville Herald*, 23 January 1948, p. 8.

23   **her English proficiency:** Margaret McManus, "Unbelieving Neighbor Happy with Role on *Bewitched*," *Lancaster (PA) Sunday News*, 2 May 1965, pp. 5, 45.

23   **the bank's Philadelphia branch:** BDE, 11 May 1922.

23 **Margaret's thirtieth birthday:** PE, 1 June 1922.

24 **Clark-LaFrance family reunion:** PE, 22 June 1922. Besides the Pearces, the guests included Joe and Sallie Clark and their children, Aunt Emma and Uncle Will Netherland and daughter, Uncle Alva and Aunt Georgia Clark, Mama Sue's four children, their spouses, and her three grand-daughters, plus Mama Sue's sister Jennie and her husband, daughter and son-in-law. The Pearces' visit coincided with Josephine Clark's graduation from Hardin College in Mexico, Missouri, which they all attended on May 31.

24 **Josephine sailed from New York:** Josephine Clark, U. S. Passport Application #249215, 6 February 1923, www.ancestry.com; PE, 22 March 1923.

24 **Josephine sailed home:** PE, 31 July 1924.

25 **"an enormous, beautifully furnished mansion":** Russell, *I'm Not Making This Up, You Know*, p. 70.

25 **"a first-class French Finishing School":** *The Spectator*, 8 April 1922.

25 **principals were two elegant ladies:** Eugénie Fanny Leona Rosine Delstanche (c. 1868–1934) and Dorothy Louise Tungate (1878–1933) were longtime business partners in Les Tourelles and resided together there. Tungate, who moved to Brussels in 1900, died of pneumonia in that city, and Delstanche followed her to the grave seven months later.

25 *Exposition des travaux du trimestre*: Unbound, makeshift scrapbook, APC, Box 1.

25 *Scene Watteau*: *Ibid.*

25 **was asked to take the role of Louison:** Howard Sigmand, "Alice Pearce; Comedienne of Clubs, Stage, Films, TV," *New York Herald Tribune*, 4 March 1966.

25 **"They nearly fell off their chairs":** "Alice Pearce Biography" prepared by publicity agent Stanley Musgrove, 1951, APC, Box 1.

27 **"I fell in love with the theater":** Barclay, *op. cit.*

28 **Bob's niece Margaret:** BDE, 10 July 1926.

28 **boarded a train for Colorado Springs:** PE, 5 August 1926.

28 *Le Loup et L'Agneau*: Unbound, makeshift scrapbook, *op. cit.*

28 **19 Rue de Crayer:** "Rue De Crayer 19," *Inventaire Du Patrimoine Architectural*, http://www.irismonument.be/fr.Bruxelles_Extension_Sud. Rue_De_Crayer.19.html, accessed 1 May 2018.

28 **"One afternoon when I was nine":** Shearer, p. 10.

28 **"Her jaw was set":** Helen Tuttle Votichenko, via her son Terry Votichenko's email response to FT, 22 September 2014.

28 **"Her mother worried":** *Ibid.*

28 **"excruciatingly shy child":** McManus, p. 5.

28 **"I know that [Margaret]":** Alexander interview, 1987.

28 **"I realized at the age of eight":** McManus, p. 45.

28 **"double for Tallulah Bankhead":** *Ibid.*, p. 5.

28 **"I gathered":** Alexander interview, 1987.

29 **it was not until she was a teenager:** Shearer, p. 10.

29 **"never had much contact":** *TV Guide*, 25 December 1965.

30 **"lived most of the time":** *Ibid.*

30 **"compete on the stage":** McManus, p.45.

30 *L'Oiseau bleu*: Unbound, makeshift scrapbook, *op. cit.*

30 **Aunt Alice Chowning:** *Hannibal Evening-Courier*, 9 May 1928; Alice Rushbrook Chowning, Missouri State Board of Health, Certificate of Death, File Number 17799, 11 May 1928.

30 **"generous woman":** PE, 17 May 1928. Aunt Alice died in the Levering Hospital after a four-night stay. Previously she had been treated for four weeks at Beaumont Hospital in St. Louis.

30 **Joe Clark:** Joseph L. Clark, Missouri State Board of Health, Certificate of Death, File Number 3058, 30 January 1929.

30 **"He contributed his share":** PE, 31 January 1929. Joe Clark left an estate valued at just over $9000, with only $150 of that in ready cash. His real property included two tracts of land on Palmyra Street and four lots in downtown Perry where the milling plant and grain elevator were located. His Ford automobile was appraised at $300.

30 **Northwestern University:** PE, 21 July 1927.

30 **Josephine had married:** PE, 29 December 1927. Josephine's gown was dark blue chiffon, accessorized with a crystal and pearl necklace and a corsage of pink roses, orchid sweet peas, and ostrich feather tips. The altar was decorated with pots of Jerusalem cherries on pedestals.

30 **"delightful trip through Yellowstone Park":** PE, 15 August 1929.

30 **"large double swing":** Williams interview.

31 **"detention camps":** Russell, p. 68.

31 **"acoustics":** *Ibid.*, p. 60.

31 **"Breakfast was at a civilized":** *Ibid.*, pp. 70–71.

31 **"There was one darling":** *Ibid.*, p. 71.

31 **"I could tell that she":** Author's interview with Miles White, 23 July 1996.

32 *Minna*: Unbound, makeshift scrapbook, *op. cit.*

Chapter Six

33 **"I suppose I had a good education":** McManus, p. 5.

33 **"never did much work":** "Peeps Chooses American College After Years in Brussels and Paris," TC, 31 January 1940.

33 **"very artsy-craftsy":** George Freedley, *The Playbill: The Magazine of the Theatre*, p. 3.

33 **"I hated living in Europe":** McManus, p. 5.

33 **"To this day":** *Ibid.*

33 **"American girls are welcomed":** Porter Sargent, *A Handbook of Private Schools for American Boys and Girls*, Volume 14, 1932, p. 636.

33 **Professor Jean Le Goff:** Unbound, makeshift scrapbook, *op. cit.*

33 **Rosemont:** APSF. Rosemont was located at 18 Rue du Calvaire. The house no longer stands, but a stable built on the estate in 1904 has been preserved. The National City Bank was located at 60 Avenue des Champs-Élysées.

34 **take piano lessons:** Margaret studied at the Institut International de Musique. An avid gardener, she also studied at the Société Nationale d'Horticulture de France.

34 **Alice's grandmother:** PE, 26 May 1932. Sallie Clark had been living with daughter and son-in-law Josephine and Paul Dillard for much of the time since her husband's death. In 1931, she had suffered a great financial loss when the Clark grain elevator and its machinery were destroyed by fire.

34 **Lucerne, London:** PE, 29 June 1933.

34 **"something awful":** TC, 31 January 1940.

34 **Mr. Kenrick Mervyn Brace:** APSF. Evidently the Masters School made it a practice of keeping up with its graduates because this file also contains transcripts from Alice's subsequent years at Sarah Lawrence College as well as newspaper clippings regarding her stage career and first marriage.

34 **"right schools":** "Minx with Three Minks," *Newsweek*, 6 October 1947, p. 76.

34 **obtained her passport:** Alice C. Pearce, Passport No. 3944, Consulate General of the United States of America at Paris, France, 23 January 1933, in the author's collection. At the time of issue, Alice stood five feet, three inches tall, with brown hair and grey-blue eyes.

34 **"I wish to select a school":** Letter from Margaret Pearce to the "Dobbs Ferry School," 9 July 1933, APSF.

34 **an incorporated secondary school:** *Dobbs Today: The Masters School, Dobbs Ferry-On-Hudson, New York*, promotional booklet, circa 1941, p. 4.

35 **"kept a high standard":** Shelton, *An American Schoolmistress*, p. 56.

35 **combined religion:** *Ibid.*, p. 118.

35 **"sound habits of scholarship":** *Ibid.*, p. 112.

35 **"good general cultural education":** *Ibid.*, p. 110.

35 **"firmly convinced":** *Ibid.*, p. 192.

35 **Wellesley:** "Certificate Recommended by The Head Mistresses Association of the East," APSF.

35 **"staunch New Englander":** Vose, *The Masters School*, page 36. Mary Evelina Pierce (1880–1972), the daughter of an attorney, was born in Portland, Maine. She came from The Potomac School in Washington, DC, to the Masters School in 1927 as associate principal, assuming the position of principal in 1928. Retiring in 1945, Miss Pierce brought the school safely through the Depression and the Second World War.

36 **Mrs. Gertrude Haff:** Letter from Mrs. Haff to Miss Evelina Pierce, 24 July 1933, APSF.

36 **"process not quite complete":** "Certificate Recommended by The Head Mistresses Association of the East," APSF.

36 **current enrollment at the Masters School was down:** Vose, p. 44.

36 **reduce faculty salaries:** *Ibid.*, p. 39.

36 **Resident tuition:** *Ibid.*, p. 44.

36 **"Extremes are to be avoided":** *Ibid.*, p. 46.

36 **"homelike feeling":** *Dobbs Today*, p. 25.

36 **"The view from the Hill Houses":** *Ibid.*, p. 30.

36 **"I was sorry":** Undated letter from Margaret Pearce to Evelina Pierce, APSF.

36 **"In a sense, I left home at about fifteen":** Swan, p. 8.

36 **"strict girls' boarding school":** *Ibid.*, p. 50.

37 **attend the weekly services:** *Ibid.*, p. 41.

37 **"proceed at their own speed":** *Dobbs Today*, p. 11.

37 **"found it terribly hard":** TC, 31 January 1940.

37 **sources of entertainment:** Blanck, *Life of a River Village*, pp. 86–87. Another place the local frequented during the Depression was the public library, which had gotten its start in 1899 in the home of a married couple, coincidentally named Robert and Margaret Pearce.

37 **spending money:** Western Union telegrams to parents in undated makeshift scrapbook, APC.

38 **"Every girl wants to be beautiful":** Shearer, p. 10.

38 **"This left Alice feeling somewhat awkward":** Votichenko email, 2014.

38 **"As a teenager I was sent":** Shearer, p. 10.

38 **"But she had beautiful eyes":** Alexander interview, 1987.

38 **"She had on a bright red coat":** Williams interview.

39 *Le Farce de Maitre Pathelin*: *The Reflector*, The Masters School newspaper, clipping in undated makeshift scrapbook, APC.

39 **bottom quarter:** "Final Data Sent to Sarah Lawrence," 2 June 1936, APSF.

40 **"Special ability":** "Alice Pearce, Dobbs, 1933–1936," Evelina Pierce-Headmistress, The Masters School, 3 September 1942, APSF.

40 **Vassar and Smith:** Vose, p. 48.

Chapter Seven

41 **"at-home" in Alice's honor:** handwritten invitation and undated newspaper clipping in undated makeshift scrapbook, APC.

41 **"well-known American resident":** undated newspaper clipping in makeshift scrapbook, APC.

41 **"from the far corners of the earth":** TC, 28 September 1936.

42 **Alice always maintained:** "Alice Pearce, '40—Comedienne," *Sarah Lawrence Alumnae Magazine*, January 1946. Bob Pearce's close friend, Howard C. Sheperd, senior vice president of the National City Bank of New York, was a longtime resident of Bronxville, and perhaps it was he who suggested Sarah Lawrence College to the Pearces.

42 **"text books playing little part":** *Look*, 6 July 1937.

42 **regular field trips into New York City:** *Life*, 6 June 1938.

42 **annual tuition:** *Look*, 6 July 1937.

42 **"They do not worry about rules":** *Buffalo Courier-Express Pictorial*, circa 1939.

42 **"comfortably careless":** *Ibid.*

42 **"educate young ladies of good families":** *Sarah Lawrence* magazine, Spring 2004.

42 **William Van Duzer Lawrence:** Lawrence was born near Elmira, New York, in 1842. At nineteen, he became engaged in the drug manufacturing trade. In five short years, he established and became president of the Davis & Lawrence Company, manufacturing chemists. In the 1890s, he played a critical role in the development of a planned community in Bronxville, which attracted a homogenous population of upper-middle-class residents.

42 **His unexpected death:** Profile of William Van Duzer Lawrence, *Sarah Lawrence College: First Year, 1927–1928* commemorative booklet, 1928, pp. 43–47.

42 **Westlands:** Lawrence's Neo-Tudor-style home Westlands was completed in 1917, the same year Alice was born. She roomed in Westlands, Room 205, during her freshman year and Room 207 during her sophomore year. Photographs from her personal album (APC) show Room 207 with its hardwood floors, leaded windows, and an elegant mantelpiece with marble surround, making a sharp contrast to the bare furnishings consisting of twin iron beds, two desks, and a phonograph on a small table. She even photographed her stockings drying on a wooden rack in the tiled bathroom.

42 **"shift the base of college education":** TC, 14 December 1936.

43 **German, ceramics, and child psychology:** Report of Alice Pearce, Sarah Lawrence College, 12 June 1937, APSF.

43 **"That [was] about all the excitement":** "Schulberg, Pearce Have Exciting Trips," TC, 18 January 1937.

43 **"unflagging interest and concentration":** Report of Alice Pearce, Sarah Lawrence College, 10 June 1938, APSF.

44 **Elizabeth "Betty" La Branche:** Betty La Branche (1917–2010), SLC Class of 1940, served overseas with the American Red Cross during World War Two. When she returned to the States, she became an elementary school teacher in New York before moving to Washington, D. C., in the early 1950s to work as a CIA analyst. After receiving counterespionage training, she was sent to Europe as a covert agent. She resigned from the agency in 1962. For her final fifty years, she resided in the Georgetown neighborhood of Washington. Never wed, she died of stroke complications at age 92.

44 **The Center for European Study:** TC, 28 September 1936.

44 **Betty's father:** The handsome George Michel Lucien La Branche (1875–1961) founded La Branche and Company, an international investment firm. He was considered a top authority on fly fishing, authoring two books on the subject.

44 **Fredrika Tuttle:** Fredrika Bremer Tuttle (1918–1990), SLC Class of 1939, married Princeton professor David Hunt Blair in 1941 but later divorced. With her second husband Jerome Hast-

ings, she traveled the country, researching the life and career of dancer Isadora Duncan, whose biography she published in 1986. She died of cancer at age 72.

44 **Helen Tuttle:** Helen Davenport Tuttle (1920–2018), SLC two-year degree, 1939, married Princeton graduate Taras "Terry" Votichenko in 1943. In 1956, the Votichenkos and their three sons moved to Tempe, Arizona, where Terry taught philosophy and psychology for more thirty years. Helen received her master's degree from Arizona State University and subsequently taught French there. She died in Paradise Valley, Arizona, at age 98.

44 **Mary Holland Gordon:** "Dutch" Gordon (1918–2014), SLC Class of 1941, married naval commander-author Arthur H. Bryant in 1946. Their union produced one child, Geraldine Mason "Melodie" Bryant, born 1949, and ended in divorce after a few years. In 1956 Arthur Bryant was killed while racing in England when his Aston Martin crashed. Dutch married again in 1964 to playwright and author Max Shulman (1919–1988), the creator of the "Dobie Gillis" character of film and television. "Dutch" died at 95 in her New York City apartment.

44 **"she was an avid reader":** Geraldine M. Bryant, "A Life Changing Education for a Future Generation," Sarah Lawrence College *Legacy News*, Spring 2015.

44 **"Her future would have been bleak":** *Ibid.*

46 **Mary Virginia Heinlein:** Following her graduation from Vassar in 1925, Miss Heinlein (1903–1961), an Ohio native, studied acting at the Theatre Guild School in New York City. She left Sarah Lawrence College in 1942 to head Vasar's Experimental Theatre, a position she held for nineteen years. According to the online "Vassar Encyclopedia," she taught her final class on 20 December 1961. She died of cancer that Christmas Day.

46 **"brilliantly and sometimes caustically witty":** TC, 7 March 1939.

46 *When We Dead Awaken:* TC, 25 April 1938.

46 **"my dearest, closest friend":** Freedley, p. 3.

46 **Alice spent the following weekend:** TC, 23 May 1938.

46 **commencement ceremony:** TC, 8 June 1938.

47 **Adirondacks:** *Ibid.*

47 **Hotel Schweizerhof:** Alice's gray photo album, Box 2, File 1, APC.

47 **"Everywhere one went in Paris":** "Pearce Describes Paris War Scene," TC, 17 October 1938.

48 **President Roosevelt:** "1938 Timeline," *World War II Database*, https://ww2db.com, accessed 23 January 2019.

48 **"It is extremely personal painting":** Report of Alice Pearce, Sarah Lawrence College, 9 June 1939, APSF.

48 **"a bad Grandma Moses":** McManus, p. 45.

48 **"unflagging and stimulating":** Report of Alice Pearce, *op. cit.*

48 **drawing classes:** TC, 14 February 1939.

48 **"Peeps":** Alice's college nickname transcended those days. Her great friend Cris Alexander, who professed not to know its origin, faithfully used it when referring to Alice, as did others who did not know Alice nearly as well as he—KayeBallard and Dominick Dunne, for instance.

48 **"Peeps Pearce":** TC, 1 October 1938.

48 **"... tan rough suede shoes":** TC, 7 November 1938.

48 **"Peeps regularly went through her wardrobe":** email message from Melodie Bryant to FT, 8 May 2018.

49 **Christa Winsloe's 1930 play:** Mennel, *Queer Cinema: Schoolgirls, Vampires, and Gay Cowboys*, p. 16. Christa Winsloe (1888–1944) was a German-Hungarian novelist-playwright who is credited with having written the first detailed play on lesbianism in the Weimar Republic. In the late 1930s, she fled Berlin and the Nazis for France where she joined the French Resistance. Later, when she and her domestic partner Simone Gentet were suspected of collaborating with the German occupation, they were shot and killed by four Frenchmen near Cluny.

49 **"the most finished piece of work":** TC, 19 December 1938.

49 **lighting, scenery, and costumes:** Veteran Broadway costume and scenic designer Raymond Sovey, known for the recent hit *Our Town*, oversaw the students' costume creations.

49 **"enticing":** TC, 28 March 1939.

49 **"with sensitivity ...":** Report of Alice Pearce, Sarah Lawrence College, 9 June 1939, APSF.

49 **"perfectly keeping [the] mood":** TC, 9 May 1939.

49 **"In everything..."**: Report of Alice Pearce, *op. cit.*

49 **"more of a party"**: TC, 2 May 1939.

49 **"It will be the culmination"**: TC, 30 May 1939.

50 **Ed Seiler:** Edwin Norton Seiler (1918–1945), Princeton Class of 1940, was the son of a New York banker. He became a U. S. Navy fighter pilot after enlisting in 1942. The following year he co-authored *Wildcats Over Casablanca*, which told the story of carrier-based aircraft employed in the invasion of North Africa. At age 26, Seiler was killed in action in the Pacific. He was unmarried.

50 **newly elected vice-president:** DP, 19 May 1939.

50 **"At the time, we thought little"**: "Intime Takes Sarah Lawrence Girls Dutch and Peeps in 'Front Page,'" TC, 4 October 1939.

50 **"I looked in the mirror"**: Shearer, p. 10.

50 **"perhaps not the most academically inclined"**: Votichenko email, 2014.

51 **Saint-Jean-de-Luz:** Margaret Pearce's red leather photo album, APC.

51 **Eleanor Rowe:** Americans Eleanor Mitchell Rowe (1880–1979) and her husband Harlan Page Rowe (1881–1950) were European buyers for the J. L. Hudson Company, a retail department store chain based in Detroit, Michigan.

51 **"The boat train"**: Margaret Pearce, "War Diary," 1 September 1939–24 June 1940, page 1, APC. According to Margaret's entry for 1 November 1939, Alice's final night with her parents on August 31 was spent "at the cinema."

51 **Howard Sheperd:** Howard Cotterill Sheperd (1894–1980) was a senior vice-president of the National City Bank and had been a resident of Bronxville since about 1920.

52 **"Her experience"**: Margaret Pearce, "War Diary," p. 7.

52 **"Alice Pearce Crosses Safely"**: PE, 21 September 1939.

52 **"I hated living in Europe"**: McManus, p. 5.

52 **blue paper and blackout curtains:** There were so many windows at Rosemont that it kept Margaret busy from September 2 until September 13, and even then, she required the services of a *tapissier* to complete the job, hanging blackout curtains over the "tall windows on the stairs. The only ladder in town tall enough was the church ladder."

52 **"Alice Perce [*sic*]"**: TC, 27 September 1939.

52 **abri:** On September 29, 1939, Margaret Pearce wrote her most descriptive diary entry ever, following a Paris air raid drill. She was with her chauffeur Martin at a cobbler's shop when the alert sounded: "We walked down the *Ave. de L'Opéra* about two blocks, and into a doorway, then down steps and steps, through a long black corridor, and into a very small room. I had forgotten my flashlight, and some kind gentleman offered to light my way. The concierge of the apartment is always in charge of the *abri*. This little concierge was buzzing around, shouting for us to get out of the corridor, and scolding us for not carrying flashlights. Then he came into the *abri* and lighted a very small electric light, and there was welcome light. I looked around this *abri*. Cedar posts had been placed all throughout the room, extending from floor to ceiling, also, the ceiling was entirely covered with these cedar posts. We were about fifty in number. I was the only American. One little man read his paper by the dim light. A clerk offered me her folding chair and she sat upon her gas mask can. French wit was ever present in their conversations. It was approaching the noon hour and everyone was afraid they would miss their luncheon. I looked at those cedar posts, hoped they were strong, they seemed to slant already a little, and the iron bars holding them up looked frail. Someone murmured, that it was a good *abri*. I wondered how in my forty-seven years, I had gotten myself in this particular place. Born on a Missouri farm, and, now in the bowels of the earth, under an old building in Paris, France, trusting to God and cedar posts that I might get out alive."

52 **"the best serious undergraduate"**: *Cincinnati Enquirer*, 4 October 1939. Theatre Intime alums include stage and screen actors Myron McCormick and James Stewart.

52 **Dick Koch:** Richard Henry Koch II (1918–2009), Princeton Class of 1940, a native of Pottsville, Pennsylvania, was the son of a lawyer. A lieutenant in the US Naval Reserve from 1942 until 1946, Koch earned his law degree from Columbia University in 1954 and practiced law until 1959 when he became deputy director of the Museum of Modern Art in NYC. He married at age 49 and later became the father of three children.

52 **"My big moment"**: TC, 4 October 1939.

52 **"[We] were whisked"**: *Ibid.*

52 **"ragged"**: DP, 13 October 1939.

52 **"You learn those lines and go on"**: Freedley, p. 3.

52 **"They did the best they could"**: DP, 10 October 1939.

53 **"field work"**: *New York Daily Mirror*, 25 June 1947.

53 **"very general and terribly sweet and gentle":** TC, 6 December 1939.

54 **"Alice Pearce accomplished":** TC, 29 November 1939.

54 **four books and some parlor games:** Margaret Pearce, "War Diary," p. 24.

54 **"flu-pneumonia":** PE, 14 December 1939. Paul Dillard (1903–1939), a pharmacist, was a native of Houstonia, Missouri, but he grew up in nearby Sedalia. After living in Mexico for a number of years, Paul and Josephine moved to Butler, Missouri, where he bought a drug store. Six months before his death, they moved to Warrensburg. Paul and Josephine were childless.

54 **promised to be very sad:** Margaret Pearce, upon receiving a cable on December 8, 1939, with the news of Paul Dillard's death, wrote, "We were terribly shocked. Our hearts ache for Josephine in this terrible hour of trouble and sorrow. Why must good men like Paul be taken, when mean men like Hitler live to bring sorrow upon the whole world?"

54 **skiing party in Quebec:** *Pelham Sun*, 29 December 1939.

54 **"very, very unathletic":** TC, 31 January 1940.

54 **"The majority of the audience":** TC, 14 February 1940.

54 **Yale-Army football game:** TC, 25 October 1939.

54 **"While I was in college":** Shearer, p. 10.

54 **"intimate musical revue":** DP, 20 March 1940.

55 **"rowdy satire on American patriotism":** DP, 11 April 1940.

55 **"these troubled times":** DP, 25 April 1940.

55 **"the Intime is not a radical":** *Ibid.*

55 **Dress rehearsals:** DP, 29 April 1940.

55 **"Tobacco Wrath":** DP, 30 April 1940.

55 **"the best production":** DP, 2 May 1940.

55 **"The mood of the evening":** DP, 1 May 1940.

56 **"the brunt of the show":** DP, 2 May 1940.

56 **"eclipsed all his former records":** *Ibid.*

56 **Bob Perry:** Harold Robert Perry, Jr. (1919–1943), the son of an executive with the G. R. Kinney Shoe Company, was born in Manchester, New Hampshire. An English major, he left Princeton in 1940 at the end of his junior year to pursue an acting career. Before enlisting in the army in 1942, Perry directed CBS radio productions in NYC. Technical Sgt. Perry was serving as a radioman during a bombing raid on May 23, 1943, when his plane was shot down over occupied France, near Saint-Nazaire. Perry was unmarried.

56 **Bill Callanan:** Malcolm Williams Callanan (1919–1993), Princeton Class of 1941, and a native of Cleveland, Ohio, was the son of the president of the Brown Rubber Company in Lafayette, Indiana. Before enrolling at Princeton, he had been educated in Saint-Cloud, France, where the Pearces resided from 1930 until 1940, and Melbourne, Australia. In 1942, he enlisted in the military, eventually being recruited for the O.S.S., posted to Algeria (where he taught himself Arabic) and slipped five times behind Nazi lines in Yugoslavia where he was instrumental in the U.S. effort to help Marshal Tito edge out others vying for partisan power. After the war, he eventually became a teacher and later the headmaster of the Solebury School in New Hope, Pennsylvania. At 73, he died of pneumonia in a Doylestown nursing home. Callanan never married.

56 **Bus Davis:** Carl Estes Davis, Jr. (1918–1987), Princeton Class of 1941, called "Buster" (generally shortened to "Bus"), was born on the Fourth of July in Johnstown, Pennsylvania, the only child of a mortician. During the war he was a musical director of an overseas USO troupe. From the 1940s through the 1980s, Bus was an active musical director and vocal arranger for many Broadway productions, including three which featured Alice in their casts: *Look, Ma, I'm Dancin'*, *John Murray Anderson's Almanac*, and *Bells Are Ringing*. He also wrote material for many television shows, winning an Emmy for music direction the year he died. Battling cancer, he moved from California to NYC shortly before the disease claimed his life at age 69. Bus never married.

56 *Mademoiselle*: *Mademoiselle*, July 1940.

56 **"We truly thought the play":** "Alice Pearce Rox '40," *Sarah Lawrence Alumnae Magazine*, Spring 1949. Alice graduated with a Bachelor of Arts degree in dramatics.

57 **"The funny old Mad Hatter":** TC, 29 May 1940.

57 **"We pick things up":** TC, 22 May 1940.

57 **"with its lively skits":** TC, 5 June 1940.

57 **"often informally consulted":** The National City Bank of New York, Monthly Letter Number 171, from the Head Office to All Managers, Overseas Division, December 1946, APC.

58 **Jack Wright:** John Stratton Wright, Jr. (1879–1965), was born in Waddington, New York. Since 1906 he had been associated with the Bell Telephone Manufacturing Company, later I. T. & T. He stayed with the Pearces for three months

during the earliest days of the war, and Margaret described Jack as "splendid company." After his retirement in 1946, he retained his post as vice president of International Standard Electric Corporation, which controlled manufacturing properties outside the States. Jack died at Roosevelt Hospital in NYC at age 85.

58 **Morgan Heiskell:** Morgan Ott Heiskell (1882–1967), a native of Wheeling, West Virginia, had lived in Europe almost exclusively since 1910. A vice president with the Commercial Cable Company, a subsidiary of I. T. & T., Heiskell had two children by his first wife Ann Hubbard, one of whom was Andrew Heiskell (1915–2003), board chairman of Time, Inc.

58 **Count Jacques Aldebert de Chambrun:** Général de Chambrun (1872–1962) was a lineal descendant of the Marquis de Lafayette (1757–1834). From 1901, the year of his marriage, until his death he was a resident of France, serving as an artillery general for the French army during the First World War and the Rif War. During the Second World War, he was appointed the governor-general of the American Hospital of Paris. Of his service to the National City Bank, his wife wrote in her 1949 memoir *Shadows Lengthen*: "For a general, I must admit he had proved himself a sufficiently competent banker."

58 **retired from military service:** de Chambrun, *Shadows Like Myself*, p. 347.

58 **Clara Longworth:** The Comtesse de Chambrun (1873–1954) was a remarkably accomplished woman, earning a doctorate from the Sorbonne in 1921. She was a founding member of the American Library in Paris, and her close connection with it perhaps explains how Robert Pearce became a library trustee. She once presented her fellow Ohioan with an autographed copy of her book on Cincinnati. Her famous sister-in-law was Alice Roosevelt Longworth, the daughter of President Theodore Roosevelt.

58 **take up golf:** Margaret Pearce, "War Diary," p. 30.

59 **joining in by making jam:** As an added protection against incendiary bombs, Margaret also helped spread sand on the attic floor at Rosemont. On September 19, she helped Emma, the cook, make fourteen bottles of tomato sauce. "We thought of Alice. She loves our *sauce tomate.* Hope she can have some this summer."

59 **"D. C. A. guns":** Margaret Pearce, "War Diary," p. 33.

59 **"We realize that the war":** *Ibid.* Elise and Emma, both young ladies born in Belgium, were the Pearces' maid and cook, respectively.

59 **"Sun shining":** *Ibid.,* p. 34.

59 **June 8, 1940:** Margaret's diary entry: "Home all day . . . Alice's graduation day, sad to be so far away."

59 **"The Tyranny of Words":** TC, 5 June 1940.

59 **bittersweet circumstances:** Unfortunately for Alice, her beloved Aunt Josephine and grandmother Sallie Clark couldn't fill in for her parents on Commencement Day due to Josephine's hospitalization at Mexico, Missouri.

59 **overexposed candid snapshot:** Unbound, makeshift scrapbook, *op. cit.*

Chapter Eight

60 **"avant la guerre":** Margaret Pearce, "War Diary," p. 13.

60 **"while hell broke over Paris":** *Ibid.,* p. 41.

60 **"certain French directors":** de Chambrun, *Shadows Lengthen*, p. 99.

60 **an ancient castle:** The Château de Lavoute-Polignac was the favorite residence of the family of Polignac, a very old French family affiliated with the castle since the ninth century.

60 **"[drove] off into the unknown":** Margaret Pearce, "War Diary," p. 44.

60 **"We leave Paris":** *Ibid.,* pp. 44–46.

61 **too ill-equipped for their use:** The Pearces and their comrades were quite dissatisfied with the Château de Lavoute-Polignac, which had no hot water or gas and "just enough electricity to light one bulb in each room," according to the Comtesse de Chambrun, who with her husband was resigned to stay there for three weeks upon finding no other accommodations by the time they reached Le Puy on June 14.

61 **"dirty, neglected house":** Margaret Pearce, "War Diary," p. 51.

61 **"I have been defeated, too":** *Ibid.,* page 52.

61 **Bob Pearce would long be commended:** The National City Bank of New York, Monthly Letter Number 171, from the Head Office to All Managers, Overseas Division, December 1946, APC.

61 **Berkshires:** "Pearces To South of France," PE, 20 June 1940.

61   **"get an apartment in New York"**: Alice (Peeps) Pearce, "Two H," *Sarah Lawrence Alumnae Magazine*, December 1940.

61   **"While [Betty and I] were taking life easy"**: *Sarah Lawrence Alumnae Magazine*, December 1940.

61   **"stopping in wherever"**: *Ibid.*

61   **signed a lease:** *New York Times*, 26 July 1940.

61   **New Kennebunkport Playhouse:** *Variety*, 10 July 1940.

62   **"three hundred comfortable seats"**: Ostrander, *Remembering the Kennebunks*, p. 110.

62   **Booth Tarkington:** *Ibid.*, page 109. Booth Tarkington (1869–1946), considered in the 1910s and 1920s to be America's greatest living author, won the Pulitzer Prize for Fiction for *The Magnificent Ambersons* and *Alice Adams*.

62   **invited all twenty-six members:** *Biddeford Daily Journal*, 13 August 1940.

62   **"facetious good-time seekers"**: *Biddeford Daily Journal*, 14 August 1940.

63   *What a Life*: *Variety*, 10 July 1940.

63   **"paint[ed] scenery and ma[de] intermission coffee"**: *TV Guide*, 25 December 1965.

63   **"was no church bazaar"**: Betty La Branche, "Shop-Worn," *Sarah Lawrence Alumnae Magazine*, December 1941.

63   **"fifth year of college"**: *Ibid.*

63   **"It had turned out quite nicely"**: *Sarah Lawrence Alumnae Magazine*, December 1940. Alice was skillful at anecdotes, and this account of settling into a new apartment is a superb example.

63   **"I wore out my shoe leather"**: *Sarah Lawrence College Alumnae Magazine*, Spring 1949.

63   **"Peeps says"**: *Sarah Lawrence Alumnae Magazine*, January 1946.

63   **"Budget Underwear"**: TC, 13 November 1940.

63   **head of the whole bra and girdle department:** *TV Radio Mirror*, September 1965.

63   **supportive of Alice's study of dramatics:** In 1939, Margaret Pearce had written in her diary: "Alice had beautiful talent for such work, and I am glad she can enjoy it."

63   **"Sarah Lawrence College would remove"**: "The Mad Miss Pearce," typewritten profile, 1948, Alice Pearce clippings file, Billy Rose Theatre Collection, The New York Public Library.

63   **"They knew so little"**: Ed Misurell, "Her Life Is Filled with Sorcery," *Tyrone Daily Herald*, 26 May 1965, p. 14.

63   **"did not approve"**: White interview.

63   **"They probably just didn't know"**: Alexander interview, 1987.

64   **"Oh, Alice was much too down-to-earth"**: Wilson interview.

64   **"Oh, how well I know that!"**: Williams interview.

64   **Bellefontaine on March 15:** BDE, 17 March 1941.

64   **Albuquerque . . . Grand Canyon:** Margaret Pearce's red leather photo album, *op. cit.*

64   **Alice joined them:** BDE, 22 March 1941.

64   *Experimental Playhouse of the Air*: "Miss Pearce in Spring Revue at Princeton," PE, 22 May 1941, page 1. Margaret Pearce would note in her makeshift scrapbook that Alice made her network radio debut on 13 December 1942, but she neglected to name the network or the program.

64   **"written by English professors"**: *New York Daily News*, 9 January 1941.

64   **Dixon taught speech classes:** TC, 4 June 1941.

65   **strolled out:** TC, 21 May 1941.

65   **"revue to end all revues"**: DP, 31 March 1941.

65   **"less distinguished"**: DP, 7 May 1941.

65   **Helen Hokinson:** Helen Hokinson (1893–1949) was a staff cartoonist for *The* wealthy, plump, ditsy society women and their foibles.

65   **Mark Lawrence:** Born in Washington, DC, Mark Lawrence (1921–1991) was educated at Phillips Academy in Andover, Massachusetts. After his graduation from Princeton in 1942, he enlisted in the U. S. Naval Reserves, serving four years in the Pacific as a deck officer on light cruisers. A bachelor until age 30, he married Nan Hoyt in 1951, and they had three children before their divorce some twenty years later. Besides being a composer, he was a theatrical and film producer, as well as an award-winning advertising copywriter. Lawrence died of prostate cancer in Boston at age 70.

65   **Nancy Lawrence:** Nancy Ellanor Lawrence (1922–1968) was a graduate of Harcum Junior College in Bryn Mawr, Pennsylvania. In 1943 she married Princeton graduate Alfred Lawrence Hart, Jr. She died of a sudden heart attack while vacationing in the Caribbean.

65   **David Lawrence:** David Lawrence (1888–1973), whose news career in Washington spanned 60 years and 11 presidential administrations, graduated from Princeton in 1910. He was one of radio's first political commentators and an author of more than a half-dozen books. In 1918, he married

Ellanor Campbell Hayes Daly (1884–1969), who grew up in Spartanburg County, South Carolina.

65 **newly elected president:** DP, 20 March 1941.

65 **Leonard Sillman:** DP, 12 May 1941. By the time of his death, Leonard Dexter Sillman (1908–1982) was widely considered to have launched the careers of more actors than any other producer in the country, among them Tyrone Power, Eve Arden, Alice Ghostley, Paul Lynde, Eartha Kitt, and Maggie Smith. Never married, Sillman died in New York City after a long struggle with cancer.

65 **stage-struck since his prepubescent days:** Sillman, *Here Lies Leonard Sillman, Straightened Out at Last*, pp. 30–31.

65 **"[He] made fierce demands":** *New York Daily News*, 7 July 1982.

66 **"small, intimate revue":** *New York Daily News*, 3 September 1941.

66 **("one of the best ..."):** DP, 12 May 1941.

66 **"natural instincts and expert timing":** Gary Brumburgh, "Alice Pearce: Beauty Inside," *Classic Images*, March 2010, p. 8.

66 **"Talent is not enough":** Robert Ullman, Radio Corporation of America, "Synopsis" for New Faces '56 record album, *Masterworks Broadway*, https://masterworksbroadway.com/music/new-faces-of-56-original-cast/, accessed 5 March 2019.

66 **come audition for him:** Sillman also signed Bill Callanan for the revue, but the advent of Pearl Harbor precipitated his military enlistment on 4 February 1942, thus ending his one shot at a Broadway debut.

66 **"My hopes were high again":** *Sarah Lawrence College Alumnae Magazine*, Spring 1949.

66 **"We would raise our money":** Sillman, p. 172.

66 **"It was never done like that":** *Ibid.*

66 **135 auditions:** *Ibid.*, p. 173.

67 *Three White Leopards:* "Alice Pearce Enlists in New Intime Production," DP, 6 December 1941.

67 **"[W]e cannot resist":** DP, 15 December 1941.

67 **31 Sutton Place South:** *New York Times*, 23 January 1942.

67 **vice president:** *New York Times*, 18 March 1942.

67 **Bob wanted Alice to be certain:** Barclay, *op. cit.*

67 **"the theater was an unreliable business":** Harold Stern, "Nosy Alice Pearce Having Bangup Time in *Bewitched*," *Dayton Journal Herald*, 21 September 1965, p. 35.

67 **agreed to allow Alice to use:** *TV Guide*, 25 December 1965.

67 **suggested that Alice:** Joan Crosby, "Parents Hope Alice Pearce to Tire of Being an Actress," *Austin Daily Herald*, 28 May 1965, "Showcase" section, p. 1.

67 **"So I went to a [YWCA]":** Stern, p. 35.

68 **"flying from one audition":** *New York Daily News*, 31 January 1943.

68 **"I called Leonard":** Letter from Alice Pearce to John Rox, 30 October 1942, APC.

68 **"every imaginable source":** *Brooklyn Daily Eagle*, 10 January 1943.

68 **"some 80 tedious auditions":** *Sarah Lawrence College Alumnae Magazine*, Spring 1949.

68 **lobbies and rest rooms:** William Hawkins, "Anita Loos and Luck Got Role," *New York World-Telegram and The Sun*, 25 May 1950.

69 **Harry Pearce died:** "Harry Pearce Dies," BDE, 19 November 1942. The ninety-one-year-old had suffered from heart disease for several years. His infirmity brought on kidney failure, with which he suffered for about a week before dying peacefully on the afternoon of November 18, 1942, at his home at 217 N. Detroit Street in Bellefontaine. He had outlived three wives and three of his five children. Surviving him were two sons, four granddaughters, and four great-grandsons. Funeral services were held on November 20 at the Kennedy Funeral Home, followed by burial at the Bellefontaine Cemetery. His estate was valued at approximately $20,000. Harry's death would essentially mark the end of any close contact Alice would share with her father's family. Mary Barbara Squires, Alice's first cousin once removed, when interviewed on 2 March 2014, explained that physical distance was the primary factor limiting the connection between Alice and her paternal cousins. However, sources firmly indicate that, despite the distance factor, Alice shared a more intimate connection with her mother's side of the family through the years.

69 **"New Faces of 1943":** *New York Daily News*, 10 December 1942.

69 **Charles Weidman:** Weidman had been a dance instructor at Sarah Lawrence College during Alice's years there, although she never studied under him.

69 **Ritz Theatre:** Located at 219 W. 48th Street, it is currently the Walter Kerr Theatre.

69 **"New Faces isn't any fun":** *Variety*, 30 December 1942.

69 **"adolescent and unclever":** *The Billboard*, 9 January 1943.

69 **"sketchy affair":** *Theatre Arts*, February 1943.

70 **Two dollars:** *New York Daily News*, 23 December 1942.

70 **$3.30 for top seats:** Bob and Margaret Pearce and Alice's Aunt Josephine paid $4.40 each for their opening night seats in the orchestra section.

70 **"This [current success]":** *New York Daily News*, 31 January 1943.

70 **"deserved some boost":** *Ibid.*

70 **Billboard gave credit to Alice:** *The Billboard*, 9 January 1943.

70 **"She was really marvelous":** Lund letter.

70 **"She's the female lead":** TC, 3 February 1943.

70 **"We limped through four months":** *Sarah Lawrence College Alumnae Magazine*, Spring 1949.

70 **"I picked 1943":** Sillman, pp. 315–316.

70 **received job offers:** *New York Daily News*, 31 January 1943.

70 **John Lund:** John Lawrence Lund (1911–1992), according to the New York Birth Index, was born in Ithaca, New York, and not Rochester, New York, as most of his online biographies state. One of eight children, Lund got his professional start on radio, mainly in soap operas like *Portia Faces Life*. He married Marie Charton, a model for New York's Conover Model Agency. He retired from acting in 1963. Outliving his wife by a decade, he was found dead of an apparent heart attack in his Coldwater Canyon home.

70 **Irwin Corey:** Irwin Corey (1914–2017), *né* Cohen, was born in Brooklyn but spent his teen years in California. He performed as the character "Professor Irwin Corey, the world's foremost authority" in vaudeville, nightclubs, and television for over seventy years.

Chapter Nine

72 **hottest day in New York City:** *New York Daily News*, 23 May 1941.

72 **"a red-letter day":** *Sarah Lawrence College Alumnae Magazine*, Spring 1949.

72 **"He was a charmer!":** Alexander interview, 1987.

72 **songwriting:** "Biographical Notes on John Rox," one-page, typewritten document prepared by publicity agent Stanley Musgrove, 1951, APC.

72 **unemployed for the past two years:** 1940 U. S. Federal Census, New York City, New York, Enumeration District No. 31-1368, Sheet 9B, 4 East 64th Street, Household No. 124, Line No. 57. Perkins Bailey, single and with an annual income of more than $5000, was listed as head of household, and John Rox, single with no annual income, was listed as a "roomer."

73 **"on his family tree somewhere":** OWH, 13 March 1949.

73 *Stuart Herald*: SH, 25 July 1902: "Born, to Mr. and Mrs. Arthur Barber of Des Moines, July 21st, a son."

73 **John Barber:** John Seth Barber (1845–1915), the paternal grandfather of John Rox, was born in Westport, NY. When eighteen years old he enlisted in Company H, 46th Infantry, New York Volunteers, serving for one year. Since 1895, his family had lived in Atlantic, where he died of heart disease at age 69.

73 **streetcar conductor:** Arthur Barber's occupation is listed on the following documentation of his son's birth: John Arthur Barber, Iowa State Department of Health-Division of Vital Statistics Birth Certificate, No. 23245, 16 October 1940.

74 **Ina Maureen Brown:** At least once, her name was spelled as "Inah Maurine," but since her niece and namesake used the more traditional spelling of the middle name, it appears in the narrative as Ina Maureen. Likewise, Ina's nickname is variously spelled "Dolly" or "Dollie," but the former, which appears on her gravestone, is used for this work.

74 **John Jefferson Brown:** J. J. Brown (1851–1909), the maternal grandfather of John Rox, was the fifth generation of his family to live in western Virginia. When Brown was a small child, his parents moved to Illinois, then Missouri, and finally settling in Guthrie County, Iowa, in 1859. He became a harness maker at a very young age, and when the town of Stuart was organized, he decided to open a harness shop there. At age 58, he died of Addison's disease in Stuart, IA.

74 **"the life of his home":** SH, 1 October 1909.

74 **Alice Cora Barringer:** Alice Barringer Brown (1856-1943), maternal grandmother of John Rox, was a steadfast caregiver to two of her adult children, and she was rarely sick. She was remembered as having a "wicked sense of humor," according to her great-granddaughter Shirley Herring Taylor. She retained all her faculties until the end, which came at the home of her granddaughter Edna Haase in Des Moines, after a three-day illness.

74 **in 1899 she clerked:** *Stuart Locomotive*, 1 December 1899.

74 **very proper young ladies:** Email message from John Higginbottom to FT, 16 March 2103.

74 **"highway robbery"**: *Glenwood Opinion*, 10 November 1898.

74 **"five years at hard labor"**: *Daily Iowa Capital*, 21 February 1899.

74 **sentence was commuted**: *Ottumwa Tri-Weekly Courier*, 21 January 1902.

74 **Earl Granville Herring**: SH, 31 December 1964.

74 **married in her parents' parlor**: Earl Herring and Dolly Brown married on April 3, 1907, in Stuart, Iowa. The bride wore a white muslin gown adorned with artificial orange blossoms, which were also "sprinkled in her hair." See *Stuart Herald*, 5 April 1907.

75 **"[John] was like my grandfather's own son"**: email message from Linda Swanson to FT, 15 March 2013.

75 **butter making and chemistry**: WM, 24 February 1910. By April 1910 the Herrings were living in Stuart with Dolly's mother Alice Brown, and Earl was unemployed. There is some indication that they lived with Earl's mother in Dexter during this interval as well.

75 **John Wayne**: Wayne was born May 26, 1907, at 224 South Second Street in Winterset, but his father Clyde moved the family to Des Moines that August, returning to Winterset within three months, according to the *Madison County Reporter* (5 December 1907). The Morrisons moved from Winterset in 1909, eventually leaving Iowa for California in 1914.

75 **contracted diphtheria**: WN, 19 November 1909.

75 **George Washington's birthday**: WN, 19 February 1913.

75 **Confederate soldier**: WM, 28 February 1917.

75 **school operetta**: WM, 2 April 1919.

76 **Charles Leech**: Charles Sloan Leech (1876–1929), a native of Winterset, graduated from the State University of Iowa in 1898. In addition, he studied voice at Simpson College in Indianola, Iowa.

76 **"high school boy"**: WM, 30 April 1919.

76 **"sacrificing sports and other fun"**: WM, 12 February 1920.

76 **"a pure Italian tenor"**: *Ibid.*

76 **"Endowed"**: *Ibid.*

76 **school productions**: On May 24 and 25, 1920, John played the leading role of Charles Marlow in *She Stoops to Conquer*, presented by the senior class. Following graduation, Dr. Leech kept John's agenda packed with engagements. His repertoire included both classical and popular pieces, which

he performed for church services, music clubs, hospital patients, and even a three-night gig at an Elks convention in Saint Paul, Minnesota. At the same time, John's friendship with Leech grew more intimate, demonstrated by the fact that he and Leech were the only witnesses in December 1920 to the marriage of Leech's sister in Des Moines, where the dentist had arranged everything, including the wedding supper. Similarly, when a sinus condition interfered with John's singing, Leech saw to it that his protégé had surgery to correct it. Following a benefit recital in Stuart in May 1921, the *Stuart Herald* recognized Dr. Leech: "Much of the credit for Mr. Herring's fine singing should be given to Dr. Leech who ... early discovered the unusual quality of Mr. Herring's voice. [He] has given freely of his time and talent in his effort to produce a singer of unusual ability."

76 **Holmes Cowper**: *The Annals of Iowa* 19, no. 6 (1934), p. 476-477. Harry Mattingly "Holmes" Cowper (1870–1934) taught singing at Drake University for twenty-five years, until his death from a brain abscess.

77 **John enrolled**: email message from Kevin Moenkhaus, Director of Student Records, Drake University, to FT, 14 February 2013.

77 **"A new baritone"**: *Des Moines Capital*, 20 April 1922.

77 **"morning and evening"**: "Millionaire to Take Young Omahan from Hollywood for Career in Opera," OWH, 3 April 1928.

77 **visited him regularly**: Apparently, John was still training with Leech during the 1923 spring semester, for he was prominently featured in a recital of Leech's students on April 27. As an encore, he sang "Little Mother of Mine," a sentimental favorite for which he was well known.

77 **Paul William Zeh**: Paul Zeh (1896–1975), whose surname rhymes with "hey," was born in Des Moines to Christian Zeh and his wife Hulda Rosa Zerr. His physical description comes from his World War I Draft Registration Card, viewable on www.ancestry.com. Prior to working for Standard Oil, Paul was a 'salesman in Des Moines' largest department store and a clerk/timekeeper for the Des Moines City Railway. Newspaper items would report that Paul and John met when both were students at Drake University, however, university officials in 2019 found no record of Paul's attendance. Unmarried and the youngest of five

children, Paul lived with his widowed mother in a small house on Ascension Street.

77   **radio debut:** WM, 11 January 1923.

77   **Melo-Blue Dance Orchestra:** *Des Moines Tribune*, 20 April 1923.

77   **"known as a team":** OWH, 13 July 1927.

77   **move Dolly:** WM, 21 June 1923. Earl, Dolly, Donald, and Robert Herring moved to Omaha in late July 1923.

77   **moved in with Paul:** Des Moines City Directory, 1924, pp. 620, 1451. Paul was evidently very close to his mother; his father had died when he was only ten. Mother Zeh could have stayed behind with any of her married children, but perhaps that was not what she or Paul wanted.

78   **1110 Twenty-ninth:** Des Moines City Directory, 1925, pp. 609, 1430.

78   **"Quittin' Time":** OWH, 13 March 1949.

78   **Encouraged by Dr. Leech:** OWH, 15 April 1928.

78   **moved to Los Angeles:** OWH, 29 March 1925.

78   **John and Paul performed:** *San Diego Evening Tribune*, 12 June 1925; *Radio Digest*, Vol. XIII, 4 July 1925.

78   **"Herring and Zeh":** OWH, 21 October 1926.

78   **act temporarily ran aground:** While waiting for a new engagement, John went to Winterset to spend several weeks with Dr. Leech. Meanwhile, Paul's visit at his sister's home in Des Moines ended sadly when his mother unexpectedly died there on December 8. John attended the funeral but returned briefly to Winterset before going back to Des Moines on December 15 in preparation for the team's new engagement at the Des Moines Theater. "They are peppy and popular, these boys," hyped the *Des Moines Register*, "and they are on their way east after a long and successful career on the west coast."

78   **paid a farewell visit:** email message from Linda Swanson to FT, 29 June 2015.

78   **brother Don:** John found the Herring household in the midst of a rather unsettling situation. John's half-brother Don, also musically talented, was eager to go with John to California to begin his own career in entertainment. However, there were significant complications. The boy had eloped the previous summer when he was seventeen, and now his young bride Doris was expecting a baby in five months. Compounding those circumstances was the issue of Don's impaired eyesight. When he was about eighteen months old, Don was accidentally poked in the face with a fishing pole, necessitating surgery, during which two pieces of gauze were negligently left inside his nose, near his eyes. This misfortune resulted in his partial blindness and disfigurement, despite thirteen subsequent surgeries to improve his condition. Given Don's physical handicap, his immaturity, and the uncertainties of gainful employment, especially in an unpredictable field such as show business, Earl and Dolly Herring thought it best for the youngsters to terminate their hasty marriage. On March 1, 1927, Dolly took the teenagers to the courthouse where Doris filed for divorce on the grounds of nonsupport. "He had no way to support a wife, much less a child at that time," reflected their younger daughter Linda Swanson in 2013. "I think that his plan was to [go to California] and break into the music world and then send for [his wife and child]." Donald Granville Herring (1908–1968) and his wife Doris Haverstock Herring (1907–1982) were born one year apart, exactly to the day—October 16— sharing birthdays with their sister-in-law Alice Pearce. They married on 24 July 1926 in Papillion, Nebraska. See SH, 6 March 1925, p. 1; OWH, 2 March 1927, p. 4.

78   **whirlwind cycle of melodies:** *Riverside Daily Press*, 21 May 1927.

78   **"epochal efforts":** Liebman, *Vitaphone Films*, p. 5.

79   **"Vitaphone was the place vaudeville went to die":** *Ibid.*

79   **Doris Duncan:** Doris Duncan Murphy (1896–1957) was the daughter of financier-cattleman James Roy Duncan. She died in Baltimore at age 61.

79   **Stanford University:** "Doris Duncan at Golden Gate," *San Francisco Examiner*, 28 April 1925.

79   **performed four selections:** Liebman, p. 174. The songs were: "From Now On," "Mine," "Come to Me Tonight," and "Side by Side." The group was paid $150.

79   **subsequent engagements:** It's possible that there was an intimate relationship between John and Paul, who lived together in the Salem Apartments at 6051 Salem Place in Los Angeles, but no proof exists. One wonders if an end to their domestic partnership precipitated the termination of their professional association. Paul's musical career appears to have sputtered out by 1930. Billed as "Paul Zey" during 1928 and 1929, he, along with another young man, was an "acrobatic dancer" in the Grace Adelphi Company, touring vaudeville houses all over the country. He later returned to an occupation he had held in his youth—men's

clothing salesman—and retired from the exclusive Oviatt haberdashery on Olive Street in downtown Los Angeles. In 1975, at a Santa Monica hospital Paul died from heart disease at age 79. At the time, his domestic partner was Hal Long (1907–1981), former Hollywood screenwriter.

79 **completion of a screen test**: "Finds the Rainbow's End," OWH, 13 April 1928.

79 **"bit work"**: OWH, 3 April 1928.

79 **"one of the most eligible bachelors"**: Hall, *Dolores del Río*, p. 28.

79 **"turned down over and over"**: *Ibid.*, p. 78.

79 **"pushing Jaime"**: *Ibid.*, p. 71.

79 **"almost immediately found favor"**: OWH, 13 April 1928. Hollywood historian DeWitt Bodeen wrote in his book *From Hollywood* (1976) that Jaime "had stifled his Latin pride and accepted a job as a script *clerk*" for Dolores' productions, in order to be near her in the studio, but this seems rather implausible.

79 **the del Ríos:** Jaime Carlos Mateo Martínez del Río (1893–1928) and Dolores del Río (1904–1983) separated in the fall of 1927 and divorced in June 1928. Six months later, he died of blood poisoning in Berlin, Germany, leaving some to say that he actually died of a broken heart and others to speculate that he had committed suicide. At his bedside was his friend Paul Mooney, who, according to the *New York Daily News* (8 December 1928), was collaborating with del Río on a play, *Barricade.* Mooney (1904–1939), possibly the lover of explorer Richard Halliburton, was lost at sea with him when Halliburton's Chinese junk met with a typhoon. See Max, *Horizon Chasers.*

80 **with whom they sailed:** Ghareeb, *Hollywood to Honolulu*, p. 178.

80 **Lloyd Pantages:** Lloyd Alexander Pantages (1907–1987), born in Seattle, became a syndicated newspaper columnist who also reported Hollywood happenings on his CBS radio program. He also wrote for *Photoplay.* At 80, he died from cardiac arrest at his Los Angeles home.

80 **"always wore an ascot"**: Deverich, *Wandering Through La La Land*, p. 18.

80 **"I was given contracts"**: *Buffalo Courier-Express*, 6 March 1929.

80 **"voice interested Post"**: OWH, 3 April 1928.

81 **"just before [John] left Hollywood"**: "Scenario Writing to Pay for Voice Study," OWH, 15 April 1928.

81 **"for enough money to pay"**: OWH, 13 April 1928.

81 *Blind Man's Bluff:* According to the *Omaha World-Herald*, actor Alec Francis (1867–1934) was likely to be a featured player in the production. In 1941, John would tell *Des Moines Tribune* reporter Mary Little that he wrote and sold a picture to the movies, but "it was never produced," even though "he received a check for his efforts."

81 **"Uplifters Ranch club"**: OWH, 13 April 1928. According to records maintained by the William Andrews Clark Memorial Library, Harrison Post and William Andrews Clark Jr. joined the Uplifters Club in 1925.

81 **"Spanish Colonial-style clubhouse"**: *Los Angeles Times*, 29 June 1994.

81 **Villa Dei Sogni:** This Uplifters Ranch house is not to be confused with another Post home, also called Villa Dei Sogni and located at 775 Kingman Avenue in the Pacific Palisades section of Santa Monica, which Post did not occupy until 1931. The Kingman Avenue property consisted of twelve acres and was formerly known as the Lester A. Scott Ranch.

81 **William Andrews Clark, Jr.:** William Clark (1877–1934), or Junior, as he was called, was born in Deer Lodge, Montana. His early childhood was spent in France, and he spoke French before he spoke English. At 22, he graduated from law school at the University of Virginia. After moving to Los Angeles, he according to Clark historian Bruce Whiteman, "acquired other residential properties contiguous to his own, so that eventually his house stood on a full city block of almost five acres." He also gathered perhaps the finest collection pertaining to Oscar Wilde. A trained violinist, he was the founder of the Los Angeles Philharmonic Orchestra. He bestowed his magnificent library building with its 13,000 books to UCLA. Harrison Post was not the only younger man whom Clark showered with gifts and cash, but their relationship was evidently the lengthiest. See Bruce Whiteman, "With These Philistines We Have No Quarrel," *Gazette of the Grolier Club*, Number 59/60.

82 **"an elaborate jewel-box Italian Renaissance library"**: Dedman, *Empty Mansions*, p. 142.

82 **"the gifts bestowed upon [him]"**: Watters, *Houses of Los Angeles*, p. 166. The Cimarron Street house and the Rolls-Royce were evidently given to Post after John Rox left for Europe.

82 **Albert Weis Harrison:** "New York, New York, Extracted Birth Index, 1878-1909," *Ancestry*, https://www.ancestry.com/search/collections/nycbirthindexes/, accessed 4 May 2019. Post's parents were Mark James Harrison (c. 1865–1916) and Genevieve "Jennie" Weis (c. 1874–?), the daughter of Albert Weis (c. 1840–1918), president of the American Theatrical Exchange in Manhattan. In 1946, five months before he died, Post charged that his half-sister, who twelve years previous had been appointed his guardian after he suffered a mental breakdown, misappropriated the fortune left to him by Clark. In his petition, Post stated that this woman sent him to a Norwegian health resort in 1939, where he was later interned by the Nazis. The suit was still underway when Post died of a heart attack in San Francisco on October 30, 1946, but was finally settled out of court in 1949. In one article linking Harrison Post to John Rox, the millionaire benefactor is unwittingly referred to as "the good fairy." See *Des Moines Register*, 3 April 1928.

82 **foster mother:** "U. S. World War I Draft Registration Cards, 1917-1918," *Ancestry*, https://search.ancestry.com/cgibin/sse.dll?indiv=try&db=WW1draft&h=33735551, accessed 4 May 2019. On his draft registration, Harrison listed Mary Annette Ostrander Post (1851–1935), who was the mother of actor Guy Bates Post (1875–1968), as his next of kin.

82 **"muckraking page-turner":** Whiteman, *op. cit.*

82 **Clark and Post met:** Mangam, *The Clarks: An American Phenomenon*, p. 204. William "Buck" Mangam (1877–1955), born in Brooklyn, New York, had known William A. Clark Jr. since their youth. Five months before Clark died, Mangam, who claimed he had been fired by Clark without being told the reason, sued Clark for slander. After Clark died, Mangam sued his estate for $29,000 for funds owed him, but settled out of court for $17,500. Mangam moved from Butte, Montana, around 1930. He died in a New York City hospital.

82 **"binge drinker":** Dedman, p. 142. Unfortunately, Mangam's account of Clark's personal life, although mean-spirited, is the only available source about Clark, whose papers were burned after his death. In 2009, Bruce Whiteman, then the director of the William Andrews Clark Memorial Library, expressed belief in Mangam's view of Clark's sexuality: "[H]is disinterest in remarrying bespoke a homosexual or bisexual nature that was more unrestrainedly indulged during the final sixteen years of his life." Today, Clark and Post are widely considered to have been lovers. See Whiteman, *op. cit.*

82 **"two-time felon then on parole":** Mangam, p. 209.

83 **New York passengers' lists:** Burgess, Post, Clark, McInerney, as well as Idaho attorney John P. Gray and his associate Robert E. Tally, all appear on manifests per those respective dates, available on the Ancestry website.

83 **sent out of the country:** It was also planned for Jack Oray to be sent to South America, but that didn't happen, according to Mangam.

83 **"homosexual subculture":** Mann, *Behind the Screen*, p. 87.

83 **"relaxed attitudes":** *Ibid.*, p. 103.

83 **"lifestyles were undisguised":** Mann, *Wisecracker*, p. 77.

83 **"markers":** Mann, *Behind the Screen*, p. xvii.

83 **"gossip, film lore, and legend":** *Ibid.*, p. xxi.

83 **"rumor and gossip":** Carson, *Multiple Voices in Feminist Film Criticism*, p. 330.

83 **Del Río endured rumors:** Hall, pp. 40, 95, 132.

84 **rumors about Buddy Rogers:** Rich, *Sweethearts*, p. 186.

84 **"In those days":** Email message to FT from a family member who requested anonymity.

84 **"a pretty good looking boy":** OWH, 13 April 1928.

84 *A Son of the Desert*: A feature film by this title, starring Merrill McCormick as a sheik, was released in February 1928.

84 **Betty Bronson:** Pretty brunette Betty Bronson (1906–1971) enjoyed a flurry of successful silents, including 1924's *Peter Pan*. John's name would not be linked in the press with any other female until he became engaged to Alice Pearce. However, the *Stuart Herald* (6 April 1928) once reported that his Winterset neighbors had watched him "glide through high school as a likeable, attractive chap who was favored by all the girls for dates."

84 **"John Rox":** OWH, 13 March 1949. John told Wilson that he had been advised to substitute another name for "Herring."

84 **planned for his vacation:** On April 29, 1928, Dr. Leech drove John from Des Moines to Chicago, where they spent four nights before John boarded the train for New York on May 3. According to the *Winterset News*, John and Dr. Leech met in

Paris in August 1928, while the *Winterset Madisonian* reported that they met in Italy. Nevertheless, it would be the final time these friends enjoyed each other's company. Leech grew ill that fall and entered the Mayo Clinic for treatment. From there he went to St. Paul for recuperation, but on March 8, 1929, he died from a heart attack.

85 **a letter of introduction:** OWH, 13 April 1928.

85 **In Vienna, John met:** OWH, 1 August 1929.

85 **"naively young":** Max, *Horizon Chasers*, p. 47.

85 **"When you're in Paris":** *Ibid.*

85 **villa at Beaulieu-sur-Mer:** Turnbull, *Mary Garden*, p. 165.

85 **sunbathing nude:** *Ibid.*, p. 159.

85 **"having a fling at the green tables":** *Ibid.*, p. 171.

85 **won three rings:** Higginbottom email, 2013.

85 **Elsa Maxwell:** After the completion of the hotel, the inveterate party-giver was recruited to draw a jet-setting crowd to Monte Carlo in the 1930s.

85 **"seduce more rich visitors":** Staggs, *Inventing Elsa Maxwell*, p. 153.

85 **"new smart beach club":** notation by John Rox on reverse side of photograph of Monte Carlo, 1929, LSC.

85 **shirtless bathing trunks:** Los Angeles rescinded its ordinance against shirtless swimsuits in 1929, but New York's municipal beaches did not permit shirtless bathing until 1936.

86 **Richard Barthélemy:** OWH, 1 August 1929.

86 **Martin Brown:** Meredith Gibson Brown (1884–1936), whose professional name was Martin Brown, was born in Montreal to insurance salesman Robert Brown and his wife Annie Spaulding. One of his best-known stage credits was the *Ziegfeld Follies of 1913*, in which he danced with one of the Dolly Sisters. While spending the winter of 1936 in New York, Brown developed bronchial pneumonia and died of that ailment at Bellevue Hospital with sister Fredrika at his side. He was 51. He had never married. A photograph of Brown, Mary Garden, and John Rox, all in beach attire, appeared in the OWH edition of 6 January 1930. Brown and John co-wrote at least one song, "Hickory Dickory Dock" (© 2 Feb. 1931).

86 **an ideal place to write:** *Santa Ana Register*, 26 November 1930.

86 **Fredrika:** Annie Fredrika Brown (1878–1952) was the older sister of Martin Brown. Following his death, she became a U. S. citizen and settled in Los Angeles. She appeared in small roles in a handful of films, including *Zaza*, *The Women*, and *Ninotchka*. Never married, she died in Los Angeles at age 74.

86 **dancer in Broadway musical comedies:** *Detroit Free Press*, 1 June 1930.

87 **"Why not Rox?":** Letter from John Rox to Don Roxy, 3 April 1930, LSC.

87 **"shortly will sail for London":** "Omahan Will Play in London Productions," *Columbus* (NE) *Telegram*, 16 July 1930.

87 *Bitter Sweet*: *Bitter Sweet*, an operetta starring Peggy Wood, ran in London for over eighteen months (1929–1931). Mary Garden could have been responsible for recommending John Rox to Noël Coward.

87 **"but he grew homesick":** "Biographical Notes on John Rox," *op. cit.*

87 **"at the crucial moments":** OWH, 13 March 1949.

87 **didn't know how to play:** "Biographical Notes on John Rox," *op. cit.*

87 **Nor was he able to write music:** Author's interview with Peggy Coburn, 21 February 2014.

88 **"John had a screen test":** Swanson email, 2015.

88 **"In those days Hollywood had a habit":** Sillman, p. 130.

88 **"deep-throated":** *Los Angeles Times*, 6 January 1931.

88 **"I Don't Want One Man":** Words and music by John Rox, © 10 January 1931, *Catalog of Copyright Entries*, Third Series, Volume 12, Part 5, Number 1, The Library of Congress, 1959. Sillman erroneously stated in his autobiography that June Sillman "had written this song herself." See Sillman, p. 132.

88 *It's All Too Wonderful*: Library of Congress Catalogue of Copyright Entries, Dramatic Compositions, 1931, Vol. 4, No. 2, p. 2387.

88 **Metro-Goldwyn-Mayer:** "Biographical Notes on John Rox," *op. cit.* This connection to M-G-M is corroborated by the 1932 California Voters Registration records for Laguna Beach Precinct No. 4, which lists John as a "writer."

88 **Robert Montgomery picture:** "Former Resident Will Star in The Movies," WM, 19 November 1931.

88 **P. G. Wodehouse's Beverly Hills home:** The poolside photograph was published in the OWH, 4 October 1931.

89 **"John worked very hard":** *Sun Coast News* clipping, 14 October 1932. LSC.

89 **"who made up in youth, charm and enthusiasm":** Sillman, p. 147.

89 **"hunky nineteen-year-old chauffeur":** Irvin, *Kay Thompson*, p. 32.

89 **"had a surprisingly progressive queer eye":** *Ibid.,* p. 33.

89 **"burst of glory":** Sillman, p. 205.

90 **resident of New York City:** SH, 15 July 1937: "John Herring of New York City and father and mother of Omaha spent the Fourth in Atlantic with Mrs. Herring's aunt Mrs. Fisher and mother Mrs. Alice Brown."

90 **"has done a lot of things":** "John Rox, Once of Des Moines, To Be Honored Sunday," *Des Moines Tribune*, 25 January 1941.

90 **Dr. Lyman Fisher:** Lyman Richard Fisher (1907–1988) was born in Spencer, New York. In 1936, he lived just outside Ithaca on the shore of Lake Cayuga, operating the Limehouse Kennels. Although Ithaca city directories are available for the 1930s, the doctor's residence was not included in the city's listings because it was not within the city limits. John Rox does not appear in any city directories of Ithaca; Dr. Fisher is only listed by his medical office address.

90 **Helen Broderick:** *Elmira Star-Gazette*, 4 January 1937.

90 **Female impersonation:** See *Cornell Daily Sun*, 5 February 1926; 26 April 1926; and *Variety*, 28 April 1926.

90 **Robert Herring:** OWH, 2 August 1936.

90 **short stories, radio scripts:** SH, 15 September 1938.

90 ***The Shadow*:** "Biographical Notes on John Rox," *op. cit.*

90 **Talon's director of design:** *South Bend Tribune*, 7 March 1946.

90 **Perkins Hillier Bailey:** Like John Rox, Perkins Bailey had endured two name changes. He was born Robert Perkins Hillier in Salt Lake City on May 27, 1906. When Perk was three years old, his mother died unexpectedly, also leaving behind his father, the vice-president of an Ogden paint and glass company, and his infant brother. Following the death of this little brother in 1911, Perk moved to South Bend, Indiana, to live with his mother's sister and her husband, who adopted him. Since the couple's natural son was also named Robert, Perk's name was legally changed to Perkins Hillier Campbell—only to be changed again three years later after the Campbells divorced and his aunt

married the county sheriff whose name was Bailey. Perk's natural parents were Glen Hillier (1882–1959) and Frances Georgianna Perkins (1884–1909). Perk's adoptive parents were Charles Elmer Bailey (1884–1947) and Louise Jane Perkins (1881–1967). Louise's first husband was Robert S. Campbell (1879–1960). Perk was an honor student during his years in the South Bend public schools, and he excelled in college as well. During his senior year at the University of Pennsylvania, he was recognized as an outstanding leader of his class when he was inducted into the Friars Senior Society.

90 **Talon's director of design:** *South Bend Tribune*, 7 March 1946.

90 **Talon Company:** During his employment with Talon, Perkins Bailey held nineteen patents, mainly for men's jackets.

91 **final vacation trip:** On the passenger list of the S. S. *Monarch of Bermuda*, which docked in New York on July 29, 1939, John and Perk listed the same home address.

91 **1940 federal census:** The enumeration of 4 East 64 Street, a seven-unit apartment house built in 1900, was completed on April 8. Perk Bailey's monthly rent was $87. Living in the same apartment building was down-on-her-luck B-movie actress Adrienne Ames, most recently divorced from film actor Bruce Cabot.

91 ***New Faces of 1940*:** *New York Times*, 22 February 1940.

91 **it was common knowledge:** Alexander interview, 1987.

91 **"In those days":** Coburn interview, 5 March 2014.

92 **casual topic of conversation":** Mann, *Behind the Screen*, p. 30.

92 **"greatest musical accompanist":** Shapiro, *Nothing Like a Dame*, p. 29.

92 **"perhaps had never been asked":** Irvin, p. 33.

92 **"drenched in gay culture":** Mann, *Behind the Screen*, p. 30.

92 **"gay in a world that didn't accept it":** Bryant email, 2018.

92 **"an artistic and high-living cafe society crowd":** *Washington Post*, 21 August 1983.

92 **snapshot:** Contained in a 1944 Valentine card made by Alice for John, APC, Box 1, Folder 1.

92 **Don had remarried Doris Haverstock:** Don and Doris married for the second time on June 29, 1936, in Arnolds Park, Iowa. Shirley Ann Herring (1927–2009) was born in Omaha. Daniel

Granville Herring (1940–2007) was born in Los Angeles, and Linda Sue Herring was born in Long Beach. Linda believes that John encouraged Don to remarry Doris. Together they shared a happy life until Don passed away from a heart attack in 1968.

92 **infectious arthritis:** While infectious arthritis is listed on Dolly Herring's death certificate as the immediate cause of death, family members claim that she was secretly suffering from cancer. The day after her burial, John was talking with Dolly's sister Nelle McKee in the Herrings' Omaha home when she suffered a debilitating stroke. Nelle would die two years later in Stuart, Iowa.

93 **Libby Holman:** Alice Pearce to John Rox, 30 October 1942.

93 **"I did fall down on your departure":** *Ibid.*

93 **"hit an all-time low":** *Ibid.*

93 **"you and I can drink them":** *Ibid.*

Chapter Ten

94 **Technician 5th Grade:** This rank carried the same weight as that of a corporal.

94 **Its mission:** Letter from Keli Schmid, 10th Mountain Division Resource Center, Denver Public Library, to FT, 17 June 2019.

94 **Pando Valley:** "How the WWII 10th Mountain Division Was Formed," *10th Mountain Division Info*, http://10thmountaindivisioninfo.com/wwii-10th-mountain-division/, accessed 29 June 2019.

94 **Camp Adair in Oregon:** Postcard from Bob Herring to Pvt. John Rox, 14 December 1942, APC.

94 **Bob Perry:** *Harrisburg Evening News*, 18 June 1943.

94 **family members engaged in warfare:** Alice's three first cousins were all females, but the oldest, Thelma Pearce White (1900–1949), had a son, William Pearce White (1924–2015), who fought as a member of the 1st Marine Raider Battalion during WWII. Alice had no first cousins on her mother's side.

94 **"[n]ever did anything but collect commissions":** *The Billboard*, 24 April 1948.

95 **"society chantoozie":** *Pottstown Mercury*, 28 June 1943.

95 **nightclub proprietor Herbert Jacoby:** Vernon Rice, "Wherever Alice Goes So Goes 'The Girl'," *New York Post*, 28 January 1948, p. 41. Herbert Jacoby (1899–1972), a native of Paris, immigrated to New York in 1937 and opened Le Ruban Bleu,

a supper club on 56th Street, where, according to writer James Gavin, he "brought together a truly cosmopolitan group of performers and audiences." On April 14, 1943, he opened The Blue Angel, remaining until 1962 when he sold his interest to Max Gordon.

95 **Gus Schirmer:** Gustave Schirmer (1918–1992) was born in Manhattan one year and two days after Alice Pearce was born. Professionally, he was known as Gus Schirmer Jr. He made his theatrical debut in *New Faces of 1934* and then spent four seasons at the Pasadena Playhouse. In 1944 and 1945, he was the producer-manager of the Stamford Theatre, where he was responsible for Clare Booth Luce's acting debut in Bernard Shaw's *Candida*. He was never married.

95 *Look, Boys!...Girls!:* *New York Daily News*, 9 April 1943.

95 **"It was a wonderful experience":** "Alice Pearce In U. S. O. Revue," PE, 25 November 1943. Alice continued to appear in the revue throughout 1944 and as late as February 1945, when she performed at Camp Shanks, near Orangetown, New York, the largest army embarkation camp used during the war.

96 **"delicious filet mignon":** *Ibid.*

96 **excelled her work:** Freedley, p. 3. Alice, Imogene Coca, Celeste Holm, and others continued to perform in Schirmer's revue throughout 1944 and into 1945. Her friend Bus Davis wrote the music for the songs they performed, while Miles White donated sketches for the costumes.

96 **"I don't think we pleased the boys":** Hal Humphrey, "She's Bewitched by Toothy Grin," *Los Angeles Times*, 16 December 1964, p. 18.

96 **"Alice always made fun of her looks":** Wilson interview.

97 **"all the money she could get her hands on":** Hawkins, *op.cit.*

97 **auditioned in New York:** Joseph F. Dinneen, "Satirist Alice Pearce," *Boston Globe*, 20 March 1944, p. 15.

97 **Arki Yavensonne:** Born Arcadie Yavensohn in Vilna (today the capital of Lithuania) in 1892, during the days of the Russian Empire, Arki immigrated to the United States in 1911 after spending much of his youth in Paris. By the time Alice auditioned for him, he had been in the hotel business for thirty years. In 1955, he died of a sudden heart attack in Los Angeles at the Hotel Clark, for which he was director of sales.

97 **Satire Room:** In 1943, the cover charge at the Satire Room was $2.50 (roughly $37.00 in 2019 dollars), and no drink was less than 90 cents, even Coca-Cola. Yavensonne proudly proposed it as the most expensive club in the country.

97 **"combs the field of entertainment":** *Boston Globe*, 29 September 1943.

97 **white carnation in his lapel:** *Boston Globe*, 13 January 1942.

97 **seventy-five dollars per week:** *The Billboard*, 24 April 1948.

97 **seated only thirty-eight:** *Boston Globe*, 29 September 1943.

97 **"The tables were so close":** Barclay, *op. cit.*

97 **"Progressive education":** Dinneen, p. 15.

97 **"weak":** *Sarah Lawrence College Alumnae Magazine*, Spring 1949.

97 **"really terrible":** Hawkins, *op. cit.*

97 **supporting Tallulah Bankhead:** *Brooklyn Daily Eagle*, 4 June 1944. Bankhead was paid $3000 for the week's work, "a transaction that may not have left any profit but which at least drew public attention to [Schirmer's] project and paid dividends later," according to syndicated New York journalist Jack Gaver.

97 **fluency in French—all dialects, no less:** Alice Pearce, 1961 resume, author's collection.

98 **John Hoysradt:** Hoysradt (1905-1991), a member of Orson Welles' Mercury Theatre, would change his professional name to John Hoyt in 1945, when his lengthy Hollywood film career began.

98 **"satirical impersonators":** *Brooklyn Daily Eagle*, 18 June 1944.

98 **"decidedly offkey":** *Pittsburgh Sun-Telegraph*, 25 June 1944. Garland dismissed Hoysradt's performance from five years earlier in *The Man Who Came to Dinner*, in which he played Beverly Carlton, a character inspired by the real-life persona of Noël Coward. "John Hoysradt seems destined to be as Noelly as possible for the rest of his career. This is a shame, for they tell me he's quite something up around the nightclubs, laying them low . . . He certainly didn't lay them low last Monday night in Stamford. He was an entertainer rather than an actor."

98 **"shrieked happily":** *New York Daily News*, 22 June 1944.

98 **Hoysradt himself was gay:** Grondahl, *Mayor Corning*, p. 100.

99 **"Alice Pearce received an ovation":** *Stamford Advocate*, 20 June 1944.

99 **Laird Cregar:** Cregar (1913-1944) died just five months following the Strand engagement. During 1941 and 1942, he had lived at 8659 Holloway Plaza Drive in West Hollywood, four doors away from 8629 Holloway Drive, where Alice Pearce lived from 1962 to 1965. See Gregory William Mank, *Laird Cregar: A Hollywood Tragedy*, McFarland & Co., Inc., 2018.

99 **Mary Wickes:** Born Mary Isabella Wickenhauser (1910-1995) in St. Louis, Wickes' professional career spanned sixty-two years, from 1933 to 1995. She worked with Alice Pearce four times between 1961 and 1963. They often played the same type of roles, which sometimes resulted with less discerning viewers mistaking Wickes as the actress who played Gladys Kravitz on *Bewitched*.

99 **"that ultimately defined her":** Taravella, *Mary Wickes*, p. 74.

99 **Cregar lacked the draw:** *Variety*, 18 July 1944.

99 **"lacked the smoothness":** *Stamford Advocate*, 11 July 1944.

99 **Dr. George K. Strode:** George King Strode (1886-1958), born in Chadds Ford, Pennsylvania, graduated from the School of Medicine, University of Pennsylvania. He received the degree of Master of Public Health from Harvard in 1927. In 1919, he married Elizabeth Coombs, a medaled First World War nurse who died in 1937. During most of the 1930s, Strode had been the head of the Paris office of the Rockefeller Foundation. At the time of his marriage to Josephine Clark Dillard, he had been decorated by the governments of Norway, Denmark, Bulgaria, Portugal, France, Romania, and Sweden.

99 **"woman of charm and personal magnetism":** PE, 17 December 1964.

100 **"Josephine was one of my favorite people":** Williams interview.

100 **wedding ceremony:** PE, 6 July 1944. The ceremony was performed by the Rev. Dr. Theodore Cuyler Speers of the Central Presbyterian Church. Josephine wore an afternoon dress of grey-blue crepe with hat and accessories of honey brown. Her shoulder bouquet was made of tiger orchids. The *Perry Enterprise* did not mention if Alice attended the ceremony. She very likely was required to remain in Stamford for rehearsals that day. Josephine and Dr. Strode made their home at 53 East 66th Street in New York.

100 **V-1 bomb explosion:** The National City Bank of New York, Monthly Letter

Number 171, from the Head Office to All Managers, Overseas Division, December 1946, APC.

100 **honorable discharge papers:** John J. Rox, Honorable Discharge, Army of the United States, 5 January 1945. APC.

100 **"My Valentine Agency":** 1944 Valentine card made by Alice for John, APC.

101 **singing and dancing lessons:** *Sarah Lawrence Alumnae Magazine*, January 1946.

101 **"that granddaddy of the stage":** *Vanity Fair*, February 2018.

101 **"classical dance, jazz, farce, and heart":** Bloom, *Broadway Musicals*, p. 241.

101 **Oliver Smith:** A native of Wisconsin, Oliver Lemuel Smith (1918–1994) designed dozens of Broadway musicals, films, and operas. He was nominated for twenty-five Tony Awards and won ten. In the early 1960s, he redesigned the ballroom of New York's famous Waldorf-Astoria Hotel. Carol Channing, in her 2002 memoir *Just Lucky I Guess*, described Smith as a "long, lean glamour boy, a beautiful, brilliant man with manly grace." Smith died of emphysema in New York City.

101 **Paul Feigay:** Manhattan native Paul Anton Feigenbaum (1918–1983) produced other Broadway shows, such as *Billion Dollar Baby* and *Me and Molly*. In the 1950s, he produced the award-winning television series *Omnibus*. He died in Brewster, New York.

101 **Smith thought the piece:** Mikotowicz, *Oliver Smith: A Bio-Bibliography*, p. 4.

101 **Bernstein then convinced Smith and Robbins:** Propst, *They Made Us Happy*, p. 20. Propst's book, a history of Comden and Green's musicals and movies, provides a detailed account of the evolution of *On the Town*.

101 **"We were all twenty-five years old":** Oja, *Bernstein Meets Broadway*, p. 89. George Abbott, smelling success, agreed to direct and was responsible for fine-tuning the script.

101 **"whirlwind tour":** Propst, p. 23.

101 **"giddily portray":** *Ibid.*, p. 26.

103 **Lucy Schmeeler:** Broadway historians Ken Bloom and Frank Vlastnik point out that the names of *On the Town*'s characters reveal Comden and Green's playful imagination." Besides Lucy Schmeeler, there are Pitkin W. Bridgework, Waldo Figment, and Maude P. Dilly. Interestingly, Alice Pearce's character was originally named "Ida Schmeeler," according to an early draft of the script, found in the APC.

103 **bronchial condition:** *Sarah Lawrence College Alumnae Magazine*, Spring 1949.

103 **raw onions:** *On the Town* souvenir program, 1945, p. 12.

103 **"a great director":** Rice, p.41.

103 **Abbott saw fit to praise Alice:** Abbott, *Mister Abbott*, p. 200.

103 **"nothing role":** Rex Reed, "The Movie Was Better: *On the Town* Revival Erases No Golden Memories of MGM Magic," *Observer*, https://observer.com/2014/10/the-movie-was-better-on-the-town-revival-erases-no-golden-memories-of-mgm-magic/, accessed 19 July 2019. Reed, unhappily reviewing the 2014 revival, compared it point by point to the MGM film, without missing "the girl with the cold": "As sneezing Lucy Schmeeler, Hildy's roommate and intended date for Gabey, the great Alice Pearce beefed up the role and stole the show in an arresting number called 'You Can Count on Me.' In the original production, Lucy is a nothing role and she doesn't even sing."

103 **"made up almost entirely of unknowns":** Mordden, *Beautiful Mornin'*, p. 129.

104 **Nancy Walker:** Born in Philadelphia as Anna Myrtle Swoyer and called "Nan" as a child growing up in New York, Walker (1922–1992) was the daughter of vaudevillian acrobat Dewey Barto. Auditioning for a straight role in *Best Foot Forward* in 1941, she sang one of her favorite melancholy numbers which produced a loud laugh from director George Abbott. He then had a comedy role ("Blind Date") written into the show for her. After *On the Town*, Walker appeared in thirteen other Broadway shows, but her greatest fame was attained on television's *Rhoda* and as "Rosie" on the Bounty Paper Towel commercials.

104 **"that incredible gnome":** *Chicago Sun-Times*, 2 April 1946.

104 **"Sainted Alice Pearce":** Letter from Cris Alexander to FT, 4 October 1986.

104 **Cris Alexander:** Born January 14, 1920, as Allen Murry Smith, Cris was the only child of Allen Ticer Smith and his wife Mary Hunt Murry. Both parents were native Mississippians; among Cris' distinguished distant relatives were William Faulkner and Tallulah Bankhead. His father, a newspaper publisher, owned the Mid-West Printing Company, retiring at age fifty. Cris graduated from Tulsa's Central High School in 1937, and for one semester he attended the University of Oklahoma. For a brief time, when he first came

to New York, he shared his apartment with the character actress Mabel Paige.

104 **"thought that they were waiting"**: Robert Hayes, "Cris Alexander the Great," *Interview*, July 1980, p 36.

104 **"But it was no soap"**: Robert Francis, "Cris Alexander Photographed Actors While Waiting to Act," *Brooklyn Daily Eagle*, 2 September 1945.

105 **"That's where I got my first real experience"**: *Ibid.*

105 **"She auditioned"**: Alexander interview, 1987.

105 **"About some rare productions"**: Jane Klain, "Cris Alexander: In Tune, In Focus," *Show Music*, Winter 1994, p. 36.

105 **"she was called 'Peeps'"**: Alexander interview, 1987.

105 **"Sister"**: Alexander letter, 1986.

105 **"I'd rather pick them myself"**: Alexander interview, 7 February 2003.

105 **"ultimate hard-luck house"**: Mordden, *Beautiful Mornin'*, p. 130.

105 **"most feeble bookings"**: *Ibid.*

105 **December 28, 1944:** Margaret Pearce and family friend Jack Wright attended the opening night performance. Their ticket stubs, pasted into Margaret's scrapbook, show that they paid $12.00 each for their seats. Bob Pearce and Josephine Strode missed opening night. He was still working in Paris, and she was recovering from a recent operation.

105 **Walter Winchell:** *Pittsburgh Sun-Telegraph*, 2 January 1945.

105 **"The main thing was the music"**: Klain, p. 36.

107 **"It looks spick and span"**: *New York Daily News*, 5 August 1945.

107 **"to no end"**: *Sarah Lawrence Alumnae Magazine*, January 1946.

107 **"Alice Pearce is kept backstage"**: *New York Daily News*, 5 August 1945.

107 **"Have you ever seen me in my green leotard?"**: Freedley, p. 4.

107 **"insufficient business"**: *New York Times*, 23 April 1946.

107 **"Alice Pearce makes a lot out of the role"**: *Chicago Sun-Times*, 2 April 1946.

Chapter Eleven

108 **hand selected a supporting cast:** *Montreal Gazette*, 22 June 1946. Susan Thompson was Alice's replacement on the tour, which included stops in Ottawa, Montreal, and Boston.

108 **"high-comedy matinee idols"**: Israel, *Miss Tallulah Bankhead*, p. 245.

108 **"bring tenderness"**: *Boston Traveler*, 23 July 1946.

108 **offstage love affair:** Israel, p. 246.

108 **police were called in:** *New York Times*, 22 June 1946.

108 **Alice pitched in:** Freedley, p. 4.

108 **largest advance sale:** *Massillon Evening Independent*, 27 June 1946.

108 **"one of the highest scales"**: *Newark Star-Ledger*, 6 June 1946.

108 **"a quiet, retiring missy"**: *New York Post*, 25 June 1946.

109 **"put her in a good humor"**: Freedley, p. 3.

109 **"be on their best behavior"**: Israel, p. 246.

109 **"thousands of her fans were haunted"**: *Screenland*, March 1949.

109 **Ethel Merman:** OWH, 13 March 1949.

109 **Men's Wear magazine:** *South Bend Tribune*, 7 March 1946.

109 **152 Bayview Avenue:** Suffolk County, New York, Deed 2559, Pages 570-71, Mary F. Jensen (grantor) to Perkins H. Bailey (grantee), 25 April 1946.

109 **John C. Smith:** Email message from Northport historian Steven King to FT, 17 July 2019.

110 **Peggy Watson:** Peggy Irene Watson (1922–2015) was born in Clearfield, Pennsylvania. Her parents were officers in the Salvation Army, and as a child Peggy sang with them on street corners. Elizabeth Van Winkle, a prominent voice teacher from Cleveland, happened to hear her and immediately offered Peggy a scholarship in voice. This association continued through Peggy's public-school education. Then she was awarded a full scholarship to Juilliard School of Music, graduating in 1946. In 1949, she married William J. Coburn (1913–1985), a master's graduate in composition from the Eastman School of Music. In 1956, the Coburns moved to the Los Angeles area, where Peggy's contralto voice became well-known through her many appearances at the Hollywood Bowl, including the yearly Rodgers and Hammerstein summer music series and Easter Sunday sunrise services. Peggy also sang with symphony orchestras at Carnegie Hall and Constitution Hall in Washington, DC.

111 **"One night in 1946"**: Coburn interview, 21 February 2014.

111 **"He was going with Alice part of the time"**: *Ibid.* By the end of 1946, John Rox seems to have been back in the picture because he appears in a snapshot taken on Christmas Day at Bob and Margaret Pearce's apartment at 29 Sutton Place South. In the photo with him are Alice, her parents, and Josephine and George Strode. Margaret's red leather photo album, APC.

111 **"It doesn't surprise me"**: Coburn interview, 5 March 2014.

111 **house dated back to 1833:** Hamilton Greene, *Birth of a Mountain Town*, Whitingham commemorative booklet, 1966. The Wheeler house, presently bearing the address of 428 Town Hill Road, was built for original owner Henry Goodnow (1809-1889), a local merchant. It stands very near the site where Mormon leader Brigham Young (1801-1877) was born. The pre-Civil War home where George and Josephine Strode lived still stands on Chase Hill Road.

111 **Eleven red barns:** From a description Margaret Pearce wrote on a piece of tree bark and mounted in her scrapbook, APC.

111 **offered $50,000:** Author's interview with Whitman James Wheeler, grandson of Whitman Jesse Wheeler, 13 June 2013. Wheeler estimated that the property acquired by Bob and Margaret Pearce totaled only 150 acres. According to Margaret Pearce's notes, the land transaction took place on July 27, 1946.

112 **military discharge:** Mark Lawrence's military service almost ended before it began. Three months after his enlistment, he was supposed to ship out to New Caledonia on the S. S. *Juneau*, but luckily for him he missed the departure. One day later, the light cruiser was torpedoed by the Japanese. Almost 700 men aboard perished, including the famous five Sullivan brothers of Waterloo, Iowa. Lawrence's parents thought he was onboard, and for three weeks, until they received news otherwise, believed he was dead. Lawrence eventually made it to Noumea, where he staged his original musical, *South Seas Scandals*. His Princeton classmate Edward Coale, who happened to catch the show in 1943, recalled: "It was a smash hit. I found it extremely nostalgic as Mark had incorporated many of the tunes he composed for the Triangle show, senior year, including that wonderful and memorable 'Keep 'Em Rolling, Keep 'Em Flying.'" Lawrence earned five battle stars

and other decorations. See *The Princeton Class of 1942 During World War II: The Individual Stories*, Impressions Book and Journal Services, Inc., 2000.

112 *It Sez Here*: Sidney Fields, "When Money Is No Obstacle," *New York Daily Mirror*, 25 June 1947.

112 **"she needed his lyrics"**: Joseph Mackey, "Silver-Spoon Scions Do Satirical Didos in Darkdom's Dipsy-Doodle Duo," *New York Sun*, 24 January 1948.

112 **"I was anxious to rectify"**: *Sarah Lawrence Alumnae Magazine*, Spring 1949.

112 **"senses of humor were identical"**: "The Mad Miss Pearce," anonymous unpublished article, Billy Rose Theatre Division, New York Public Library.

112 **live-in governess:** 1930 U. S. Federal Census, Washington, District of Columbia, Enumeration District No. 388, Sheet 72A, 3900 Nebraska Avenue, Lines 7-15.

112 **home state of South Carolina:** Marie Torre, "Pearce and Lawrence Cure Their Own Ham," *New York World-Telegram*, 23 October 1947.

112 **portraying an elf:** Mackey, *op. cit.*

112 **"Some people are born funny"**: Fields, *op. cit.*

112 **"When Alice and I decided"**: Torre, *op. cit.*

113 **"It was his taste"**: James Gavin, *Intimate Nights*, p. 59.

113 **"usually indisputable"**: *Ibid.*

114 **"the Prince of Darkness"**: Lorraine Gordon, *Alive at the Village Vanguard*, p. 107.

114 **"acts that were looking to go places"**: Max Gordon, *Live at the Village Vanguard*, p. 66.

114 **an old carriage house:** Lorraine Gordon, p. 108.

114 **"If you lived in the neighborhood"**: Max Gordon, p. 68.

114 **Max Gordon:** Not to be confused with the Broadway producer by the same name, Gordon (1903–1989) founded the Village Vanguard as a cabaret in 1934. He gave major career boosts to Judy Holliday, Betty Comden, Adolph Green, Pearl Bailey, and Lenny Bruce.

114 **"But the club itself had an electricity"**: Gavin, p. 57.

114 **"an adorable tiny stage"**: Lorraine Gordon, p. 108.

114 **"fine talent with commercial appeal"**: Gavin, p. 57.

114 **$300 per week:** The terms of the original agreement which Alice and Mark signed were reiterated in a later contract with Jacoby, dated 25 August 1947, which is now in the author's possession. (In

2019 dollars, the weekly pay would equal approximately $3450.)

114 **"convey that she is insanely happy"**: H. H. Wildman, "Sutton Place Pixie," *New York Times Magazine*, 2 November 1947, p. 28.

115 **"to the screams of a hep audience"**: "The Mad Miss Pearce," *op. cit.*

115 **"Bikini Atoll hair-do"**: Freedley, p. 3.

115 **"In 1937, Mother had ordered the dress"**: *New York Herald Tribune*, 24 March 1948.

116 **mink head bandage from Betty**: Wildman, p. 30. At one point, Betty La Branche's mother suggested that maybe the minks should be returned. "I told her," Alice said severely, "that I think of them as pets."

116 **first paycheck from *New Faces of 1943***: *Newsweek*, 6 October 1947.

116 **fradous**: Mackey, *op. cit.* Mark Lawrence told journalist Mackey that he borrowed "fradou," the word used for "sweater" by the small son of his sister's black cook.

116 **"see something funny in any situation"**: Margaret Mara, "She's Only a Banker's Daughter—But What a Role She Coined!" *Brooklyn Daily Eagle*, 27 February 1948, p. 13.

117 **"The most exciting thing"**: *New York Herald Tribune*, April 30, 1947.

117 **"weird mangling of song and words"**: *Brooklyn Daily Eagle*, 29 April 1947. Sheaffer preferred Blue Angel singer Rose Murphy—"a buxom Negro woman with a squeaky voice that belies her size and the jolliest face you've ever seen"—over Alice.

117 **"In a café year"**: *New York World-Telegram*, 16 June 1947.

117 **"the purlieus of night club life"**: George Freedley, "Stage Today: Alice Pearce Scores Again," *New York Morning Telegraph*, 6 May 1947.

118 **extended their engagement**: "Zany Team at Blue Angel Writing New Musical," *Brooklyn Daily Eagle*, 11 May 1947.

118 **Alexis "Lex" Thompson**: *New York Evening Post*, 1 May 1947.

118 **"a cold, shrewd businessman"**: Gavin, p. 26.

118 **personal management contract**: *Variety*, 14 May 1947.

118 **"counsel and advise"**: Photocopy of personal management contract between Alice Pearce and Herbert Jacoby, 7 June 1947, Alice Pearce clippings file, Billy Rose Theatre Collection, The New York Public Library. Alice and Mark's first Blue Angel engagement closed on July 3, 1947.

118 **Phil Gordon:** Born Philemon Hodges Gulley Jr. (1916–2010) in Meridian, Mississippi, Gordon served in the US Navy during WWII before performing with the USO. Following his Blue Angel stint, he toured as a jazz musician, settling in California where he performed small roles on TV shows such as *The Beverly Hillbillies*, *Petticoat Junction*, and *Green Acres*. He died in Mobile at age 94.

119 **Gordon considered pure "genius":** Letter from Phil Gordon to FT, 6 October 1988.

119 **piano "whimsyist":** *Chicago Tribune*, 31 July 1955.

119 **"She sang in this real high, Mrs. Roosevelt type voice":** Author's interview with Phil Gordon, 30 October 1988.

119 **"Alice was also one of the dearest":** Gordon letter, 1988.

119 **"We must have taken a thousand pictures":** Alexander letter, 1986.

119 **"That was where she used to live":** Alexander interview, 1987.

120 **"She was wearing my best lace dress":** *Ibid.*

120 **Alice was courted:** *New York Times*, 18 June 1947.

120 **delete Alice's part:** *New York Times*, 30 July 1947. *Free for All* was renamed *Bonanza Bound!* which died during tryouts in Philadelphia in December 1947.

122 **"not content just to play in nightclubs":** Torre, *op. cit.*

122 **"Alice was one of the most charming":** Letter from Hugh Martin to FT, 4 April 2003.

122 **George Abbott paid Mark Lawrence:** Original agreement signed and dated July 15, 1947, from the estate of Arnold Weissberger, now in the author's collection.

122 **snapped photos of Alice:** Weissberger, *Famous Faces*, pp. 24–25.

122 **vacationing without John:** *Kingston Daily Gleaner*, 19 January 1947.

122 **"They had really fallen apart anyway":** Alexander interview, 1987.

122 **Alice and Mark signed a contract:** Original contract, dated 25 August 1947, and signed by Alice, Mark, and Jacoby, from the estate of Arnold Weissberger, now in the author's collection.

122 **"capacity crowd":** *Syracuse Herald-Journal*, 9 September 1947.

122 **they packed the house:** *The Billboard* reported on 20 September 1947: "Reopening of small East Side room jammed it to the doors. Outer bar did a big biz from customers waiting to get in the

main room. Show itself was on par with previous bills here. The use of smart talent, rather than name talent has proven successful, and from a customer viewpoint eminently satisfactory. Alice Pearce, back on a return date, was the same unpredictable mad comedienne. Her routines, bouncyish, bubblish, affairs, salted down with bits of business, pulled some of the heftiest yocks heard in a long time. Phil Gordon, the fresh looking, crewcut kid, also doing a return date, is a far cry from the scared looking youngster who opened here two seasons ago. He still has that Southern drawl, but with it he's added a platform polish that heightens his infectious personality and now makes him a real seller. Gordon's voice isn't distinguished, but it's pleasant. With his piano playing, incidentally of a high order, he had them in his hands, winding up with a terrific mitt."

123 **"Lest you be intimidated"**: *New York Herald Tribune*, 10 September 1947.

123 **"Once in a blue moon"**: *Cue*, 20 September 1947.

123 **"Alice Pearce presents herself"**: *The New Yorker*, 4 October 1947.

124 **With the rave reviews coming in each week:** *The Billboard* wrote on November 15, 1947: "Alice Pearce, with Mark Lawrence on the piano, is still one of the maddest acts around. Appeal, however, is limited and requires an audience that can laugh at deliberate nonsense. Gal's high-pitched giggle is at first startling, even embarrassing. Later it becomes infectious and pulls yocks regularly."

124 **a world-famous playwright:** *Scranton Times-Tribune*, 4 October 1947.

124 **"a noble artist":** Wildman, p. 30.

124 **"She had just gotten back from Fire Island":** Gordon interview. (Actually, Alice had acquired her suntan during her week at East Hampton.)

125 **Beethoven's Fifth:** *Newsweek*, 6 October 1947.

125 **"I just don't want a new dress":** *New York Herald Tribune*, 24 March 1948.

125 **"the horn might knock over":** Wildman, p. 28.

125 **"I received some fans":** Mackey, *op. cit.*

125 **Jacoby hired a new janitor:** *New York Herald-Tribune*, 12 November 1947.

125 **her first show began at eleven-thirty:** Nina Phillips Washburn, "Goon Girl," *Sarah Lawrence Alumni Magazine*, Fall 1947.

125 **Some [customers]:** Barclay, *op. cit.*

125 **fellow who stood up and urinated:** Gavin, p. 63.

125 **favorite work to date:** *Sarah Lawrence College Alumnae Magazine*, Spring 1949.

125 **Naturally [we] feel much closer to it:** Barclay, *op. cit.*

125 **"Next to the roar of the ocean":** Wildman, p. 28.

Chapter Twelve

126 **an idea conceived by choreographer Jerome Robbins:** *Windsor Star*, 13 December 1945.

126 **"brash and manipulative":** Vaill, *Somewhere: The Life of Jerome Robbins*, p. 134.

126 **"sprang back to life, resuscitated":** *Ibid.*, p. 145.

126 **Nancy Walker had been seriously considered:** *Windsor Star*, 4 July 1946.

126 **"tough-talking, tenderhearted, unaffected broad":** Vaill, p. 135.

126 **"a camped-up caricature of Lucia Chase":** *Ibid.*, p. 146. Lucia Chase founded the Ballet Theatre as its principal dancer and prime financial backer.

126 **"The role was tailor-made":** *Ibid.*, p. 147.

126 **aggressively pushed:** Martin, *Hugh Martin*, p. 269.

126 **Harold Lang:** Harold Richard Lang (1920–1985), born in Daly City, California, studied at the San Francisco School of Ballet before touring the country with the Ballet Russe de Monte Carlo. At age 22, he joined New York's Ballet Theatre as a means to begin a theatrical career, which included nine Broadway musicals including *Kiss Me, Kate* and *Pal Joey*. Alcoholism essentially ended his career as a performer, and for the final fifteen years of his life, he taught dance at California State University in Chico, where at 64 he died from—according to the official record—metastatic carcinoma caused by pancreatic cancer, and not from AIDS as speculated by Gore Vidal in *Palimpsest* (p. 132).

127 **former lover Laurents:** Laurents, *Original Story*, p. 47.

127 **having affairs with both Nancy Walker and Gore Vidal:** Vidal, *Palimpsest*, p. 151. According to Vidal, Lang had once been the lover of Leonard Bernstein. Vidal's biographer Fred Kaplan (*Gore Vidal*, Doubleday, 1999) asserts that Lang and Vidal met in August 1947 when Lang was performing in *Best Foot Forward* with Alice Pearce at East Hampton. Presumably this is when Nancy Walker pursued Lang. Lang and Vidal, however, continued their affair after Labor Day when they flew to Bermuda for a month's stay. Walker's sexual pursuits, which included Robbins, were rather notorious in those days, according to Cris Alexander, who told Robbins biographer Greg Law-

rence (*Dance with Demons*, G. P. Putnam's Sons, 2001): "Nancy went after every queen in reaching distance. All she had to do was catch sight of an attractive gay man and she wanted to fuck him. She had an appalling number of conquests."

127 **"Build that part up"**: Martin, p. 272. Kay Thompson, a radio singer who had become M-G-M's top vocal arranger/coach, introduced Martin to his future songwriting partner, Ralph Blane. Martin considered Thompson his guru.

127 **"a lovely Southern girl"**: Wildman, p. 30.

127 **"a revolutionary standard"**: Vaill, p. 147.

127 **Actors' Equity standard contract**: Original document, dated 10 November 1947 and signed by Alice Pearce and George Abbott, author's collection.

128 **By the time of her mother's death**: *Passaic Herald-News*, 13 February 1942.

128 **"He would give me money each day"**: *Brooklyn Citizen*, 2 May 1942.

128 **"jazzy swagger. . . [spoke] a breezy, highly specialized language"**: *Ibid.*

128 **"wildly profane"**: Martin, p. 148.

128 **"needs only the addition of a cigar"**: *Sioux City Journal*, 14 March 1948.

129 **"I told her that not since Alice Pearce"**: *Poughkeepsie Journal*, 18 August 1976.

129 **"Not since I worked with Alice Pearce"**: *Hartford Courant*, 13 November 1977.

129 **"No critique of *Look, Ma, I'm Dancin'!*"**: *Camden Courier-Post*, 14 January 1948.

130 **"some ancient and rotting finery"**: *New York Daily News*, 8 February 1948.

130 **"has nothing to do with anything or anyone"**: *New Orleans Times-Picayune*, 8 February 1948.

130 **"It was not really as strong"**: Martin letter.

130 **the soundtrack was hurriedly recorded**: *Ibid.*

130 **"The New Look"**: In February 1948, Alice performed "The New Look" at dress designer Adele Simpson's fashion show for the New York press. It is not known if she wore the shower curtain and sausages.

130 ***Look, Ma, I'm Dancin'!* opened on Broadway at the Adelphi**: In the audience that night also were Alice's parents, her grandmother Sallie Clark, her aunt Josephine Strode, and "Uncle" Jack Wright, according to Margaret Pearce's notation in a brown leather scrapbook, Box 1, APC.

130 **"I was much too uncritical of my own work"**: Martin, p. 271.

130 **"a grotesque comedienne"**: *Pittsburgh Press*, 15 February 1948.

130 **"It is my morbid"**: *New York Evening Post*, 30 January 1948.

130 **"Three-Eye League Paula Laurence"**: Watts jokingly alters the spelling of the Three-I League (Illinois-Indiana-Iowa League), a minor league baseball organization. Paula Laurence was a Broadway comedienne who sometimes performed at Herbert Jacoby's Le Ruban Bleu, specializing in parodies of popular songs while wearing fruit and flowers on her head and utilizing a box of props.

130 **"Just at a time when things were beginning to roll"**: Abbott, p. 222.

130 **"The Adelphi is much too big"**: *New York Daily News*, 30 January 1948.

130 **"Maybe it was the butterflies"**: *The Billboard*, 6 March 1948.

131 **"projected to star proportions"**: *Variety*, 10 March 1948.

131 **splitting $750 per week**: *The Billboard*, 24 April 1948.

131 **"I'd do a breakfast show"**: Mara, p. 13.

131 **"I'd come dashing out of the stage door"**: Barclay, *op. cit.*

132 **"Over at the Blue Angel"**: *The New Yorker*, 17 April 1948.

132 **"they don't seem quite as funny"**: *New York World-Telegram*, 27 March 1948.

132 **"Alice pretended like she was Miss Sallie"**: Williams interview.

132 **"New York Easter Parade"**: *Cue*, 20 March 1948.

132 **"tremendous potentialities"**: *Variety*, 21 April 1948.

132 **"in the same class"**: Gordon letter, 1988.

132 **"helped pave the way"**: Gavin, p. 51.

132 **Imogene Coca**: More than one person confused Alice with Coca, including Lorraine Gordon, the wife of Herbert Jacoby's partner, who frequented the club after her marriage in 1949. Gordon wrote in her 2006 memoir: "I used to sit with Imogene Coca's husband, John Rox. I was always the person to take care of the husbands so they shouldn't sit alone."

133 **"one of the foremost midtown showcases for black talent"**: Gavin, p. 84.

133 **"office boy"**: *Syracuse Post-Standard*, 26 December 1947.

133 **difficulty he'd encountered in getting vocalists to record his songs**: By this point, at least one of

John's songs had been recorded on film. "Ridin' Double" was used in the 1946 Republic Pictures release *Sioux City Sue*, starring Gene Autry and Sterling Holloway. See SH, 5 June 1947.

133 **Harry Noble and Frances King:** *Pittsburgh Post-Gazette*, 29 September 1949.

133 **Clark's recording:** By 1951, fourteen other artists recorded "It's a Big, Wide Wonderful World," including Hildegarde, Larry Green, and Margaret Whiting.

133 **"I know you feel so much better than before":** Letter from Pearl Bailey to John Rox, 29 January 1948, signed "Pearlie Mae," APC. The letter also reveals that Bailey and John may have shared a common interest in Christian Science.

134 **Phil Bloom:** Phillip I. Bloom (1916–1996) was born in the Bronx. Before his military service in WWII, he wrote radio scripts and co-authored a comedy-drama with Jean Dalrymple.

134 **"Society of Tasteful Men":** "How to Sell a Sow's Ear . . . And Throw a Great Party," *Key West Wind*, https://keywestwind.blogspot.com/2012/, accessed 30 September 2019. Franklin Garfield Marshall (1933–2017) formed Reeves Communication which produced successful TV shows such as *Sesame Street*.

134 **"The revulsion against gay life":** Chauncey, *Gay New York*, p. 353.

134 **"laws and regulations were enacted":** *Ibid.,* p. 8.

134 **"Newspapers stepped up publica‑on":** Schanke, *Passing Performances*, pp. 184‾185.

134 **"Senator Joseph McCarthy warned":** Chauncey, pp. 8–9.

134 **"a rarified breed":** Lorraine Gordon, p. 112.

135 **"high quota of homosexual customers":** Gavin, p. 59.

135 **"Nowhere else in popular culture":** Bronski, *Culture Clash,* p .111.

135 **"Every man is in business for himself":** *Springfield Union*, 20 January 1957.

135 **Perk was vacationing alone:** *Palm Beach Post*, 30 January 1948.

135 **"It took John a long time to decide":** Coburn interview, 21 February 2014.

135 **item scooped the day before:** *New York Daily Mirror*, 23 March 1948.

135 **wedding would take place that autumn:** *New York Herald Tribune*, 27 March 1948.

135 **John scratched an accompanying note:** Undated letter from John Rox to Don Herring, LSC.

136 **guest list:** Notes in Margaret Pearce's hand, APC. Margaret also invited Jack Wright and Mr. and Mrs. Jay Arthur Whitecotton, recently returned to the States from Europe where he was the head of the French division of Socony-Mobile Oil Company. The only Clark relations attending, besides Josephine and George Strode, were Margaret's first cousin Gertrude Netherland (who lived in nearby Scarsdale with her husband Elmer Helferich) and her second cousin once removed Edward Alford (an electrical engineer for Bell Telephone, who lived with his wife Alice in New Jersey). Sallie Clark did not return from Missouri to attend the wedding. Likewise, John Rox's stepfather, brother Don, and first cousin Edna Haase were unable to make the trip from the Midwest, but brother Bob and his wife attended the ceremony, along with Bill Coburn and Peggy Watson. Curiously, Cris Alexander was omitted from the guest list, as was Alice's favorite professor, Mary Virginia Heinlein.

136 **June Kent:** A first-generation American, June Kent (1907–2007) was born in Manhattan to an Austrian-born cabinetmaker and his Hungarian wife. The Kuntschke family had also lived in Brooklyn and Yonkers. In 1930, June married bond salesman Charles S. White (1901–1971), remaining with him for at least a decade. Her name change was approved in 1946, but she did not seek a divorce from White until two years later, granted in Reno that year on March 18, 1948. See Birth Certificate #32154, Department of Health, City of New York; Marriage License #21237, Westchester County, New York State Department of Health; Marriage License #14533, New York County, New York State Department of Health.

136 **her husband wanted children while she did not:** Author's interview with Anne Richards, 4 March 2014.

137 **Perk and June applied for their marriage license on May 20:** Alice and John had applied for theirs on May 17, making the Baileys' application appear quite rushed.

138 **"Rumors are quick about a man who marries late":** Laurents, p. 72.

138 **"bearded marriages":** Schanke, p. 11.

138 **such as Guthrie's with stage star Katherine Cornell:** *Ibid.,* p. 198.

138 **"Oh, she was very open about it":** Wilson interview.

138 **"When acknowledged, the facet of sexuality":** Schanke, p. 4.

138 **"There's no question in my mind":** Email message from Linda Swanson to FT, 8 September 2019.

138 **"I do know that she was very, very fond of him":** Wilson interview.

138 **"Oh, how she loved him!":** Alexander interview, 2003.

138 **Alice withdrew from *Look, Ma, I'm Dancin'!*:** Alice's replacement was redhaired Marie Foster, drafted by George Abbott who had directed her in the touring version of *High Button Shoes*.

139 **Collegiate Church of St. Nicholas:** Amid great controversy, the church property was sold in early 1949, and by October of that year, demolition of the structure had begun. Brick by brick the brownstones came down. It took two and one-half months just to demolish the spire. In its place was built the Sinclair Oil Company Building, standing at twenty-six stories.

139 **The living room was decorated:** PE, 27 May 1948.

139 **At John and Alice's sides were Perk and June:** When Perk and June signed as witnesses to John and Alice's marriage, June, who had been Mrs. Perkins Bailey for scarcely a day, signed as "June Kent White," then traced back over it to show her new surname.

139 **"I shall always remember my wonderful wedding":** Letter from Alice Rox to Robert and Margaret Pearce, 31 May 1948, APC.

140 **The menu was fittingly French:** Margaret's wine-colored scrapbook, Box 1, APC.

140 **When [the Pearces] left [France during the first year of Nazi occupation]:** *New York Herald Tribune*, 21 June 1948.

141 **"We have dipped into all your supplies":** Letter from Alice Rox to Robert and Margaret Pearce, 31 May 1948, APC. *Je suis si heureuse* (I am so happy). Monk *et son mari* (Monk and her husband).

141 **Bob and Rae [Herring]:** John's half-brother Robert Eugene Herring (1913–1969) married Rachel Schoessler (1919–2007) on 26 December 1943 in Burley, Idaho. In 1944, they settled in New York City. They divorced in 1949.

141 **"Alice and I thank you for your good wishes":** Letter from John Rox to Marjorie McKee Fitzgerald, 7 June 1948, John Higginbottom collection.

142 **Arthur Barber:** *Des Moines Register*, 10 July 1948. It isn't known if John attended his father's funeral,

but perhaps the four-day span between Barber's death and the services allowed him to travel to Des Moines.

142 **the eminent Barbara Karinska:** Barbara Karinska (1886–1983) was born Varvara Jmoudsky, the daughter of a successful textile manufacturer. She won an Academy Award in 1948 for her costume design for *Joan of Arc*.

142 **"flung westward from czarist Russia by the Bolsheviks":** Bentley, *Costumes by Karinska*, p. 9.

142 **"discoursing earnestly":** *Boston Herald*, 31 August 1948.

143 **"his turned-up nose":** *Boston Globe*, 31 August 1948.

143 **"two 'tetched' individuals":** *Boston Herald*, 31 August 1948.

143 **"Pistachio":** Titled "Ice Cream Song," a typewritten copy exists in the APC.

143 **"proves herself a splendid pantomimist":** *New York World Telegram*, 16 September 1948, clipping, APC.

143 **"Alice Pearce gets in a good evening's work:** *New York Sun*, 16 September 1948, clipping, APC.

144 **"*Small Wonder* team is captained":** *Pottstown Mercury*, 19 October 1948.

144 **"Alice Pearce has set her performance":** *New York Morning Telegram*, 11 November 1948, clipping, APC. George Reynolds Freedley (1904–1967), born in Richmond, Virginia, was a former actor, author, librarian, lecturer, educator, and theatre critic. He founded the New York Public Library's theatre collection in 1931, serving as its curator from 1938 until 1965. Freedley, a bachelor who lived at 19 East Fifty-fifth Street, maintained a summer home on Fire Island where he suffered a fall on September 7, 1967, and died four days later in a Bay Shore hospital.

144 **"First of all, a *desire* to make people laugh":** Barclay, *op. cit.*

144 **"From the producer and the director":** *New York Herald Tribune*, 24 October 1948, clipping, APC. (Forty years later when responding to the author, Ewell, unprompted, recounted the same anecdote about Alice's response to the photograph request.)

144 **"In my life time":** Letter from Tom Ewell to FT, 11 April 1988.

145 **"It will probably run until next June":** Letter from John Rox to Shirley Taylor, 6 December 1948, LSC. John reports that the Buddy Clark recording of "It's a Big, Wide, Wonderful World" has not yet been released.

Chapter Thirteen

146 **"television was still the stepchild of radio"**: Krampner, *The Man in the Shadows*, p. 31.

146 **"I was one of a group"**: Misurell, p. 14.

146 **performed part of their act on radio:** Alice and Mark were guest artists on "On Stage America: Paul Whiteman" over WJZ on October 27, 1947, and appeared along with Marlene Dietrich on "We, the People" over WCBS radio on November 4, 1947, per a clipping from the *New York World-Telegram*, APC.

146 **thereafter featured both black and white players:** Brooks, *The Complete Directory to Prime Time Network TV Shows*, p. 87.

146 **"Television couldn't find a funnier entertainer"**: *New York World-Telegram*, 30 June 1948, clipping, APC.

147 **"in her typical dissonant style"**: *Variety*, 2 February 1949.

147 **"It was a little campy"**: Gordon interview.

148 **"a fifteen-minute nonsense"**: *TV Radio Mirror*, September 1965. (Alice would state in the Spring 1949 issue of the Sarah Lawrence *Alumni Magazine* that her own television show ran for seven weeks, but given that she reported to work at M-G-M on March 7, she was undoubtedly in error. The show does appear in newspaper television listings for March 11 and March 18, but perhaps these were kinescope telecasts of previous live telecasts.)

148 **"the Ziegfeld of M-G-M"**: Kobal, *People Will Talk*, p. 635.

148 **"surrounded himself with the finest M-G-M craftsmen"**: Phillips, *Charles Walters*, p. 59.

148 **"first theatrical property to be sold to Hollywood"**: Silverman, *Dancing on the Ceiling: Stanley Donen and His Movies*, p. 108.

148 **"too symphonic"**: Oja, p. 113.

148 **most of the Bernstein score was scrapped:** The dispute regarding the decision to greatly alter the stage version for the film adaptation rages on today. See Silverman (pp. 108–109) for a view supporting Freed's decision. See also Oja (p. 114) for a rationalization which cites America as being in a much different place in 1949 than it was five years earlier.

148 **"tidying up loose business"**: Silverman, pp. 105-106; *Variety*, 26 January 1949.

148 **having seen the stage version of *On the Town* in 1945:** According to Silverman (p. 110), Gene Kelly "told a Bernstein Archive Oral History interviewer that he saw [*On the Town* on] opening night." This seems unlikely because, at the time of the show's debut on December 28, 1944, Kelly was in boot camp at the U. S. Naval Training Center in San Diego. Furthermore, Hedda Hopper reported on December 30 that Kelly had spent the Christmas holidays in Beverly Hills. By January 1, he was back in San Diego.

148 **Kelly wanted Alice to repeat her role:** *Los Angeles Times*, 11 March 1949. Another source asserted that Kelly demanded that Alice be cast as Lucy.

148 **Alice was "going to Hollywood"**: *Camden Courier-Post*, 16 February 1949.

148 **"With Gene as [Gabey]"**: Fordin, *The World of Entertainment*, p. 259.

149 **"to suit Green's own performance style"**: Propst, p. 58.

149 **"assertive female voices"**: Oja, p. 112.

149 **"radiated a boisterous sunniness"**: Propst, p. 58.

149 **surname was changed by a single letter:** Silverman, p. 112.

149 **became a little less one-dimensional:** The character of Pitkin, deemed "too operatic for Hollywood," was dropped, allowing Lucy more screen time.

149 **"Who are you going to replace Alice with?"**: Cimber interview.

149 **"M-G-M feels it has scored a coup"**: *Los Angeles Times*, 11 March 1949.

149 **"Sinatra was as popular as all four Beatles"**: Silverman, p. 113. Kelly and Sinatra were just two of Metro's illustrious stars who, on February 10, 1949, had gathered on the studio's largest sound stage for a lavish luncheon celebrating M-G-M's twenty-fifth anniversary. Fifty-eight contract players—including Lionel and Ethel Barrymore, Clark Gable, Ava Gardner, Judy Garland, Katharine Hepburn, and Spencer Tracy—were seated on a four-tier dais nearly fifty yards long, where they were served squab stuffed with wild rice. They were joined by 150 members of the press and almost as many sales executives and studio brass.

150 **Alice, accompanied by John, flew to Los Angeles that weekend:** Arrangements had been made by her New York agent Gloria Safier to have a car waiting at the airport to take the Roxes to the hotel handling their reservations. Once their plane landed, Alice and John found no one waiting for them. They took a taxi to the hotel where they stayed during Alice's eight weeks working at

M-G-M. On her last day at the studio, Alice took her packed bags with her, so that she could leave immediately for another hotel in the area where she and John would spend a vacation before going back to New York. She received an urgent message to rush to her agent's west coast office. As Alice was ushered in, the agent rose and said, "Welcome to Hollywood." (By 1949, Safier was an associate of Lillie Messinger, once employed in M-G-M's story department, who had convinced Louis B. Mayer to buy the film rights to *On the Town*.)

150 **rehearsed a total of eighteen days:** University of Southern California, Cinematic Arts Library, Arthur Freed Collection, Box 17, Folder 2 (*On the Town*, Assistant Director's Reports).

150 **Alice's weekly pay was $750:** Silverman, p. 111. Alice received the same weekly pay as contract player Vera-Ellen whose total compensation was $8,875. As for other supporting players, who were largely uncredited, the highest paid "day players" were Bea Benaderet (as the Brooklyn girl on the subway train), whose pay for one day was $300, and Hans Conried (as headwaiter François) who earned $500 for two days' work.

150 **cooch:** a type of dance performed by women that was common in carnivals and fairs and marked by suggestive twisting and shaking of the torso and limbs.

151 **"You Can Count on Me":** Filming this number began on April 21, 1949, and concluded the following day. Alice's final scene, her goodnight kiss from Gene Kelly, was filmed on the morning of April 25. She was called back to the studio to record some dubbing on May 2.

151 **"the classic (under) dog":** Nissen, p. 157.

152 **"Alice was one of the loveliest ladies that one could know":** Letter from Gene Kelly to FT, 18 August 1982.

152 **"Alice Pearce was one of my favorite people":** Letter from Betty Garrett to FT, 1 October 1982.

152 **"rather adored Alice":** Cimber interview.

152 **"I am returning to New York today":** Fordin, p. 268. Alice's note, dated 10 May 1949, was written on The Garden of Allah stationery.

152 **"Give my love to Alice":** Letter from Gene Kelly to John Rox, 15 August 1949, APC.

153 **"A special award is reserved":** *Cue*, 10 December 1949, APC.

153 **Lucy Shmeeler would forever be synonymous with Alice Pearce:** Other character actresses had preceded Alice in creating unforgettable film

debut performances, including veteran scene-stealers Beulah Bondi in *Street Scene*, Margaret Hamilton in *Another Language*, and Alice's *On the Town* castmate Florence Bates in *Rebecca*. Bates (1888–1954), who had fifty film roles under her belt by the time *On the Town* premiered, was seventh billed to Alice's eighth, but Alice's onscreen minutes doubled those of her adept elder.

153 **"tropical plants, ferns, fruit trees":** Graham, *The Garden of Allah*, p. 13.

154 **"The Garden was one of the few places":** *Ibid.*, p. 72.

154 **"The walls were dirty":** *Ibid.*, p. 230.

154 **"No one who was anyone":** *Ibid.*, p. 48.

154 **where all of the Herrings had since resettled:** Don and Doris Herring, with their children Danny and Linda Sue, made a permanent move to the Los Angeles area in late July 1949. Don's father Earl and older daughter Shirley and her family would eventually follow them.

154 **"We cannot make plans to go to the coast":** Letter from Alice Pearce to Shirley Taylor, 8 August 1949, LSC. "I have been working hard on television and radio," Alice wrote. "Johnnie is hard at work on some new songs. He's a very talented boy!"

155 **"I put it inside my little white Bible":** Coburn interview, 21 February 2014.

156 **The pressure:** *Baltimore Evening Sun*, 16 September 1949. The show's choreographer was John Butler, Cris Alexander's former lover. Other guest performers included Bill "Bojangles" Robinson and Elaine Stritch.

156 **"Gay Paree":** *Birmingham News*, 23 June 1949.

156 **lampooning the ways of Hollywood:** "Alice Pierce [*sic*] TV Guest Twice in Two Weeks," *Baltimore Evening Sun*, 30 June 1949.

156 **"the darling of his generation's rebels and thinkers":** Dunning, *On the Air*, p. 316.

157 **Alice was hired to fill the vacancy:** *Newark Star-Ledger*, 6 July 1949.

157 **"the girl with a perpetual cold":** Lackmann, *Same Time . . . Same Station*, p. 130.

157 **"Henry Morgan isn't funny anymore":** *New York World-Telegram*, 22 July 1949. Clipping, APC.

157 **vacation at her parents' summer home:** *Brattleboro Daily Reformer*, 3 January 1950.

158 **"biggest booster":** Hawkins, *op. cit.*

158 **"The only disappointment of the whole evening":** *Courier-Post*, 18 November 1949. The same sentiment was shared by lyricist Johnny Mercer,

writing to John Rox: "I happened to see *Gentlemen* in Philadelphia and, of course, loved Alice though she hasn't much to do." See letter from Mercer to Rox, 15 February 1950, APC.

159 **"The comical Alice Pearce"**: *Latrobe Bulletin*, 22 December 1949.

159 **"A gal who hasn't had half enough praise"**: *Durham Morning Herald*, 27 December 1949.

159 **"Finally, I've come around to the admission"**: *New York Sun*, 9 December 1949. See Rex Evans Papers, Box 1, Folder 17, UCLA Library, Department of Special Collections.

159 **"No one will ever forget her"**: *The Saturday Review*, 31 December 1949.

159 **"ranges facilely from the squeak"**: *Newsweek*, 19 December 1949.

160 **"slightly overwhelmed by the Channing personality"**: *Ibid.*

160 **"Alice and her husband John Rox were a very definite part of my life"**: Letter from Carol Channing to FT, 7 September 1982. (Channing, however, did not mention Alice in her 2002 memoir *Just Lucky I Guess*.)

160 **"We also had Alice Pearce"**: John C. Wilson, *Noel, Tallulah, Cole, and Me*, p. 185.

160 **Rex Evans**: Born in Southport, England, Reginald Llewelyn Evans (1903–1969), the son of a solicitor, became a United States citizen in 1947. A close friend of George Cukor, Evans appeared in ten of the director's films. For almost twenty years, his domestic partner was James Swift Weatherford (1918–2007), with whom he opened the Rex Evans Gallery on North La Cienega Boulevard in West Hollywood in 1960. Evans and Weatherford lived at 1171 North Doheny Drive in Los Angeles until Evans' death, which resulted from hernia surgery.

161 **Miles White**: Born in Oakland, California, Miles Edgren White (1914–2000) was the son of an attorney. An early desire to become a couturier led him to study at the California School of Fine Arts in San Francisco and the California School of Arts and Crafts in Oakland before attending UC Berkeley. He broke into the business by designing costumes for nightclub shows in New York. This led to his Broadway debut in 1938. In a career that spanned seven decades, White's Broadway credits included *Pal Joey*, *Bye Birdie*, and *The Unsinkable Molly Brown*, while *The Greatest Show on Earth* and *Around the World in Eighty Days* were among his film achievements. According to William J. Mann, Tony winner White was always "circumspect and discreet," but his gayness was "hardly a secret." (See *Behind the Screen*, p. 246.) White's friend Jay Blotcher shared with the author: "Miles had casual relationships or restrained ones, owing to the times he lived in. I recall him talking about one man whom he loved dearly, but I don't recall that they lived together." White died in New York City at age 85. At the time, he lived at 360 East Fifty-fifth Street, less than two blocks from where Alice had lived on Sutton Place South.

161 **"costumes are brilliantly satiric"**: *The Saturday Review*, 31 December 1949.

161 **"White [has] seemed to lean over backwards"**: *The Commonweal*, 30 December 1949.

161 **"Alice stole the show. A perfect role for her!"**: White interview.

161 **"In the theatre, when you do one show"**: Pecktal, *Costume Design*, p. 231.

161 **"I've just heard with the greatest grief"**: Letter from Anita Loos to Alice Pearce, 14 May 1951, APC.

161 **Alice departed *Blondes***: Alice's replacement was Paula Trueman, who in turn was replaced on July 9, 1951, by Mary Finney. Finney continued with the national tour.

161 **"We talk about you all the time"**: Postcard from Carol Channing to Mr. and Mrs. John Rox, 8 February 1952, APC.

Chapter Fourteen

162 **"a nervous breakdown"**: Letter from Alice Pearce to Shirley Taylor, 28 August 1950, LSC.

162 **"We were tied down with family all spring"**: *Ibid.*

162 **"some sort of difficulty with the bank"**: Coburn interview, 5 March 2014.

163 **"He seemed to suffer"**: Wheeler interview. When Bob suffered another setback requiring prolonged hospitalization in early 1951, Wheeler's father and grandfather drove to the city to fetch him and Margaret home. See *The Brattleboro Reformer*, 8 February 1951.

163 **an apparent suicide**: BDE, 1 November 1930.

163 **on the second weekend in June**: *North Adams Transcript*, 13 June 1950; *New York Times*, 5 July 1950; Letter from Alice Pearce to Shirley Taylor. Margaret Pearce's siblings LaFrance and Josephine had appendectomies, but it is not clear whether

the third sibling was Mary Emma or Margaret. See PE, 20 September 1928.

163 **"I am very well now"**: Alice Pearce to Shirley Taylor, 1950.

163 **"just plain lucky"**: *Philadelphia Inquirer*, 6 August 1950.

163 **'Cincinnati Dancing Pig'**: Recorded by Red Foley, this song was a recent release when Alice wrote to Shirley.

164 **"socked across her own particular brand"**: *Variety*, 1 February 1950.

164 **unflattering look**: Alice had worn this same hairstyle in the film version of *On the Town* but enhanced it with hairpieces to thicken her bangs and topknot. She had worn the same attachments for her wedding ceremony in 1948. Rarely after 1952 would Alice appear on film or stage without some type of hairpiece or hat to camouflage her thinning hair.

165 *The Faye Emerson Show*: By this point, Alice had been performing in *Gentlemen Prefer Blondes* for fourteen months. When Emerson asked why she would like to host a talk show, Alice "breaks character" and responds, "Well, I'll tell ya, if you're in a show, you see the same people every night, and in *your* show, you see different people every day and I think that must be great fun. We see the same faces every night and say the same things every night and just to get a chance to see somebody new and then do a little different talk, I'm excited."

165 **"Mammy's little baby loves blubber soup"**: *New York World-Telegram and Sun*, 14 April 1951.

165 **"a gem of invention"**: *New York Daily News*, 10 May 1951. Mark had written the MIT song back in 1947, but it was still popular during Alice's 1951 gig.

166 **"Miss Pearce purveys a brand of comedy"**: *Variety*, 11 April 1951.

166 **twelve bows on opening night**: *Camden Courier-Post*, 7 April 1951.

166 **"heavy schedule"**: Note from John Rox to Shirley Taylor, not dated, LSC.

166 **"a Salvation Army lass"**: Mueller, *Astaire Dancing*, p. 335.

166 **"fanciful signal of interior emotional states"**: *Ibid.*, p. 334.

166 **"the initial idea was good"**: Phillips, p. 139.

167 **"wanted too much money"**: Fordin, p. 364.

167 **Charles Walters**: Born in Pasadena in 1911 as Charles Powell *Walter*, the future director-choreographer grew up in Anaheim. After being befriended by Leonard Sillman in 1930, Walters studied dance in order to fulfill his dream of becoming a film star at M-G-M. That wasn't to be, but eventually he staged many of the iconic musical sequences of Hollywood's golden age. In 1982, Walters died in his Malibu condo, a victim of mesothelioma, perhaps stemmed from exposure to the asbestos-lined walls at M-G-M. Though their domestic partnership ended around 1955, Walters still considered Darrow his best friend.

167 **known the Roxes socially**: Walters had also known John's brother Bob Herring, as they both appeared in the 1939 Broadway production of *DuBarry Was a Lady*.

167 **John Darrow**: Born as Harry L. Simpson, Darrow (1904–1980), a New Jersey native, followed in the footsteps of his two brothers and twin sister, all actors. Darrow appeared in forty feature films between 1927 and 1936. A shrewd businessman, he later represented such artists as Gene Kelly, Leif Erickson, Scott Brady, Ellen Corby, Madge Blake, and *Belle of New York* player Gale Robbins.

167 **"It was in the area of the [Malibu] Colony"**: White interview. A secluded one-mile stretch of beachfront property first developed in 1926, the Colony has been long known as a popular private enclave for wealthy celebrities.

167 **"begun purchasing land around Malibu"**: Phillips, p. 103.

167 **"committed relationship"**: *Ibid.*, p. 29.

168 **feted on separate occasions**: *Los Angeles Herald-Express*, 13 June 1951, clipping, APC.

168 **"Edens' right hand and Freed's left"**: Fordin, p. 121.

168 **"My brother Danny and I"**: Linda Swanson, "Memories of Alice and John," unpublished account, 2013.

168 **"The less said about it the better"**: Mueller, p. 333.

168 **"That picture was a duty"**: Phillips, p. 137. Phillips has noted that some of Walters's "disinterest in *Belle* stemmed from his preoccupation with a much more appealing project," the staging of *Judy Garland at the Palace*.

168 **("like a piece of moving putty")**: Mueller, p. 334.

168 **"I couldn't stand Vera-Ellen"**: Phillips, p. 137.

168 **"There were no conferences"**: *Ibid.*, p. 138.

168 **six weeks swelled to sixteen**: *Franklin News-Herald*, 11 October 1951. Alice was on salary the entire sixteen weeks, although her days on the lot totaled only thirty-four.

169 **"a section boss stride"**: *Wilkes-Barre Times Leader*, 19 September 1940.

169 **"Character actors are best"**: Parish, *The Slapstick Queens*, p. 23.

170 **"Marjorie Main was always afraid of Alice Pearce"**: Fordin, p. 365. In 2013, one observing fan noted the opening scene in which Alice carried an immense marching drum: "And even before she opens her mouth, she gets to deliver one big bang on that thing, inadvertently serving notice that Main had better look to her laurels."

170 **musical number designed especially for her:** *Variety* reported on June 11, 1951, that Main "will warble a tune custom-cleffed for her by Harry Warren and Johnny Mercer." Alice's screen minutes totaled eighteen to Main's nine.

170 **Alice's final day of filming:** University of Southern California, Cinematic Arts Library, Arthur Freed Collection, Box 6, Folder 3 (*Belle of New York*, Assistant Director's Reports and Daily Progress Reports). A major delay was caused by Walters's eight-day sabbatical in late August. Main contributed to some minor delays, quibbling over hats, hairstyles, and furs, not to mention arriving late to the set several times. On the morning of September 4, when she should have been on the sound stage at 8 o'clock, Main was still at her home, causing a two-hour filming delay.

170 **"dramatically boneless"**: *New York Times*, 6 March 1952.

170 **"drab atmosphere"**: *Windsor Star*, 27 March 1952.

170 **"entertainment and humor are jolted"**: *New York Daily News*, 6 March 1952.

170 **"The show is stolen"**: *Oakland Tribune*, 17 March 1952.

170 **"Alice Pearce contributes"**: *Democrat and Chronicle*, 7 March 1952.

170 **"Alice Pearce turns out"**: *Los Angeles Times*, 10 March 1952.

170 **"a homely Judy Canova"**: *Dallas Morning News*, 30 March 1952.

170 **"all she does is beat a great big drum"**: *The Journal Herald*, 7 March 1952.

170 **"delivered in a throwaway manner"**: Mueller, p. 333. The blustery Marjorie Main —and sometimes Alice—is guilty of delivering casual lines.

170 **"companion portrayal"**: Douglas McVay, "The Belle of New York," *The Velvet Light Trap*, No. 14 (Winter 1975), p. 30. Author Tom Vallance (*The American Musical*, Castle Books, 1970) found Alice "even more appealing" in *The Belle of New York* than she was in *On the Town*.

171 **"the comedy is heavy and badly timed"**: Mueller, p. 347.

171 **"a lumpish parody"**: Mueller, p. 346. Actually, Alice sings two songs in the film. The other, "Let a Little Love Come In," was written by Roger Edens.

171 **"mug without offending"**: "I'm Out with the Belle of New York," *Canadian Ken On . . .*, https://canadianken.blogspot.com/2013/07/im-out-with-belle-of-new-york.html, accessed 30 January 2020.

171 **Barron Polan:** Barron Reynolds Polan (1914–1986), born in West Virginia, once represented Judy Garland, Kay Thompson, Jane Morgan, and Julie Wilson, to whom he was married for only six months. Polan never rewed and died of metastatic prostate cancer at the Beverly Hills home of his sister Connie Wald.

172 ***Lend An Ear:*** *Variety*, 11 June 1951. Around the same time, Ed Sullivan reported that Alice was being considered for "the top comedy spot" in the fledgling revue *Curtain Going Up*, to be produced by Daniel Melnick and directed by Mervyn Nelson, which never got off the ground. It seems that "too much temperament [kept] the curtain from going up," according to columnist Danton Walker. See *New York Daily News*, 22 September 1951.

172 **Ciro's:** *Variety*, 8 August 1951.

172 **"All that Bromfield and Cobey need"**: *New York Daily News*, 7 February 1951.

172 **"The script is finished"**: Letter from Bromfield to Alice and John, undated, APC.

172 **"at a London music hall"**: *Glens Falls Post-Star*, 24 September 1951.

172 **"It would be wonderful"**: Letter from Anita Loos to Alice Pearce, undated, APC.

173 **society impresario Earl Blackwell:** In 1938, Atlanta native Samuel Earl Blackwell, Jr. (1909–1995), a frustrated playwright, and his then domestic partner, Bostonian Ted Strong (1910–1985), a frustrated novelist, founded Celebrity Service in New York as a clearinghouse for information about celebrities. Their partnership ended in 1950 when Blackwell bought out Strong. (Tallulah Bankhead once rang them up to ask, "Is this Celebrity Service?" Blackwell answered, "Yes, Tallu." She growled in reply, "Well, I'm a celebrity and I want some service. Get me an apartment." Blackwell did.) See Earl Blackwell, *Mr. Celebrity*, C.I.P.R, Ltd., 1991.

173 **Judy Garland's act:** Garland's smash hit opened on Tuesday, October 16—Alice Pearce's thirty-fourth birthday.

173 **"Ralph Blane and Hugh Martin played":** *Gotham Guide*, undated clipping, APC. Also attending the party were Nancy Walker, Audrey Christie, Eva Gabor, and journalists Danton Walker, William Hawkins, and Dorothy Manners.

173 **"The young medium":** Krampner, p. 54.

174 **auditioning "more players":** *Theatre Arts*, September 1952, p. 94.

174 **"the darling of half of Manhattan":** Clarke, *Capote*, p. 133. Capote had also seen Alice in *Look, Ma, I'm Dancin'!* on opening night.

174 **"blunt-talking Negro woman":** *Brooklyn Daily Eagle*, 28 March 1952.

175 **Saint Subber:** Arnold Saint-Subber (1918–1994), born in Washington, DC, and raised in New York City, gained fame as a co-producer of *Kiss Me, Kate* (1948). He went on to produce several Neil Simon plays, including *Barefoot in the Park* and *The Odd Couple*. He died of heart failure in Berkeley, California.

175 **"crazy proposition":** Clarke, *Too Brief a Treat*, p. 176.

175 **"substantial changes":** Clarke, *Capote*, p. 226.

175 **"top-flight production":** Clarke, *Too Brief a Treat*, p. 185.

175 **"charming, fanciful, funny, and moving":** Lewis, *Slings and Arrows*, p. 222.

175 **"taking the recommendation":** Clarke, *Capote*, p. 228. Some newspapers reported that the Gish sisters opted out because their salary demands were not met.

175 **"Honey, you [will] know":** Clarke, *Capote*, p. 228.

175 **"biggest [tree] ever yet constructed":** *Boston Globe*, 9 March 1952.

175 **"Because we were opening in Boston":** Thomson, *Virgil Thomson*, p. 397.

176 **"the perfect background":** *Variety*, 19 March 1952.

176 **"Her scene was a capricious vaudeville turn":** Lewis, pp. 222–223.

176 **the "disruptive" Miss Baby Love Dallas:** In 1953, when *The Grass Harp* was staged off Broadway at the Circle in the Square, the character was excised from the script.

177 **"had never understood his work at all":** Clarke, *Capote*, p. 230.

177 ***Île de France:*** Capote and his lover Jack Dunphy sailed on April 9, 1952.

177 **"You were angels":** Letter from Truman Capote to John and Alice Rox, 20 April 1952, APC.

177 **"I want you to be in *Flowers*":** Letter from Truman Capote to John and Alice Rox, 20 May 1952, APC.

177 ***House of Flowers:*** With music by Harold Arlen and lyrics by Capote and Arlen, the musical finally opened at the Alvin Theatre on December 30, 1954. In the cast were Pearl Bailey, Juanita Hall, and Diahann Carroll. It ran for 165 performances. (In early 1953, Capote was considering Eartha Kitt for a role in the play, which "upset" Alice, he said—most likely because she knew of Kitt's backstage reputation at the Blue Angel, that of a temperamental tigress.)

177 **"If only we had some money":** Letter from John Rox to Don Herring, 18 September 1952, LSC. (The play John mentioned was most probably *See How They Run*, a farce slated to feature Alice, Arthur Treacher, and Douglass Watson. However, it never found enough backers.)

178 **"Oh, they had a very good marriage":** Alexander interview, 1987.

178 **"She was very proud of him":** Wilson interview.

178 **"Every New Year's Eve":** Smith, *Natural Blonde*, p. 97.

178 **"life-saver":** Kobal, p. 675.

179 **Kaye Ballard:** When interviewed by performer-writer Gary Brumburgh in 2017, Ballard (1925-2019) gleefully recalled Alice's nightclub staple "Wait for the Dial Tone, Nellie." "She was one of the funniest ladies I ever knew," Ballard told Brumburgh. "My God, she could sing the phone book and leave people rolling in the aisles." See Brumburgh's article "Kaye Ballard: The Songs and the Laughs Are on Me," *Films of the Golden Age*, Number 92, Spring 2018.

179 **"probably tied with Imogene Coca":** *New Haven Evening Register*, 8 July 1952, clipping, APC.

179 **"miserable":** Letter from Capote to Alice, 25 August 1952, APC. Alice earned $350 for the week at the Westport Country Playhouse. She and Ballard subsequently appeared in *Three to One* at a theater in East Hampton, NY, July 21-26, 1952.

179 ***Broadway Television Theater:*** The episode "The Bishop Misbehaves" aired on September 22, 1952, starring Gene Lockhart. Alice played Lady Emily Lyons, sister of the title character.

179 **lampooned columnist Dorothy Kilgallen:** At the skit's conclusion, gutsy Capp commented: "You

know, in the old New England days, they used to dunk this kind of vicious town gossip into the nearest river—have you ever noticed what fine rivers we have around here?" Alice may have taken special pleasure in satirizing Kilgallen, who three years earlier had referred to Alice in her column as a "weird comedienne."

179 **"average good actor"**: *Theatre Arts*, September 1952.

180 **"It is very hard to make ends meet"**: Letter from Alice to Shirley Taylor, 28 August 1950, LSC.

Chapter Fifteen

181 **"great era of nightclub entertainment flourished"**: Gavin, p. 7.

181 **Julius Monk:** Julius Withers Monk (1912–1995), the son of a surgeon, was born in Spencer, North Carolina. He moved to New York in 1934 and despite his homosexuality, he wed sculptress Eliza Allen with whom he shared a roof for only two years. Their union—in Monk's own words, a *mariage de raison*—ended officially in 1942. He spent the late 1930s racketing back and forth between Europe and New York as an itinerant pianist and boulevardier, frequently hobnobbing with the Duke of Kent. After he was abruptly dismissed from the Ruban Bleu in 1956, Monk went on to produce fourteen revues during the next twelve years before his career began to fizzle out in the late 1960s. Realizing that the end of an era had arrived, Monk spent his retirement residing in "genteel, cluttered Edwardian splendor in a small aerie on West Fifty-seventh Street." See Whitney Balliett, "Régisseur," *The New Yorker*, 6 April 1992, pp. 38–40, 42–44.

181 **"an upper-class North Carolina drawl"**: Balliett, p. 39.

181 **"East Siders would have never ventured"**: Gavin, p. 56.

181 **"He exuded an authority"**: *Ibid.*, pp. 59–60.

181 **"This showstop has returned"**: *The New Yorker*, 7 February 1953.

181 **Alice Ghostley:** Alice Margaret Ghostley (1923–2007), who was born in Eve, Missouri but grew up in Henryetta, Oklahoma, dropped out of college to pursue a theatrical career. Trained as an opera singer, she filled in the spot Charlotte Rae vacated before *New Faces* opened on Broadway. She wed actor Felice Orlandi in October 1951. The couple had no children.

182 **"They were a tough breed"**: Gavin, p. 112.

182 **"They were great"**: *Sioux Falls Argus-Leader*, 5 September 1979.

182 **"sweet Alice Pearce"**: Letter from Alice Ghostley to FT, 13 August 1989.

182 **Alice returned to the Blue Angel:** Her accompanist was Bart Howard, the club's pianist and emcee. Between her two 1953 engagements, Alice appeared for one week in *Lend an Ear* at the Palm Beach Playhouse in Florida.

182 **McManus, John & Adams:** An advertising executive had heard Lawrence "doodling on the piano at a night spot" and had lured him into the industry because "he was impressed by the ease with which Lawrence could turn out a set of words and a tune." See *Rochester Democrat and Chronicle*, 14 July 1956, p. 8.

182 **Lawrence would never again perform professionally:** Lawrence left the ad agency in 1961. He composed the score for the 1962 film *David and Lisa*. He was also known for his award-winning jingle "Wouldn't You Really Rather Have a Buick." After a stint at his father's magazine *U. S. News & World Report*, Lawrence worked for several Boston ad agencies.

182 **"That redoubtable and penetrating"**: *The New Yorker*, 23 May 1953.

182 **"Alice Pearce goes with the lease"**: *Variety*, 20 May 1953.

183 **"In nightclubs, [patrons]"**: Gavin, p. 51.

183 **"Saturdays were the worst"**: Gavin, p. 11.

183 **"The inebriated customer"**: *Screenland*, September 1953.

183 **"an audience darling"**: *Dallas Morning News*, 23 June 1953.

183 **"We were all so frightened"**: *Dallas Times Herald*, 30 August 1959, clipping, APC.

184 **"I was hardly alone in loving Alice"**: Kathleen Post, "Sunshine Before the Dark," *TV Radio Mirror*, June 1966, p. 81.

184 **"invited by some admirers"**: Balliett, p. 43.

185 *Stock in Trade:* Halfway through the run, John joined Alice in Bermuda. On August 24, they, along with Imogene Coca, attended the opening of a lavish outdoor production of *Macbeth*, directed by Burgess Meredith and starring Charlton Heston. The Roxes flew back to New York on August 30. Three weeks later, *The Billboard* reported that Bing Crosby Enterprises was interested in producing a television pilot based on Mike Angelo's comic panel "Emily and Mabel," starring Alice and

Bibi Osterwald as two lovable spinsters who realize late in life that they've missed something and are generally looking for a man. This project never came to fruition.

185 **"He had a great sense of humor"**: Gavin, pp. 49–50.

185 **"[Her agents] didn't push her at all"**: Alexander interview, 1987.

185 **"in addition to his ever-expanding list"**: Irvin, pp. 185–186.

185 *The Body in the Seine*: The recording failed to attract a playwright, but the long-playing album's limited release made it a rarity. Collectors of original cast albums came to consider it the "holy grail" of recordings. In 2018, the recording was at last reproduced on compact disc.

185 **"was obviously an admirer"**: *New York Times*, 13 June 1954.

186 **second appearance in a situation comedy:** Alice's debut performance in a television sitcom was "The Eye Examination," a segment of NBC's *The Aldrich Family*, broadcast live on April 24, 1953.

186 **"Aunt Laurie's New Assistant"**: *TV Guide* (Chicago edition), 30 October 1953, p. A–29. The pilot for *Jamie*, which aired as an episode of anthology series *ABC Album*, on April 26, 1953, was written by David Swift of *Mister Peepers* fame. Other regular members of the cast for the *Jamie* series were Polly Rowles (Aunt Laurie) and Kathy Nolan (Cousin Liz). Brandon De Wilde had first achieved fame in the Broadway production of *The Member of the Wedding*. During *Jamie*'s run, he was nominated for an Academy Award for *Shane*. His character's full name in *Jamie* was Jamison John Francis McHummer. Grandpa's full name was Frank L. Dimmer. The series was renewed for a second season, but only two episodes were produced due to a disagreement between the network and the show's sponsor.

186 **"slob of a husband"**: *Long Island Star-Journal*, 11 November 1953.

187 **"Alice Pearce sparked"**: *Variety*, 11 November 1953.

187 **network's files from this period:** Letter from Tim Brooks to FT, 28 January 1988.

187 **"dreadfully miscast"**: Leszczak, *Single Season Sitcoms*, p. 179.

187 *Take It from Me:* No kinescopes of *Take It from Me* are known to exist, but there are a few kinescopes of *Jamie* which are available to researchers at the UCLA Film & Television Archive.

187 **"You don't have the sort of rehearsal time"**: *Santa Rose Press-Democrat*, 28 June 1954.

187 **Fridays and Sundays:** *Philadelphia Inquirer*, 2 February 1954.

187 **rehearsed its plays for eight days:** *Brooklyn Daily Eagle*, 6 August 1952.

187 **yesteryear's top plays in their entirety:** The producers of *Broadway Television Theater* typically made no adaptations or deletions from the original works, except in the case of profanity or questionable words, lines, or situations. The productions aired Monday through Friday from 7:30 to 9 p.m., or longer when necessary.

188 **"Thanks to the deft acting"**: *Life,* 11 January 1954.

189 **lacking in "charm and warmth"**: *Variety,* 6 January 1954.

189 **"too small for a comedienne of her stature"**: *New York Morning Telegraph*, 31 March 1954.

189 **"small army of composers"**: *Brooklyn Daily Eagle*, 11 December 1953.

190 **"jealous about who bowed"**: *Hazleton Standard-Speaker*, 31 March 1954.

190 **"While we were doing *Almanac*"**: Carpenter, *The Absolute Joy of Work*, p. 174. According to *Variety* (4 August 1961), Alice was chosen to star in *Untitled*, a musical revue written by Carpenter, but it was postponed due to her commitment to Noël Coward's *Sail Away*.

190 **$3,000 to $4,000 annually:** *Des Moines Register*, 28 December 1953.

190 **"'Two Lovers' is not worth listening to"**: Letter from John Rox to Donald Herring, 16 July 1953, LSC.

190 **"I Want a Hippopotamus for Christmas"**: A shrill, inescapable earworm, the song may be one of the most celebrated oddities in all of holiday music, although it was largely forgotten for about fifty years. In 2016, the United States Postal Service used the song for their Christmas ad campaign. Since 2008, Hallmark Cards has produced "I Want a Hippopotamus for Christmas" ornaments.

190 **"My husband wrote a lot of [John's] music"**: Coburn interview, 21 February 2014. John and Bill appeared together in a men's fashion photo feature coordinated by Perk Bailey for *Look* (13 January 1953).

191 **Sarah Lawrence College alumnae:** In the years since her graduation, Alice had been quite faithful to her alma mater. In the spring of 1953, she had headed the entertainment for a similar event

which featured a 1920s theme. In 1955, Alice would serve as head of the college's alumnae fund drive to benefit its drama department.

191 **volumes filled an entire bookshelf:** Mara, p. 13. One of Alice's copies of *Alice in Wonderland*, dating to the 1920s when she was a girl in Brussels, is now in the author's collection. Alice also informed Mara that there had been an "Alice" in her family for generations, including her mother Margaret whose middle name was Alice. Actually, Alice and Margaret shared the same namesake: Aunt Alice Chowning. Aunt Alice was on the Clark side of the family, but much earlier, there was an "Alice" on the Pearce side—whether Alice knew it or not. Her grandfather Harry Pearce had a paternal aunt named Alice who was born in Cornwall in 1824.

191 **"Peeps had convinced me":** Carpenter, p. 174.

191 *The Torch-Bearers: New York Times*, 2 July 1954.

191 **one-time "tryout":** The topics that evening included beekeeping, billy goats, ogling, bronco busting, and dressing in an upper berth.

191 **"*One Minute Please* could be an immensely amusing program":** *New York Times*, 11 July 1954. Future topics included whale blubber, jellied eels, growing poison ivy, making glue, and joining a Liberace fan club.

193 **Peter Turgeon:** Turgeon (1919–2000) was born as Boyd Higginson Turgeon on Christmas Day in Hinsdale, Illinois. He began his theatrical career playing in a 1940 touring production of *Life with Father*. Ten years later he made his Broadway debut in *Brigadoon*. Turgeon was active in early live television in New York, including seven episodes of his friend Wally Cox's show *Mister Peepers*. He later appeared in a regular role on the Gothic soap opera *Dark Shadows*. He died at the Long Island State Veterans Home in Stony Brook, NY.

193 **"Any man who doesn't want to earn":** *Illustrated Buffalo Press*, 27 May 1923.

193 **"sophomoric flop":** *Chicago Daily News*, 10 August 1954.

193 **"cracks about the Roosevelts":** *Boston Traveler*, 3 August 1954.

193 **"considerable alteration":** *Boston Daily Record*, 4 August 1954.

193 **Mr. Cox and Miss Pearce contribute:** *Christian Science Monitor*, 24 August 1954.

193 **burden he felt while directing, producing, and acting:** According to Adam Redfield, the son of William "Billy" Redfield, whom the author

interviewed on June 27, 2103, an uncertainty exists regarding Turgeon's directorial credit. "Peter Turgeon, who was a wonderful guy, is listed as the director," Redfield explained, "but the credits also indicate that the entire production was under Billy's supervision, and Billy always told me he directed it. The only story I can recall about [the production] is that Wally [Cox] invented a word. He was supposed to say to his wife, 'because you nag me, nag, nag, nag.' Wally thought this was flat and inserted the made-up word 'ginch.' [changing it to] 'because you ginch me, ginch, ginch, ginch."

193 **"I found myself suffering":** "Don't Wait for Smiles," *PaulTurgeon-Dot-Com*, http://www.paulturgeon.com/PT/, accessed 20 February 2020.

194 **William "Bill" LeMassena:** William Henry LeMassena III (1916–1993) was the son of W. H. LeMassena, Jr. and his wife Margery Lockwood, both of whom died during the course of the Second World War. Bill's ancestry was mainly French and English. His great-grandfather Andrew LeMassena (1808–1885) was a first-generation American who led the way for the next two generations to carry on his brokerage firm. Stage-struck Bill would have none of that, nor of the steel business on his maternal side. His grandfather Arthur Lockwood told him he was choosing the lowest paid profession in the world, but that if the theater remained his choice the family would help him get the proper training. Bill's Broadway credits numbered more than twenty, and he was quite active in regional and summer theatre. He never married, and it's not known if he ever had a long-term relationship. His most famous lover, however, was Montgomery Clift, whom he met as a fellow actor in the Lunts' production of *There Shall Be No Night*. Bill remained close to the Lunts until their deaths, inheriting many of Alfred Lunt's suits and formal wear, which fit him perfectly. Late in his career, he gained a certain amount of fame on the CBS soap *As the World Turns*. Bill died of lung cancer at his New Suffolk home on Long Island, which he shared with a companion, the widowed Marian Tuthill Connolly.

194 **"It was *Dracula*":** *Passaic Herald-News*, 2 August 1954.

194 **"staked [him] to four years majoring in drama":** William LeMassena, autobiographical document, 1970, author's collection.

194 **"the most powerful people in the theatre":** Brown, *The Fabulous Lunts*, p. 303.

195 **a rather checkered past:** *Dear Charles* was the third incarnation of an American work originally titled *Slightly Scandalous* (1944) which was adapted into French as *Les Enfants d'Eduoard* only to be adapted back into English by British playwright Alan Melville, enjoying great success on the London stage in 1952.

195 **join the final week of Bankhead's tour:** Alice replaced Hope Sansberry (1894–1990), who was perhaps a little too old to play the part of Madame Bouchemin.

197 **"behavior was good":** Lobenthal, *Talllulah! The Life and Times of a Leading Lady*, p. 442.

197 **"On my own I want to thank you, kind sir":** Letter from Tallulah Bankhead to John Rox, 23 October 1954, APC.

197 **Nunnally Johnson had handpicked her:** *New York Daily News*, 28 January 1955. (Bankhead's pal Patsy Kelly replaced Alice as Mme. Bouchemin in the *Dear Charles* tour.)

Chapter Sixteen

198 **"played two self-centered old dowagers":** Gingold, *How to Grow Old Disgracefully*, p. 136.

200 **"a better description":** *Chicago Tribune*, 23 August 1955.

200 **"waxes a little thin":** *Variety*, 15 July 1955.

200 **"This five-foot-two actress":** *Valley Times*, 1 April 1955.

200 **"Spigelgass and . . . Toomey":** *Los Angeles Times*, 9 April 1955. For more information on Spigelgass (1908–1985) and Toomey (1930–1989), see Mann, *Behind the Screen*, p. 212-215.

200 **"very well connected, very influential":** Mann, *Behind the Screen*, p. 212.

200 **"Danny and I spoke to Aunt Alice":** Swanson account, 2013. Linda's sister Shirley Taylor, in an undated memoir, also mentioned John's voice: "My mother [Doris Herring] used to feel that Grandma [Dolly] Herring did not really like the way John put on his sophisticated New York talk with her . . . guess she felt it wasn't genuine."

200 **"her 'funny' voice":** In 1987, Cris Alexander also mentioned Alice's voice: "When she spoke in life, she spoke a *little bit* like the way she did onscreen, but she cranked it up, very much exaggerated it [for the camera], but I couldn't say she was a *different* person." Forty years earlier, journalist Vernon Rice described Alice's natural voice as "well-modulated."

201 **"Knowing that he had booked":** Wilson interview.

201 **Patricia Wilson:** Patricia Jean Wilson, a third-generation actress born in Ohio in 1929, graduated from Ohio State University in 1950. She would go on to star in Broadway's *Fiorello!* with Tom Bosley. At the time she met Alice Pearce, Wilson was married to pianist Richard Greenwald (1924–1978), whom she later divorced.

201 **"He was blunt":** Patricia Wilson, *Yesterday's Mashed Potatoes*, p. 26. By 1958, Schirmer also represented Shirley Jones, Lee Remick, and Miles White.

202 **"great comedienne":** *Pittsburgh Post-Gazette*, 20 July 1955.

202 **"vintage comedy":** *Pittsburgh Sun-Telegraph*, 20 July 1955.

202 **"the wrangle over who should get what":** *New York Times*, 10 November 1955. According to an undated clipping in the APC, "Alice Pearce will wear the same ratty red fox fur piece she wore in *The Grass Harp* when she appears on the *Kraft Television Theater*. Director Bob McIntosh, after much searching, found it for her."

202 **color presentation:** An overwhelming majority of Americans did not own color television sets in 1955. That year, for instance, an RCA color set sold for about $400, a figure, when adjusted for inflation, which would equate with almost ten times that in 2020 dollars.

203 **"costumes that hued to the spirit":** *Philadelphia Inquirer*, 24 October 1955.

203 **"essence of Carroll's humor and whimsy":** *Daily News*, 24 October 1955.

203 **"the inherent simplicity":** *Broadcasting*, 31 October 1955.

203 **"to head the feminine contingent":** *New York Times*, 4 September 1955.

203 **"It seems I can't write anything good for her":** *Des Moines Register*, 21 November 1955.

204 **"I never remember going to the general store":** Wheeler interview.

205 **"Alice never mentioned her parents":** Wilson interview.

205 **"I know that Alice was not close to them":** Alexander interview, 1987.

205 **"It's so hard to find the right material":** "Miss Persimmon Hunting a Play," *New York World-Telegram*, 17 April 1956.

205 **"an *actress* of the highest grade":** Crespy, *Richard Barr*, p. 72.

205 **"They are both good actresses"**: Payn, *The Noël Coward Diaries*, p. 277.

206 **"radiate[d]" comedy**: *New York Times*, 18 January 1956.

206 **"Ladies and Gentlemen"**: Crespy, p. 74.

206 **"Strange to say"**: Payn, p. 305.

207 **Outer Circle:** The Outer Circle, which is currently known as the Outer Critics Circle, was a reaction to the already prestigious Drama Critics Circle, which included first-string critics from Manhattan's major newspapers and other important publications like *The Saturday Review of Literature*. Prior to Alice, winners in the supporting actress category included actresses Kim Stanley, Bibi Osterwald, and Eva Marie Saint.

207 **"We have an absolute ball"**: *Rochester Democrat and Chronicle*, 18 March 1956.

207 **"I can't really play well"**: *New York World-Telegram*, 17 April 1956.

208 **"Nancy Walker . . . Edmund Baylies"**: Letter from William Windom to FT, 21 April 2003.

208 **"no big dream of an ideal role or play"**: "Bill LeMassena Followed a Star," 16 April 1956, unsourced newspaper clipping, William LeMassena's personal scrapbook in the author's possession. LeMassena was handpicked for *Fallen Angels* by producer Charles Bowden, who had acted with LeMassena in the 1939 tour of *The Taming of the Shrew*. In the postwar years, LeMassena first lived at 132 Bank Street, then 26 Bank Street, and finally at 132 West Eleventh Street, where he remained for many decades.

208 **"Alice left yesterday"**: Letter from John Rox to Don Herring, 6 February 1956, LSC. Alice had signed to make *The Opposite Sex* before *Fallen Angels* opened on Broadway.

208 **Pasternak assembled an all-star cast:** According to a press release, 246 actresses were considered for the eight leading roles as well as for three featured parts. Over four months were devoted to interviews and tests for the roles eventually played by Allyson, Collins, Gray, Sheridan, Miller, Joan Blondell, Agnes Moorehead, Charlotte Greenwood, Alice Pearce, Barbara Jo Allen, and Carolyn Jones.

209 **Allyson burned her arm:** Dorothy Kilgallen, unsourced clipping, 22 February 1956, APC.

209 **"it was a rat race"**: Letter from Alice Pearce to Don and Doris Herring, 23 February 1956, LSC.

210 **six months' notice to vacate:** *New York Daily News*, 8 April 1956; Letter from John Rox to Suzie Herring, 18 July 1956, LSC.

210 **"Her Sutton Place apartment was *so* charming"**: Alexander interview, 2003.

210 **city-bred Roxy:** *New York Journal-American*, 3 March 1956.

210 **"an uptown Greenwich Village"**: *The New Yorker*, 29 September 1975.

210 **John's hospitalization in April:** *Fort Worth Star-Telegram*, 27 April 1956.

210 **Jan Sterling:** In order to corroborate Alexander's account, the author made unsuccessful attempts to communicate with Sterling. Nevertheless, Sterling's interest in astrology was widely known. In 1964, she appeared with three prominent astrologers and a physicist on David Susskind's television program *Open End* to discuss astrology and metaphysics. Six years later, journalist Rebecca Morehouse reported that Sterling had "some expertise at numerology and astrology." "I don't run my life by astrology, but I find it very interesting," Sterling told Morehouse. Sterling and Peggy Cass had been best friends since 1947 when Cass, as Sterling's understudy, took over the role of Billie Dawn in the touring production of *Born Yesterday*.

211 **somewhat embellished:** Cris' version included unlikely details. He said that six months prior to John's hospitalization, Sterling and Alice visited a female "fortune teller" in California "where John and Alice were at the time." However, the final time John and Alice were in California together was 1951, five years previous to John's hospitalization. Cris admitted that Sterling and Alice were not particularly close. Given that, it's plausible that Sterling had heard about Peacock's astrological report from someone besides Alice. Then again, there is the possibility that sometime after Alice received Peacock's 1955 report, she may have consulted yet another astrologer— perhaps in the company of Sterling, or perhaps not—and that it was this report that Sterling may have shared with Cris. Moreover, Cris stated that the "fortune teller" predicted that John would die within six months. Peacock's report does not mention any specific lapse of time.

211 **eight-page handwritten document:** It is part of the APC.

211 **Charles A. Peacock:** Peacock's true surname was Peacox. For many years prior to 1955, he managed laundries both in Yonkers and Tarrytown. He

died in Valhalla, NY, in 1964 at age seventy-two. Peacock gained a bit of notoriety in 1931 when his marital misdeeds, brought forth in divorce court, became front page news in Yonkers. According to the *Yonkers Statesman*, when his wife unexpectedly returned home from an out-of-town trip, she found Peacock in bed with a strange woman. "Before she could do or say anything, Mrs. Peacox declared, her husband jumped from bed, tied her up, and threw her in a corner and then ordered the other woman to dress and leave the house. 'I'll murder you if you make any trouble for me on account of this,' Peacock told his wife." Those words were especially chilling to readers who knew that Peacock's younger brother Earl, whom the papers called "the torch slayer," had been convicted in 1929 of murdering his own wife during their honeymoon and setting fire to her body.

211 **coffee pot suddenly exploded:** William Peper, " 'Lovable Nut' Lives Her Role," *New York World-Telegram and Sun*, 13 May 1960.

213 **"most outstanding and longest-running cultural series":** Brooks, p. 457.

213 **"I have one word of advice":** *St. Louis Post-Dispatch*, 18 December 1956.

213 **"There's nothing so crushing":** *Los Angeles Times*, 3 May 1951.

213 **"I get fascinated by titles":** *Des Moines Register*, 10 September 1956.

214 **"a man condemned to death":** "One More Sunrise" was recorded by Georgie Shaw and released by Decca in January 1957.

Chapter Seventeen

215 **"a very funny young woman":** *The New Yorker*, 16 March 1957.

215 **"It was a scary thing":** Gavin, p. 175.

215 **"They were hard work":** *Ibid.*, p. 15.

216 **"There's nothing quite as strange":** *New York World-Telegram & Sun*, 26 March 1957, clipping, APC.

216 **several of his songs:** "Unbelievable" was not recorded by the Hilltoppers, but instead by the King Sisters for Capitol Records in 1958. "Where's the Boy I Saved for a Rainy Day?" was chosen for Polly Bergen's LP "The Party's Over" (Columbia Records, 1957).

216 **"Rock 'n' Roll groove":** Letter from John Rox to Don Herring, 25 May 1957, LSC.

216 **opted out of *Rose Marie*:** Alice's replacement was Alice Ghostley. The production, running from August 19 until September 1, starred Anna Maria Alberghetti and John Reardon, supported by Alice's friend William LeMassena and Ghostley's night club partner G. Wood.

216 **"Leja Beach on Fire Island":** *New York Times*, 21 July 1957.

216 **fill his birdbath:** Email message from Linda Swanson to FT, 15 March 2013.

217 **"coronary atherosclerosis":** John J. Rox, New York State Department of Health, Certificate of Death, #56072, 6 August 1957.

217 **"like his own son":** Linda Sue Swanson, "The Herring Boys," unpublished memoir, 2013.

217 **"I called Alice immediately":** Wilson interview.

217 **"Of course, Peeps was just demolished":** Alexander interview, 1987.

217 **John's funeral:** PE, 8 August 1957.

217 **Frank E. Campbell Funeral Chapel:** Future clients of the funeral parlor would include Joan Crawford, Greta Garbo, Judy Garland, Oscar Hammerstein II, Robert F. Kennedy, Dorothy Kilgallen, John Lennon, Margaret Mead, Jacqueline Onassis, and Tennessee Williams, to name but a few.

217 **"a surprisingly large number":** *New York Daily News*, 2 August 1966.

218 **"while she endeavor[ed] to recover":** *Scranton Times-Tribune*, 13 August 1957.

218 **she sought counseling:** Florenski, *Center Square*, p. 58.

218 **"If I hadn't been working, I would have lost my sanity":** *TV Guide*, 25 December 1965.

218 **"both metals gleamed only fitfully":** *Philadelphia Inquirer*, 26 September 1957.

219 **"One of the funniest bits":** *Meriden Record*, 18 September 1957, clipping, APC.

219 **"the mistake of the century":** *Boston Daily Record*, 25 September 1957.

220 **"breathlessly unfunny book":** *New York Times*, 18 October 1957.

220 **"You have to be a grown-up":** *Honolulu Star-Bulletin*, 1 March 1970.

221 **"decline of the live 60-minute dramatic showcase":** *Variety*, 5 June 1957.

221 **signed as her personal manager Bob Kohler:** *Variety*, 1 April 1959.

221 **"Don't make me out to be a big shot":** "Bob Kohler, Gay Rights Pioneer, 1926-2007," *The Village Voice*, https://www.villagevoice.

com/2007/12/06/bob-kohler-gay-rights-pio-neer-1926-2007/, accessed 26 March 2020.

221 **"Alice Pearce is perfectly cast"**: Ralph Porter, "Commercials This Month: The Big Spoof," *The Magazine of Creative Advertising*, undated clipping, APC.

221 **"With the battle cry"**: *Sponsor*, 11 March 1963.

221 **Ritalin pamphlet:** Dated 1961, the advertising pamphlet is part of the APC.

222 **Jule Styne:** Douglas Watt of the *Daily News* reported on April 30, 1958, that Styne was currently writing songs for a show called *Many Happy Returns*. "Charlie Gaynor is doing the lyrics," said Styne. "Rehearsals start in October with Carol Channing, Alice Pearce and, if we can get him, Louis Armstrong." Of course, this project proved to be yet another one that failed to materialize.

223 **"Only Alice Pearce succeeded"**: *New York Times*, 15 February 1958.

223 **"This week's Sinatra show"**: *Milwaukee Sentinel*, 14 February 1958.

223 **little Tina got stage fright:** *St. Louis Post-Dispatch*, 15 February 1958.

223 **"One of those garrulous and theatre-wise cab drivers"**: Letter from Hume Cronyn to Alice Pearce, 26 April 1958, APC.

224 **recently demoted Goodman:** By February 1958, Goodman was asked to give up her place as a regular member of Paar's show. Nor did she join Alice, Genevieve, Arquette, and five hundred others when they celebrated Paar at the Plaza Hotel on March 29. However, Goodman would continue to appear sporadically on Paar's show until 1962.

224 **"alerted the nation"**: Gavin, p. 92.

224 **"By 1959, Herbert Jacoby was having trouble booking acts"**: *Ibid.*, p. 236.

224 **"People wanted to hear the rock singers"**: *Ibid.*, p. 237. By 1962, the Blue Angel was nearly bankrupt, and Herbert Jacoby asked Max Gordon to buy out his half interest. Gordon was forced to cut his losses and sell the club in mid-1964.

225 **embarrassingly silent:** Film/television historian Charles Stumpf provided the author with an audiotape of two live appearances of Alice Pearce on *The Jack Paar Show*. He had recorded them on the nights of their original telecasts. Besides the songs mentioned, the tape includes an abbreviated version of "If I Were as High as a Bird in the Sky."

225 **"She was playing at the Shubert"**: Alexander interview, 1987.

225 **171 East Seventy-first Street:** The Baileys' neighbors, Hume Cronyn and Jessica Tandy, lived up the street at Number 136.

225 **"They sort of banged around in that big house"**: Wheeler interview.

225 **garbage in a large chest freezer:** Author's interview with Reginald and Elaine Maynard, June 2004.

Chapter Eighteen

227 **Mike Rayhill:** Robert Michael Rayhill (1930–1981), called "Bob" back home in Utica, dropped out of Michigan State University in 1949 to pursue an acting career. Two years later, after sailing to Europe on the *Queen Mary*, he found work singing in clubs like Le Drap d'Or and Spivy's East Side. While there, he landed a bit part in John Huston's film *Moulin Rouge*. His only other film appearance was another bit in *The Bold and the Brave* (1956) starring Mickey Rooney. Rayhill attempted to reignite his Hollywood career in 1959, and when this failed, he joined Gramercy Tours, Inc., which specialized in "bachelor party" tours of Mexico and Europe. His last known job was cruise director on the U. S. S. *United States*, the last American luxury liner, which operated until 1970. Rayhill died in New York City following a brief illness. He was 51.

227 **"parked a couple of blocks from the theater"**: *Scranton Times-Tribune*, 30 April 1957.

227 **boyfriend of television producer-director Ralph Levy:** Holley, *Mike Connolly and the Manly Art of Hollywood Gossip*, p. 15. Levy (1919–2001) helped Rayhill win bit parts on two episodes of *The Jack Benny Program* during the 1955-56 television season. Before moving to Hollywood, Levy had directed Alice Pearce in *The 54th Street Revue* at CBS Studio 52 on West Fifty-fourth Street in New York. In 1958, he married Miranda Masocco (1915–2011) in Santa Fe, New Mexico.

227 **Chateau Marmont:** Rayhill's friend, Mike Connolly, shared the following anecdote with his readers in May 1956: "Marilyn Monroe moved away from the house on Beverly Glen Drive and into the Chateau Marmont in Hollywood, incognito, of course. I learned that Marilyn had moved through singer Mike Rayhill. Mike lives in the apartment below Marilyn's. Marilyn was cooking some hamburger for her dog and put it on a ledge of the Marmont to cool. It fell and splattered Mike who

was sunbathing on the balcony below Marilyn's. Marilyn leaned over to apologize and then came down in blue jeans and shirt to mop up."

228 **help her write a musical comedy:** *Scranton Times-Tribune*, 22 August 1958; *Pittsburgh Post-Gazette*, 23 September 1958.

228 **"Alice Pearce, femmedian":** *Lebanon Daily News*, 4 May 1959.

228 **"But my uncle was gay!":** Author's interview with Nancy Cummings, 3 November 2015.

228 **"The late William LeMassena":** Letter from Tom Monsell to FT, 1 August 2003.

229 **Ralph Roberts replaced Heywood Hale Broun:** *Salisbury Post*, 3 January 1960.

229 **"old flame" Davis:** *Boston Daily Record*, 4 November 1958.

229 **Ralph Roberts:** Ralph Leonard Roberts (1916–1999), born in Salisbury, North Carolina, was one of ten children born to a cotton broker who had worked his way up from being a carder in area textile mills. As a youth, Ralph loved literature, music and movies, wrote poetry, and enjoyed dramatics. He attended both Catawba College and the University of North Carolina prior to a stint working in a textile mill. At 24, he joined the army and rose to the rank of major, becoming Gen. Joseph Stillwell's personnel officer in the China-Burma theater. After moving to New York, he lived first at 315 West Fourth Street, later moving to 409 East Fifty-first where he lived for many years. In 1948, Ralph made his Broadway debut in an unsuccessful revival of *Angel Street*. His film debut was M-G-M's *Dial 1119* (1950). With actress Julie Harris, whom he supported in *The Lark*, he was featured on the cover of *Time* in 1955. Marilyn Monroe became his most famous massage client in 1959, and for the final three years of her life, Ralph was considered by many as her most intimate friend. He continued acting into the late 1980s, but being a masseur remained his primary career. Ralph, who never married, spent the final three years of his life in Salisbury, where he died of a heart attack at his home on April 30, 1999. "None of the people at his funeral," said old friend Rose Post, "wanted to leave." See *Salisbury Post*, 23 October 2006.

229 **"looked like the Indian on the old buffalo nickel":** Shayne, *Double Life*, p. 54.

229 **"I really wanted to be an actor":** *Salisbury Post*, circa December 1956.

230 **"solid reputation as a Southern gentleman":** Spoto, *Marilyn Monroe: The Biography*, p. 412.

230 **Paul Davis:** Paul Ralph Davis was the son of Max and Sarah Raphel Davis. During the 1930s and 40s, he lived with his parents and siblings at 47 Withington Street, a large two-family home in Dorchester owned by his maternal grandfather Sol Raphel, a tailor who occupied the other half with his wife Fannie and their younger children. Paul lived at 332 West Twenty-eighth Street in Manhattan during the war years. Postwar, for more than a decade, he lived in an apartment at 11 East Eightieth Street, concurrently renting an apartment at 833 ½ Sweetzer Avenue, Los Angeles, for the latter part of that period.

230 **three ringleaders:** Paul's fellow autograph hounds were William Joseph Coleman (1919–1993) of Chelsea and Frederick Howard Davis (1920–1999) of Framingham, the latter being of no relation to Paul.

230 **"We give [the actors] gifts":** *Boston Globe*, 16 November 1939. One of Paul's autograph books (1937–38) is part of the APC. It includes the signatures of Jon Hall, Ezio Pinza, Evelyn Keyes, Mischa Auer, Rex O'Malley, and Clifton Webb.

230 **Bishop-Lee School of Theatre:** First located at 73 Mount Vernon Street, the school was established by Emily Bishop and Adele Lee in the fall of 1934. In 1940, the school was relocated to 6 Byron Street.

230 **"Paul and Ruth Roman had done summer stock":** Email message from Renee Summers to FT, 13 April 2010; author's interview with Summers, 24 January 2013. Paul was eleven years older than Summers.

231 **Paul was drafted:** *New York Times*, 10 April 1943.

232 *War and Peace*: Paul filmed three other films in Italy during this period. Reportedly, one starred Sophia Loren, while another one, *Conescete La Bella Gina*, featured Paul in a leading role. See *Boston Daily Record*, 13 March 1956.

232 *The Teahouse of the August Moon*: Paul was a replacement in the role of Sgt. Gregovich during the final two weeks the show played at the Martin Beck. This marked his second and final acting experience on the Broadway stage. In November 1956, he would repeat his role at New York City Center.

232 **"Paul Davis couldn't find a job in Hollywood":** *Pasadena Independent*, 7 January 1959. Paul served as a stage manager for three other Broadway pro-

ductions: *Kiss and Tell* (1943), *Good as Gold* (1957), and *Hot Spot* (1963).

232 **"tidy total of $280,000":** *Washington Evening Star,* 1 April 1959.

232 **"That day the interest was in the audience":** *Salisbury Post,* 3 January 1960.

232 **The Washington run of *Bells*:** On March 31, Alice, along with fellow player Hal Linden, entertained at a luncheon to kick off a fundraising campaign for the American Cancer Society at the Sheraton Park Hotel.

233 **"Hundreds of dinner parties":** *Los Angeles Times,* 21 April 1959.

233 **"Alice Pearce is excellent":** *Valley Times,* 22 April 1959.

233 **"Alice took us to the cast's hangout":** Swanson account, 2013.

233 **"a Broadway person":** "An Interview with Eddie The Old Philosopher Lawrence," *Classic Television Showbiz,* http://classicshowbiz.blogspot. com/2011/07/eddie-bold-draft.html, accessed 9 April 2020.

233 **"I learned that the MGMoguls":** *Philadelphia Inquirer,* 28 April 1959.

233 **"Most good actors also enjoy":** Brown, p. xiv.

234 **Alice received nothing but praise:** *Oakland Tribune,* 2 June 1959; *Sacramento Bee,* 7 June 1959; *San Francisco Examiner,* 3 June 1959. Glackin described Ralph Roberts as "easily the most disquietingly likable giant of a police subaltern to show up onstage since Gilbert and Sullivan gave up the ghost."

234 **rented an apartment together:** "Ralph's Manuscript," *Ralph L. Roberts.com,* http://www.ralphl-roberts.com/Manuscript/manuscriptpage19.htm, accessed 10 April 2020.

234 **"the society of tasteful men":** In David Marshall's *The DD Group: An Online Investigation into the Death of Marilyn Monroe* (iUniverse, Inc., 2005), Monroe researcher Eric Woodard identified Ralph Roberts as a gay man. When contacted by the author in 2020, Woodard confirmed his source for this statement as James Haspiel, Monroe's intimate friend who also knew Roberts.

234 **an astonishing 2,000:** unsourced newspaper clipping, 1959, APC.

234 **part of her weekly paycheck:** "Revue Star Collects Hats—All the Same Style," unsourced Bermuda newspaper clipping, 1953, APC.

235 **"Peggy played my sister":** *Dallas Times Herald,* 12 August 1959, clipping, APC.

235 **Cass would echo that sentiment:** *TV Radio Mirror,* November 1961.

235 **"Miss Pearce manages to give":** *Dallas Morning News,* 22 August 1959.

235 **"Since everybody in the world":** *Dallas Times Herald,* 8 September 1959, clipping, APC.

235 **Jean Stapleton:** For the film version of *Bells,* Holliday and Stapleton were joined by four others from the Broadway and touring productions: Dort Clark, Bernie West, Ralph Roberts, and in a small role, Hal Linden. Dean Martin was Holliday's leading man.

236 **"one constant struggle":** Fordin, p. 508.

236 **"We watched as it sank like a stone":** *Films of the Golden Age,* Summer 2016.

236 **Mayfair Supper Dance:** *Ballroom Dance Magazine,* February 1960.

236 **Milton Lyon:** Milton Neeson Levine (1923–1995), a native of Pittsburgh, was a graduate of Carnegie-Mellon University. For more than thirty years he directed the Triangle Club's annual musicals, having founded the McCarter Theatre at Princeton in 1960. When once asked why he chose to work with college students instead of being a professional actor, Lyon smiled and said he was "married to Princeton." However, in early 1959, he was briefly married to Elaine Frueauff, the daughter of Antoinette Perry, for whom the Tony Awards were named.

Chapter Nineteen

237 **"Honey! What do you think was the reason?":** *San Antonio Light,* 6 March 1959.

237 **"a good idea carried to extreme lengths":** *Variety,* 11 February 1959.

237 **"salon of eccentrics":** Staggs, p. 265.

237 **"a blabber-mouth":** *Atlanta Constitution,* 26 January 1960.

237 **"intelligent, literate conversations":** Staggs, p. 265.

238 **"was to prove an agonizing misnomer":** *New York Times,* 27 January 1960.

238 **"pour the special magic":** *Boston Globe,* 27 January 1960.

238 **"delightful whimsy and satire":** *Valley Times,* 29 January 1960.

238 **"regularly cackling off":** *New York Journal-American,* 27 January 1960.

238 **Angel in the Wings:** After the evening performance on March 5, Alice and Hartman were among the

hundreds of entertainers appearing at the Miami Beach Municipal Auditorium in the Dade County United Cerebral Palsy Telethon, telecast over WCKT.

239 **"Alice Pearce brings down the house":** *Miami Herald*, 25 February 1960.

239 **her solo number:** "If I Were as High as a Bird in the Sky."

239 **"All [Miss Pearce] has to do":** *Miami News*, 24 February 1960.

239 **"a bright red wool unbelted tunic":** "Gamin Chapeau, a 'Pearcing' Look—It's Alice Doing Fashion Poses," *Miami Herald*, 24 February 1960.

239 **"kooky little touch":** Post, p. 82.

240 **"I'm writing an intimate revue":** Peper, p. 22. Neither project came to fruition. Nor did plans for Alice to appear in *I've Got It*, a television panel show with Marc Connelly and Hermione Gingold.

240 **Matt Cimber:** Born in the Bronx on January 12, 1936, Cimber's real name was Thomas Vitale Ottaviano. He was sometimes credited as Matteo Ottaviano. In 1964, he married actress Jayne Mansfield, whom he divorced almost two years later.

240 **William Guthrie:** William Alexander Guthrie (1925–2011), Princeton University Class of 1947, was born in Baltimore. For many years he was a struggling playwright in New York City. He moved to Boston in the 1970s to join the advertising department at Little, Brown and Company. Later, he moved to Cambridge, Massachusetts and summered in a small cottage in Kennebunkport, Maine. After a seventeen-year battle with dementia and heart disease, the never-wed Guthrie died at 85 in Princeton. *The Ignorants Abroad* was his first and only New York production. "Logic, language, and literature were the pillars of [his] life," according to a memorial in the *Princeton Alumni Weekly* (16 May 2012).

241 **"trifling paradoxes":** *Long Island Star-Journal*, 24 May 1960.

241 **"I think it was the first comedy I had ever tackled":** Cimber interview.

241 **"Cimber has permitted":** *New York Herald Tribune*, 24 May 1960, p. 18. Crist could not avoid this nugget as her summation: "Mr. Guthrie has not made a play, except on words . . . oops. Sorry."

242 **"The dauntless Miss Bevans":** *Long Island Star-Journal*, 24 May 1960.

242 **"Accepting the script":** *Variety*, 1 June 1960, p. 72. The reviewer gave Alice a nod ("broad but vital") and noted: "When Guthrie does abandon the epigram, he often comes up with a genuinely funny observation on a world he himself live in. There is this anguish expressed by Miss Pearce when she hears that her daughter has eloped, 'I gave her the best years of my life, the best comic books money could buy. It was I who saw that she had her first permanent as soon as her hair was thick enough to absorb the chemicals.' An unwieldy, un-Wildey line, but one that expresses more truth than many abstract witticisms on fashion and respectability."

242 **"in a style of antithesis":** *New York Times*, 24 May 1960. Guthrie did allow Mrs. Oxslip a few zingers, such as: "Incompatibility is when one partner in a marriage wants to commit adultery and the other does not."

242 ***Hotel Paradiso*:** The farce had been staged in 1957 at Henry Miller's Theatre, featuring Bert Lahr, John Emery, Angela Lansbury, and Alice's friend Carleton Carpenter.

242 **"There are so few straight comedies":** Peper, p. 22.

242 **June Harding:** June Allison Harding (1937–2019) hailed from Emporia, Virginia. A 1959 graduate of the Richmond Professional Institute of the College of William and Mary, she made her Broadway debut two years later in *Take Her, She's Mine*. Harding went on to appear in Hollywood-based television shows and at least one film, *The Trouble with Angels* (1966), co-starring Hayley Mills. She retired to New England where she took up painting landscapes, still lifes, and abstracts. She died at 81 of natural causes while under hospice care in Deer Isle, Maine.

243 **"I had worked with other professional actors":** Email message from June Harding to FT, 23 June 2013.

243 **"I was a fledgling director":** Cimber interview.

243 **"our character man":** Letter from June Harding to Virginia Harding, 20 May 1960, shared by June Harding via email with FT, 10 May 2013. The "character man" was Charles Gerald (1920–1988) who played Lady Valerie's long-lost husband. In 2014, Guthrie Sayen, the nephew of playwright William Guthrie, shared the following via email with FT: "I remember a story of my uncle punching the director on Fifth Avenue, NYC. If this is true, it must be the only act of violence in my uncle's life."

243 **wooden cricket in a cage:** Email message from June Harding to FT, 16 June 2013. Valerie is Philippa Bevans, who evidently once saw a roach when entering Theatre East.

243 **"I worked on the hem":** Letter from June Harding to Virginia Harding, mid-June 1960, shared by June Harding via email with FT, 16 June 2013.

243 **"Alice made me promise to call her":** Letter from June Harding to Virginia Harding, 25 June 1960, shared by June Harding via email with FT, 16 June 2013.

243 *Redhead:* Alice was reunited in Dallas with Carol Channing who was appearing in her revue *Show Business* at the State Fair Music Hall during Alice's rehearsals at the same venue.

244 **"rollicking murder mystery":** *Dallas Morning News,* 10 July 1960.

244 **"When the show tries to be clever":** *Denton Record-Chronicle,* 12 July 1960.

245 *Full Circle:* Alice's 1961 resume is the only known evidence proving that Alice appeared on this soap opera.

246 **"Static":** Most episodes of *The Twilight Zone* were filmed at the M-G-M studios, but "Static" was the second of six consecutive episodes which, in the effort to cut costs, were instead videotaped in the manner of a live drama. However, the savings were judged to be insufficient to offset the loss of depth of visual perspective which only film could offer. The experiment was deemed a failure and never tried again.

246 **"Operation Pudney":** When Katy hears that Ethel is engaged, she responds, "But she must be past fifty-five!" Sothern, nearing fifty-two, was closer to Ethel's age than Alice, who was forty-three, but as star of the show, she required filtered lenses for her close-ups—despite a noticeable contrast when the shots alternated with close-ups of Alice and Jesse White.

247 **"considerably less experience":** Lobenthal, p. 493.

247 **"The play wasn't right from the beginning":** Israel, p. 327.

247 **"one of the most original comedy minds":** Lobenthal, p. 493.

247 **"started with a germ":** Howard Taubman, *New York Times* 2 February 1961.

247 **"sharp wit and offbeat imagination":** Meredith, *So Far, So Good,* p. 69.

247 **"only intermittently funny":** *Philadelphia Inquirer,* 27 December 1960.

247 **"seem to be long for this world":** *Philadelphia Daily News,* 27 December 1960.

248 **"running away with her or from us":** *Evening Star,* 11 January 1961.

248 **"Dear, dear Alice Pearce":** Letter from Mary Chase to Alice Pearce, undated, APC.

248 **"She continued to accept new material":** Lobenthal, p. 494.

248 **"Everyone's performance suffered":** Meredith, p. 70.

249 **"I thought she was terrific":** Carrier, *Tallulah Bankhead: A Bio-Bibliography,* p. 104.

249 **"I remember being surprised":** Letter from Janice Mars to FT, 10 April 2003.

249 **Janice Mars:** Born Janice Maxine Marx in Lincoln, Nebraska, in 1924, Mars left her native state in 1944 to pursue an acting career in New York. She studied at Lee Strasberg's Actors Studio and met Marlon Brando who became an intimate lifelong friend. *Midgie Purvis* reunited Mars with William Redfield and Nydia Westman, whom she (and Brando) supported in a 1953 New England summer tour of *Arms and the Man.* In 1960, after the Baq Room closed for good, Mars recorded eleven of her most popular songs. Brando kept the master tapes in his own home for safekeeping until 1999 when they were given to Mars' relatives and then released on CD in 2001. In the early 1970s, Mars moved to New Mexico where she enjoyed writing songs and poetry and tending her garden. She died there at age 79 on April 9, 2004. Her first husband was lyricist and author Benedict Ross Berenberg (1911–1997) whom she married in 1958. Her second husband was composer-arranger Hampton St. Paul Reese (1925–1994) whom she divorced in 1971.

249 **"a dark, dank little box":** Gavin, p. 137.

249 **"unmistakable singing voice":** Israel, p. 327.

250 **"Except for Pia Zadora":** *Variety,* 8 February 1961.

250 **"wastes time on a batch of snoopy [women]":** *New York Herald Tribune,* 2 February 1961.

250 **largely sank without a trace:** It is difficult to justly critique *Midgie,* aside from the contemporary reviews, as there seem to be no extant copies of the script used in the Broadway production. Searches of the respective archived papers of Chase, Whitehead, and Bankhead yield no such text. The only script for *Midgie Purvis* among Chase's papers at the University of Oregon is the one she submitted for publication in 1963. This revamped edition does not include the character played by Alice

Pearce in the 1961 Broadway version. However, in 2020, the son of actor William Redfield discovered among his father's papers a bound copy of what must have been the script employed for the initial rehearsals in November 1960. Redfield's script is heavily marked, showing excised portions of dialogue and crowded substitutions in the margins.

250 **"The play was rather charming"**: Mars letter.

250 **"if Buzz Meredith hadn't"**: Lobenthal, p. 496. Ted Hook (1930–1995), a former chorus dancer whose film credits numbered in the hundreds, served as Tallulah Bankhead's manager and social secretary from 1958 until 1962. He subsequently opened a restaurant called Backstage next to the Martin Beck Theatre where *Midgie Purvis* had its brief run. Regarding the play, Hook told Lobenthal, "I knew there was magic there."

251 **modeled for *Look* magazine**: *Look*, 9 May 1961. Perkins Bailey, still employed by *Look*, may have been instrumental in securing this job for Alice.

251 **"It wasn't until Pat [Tanner] took"**: Dennis, *Little Me*, p. xiii.

251 **"I never had no trainin' nowhere!"**: Alexander interview, 2003.

251 **"phony autobiography"**: Myers, p. 165.

251 **"The whole thing was marvelous fun"**: *Ibid.*, p. 168.

252 **"The place was inhabited"**: Carpenter, p. 205.

254 **General Foods**: *Variety*, 15 February 1961. Ironically, the cancellation of *The Ann Sothern Show* proved that "what goes around, comes around." In 1958, when Sothern's show debuted, General Foods bumped Desilu sitcom *December Bride* from its four-year Monday night spot, replacing it with *Ann Sothern*. *Bride* was moved to a Thursday slot, where it languished for one season until it was cancelled. Two years later, the same happened to *The Ann Sothern Show* which—in a final twist— was replaced by reruns of *December Bride*.

255 **Principal photography**: Alice's final scene was filmed at the Warner Brothers Burbank studio on May 17. She was called back twice for post-recording on May 25 and 29. Details of this production are from the "Daily Production and Progress Reports" of the Warner Brothers Archives, managed by USC's Cinematic Arts Library in Los Angeles.

255 **as soggy as a dish of dog food**: *Boston Globe*, 7 June 1962.

Chapter Twenty

256 **"chubby sheepdog of a youth"**: Plummer, *In Spite of Myself*, p. 120.

256 **Jane Broder**: Active in the entertainment world for more than sixty years, Jane Broder (1894–1977) aided the careers of scores of actors, including Bette Davis, Rosalind Russell, and Colleen Dewhurst. She was also the personal representative and close friend of Marion Lorne.

256 **"for a few minutes"**: *Screen Actor*, May–June 1970.

256 **"George went to New York"**: Email message from Carolyn Roesner to FT, 3 April 2018.

256 **Neighborhood Playhouse**: The Playhouse was a professional conservatory for actors, at the time headed by Sanford Meisner.

256 **"Never regret!"**: *Screen Actor*, May–June 1970.

256 **relocating to Los Angeles**: "His road trip across the country is its own story," insisted George's niece Carolyn Roesner. He was accompanied by the endearing Maude Franchot (who had married the uncle of actor Franchot Tone) and her tiny dog.

256 **George Morris**: George Edward Morris (1923–1969) was born in Havana, Cuba, where his father Henry was the manager of the Havana office of Swift & Company, one of America's leading meatpackers. In 1925, when George was seventeen months old, a deranged stenographer entered his father's office and shot him four times, killing him. George's mother, who was then pregnant, returned to the States with George and his older brother. Their baby sister was born that same year, the day after Christmas. George, who never married, was especially close to his mother, and they wrote to each daily during World War II. "My grandmother always referred to him as a 'bachelor,'" said Carolyn Roesner, "but I think he was probably gay, but conflicted—in those days it wasn't easy to come out—however, I have absolutely no proof of this." George, who was a smoker, had high blood pressure, a factor that may have led to his sudden death, which occurred at his home, 12661 Sarah Street in Studio City, California.

257 **"My mother told me"**: Email message from Channing Lowe to FT, 28 March 2013.

257 **Chan's godmother**: Channing letter.

257 **"I don't remember exactly how it happened"**: Lowe email.

257 **both in print and on the Broadway stage:** Dennis, *Auntie Mame*, p. 13; Mordden, *All That Glittered*, p. 300.

258 **my family moved to New York City:** On December 9, 1960, Carol Channing won complete custody of her son Channing Lowe. Around this same time, the move to Manhattan was accomplished. Due to Alice's busy schedule from October 1960 until June 1961, there was little chance to rendezvous with Chan until the summer of 1961.

258 **House of Chan:** Founded in 1938 by Sou Chan, the restaurant was located at Fifty-second Street and Seventh Avenue.

258 **Goldie Hawkins:** Louis Golson Hawkins (1917–2000) operated Goldie's New York, the "breeziest piano hangout of the '50s and '60s," at 232 East Fifty-third Street. Hawkins, a native of Fort Deposit, Alabama, seemed to "populate his room exclusively with old friends," said the *New York Times* in 1960. Regulars included Ethel Merman, Judy Holliday, Betty Comden and Adolph Green. Chan Lowe added, "My understanding is that Alice, Charlie [Gaynor], Goldie, the Broadway set designer Oliver Smith, and my mother belonged to the same coterie of theatre people that ran around together before I was born."

258 **"I spent the whole day with Alice":** Most likely this occasion occurred during June or July of 1961 before Alice began rehearsals for *Sail Away*. Channing Lowe was born March 25, 1953, and would have been eight years old that summer.

259 **"Everyone loved Alice, *except* Noël Coward":** Deacon letter.

259 **"a well-disposed megalomaniac":** Noël Coward, *Sail Away* script, Joe Layton Papers, Billy Rose Theatre Division, New York Public Library.

259 **"old-fashioned heart-throb trash":** *Boston Globe*, 10 August 1961.

259 **"I've tried to keep the dialogue":** *Theatre Arts*, September 1961.

260 **"anything even half so ambitious":** Marchant, *The Privilege of His Company*, p. 125.

260 **"I don't remember, since *Bitter Sweet*":** Ibid., p. 475. Coward's operetta *Bitter Sweet* debuted in London in 1929.

260 **"Before Alice went into rehearsals":** Alexander interview, 1987.

260 **"Coward, the kind of director":** *New York Herald Tribune*, 22 July 1961.

260 **William Marchant:** William Marchant Davis (1923–1995), born in Allentown, Pennsylvania,

attended Temple University and Yale University. After serving in the Air Force during World War Two, he turned to writing in 1948. His only hit was *The Desk Set*, which ran on Broadway for 297 performances in 1955-56. He died in obscurity in a New Jersey hospital, where his body lay unclaimed in the morgue for six weeks. Although his only brother survived him, his next of kin was listed as actress Dorothy Stickney, then ninety-nine years old and no longer living at the address on file.

260 **"One hot July Sunday afternoon":** Marchant, pp. 127-130.

261 **"I can only tell you":** Letter from Elaine Stritch to FT, 16 January 1989.

261 **"surprised that she had issues with Coward":** Email message from Grover Dale to FT, 23 July 2018.

261 **"I recall [Alice] as cheerful":** Email message from Alan Helms to FT, 3 July 2010.

262 **the name of Alice Pearce is absent:** Coward's first entry following Alice's daring "interpolations" of July 30 is dated August 13 and concentrates on the Boston premiere of August 9.

262 **"the one and only Alice Pearce":** *Boston Evening American*, 4 August 1961. "Pass the mustard" seems to have been one of Coward's stock phrases. When screenwriter Ben Hecht radically rewrote Coward's *Design for Living*, Coward reportedly quipped, "I am told that there are three of my original lines left in the film—such original ones as 'Pass the mustard.'" Marchant, relating Coward's standard practice of weekend rest when engaged in a production, also quotes Coward: "I speak literally to nobody from the time the curtain falls on Saturday night until it rises again the Monday evening following. Except to say 'Pass the mustard' or something equally imperative . . ."

262 **"nearly every star of one of his plays":** Lobenthal, p. 95.

262 **"a brittle man":** *Chicago Tribune*, 27 April 1975.

263 **"she is greeted by warm applause":** *Boston American*, 16 August 1961.

263 **"Alice Pearce needs funnier lines":** *Boston Globe*, 10 August 1961.

263 **"No woman writer ever talked like that":** Day, *The Letters of Noël Coward*, p. 679.

263 **The tryout in Philadelphia:** Jerry Gaghan of the *Philadelphia Daily News* (6 September 1961) noted: "The playwright in his attempt to show the cruise passengers as bores has overworked some

of them to just that point. Alice Pearce, a sight comic, finds little rewarding in her role of a traveling novelist."

263 **"First they cut her hair"**: *New York Times*, 2 November 1999. Alice's observation was included in Elaine Stritch's reminiscences of *Sail Away* when she was interviewed in conjunction with its restaging at Weill Recital Hall in November 1999. Walter Winchell offered this contemporary summation: "The Noël Coward *Sail Away* cast tells chums that Jean Fenn got an ultimatum from Noël: 'Cut your hair or get fired!' He thought, they say, she'd rather cut it (it fell to her waistline) than lose the featured role. So she cut it. Coward fired her, anyway." See *Philadelphia Inquirer*, 27 September 1961.

263 **Joe Layton**: Layton (1931–1994) explained: "Noël made the decision [to cut Fenn's role] on Thursday, September 7. He did the rewriting Friday and Saturday. We rehearsed Sunday and Monday and played it Monday night. Good, bad, or indifferent, it was the most exciting evening I've ever experienced in the theater." See *Philadelphia Inquirer*, 17 September 1961.

263 **"there was nothing against the idea"**: Payn, p. 478.

264 **"Listen hard"**: *Theatre Arts*, December 1961.

264 **"Some of the comic lines"**: *The New Yorker*, 14 October 1961.

264 **"Looking like an irascible macaw"**: *New York Times*, 4 October 1961.

264 **"*Sail Away* got jumbled notices"**: *Wilkes-Barre Times Leader*, 10 October 1961.

264 **"Margalo Gillmore"**: *Mt. Kisco Patent Trader*, 15 October 1961.

264 **"mildly funny"**: *Variety*, 11 October 1961.

264 **"there is something about *Sail Away*"**: Payn, p. 484.

264 **"I am sick to death of poor *Sail Away*"**: *Ibid.*, p. 497.

264 **"Dearest Alice, Gallop into the paddock"**: Note from Noël Coward to Alice Pearce, APC.

264 **"she had never been so disappointed"**: Alexander interview, 2003.

264 **"For those of us who love Alice Pearce"**: *Kane Republican*, 16 November 1961. The actress Joan Crawford was a fan. She wrote to Alice on October 12 after seeing the show: "Dear Alice, Dammit, you are but the greatest! With such devotion and respect, Joan." (APC.)

265 **Josephine sold her 140-acre property**: *Brattleboro Reformer*, 24 June 1961 and 27 June 1961. The

seven-room clapboard house at Whitingham, built around 1843, featured a 31-foot living room with a fireplace of decorative tile. All bedrooms and the bathroom were on the second floor. Half the acreage was in pasture, the balance in woodland. The buyer was Hans Winkler of Scarsdale, New York.

265 **"she possessed a beauty of mind"**: PE, 21 September 1961.

265 **"When a show closes"**: McManus, p. 45.

265 **"[The contract] means something"**: *TV Radio Mirror*, November 1961.

265 **Acres and Pains**: Filming began February 5, 1962, at the Ziv-United Artists studio in New York. On February 15, thirty-five members of the cast and crew filmed exteriors for eight hours on location in Doylestown, Pennsylvania, at an authentic ramshackle farmhouse. See *Bristol Daily Courier*, 10 March 1962. If the premise of *Acres and Pains* sounds familiar, that's because the CBS sitcom *Green Acres* (1965-1971) shared its theme with Perelman's. Whether Sommers was inspired by Perelman's work remains debatable, but in 1950 he developed a short-lived radio comedy for CBS called *Granby's Green Acres*, starring Gale Gordon as a blustery bank clerk who leaves his job to buy a farm. Bea Benaderet played his wife. Years later, Sommers pitched his idea to adapt *Granby's* for television to producer Paul Henning, who snapped it up and integrated it with his current hits, *The Beverly Hillbillies* and *Petticoat Junction*.

266 **"a far cut above"**: *Variety*, 15 May 1962.

266 **"may look funny on paper"**: *Des Moines Register*, 14 May 1962.

266 **"Perelman just doesn't seem to translate"**: Stern, p. 35.

267 **"These parody memoirs are a cinch"**: *The Saturday Review*, 1 August 1964.

267 **"I had a wonderful time"**: Myers, p. 200.

267 **"Many of the pictures were taken"**: Dennis, *Little Me*, pp. xviii–xix.

267 **"Peeps and I were having dinner"**: Alexander interview, 1987.

267 **Butterfield brothers**: Besides Robert Locklin whom he met that evening at 21, Cris eventually rounded up seven other men to pose as the younger Butterfield brothers. For the record, they were: ballet dancer Eugene Tanner (1929–1986), set designer Merrill Sindler (1931–2014), singer Del Hanley (1931–2005), composer Harry Percer (1932–1995), dancer Lorenzo Bianco (1932–1994), photographer Steve Schapiro (born

1934), and actor Johnny Kuhl (1935–2003). Actor William Martel (1916–1997) depicted the oldest brother, President George Butterfield. Cris had known Bianco, whose birth name was Lorenzo Bianco Schlick, since he was a boy. Bianco was the grandson of author Margery Williams (*The Velveteen Rabbit*). Schapiro had often photographed Pat Tanner. According to Cris, Kuhl was a friend of Harold Lang and Hanley was the lover of Hugh Martin.

268 **"Those two books with Pat"**: Alexander letter, 1986.

268 **"The story was not very complicated"**: Alexander interview, 1987.

269 **Hal Vursell:** Harold Dean Vursell (1908–1977), born in Salem, Illinois, graduated from the University of Illinois. He became a vice-president at Farrar, Straus and Giroux where, according to Boris Kachka, author of *Hothouse* (Simon & Schuster, 2013), he was "a jack-of-all-trades who could move fluidly from production to copyediting to acquisitions." Besides Patrick Dennis, Vursell worked with other writers, including Colette and Madeleine L'Engle. His life partner was financier Franklin Haase Kissner (1909–1988), with whom he shared a home at 24 Gramercy Park South—filled with 4,500 rare books.

269 **Sterling Jensen:** Native Californian Sterling Brown Jensen (1925–1993) graduated from San Diego State University following a stint in the Philippines during WWII. He married at age 48. Jensen died of congestive heart failure in New Orleans.

269 **Dal Jenkins:** William Dal Jenkins (born 1935) appeared in supporting roles on television programs from 1961 until 1983. His television credits include *Bonanza*, *Batman*, and *The Wild, Wild West*.

273 **"It's a friendly country"**: *Philadelphia Daily News*, 6 December 1962.

273 **Harry Percer:** Tennessee native Harry Harsson Percer (1932–1995) was a 1955 graduate of Memphis State College, majoring in education. He later moved to New York City after meeting Walter Pistole, who became his life partner. Percer died of AIDS-related pneumonia in Los Angeles.

273 **Walter Pistole:** Memphis-born Walter Hiram Pistole (1921–1994), the son of a physician, graduated from Harvard in 1944 with a degree in English. In New York, Pistole became an editor for the publishers Reynal and Hitchcock and was later an assistant editor for the *Sunday Times Book Review*. At the time of Patrick Dennis' *High Life*, he was an "editor in search of plays" for the Robert Fryer-Lawrence Carr production office. He was also the author of a three-act farce called *Welcome, Senator!* (1946). Pistole died in Los Angeles of an electrolyte imbalance precipitated by Hepatitis B.

273 **"Pat took [*High Life*] around to investors"**: Alexander interview, 1987.

273 **"It's like a New York convention"**: *Newsweek*, 16 December 1957.

273 **"I [had become] discouraged"**: Stern, p. 35.

273 **"stepping off a dock"**: *TV Radio Mirror*, November 1961.

Chapter Twenty-One

274 **On March 14, 1962:** *Variety*, 15 March 1962.

274 **"It was offered to me"**: Stern, p. 35.

274 **"Well, in her first scene"**: Post, p. 81.

275 **"Better I should walk"**: *Los Angeles Times*, 28 March 1963. In 1965, Alice told journalist Harold Stern that the experience scared her so badly that she never again attempted to drive.

275 **"as syrupy-sentimental as you can get"**: *Cincinnati Enquirer*, 11 April 1963.

276 **"the real loves here"**: *New York Times*, 4 April 1963. According to *Variety* (11 January 1962), producer Gant Gaither originally considered Elizabeth Montgomery for the role ultimately played by Eileen Heckart.

276 **"Nearly did me in"**: *Palm Beach Daily News*, 12 November 1976.

276 **8629 Holloway Drive:** Although Alice may not have known it, Laird Cregar, with whom she had appeared in a stage production of *The Man Who Came to Dinner* back in 1944, lived in a nearby bungalow at 8659 Holloway Plaza Drive during 1941 and 1942. Actor Sal Mineo's final residence was 8563 Holloway Drive, just one tenth of a mile from Alice's door. Mineo was knifed to death in his apartment's parking lot in 1976.

276 **"West Hollywood was like a small, comfy village"**: Carpenter, p. 214.

276 **"That whole freer, more theatrical sense"**: Mann, *Behind the Screen*, p. 334.

277 **Francis Lederer:** *Boston Globe*, 16 November 1939; *Boston Traveler*, 23 December 1959.

277 **Desilu Workshop Theatre:** Located on the Desilu-Gower lot, the theatre building—formerly RKO's two-hundred-seat Studio Club Little Theatre—was renovated by Ball in late 1958.

277 **"a stock company"**: Sanders, *Desilu: The Story of Lucille Ball and Desi Arnaz*, p. 170.

277 **"Lucy was very naïve about the stage"**: Author's interview with Carole Cook, 16 November 2019.

277 **"Pesha Darshefsky"**: *Variety* announced that Ball was producing *The Desilu Revue* with the assistance of Pesha Darshefsky. A few days earlier, columnist Mike Connolly reported that he "had a ball with Lucy Ball" at the Interlude, a nightclub on the Sunset Strip: "Lucy got her jollies out of introducing the near-unpronounceable HJORDIS NIVEN, David's estranged spouse, to the near-unpronounceable PESHA DARSHEFSKY, an actor." For an interview with the *Los Angeles Times*, Paul identified himself as Pesha Darshefsky, associate producer of *The Desilu Revue*. In 1965, Paul told *TV Guide* that his real name was Pesha Darshefsky. See *Variety*, 4 September 1959; *Daily Illinois State Journal*, 29 August 1959; *Los Angeles Times*, 18 October 1959; *TV Guide*, 25 December 1965.

277 **"Paul was named for a man"**: Summers interview.

277 **first-generation American:** In 1906, Paul's mother, née Sarah Raphel, also claiming Russian ancestry, immigrated to New York from her birthplace of London, England.

277 **Chaim Dashefsky:** Sponsored by banker Meier A. Slobodkin, the assistant treasurer for a federation of Jewish fraternal societies of Boston, Dashefsky arrived in America around 1900. His wife and two of his sons immigrated in October 1904, but two others, including Paul's father, were detained until January 1905 due to "eye problems," according to Paul's sister Renee Summers. Dashefsky was later known as Hyman Davis (c. 1866–1949), finally settling in Revere, Massachusetts.

277 **"My grandparents came to this country"**: "Letters to the Editor, 16 August 2005," *Portsmouth Herald*, www.seacoastonline.com, accessed 18 April 2016.

277 **"Paul always wanted to be a successful actor"**: Email message from Milton Davis to FT, 12 May 2016.

278 **"Lucille did everything for this show"**: Fidelman, *The Lucy Book*, p. 137.

278 **"I was just a kid"**: Author's interview with Jonathan Oppenheim, 31 March 2018. Despite the passage of almost sixty years—not to mention his being very young when he knew Paul—Oppenheim remembered without being prompted that Paul had lived on Sweetzer Avenue in West Hollywood. He also recalled that Paul told him that his real name was "Pesha Darshefsky." The accuracy of these particular recollections lends credence to Oppenheim's other memories of Paul Davis.

278 **Paul and Ball:** Carole Cook related an amusing anecdote: "We were at Lucy's house, all of us. And Paul reached down to get an electric plug out of the wall and his back went out, and he had to stay for the night there. And we're going, 'Oh my God, he has to stay with Lucille Ball! How do you do that? What's that like?' I was living with her, but I was out in the guesthouse. I said, 'Lucy, he's all nervous because he's gonna have to be sure he does right.' Of all people, you didn't have to worry about Lucy."

278 **"secretary and general factotum"**: Carey, *Judy Holliday*, p. 215.

278 **"My grandmother, for some reason, didn't like him"**: Helen Tuvim (1885–1973), the mother of Judy Holliday, mainly lived at the Dakota Apartments with her daughter and grandson, but she maintained a small apartment on West Seventy-fifth Street. Oppenheim recalled that at some point when Tuvim wasn't using it, Paul Davis stayed there for a time."

279 **"You Go Your Way"**: Screen Gems executive producer Harry Ackerman, in a 1962 letter to Nicholas Keesely of the Madison Avenue advertising agency Lennen & Newell, explained that the "Mary Wickes-Alice Pearce types of shows" were created as "contrast programming" to the series' cardinal element: Dennis' good intentions running afoul of Mr. Wilson. [Harry Ackerman Papers, Box 6, Folder 5, American Heritage Center, University of Wyoming.]

280 **Columbia Ranch:** Perry, *Screen Gems*, p. 4.

280 **a total cost of $730,000:** *Variety*, 20 August 1962.

280 **"Alice Pearce has a funny moment or two"**: *Variety*, 6 May 1963.

280 **"kids wouldn't have anything else to see"**: *Variety*, 23 September 1963.

281 **"I was a great fan of hers"**: Deacon letter.

282 **"[the pilot] reeked"**: "Memories of Ann Sothern by Jim Bawden," *The Columnists*, www.thecolumnists.com/bawden/bawden55.html, accessed 28 February 2013.

282 **George Schaefer:** Schaefer (1920–1997) had directed the first live television productions of *Hamlet* and *Richard III*. He also directed Alice in the 1955 production of "Alice in Wonderland" for *Hallmark Hall of Fame*.

282 **A-line evening coat of hot pink silk:** The same year, actress Jill Haworth was photographed (with Sal Mineo) wearing an identical coat. Alice's coat is currently in the possession of the author.

282 **"We need to have something running":** *Los Angeles Times*, 8 October 1962.

283 **a cigarette from her refrigerator:** Peper, p. 22.

283 **"I felt that was the dumbest casting":** Cook interview. "And Now a Word from Our Sponsor" was filmed the week of October 8, 1962.

283 **second guest spot on *Dennis the Menace*:** The episode "Jane Butterfield Says" was filmed between October 15 and 18, 1962. Alice and Mary Wickes were each paid $750 for four days' work. George Cisar was paid $650 for four days. See Harry Ackerman Papers, Box 5, Folder 6, American Heritage Center, University of Wyoming.

283 **"Dear ones":** Letter from Alice P. Rox to Mr. and Mrs. Don Herring, 15 October 1962, LSC.

284 **"It doesn't seem likely":** Alexander interview, 2003.

284 **a shrew stalled in a traffic jam:** Hunter had planned for part of the traffic jam scene to include location shooting on New York's FDR East River Drive in October 1962. However, after it rained for ten of the twelve days the crew was there, a section of the drive was simulated on Stage 12 back at Universal.

284 **"an expensive glamorous sheen":** *Variety*, 10 June 1963.

285 **"The lines and situations are fresh":** *Houston Chronicle*, 2 August 1963.

285 **"We met through a mutual friend":** Post, p. 82. Richard Lewis Deacon (1922–1984) was born in Philadelphia but grew up in Binghamton, New York. From the age of six, he knew he wanted to become an actor. "The people I idolized," he told *TV Guide* in 1969, "were the character actors, the backbone of the industry . . . Arthur Treacher, Donald Meek, Franklin Pangborn, Edmund Gwenn, Eric Blore." Deacon studied drama for two years at Ithaca College before finally moving to Hollywood in 1953. He achieved fame and fortune on the small screen, appearing in a regular role on seven series, including *A Date with the Angels*, *Leave It to Beaver*, *The Dick Van Dyke Show*, and *The Mothers-in-Law*. A lifelong bachelor, Deacon was an avid art collector and an expert on cuisine. When he unexpectedly died of a heart attack, he was just about to begin a home video on microwave cooking.

285 **"The first night I had to step in for Nancy":** *Ibid.* Jane Dulo (1917–1994) was born as Bernice Dewlow in Baltimore, Maryland, on October 13, 1917, just three days prior to Alice Pearce's birth in Manhattan. When just a kid, she was nicknamed "Ginger" because of her hair color. After high school, Dulo tried to break into show business, first in musicals and vaudeville revues. In 1942, she settled in New York after landing several bookings in clubs like the Village Vanguard and Le Ruban Bleu. Around 1956, Dulo made the move to California where she appeared in many sitcoms including *McHale's Navy*, *The Jack Benny Program*, and *The Andy Griffith Show* (with Reta Shaw and Jean Carson as her fellow escaped convicts.) Her final credit was a 1992 episode of *The Golden Girls*. She died at Cedars-Sinai Medical Center following coronary bypass surgery. Never married, Dulo had once quipped, "Love ain't for me."

286 **"Alice was one of the few ladies":** Deacon letter. Thirty-seven years later, when the author shared Deacon's statement with Carole Cook, she enthused, "Don't you love it? You know, it's funny. When you say Alice's name, I visualize her in a hat."

286 **"Since Alice didn't drive":** Post, p. 82.

286 **"I don't mean that he was a loner in a reclusive way":** Cook interview.

Chapter Twenty-Two

287 **"It doesn't do any good sometimes":** Humphrey, p. 18.

287 **Edward Montagne:** *Variety*, 2 January 1963.

287 **"[Wills] and I were sharing a dressing room":** "Ann B. Davis," *The Interviews: An Oral History of Television,* www.interviews.televisionacademy.com, accessed 20 July 2020.

287 **Beverly Wills:** Wills (1933–1963), the daughter of television star Joan Davis, died along with her sons and grandmother in a housefire later that year.

287 **"The more undisciplined members of the crew":** Letter from Ann B. Davis to FT, 29 May 2013.

287 **large house in Whitingham had finally sold:** Pearce Place was purchased by Mrs. Lovilla Bromley whose plans were to convert it into a ski lodge and guest house she had named Blueberry Hill. Bromley's venture appears to have been unsuccessful. In June 1964, she sold the house to Mildred Schenck who renamed it Eva's Lakeview

Inn. Schenck operated the inn, which featured "New England cooking" by chef Eva Jennison, at least through 1966. Schenck sold the property in 1976, and it became a private residence once again. When the author visited the house in 2004, it was undergoing renovations by its new owner Dana Friedman. See *North Adams Transcript*, 9 January 1963; *Brattleboro Reformer*, 12 June 1964 and 28 September 1976.

288 **"Dearest Bro":** Letter from Alice Pearce to Cris Alexander, 12 March 1963, author's collection.

288 **La Valencia Hotel:** Built in 1926, the hotel, commanding an oceanfront view, had long offered a hideaway for Hollywood stars, particularly those appearing at the La Jolla Playhouse.

288 **Bob and Margaret moved in on May 15:** PE, 25 April 1963.

288 **"Your wedding invitation was forwarded to me":** Letter from Alice Rox to Linda Sue Herring, June 1963, LSC.

288 **"a major depressive episode":** Myers, p. 192.

288 **"Patrick had rewritten a section for Peeps":** Alexander interview, 2003.

289 **"appear in the offering":** *New York Times*, 8 November 1963.

289 **"It was a big, lavishly produced extravaganza":** Myers, p. 201.

289 **"I hope you had a happy Fourth":** Note from Alice Pearce to Ross Hunter, July 1963, author's collection.

289 **"I first met her at an audition":** Author's interview with John Fiedler, 9 February 2003.

289 **"had many lifelong friends":** Roesner email.

290 **"do [his] own thing":** *Palm Beach Daily News*, 12 November 1976.

291 **"The Groupers":** *Marietta Journal*, 8 September 1963. "The Groupers" was a tidbit in Mike Connolly's column.

291 **"a talented actress with home appeal":** *Sponsor* magazine, March 1963.

291 **"The performer hates himself":** *Television Magazine*, January 1964.

291 **"I had no idea the Procter & Gamble people":** Humphrey, p. 18.

291 **"I couldn't stand that thing":** *TV Radio Mirror*, September 1965.

292 **"I wanted double the residuals":** Humphrey, p. 18.

292 **"premiere of *The Thrill of It All*":** *Los Angeles Times*, 6 August 1963.

293 **"Jack Warner said *The Out-of-Towners* was the worst title":** Letter from Tad Mosel to FT, 1 January 1991. Mosel shared more in his letter: "Apparently, Mr. Warner changed his mind about the title, because when Neil Simon came along a few years later with *his* movie of that name, there was no stopping him. But the title was registered with the Writers Guild, and Doc Simon had to buy it from me for five dollars, which he still owes me." Mosel enjoyed a bit part in one of the closing scenes of the movie: "I was the man on his way to the men's room, with a carefully worked out characterization—the raincoat, the thick biography of Renoir, with my finger marking my place. The extras' union wouldn't let me do it, so I had to enroll in the bit players' union, which meant I had to speak. I consented to write one word for myself—'Jackson,' in repetition of [Page's character's] name, but on the first take, I added a few noises, and Delbert Mann, the director, stopped filming to say loudly, in front of the cast, 'In this movie we are endeavoring to stick to the script, to the exact words the author wrote, so on the next take please do not embellish your part.' The cast was shocked to hear this gentle, loving man berate a poor bit player, and didn't even catch on when I hung my head and promised to be good if he'd give me one more chance. Then, I think, we giggled and the tension was broken."

294 **"A half century of emotion":** Diehl, *The Late, Great Pennsylvania Station*, p. 18.

294 **"Geraldine Page arrived for filming":** Mosel letter.

295 **Mancini then told Warner:** *Variety*, 10 March 1965. Warner had changed the film title from *The Out-of-Towners* to *The Big Weekend*, an impossible choice, said Mosel, as the story takes place on a Tuesday and Wednesday.

295 **"a waltz right straight down":** Mancini, *Did They Mention the Music?*, p. 150.

295 **"funny and touching":** *Los Angeles Times*, 4 December 1964.

295 **"human without being sentimental":** *Valley Times*, 3 December 1964.

295 **"play[ed] their respective parts":** *Variety*, 2 December 1964.

295 **"It received rave notices":** Mosel letter.

295 **"stale, dull and humorless":** *New York Times*, 8 March 1965.

295 **"I take the blame for it":** Mosel letter.

295 **took three days to film:** Warner Brothers production files show that Alice was required to film a total of six days (October 23–25, October 28–29, and November 5) at a compensation of $1,000 per week with a three-week guarantee. Mary Wickes was paid the same, but Ruth McDevitt commanded $1,500 per week with the same guarantee. Other comparative totals: Patricia Barry (2 weeks, $5,000); Barbara Nichols (2 weeks, $3,500); Charles Drake (2 days, $2,500); Richard Deacon (1 week, $1,750); Ken Lynch (2 days, $1,250); Peter Turgeon (3 days, $1,250); Sandra Gould (3 days, $750).

295 **affords Alice a comical closeup:** The closeup reveals the character's full name on her badge: Agnes Moore.

295 **trio of actresses presented quite a contrast:** In September 1961, Wickes stated her height (and weight: 136) on a biographical press release for her sitcom *Mrs. G. Goes to College.* Alice's height is found on a similar press release during the second season of *Bewitched.* She had stated the same measurement on her 1933 passport.

295 **"We cast the roles":** Letter from Delbert Mann to FT, 13 January 1989. Mann added, "We had great fun. Alice, Ruth, and Mary brought laughs from everyone on the set. It was a lovely experience."

296 **"I knew them only briefly":** Letter from Mary Wickes to FT, 13 May 1982.

297 **"This is simply how Mary responded":** Email message from Steve Taravella to FT, 9 June 2013.

297 **she lopped ten years off:** For other examples of Wickes' absurd measures to hide her age, see Taravella, pp. 156–158.

297 **"those who showed greatest interest":** Taravella, p. 170.

297 **"a strong desire to keep secret":** *Ibid.*, p. 171.

298 **"She wasn't a warm and cozy person":** *Ibid.*, p. 82.

298 **"Mary never pushed a button":** *Ibid.*

298 **"Mary Wickes was a character":** Cook interview.

299 **"They all seemed so terribly funny":** Stern, p. 35.

299 **President Kennedy's assassination:** John F. Kennedy and Alice Pearce were born the same year. He was almost five months older than she. Alice seems to have rarely mentioned politics in interviews, but it's possible that she was a Kennedy supporter.

299 **"Hot Potato à la Hazel":** The production of this episode may have been interrupted by the ensuing events of the Kennedy assassination, given certain discrepancies of the finished product. During the

final scene the police detective identifies himself as Sgt. Lewis, but the end credits list him as "Policeman Murphy." In addition, actress Ellen Corby (as Miss Elsie's sister Minnie) is included among the "Hot Potato" cast in television listings found in various magazines and newspapers, but she does not appear in the episode (or the film credits) although her character is mentioned. Moreover, the seemingly generic teaser which precedes the opening credits has nothing to do with the episode's subsequent plot, leaving one to wonder if Corby's scene(s) included a teaser which was later deleted.

299 **"I never thought I'd say this":** McManus, p. 5.

Chapter Twenty-Three

300 **"Ken wanted to do television":** Cox, *The Addams Chronicles,* p. 100.

300 **she was told that she was too young:** Humphrey, p. 18. Alice's test would have taken place in late February 1964. Filming for the pilot began on March 10.

301 **"Most of the laughs come from Alice Pearce":** *Pittsburgh Press,* 21 March 1964.

301 **"the most influential columnist":** Holley, p. 1.

301 **"the pick of the trade items":** *Newsweek,* 2 February 1954. Connolly was often ahead of *Variety* with casting news. For instance, his syndicated column, appearing in the *Pasadena Independent* on August 10, 1965, included a blurb that Alice and George Tobias had been cast for M-G-M's *The Glass Bottom Boat. Variety* reported the same item on October 20.

302 **Stanley Musgrove:** Stanley Eugene Musgrove (1924–1986), a native of Yuma, Arizona, was a 1947 graduate of USC's School of Cinema-Television. He had tried his hand at acting in the 1940s but soon resorted to being a publicity agent. As part of Mike Connolly's coterie of influential gay friends, Musgrove often supplied the columnist with items about his clients who included Cole Porter, Moss Hart, Guy Madison, Susan Hayward, and Mae West. With George Eells, Musgrove authored a biography of West, which he was preparing to produce as a telefilm at the time of his death from AIDS-related adenocarcinoma. He was never married.

302 **"Much of the column":** Holley, p. 98.

302 **"The silly-season singing sister trio":** *Pasadena Independent Star-News,* 9 February 1964. Sultan

and Worth finally abandoned "One More Time" in 1965 after the Beatles turned down a cameo appearance in the proposed film.

302 **Tom Troupe and Carole Cook:** "You might say our wedding was more like an old Ziegfeld show," Carole told the *Sacramento Bee* in 1964. "It was supposed to be a small affair and all I wanted was a train longer than Grace Kelly's. I had that and Lucy was my only attendant, but somehow we ended up with 12 ushers and about 700 guests. It was quite a show."

302 **"'Twas strictly one of those":** *Pasadena Star News*, 16 March 1964. The First Baptist Church of Beverly Hills was actually located in West Hollywood on Cynthia Street, seven-tenths of a mile from Alice Pearce's apartment.

303 **sharing the apartment on Holloway Drive:** "I really think they lived together until they got married," John Fiedler said in an interview with FT, 2003.

303 **"I would always see them together":** Cook interview.

303 **Alice was simply "a friend of a friend":** Oppenheim refutes a claim by his mother's biographer Gary Carey that Alice and Holliday were close friends. Oppenheim maintains that while the *Bells Are Ringing* cast, including Alice, was "kind of an extended family," there was no regular interaction between Holliday and Alice after the touring production ended in 1959.

303 **"One thing that I heard":** Oppenheim interview.

303 **"Desilu actor Paul Darshefsky":** *Daily Illinois State Journal*, 2 January 1960.

303 **"a virtuoso":** Holley, p. xiii.

304 **"He rendered the same service":** *Ibid.*, p. 4.

304 **"Ruth Roman's not-so-ever-lovin' mate":** *Pasadena Independent*, 9 February 1960.

304 **"I think that Alice and Paul were just buddies":** Cook interview.

304 **"Alice dear":** Letter to Alice Pearce from Debbie Reynolds, 8 January 1964, APC.

304 **"I remember it to this day":** Cook interview. "I've always felt a kinship of some kind with Alice Pearce," Cook confesses, "because Tom and I did send her to the doctor."

305 **Hilard Kravitz:** Hilard Leonard Kravitz (1917–2006), a native of Dayton, Ohio, earned his medical degree at the University of Cincinnati. From 1955 until 2000, he specialized in internal medicine and cardiology in Los Angeles.

305 **"was inclined to be a tubby":** Deacon letter. Just two years earlier, when Alice was performing in *Sail Away*, she showed no signs of a serious weight gain. One afternoon following a matinee, journalist Robert Wahls climbed three flights backstage at the Broadhurst to interview Patricia Harty, with whom Alice shared a dressing room. When Wahls walked in without permission, "a Pearcing scream ricocheted down the corridor." Wahls had surprised Alice, standing there in nothing but panties and bra. "I have shared cabs, cocktail party chit chat and night club nods with Alice," Wahls admitted, "but never have I seen so much of Alice. I swear she is miscast as the weedy, padded Elinor Spencer-Bollard. She doesn't have a chaperone's figure." See *New York Daily News*, 29 October 1961.

305 **"I was pretty embarrassed":** Post, p. 82.

305 **he knew immediately:** Carole Cook called Dr. Kravitz to learn Alice's diagnosis, but naturally he refused to disclose anything. After Alice's death, Cook again questioned Kravitz, who confided that he had immediately suspected cancer. "Evidently, it was pretty fierce already," Cook says.

305 **"Alice wanted to keep working":** Letter from Terry Votichenko to FT, 12 August 2014.

306 **"When we signed Ann-Margret":** *Variety*, 19 March 1965.

306 **Natalie Schafer:** McClelland, *The Unkindest Cuts*, p. 171.

306 **"uncorks a set of James Dean mannerisms":** *New York Times*, 8 April 1965.

307 **Principal photography with Sellers:** Billy Wilder "held out" for shooting *Kiss Me, Stupid* in black and white. *Dear Heart* and *Kiss Me, Stupid* would be the only black-and-white films Alice Pearce made. See Gene Phillips, *Some Like It Wilder*, The University Press of Kentucky, 2010, p. 270.

308 **"Alice and I were just about to report":** Fiedler interview. Sellers had his heart attack on April 6, 1964; Walston filmed his first scene exactly one week later. Alice reported to the studio the first week of May.

308 **"At issue was the intentional coarseness":** "Kiss Me, Stupid," Turner Classic Movies, http://www.tcm.com/tcmdb/title/17189/Kiss-Me-Stupid/articles.html , accessed 11 August 2020.

308 **"it quietly turned the picture over":** *Life*, 15 January 1965.

308 **"contrived double adultery"**: *Variety*, 16 December 1964.

308 **"exceedingly larger stigma"**: *New York Times*, 23 December 1964.

308 **"a comedy which deals with human dignity"**: *Life*, 15 January 1965.

308 **"When it came out, it was the biggest flop"**: Fiedler interview. For modern appraisals of Kiss Me, Stupid, see Michael Scheinfeld's TV Guide review https://www.tvguide.com/movies/kiss-stupid/review/103317/ and Michael Barrett's review https://www.popmatters.com/192753-kiss-me-stupid-aint-so-dumb-2495537969.html.

309 **"Delay in ovarian cancer diagnosis"**: *Kansas City Times*, 24 April 1964.

309 **"But it is important to guard"**: Letter from Barron Polan to Agnes Moorehead, 2 May 1966, Agnes Moorehead Papers, Wisconsin Historical Society, Box 88.

309 **"I remember thinking then"**: Cook interview.

309 **"Although very warm and congenial"**: Letter from Jane Dulo to FT, 27 November 1984. In 1966, Dulo told *TV Radio Mirror*: "I'd say [Alice] was a loner . . . I knew her a year before I went to visit her in her apartment. That's when I discovered her talent as a painter. She'd never mentioned it before." See Post, p. 82.

310 **"She once told my mother"**: Votichenko email, 2014.

310 **"film's funniest sequence"**: *San Francisco Examiner*, 11 February 1965. *Variety* (28 January 1965) was also pleased: "Alice Pearce does smash bit as bureaucratic clerk, a highlight segment."

311 **signed a contract to appear in *The Disorderly Orderly***: Screen Actors Guild, Inc. Minimum Free Lance Contract, 4 June 1964. Under its terms, Alice was paid $2500 per week with a one-week guarantee and she agreed to furnish her own wardrobe. Original contract signed by Alice Pearce, Jerry Lewis, and Paramount casting director Edward R. Morse, author's collection. Alice began filming on June 11.

311 **"Tashlin had played a pivotal role"**: Garcia, *Frank Tashlin*, p. 44.

311 **"it contains minimal amounts"**: de Seife, *Tashlinesque*, p. 161.

313 three **"cameo guest stars"**: *The Disorderly Orderly*, Screenplay by Frank Tashlin, Patti Enterprises, Inc., Preliminary Script, 19 February 1964. Photocopy, author's collection. Despite her reduced billing, Alice is on screen longer (six min-utes) than either Leonard (one minute) or Nichols (two and one-half minutes).

313 **"the one comic moment"**: Brumburgh, p. 13.

313 **"screamingly funny"**: *New York Times*, 24 December 1964.

313 ***The Disorderly Orderly* wrapped on August 24**: Alice's friend Richard Deacon, who filmed a scene as hospital patient Mr. Courtney, was concerned that his own family wouldn't recognize him in the film, which required him to wear a toupee, a mustache, and a full beard. His worries were unnecessary—his part was completely excised from the final print. See *Pittsburgh Post-Gazette*, 19 November 1964.

313 **the sole beneficiary of her pensions:** A note, dated 27 January 1966, written in Alice Pearce's hand, lists the three pensions and their corresponding account numbers with the notation "death benefits made out to Paul Davis in June 1964." APC, Box 1, File 1.

313 **"I made a pact with Alice"**: Landy, p. 80.

Chapter Twenty-Four

314 **"the year of the chuckle"**: *TV Guide*, 19 September 1964.

314 **"It's not the type of show"**: *Variety*, 27 May 1964.

314 **ordered Levy to reshape storylines:** *Los Angeles Times*, 22 January 1965.

314 **"a running feud"**: *Los Angeles Times*, 23 December 1964. In October 1964, CBS and Benton & Bowles, the ad agency representing General Foods, initiated negotiations to buy out Parke Levy because they wanted "new creative guidance" for *Many Happy Returns*. When their efforts failed, they briefly considered but later nixed moving the show to a less important time slot—it continued to follow *The Lucy Show* on Monday nights at 9. See *Variety*, 21 October 1964.

315 **"That was a mean set"**: Hyatt, *Short-Lived Television Series*, p. 145.

315 **extremely obnoxious by getting tipsy:** Naturally, Alice could play both obnoxious and tipsy, but her casting was a bit curious, considering her character's description in the script's final draft: "Mrs. Walsh is a woman in her late fifties. She is rather nondescript, neither striking nor unattractive, and is a little inclined on the heavy side. She is a little shy by nature." By this time, Alice, forty-six, was far from "heavy," having lost a considerable amount of weight due to the stress of her adverse

315 **"the only comedy writer in the millionaire class"**: *Variety*, 23 December 1964. Parke Levy (1908–1993) kept busy during his retirement years with investments, travel, gardening and painting. In 1992, he told author Jordan R. Young: "Three out of every five people I know in [show] business either have nervous tics, bad stomachs or they drink like fish. There's a great deal of tension in this kind of work. I got out before it got to me." See Jordan R. Young, *The Laugh Crafters*, Past Times Publishing Company, 1999.

315 **"almost single-handedly responsible"**: Perry, p. 10.

315 **"was essentially a silent producer"**: Pilato, *The Bewitched Book*, p. 16. Asher was listed as a "production consultant" in the show's closing credits.

315 **"a few cuts above"**: *Variety*, 11 June 1964. Arnold joined the *Bewitched* team after the departure of Sol Saks who had written the pilot but was deemed by Ackerman as unsuitable as a producer.

316 **"A writer-turned producer"**: *Variety*, 30 November 1964.

316 **"glove-fitted for their roles"**: *Variety*, 11 June 1964.

316 **eighteen candidates for Abner**: Seven of those actors considered for the Abner Kravitz role eventually appeared in guest shots on *Bewitched*: Phil Arnold, Parley Baer, Paul Barselow, Lennie Bremen, Henry Corden, Frank Maxwell, and Jack Weston. Other prospective "Abners" who had previously appeared on at least one Screen Gems sitcom included Stanley Adams, Murray Alper, Benny Baker, Alan Carney, Jerry Hausner, Bill McLean, and Robert B. Williams.

316 **George Tobias**: Born on Manhattan's Lower East Side, George Tobias (1901–1980), the son of repertory players in the Yiddish theater, became an actor at age fifteen when he appeared in a play at the Neighborhood Playhouse on Grand Street in New York City. He made his Broadway debut in 1924, and remained a stage actor until moving to Hollywood in 1939. For seven years, Tobias was under contract to Warner Brothers, appearing in

Sergeant York, Yankee Doodle Dandy, and *My Sister Eileen*, among others. By the time he was cast as Abner Kravitz, six-foot Tobias had trimmed off seventy pounds by jogging daily, playing handball and tennis, and swimming. The solitudinarian lived on an isolated twenty-acre ranch in the Lucerne Valley but stayed with friends in Encino when filming episodes of *Bewitched*. Never wed, Tobias died of metastatic colon cancer at Cedars-Sinai Medical Center on February 27, 1980. That night, when his body was transported from the hospital to the mortuary, the driver was involved in a minor traffic accident. While he was exchanging information with the other driver, a couple of young men hijacked the station wagon carrying Tobias' casket. Moments later, a witness reported seeing the car pull abruptly to the curb at Sierra Bonita and Franklin Avenues. The pair scrambled out of the vehicle and proceeded to "run like hell." See *Variety*, 29 February 1980.

316 **According to Tobias**: *TV Radio Mirror*, November 1968, p. 16.

316 **Ackerman's list of actresses**: The list also included Helene Winston, Florence Halop, seventy-five-year-old Alma Murphy, and Ruth Perrott (whom Ackerman had known from Lucille Ball's radio program *My Favorite Husband*). Winston and Helen Kleeb would eventually appear on *Bewitched* in guest roles. Ackerman's list can be found in the Harry Ackerman Papers, Box 64, Folder 11, at the American Heritage Center, University of Wyoming.

316 **"Mrs. Rich-Bitch"**: *New York Post*, 19 March 1986.

316 **Enid Markey and Doro Merande**: During a 2007 interview with the author, the actresses' *Bringing Up Buddy* co-star Frank Aletter discussed their feud, calling Markey "a pussycat from the time she got up in the morning" and Merande "a pain in the ass."

317 **"a kooky neighbor"**: Humphrey, p. 18.

317 **only for two guest appearances**: Stern, p. 35.

317 **"Alice was offered"**: Letter from Harry Ackerman to FT, 5 December 1986. Asher had known Alice four years earlier when he produced "The Reluctant Dragon" episode of *The Shirley Temple Show*.

317 **"the most promising pilot"**: *Variety*, 15 July 1964.

317 **"When I first heard"**: *TV Radio Mirror*, September 1965.

317 **no one was the wiser**: Carole Cook knew the real story, but by the time Alice shared her "Dr.

Kravitz" anecdote, Cook was across the globe, performing the lead in the Australian production of *Hello, Dolly!*

319 **"somehow never felt ready for a second marriage":** Post, p. 43.

319 **"always planned to be married":** Landy, p. 81.

319 **"Paul and I have had long discussions":** Letter from Alice Pearce Rox to Mr. and Mrs. Robert Pearce, 11 September 1964, APC, Box 1. The *Bewitched* episode which Alice mentions is "Little Pitchers Have Big Fears."

320 **"They phoned me from San Diego":** Email message from Milton Davis to FT, 1 May 2016.

321 **"The most perfect part":** Letter from Alice Pearce Davis to Mr. and Mrs. Robert Pearce, 21 September 1964, APC, Box 1. The wedding dinner at the Pearces' home included only three guests: Alice, Paul, and Josephine Strode who flew back home to Vermont three days later.

321 **a call from George Morris:** Landy, p. 80.

321 **"This is the one to watch":** *Variety*, 21 September 1964.

322 **"bewitched by *Bewitched*":** *TV Guide*, 24 October 1964.

322 **"our favorite other people's neighbors":** *Arizona Republic*, 1 October 1964. The previous week, the same reviewer wrote: "The neighbor and her husband are deliciously played by Alice Pearce and George Tobias, and the interplay between them is good for several howls."

322 **"if available" agreement:** On September 4, 1964, Phil Rogers of the Screen Gems casting department sent an inter-office memo to his fellow casting director Mildred Gusse, stating: "As of this date, we have entered in 'if available' agreements with George Tobias . . . and Alice Pearce." On a sliding scale, Tobias was to receive $350 for one day's work or $550 for two days' work, compared to Alice's $300 for one day and $600 for two days. For three, four, or five days' work, each would receive $750, $850, and $1000, respectively. On October 6, Fries noted that "we have examined our production records and find that they work one day in each picture in which they appear. Accordingly, their salaries were $650 per one day per film where they will now amount to $1900 per picture." See Harry Ackerman Papers, Box 65, Folder 12, American Heritage Center, University of Wyoming.

322 **"I believe we should review":** Harry Ackerman Papers, Box 65, Folder 12, American Heritage Center, University of Wyoming.

322 **"While I realize the costs":** *Ibid.*

322 **Her compensation per "picture":** *Ibid.* Alice's 1964 contract detailed that she would receive $1250 per episode for *Bewitched*'s second season, $1400 for the third, $1550 for the fourth, and $1700 for the fifth. For these four subsequent seasons, Alice was guaranteed a minimum of seven out of thirteen episodes. Another stipulation in Alice's contract was that she would receive first or second position in the end credits [below Agnes Moorehead or below Dick York if Moorehead did not appear in the episode], alternating with George Tobias every other episode in which they appeared together.

322 **five out of nine:** *Ibid.* Charles Fries, in a memo to Harry Ackerman on October 28, 1964, expressed concern that "we may not be able to meet this commitment on the basis of scripts planned." Fries was right. By December 18, the Screen Gems executives found themselves in a somewhat sticky situation. Alice and George Tobias had only appeared in three of the nine episodes produced since signing their contracts. Regarding Alice's contract, Arthur Frankel of the company's legal department proposed a possible course of action to Fries. Since Alice had agreed to waive her pay for episodes in which she didn't appear, Frankel suggested asking the Screen Actors Guild for permission to pay her for the three episodes and add the remaining two to the next group of sixteen. However, this would necessitate using Alice in eleven of the sixteen, a possibility Frankel considered tenuous. Furthermore, Tobias had refused to give Screen Gems the waiver, meaning that—regardless of Alice's situation—they would have to pay him for two episodes in which he did not appear. In the end, Frankel, who had not informed SAG of Tobias' refusal, reasoned that the Guild would not grant the waiver "once they learn that it is to be confined to Pearce." The matter was dropped, and Alice and Tobias each received pay for five episodes. Subsequently, they appeared in ten of the next sixteen segments of the 1964-65 season.

322 ***Inside Daisy Clover*:** As things turned out, Alice was not hired for this film.

322 **guest list for a cocktail and dinner party:** *Los Angeles Herald-Examiner*, 28 October 1964. Other party guests mentioned in Parsons' column were

Montgomery, Moorehead, Asher, Jackie Cooper, Suzanne Pleshette, and Ackerman's wife Elinor Donahue.

322 **"there'd be no Christmas hiatus":** *Variety*, 26 October 1964.

323 **"It's a lovely place":** *New York World-Telegram*, 3 October 1964.

323 **Many of Alice's friends ... were caught unawares:** It seems that Alice did not maintain close contact with her friends in New York, a circumstance that seems quite mutual. "I don't imagine her correspondence was very voluminous, and I know mine's not!" laughed Cris Alexander in 1987. "Oh, I don't think I have more than a couple of letters from her." Likewise, Carol Channing professed that she wrote Alice only once a year.

323 **"I really didn't know anybody who knew him":** Alexander interview, 1987.

323 **"When they married, I was kind of surprised":** Cook interview.

323 **"It took Chan two days to adjust":** Letter from Mrs. Charles Lowe to Mrs. Paul Davis, 2 November 1964, APC. Channing was then starring on Broadway in *Hello, Dolly!*

323 **"Paul is a great guy":** Letter from Mrs. Paul Davis to Mr. Don Herring, 3 November 1964. Shirley Taylor and Susie Swanson were Don's daughters.

323 **"We are very happy for you":** Letter from Doris Herring to Alice Pearce Davis, 7 November 1964.

323 **Although Mike Connolly scooped:** Ed Sullivan announced Alice's marriage on October 9, 1964, but Walter Winchell didn't report it until December 8.

323 **"Alice Pearce made the happiest move":** *San Antonio Light*, 11 November 1964.

324 **"It was one of the laughing-est":** Dorothy Manners, "Alice: Courage, Love," *Los Angeles Herald-Examiner*, 9 March 1966, p. A–19.

324 **"very aristocratic":** Mann, *Behind the Screen*, p. 324. For more about Rupert Allan (1912–1991) and his lover, the retired brigadier general-film producer Frank McCarthy (1912–1986), see *Behind the Screen*, pp. 296–303.

324 **"Alice Pearce: The Chinless Wonder":** The article focuses not on Alice's acting career but her philosophy regarding female beauty versus character.

324   **"six-week closing date":** *El Paso Times*, 18 February 1964.

324 **the journalist's own tenacious curiosity:** The eccentric Lloyd Shearer (1916–2001) was grounded in reporting and loved chasing down a story,

tapping his network of sources including everyone from studio heads to secretaries and hotel desk clerks. In 1958, under the pseudonym of Walter Scott, Shearer launched *Parade*'s weekly column "Personality Parade," best known for celebrity tidbits written in question-and-answer form, which he banged out until 1991.

325 **"I'm learning about soft-sell":** *Pasadena Independent*, 4 December 1964.

325 **Josephine Strode died:** Josephine C. Strode, Certificate of Death, State of Vermont, 13 December 1964. Josephine's funeral and burial took place in Perry, Missouri, on December 16.

325 **homey patients' rooms:** *Brattleboro Reformer*, 2 August 1961.

326 **delectable sugar-cured hams:** Elaine Leake Wicken to FT, via Facebook, May 2014.

326 **"He is not very well":** Letter from Doris Herring to Alice Pearce Davis, 7 November 1964. Earl Herring died in Orange, California on December 18.

326 **"Because of my own loss":** Telegram from Alice Pearce to Mr. and Mrs. Don Herring, 22 December 1964, LSC.

326 **"I've always wanted a series":** Stern, p. 35.

326 **"I still have a lot to learn about it":** Misurell, p. 14.

328 **"pick up shots":** close-up shots filmed after principal photography has been completed for an episode or additional shots for a scene previously filmed.

328 **"This is the treadmill":** *TV Guide*, 17 July 1965.

328 **"I would drive [Alice] to the studio":** Landy, p. 80.

328 **"I felt closer to Alice":** Post, p. 81.

328 **"they liked each other":** Landy, p. 82.

328 **"got along splendidly with other cast members":** Ackerman letter.

328 **"It was impossible":** Post, p. 82.

328 **"If Endora was the conflict":** Tranberg, *I Love the Illusion*, p. 236.

328 **"a peculiar mix":** "The Magic Unveiled," bonus featurette for the 2005 Sony Pictures Home Entertainment DVD "Bewitched: The Complete First Season."

329 **"Miss Pearce makes all of her lines":** *Lima News*, 2 September 1965.

329 **black lace negligee:** Alice generally provided her own wardrobe, but sometimes she took advantage of the Screen Gems costume department. For "Illegal Separation," she chose a fussy floral dress

which her old friend Imogene Coca had worn the previous season in *Grindl*.

329 **more recognition on the street:** Alice's exposure on *Bewitched* suddenly garnered more attention from film critics who might have otherwise ignored her incidental roles in the five films released during the show's first season, most particularly *Dear Heart*. The *Baltimore Evening Sun* (25 March 1965) singled out Alice (and Barbara Nichols) for providing the film's "very solid comedy roles." More curiously, reviews in the *Boston Traveler* (25 March 1965) and London's Sunday newspaper *The Observer* (2 May 1965) name only three members of the films' gem-studded cast: Geraldine Page, Glenn Ford, and Alice Pearce. In both, Alice was saluted for the drunken postmasters scene.

329 **"I've been in show business":** Maureen James, "Alice Pearce: Comic Bewitched into Recognition," *Boston Record American*, 19 September 1965, p. 144.

329 **"I was just a face":** *TV Radio Mirror*, September 1965.

329 **"There's a bewitched!":** Humphrey, p. 18.

329 **"I'm playing someone":** *TV Radio Mirror*, September 1965.

329 **"Bless my series":** McManus, p. 45. In April 1965, Alice told journalist Ed Misurell that Screen Gems had recently renewed her contract for five years.

331 **The sale was completed on March 9, 1965:** Alice Pearce Davis, Probate Case #506667, Superior Court, County of Los Angeles, State of California.

331 **"a small house, made of adobe brick":** McManus, p. 5. The studio, glamorized by the prose of McManus, was actually a detached garage. According to Alice Pearce's probate file, the 1966 estimated value of 8242 Hillside Avenue was $55,000. The house, later enlarged to 1,970 square feet, sold for $2.45 million in 2017.

331 **"a little cement-block house":** Weaver, *Glad Tidings*, p. 6.

331 **"I can't think of a place":** *Ibid.*, p. 171.

331 **"It was more difficult":** *Ibid.*, p. 181.

331 **"millions of affluent aunts":** *Ibid.*, p. 180. Mary Winternitz Cheever (1918–2014), Sarah Lawrence College Class of 1939, was Alice's fellow member in the German and French clubs.

332 **"She took me out":** Alexander interview, 1987.

332 **"By then, I had two children":** Davis email, 2016. Davis' children were sons Geoffrey, three, and Gregory, one.

333 **"tangible personal property":** Last will and testament of Josephine C. Strode, recorded in Marlboro County Probate Court, Volume 83, p. 2. The household furniture was appraised at $5,377; the jewelry at $1,122; and Josephine's jeep at $50. As of 27 November 1965, Josephine's notes, bonds, stocks, and cash amounted to approximately $89,787.

333 **"It will be one glorious chaos":** McManus, p. 5.

333 **"It was like marrying my wonderful Paul":** Elizabeth Sullivan, "Doting In-Laws Welcome Alice Pearce to Boston," *Boston Sunday Globe*, 9 May 1965.

333 **"He wanted a memento":** Renee Summers, "Renee Bids Farewell to Well-Loved Star," *The Sentinel*, 26 May 1966.

333 **"Oh, Alice was very lovely":** Summers interview.

333 **Sarah Davis:** Born Sarah Raphel (1903–1972), she was the oldest of seven children of Samuel "Sol" Raphel and his wife Fannie Margil. Sarah and Max Dashefsky married in the Bronx on August 16, 1921. Besides Paul, their children included Stanley Norris Davis (1928–2016), Renee Sonia Davis Summers (1933–2020), and Milton Simon Davis (born 1936). For immigration documentation, see New York Passenger and Crew Lists, 1820–1957 for Fanny Rafel (mother of Sarah Davis), 7 April 1906, www.ancestry.com.

333 **Max Dashefsky:** Listed as "Meyer Daschefski" on the passenger list for the S. S. *Saxonia* when it docked in Boston Harbor on January 12, 1905, he later went by the name Max Davis (1899–1988). In 1970, he retired from the *Boston Globe* after more than fifty years as a truckdriver. Max died of a heart attack at New England Deaconess Hospital, outliving both his wife Sarah and son Paul. At the time, he was a resident of Boston's Hyde Park neighborhood.

333 **"They were caught up":** Email message from Renee Summers to FT, 15 March 2013.

334 **"Listen, I don't think":** Summers interview.

334 **"It's the first time":** McManus, p. 5.

334 **"It's the first real home":** *TV Guide*, 25 December 1965.

Chapter Twenty-Five

335 **"let out a screech"**: *TV Radio Mirror*, August 1965.

335 **"Our TV cast"**: Sullivan, *op. cit.*

335 **"Alias Darrin Stephens"**: Alice Pearce's copy of the "revised final draft" script, dated April 30, 1965, bears her handwritten notes indicating that her interior scenes were filmed on Stages 7 (Kravitz home) and 4 (Stephens home) at Columbia Studios on May 18, and that her exterior scene at the Columbia ranch was filmed the following day. APC.

336 **"She never admitted"**: Ackerman letter.

336 **"Husbands do not"**: Landy, p. 80.

336 **were not telecast in the order of their production:** Alice's first seven episodes are listed here in order of filming with their corresponding telecast ranks in parentheses: "Alias Darrin Stephens" (1); "Prodigy" (36); "My Grandson, the Warlock" (4); "A Strange Little Visitor" (12); "And Then I Wrote" (9); "Aunt Clara's Old Flame" (11); "Take Two Aspirins and Half a Pint of Porpoise Milk" (6). The last two on this list—both written by Bernard Slade—are perhaps the most appealing and have qualities reminiscent of first-season episodes.

336 **"After appearing in a dozen"**: James, *op. cit.*

336 **"Playing Gladys"**: *Ibid.*

336 **"I'm [there] every minute"**: McManus, p. 45. Besides hanging out at the framing shop, the couple continued to see plays and movies, sometimes in the company of her old friends. In a 1989 letter to the author, actor John Lund recalled, "Her second husband was a man named Speha [*sic*], or something like that. As I recall, he owned an art supplies shop. I met him only once when he and Alice and my wife and I attended a performance together at the Biltmore Theatre in Los Angeles. That was also the last time I saw Alice herself."

336 **"Raymond Burr has an art gallery"**: Sullivan, *op. cit.*

337 **"He's got some now"**: *TV Radio Mirror*, September 1965.

337 **"Now that they know its worth"**: *New York Daily News*, 10 September 1965.

337 **"Alice and Pesha's"**: McManus, p. 45.

337 **"Her home was furnished"**: Deacon letter.

337 **"We're going to one of the small islands"**: Manners, p. A-19.

337 **"Paul gave me an anniversary present"**: Postcard from Alice Pearce to Agnes Moorehead, postmarked Lahaina, Hawaii, 23 September 1965, Box 80, Agnes Moorehead Papers, Wisconsin Center for Film and Theater Research. Actually, Alice paid for the Hawaiian vacation, charging it to her Carte Blanche credit card. See Alice Pearce Davis, Probate Case #506667, Superior Court, County of Los Angeles, State of California.

337 **painting up a storm**: *Anderson Daily Bulletin*, 15 October 1965.

337 **"dining out every night"**: *Boston Herald*, 10 October 1965.

337 **"that charity work"**: *Eureka Humboldt Standard*, 14 September 1965.

338 **"derived from the work"**: *Los Angeles Times*, 4 October 1965.

338 **Baby Jane Hudson:** The title character in *Whatever Happened to Baby Jane?* (1962) often dressed as she had forty-five years earlier when she was a girl.

338 **"I said that she was looking"**: Post, p. 82. Post also revealed that when "an unknowing actress friend asked [Alice] for her reducing diet, [she] merely laughed heartily and, without blinking an eye, replied that it was a 'secret that she couldn't divulge.'"

338 **"No, I consider myself a sex symbol"**: *Boston Record-American*, 30 August 1965.

338 **"Being beautiful"**: *Cedar Rapids Gazette*, 26 September 1965. Dahl's feature on Alice appeared in shortened form two months earlier in various newspapers, such as the *Alabama Journal* (21 July 1965). When Dahl commented on Alice's simple hairstyle, she joked about current hairdos: "Aren't those mile-high hair styles ridiculous? In the theater I'm tempted to say to the lady in front of me, 'Would you take your hair off, please?'"

339 **flair for fashion:** Alice usually chose dowdy dresses from thrift shops to wear as Gladys Kravitz, but once in a while she slipped in a chic ensemble from her own wardrobe, particularly a blue knit suit and a two-piece apricot wool dress, seen in "Fastest Gun on Madison Avenue" and "Samantha, the Dressmaker."

339 **"I feel the progress of the disease"**: Manners, p. A-19.

340 **"Alice Pearce and George Tobias"**: *Springfield Union*, 16 August 1965. The movie's title had little to do with the plot, except that Day posed as a mermaid for the benefit of tourists on her father's glass bottom boat. The bottom half of her costume is snagged by fisherman Rod Taylor who returns

her "tail" to neighbors Pearce and Tobias while Day's away at her workplace.

340 **changes were indeed made during filming:** Besides dialogue revisions, two characters' names were changed on July 26. "Homer Cook" became "Homer Cripps" and "Anna Muir" was switched to "Anna Miller." Shamroy's copy of the script is in the author's possession.

342 **frail but gutsy Mabel:** Alice attempted to disguise her rail-thin frame in all three of her scenes, first using a sky-blue afternoon dress with a ruffled bodice. For her second scene, she covers herself in a bulky wool cardigan, and for the bedroom scene she chose a nightgown with long lacy collar ties.

342 **"a cynicism":** Garcia, p. 175.

342 **final visit to her native city:** During her brief stay in Manhattan, Alice shied from visiting old friends. She was afraid that her weight loss would arouse too many questions. It's likely that none of them even knew she was in the city. On October 27, 1965, she did make a stop at Bonwit Teller on Fifth Avenue to shop in their junior sportswear department.

343 **"On the assumption":** Lois, *What's the Big Idea?*, p. 148.

343 **"A Coty Cremestick turned Alice Pearce":** *Cosmopolitan*, April 1966.

343 **"We're all suckers":** Lois, *$ellebrity.*

343 **"So, I sadly cast Alice Ghostley":** Lois, *George Lois on His Creation of the Big Idea.*

343 **"At all times, good or bad":** Post, p. 81.

344 **"It was thrilling":** *Ibid.*, p. 82.

344 **a matching feather boa:** Alice's probate file reveals that she paid $31.20 for the pink feather boa on December 23, 1965.

344 **"But I have never worked":** *Elmira (NY) Star-Gazette*, 5 June 1965.

344 **When she wrote Moorehead from Hawaii:** "Hope you are enjoying your picture. Shall see you on the lot. I am going to be in Glass Bottom B." Moorehead was filming *The Singing Nun* at M-G-M at the same time *The Glass Bottom Boat* was in production.

345 **she shared alone with Moorehead:** As Gladys and Endora trade a few barbs, Alice's face is noticeably more drawn than in the episode's other scenes.

345 **"the day she could no longer stand on her feet":** Post, p. 82.

345 **Screen Gems' "production summary" records:** See "Original Filming/Telecast Dates," *The*

Bewitched and Elizabeth Montgomery Web Site, http://www.bewitched.net/filmdates.htm.

345 **"Disappearing Samantha":** According to Alice's copy of the script's first revised draft—dated 5 January 1966—this was to be the first episode to feature Gladys but not Abner. The tag scene at the end called for Gladys to dive over Samantha's fence "head-first," an absurd plan considering Alice's physical condition by that time.

345 **call sheets:** The Screen Gems-*Bewitched* call sheets for January 27 and February 4, 1966, were both offered for sale on eBay in 2016 and 2017.

345 **"hit TV paydirt":** *World Telegram and Sun*, 9 March 1966. Columnist Al Salerno noted that Alice and George Tobias' television commercial for a margarine spread were still airing after her death.

345 **"I like earthy parts":** *TV Guide*, 25 December 1965.

345 **"Gladys Kravitz is an enigma":** Alice Pearce, "She Doesn't Mean to Pry, But—," ABC News press release, 29 December 1965, author's collection.

346 **"Alice Pearce's loss of weight":** *Hollywood Reporter*, 24 February 1966.

346 **"During the last month":** Davis email, 1 May 2016.

346 **"Alice wouldn't allow me":** White interview.

346 **"I addressed the card":** Post, p. 82. Deacon was also among the few honored to be left a goodbye note from Alice. She wrote, "Thank you for being a wonderful friend. Please look after my Pesha as he will need friends now. And please give my love to the two great ladies Jane Dulo and Cynthia Lindsay." Lindsay, the former wife of actor Russell Gleason, wrote teleplays and authored books. (On February 12, 1966, Alice sent flowers for Valentine's Day to her parents in La Jolla.)

346 **"I just want you to know":** Letter from Kaye Ballard to Alice Pearce, 23 February 1966, APC. The actresses' lack of communication is evident by the address to which Ballard mailed her greeting. Alice had vacated Holloway Drive ten months previously.

346 **"My mother told me":** Bryant email, 2018.

347 **Helen Farrell:** Helen Frances O'Connell Farrell Hoyt (1911–2003) was born in Ayers, Massachusetts and grew up in Nashua, New Hampshire. After retirement, she volunteered at Scripps Clinic in Rancho Bernardo from 1984 until 1991. See *North County Blade-Citizen*, 2 February 2003.

347 **"Alice never went into coma":** Post, p. 82. Alice Pearce died in Room 528 at Cedars of Lebanon

Hospital at 4:15 a. m. on March 3, 1966 (Alice Pearce Davis, Probate Case #506667).

347 **Only one newspaper in the nation:** Most of Alice's obituaries gave 47 as her age. Some reported it as 45. Noting the discrepancies, *Variety* played it safe and omitted Alice's age from its obituary.

347 **"I couldn't believe it":** Ghostley letter. Ghostley had wintered in Los Angeles, filming guest appearances on TV's *Please Don't Eat the Daisies* and *The Farmer's Daughter*. She had filmed an episode of *Bewitched* the previous September, but Alice was not on the set that week.

347 **"I remember the *shock*":** Wilson interview. Wilson, whose father died the same day as Alice, was also unaware that Alice had married Paul Davis.

347 **pasted Alice's *New York Times* obituary:** Later that year, LeMassena added to the same page an obituary for his close friend Montgomery Clift. The scrapbook is now in the author's possession.

348 **"Still following Alice's wishes":** Post, p. 82.

348 **"One thing Alice disliked":** "Don't Wait for Smiles," *op. cit.* Turgeon does not cite any sources for this particular anecdote, but he does list individuals who shared with him the stories in his collection, including Alice's friends William LeMassena and Peggy Cass. "Peter Turgeon said he thought that Alice was one of the most beautiful human beings he'd ever known," remembered Patricia Wilson in 2019.

348 **"Alice Pearce was one of my closest friends":** Letter from John Fiedler to FT, 2 January 1989.

348 **"She was the perfect lady":** Letter from Debbie Reynolds to FT, 7 December 1982.

348 **"Knowing her was a joy":** Dulo letter.

348 **"Alice and I had many things in common":** Post, p. 82.

348 **"They were devastated":** Email message from Herbie J Pilato to FT, 12 July 2014.

348 **"One of the few true-blue ladies":** *Miami News*, 14 September 1971.

348 **"Ladies are a rarity":** Landy, p. 81.

348 **"She was never bitter":** Post, p. 82.

349 **would film only three episodes:** Canfield actually appeared in four episodes, but her brief scene in "Follow That Witch!" (Part Two) was actually a replay from "Follow That Witch!" (Part One).

349 **"I was dropped":** Letter from Mary Grace Canfield to FT, 22 November 1986.

350 **"decide[d] against giving him":** *World Telegram and Sun*, 9 March 1966. *Bewitched* associate pro-

ducer Richard Michaels later recalled the situation: "We were either going to hire someone new to play Gladys after Alice passed away or move in new neighbors to replace the Kravitzes altogether. Obviously, we opted for the former due to the fact that Gladys's interplay with Abner was too funny, and, yes, too essential to the show's format." See Pilato, p. 111.

350 **"All of us watched it":** Post, p. 82.

350 **"most gala ceremony":** Rod Serling to Paul Davis, 25 April 1966, APC.

350 **"would be handled as an event":** *Valley Times*, 23 May 1966.

350 **"very few awkward stage waits":** *Hollywood Reporter*, 23 May 1966.

350 **Debbie Reynolds:** After Alice's Emmy win, Reynolds wrote to Moorehead, who was recovering from surgery in Wisconsin: "I know you were pleased for Alice, but everyone knows you deserved it." See Tranberg, p. 260.

351 **"I think the best thing":** Paul Davis' acceptance speech is quoted directly from a videotape supplied by the UCLA Film & Television Archive in conjunction with the Academy of Television Arts & Sciences. In their reviews of the ceremony, many newspaper editors would substitute the words "wonderful" or "delightful" for Paul's interesting choice of adjectives: "delicious."

351 **Alice's win:** There were those who considered Alice's posthumous win as a result of sentimentality or sympathy. Rose Marie, in her 2002 autobiography *Hold the Roses*, groused—in error—that all three of her Emmy losses were due to posthumous winners. In 1963, she lost to Glenda Farrell, and the following year to Ruth White, both of whom were very much alive at the time. Therefore, Marie's dissatisfaction seems to stem from having lost to Alice in 1966, the final year Marie was nominated.

351 **"She was just following instructions":** *Bridgewater Courier-News*, 13 June 1966.

351 **"Your loss is shared":** Rod Serling to Paul Davis, 27 May 1966, APC.

351 **"If the recognition":** Carl Uren to Paul Davis, 27 May 1966, APC.

352 **"I cannot tell you":** Dominick Dunne to Paul Davis, 23 May 1966, APC.

352 **"'Prodigy' was one of those incredible":** Ackerman letter.

352 **The program topic was Alice Pearce:** PE, 6 October 1966. Mrs. Hiram Biggers was married to Alice's second cousin twice removed.

352 **"I recently watched *On the Town*":** Lowe email.

Epilogue

354 **Sandra Gould:** Born in Manhattan as Sylvia Goldfarb, Gould (1916–1999) grew up in Brooklyn where her father Moses was a letter carrier for the U. S. Postal Service. She made her Broadway debut in *New Faces of 1934*. In 1938, Gould married Larry Berns (born Solomon Louis Bernstein), a 1930 graduate of the University of Pennsylvania who later became producer of television's *Our Miss Brooks*. During *Bewitched*'s fourth season, Gould married for a second time to director Hollingsworth Morse. Widowed twice, she died of a massive heart attack following heart surgery in a Burbank hospital.

354 **"I was so numb":** *Edwardsville Intelligencer*, 24 August 1967.

354 **"They had already read sixty actresses":** *Syracuse Herald-American*, 30 October 1966.

354 **"We shared a dressing room":** *Ibid.*

354 **"Elizabeth Montgomery was still heartbroken":** Ed Gross, "Here's What Happened to Bewitched Actress Alice Pearce," Do You Remember?, https://doyouremember.com/126352/what-happened-mrs-kravitz-from-bewitched, accessed 12 November 2020.

354 **"Elizabeth did not like Sandy at all":** Pilato email.

354 **absentmindedly called her "Alice":** *TV Guide*, 11 July 1970.

354 **"but what she could not do":** Gross, *op. cit.*

355 **"one of those insane comedies":** *Los Angeles Times*, 17 August 1966.

355 **"Given to sight gags":** *Variety*, 20 April 1966.

355 **"what we used to call a 'good family'":** Letter from Dominick Dunne to FT, 3 April 2003. Dunne also recalled Alice's nickname "Peeps" but was embarrassed to admit that he didn't remember Paul Davis at all. In his 1999 memoir *The Way We Lived Then*, Dunne referred to the marble top table as "a lovely French chest." Film producer Dodi Fayed was killed in the car crash with Princess Diana in 1997.

355 **Tommy Sand:** *California Business*, Volume 18, 1983.

355 **LaFrance Clark:** After several years of declining health, Alice's maternal uncle died at age seventy-three in the Veterans Hospital in Portland, Oregon, on March 17, 1969. None of the family had seen him for years. In 1930, he had married Phoebe Mae Franz in Evanston, Illinois. Around 1939, they moved to Salem, Oregon, where LaFrance was employed as a clerk in the state unemployment compensation commission. In 1947, he began studying dentistry, which he later practiced in Salem until his retirement. His widow died five months after he did.

355 **agreed to withdraw their appeals:** The decree of distribution of the estate of Josephine Clark Strode is recorded in Marlboro County Probate Court, Volume 94, p. 337. Josephine's estate, totaling almost $87,000, was divided in four equal shares among her late husband's nephews and nieces.

355 **"Paul kind of went into seclusion":** Cook interview.

355 **"I was never in touch":** Alexander interview, 1987.

356 **"Everyone was wonderful to me":** Landy, p. 22.

356 **"It's Wishcraft":** On March 29, 1967, Paul took out a one-page ad in the *Hollywood Reporter* featuring a large photo of himself and announcing the telecast of "It's Wishcraft."

356 **"far ahead of its time":** "Dinah East 1970," Dreams Are What Le Cinema Is For, https://lecinemadreams.blogspot.com/search?q=dinah+east, accessed 17 November 2020.

356 **"The view was as magnificent":** Weaver, pp. 311–312.

356 **"My wife and I took care of him":** Davis email, 12 May 2016.

356 **"Paul phoned me once":** Summers interview.

356 **transferred all of Alice's assets:** Once Alice's debts had been paid, her assets—including jewelry, furniture, and a claim for interest under a contract with music publisher Edwin H. Morris—totaled $12,644.09. This figure did not include her joint tenancy in 8242 Hillside Avenue.

357 **"He was a wonderful man":** *Tampa Bay Times*, 16 February 1972.

357 **"She was a character":** Richards interview.

357 **"My [photography] studio":** Klain, p. 39.

358 **"These Clark papers":** Letter from Margaret Pearce to Edward and Alice Alford, 24 September 1967, Barbara Alford Torbjornsen collection.

358 **Bob died:** State of California, Department of Health Services, Certificate of Death, #71-109174.

358 **"Mrs. Pearce is an eccentric old woman":** Letter from Milton Davis to FT, 31 October 1984.

Margaret lived at Culver Village, a senior care community located at 10955 West Washington Boulevard in Culver City.

358 **Margaret Pearce:** State of California, Department of Health Services, Certificate of Death, #38619019530.

358 **"It is amazing":** Wheeler interview.

Bibliography

This is a general list of books; for articles and other sources, published and unpublished, see Notes.

Abbott, George. *Mister Abbott.* New York: Random House, 1963.

Bentley, Toni. *Costumes by Karinska.* New York: Harry N. Abrams, 1995.

Blanck, William J. (ed.). *Life of a River Village: Dobbs Ferry.* Dobbs Ferry: Morgan, 1974.

Bloom, Ken, and Frank Vlastnik. *Broadway Musicals.* New York: Black Dog & Leventhal, 2004.

Bordman, Gerald. *American Theatre: A Chronicle of Comedy and Drama, 1914–1930.* New York: Oxford University Press, 1995.

Bronski, Michael. *Culture Clash: The Making of Gay Sensibility.* Brooklyn: South End, 1984.

Brooks, Tim, and Earle Marsh. *The Complete Directory to Prime Time Network TV Shows.* New York: Ballantine, 1979.

Brown, Jared. *The Fabulous Lunts.* New York: Atheneum, 1986.

Carey, Gary. *Judy Holliday.* New York: Seaview, 1982.

Carpenter, Carleton. *The Absolute Joy of Work.* Albany, GA: BearManor Media, 2016.

Carrier, Jeffrey L. *Tallulah Bankhead: A Bio-Bibliography.* Santa Barbara: Greenwood, 1991.

Carson, Diane, Linda Dittmar and Janice R. Welsh (eds.). *Multiple Voices in Feminist Film Criticism.* Minneapolis: University of Minnesota Press, 1994.

Chauncey, George. *Gay New York.* New York: BasicBooks, 1994.

Clarke, Gerald. *Capote: A Biography.* New York: Simon & Schuster, 1988.

———. *Too Brief a Treat: The Letters of Truman Capote.* New York: Random House, 2004.

Cox, Stephen. *The Addams Chronicles.* New York: Harper Perennial, 1991.

Crespy, David A. *Richard Barr: The Playwright's Producer.* Carbondale: Southern Illinois University Press, 2013.

Day, Barry (ed.). *The Letters of Noël Coward.* New York: Knopf, 2008.

de Chambrun, Clara Longworth. *Shadows Lengthen: The Story of My Life.* New York: Scribner's, 1949.

de Chambrun, Comtesse. *Shadows Like Myself.* New York: Scribner's, 1936.

de Seife, Ethan. *Tashlinesque: The Hollywood Comedies of Frank Tashlin.* Middletown: Wesleyan University Press, 2012.

Dedman, Bill, and Paul Clark Newell, Jr. *Empty Mansions.* New York: Ballantine, 2013.

Dennis, Patrick. *Auntie Mame.* New York: Vanguard, 1955.

———. *Little Me.* New York: Broadway Books, 2002.

Deverich, Linsey. *Wandering Through La La Land with the Last Warner Brother.* Bloomington: AuthorHouse, 2007.

Diehl, Lorraine B. *The Late, Great Pennsylvania Station.* Rockville: American Heritage, 1985.

Dunning, John. *On the Air: The Encyclopedia of Old-Time Radio.* New York: Oxford University Press, 1998.

Fidelman, Geoffrey Mark. *The Lucy Book.* Los Angeles: Renaissance, 1999.

Florenski, Joe, and Steve Wilson. *Center Square: The Paul Lynde Story.* Los Angeles: Advocate Books, 2005.

Fordin, Hugh. *The World of Entertainment.* New York: Doubleday, 1975.

Garcia, Roger (ed.). *Frank Tashlin.* London: British Film Institute, 1994.

Gavin, James. *Intimate Nights.* New York: Limelight, 1992.

Ghareeb, Gordon, and Martin Cox. *Hollywood to Honolulu.* El Cerrito: Glencannon, 2009.

Gingold, Hermione. *How to Grow Old Disgracefully.* New York: St. Martin's, 1988.

Gordon, Lorraine, and Barry Singer. *Alive at the Village Vanguard.* Milwaukee: Hal Leonard, 2006.

Gordon, Max. *Live at the Village Vanguard.* New York: St. Martin's, 1980.

Graham, Sheilah. *The Garden of Allah.* New York: Crown, 1970.

Grondahl, Paul. *Mayor Corning: Albany Icon, Albany Enigma.* Albany: State University of New York Press, 2007.

Hall, Linda B. *Dolores de Río: Beauty in Light and Shade.* Redwood City: Stanford University Press, 2013.

Holley, Val. *Mike Connolly and the Manly Art of Hollywood Gossip.* Jefferson, NC: McFarland, 2003.

Hover, John C., et al. *Memoirs of the Miami Valley, Volume III.* Chicago: Robert O. Law Company, 1920.

Hyatt, Wesley. *Short-Lived Television Series, 1948–1978.* Jefferson, NC: McFarland, 2003.

Irvin, Sam. *Kay Thompson: From Funny Face to Eloise.* New York: Simon & Schuster, 2010.

Israel, Lee. *Miss Tallulah Bankhead.* New York: Putnam's, 1972.

Kobal, John. *People Will Talk.* New York: Knopf, 1985.

Krampner, Jon. *The Man in the Shadows: Fred Coe and the Golden Age of Television.* New Brunswick: Rutgers University Press, 1997.

Lackmann, Ron. *Same Time . . . Same Station.* New York: Facts on File, 1996.

Laurents, Arthur. *Original Story.* New York: Knopf, 2000.

Leszczak, Bob. *Single Season Sitcoms, 1948–1979.* Jefferson, NC: McFarland, 2012.

Lewis, Robert. *Slings and Arrows.* New York: Stein & Day, 1984.

Liebman, Roy. *Vitaphone Films: A Catalogue of the Features and Shorts.* Jefferson, NC: McFarland, 2003.

Lobenthal, Joel. *Tallulah! The Life and Times of a Leading Lady.* New York: Regan Books, 2004.

Lois, George. *George Lois on His Creation of the Big Idea.* New York: Assouline, 2008.

———. *$ellebrity: My Angling and Tangling with Famous People.* New York: Phaidon, 2003.

———. *What's the Big Idea?* New York: Plume, 1993.

Mancini, Henry. *Did They Mention the Music?* New York: Contemporary, 1989.

Mangam, William D. *The Clarks: An American Phenomenon.* New York: Silver Bow Press, 1941.

Mann, William J. *Behind the Screen: How Gays and Lesbians Shaped Hollywood.* New York: Viking, 2001.

———. *Wisecracker: The Life and Times of William Haines.* New York: Viking, 1998.

Marchant, William. *The Privilege of His Company.* Indianapolis: Bobbs-Merrill, 1975.

Martin, Hugh. *Hugh Martin: The Boy Next Door.* Encinitas: Trolley, 2010.

Max, Gerry. *Horizon Chasers.* Jefferson, NC: McFarland, 2007.

Mayer, Robert Stanley. *The Influence of Frank A. Vanderlip and the National City Bank on American Commerce and Foreign Policy, 1910–1920.* New York: Garland, 1987.

McClelland, Doug. *The Unkindest Cuts.* New York: A. S. Barnes, 1972.

Mennel, Barbara. *Queer Cinema: Schoolgirls, Vampires, and Gay Cowboys.* New York: Columbia University Press, 2012.

Meredith, Burgess. *So Far, So Good.* New York: Little, Brown and Company, 1994.

Mikotowicz, Tom. *Oliver Smith: A Bio-Bibliography.* Westport: Greenwood, 1993.

Mordden, Ethan. *All That Glittered.* New York: St. Martin's, 2007.

———. *Beautiful Mornin': The Broadway Musical of the 1940s.* New York: Oxford University Press, 1999.

Mueller, John. *Astaire Dancing.* New York: Knopf, 1985.

Myers, Eric. *Uncle Mame.* New York: St. Martin's, 2000.

Nissen, Alex. *Actresses of a Certain Character.* Jefferson, NC: McFarland, 2007.

Oja, Carol J. *Bernstein Meets Broadway.* New York: Oxford University Press, 2014.

Ostrander, Kathleen. *Remembering the Kennebunks.* Charleston: History Press, 2009.

Parish, James Robert. *The Slapstick Queens.* New York: A. S. Barnes, 1973.

Payn, Graham, and Sheridan Morley (eds.). *The Noël Coward Diaries.* New York: Macmillan, 1985.

Pecktal, Lynn. *Costume Design.* New York: Back Stage, 1993.

Perry, Jeb H. *Screen Gems.* Lanham, MD: Scarecrow, 1991.

Phillips, Brent. *Charles Walters: The Director Who Made Hollywood Dance.* Lexington: University Press of Kentucky, 2014.

Pilato, Herbie J. *The Bewitched Book.* New York: Delta, 1992.

Plummer, Christopher. *In Spite of Myself: A Memoir.* New York: Knopf, 2008.

Propst, Andy. *They Made Us Happy.* New York: Oxford University Press, 2019.

Rich, Sharon. *Sweethearts.* New York: Penguin, 1994.

Russell, Anna. *I'm Not Making This Up, You Know.* New York: Continuum, 1985.

Sanders, Steven Coyne, and Tom Gilbert. *Desilu: The Story of Lucille Ball and Desi Arnaz.* New York: William Morrow, 1993.

Schanke, Robert A., and Kim Marra (eds.). *Passing Performances: Queer Readings of Leading Players in*

American Theater History. Ann Arbor: University of Michigan Press, 1998.

Shapiro, Eddie. *Nothing Like a Dame.* New York: Oxford University Press, 2014.

Shayne, Alan, and Norman Sunshine. *Double Life: A Love Story, from Broadway to Hollywood.* New York: Magnus, 2011.

Shelton, Marion Brown. *An American Schoolmistress: The Life of Eliza B. Masters.* New York: Putnam's, 1927.

Sillman, Leonard. *Here Lies Leonard Sillman, Straightened Out at Last.* New York: Citadel, 1959.

Silverman, Stephen M. *Dancing on the Ceiling: Stanley Donen and His Movies.* New York: Knopf, 1996.

Smith, Liz. *Natural Blonde.* New York: Hyperion, 2000.

Spoto, Donald. *Marilyn Monroe: The Biography.* New York: HarperCollins, 1993.

Staggs, Sam. *Inventing Elsa Maxwell.* New York: St. Martin's, 2012.

Taravella, Steve. *Mary Wickes: I Know I've Seen That Face Before.* Jackson: University Press of Mississippi, 2013.

Thomas, Lawrence B. *The MGM Years.* New York: Columbia House, 1972.

Thomson, Virgil. *Virgil Thomson.* New York: Knopf, 1966.

Tranberg, Charles. *I Love the Illusion.* Albany, GA: BearManor Media, 2005.

Turnbull, Michael T. R. B. *Mary Garden.* Portland: Amadeus, 1997.

Vaill, Amanda. *Somewhere: The Life of Jerome Robbins.* New York: Broadway Books, 2006.

Vaughn, Barbara Biggers. *Lick Creek Beckoned.* Decorah, IA: Anundsen, 1995.

Vidal, Gore. *Palimpsest: A Memoir.* New York: Random House, 1995.

Vose, Pamela Daly. *The Masters School, 1877–1977: A Retrospective Portrait.* New York: Georgian Press, 1977.

Watters, Sam. *Houses of Los Angeles, 1885–1919.* New York: Acanthus, 2007.

Weaver, John D. *Glad Tidings: A Friendship in Letters.* New York: HarperCollins, 1993.

Wecter, Dixon. *Sam Clemens of Hannibal.* Boston: Houghton Mifflin, 1952.

Weissberger, L. Arnold. *Famous Faces.* New York: Harry N. Abrams, 1973.

Williams, Walter. *A History of Northeast Missouri.* Chicago: Lewis, 1913.

Wilson, John C., Thomas S. Hischak and Jack Macauley. *Noel, Tallulah, Cole, and Me.* Lanham, MD: Rowan & Littlefield, 2015.

Wilson, Patricia. *Yesterday's Mashed Potatoes.* Indianapolis: Dog Ear Publishing, 2009.

Appendix:
Alice Pearce Professional Credits

Broadway Productions

1942–1943	*New Faces of 1943*, Ritz Theatre
1944–1946	*On the Town*, Adelphi Theatre, 44th Street Theatre, Martin Beck Theatre
1948	*Look, Ma, I'm Dancin'!*, Adelphi Theatre
1948–1949	*Small Wonder*, Coronet Theatre
1949–1951	*Gentlemen Prefer Blondes*, Ziegfeld Theatre
1952	*The Grass Harp*, Martin Beck Theatre
1953–1954	*John Murray Anderson's Almanac*, Imperial Theatre
1954–1955	*Dear Charles*, Morosco Theatre
1956	*Fallen Angels*, Playhouse Theatre
1957	*Copper and Brass*, Martin Beck Theatre
1957–1959	*Bells Are Ringing*, Shubert Theatre, Alvin Theatre
1961	*Midgie Purvis*, Martin Beck Theatre
1961–1962	*Sail Away*, Broadhurst Theatre

Broadway Tours

1946	*On the Town*
1959	*Bells Are Ringing*

Off-Broadway Production

1960	*The Ignorants Abroad*, Theatre East

Summer Theatre Productions

1940	New Kennebunkport Playhouse, Maine (apprenticeship)
1944	Strand Theatre, Stamford, Connecticut (summer stock, 11 weeks)
1946	*Private Lives*, Royal Alexandra Theatre, Toronto
1946	*Private Lives*, Greenwich Playhouse, Connecticut (2 weeks)
1946	Greenwich Playhouse, Connecticut (summer stock)

1947	*Best Foot Forward*, John Drew Theatre, East Hampton, Long Island
1952	*Three to One*, Westport Country Playhouse, Connecticut
1953	*Best Foot Forward*, State Fair Musicals, Dallas
1953	*Stock in Trade*, Bermudiana Theatre, Bermuda
1954	*The Vegetable*, Marblehead, Mass.; Hinsdale, Ill.; Boston, Mass.
1954	*Dear Charles*, Ogunquit Playhouse, Maine
1955	*Best Foot Forward*, Civic Light Opera Association, Pittsburgh Stadium
1959	*Bells Are Ringing*, State Fair Musicals, Dallas
1960	*Redhead*, State Fair Musicals, Dallas

Other Theatrical Engagements

1953	*Lend an Ear*, Palm Beach Playhouse
1957	*Fallen Angels; Witness for the Prosecution*, Palm Beach Playhouse
1960	*Angel in the Wings*, Coconut Grove Playhouse, Miami

Nightclub Engagements

1944	The Satire Room, Boston, 8 weeks
Spring/Summer 1947	The Blue Angel, 10 weeks
Fall 1947	The Blue Angel, 12 weeks
Winter/ Spring 1948	The Blue Angel, 13 weeks
Spring 1951	The Blue Angel, 6 weeks
Winter 1953	The Blue Angel, 7 weeks
Spring 1953	The Blue Angel, 5 weeks
Winter 1957	The Blue Angel, 5 weeks
September 1959	The Tree Club, Dallas, 2 weeks
April 1960	Colonial Inn, St. Petersburg, 1 week

Discography

1949   *Gentlemen Prefer Blondes* (Original Broad way Cast), LP, Columbia, ML-4290
1954   *The Body in the Seine*, LP, Alden-Shaw Productions, VB-001
1959   *Monster Rally*, LP, RCA Victor, LPM-1923

Radio Appearances

1941   *The Experimental Playhouse of the Air* (WOV, New York)
13 December 1942   Network debut, unknown program/network
27 October 1947   *On Stage America* (ABC)
4 November 194   *We, the People* (CBS)
28 March 1949   *The Railroad Hour*: "Best Foot For ward" with Betty Garrett (ABC)
July–Sept. 1949   *The Henry Morgan Show* (NBC), regular cast member
15 June 1953   *Brandeis University Festival of Creative Arts*: "The Comic Performer" with Fred Allen and Jack Pearl (WNBC)
29 October 1954   *Make Up Your Mind* (CBS). As a guest on this panel show, Alice was required to decide whether or not she would pursue a theatrical career against her husband's wishes.
12 November 1957   *Robert Q. Lewis* (CBS)
21 December 1962   *Flair* (ABC) with host Dick Van Dyke and fellow guests Carl Sandburg, Don McNeill, and Ruth Olami.
25 February 1963   *Flair* (ABC) with host Dick Van Dyke and fellow guests Betsy Palmer, Don McNeill, and Bonnie Prudden.

Motion Picture Appearances
(in order of release)

1949 *On the Town* (M-G-M). Producer: Arthur Freed. Directors: Gene Kelly and Stanley Donen. Cast: Gabey (Gene Kelly), Chip (Frank Sinatra), Brunhilde Esterhazy (Betty Garrett), Claire Huddesen (Ann Miller), Ozzie (Jules Munshin), Ivy Smith (Vera-Ellen), Madame Dilyovska (Florence Bates), Lucy Shmeeler (Alice Pearce), Professor (George Meader), Shipyard Singer (Bern Hoffman), Brooklyn Working Girl (Bea Benaderet), François,

the headwaiter (Hans Conried), Working Girl's Friend (Gladys Blake), Sign Poster (Milton Kibbee), First Man in Subway Station (Lester Dorr), Second Man in Subway Station (Robert R. Stephenson), Spud (Sid Melton), Cab Company Owner (Murray Alper), Police Sergeant, Car 44 (Robert B. Williams), Officer Tracy, Car 44 (Tom Dugan), First Class Sea man Simpkins (William "Bill" Phillips), First Class Seaman Kovarsky (Dick Wessel), Shanghai Club Bartender (Peter Chong), Waiter (Eugene Borden), Redheaded Flirt (Claire Carleton), Man Reading Poetry (Richard Kean), Little Girl at Symphonic Hall (Diane Nance), Little Girl's Mother (Helen Eby-Rock), Boys on Subway (Timmy Hawkins, Curtis Jackson, Norman Ollestad), Photo Layout Man in Subway Station (Don Brodie), Max, the Photographer in Subway Station (Hank Mann), Tough Marine in Subway Station (Jack Shea), Coney Island Barker (Royal Raymond), Officer Mulrooney (Frank Scannell), Speed Cops (Jack G. Lee, Bud Wolfe).

1952 *The Belle of New York* (M-G-M). Producer: Arthur Freed. Director: Charles Walters. Cast: Charlie Hill (Fred Astaire), Angela Bonfils (Vera-Ellen), Mrs. Phineas Hill (Marjorie Main), Max Ferris (Keenan Wynn), Elsie Wilkins (Alice Pearce), Gilfred Spivak (Clinton Sundberg), Dixie McCoy (Gale Robbins), Officer Clancy (Henry Slate), Bow ery Bums (Tom Dugan, Percy Helton, Dick Wessel), Frenchie (Lisa Ferraday), Judkins, the butler (Roger Davis), Harris, the Hills' Driver (Buddy Roosevelt), Mr. Currier (Oliver Blake), Mr. Ives (Billy Griffith), Police Officer (Shep Houghton).

1955 *How to Be Very, Very Popular* (20th Century Fox). Producer/Director: Nunnally Johnson. Cast: Stormy Tornado (Betty Grable), Curly Flagg (Sheree North), Fillmore Wedgewood (Bob Cummings), Dr. Tweed (Charles Coburn), Eddie Jones (Tommy Noonan), Toby Marshall (Orson Bean), B. J. Marshall (Fred Clark), Midge (Charlotte Austin), Miss Sylvester (Alice Pearce), Cedric Flagg (Rhys Williams), Police Sgt. Moon (Andrew Tombes), Chief of Police (Emory Parnell), Bus Driver (Harry Carter), Music Teacher (Jesslyn Fax), Graduation Speaker (Jack Raine), First Police Detective (Jack Mather), Second Police Detective (Michael Lally), Introductory Graduation Speaker (Stanley Farrar), Mr. X, Bald Barber (Milton Parsons), Desk Sergeant (Howard Petrie), Airport Attendant (Anthony Redondo), Cop at Graduation (Edmund Cobb), Bar Patron in Hawaiian Shirt (Richard Collier), News Vendor

(Hank Mann), Bartender (Colin Kenny), Student in Graduation Line (Ralph Moratz), Telephone Operator's Voice (Jean Walters), Cherry Blossom Wang (Noel Toy), Yawning Man in Strip Bar (Heinie Conklin), Girl on Bus (Leslie Parrish).

1956 *The Opposite Sex* (M-G-M). Producer: Joe Pasternak. Director: David Miller. Cast: Kay Hilliard (June Allyson), Crystal Allen (Joan Collins), Sylvia Fowler (Dolores Gray), Amanda Penrose (Ann Sheridan), Gloria Dahl (Ann Miller), Steve Hilliard (Leslie Nielsen), Buck Winston (Jeff Richards), Countess de Brion (Agnes Moorehead), Charlotte Greenwood (Lucy), Edith Potter (Joan Blondell), Mike Pearl (Sam Levene), Howard Fowler (Bill Goodwin), Olga (Alice Pearce), Dolly DeHaven (Barbara Jo Allen), Debbie Hilliard (Sandy Descher), Pat (Carolyn Jones), Jerry Antes (Leading Male Dancer-Banana Number), Ted (Alan Marshal), Phelps Potter (Jonathan Hole), Themselves (Harry James, Art Mooney, Dick Shawn), Psychiatrist (Jim Backus), Women Exiting Sydney's (Jean Andren, Gail Bonney, Maxine Semon), Store Clerk Stampeded by Women (Hal Taggart), Sydney's Receptionist (Ann Morriss), Violet (Maidie Norman), Steam Room Attendant (Jo Gilbert), Annoyed Theatre Patron (Lillian Powell), Assistant Stage Manager (Dean Jones), Man Leaving Phone Booth (Jeffrey Sayre), Ralph the counterman (Wayne Taylor), Delivery Boy (Harry Harvey Jr.), Marie the manicurist (Charlotte Lawrence), Friendly Client at Sydney's (Lela Bliss), John the Hilliards' Butler (Gordon Richards), Army officer acting as Emcee (Joe Corey), Joe the pianist at party (Joe Karnes), Popsicle Vendor (Joe McTurk), Al the Stage Manager for Benefit (Jess Kirkpatrick), First Specialty Dancer (Ellen Ray), Second Specialty Dancer (Barrie Chase), Drunk on Sidewalk (Jack Daly), Drunk's Wife (Trude Wyler), Mrs. Wilson (Janet Lake), Club Car Bartender (Joel Fluellen), Women Departing Ranch (Eve McVeagh, Elizabeth Flournoy, Doris Simons), Ralph the divorce lawyer (Vernon Rich), Lutsi (Celia Lovsky), Television Stage Manager (Richard Grant), Sylvia's maid Helene (Karine Nordman), Maitre d' (Gabor Curtiz), Headwaiter (Jan Arvan), Hughie (Harry Tom McKenna), Powder Room Attendant (Juanita Moore), Messenger at Nightclub (Wilson Wood), Nightclub Waiter (Sid Tomack), Backstage Well-wishers (Robert Carson, Frank Scannell).

1962 *Lad: A Dog* (Warner Brothers). Producer: Max J. Rosenberg. Directors: Adam Avakian, Leslie H. Martinson. Cast: Stephen Tremayne (Peter Breck), Elizabeth Tremayne (Peggy McCay), Hamilcar Q. Glure (Carroll O'Connor), Angela Glure (Angela Cartwright), Lester (Maurice Dallimore), Hilda (Alice Pearce), Jackson White, the Poacher (Jack Daly), Sheriff (Charles Fredericks), Constable (Tim Graham), Miss Woodward (Lillian Buyeff), Dr. Maxwell (Harry Holcombe), Dog Show Judge (Nelson Olmsted), Glure's Dog Trainer (Peter Forster), Dog Show Official (Vincent Perry), Boy at Dog Show (Johnny Bangert), Congratulatory Friend (Budd Albright), Woman at Dog Show (Patricia Basch), Lad (Lord Byron).

1963 *My Six Loves* (Paramount). Producer: Gant Gaither. Director: Gower Champion. Cast: Janice Courtney (Debbie Reynolds), Rev. Jim Larkin (Cliff Robertson), Martin Bliss (David Janssen), Ethel Swenson (Eileen Heckart), Kingsley Cross (Hans Conried), Doreen Smith (Mary McCarty), Tom, the sheriff (Jim Backus), Judge Harris (John McGiver), B. J. Smith (Max Showalter), Selina Johnson (Alice Ghostley), Bus Driver (Alice Pearce), Diane Soper (Pippa Scott), Dr. Ben Miller (Claude Stroud), Ava Johnson (Darlene Tompkins), Mario (Leon Belasco), Leo Smith (Billy Hughes), Sherman Smith (Barry Livingston), Sonny Smith (Teddy Eccles), Amy Smith (Colleen Peters), Brenda Smith (Sally Smith), Dulcie Smith (Debbie Price), Harry, the studio representative (Tommy Farrell), Photographers (Larry Alderette, Robert Cole, Cass Jaeger, Robert Karl, Frank Radcliff, Paul Rees, Terry Terrill), First Reporter (Ted Bergen), Second Reporter (Ted Quillin), Nina, the columnist (Yvonne Peattie), Third Reporter (William Hudson), Party Crasher (Victor Buono), Armed Forces Radio Interviewer (Maurice Kelly), Bill Carson (Leon Tyler), First Woman at Auction (Georgine Cleveland), Second Woman (Molly Dodd), Third Woman (Freda Jones), Old Lady in Wheelchair (Minta Durfee), Oliver Dodds (Sterling Holloway), Judge's Clerk (William Wood), Bus Driver's Son (Gary Goetzman), Nurse (Mimi Dillard), Stage Manager (Thomas Thomas), Actor (Richard Fitzgerald).

1963 *Tammy and the Doctor* (Universal-International). Producer: Ross Hunter. Director: Harry Keller. Cast: Tammy Tyree (Sandra Dee), Dr. Mark Cheswick (Peter Fonda), Dr. Wayne Bentley (MacDonald Carey), Rachel Coleman (Margaret Lindsay), Annie Call (Beulah Bondi), Jason Tripp (Reginald Owen), Millie Baxter (Alice Pearce), Dr. Eric Hassler (Adam West), Vera Parker (Joan Marshall), Wally Day (Stanley Clements), Traction patient (Doodles

Weaver), Pamela Burke (Mitzi Hoag), Chief of Staff (Alex Gerry), Dr. Smithers (Charles Seel), Surgeon (Robert Foulk), Surgical Nurse (Connie Madison), Assistant Surgeon (Jill Jackson), Dr. Crandall (Forrest Lewis), Surgical Nurse assisting Bentley (Sondra Rodgers), Dora, college co-ed (Suzie Kaye), David, college co-ed (Paul Nesbitt), College Co-ed (Barbara Gayle), Young Boy (David Nelson Crawford), Orderly (Robert Biheller), Hospital Administrator (Henry Hunter), First Maternity Patient (Janice Carroll), Second Maternity Patient (Mimi Dillard), Mrs. Call's Nurse (Dale Hogan), Nurse in Hallway (Joan Young).

1963 *The Thrill of It All* (Universal-International). Producer: Ross Hunter. Director: Norman Jewison. Cast: Beverly Boyer (Doris Day), Dr. Gerald Boyer (James Garner), Mrs. Fraleigh (Arlene Francis), Gardiner Fraleigh (Edward Andrews), Old Tom Fraleigh (Reginald Owen), Olivia (ZaSu Pitts), Mike Palmer (Elliott Reid), Woman (Alice Pearce), Maggie Boyer (Kym Karath), Andy Boyer (Brian Nash), Mrs. Goethe (Lucy Landau), Dr. Taylor (Paul Hartman), Billings (Hayden Rorke), Stokely (Alex Gerry), Van Camp (Robert Gallagher), Miss Thompson (Anne Newman), Butler (Burt Mustin), Sidney, the chauffeur (Hedley Mattingly), Garbage Truck Foreman (Robert Strauss), Garbage Truck Crewman (Maurice Gosfield), Angry Driver (William Bramley), Spot Checker (Pamela Curran), Irving (Herbie Faye), Cabbie (Lenny Kent), Mr. Caputo (John Alderman), Second Garbage Truck Crewman (Lennie Weinrib), Third Garbage Truck Crewman (Karl Lukas), Fourth Garbage Truck Crewman (Joe Higgins), Crane Operator (Buddy Lewis), First Neighbor (Dorothy Neumann), Second Neighbor (Hallene Hill), Studio Guard (Tim Graham), Maitre d' (Jacques Foti), TV Announcer's Voice (Paul Frees), Dr. Frederick Erlich (Irwin Charone), First Autograph Seeker (Hope Sansberry), Second Autograph Seeker (Lillian Culver), Third Autograph Seeker (Gertrude Flynn), Fourth Autograph Seeker (Jeane Wood), State Policeman (Kelly Thorsden), Motorcycle Cop (Mickey Finn), Commercial Director (Bernie Kopell), Nurse (Jan March), Mounted Policeman (John Daheim), First Actress (Lisa Seagram), Second Actress (Pamela Searle), Third Actress (Patricia Krest), Nazi Officer/Cad/Cowboy (Carl Reiner).

1964 *Dear Heart* (Warner Brothers). Producer: Martin Manulis. Director: Delbert Mann. Cast: Harry Mork (Glenn Ford), Evie Jackson (Geraldine Page), Phyllis (Angela Lansbury), Patrick (Michael Anderson, Jr.), June Loveland (Barbara Nichols), Daphne Mitchell (Patricia Barry), Frank Taylor (Charles Drake), Miss Tait (Ruth McDevitt), Connie Templeton (Neva Patterson), Miss Moore (Alice Pearce), Mr. Cruikshank (Richard Deacon), Emile Zola Bernkrant (Joanna Crawford), Peterson (Peter Turgeon), The Masher (Ken Lynch), Miss Fox (Mary Wickes), Marvin (James O'Rear), Herb (Nelson Olmsted), Mrs. Sloan (Sandra Gould), Chester (Steven Bell), Jerry (William Cort), Restaurant Proprietor (Ralph Manza), Unpleasant Waitress (Maxine Stuart), Mr. Grove (Robert Kenneally), Mr. Weinstock (Tom Palmer), Florist (Pauline Myers), Penn Station Information Counter Attendant (Parker McCormick), Man in Lobby (Tad Mosel), Stubby (Hal Smith), Stu (Billy Benedict), Millicent (Patsy Garrett), Veronica (Dorothy Abbott), Woman Looking for Badge (Mary Carroll), Joe (Fletcher Allen), Coffee Shop Hostess (Karen Norris), Vernon (Robert Casper), Shorty (Peter Ford), Zanzibar Kentucky (Charles Alvin Bell), Miss Carmichael (Barbara Luddy), Penn Station Porter (George Wiltshire), Jeannie (Nanette Leonard), Maurice (John Wilson), Fred (Martin Bolger), Joyce (Allyson Ames), Henry (Ronnie Knox), Rita (Jeanne Arnold), Minerva's Voice (Juanita Field), Metropolitan Hotel Bellboy (Dick Balduzzi), Magazine Counter Clerk (Louise de Carlo), Barber (Irving Steinberg).

1964 *The Disorderly Orderly* (Paramount). Producer: Paul Jones. Director/Screenplay: Frank Tashlin. Cast: Jerome Littlefield (Jerry Lewis), Susan Andrews (Susan Oliver), Dr. Jean Howard (Glenda Farrell), Mr. Tuffington (Everett Sloane), Julie Blair (Karen Sharpe), Maggie Higgins (Kathleen Freeman), Dr. Davenport (Del Moore), Mrs. Fuzzyby (Alice Pearce), Fat Jack (Jack E. Leonard), Miss Marlowe (Barbara Nichols), Opening Narrator's voice (Paul Frees), Intern in Opening Narration (Kent McCord), Gout Patient in Opening Credits (Jack Fife), First Ambulance Intern (Michael Ross), First Ambulance Driver (Danny Costello), Francine, nurse (Francine York), Janet, nurse (Cissy Wellman), Miss Marlowe's nurse (Carol Andreson), Millicent (Audrey Betz), Mr. Welles (Herbie Faye), Patient in orange pantsuit (Ethelreda Leopold), Middle-aged patient (Murray Alper), Middle-aged patient's redheaded wife (Muriel Landers), Second Ambulance Orderly (Robert Donner), First Policeman (Tommy Farrell), Second Policeman (Dave Willock), Emergency Room Nurse (Kim January), Dr. Smathers (William Wellman Jr.), Candy Striper

(Barbara Bellino), Waiter (Benny Rubin), Nurse assisting with Bandaging (Allyson Ames), Tuffington's Chauffeur (Tim Herbert), Board Members (Milton Frome, Frankie Darro), Orderlies (John Macchia, Bob Harvey, Ron Schmidt, Frank Alesia), Singing French Nurse (Gabrielle Rossillon), Milton M. Mealy (Frank J. Scannell), Moving Van Driver (Mike Mahoney), Moving Van Passenger (Mike Mazurki), Older Lady in Pink outside Supermarket (Minta Durfee).

1964 *Kiss Me, Stupid* (United Artists). Producer/Director: Billy Wilder. Writers: Billy Wilder, I. A. L. Diamond. Cast: Dino (Dean Martin), Polly the Pistol (Kim Novak), Orville J. Spooner (Ray Walston), Zelda Spooner (Felicia Farr), Barney Millsap (Cliff Osmond), Big Bertha (Barbara Pepper), Milkman (James Ward), Mamie Pettibone (Doro Merande), Waitress (Bobo Lewis), Johnnie Mulligan (Tommy Nolan), Mrs. Mulligan (Alice Pearce), Rev. Carruthers (John Fiedler), Rosalie Schultz (Arlen Stuart), Henry Pettibone (Howard McNear), Mack Gray (Cliff Norton), Dr. Sheldrake (Mel Blanc), Sylvia (Eileen O'Neill), Mitzi (Susan Wedell), Belly Button Bartender (Bern Hoffman), Smith (Henry Gibson), Wesson (Alan Dexter), Truck Driver (Henry Beckman), Nevada State Trooper (Gene Darfler), Guffawing Desert Sands Waiters (James Jeter, Richard Reeves), Stoic Desert Sands Waiter (Billy Beck), Autograph Seekers (Lori Fontaine, Kathy Garver, Jill Hill, Mary Jane Saunders).

1965 *Dear Brigitte* (20th Century Fox). Producers: Fred Kohlmar, Henry Koster. Director: Henry Koster. Screenplay: Hal Kanter. Cast: Dr. Robert Leaf (James Stewart), Kenneth Taylor (Fabian), Vina Leaf (Glynis Johns), Pandora Leaf (Cindy Carol), Erasmus Leaf (Billy Mumy), Peregrine Upjohn (John Williams), Dr. Volker (Jack Kruschen), The Captain (Ed Wynn), George (Charles Robinson), Dean Sawyer (Howard Freeman), Terry (Jane Wald), Employment Office Clerk (Alice Pearce), Chris Argyle (Jesse White), Police Lt. Rink (Gene O'Donnell), Von Schlogg (Orville Sherman), Miss Eva (Maida Severn), Nunnally (Sid Kane), Elderly Professor (William Fawcett), Student in Lecture (Lyn Edgington), Bank Manager (Pitt Herbert), Bank Teller (John Stevens), Orville (Robert Biheller), Computer Operator (Sherwood Keith), Professor Burns (Gloria Clark), Mr. Kraft (Percy Helton), Dress Shop Manager (Louise Lane), Saleslady (Adair Jameson), Eugenia Clove (Paula Lane), Students at Leaf Rally (James Brolin, Clive

Clerk, Robert Fitzpatrick), Bartender (Harry Rose), Upjohn's Brunette Date (Marissa Mathes), Mailman (Ted Mapes), Paris Taxi Driver (Marcel De la Brosse), Racetrack Ticket Seller (Jack Daly), Racetrack Cashier (William Henry), Racetrack Announcer's voice (Richard Lane), Upjohn's Blonde Doll (Susanne Cramer), U. S. Treasury Agent (Harry Fleer), and Brigitte Bardot.

1965 *Bus Riley's Back in Town* (Universal). Producer: Elliott Kastner. Director: Harvey Hart. Writer: William Inge. Cast: Laurel Aiken (Ann-Margret), Bus Riley (Michael Parks), Judy Nichols (Janet Margolin), Walter Slocum (Brad Dexter), Mrs. Riley (Jocelyn Brando), Howie (Larry Storch), Mr. Spencer (Crahan Denton), Gussie Riley (Kim Darby), Carlotta McElhaney (Brett Somers), Paula Riley (Mimsy Farmer), Mrs. Nichols (Nan Martin), Joy (Lisabeth Hush), Mrs. Spencer Sr. (Ethel Griffies), Housewife (Alice Pearce), Benji (Chet Stratton), Stretch (David Carradine), Egg Foo (Marc Cavell), Jules Griswald (Parley Baer), Mrs. Jules Griswald (Claire Carleton), Les (James Doohan), Naomi (Barbara Fuller), Country Club Bartender (William Hudson), Simmons (Maurice Manson), Larry O'Brien (Barne Williams), Mr. Spencer Sr. (Leslie Nielsen Sr.).

1966 *The Glass Bottom Boat* (M-G-M). Producers: Martin Melcher, Everett Freeman. Director: Frank Tashlin. Writer: Everett Freeman. Cast: Jennifer Nelson (Doris Day), Bruce Templeton (Rod Taylor), Axel Nordstrom (Arthur Godfrey), Zack Molloy (Dick Martin), Ralph Goodwin (John McGiver), Homer Cripps (Paul Lynde), Gen. Wallace Bleecker (Edward Andrews), Edgar Hill (Eric Fleming), Julius Pritter (Dom DeLuise), Nina Bailey (Elisabeth Fraser), Mabel Fenimore (Alice Pearce), Norman Fenimore (George Tobias), Anna Miller (Ellen Corby), Donna (Dee J. Thompson), Queasy Man on Glass Bottom Boat (George Cisar), First Reporter (Mike Mahoney), Second Reporter (Rachel Romen), Paul Valenti (Robert Kilgallen), Third Reporter (Joe Haworth), Fourth Reporter (Charles Stewart), Secretary (Pat Casella), Miss Perkins (Leslie Vallen), Engineer at Space Center (Larry Strong), Gregor (Theodore Marcuse), Henchman (Maroun Hakim), Russian (Gregg Martell), American (Bill Cord), Blonde Man dancing at Party (Richard Alden), Screaming Party Guest (Ellen Atterbury), Her Husband (Michael Romanoff), Man answering phone (Joe Ploski), His sleeping wife (Bella Bruck), Woman answering phone (Florence Halop), Napoleon Solo (Robert Vaughn), Captured Undercover Men (Tony Regan, Shep Houghton), Policemen (John Dennis, James Macklin).

Television Appearances
(excluding *Bewitched* episodes)

This list is not comprehensive. It's possible that Alice Pearce made additional television appearances not listed here. Detailed credits are provided for certain productions, particularly if their entries on the Internet Movie Database (www.imdb.com) or The Classic TV Archive (www.ctva.biz) are incomplete or erroneous.

28 June 1948	*Broadway Jamboree*
28 January 1949	*The Alice Pearce Show*
4 February 1949	*The Alice Pearce Show*
11 February 1949	*The Alice Pearce Show*
18 February 1949	*The Alice Pearce Show*
25 February 1949	*The Alice Pearce Show*
4 March 1949	*The Alice Pearce Show*
23 June 1949	*The 54th Street Revue*
30 June 1949	*The 54th Street Revue*

31 July 1949 *The Meredith Willson Show.* Alice was the guest star on the first of four installments of Willson's Sunday-night summer show. Set on a small-town front porch, the material, said the *New York Daily News*, "had a naïve and yet sophisticated freshness about it and the program offered a novelty in daring to end with the singing of a hymn."

15 October 1949	*Cavalcade of Stars*
c. 1949	*Tex and Jinx*
c. 1950	*Club Seven*
c. 1950	*The Stork Club*
c. 1950	*Tex McCrary and Jinx Falkenburg*
c. 1950	*Celebrity Time* (three appearances)
29 January 1950	*Toast of the Town (Ed Sullivan)*
13 August 1950	*Toast of the Town (Ed Sullivan)*
5 September 1950	*Van Camp's Little Show*
19 September 1950	*Eloise Salutes the Stars*

10 October 1950 *Texaco Star Theater (Milton Berle).* Alice and comic Bert Gordon play contestants.

31 October 1950 *Texaco Star Theater (Milton Berle)*

20 November 1950 *The Kate Smith Hour*

21 November 1950 *The Faye Emerson Show.* On this fifteen-minute telecast, guest performer Alice sings "Constantinople" and the M.I.T. song. Emerson and Alice model various fur pieces.

12 February 1951 *The Faye Emerson Show* (with fellow guests Peter Donald and Richard Cleary)

17 October 1951 *The Kate Smith Evening Hour*

27 October 1951 *Faye Emerson's Wonderful Town* (with Abe Burrows, Nora Kaye, and Donald Richards in a salute to the Bronx).

29 December 1951 *Faye Emerson's Wonderful Town*: "New Year's Town" (with fellow guests Rosemary Clooney, Nora Kaye, and Tommy Rall).

6 November 1951 *The Garry Moore Show* (daytime series)

22 November 1951 *The Garry Moore Show* (daytime series)

26 November 1951 *Lux Video Theatre*: "Dames Are Poison"

3 December 1951 *The Kate Smith Show* (daytime series)

9 December 1951 *Goodyear Television Playhouse*: "Money to Burn"

10 April 1952 *The Garry Moore Show* (daytime series)

22 September 1952 *Broadway Television Theatre*: "The Bishop Misbehaves"

9 November 1952 *The Al Capp Show* (weekly daytime series, WNBT). Writer/Producer: Al Capp. Director: Bill Harbach. Cast: Al Capp, Alice Pearce, Mort Marshall, Larry Blyden.

25 November 1952 *Mike and Buff* (In this CBS daytime talk show, Alice performs an original skit about a nightclub entertainer who cleans her hats in a washing machine.)

8 February 1953 *The Red Buttons Show*

16 February 1953 *Robert Montgomery Presents*: "The Burtons" (with fellow players Gene Lockhart, Kathleen Lockhart, June Lockhart, Art Carney, Parker Fennelly, and Milton Parsons).

24 April 1953 *The Aldrich Family*: "The Eye Examination" (with fellow guest player Royal Beal). Summary: Henry Aldrich proves that love is blind after an oculist puts drops in his eyes. He falls for his sister's homely houseguest, played by Alice.

29 September 1953 *One Minute Please* (tryout)

2 November 1953 *Jamie*: "Aunt Laurie's New Assistant"

4 November 1953 *Take It from Me* (with fellow guests Mildred Clinton, Myrtle Ferguson, Dortha Coe, Harold Grau, Edith Gresham, and Maxine Stuart).

23 November 1953 *Broadway Television Theatre*: "The Bat"

2 December 1953 *Kraft Television Theatre*: "The Rose Garden." Cast: Rose Frobisher (Enid Markey), Leila Frobisher (Mary James), Barbara Parris (Barbara Baxley), Maxine (Alice Pearce), Mr. Jones (Fred

Stewart), Violet (Brett Somers), Gloria (Martine Bartlett), Charlie Gordon (Herbert Patterson).

21 December 1953 *Jamie*: "Jamie and the Wallflower" (with fellow guests Mary Finney, Bruce Marshall, Shirley Enker, Susan Lee Zeller).

29 December 1953 *The Motorola Television Hour*: "The Thirteen Clocks"

11 January 1954 *Jamie*: "Love Comes to Annie Mokum" (with fellow guest player Nathaniel Frey).

28 February 1954 *The Man Behind the Badge*: "The Dade County, Florida Story" (aka "The Miami Story"). Summary: A building inspector fights for stricter standards in home construction. Cast: Murray Hamilton, Alice Pearce, Edgar Stehli, Bernard Grant, Will Scholz, Andy Sabilia, Harry Worth, Tom Gorman, Stewart Bradley, Dorothy Sands, Patsy Campbell, Doris Davis.

6 July 1954   *One Minute Please*
13 July 1954   *One Minute Please*
20 July 1954   *One Minute Please*
27 July 1954   *One Minute Please*
1955   *Norby*. The first network series filmed entirely in color by Eastman Kodak, *Norby* was a sitcom starring David Wayne.

16 January 1955 *The Ed Sullivan Show*

13 February 1955 *Mister Peepers*. Cast: Robinson Peepers (Wally Cox), Wilma Potts (Alice Pearce), Lawyer (Victor Wood), Uncle Spencer (Robin Craven), Aunt Elizabeth (Jenny Egan), Peter Rhodes-Downing (Cyril Ritchard).

4 May 1955   *Kraft Television Theatre*: "Flowers for 2-B." Cast: Benny Baker, Virginia Vincent (as "Tillie Silver"), Alice Pearce (as "Judy"), Harold Stone, Augusta Merighi, Anna Appel, Carolyn King, James Lacirignola, Leo Bayard, Pat DeSimone.

6 June 1955   *Studio One*: "The Spongers." Original story by James Yaffe. Cast: Monty Gravenhurst (Cyril Ritchard), Fred Bristol (Ernest Truex), Regina Gravenhurst (Alice Pearce), Joe Bristol (Murray Hamilton), Amy Bristol (Judith Parrish), Margaret (Carole Somers).

23 October 1955 *Hallmark Hall of Fame*: "Alice in Wonderland"

9 November 1955 *Kraft Television Theatre*: "The Ticket and the Tempest." Cast: Sean (Arthur Shields), Liam (J. Pat O'Malley), Kate (Alice Pearce), Father Duffy (Cameron Prud'homme), Lawyer (Tom McElhany), Sean's wife (Mabel Taliaferro).

11 December 1955 *Frontiers in Faith*: "The Enchanted Top" (an episode of *The Eternal Light*). Adaptation by James Yaffe from the original story by Judah

Steinberg. Cast: Jimmy Oster, Peter Lazar, Margaret Hamilton, Alice Pearce, Viola Harris, Robert Harris.

1 January 1956   *Omnibus*. Besides Alice's solo, other segments included the Azuma Kabuki Dancers, the documentary *The Private Life of a Cat*, and William Saroyan's comedy play *The Best Year in the History of the World*, directed by Delbert Mann, with actors Paul Hartman, Orson Bean, Jean Stapleton, Georgann Johnson, Ruth McDevitt, and Howard Freeman.

26 April 1956   *The Goldbergs*: "The Milk Farm." Director: Marc Daniels. Cast: Molly Goldberg (Gertrude Berg), Uncle David (Eli Mintz), Rosalie Goldberg (Arlene McQuade), Sammy Goldberg (Tom Taylor), Hortense Lang (Natalie Schafer), Beatrice (Alice Pearce), Louise Harper (Nina Varela), Nurse (Pat Parker), Eva (Lucille Rogers), Martha (Eva Gerson), Dolly (Evelyn Wall), Fantasia (Laura Prikovits), Lulu (Gertrude Kinnell). Filmed 1955. First-run airdate in syndication: 26 April 1956, WABD-TV, New York.

24 May 1956   *The Jack Paar Show* (CBS daytime series)

10 June 1956   *Camera Three*: "What Price Nonsense?" Cast: Archie Smith, Alice Pearce, Tommy White, Rex Everhart, Dorothy Sands. Alice reads selections from the works of Edward Lear.

3 July 1956   *Tonight!* (with guest host Jack Paar, Louis Nye, and Elise Rhodes)

9 July 1956   *Tonight!* (with guest host Bill Cullen and Arlene Francis)

27 August 1956   *Tonight!* (with guest host Tony Randall, and Enid Markey; Louis Nye and Alice parodied TV serial dramas in a skit.)

4 September 1956 *Tonight!* (with guest host Jack Paar and Sister Rosetta Tharpe)

17 September 1956 *Tonight!* (with guest host Tony Randall, Louis Nye, and Einar Hanson)

18 September 1956 *Tonight!* (with guest host Tony Randall, Louis Nye, and Ray de la Torre)

24 September 1956 *Tonight!* (with guest host Tony Randall, Louis Nye, and Diahann Carroll)

25 September 1956 *Tonight!* (with guest host Tony Randall, Louis Nye, and Virginia Graham)

3 October 1956   *Good Morning! With Will Rogers, Jr.*
15 October 1956   *Good Morning! With Will Rogers, Jr.*
22 October 1956   *Studio One*: "The Crimes of Peter Page." Summary: A question is raised about the authenticity of the priceless objects housed in the Americana museum of which Peter is the dignified curator. Original story by Kathleen and Robert

Howard Lindsay. Director: Paul Nickell. Cast: Barry Jones, Luella Gear, Priscilla Gillette, Norman Lloyd, Don Murphy, Alice Pearce, George Maharis, Norman Rose, Wyatt Cooper, Fred Stewart.

2 December 1956 *The Alcoa Hour*: "Merry Christmas, Mr. Baxter." Director: Herbert Hirschman. Cast: George Baxter (Dennis King), Susan Baxter (Cornelia Otis Skinner), Polly (Patricia Benoit), Miss Gillyard (Margaret Hamilton), Housewares Lady (Alice Pearce), Herbert (Rex O'Malley), Bobby (Jimmy Rogers), Cora (Eulabelle Moore), Policeman (Tom Pedi), Lingerie Lady (Margaret O'Neil), Perfume Lady (Ann Wedgeworth), Mr. Malone (Mort Marshall), Mink Lady (Moyna MacGill), Mr. Hickenlooper (Roy Johnson), Doorman (Joe Silver), Mr. Bernhard (John McGiver).

9 December 1956 *Omnibus*. Besides Alice's segment, the telecast included Sidney Carroll's play *The Fine Art of Murder* with James Daly, Rex Stout, Dennis Hoey, Felix Munso, Herbert Voland, Robert Echols, Gene Reynolds, Jane McArthur, Bruce Kirby, Jack Sydow, Truman Smith, Ludie Claire, and Dan Ocko.

25 December 1956 *Good Morning! With Will Rogers, Jr.*

7 November 1957 *The Jack Paar Tonight Show* (with Danny Scholl and Florian Zabach)

28 November 1957 *The Jack Paar Tonight Show* (with Fran Allison)

31 December 1957 *The Jack Paar Tonight Show* (with Carol Burnett and Dody Goodman)

14 February 1958 *The Frank Sinatra Show* (with Shirley Jones and Jesse White)

4 April 1958 *The Patrice Munsel Show*. On Good Friday, Munsel, Alice, and fellow guest Julius La Rosa teamed up for a folk song medley including "Raise a Ruckus," "Sweet Betsy from Pike," and "Coffee Grows on White Oak Trees." Alice had an amusing bit as a prim schoolmarm who sings "Constantinople" and asks for refills on the spiked tea she ordered. Munsel sings "Bird in a Gilded Cage," "Happy Easter," and "The Lord's Prayer." Munsel also sings "It's a Big, Wide Wonderful World" as a tribute to John Rox.

3 July 1958 *The Jack Paar Tonight Show* (with Florence Henderson and Orson Bean)

4 July 1958 *The Jack Paar Tonight Show* (with Lou Holtz and Johnny Desmond)

31 July 1958 *The Jack Paar Tonight Show* (with Kay Medford and Viveca Lindfors)

16 September 1958 *The Jack Paar Tonight Show* (with Elsa Maxwell)

18 September 1958 *The Jack Paar Tonight Show* (with Peggy Cass and Cliff Arquette)

26 December 1958 *The Jack Paar Tonight Show* (with Ann B. Davis and Hermione Gingold)

8 February 1959 *The Paul Winchell Show* (with juggler Eric Badicton, aerialists Les Oriols)

28 February 1959 *Pontiac Star Parade*: "Accent on Love" (Television special featuring Alice in a Pontiac commercial)

8 October 1959 *The Real McCoys*: "Work No More, My Lady"

13 December 1959 *Hallmark Hall of Fame*: "A Christmas Festival." One segment of the hour-long telecast featured an adaptation of Ludwig Bemelmans' "A Borrowed Christmas," the story of a rich, spiritually bankrupt financier who dies on Christmas Day, goes to hell, and begs for a chance to come back for a few moments in order to talk to his grandson about what really matters in life. Cast: Mr. Reallybig (Walter Slezak), The Manager (Jules Munshin), Miss Talmey (Alice Pearce), Billy (David Francis), Officer Flannelly (John C. Becher). Ben Gross of the *New York Daily News* described Slezak as "outstanding," Francis as "appealing," and Alice as "truly funny."

26 January 1960 *Startime*: "The Wonderful World of Jack Paar"

9 August 1960 *The Jack Paar Tonight Show* (with Dorothy Lamour and Charley Weaver)

21 August 1960 *Camera Three: "A Night with Chichikov."* Cast: Chichikov (Myron McCormick), Petrushka (Gerald Hiken), Sasha/Mischa/Ana (Dorothy Greener), Manilov (Bernie West), Madame Manilov (Alice Pearce), Korobochka (Edith King), Nozdryov (Salem Ludwig). Host: James Macandrew. Dramatization of an excerpt from Nikolai Gogol's *Dead Souls*. Alice plays the silly, doting wife of an ingratiating landowner. The ensemble cast of character actors delivers fine performances.

November 1960 *Full Circle* (CBS daytime serial, live from Hollywood)

13 November 1960 *The Shirley Temple Show*: "The Reluctant Dragon." Producer: William Asher. Director: Richard Dunlap. Cast: Gillian Potter (Shirley Temple), St. George (John Raitt), Jeremy Potter (Charles Herbert), Amos Overmuch (Jack Weston), Dragon's voice (Jonathan Harris), Mayor Godfrey (J. Pat O'Malley), Samuel (Dabbs Greer), Rebecca Free (Alice Pearce), Mistress Becket (Barbara Pepper), Vacant (Johnny Melfi), Simon (Grady Sutton), Alfred Potter (Lester Dorr), Noah (John Craig), Dragon's body (Don Weismuller), Worthy Shoemaker (Hoyt Wertz), Villager in Purple Hood (Edward Knight).

5 January 1961   *The Ann Sothern Show*: "Operation Pudney." Director: Richard Whorf. Writer: Bob Barbash. Cast: Katy O'Connor (Ann Sothern), James Devery (Don Porter), Olive Smith (Ann Tyrell), Oscar Pudney (Jesse White), Woody Hamilton (Ken Berry), Ethel (Alice Pearce), Michel (Paul Dubov), Mrs. Hall (Phillis Coghlan), Linen Salesman (Kenny Jackson), Jeweler (George Ives), Hodges (Joe Brown).

10 March 1961   *The Twilight Zone*: "Static"

19 March 1961   *The Shirley Temple Show*: "The Princess and the Goblins." Director: Robert Ellis Miller. Adapted for television by Richard DeRoy. Cast: Princess Irene (Shirley Temple), Curdie Peterson (Jack Ging), Goblin King (Jack Weston), Esperanza (Irene Hervey), Lootie (Mary Wickes), Prince Gripe (Arte Johnson), Goblin Queen (Alice Pearce), Mrs. Clump (Barbara Perry), Mr. Clump (Bob Hastings), King Charles (Herb Vigran), Chamberlain (Arthur Malet), Miner (Don Harvey).

30 March 1961   *The Ann Sothern Show*: "The Beginning." Director: Richard Whorf. Writer: Bob Van Scoyk. Cast: Katy O'Connor (Ann Sothern), James Devery (Don Porter), Olive Gray (Ann Tyrell), Delbert Gray (Louis Nye), Floyd Crowley (Tod Andrews), Lahoma St. Cyr (Alice Pearce), Stewardess (Wanda Shannon).

24 May 1961   *Angel*: "Angel of Mercy." Director: Ezra Stone. Writer: Joe Quillan. Cast: Angelique Smith (Annie Fargé), John Smith (Marshall Thompson), Susie Carpenter (Doris Singleton), Cassie Turnbull (Alice Pearce), J. O. Clyde (Alan Hewitt), Fred Barnsdale (Robert Jellison), Herbert (Terence De Marney), Charles Turnbull (Lester Matthews), Mr. Nelson (Tyler McVey), Maître d' (Jan Arvan), Restaurant Patrons (David Leland, Don Lutz, George Taylor). Pre-empted from its planned air date of January 12, 1961, this episode was not telecast until nineteen weeks later. However, it aired on Canadian stations on January 15, 1961.

22 October 1961   *Look Up and Live*: "A Likely Story." Cast: Matt Batts (Roger C. Carmel), Miss Flip (Alice Pearce), Nurse (Kathryn Eames), with Ted Chapman and Dick O'Neill. An expectant father becomes involved with an advertising man while awaiting what he is told will be a "multiple" birth by his wife.

25 April 1962   *Calendar* (CBS morning talk show with fellow guests Nancy Walker and Vivian Vance, discussing female comics)

13 May 1962   *General Electric Theater*: "Acres and Pains." Producer/Director: Perry Lafferty. Writers: Harvey Orkin, David Schwartz. Cast: Tom Dutton (Walter Matthau), Jenny Dutton (Anne Jackson), Paul Goodlove (Edward Andrews), Maude Ledbetter (Alice Pearce), Jud Ledbetter (Philip Coolidge), Harold (Jerry Stiller), Burton Fairbanks (David Doyle), also with Mickey Freeman.

7 October 1962   *Dennis the Menace*: "You Go Your Way." Director: Charles Barton. Writers: John Elliotte, Clifford Goldsmith. Cast: Dennis Mitchell (Jay North), John Wilson (Gale Gordon), Henry Mitchell (Herbert Anderson), Alice Mitchell (Gloria Henry), Eloise Wilson (Sara Seegar), Esther Cathcart (Mary Wickes), Miss Tarbell (Alice Pearce), Mrs. Drum (Helen Kleeb), Katherine Prescott (Viola Harris), Mabel Simms (Carol Hill).

29 November 1962 *Alcoa Premiere*: "The Hands of Danofrio." Director: George Schaefer. Teleplay: Larry Marcus, James Gunn. Cast: Caleb Burlington (John Williams), Mario Lombardi (Telly Savalas), Marc Malatesta (Joseph Campanella), Mrs. Murrow (Beulah Bondi), Isis Flemington (Alice Pearce), Rosa Lombardi (Janet Margolin), Ted Rayburn (James Bonnet), Doctor (Lauren Gilbert), Lovely Redhead (Lory Patrick), Chauffeur (Vince Williams), Girl (Joan Swift).

23 December 1962 *Dennis the Menace*: "Jane Butterfield Says." Director: Charles Barton. Writer: John Elliotte. Cast: Dennis Mitchell (Jay North), John Wilson (Gale Gordon), Henry Mitchell (Herbert Anderson), Alice Mitchell (Gloria Henry), Eloise Wilson (Sara Seegar), Esther Cathcart (Mary Wickes), Lucy Tarbell (Alice Pearce), Sgt. Harold Mooney (George Cisar), Police Chief Doyle (Stafford Repp), Mr. Krinkie (Charles Seel).

30 January 1963   *The Many Loves of Dobie Gillis*: "And Now a Word from Our Sponsor." Director: Rod Amateau. Writer: Arnold Horwitt. Cast: Dobie Gillis (Dwayne Hickman), Maynard G. Krebs (Bob Denver), Zelda Gilroy (Sheila James), Dr. Imogene Burkhart (Jean Byron), Mom Baker (Alice Pearce), Fifi Laverne (Carole Cook), Eddie Baker (Lennie Weinrib).

5 December 1963 *The Donna Reed Show*: "A Touch of Glamour." Director: Barry Shear. Writer: Erna Lazarus. Cast: Donna Stone (Donna Reed), Alex Stone (Carl Betz), Jeff Stone (Paul Petersen), Trisha

Stone (Patty Petersen), Dave Kelsey (Bob Crane), Midge Kelsey (Ann McCrea), Adele Collins (Alice Pearce), Mr. Herbert (Steven Geray), Miss Forsythe (Myrna Dell), Messenger (Sheila James).

13 December 1963 *The Alfred Hitchcock Hour*: "Good-Bye, George." Director: Robert Stevens. Writer: William Fay, based on Robert Arthur's 1959 short story "Getting Rid of George." Cast: Lana Layne (Patricia Barry), Harry Lawrence (Robert Culp), George Layne (Stubby Kaye), Dave Dennis (Elliott Reid), Haila French (Alice Pearce), Patrolman (Kreg Martin), Al the bartender (Mike Ragan), Sally Jason the starlet (Sally Carter), Photographer (Jimmy Joyce), Film Director (Bernie Kopell).

9 January 1964 *Hazel*: "Hot Potato à la Hazel." Director: William D. Russell. Writer: Robert Riley Crutcher. Cast: Hazel Burke (Shirley Booth), George Baxter (Don DeFore), Dorothy Baxter (Whitney Blake), Harold Baxter (Bobby Buntrock), Miss Elsie (Alice Pearce), Charlie Carlotti (Mario Siletti), Julia Hanson (Alice Frost), Edna Hanson (Hope Summers), Charles Drake (Howard Wendell), Detective Sgt. Lewis (Dick Wilson), Policeman (Jeff Burton).

21 March 1964 *The New Phil Silvers Show*: "Auntie Up." Director: David Davis. Writers: Bill Raynor, Myles Wilder. Cast: Harry Grafton (Phil Silvers), Audrey Cooper (Elena Verdugo), Susan Cooper (Sandy Descher), Andy Cooper (Ronnie Dapo), Minnie Tolliver (Alice Pearce), Sam (Bob Jellison), Schrieber (Tommy Farrell), Eddie the milkman (Ed Deemer), Eddie's wife (Joyce Van Patten), Charlie the neighbor (Gene O'Donnell), Ingrid (Gertrude Astor).

19 November 1964 *An Hour with Robert Goulet* (TV Special). Director: Clark Jones. Writer: Arthur Alsberg. Cast: Robert Goulet, Leslie Caron, Terry-Thomas, Peter Gennaro, Fredd Wayne, Mabel Albertson, Alice Pearce, Carol Veazie, Joseph Mell, Eddie Firestone, Linda Scott, Earl Wilson. Cameos: Ed Sullivan, Phil Silvers.

11 December 1964 *The Regis Philbin Show* (with Gisele MacKenzie, Earl Wilson, Tex Terry, Lance LeGault, and Melody Patterson)

29 March 1965 *Many Happy Returns*: "A Date for Walter." Director: Marc Daniels. Writers: Ray Singer, Dick Chevillat. Cast: Walter Burnley (John McGiver), Wilma Fritter (Jesslyn Fax), Joe Foley (Mickey Manners), Lynn Hall (Elena Verdugo), Harry Price (Richard Collier), Owen Sharp (Russell Collins), Ruby Walsh (Alice Pearce), Marilyn

Walsh (Shirley Bonne), Woman (Norma Varden), Flo Handman (Patsy Garrett), Captain (Gil Frye), Violinist (Barry Brooks).

8 July 1965 *Hazel*: "Hot Potato à la Hazel." (prime time repeat from previous season)

19 July 1965 *Summer Playhouse*: "Acres and Pains" (see 13 May 1962)

August 1965 *Girl Talk* (This syndicated show, hosted by Virginia Graham, also featured guests Hermione Gingold and Alice Leone Moates. It was taped during Alice's visit to New York in April 1965.)

October 1965 *Gypsy* (syndicated, with Pat Carroll and Else Tyroler)

November 1965 *Gypsy* (syndicated, with Mei Mei Quong)

24 July 1967 *Vacation Playhouse*: "My Boy Goggle." Director: Ralph Levy. Writer: Bill Manhoff. Cast: Bill Wallace (Jerry Van Dyke), Cameron "Goggle" Wallace (Teddy Eccles), Kate Wallace (Jeanne Rainier), Fanny Carter (Pamela Dapo), Mrs. Audubon (Alice Pearce), Mr. Walker (Lee Goodman), Mrs. Carter (Frances Robinson).

Appearances on ABC's *Bewitched* series

Season One:

24 September 1964	"Be It Ever So Mortgaged"
8 October 1964	"Mother, Meet What's His Name"
22 October 1964	"Little Pitchers Have Big Fears"
3 December 1964	"And Something Makes Three"
24 December 1964	"A Vision of Sugar Plums"
7 January 1965	"It's Magic"
11 February 1965	"Ling Ling"
4 March 1965	"Red Light, Green Light"
11 March 1965	"Which Witch Is Which?"
18 March 1965	"Pleasure O'Riley"
8 April 1965	"Open the Door, Witchcraft"
15 April 1965	"Abner Kadabra"
29 April 1965	"That Was My Wife"
6 May 1965	"Illegal Separation"
13 May 1965	"A Change of Face"
20 May 1965	"Remember the Main"
17 June 1965	"Little Pitchers Have Big Fears" (repeat)
12 August 1965	"Ling Ling" (repeat)
19 August 1965	"A Change of Face" (repeat)
2 September 1965	"Abner Kadabra" (repeat)

9 September 1965 (repeat)	"Which Witch is Which?"

Season Two:

16 September 1965	"Alias Darrin Stephens"
7 October 1965	"My Grandson, the Warlock"
21 October 1965	"Take Two Aspirins and Half a Pint of Porpoise Milk"
11 November 1965	"...And Then I Wrote"
25 November 1965	"Aunt Clara's Old Flame"
2 December 1965	"A Strange Little Visitor"
23 December 1965	"A Vision of Sugar Plums" (recut version from previous season)
20 January 1966	"My Baby, the Tycoon"
3 February 1966	"Fastest Gun on Madison Avenue"
24 February 1966	"Samantha the Dressmaker"
10 March 1966	"Baby's First Paragraph"
9 June 1966	"Prodigy"
16 June 1966	"My Grandson, the Warlock" (repeat)
23 June 1966	"Aunt Clara's Old Flame" (repeat)
30 June 1966	"A Strange Little Visitor" (repeat)
14 July 1966	"Take Two Aspirins and Half a Pint of Porpoise Milk" (repeat)
4 August 1966	"My Baby the Tycoon" (repeat)

Unsold Television Pilots

1962   *Acres and Pains.* Director: Perry Laferty. Writers: Harvey Yorkin, Dave Schwartz. Cast: Walter Matthau, Anne Jackson, Edward Andrews, Alice Pearce, Philip Coolidge, Jerry Stiller, David Doyle, Mickey Freeman.

1962   *Atta Boy, Mama!* Director: Ida Lupino. Writer: Mac Benoff. Cast: Ann Sothern, Martin Braddock, Alice Pearce, Arthur Peterson, et al.

1963   *Shape Up, Sergeant!* Director: Stanley Cherry. Writers: John Bradford, Barry Blitzer. Cast: Ann B. Davis, Alice Pearce, Beverly Wills, Murvyn Vye, Janice Carroll, Maurine Dawson, Joi Lansing, Reva Rose.

1963   *My Boy Goggle.* Director: Ralph Levy. Writer: Bill Manhoff. Cast: Jerry Van Dyke, Teddy Eccles, Jeanne Rainier, Pamela Dapo, Alice Pearce, Lee Goodman, Frances Robinson.

Television Commercials

Various Years	Scotkin Napkins, Ajax, Scotch Brand Tape, L & M Cigarettes, Oxydol, Hudson Paper Towels, Chevron Supreme, Gleem, Chevrolet, etc.

Index

CPSIA information can be obtained
at www.ICGtesting.com
Printed in the USA
JSHW042034280521
15332JS00003B/28

9 781629 337364